THE PLAYS OF
EUGENE O'NEILL

THE RANDOM HOUSE

Lifetime Library

MOURNING BECOMES ELECTRA

AH, WILDERNESS!

ALL GOD'S CHILLUN GOT WINGS

MARCO MILLIONS

WELDED

DIFF'RENT

THE FIRST MAN

GOLD

THE PLAYS
OF
EUGENE
O'NEILL

RANDOM HOUSE · NEW YORK

CONTENTS

MOURNING BECOMES ELECTRA

A TRILOGY

To Carlotta, my wife

Part One

HOMECOMING

A Play in Four Acts

Part Two

THE HUNTED

A Play in Five Acts

Part Three

THE HAUNTED

A Play in Four Acts

THE action of the trilogy, with the exception of an act of the second play, takes place in or immediately outside the Mannon residence, on the outskirts of one of the small New England seaport towns.

A special curtain shows the house as seen from the street. From this, in each play, one comes to the exterior of the house in the opening act and enters it in the following act.

This curtain reveals the extensive grounds—about thirty acres—which surround the house, a heavily wooded ridge in the background, orchards at the right and in the immediate rear, a large flower garden and a greenhouse to the left.

In the foreground, along the street, is a line of locust and elm trees. The property is enclosed by a white picket fence and a tall hedge. A driveway curves up to the house from two entrances with white gates. Between the house and the street is a lawn. By the right corner of the house is a grove of pine trees. Farther forward, along the driveway, maples and locusts. By the left corner of the house is a big clump of lilacs and syringas.

The house is placed back on a slight rise of ground about three hundred feet from the street. It is a large building of the Greek temple type that was the vogue in the first half of the nineteenth century. A white wooden portico with six tall columns contrasts with the wall of the house proper which is of gray cut stone. There are five windows on the upper floor and four on the ground floor, with the main entrance in the middle, a doorway with squared transom and sidelights flanked by intermediate columns. The window shutters are painted a dark green. Before the doorway a flight of four steps leads from the ground to the portico.

The three plays take place in either spring or summer of the years 1865-1866.

HOMECOMING

CHARACTERS

BRIGADIER-GENERAL EZRA MANNON

CHRISTINE, *his wife*

LAVINIA, *their daughter*

CAPTAIN ADAM BRANT, *of the clipper "Flying Trades"*

CAPTAIN PETER NILES, *U. S. Artillery*

HAZEL NILES, *his sister*

SETH BECKWITH

AMOS AMES

LOUISA, *his wife*

MINNIE, *her cousin*

SCENES

ACT ONE: Exterior of the Mannon house in New England—April, 1865.

ACT TWO: Ezra Mannon's study in the house—no time has elapsed.

ACT THREE: The same as Act One—exterior of the house—a night a week later.

ACT FOUR: A bedroom in the house—later the same night.

HOMECOMING

ACT ONE

Scene—*Exterior of the Mannon house on a late afternoon in April, 1865. At front is the driveway which leads up to the house from the two entrances on the street. Behind the driveway the white Grecian temple portico with its six tall columns extends across the stage. A big pine tree is on the lawn at the edge of the drive before the right corner of the house. Its trunk is a black column in striking contrast to the white columns of the portico. By the edge of the drive, left front, is a thick clump of lilacs and syringas. A bench is placed on the lawn at front of this shrubbery which partly screens anyone sitting on it from the front of the house.*

It is shortly before sunset and the soft light of the declining sun shines directly on the front of the house, shimmering in a luminous mist on the white portico and the gray stone wall behind, intensifying the whiteness of the columns, the somber grayness of the wall, the green of the open shutters, the green of the lawn and shrubbery, the black and green of the pine tree. The white columns cast black bars of shadow on the gray wall behind them. The windows of the lower floor reflect the sun's rays in a resentful glare. The temple portico is like an incongruous white mask fixed on the house to hide its somber gray ugliness.

In the distance, from the town, a band is heard playing "John Brown's Body." Borne on the light puffs of wind this music is at times quite loud, then sinks into faintness as the wind dies.

From the left rear, a man's voice is heard singing the chanty "Shenandoah"—a song that more than any other holds in it the

5

brooding rhythm of the sea. The voice grows quickly nearer. It is thin and aged, the wraith of what must once have been a good baritone.

> *"Oh, Shenandoah, I long to hear you*
> *A-way, my rolling river*
> *Oh, Shenandoah, I can't get near you*
> *Way-ay, I'm bound away*
> *Across the wide Missouri."*

The singer, SETH BECKWITH, *finishes the last line as he enters from around the corner of the house. Closely following him are* AMOS AMES, *his wife* LOUISA, *and her cousin* MINNIE.

SETH BECKWITH, *the Mannons' gardener and man of all work, is an old man of seventy-five with white hair and beard, tall, raw-boned and stoop-shouldered, his joints stiffened by rheumatism, but still sound and hale. He has a gaunt face that in repose gives one the strange impression of a life-like mask. It is set in a grim expression, but his small, sharp eyes still peer at life with a shrewd prying avidity and his loose mouth has a strong suggestion of ribald humor. He wears his earth-stained working clothes.*

AMOS AMES, *carpenter by trade but now taking a holiday and dressed in his Sunday best, as are his wife and her cousin, is a fat man in his fifties. In character he is the townsfolk type of garrulous gossip-monger who is at the same time devoid of evil intent, scandal being for him merely the subject most popular with his audience.*

His wife, LOUISA, *is taller and stouter than he and about the same age. Of a similar scandal-bearing type, her tongue is sharpened by malice.*

Her cousin, MINNIE, *is a plump little woman of forty, of the meek, eager-listener type, with a small round face, round stupid eyes, and a round mouth pursed out to drink in gossip.*

These last three are types of townsfolk rather than individuals, a

6

chorus representing the town come to look and listen and spy on the rich and exclusive Mannons.

Led by SETH, *they come forward as far as the lilac clump and stand staring at the house.* SETH, *in a mood of aged playfulness, is trying to make an impression on* MINNIE. *His singing has been for her benefit. He nudges her with his elbow, grinning.*

SETH. How's that fur singin' fur an old feller? I used to be noted fur my chanties. (*Seeing she is paying no attention to him but is staring with open-mouthed awe at the house, he turns to* AMES— *jubilantly*) By jingo, Amos, if that news is true, there won't be a sober man in town tonight! It's our patriotic duty to celebrate!

AMES. (*with a grin*) We'd ought to, that's sartin!

LOUISA. You ain't goin' to git Amos drunk tonight, surrender or no surrender! An old reprobate, that's what you be!

SETH. (*pleased*) Old nothin'! On'y seventy-five! My old man lived to be ninety! Licker can't kill the Beckwiths! (*He and* AMES *laugh.* LOUISA *smiles in spite of herself.* MINNIE *is oblivious, still staring at the house.*)

MINNIE. My sakes! What a purty house!

SETH. Wal, I promised Amos I'd help show ye the sights when you came to visit him. 'Taint everyone can git to see the Mannon place close to. They're strict about trespassin'.

MINNIE. My! They must be rich! How'd they make their money?

SETH. Ezra's made a pile, and before him, his father, Abe Mannon, he inherited some and made a pile more in shippin'. Started one of the fust Western Ocean packet lines.

MINNIE. Ezra's the General, ain't he?

SETH. (*proudly*) Ayeh. The best fighter in the hull of Grant's army!

MINNIE. What kind is he?

SETH. (*boastfully expanding*) He's able, Ezra is! Folks think he's cold-blooded and uppish, 'cause he's never got much to say to 'em.

7

But that's only the Mannons' way. They've been top dog around here for near on two hundred years and don't let folks fergit it.

MINNIE. How'd he come to jine the army if he's so rich?

SETH. Oh, he'd been a soldier afore this war. His paw made him go to West P'int. He went to the Mexican war and come out a major. Abe died that same year and Ezra give up the army and took holt of the shippin' business here. But he didn't stop there. He learned law on the side and got made a judge. Went in fur politics and got 'lected mayor. He was mayor when this war broke out but he resigned to once and jined the army again. And now he's riz to be General. Oh, he's able, Ezra is!

AMES. Ayeh. This town's real proud of Ezra.

LOUISA. Which is more'n you kin say fur his wife. Folks all hates her! She ain't the Mannon kind. French and Dutch descended, she is. Furrin lookin' and queer. Her father's a doctor in New York, but he can't be much of a one 'cause she didn't bring no money when Ezra married her.

SETH. (*his face growing grim—sharply*) Never mind her. We ain't talkin' 'bout her. (*Then abruptly changing the subject*) Wal, I've got to see Vinnie. I'm goin' round by the kitchen. You wait here. And if Ezra's wife starts to run you off fur trespassin', you tell her I got permission from Vinnie to show you round. (*He goes off around the corner of the house, left. The three stare about them gawkily, awed and uncomfortable. They talk in low voices.*)

LOUISA. Seth is so proud of his durned old Mannons! I couldn't help givin' him a dig about Ezra's wife.

AMES. Wal, don't matter much. He's allus hated her.

LOUISA. Ssshh! Someone's comin' out. Let's get back here! (*They crowd to the rear of the bench by the lilac clump and peer through the leaves as the front door is opened and* CHRISTINE MANNON *comes out to the edge of the portico at the top of the steps.* LOUISA *prods her cousin and whispers excitedly*) That's her! (CHRISTINE MANNON *is a tall striking-looking woman of forty but she appears younger.*

8

She has a fine, voluptuous figure and she moves with a flowing animal grace. She wears a green satin dress, smartly cut and expensive, which brings out the peculiar color of her thick curly hair, partly a copper brown, partly a bronze gold, each shade distinct and yet blending with the other. Her face is unusual, handsome rather than beautiful. One is struck at once by the strange impression it gives in repose of being not living flesh but a wonderfully lifelike pale mask, in which only the deep-set eyes, of a dark violet blue, are alive. Her black eyebrows meet in a pronounced straight line above her strong nose. Her chin is heavy, her mouth large and sensual, the lower lip full, the upper a thin bow, shadowed by a line of hair. She stands and listens defensively, as if the music held some meaning that threatened her. But at once she shrugs her shoulders with disdain and comes down the steps and walks off toward the flower garden, passing behind the lilac clump without having noticed AMES *and the women.)*

MINNIE. (*in an awed whisper*) My! She's awful handsome, ain't she?

LOUISE. Too furrin lookin' fur my taste.

MINNIE. Ayeh. There's somethin' queer lookin' about her face.

AMES. Secret lookin'—'s if it was a mask she'd put on. That's the Mannon look. They all has it. They grow it on their wives. Seth's growed it on, too, didn't you notice—from bein' with 'em all his life. They don't want folks to guess their secrets.

MINNIE. (*breathlessly eager*) Secrets?

LOUISA. The Mannons got skeletons in their closets same as others! Worse ones. (*Lowering her voice almost to a whisper—to her husband*) Tell Minnie about old Abe Mannon's brother David marryin' that French Canuck nurse girl he'd got into trouble.

AMES. Ssshh! Shet up, can't you? Here's Seth comin'. (*But he whispers quickly to* MINNIE) That happened way back when I was a youngster. I'll tell you later. (SETH *has appeared from around the left corner of the house and now joins them.*)

SETH. That durned nigger cook is allus askin' me to fetch wood fur her! You'd think I was her slave! That's what we get fur freein' 'em! (*Then briskly*) Wal, come along, folks. I'll show you the peach orchard and then we'll go to my greenhouse. I couldn't find Vinnie. (*They are about to start when the front door of the house is opened and* LAVINIA *comes out to the top of the steps where her mother had stood. She is twenty-three but looks considerably older. Tall, like her mother, her body is thin, flat-breasted and angular, and its unattractiveness is accentuated by her plain black dress. Her movements are stiff and she carries herself with a wooden, square-shouldered, military bearing. She has a flat dry voice and a habit of snapping out her words like an officer giving orders. But in spite of these dissimilarities, one is immediately struck by her facial resemblance to her mother. She has the same peculiar shade of copper-gold hair, the same pallor and dark violet-blue eyes, the black eyebrows meeting in a straight line above her nose, the same sensual mouth, the same heavy jaw. Above all, one is struck by the same strange, lifelike mask impression her face gives in repose. But it is evident* LAVINIA *does all in her power to emphasize the dissimilarity rather than the resemblance to her parent. She wears her hair pulled tightly back, as if to conceal its natural curliness, and there is not a touch of feminine allurement to her severely plain get-up. Her head is the same size as her mother's, but on her thin body it looks too large and heavy.*)

SETH. (*seeing her*) There she be now. (*He starts for the steps— then sees she has not noticed their presence, and stops and stands waiting, struck by something in her manner. She is looking off right, watching her mother as she strolls through the garden to the greenhouse. Her eyes are bleak and hard with an intense, bitter enmity. Then her mother evidently disappears in the greenhouse, for* LAVINIA *turns her head, still oblivious to* SETH *and his friends, and looks off left, her attention caught by the band, the music of which, borne on a freshening breeze, has suddenly become louder.*)

It is still playing "John Brown's Body." LAVINIA *listens, as her mother had a moment before, but her reaction is the direct opposite to what her mother's had been. Her eyes light up with a grim satisfaction, and an expression of strange vindictive triumph comes into her face.*)

LOUISA. (*in a quick whisper to* MINNIE) That's Lavinia!

MINNIE. She looks like her mother in face—queer lookin'—but she ain't purty like her.

SETH. You git along to the orchard, folks. I'll jine you there. (*They walk back around the left of the house and disappear. He goes to* LAVINIA *eagerly*) Say, I got fine news fur you, Vinnie. The telegraph feller says Lee is a goner sure this time! They're only waitin' now fur the news to be made official. You can count on your paw comin' home!

LAVINIA. (*grimly*) I hope so. It's time.

SETH. (*with a keen glance at her—slowly*) Ayeh.

LAVINIA. (*turning on him sharply*) What do you mean, Seth?

SETH. (*avoiding her eyes—evasively*) Nothin'—'cept what you mean. (LAVINIA *stares at him. He avoids her eyes—then heavily casual*) Where was you gallivantin' night afore last and all yesterday?

LAVINIA. (*starts*) Over to Hazel and Peter's house.

SETH. Ayeh. There's where Hannah said you'd told her you was goin'. That's funny now—'cause I seen Peter upstreet yesterday and he asked me where you was keepin' yourself.

LAVINIA. (*again starts—then slowly as if admitting a secret understanding between them*) I went to New York, Seth.

SETH. Ayeh. That's where I thought you'd gone, mebbe. (*Then with deep sympathy*) It's durned hard on you, Vinnie. It's a durned shame.

LAVINIA. (*stiffening—curtly*) I don't know what you're talking about.

SETH. (*nods comprehendingly*) All right, Vinnie. Just as you say.

(*He pauses—then after hesitating frowningly for a moment, blurts out*) There's somethin' been on my mind lately I want to warn you about. It's got to do with what's worryin' you—that is, if there's anythin' in it.

LAVINIA. (*stiffly*) There's nothing worrying me. (*Then sharply*) Warn me? About what?

SETH. Mebbe it's nothin'—and then again mebbe I'm right, and if I'm right, then you'd ought t'be warned. It's to do with that Captain Brant.

LAVINIA. (*starts again but keeps her tone cold and collected*) What about him?

SETH. Somethin' I calc'late no one'd notice 'specially 'ceptin' me, because— (*Then hastily as he sees someone coming up the drive*) Here's Peter and Hazel comin'. I'll tell you later, Vinnie. I ain't got time now anyways. Those folks are waitin' for me.

LAVINIA. I'll be sitting here. You come back afterwards. (*Then her cold disciplined mask breaking for a moment—tensely*) Oh, why do Peter and Hazel have to come now? I don't want to see anyone! (*She starts as if to go into the house.*)

SETH. You run in. I'll git rid of 'em fur you.

LAVINIA. (*recovering herself—curtly*) No. I'll see them. (SETH *goes back around the corner of the house, left. A moment later* HAZEL *and* PETER NILES *enter along the drive from left, front.* HAZEL *is a pretty, healthy girl of nineteen, with dark hair and eyes. Her features are small but clearly modeled. She has a strong chin and a capable smiling mouth. One gets a sure impression of her character at a glance—frank, innocent, amiable and good—not in a negative but in a positive, self-possessed way. Her brother,* PETER, *is very like her in character—straightforward, guileless and good-natured. He is a heavily built young fellow of twenty-two, awkward in movement and hesitating in speech. His face is broad, plain, with a snubby nose, curly brown hair, fine gray eyes and a big mouth. He wears the uniform of an artillery captain in the Union Army.*)

12

LAVINIA. (*with forced cordiality*) Good afternoon. How are you? (*She and* HAZEL *kiss and she shakes hands with* PETER.)

HAZEL. Oh, we're all right. But how are you, Vinnie, that's the question? Seems as if we hadn't seen you in ages! You haven't been sick, I hope!

LAVINIA. Well—if you call a pesky cold sick.

PETER. Gosh, that's too bad! All over it now?

LAVINIA. Yes—almost. Do sit down, won't you? (HAZEL *sits at left of bench,* LAVINIA *beside her in the middle.* PETER *sits gingerly on the right edge so that there is an open space between him and* LAVINIA.)

HAZEL. Peter can stay a while if you want him to, but I just dropped in for a second to find out if you'd had any more news from Orin.

LAVINIA. Not since the letter I showed you.

HAZEL. But that was ages ago! And I haven't had a letter in months. I guess he must have met another girl some place and given me the go by. (*She forces a smile but her tone is really hurt.*)

PETER. Orin not writing doesn't mean anything. He never was much of a hand for letters.

HAZEL. I know that, but—you don't think he's been wounded, do you, Vinnie?

LAVINIA. Of course not. Father would have let us know.

PETER. Sure he would. Don't be foolish, Hazel! (*Then after a little pause*) Orin ought to be home before long now. You've heard the good news, of course, Vinnie?

HAZEL. Peter won't have to go back. Isn't that fine?

PETER. My wound is healed and I've got orders to leave tomorrow but they'll be cancelled, I guess. (*Grinning*) I won't pretend I'm the sort of hero that wants to go back, either! I've had enough!

HAZEL. (*impulsively*) Oh, it will be so good to see Orin again. (*Then embarrassed, forces a self-conscious laugh and gets up and kisses* LAVINIA) Well, I must run. I've got to meet Emily. Good-bye, Vinnie. Do take care of yourself and come to see us soon. (*With a teasing glance at her brother*) And be kind to Peter. He's nice—

when he's asleep. And he has something he's just dying to ask you!

PETER. (*horribly embarrassed*) Darn you! (HAZEL *laughs and goes off down the drive, left front.* PETER *fidgets, his eyes on the ground.* LAVINIA *watches him. Since* HAZEL'S *teasing statement, she has visibly withdrawn into herself and is on the defensive. Finally* PETER *looks up and blurts out awkwardly*) Hazel feels bad about Orin not writing. Do you think he really—loves her?

LAVINIA. (*stiffening—brusquely*) I don't know anything about love! I don't want to know anything! (*Intensely*) I hate love!

PETER. (*crushed by this but trying bravely to joke*) Gosh, then, if that's the mood you're in, I guess I better not ask—something I'd made up my mind to ask you today.

LAVINIA. It's what you asked me a year ago when you were home on leave, isn't it?

PETER. And you said wait till the war was over. Well, it's over now.

LAVINIA. (*slowly*) I can't marry anyone, Peter. I've got to stay home. Father needs me.

PETER. He's got your mother.

LAVINIA. (*sharply*) He needs me more! (*A pause. Then she turns pityingly and puts her hand on his shoulder*) I'm sorry, Peter.

PETER. (*gruffly*) Oh, that's all right.

LAVINIA. I know it's what girls always say in books, but I do love you as a brother, Peter. I wouldn't lose you as a brother for anything. We've been like that ever since we were little and started playing together—you and Orin and Hazel and I. So please don't let this come between us.

PETER. 'Course it won't. What do you think I am? (*Doggedly*) Besides, I'm not giving up hope but what you'll change your mind in time. That is, unless it's because you love someone else—

LAVINIA. (*snatching her hand back*) Don't be stupid, Peter!

PETER. But how about this mysterious clipper captain that's been calling?

14

LAVINIA. (*angrily*) Do you think I care anything about that—that—!

PETER. Don't get mad. I only meant, folks say he's courting you.

LAVINIA. Folks say more than their prayers!

PETER. Then you don't—care for him?

LAVINIA. (*intensely*) I hate the sight of him!

PETER. Gosh! I'm glad to hear you say that, Vinnie. I was afraid—I imagined girls all liked him. He's such a darned romantic-looking cuss. Looks more like a gambler or a poet than a ship captain. I got a look as he was coming out of your gate—I guess it was the last time he was here. Funny, too. He reminded me of someone. But I couldn't place who it was.

LAVINIA. (*startled, glances at him uneasily*) No one around here, that's sure. He comes from out West. Grandfather Hamel happened to meet him in New York and took a fancy to him, and Mother met him at Grandfather's house.

PETER. Who is he, anyway, Vinnie?

LAVINIA. I don't know much about him in spite of what you think. Oh, he did tell me the story of his life to make himself out romantic, but I didn't pay much attention. He went to sea when he was young and was in California for the Gold Rush. He's sailed all over the world—he lived on a South Sea island once, so he says.

PETER. (*grumpily*) He seems to have had plenty of romantic experience, if you can believe him!

LAVINIA. (*bitterly*) That's his trade—being romantic! (*Then agitatedly*) But I don't want to talk any more about him. (*She gets up and walks toward right to conceal her agitation, keeping her back turned to* PETER.)

PETER. (*with a grin*) Well, I don't either. I can think of more interesting subjects. (CHRISTINE MANNON *appears from left, between the clump of lilacs and the house. She is carrying a big bunch of flowers.* LAVINIA *senses her presence and whirls around. For a moment, mother and daughter stare into each other's eyes. In their*

whole tense attitudes is clearly revealed the bitter antagonism be-
tween them. But CHRISTINE *quickly recovers herself and her air*
resumes its disdainful aloofness.)

CHRISTINE. Ah, here you are at last! (*Then she sees* PETER, *who is*
visibly embarrassed by her presence) Why, good afternoon, Peter, I
didn't see you at first.

PETER. Good afternoon, Mrs. Mannon. I was just passing and
dropped in for a second. I guess I better run along now, Vinnie.

LAVINIA. (*with an obvious eagerness to get him off—quickly*) All
right. Good-bye, Peter.

PETER. Good-bye. Good-bye, Mrs. Mannon.

CHRISTINE. Good-bye, Peter. (*He disappears from the drive, left.*
CHRISTINE *comes forward*) I must say you treat your one devoted
swain pretty rudely. (LAVINIA *doesn't reply.* CHRISTINE *goes on coolly*)
I was wondering when I was going to see you. When I returned
from New York last night you seemed to have gone to bed.

LAVINIA. I had gone to bed.

CHRISTINE. You usually read long after that. I tried your door—but
you had locked yourself in. When you kept yourself locked in all
day I was sure you were intentionally avoiding me. But Annie said
you had a headache. (*While she has been speaking she has come*
toward LAVINIA *until she is now within arm's reach of her. The*
facial resemblance, as they stand there, is extraordinary. CHRISTINE
stares at her coolly, but one senses an uneasy wariness beneath her
pose) Did you have a headache?

LAVINIA. No. I wanted to be alone—to think over things.

CHRISTINE. What things, if I may ask? (*Then, as if she were afraid*
of an answer to this question, she abruptly changes the subject)
Who are those people I saw wandering about the grounds?

LAVINIA. Some friends of Seth's.

CHRISTINE. Because they know that lazy old sot, does it give them
the privilege of trespassing?

LAVINIA. I gave Seth permission to show them around.

CHRISTINE. And since when have you the right without consulting me?

LAVINIA. I couldn't very well consult you when Seth asked me. You had gone to New York— (*She pauses a second—then adds slowly, staring fixedly at her mother*) to see Grandfather. Is he feeling any better? He seems to have been sick so much this past year.

CHRISTINE. (*casually, avoiding her eyes*) Yes. He's much better now. He'll soon be going the rounds to his patients again, he hopes. (*As if anxious to change the subject, looking at the flowers she carries*) I've been to the greenhouse to pick these. I felt our tomb needed a little brightening. (*She nods scornfully toward the house*) Each time I come back after being away it appears more like a sepulchre! The "whited" one of the Bible—pagan temple front stuck like a mask on Puritan gray ugliness! It was just like old Abe Mannon to build such a monstrosity—as a temple for his hatred. (*Then with a little mocking laugh*) Forgive me, Vinnie. I forgot you liked it. And you ought to. It suits your temperament. (LAVINIA *stares at her but remains silent.* CHRISTINE *glances at her flowers again and turns toward the house*) I must put these in water. (*She moves a few steps toward the house—then turns again—with a studied casualness*) By the way, before I forget, I happened to run into Captain Brant on the street in New York. He said he was coming up here today to take over his ship and asked me if he might drop in to see you. I told him he could—and stay to supper with us. (*Without looking at* LAVINIA, *who is staring at her with a face grown grim and hard*) Doesn't that please you, Vinnie? Or do you remain true to your one and only beau, Peter?

LAVINIA. Is that why you picked the flowers—because he is coming? (*Her mother does not answer. She goes on with a threatening undercurrent in her voice*) You have heard the news, I suppose? It means Father will be home soon!

CHRISTINE. (*without looking at her—coolly*) We've had so many rumors lately. This report hasn't been confirmed yet, has it? I haven't heard the fort firing a salute.

LAVINIA. You will before long!

CHRISTINE. I'm sure I hope so as much as you.

LAVINIA. You can say that!

CHRISTINE. (*concealing her alarm—coldly*) What do you mean? You will kindly not take that tone with me, please! (*Cuttingly*) If you are determined to quarrel, let us go into the house. We might be overheard out here. (*She turns and sees* SETH *who has just come to the corner of the house, left, and is standing there watching them*) See. There is your old crony doing his best to listen now! (*Moving to the steps*) I am going in and rest a while. (*She walks up the steps.*)

LAVINIA. (*harshly*) I've got to have a talk with you, Mother— before long!

CHRISTINE. (*turning defiantly*) Whenever you wish. Tonight after the Captain leaves you, if you like. But what is it you want to talk about?

LAVINIA. You'll know soon enough!

CHRISTINE. (*staring at her with a questioning dread—forcing a scornful smile*) You always make such a mystery of things, Vinnie. (*She goes into the house and closes the door behind her.* SETH *comes forward from where he had withdrawn around the corner of the house.* LAVINIA *makes a motion for him to follow her, and goes and sits on the bench at left. A pause. She stares straight ahead, her face frozen, her eyes hard. He regards her understandingly.*)

LAVINIA. (*abruptly*) Well? What is it about Captain Brant you want to warn me against? (*Then as if she felt she must defend her question from some suspicion that she knows is in his mind*) I want to know all I can about him because—he seems to be calling to court me.

SETH. (*managing to convey his entire disbelief of this statement in one word*) Ayeh.

18

HOMECOMING

LAVINIA. (*sharply*) You say that as if you didn't believe me.

SETH. I believe anything you tell me to believe. I ain't been with the Mannons for sixty years without learning that. (*A pause. Then he asks slowly*) Ain't you noticed this Brant reminds you of someone in looks?

LAVINIA. (*struck by this*) Yes. I have—ever since I first saw him—but I've never been able to place who— Who do you mean?

SETH. Your Paw, ain't it, Vinnie?

LAVINIA. (*startled—agitatedly*) Father? No! It can't be! (*Then as if the conviction were forcing itself on her in spite of herself*) Yes! He does—something about his face—that must be why I've had the strange feeling I've known him before—why I've felt— (*Then tensely as if she were about to break down*) Oh! I won't believe it! You must be mistaken, Seth! That would be too—!

SETH. He ain't only like your Paw. He's like Orin, too—and all the Mannons I've known.

LAVINIA. (*frightenedly*) But why—why should he—?

SETH. More speshully he calls to my mind your Grandpaw's brother, David. How much do you know about David Mannon, Vinnie? I know his name's never been allowed to be spoke among Mannons since the day he left—but you've likely heard gossip, ain't you—even if it all happened before you was born.

LAVINIA. I've heard that he loved the Canuck nurse girl who was taking care of Father's little sister who died, and had to marry her because she was going to have a baby; and that Grandfather put them both out of the house and then afterwards tore it down and built this one because he wouldn't live where his brother had disgraced the family. But what has that old scandal got to do with—

SETH. Wait. Right after they was throwed out they married and went away. There was talk they'd gone out West, but no one knew nothin' about 'em afterwards—'ceptin' your Grandpaw let out to me one time she'd had the baby—a boy. He was cussin' it. (*Then impressively*) It's about her baby I've been thinkin', Vinnie.

19

LAVINIA. (*a look of appalled comprehension growing on her face*) Oh!

SETH. How old is that Brant, Vinnie?

LAVINIA. Thirty-six, I think.

SETH. Ayeh! That'd make it right. And here's another funny thing —his name. Brant's sort of queer fur a name. I ain't never heard tell of it before. Sounds made up to me—like short fur somethin' else. Remember what that Canuck girl's name was, do you, Vinnie? Marie Brantôme! See what I'm drivin' at?

LAVINIA. (*agitatedly, fighting against a growing conviction*) But— don't be stupid, Seth—his name would be Mannon and he'd be only too proud of it.

SETH. He'd have good reason not to use the name of Mannon when he came callin' here, wouldn't he? If your Paw ever guessed—!

LAVINIA. (*breaking out violently*) No! It can't be! God wouldn't let it! It would be too horrible—on top of—! I won't even think of it, do you hear? Why did you have to tell me?

SETH. (*calmingly*) There now! Don't take on, Vinnie. No need gettin' riled at me. (*He waits—then goes on insistently*) All I'm drivin' at is that it's durned funny—his looks and the name—and you'd ought fur your Paw's sake to make sartin.

LAVINIA. How can I make certain?

SETH. Catch him off guard sometime and put it up to him strong —as if you knowed it—and see if mebbe he don't give himself away. (*He starts to go—looks down the drive at left*) Looks like him comin' up the drive now, Vinnie. There's somethin' about his walk calls back David Mannon, too. If I didn't know it was him I'd think it was David's ghost comin' home. (*He turns away abruptly*) Wal, calc'late I better git back to work. (*He walks around the left corner of the house. A pause. Then* CAPTAIN ADAM BRANT *enters from the drive, left, front. He starts on seeing* LAVINIA *but immediately puts on his most polite, winning air. One is struck at a glance by the peculiar quality his face in repose has of being a lifelike mask rather than living flesh. He has a broad, low forehead, framed by coal-black straight hair which he wears noticeably long, pushed back carelessly from his forehead as a poet's might be. He has a big aquiline nose, bushy eyebrows, swarthy complexion, hazel eyes. His wide mouth is sensual and moody—a mouth that can be strong and weak by turns. He wears a mustache, but his heavy cleft chin is clean-shaven. In figure he is tall, broad-shouldered and powerful. He gives the impression of being always on the offensive or defensive, always fighting life. He is dressed with an almost foppish extravagance, with touches of studied carelessness, as if a romantic Byronic appearance were the ideal in mind. There is little of the obvious ship captain about him, except his big, strong hands and his deep voice.)*

BRANT. (*bowing with an exaggerated politeness*) Good afternoon. (*Coming and taking her hand which she forces herself to hold out to him*) Hope you don't mind my walking in on you without ceremony. Your mother told me—

LAVINIA. I know. She had to go out for a while and she said I was to keep you company until she returned.

BRANT. (*gallantly*) Well, I'm in good luck, then. I hope she doesn't hurry back to stand watch over us. I haven't had a chance to be alone with you since—that night we went walking in the moonlight, do you remember? (*He has kept her hand and he drops his voice to a low, lover-like tone.* LAVINIA *cannot repress a start, agitatedly snatching her hand from his and turning away from him.*)

LAVINIA. (*regaining command of herself—slowly*) What do you think of the news of Lee surrendering, Captain? We expect my father home very soon now. (*At something in her tone he stares at her suspiciously, but she is looking straight before her*) Why don't you sit down?

BRANT. Thank you. (*He sits on the bench at her right. He has become wary now, feeling something strange in her attitude but not able to make her out—casually*) Yes, you must be very happy at the prospect of seeing your father again. Your mother has told me how close you've always been to him.

LAVINIA. Did she? (*Then with intensity*) I love Father better than anyone in the world. There is nothing I wouldn't do—to protect him from hurt!

BRANT. (*watching her carefully—keeping his casual tone*) You care more for him than for your mother?

LAVINIA. Yes.

BRANT. Well, I suppose that's the usual way of it. A daughter feels closer to her father and a son to his mother. But I should think you ought to be a born exception to that rule.

LAVINIA. Why?

BRANT. You're so like your mother in some ways. Your face is the dead image of hers. And look at your hair. You won't meet hair like yours and hers again in a month of Sundays. I only know of one other woman who had it. You'll think it strange when I tell you. It was my mother.

LAVINIA. (*with a start*) Ah!

BRANT. (*dropping his voice to a reverent, hushed tone*) Yes, she had beautiful hair like your mother's, that hung down to her knees, and big, deep, sad eyes that were blue as the Caribbean Sea!

LAVINIA. (*harshly*) What do looks amount to? I'm not a bit like her! Everybody knows I take after Father!

BRANT. (*brought back with a shock, astonished at her tone*) But— you're not angry at me for saying that, are you? (*Then filled with uneasiness and resolving he must establish himself on an intimate footing with her again—with engaging bluntness*) You're puzzling today, Miss Lavinia. You'll excuse me if I come out with it bluntly. I've lived most of my life at sea and in camps and I'm used to straight speaking. What are you holding against me? If I've done anything to offend you, I swear it wasn't meant. (*She is silent, staring before her with hard eyes, rigidly upright. He appraises her with a calculating look, then goes on*) I wouldn't have bad feeling come between us for the world. I may only be flattering myself, but I thought you liked me. Have you forgotten that night walking along the shore?

LAVINIA. (*in a cold, hard voice*) I haven't forgotten. Did Mother tell you you could kiss me?

BRANT. What—what do you mean? (*But he at once attributes the question to her naïveté—laughingly*) Oh! I see! But, come now, Lavinia, you can't mean, can you, I should have asked her permission?

LAVINIA. Shouldn't you?

BRANT. (*again uneasy—trying to joke it off*) Well, I wasn't brought up that strictly and, should or shouldn't, at any rate, I didn't—and it wasn't the less sweet for that! (*Then at something in her face he hurriedly goes off on another tack*) I'm afraid I gabbed too much that night. Maybe I bored you with my talk of clipper ships and my love for them?

LAVINIA. (*dryly*) "Tall, white clippers," you called them. You said they were like beautiful, pale women to you. You said you loved them more than you'd ever loved a woman. Is that true, Captain?

BRANT. (*with forced gallantry*) Aye. But I meant, before I met you. (*Then thinking he has at last hit on the cause of her changed attitude toward him—with a laugh*) So that's what you're holding against me, is it? Well, I might have guessed. Women are jealous of ships. They always suspect the sea. They know they're three of a kind when it comes to a man! (*He laughs again but less certainly this time, as he regards her grim, set expression*) Yes, I might have seen you didn't appear much taken by my sea gamming that night. I suppose clippers are too old a story to the daughter of a shipbuilder. But unless I'm much mistaken, you were interested when I told you of the islands in the South Seas where I was shipwrecked my first voyage at sea.

LAVINIA. (*in a dry, brittle tone*) I remember your admiration for

23

the naked native women. You said they had found the secret of happiness because they had never heard that love can be a sin.

BRANT. (*surprised—sizing her up puzzledly*) So you remember that, do you? (*Then romantically*) Aye! And they live in as near the Garden of Paradise before sin was discovered as you'll find on this earth! Unless you've seen it, you can't picture the green beauty of their land set in the blue of the sea! The clouds like down on the mountain tops, the sun drowsing in your blood, and always the surf on the barrier reef singing a croon in your ears like a lullaby! The Blessed Isles, I'd call them! You can forget there all men's dirty dreams of greed and power!

LAVINIA. And their dirty dreams—of love?

BRANT. (*startled again—staring at her uneasily*) Why do you say that? What do you mean, Lavinia?

LAVINIA. Nothing. I was only thinking—of your Blessed Isles.

BRANT. (*uncertainly*) Oh! But you said— (*Then with a confused, stupid persistence he comes closer to her, dropping his voice again to his love-making tone*) Whenever I remember those islands now, I will always think of you, as you walked beside me that night with your hair blowing in the sea wind and the moonlight in your eyes! (*He tries to take her hand, but at his touch she pulls away and springs to her feet.*)

LAVINIA. (*with cold fury*) Don't you touch me! Don't you dare—! You liar! You— (*Then as he starts back in confusion, she seizes this opportunity to follow* SETH's *advice—staring at him with deliberately insulting scorn*) But I suppose it would be foolish to expect anything but cheap romantic lies from the son of a low Canuck nurse girl!

BRANT. (*stunned*) What's that? (*Then rage at the insult to his mother overcoming all prudence—springs to his feet threateningly*) Belay, damn you!—or I'll forget you're a woman—no Mannon can insult her while I—

24

LAVINIA. (*appalled now she knows the truth*) So—it is true— You are her son! Oh!

BRANT. (*fighting to control himself—with harsh defiance*) And what if I am? I'm proud to be! My only shame is my dirty Mannon blood! So that's why you couldn't stand my touching you just now, is it? You're too good for the son of a servant, eh? By God, you were glad enough before—!

LAVINIA. (*fiercely*) It's not true! I was only leading you on to find out things!

BRANT. Oh, no! It's only since you suspected who I was! I suppose your father has stuffed you with his lies about my mother! But, by God, you'll hear the truth of it, now you know who I am— And you'll see if you or any Mannon has the right to look down on her!

LAVINIA. I don't want to hear— (*She starts to go toward the house.*)

BRANT. (*grabbing her by the arm—tauntingly*) You're a coward, are you, like all Mannons, when it comes to facing the truth about themselves? (*She turns on him defiantly. He drops her arm and goes on harshly*) I'll bet he never told you your grandfather, Abe Mannon, as well as his brother, loved my mother!

LAVINIA. It's a lie!

BRANT. It's the truth. It was his jealous revenge made him disown my father and cheat him out of his share of the business they'd inherited!

LAVINIA. He didn't cheat him! He bought him out!

BRANT. Forced him to sell for one-tenth its worth, you mean! He knew my father and mother were starving! But the money didn't last my father long! He'd taken to drink. He was a coward—like all Mannons—once he felt the world looked down on him. He skulked and avoided people. He grew ashamed of my mother—and me. He sank down and down and my mother worked and supported him. I can remember when men from the corner saloon would drag him home and he'd fall in the door, a sodden carcass. One night when I was seven he came home crazy drunk and hit my mother in the face. It was the first time he'd ever struck her. It made me blind mad. I hit at him with the poker and cut his head. My mother pulled me back and gave me a hiding. Then she cried over him. She'd never stopped loving him.

LAVINIA. Why do you tell me this? I told you once I don't want to hear—

BRANT. (*grimly*) You'll see the point of it damned soon! (*Unheeding—as if the scene were still before his eyes*) For days after, he sat and stared at nothing. One time when we were alone he asked me to forgive him hitting her. But I hated him and I wouldn't forgive him. Then one night he went out and he didn't come back. The next morning they found him hanging in a barn!

LAVINIA. (*with a shudder*) Oh!

BRANT. (*savagely*) The only decent thing he ever did!

LAVINIA. You're lying! No Mannon would ever—

BRANT. Oh, wouldn't they? They are all fine, honorable gentlemen, you think! Then listen a bit and you'll hear something about another of them! (*Then going on bitterly with his story*) My mother sewed for a living and sent me to school. She was very strict with me. She blamed me for his killing himself. But she was bound she'd make a gentleman of me—like he was!—if it took her last cent and her last strap! (*With a grim smile*) She didn't succeed, as you notice! At seventeen I ran away to sea—and forgot I had a mother, except I took part of her name—Brant was short and easy on ships—and I wouldn't wear the name of Mannon. I forgot her until two years ago when I came back from the East. Oh, I'd written to her now and then and sent her money when I happened to have any. But I'd forgotten her just the same—and when I got to New York I found her dying—of sickness and starvation! And I found out that when she'd been laid up, not able to work, not knowing where to reach me, she'd sunk her last shred of pride and written to your father asking for a loan. He never answered her. And I came too late. She died in my arms. (*With vindictive passion*) He could have saved her—and he

26

deliberately let her die! He's as guilty of murder as anyone he ever sent to the rope when he was a judge!

LAVINIA. (*springing to her feet—furiously*) You dare say that about Father! If he were here—

BRANT. I wish to God he was! I'd tell him what I tell you now—that I swore on my mother's body I'd revenge her death on him.

LAVINIA. (*with cold deadly intensity*) And I suppose you boast that now you've done so, don't you?—in the vilest, most cowardly way—like the son of a servant you are!

BRANT. (*again thrown off guard—furiously*) Belay, I told you, with that kind of talk!

LAVINIA. She is only your means of revenge on Father, is that it?

BRANT. (*stunned—stammers in guilty confusion*) What?—She?—Who?—I don't know what you're talking about!

LAVINIA. Then you soon will know! And so will she! I've found out all I wanted to from you. I'm going in to talk to her now. You wait here until I call you!

BRANT. (*furious at her tone*) No! Be damned if you can order me about as if I was your servant!

LAVINIA. (*icily*) If you have any consideration for her, you'll do as I say and not force me to write my father. (*She turns her back on him and walks to the steps woodenly erect and square-shouldered.*)

BRANT. (*desperately now—with a grotesque catching at his lover's manner*) I don't know what you mean, Lavinia. I swear before God it is only you I— (*She turns at the top of the steps at this and stares at him with such a passion of hatred that he is silenced. Her lips move as if she were going to speak, but she fights back the words, turns stiffly and goes into the house and closes the door behind her.*)

CURTAIN

ACT TWO

SCENE—*In the house*—EZRA MANNON's *study. No time has elapsed. The study is a large room with a stiff, austere atmosphere. The furniture is old colonial. The walls are plain plastered surfaces tinted a dull gray with a flat white trim. At rear, right, is a door leading to the hall. On the right wall is a painting of George Washington in a gilt frame, flanked by smaller portraits of Alexander Hamilton and John Marshall. At rear, center, is an open fireplace. At left of fireplace, a bookcase filled with law books. Above the fireplace, in a plain frame, is a large portrait of* EZRA MANNON *himself, painted ten years previously. One is at once struck by the startling likeness between him and* ADAM BRANT. *He is a tall man in his early forties, with a spare, wiry frame, seated stiffly in an armchair, his hands on the arms, wearing his black judge's robe. His face is handsome in a stern, aloof fashion. It is cold and emotionless and has the same strange semblance of a lifelike mask that we have already seen in the faces of his wife and daughter and* BRANT.

On the left are two windows. Between them a desk. A large table with an armchair on either side, right and left, stands at left center, front. At right center is another chair. There are hooked rugs on the floor.

Outside the sun is beginning to set and its glow fills the room with a golden mist. As the action progresses this becomes brighter, then turns to crimson, which darkens to somberness at the end.

LAVINIA *is discovered standing by the table. She is fighting to control herself, but her face is torn by a look of stricken anguish. She turns slowly to her father's portrait and for a moment stares at it fixedly. Then she goes to it and puts her hand over one of his hands with a loving, protecting gesture.*

28

LAVINIA. Poor Father! (*She hears a noise in the hall and moves hastily away. The door from the hall is opened and* CHRISTINE *enters. She is uneasy underneath, but affects a scornful indignation.*)

CHRISTINE. Really, this unconfirmed report must have turned your head—otherwise I'd find it difficult to understand your sending Annie to disturb me when you knew I was resting.

LAVINIA. I told you I had to talk to you.

CHRISTINE. (*looking around the room with aversion*) But why in this musty room, of all places?

LAVINIA. (*indicating the portrait—quietly*) Because it's Father's room.

CHRISTINE. (*starts, looks at the portrait and quickly drops her eyes.* LAVINIA *goes to the door and closes it.* CHRISTINE *says with forced scorn*) More mystery?

LAVINIA. You better sit down. (CHRISTINE *sits in the chair at rear center.* LAVINIA *goes back to her father's chair at left of table.*)

CHRISTINE. Well—if you're quite ready, perhaps you will explain.

LAVINIA. I suppose Annie told you I'd been to visit Hazel and Peter while you were away.

CHRISTINE. Yes. I thought it peculiar. You never visit anyone overnight. Why did you suddenly take that notion?

LAVINIA. I didn't.

CHRISTINE. You didn't visit them?

LAVINIA. No.

CHRISTINE. Then where did you go?

LAVINIA. (*accusingly*) To New York! (CHRISTINE *starts.* LAVINIA *hurries on a bit incoherently*) I've suspected something—lately—the excuse you've made for all your trips there the past year, that Grandfather was sick— (*As* CHRISTINE *is about to protest indignantly*) Oh! I know he has been—and you've stayed at his house—but I've suspected lately that wasn't the real reason—and now I can prove it isn't! Because I waited outside Grandfather's house and followed you. I saw you meet Brant!

CHRISTINE. (*alarmed but concealing it—coolly*) Well, what if you did? I told you myself I ran into him by accident—

LAVINIA. You went to his room!

CHRISTINE. (*shaken*) He asked me to meet a friend of his—a lady. It was her house we went to.

LAVINIA. I asked the woman in the basement. He had hired the room under another name, but she recognized his description. And yours too. She said you had come there often in the past year.

CHRISTINE. (*desperately*) It was the first time I had ever been there. He insisted on my going. He said he had to talk to me about you. He wanted my help to approach your father—

LAVINIA. (*furiously*) How can you lie like that? How can you be so vile as to try to use me to hide your adultery?

CHRISTINE. (*springing up—with weak indignation*) Vinnie!

LAVINIA. Your adultery, I said!

CHRISTINE. No!

LAVINIA. Stop lying, I tell you! I went upstairs! I heard you telling him—"I love you, Adam"—and kissing him! (*With a cold bitter fury*) You vile—! You're shameless and evil! Even if you are my mother, I say it! (CHRISTINE *stares at her, overwhelmed by this onslaught, her poise shattered for the moment. She tries to keep her voice indifferent but it trembles a little.*)

CHRISTINE. I—I knew you hated me, Vinnie—but not as bitterly as that! (*Then with a return of her defiant coolness*) Very well! I love Adam Brant. What are you going to do?

LAVINIA. How you say that—without any shame! You don't give one thought to Father—who is so good—who trusts you! Oh, how could you do this to Father? How could you?

CHRISTINE. (*with strident intensity*) You would understand if you were the wife of a man you hated!

LAVINIA. (*horrified—with a glance at the portrait*) Don't! Don't say that—before him! I won't listen!

CHRISTINE. (*grabbing her by the arm*) You will listen! I'm talking to you as a woman now, not as mother to daughter! That relationship has no meaning between us! You've called me vile and shameless! Well, I want you to know that's what I've felt about myself for over twenty years, giving my body to a man I—

LAVINIA. (*trying to break away from her, half putting her hands up to her ears*) Stop telling me such things! Let me go! (*She breaks away, shrinking from her mother with a look of sick repulsion. A pause. She stammers*) You—then you've always hated Father?

CHRISTINE. (*bitterly*) No. I loved him once—before I married him —incredible as that seems now! He was handsome in his lieutenant's uniform! He was silent and mysterious and romantic! But marriage soon turned his romance into—disgust!

LAVINIA. (*wincing again—stammers harshly*) So I was born of your disgust! I've always guessed that, Mother—ever since I was little— when I used to come to you—with love—but you would always push me away! I've felt it ever since I can remember—your disgust! (*Then with a flare-up of bitter hatred*) Oh, I hate you! It's only right I should hate you!

CHRISTINE. (*shaken—defensively*) I tried to love you. I told myself it wasn't human not to love my own child, born of my body. But I never could make myself feel you were born of any body but his! You were always my wedding night to me—and my honeymoon!

LAVINIA. Stop saying that! How can you be so—! (*Then suddenly —with a strange jealous bitterness*) You've loved Orin! Why didn't you hate him, too?

CHRISTINE. Because by then I had forced myself to become resigned in order to live! And most of the time I was carrying him, your father was with the army in Mexico. I had forgotten him. And when Orin was born he seemed my child, only mine, and I loved him for that! (*Bitterly*) I loved him until he let you and your father nag him into the war, in spite of my begging him not to leave me alone. (*Staring at* LAVINIA *with hatred*) I know his leaving me was your doing principally, Vinnie!

31

LAVINIA. (*sternly*) It was his duty as a Mannon to go! He'd have been sorry the rest of his life if he hadn't! I love him better than you! I was thinking of him!

CHRISTINE. Well, I hope you realize I never would have fallen in love with Adam if I'd had Orin with me. When he had gone there was nothing left—but hate and a desire to be revenged—and a longing for love! And it was then I met Adam. I saw he loved me—

LAVINIA. (*with taunting scorn*) He doesn't love you! You're only his revenge on Father! Do you know who he really is? He's the son of that low nurse girl Grandfather put out of our house!

CHRISTINE. (*concealing a start—coolly*) So you've found that out? Were you hoping it would be a crushing surprise to me? I've known it all along. He told me when he said he loved me.

LAVINIA. Oh! And I suppose knowing who he was gave you all the more satisfaction—to add that disgrace!

CHRISTINE. (*cuttingly*) Will you kindly come to the point and tell me what you intend doing? I suppose you'll hardly let your father get in the door before you tell him!

LAVINIA. (*suddenly becoming rigid and cold again—slowly*) No. Not unless you force me to. (*Then as she sees her mother's astonishment—grimly*) I don't wonder you're surprised! You know you deserve the worst punishment you could get. And Father would disown you publicly, no matter how much the scandal cost him!

CHRISTINE. I realize that. I know him even better than you do!

LAVINIA. And I'd like to see you punished for your wickedness! So please understand this isn't for your sake. It's for Father's. He hasn't been well lately. I'm not going to have him hurt! It's my first duty to protect him from you!

CHRISTINE. I know better than to expect any generosity on my account.

LAVINIA. I won't tell him, provided you give up Brant and never see him again—and promise to be a dutiful wife to Father and make up for the wrong you've done him!

32

CHRISTINE. (*stares at her daughter—a pause—then she laughs dryly*) What a fraud you are, with your talk of your father and your duty! Oh, I'm not denying you want to save his pride—and I know how anxious you are to keep the family from more scandal! But all the same, that's not your real reason for sparing me!

LAVINIA. (*confused—guiltily*) It is!

CHRISTINE. You wanted Adam Brant yourself!

LAVINIA. That's a lie!

CHRISTINE. And now you know you can't have him, you're determined that at least you'll take him from me!

LAVINIA. No!

CHRISTINE. But if you told your father, I'd have to go away with Adam. He'd be mine still. You can't bear that thought, even at the price of my disgrace, can you?

LAVINIA. It's your evil mind!

CHRISTINE. I know you, Vinnie! I've watched you ever since you were little, trying to do exactly what you're doing now! You've tried to become the wife of your father and the mother of Orin! You've always schemed to steal my place!

LAVINIA. (*wildly*) No! It's you who have stolen all love from me since the time I was born! (*Then her manner becoming threatening*) But I don't want to listen to any more of your lies and excuses! I want to know right now whether you're going to do what I told you or not!

CHRISTINE. Suppose I refuse! Suppose I go off openly with Adam! Where will you and your father and the family name be after that scandal? And what if I were disgraced myself? I'd have the man I love, at least!

LAVINIA. (*grimly*) Not for long! Father would use all his influence and get Brant blacklisted so he'd lose his command and never get another! You know how much the "Flying Trades" means to him. And Father would never divorce you. You could never marry. You'd be an anchor around his neck. Don't forget you're five years older

33

than he is! He'll still be in his prime when you're an old woman with all your looks gone! He'd grow to hate the sight of you!

CHRISTINE. (*stung beyond bearing—makes a threatening move as if to strike her daughter's face*) You devil! You mean little—! (*But* LAVINIA *stares back coldly into her eyes and she controls herself and drops her hand.*)

LAVINIA. I wouldn't call names if I were you! There is one you deserve!

CHRISTINE. (*turning away—her voice still trembling*) I'm a fool to let you make me lose my temper—over your jealous spite! (*A pause.* LAVINIA *stares at her.* CHRISTINE *seems considering something. A sinister expression comes to her face. Then she turns back to* LAVINIA—*coldly*) But you wanted my answer, didn't you? Well, I agree to do as you said. I promise you I'll never see Adam again after he calls this evening. Are you satisfied?

LAVINIA. (*stares at her with cold suspicion*) You seem to take giving him up pretty easily!

CHRISTINE. (*hastily*) Do you think I'll ever give you the satisfaction of seeing me grieve? Oh, no, Vinnie! You'll never have a chance to gloat!

LAVINIA. (*still suspiciously—with a touch of scorn*) If I loved anyone—!

CHRISTINE. (*tauntingly*) If? I think you do love him—as much as you can love! (*With a sudden flurry of jealousy*) You little fool! Don't you know I made him flirt with you, so you wouldn't be suspicious?

LAVINIA. (*gives a little shudder—then fiercely*) He didn't fool me! I saw what a liar he was! I just led him on—to find out things! I always hated him! (CHRISTINE *smiles mockingly and turns away, as if to go out of the room.* LAVINIA'S *manner becomes threatening again*) Wait! I don't trust you! I know you're thinking already how you can fool me and break the promise you've just made! But you better not try it! I'll be watching you every minute! And I won't be the only

34

one! I wrote to Father and Orin as soon as I got back from New York!

CHRISTINE. (*startled*) About Adam?

LAVINIA. Only enough so they'd be suspicious and watch you too. I said a Captain Brant had been calling and folks had begun to gossip.

CHRISTINE. Ah! I see what it's going to mean—that you'll always have this to hold over me and I'll be under your thumb for the rest of my life! (*She cannot restrain her rage—threateningly*) Take care, Vinnie! You'll be responsible if—! (*She checks herself abruptly.*)

LAVINIA. (*suspiciously*) If what?

CHRISTINE. (*quickly*) Nothing. I only meant if I went off with Adam. But of course you know I won't do that. You know there's nothing I can do now—but obey your orders!

LAVINIA. (*continues to stare at her suspiciously—grimly*) You ought to see it's your duty to Father, not my orders—if you had any honor or decency! (*Then brusquely*) Brant is waiting outside. You can tell him what you've got to do—and tell him if he ever dares come here again—! (*Forcing back her anger*) And see that you get rid of him right now! I'm going upstreet to get the latest news. I won't be gone more than a half-hour and I want him out of the house by the time I get back, do you hear? If he isn't, I'll write Father again. I won't even wait for him to come home! (*She turns her back on her mother and marches out the door, square-shouldered and stiff, without a backward glance.* CHRISTINE *looks after her, waiting until she hears the side door of the house close after her. Then she turns and stands in tense calculating thought. Her face has become like a sinister evil mask. Finally, as if making up her mind irrevocably, she comes to the table, tears off a slip of paper and writes two words on it. She tucks this paper in the sleeve of her dress and goes to the open window and calls.*)

CHRISTINE. Adam! (*She moves toward the door to wait for him. Her eyes are caught by the eyes of her husband in the portrait over the fireplace. She stares at him with hatred and addresses him vindictively, half under her breath*) You can thank Vinnie, Ezra! (*She *goes to the door and reaches it just as* BRANT *appears from the hall. She takes his hand and draws him into the room, closing the door behind him. One is immediately struck by the resemblance between his face and that of the portrait of* EZRA MANNON.)

BRANT. (*glancing uneasily at her, as they come to the center of the room*) She knows—?

CHRISTINE. Yes. She followed me to New York. And she's found out who you are too, Adam.

BRANT. (*with a grim smile*) I know. She got that out of me—the proof of it, at any rate. Before I knew what was up I'd given myself away.

CHRISTINE. She must have noticed your resemblance to Orin. I was afraid that might start her thinking.

BRANT. (*sees the portrait for the first time. Instantly his body shifts to a fighting tenseness. It is as if he were going to spring at the figure in the painting. He says slowly*) That, I take it, is General Mannon?

CHRISTINE. Judge Mannon then. Don't forget he used to be a judge. He won't forget it.

BRANT. (*his eyes still fixed on the portrait—comes and sits in* MANNON's *chair on the left of table. Unconsciously he takes the same attitude as* MANNON, *sitting erect, his hands on the arms of the chair— slowly*) Does Orin by any chance resemble his father?

CHRISTINE. (*stares at him—agitatedly*) No! Of course not! What put such a stupid idea in your head?

BRANT. It would be damned queer if you fell in love with me because I recalled Ezra Mannon to you!

CHRISTINE. (*going to him and putting an arm around his shoulder*) No, no, I tell you! It was Orin you made me think of! It was Orin!

BRANT. I remember that night we were introduced and I heard the name Mrs. Ezra Mannon! By God, how I hated you then for being his! I thought, by God, I'll take her from him and that'll be part of my revenge! And out of that hatred my love came! It's damned queer, isn't it?

CHRISTINE. (*hugging him to her*) Are you going to let him take me from you now, Adam?

BRANT. (*passionately*) You ask that!

CHRISTINE. You swear you won't—no matter what you must do?

BRANT. By God, I swear it!

CHRISTINE. (*kisses him*) Remember that oath! (*She glances at the portrait—then turns back to* BRANT *with a little shiver—nervously*) What made you sit there? It's his chair. I've so often seen him sitting there— (*Forcing a little laugh*) Your silly talk about resemblances— Don't sit there. Come. Bring that chair over here. (*She moves to the chair at right center. He brings the chair at right of table close to hers.*)

BRANT. We've got to decide what we must do. The time for skulking and lying is over—and by God I'm glad of it! It's a coward's game I have no stomach for! (*He has placed the chair beside hers. She is staring at the portrait*) Why don't you sit down, Christine?

CHRISTINE. (*slowly*) I was thinking—perhaps we had better go to the sitting-room. (*Then defiantly*) No! I've been afraid of you long enough, Ezra! (*She sits down.*)

BRANT. I felt there was something wrong the moment I saw her. I tried my damndest to put her off the course by giving her some soft soap—as you'd told me to do to blind her. (*Frowning*) That was a mistake, Christine. It made her pay too much attention to me—and opened her eyes!

CHRISTINE. Oh, I know I've made one blunder after another. It's as if love drove me on to do everything I shouldn't. I never should have brought you to this house. Seeing you in New York should have been enough for me. But I loved you too much. I wanted you every possible moment we could steal! And I simply couldn't believe that he ever would come home. I prayed that he should be killed in the war so intensely that I finally believed it would surely happen! (*With savage intensity*) Oh, if he were only dead!

BRANT. That chance is finished now.

CHRISTINE. (*slowly—without looking at him*) Yes—in that way.

37

BRANT. (*stares at her*) What do you mean? (*She remains silent. He changes the subject uneasily*) There's only one thing to do! When he comes home I'll wait for him and not give Vinnie the satisfaction of telling him. I'll tell him myself. (*Vindictively*) By God! I'd give my soul to see his face when he knows you love Marie Brantôme's son! And then I'll take you away openly and laugh at him! And if he tries to stop me—! (*He stops and glances with savage hatred at the portrait.*)

CHRISTINE. What would you do then?

BRANT. If ever I laid hands on him, I'd kill him!

CHRISTINE. And then? You would be hanged for murder! And where would I be? There would be nothing left for me but to kill myself!

BRANT. If I could catch him alone, where no one would interfere, and let the best man come out alive—as I've often seen it done in the West!

CHRISTINE. This isn't the West.

BRANT. I could insult him on the street before everyone and make him fight me! I could let him shoot first and then kill him in self-defense.

CHRISTINE. (*scornfully*) Do you imagine you could force him to fight a duel with you? Don't you know duelling is illegal? Oh, no! He'd simply feel bound to do his duty as a former judge and have you arrested! (*She adds calculatingly, seeing he is boiling inside*) It would be a poor revenge for your mother's death to let him make you a laughingstock!

BRANT. But when I take you off, the laugh will be on him! You can come on the "Flying Trades."

CHRISTINE. (*calculatingly reproachful*) I don't think you'd propose that, Adam, if you stopped thinking of your revenge for a moment and thought of me! Don't you realize he would never divorce me, out of spite? What would I be in the world's eyes? My life would be ruined and I would ruin yours! You'd grow to hate me!

38

BRANT. (*passionately*) Don't talk like that! It's a lie and you know it!

CHRISTINE. (*with bitter yearning*) If I could only believe that, Adam! But I'll grow old so soon! And I'm afraid of time! (*Then abruptly changing tone*) As for my sailing on your ship, you'll find you won't have a ship! He'll see to it you lose this command and get you blacklisted so you'll have no chance of getting another.

BRANT. (*angrily*) Aye! He can do that if he sets about it. There are twice as many skippers as ships these days.

CHRISTINE. (*calculatingly—without looking at him*) If he had only been killed, we could be married now and I would bring you my share of the Mannon estate. That would only be justice. It's yours by right. It's what his father stole from yours.

BRANT. That's true enough, damn him!

CHRISTINE. You wouldn't have to worry about commands or owners' favors then. You could buy your own ship and be your own master!

BRANT. (*yearningly*) That's always been my dream—some day to own my own clipper! And Clark and Dawson would be willing to sell the "Flying Trades." (*Then forgetting everything in his enthusiasm*) You've seen her, Christine. She's as beautiful a ship as you're a woman. Aye, the two of you are like sisters. If she was mine, I'd take you on a honeymoon then! To China—and on the voyage back, we'd stop at the South Pacific Islands I've told you about. By God, there's the right place for love and a honeymoon!

CHRISTINE. (*slowly*) Yes—but Ezra is alive!

BRANT. (*brought back to earth—gloomily*) I know it's only a dream.

CHRISTINE. (*turning to stare at him—slowly*) You can have your dream—and I can have mine. There is a way. (*Then turning away again*) You remember my telling you he had written complaining of pains about his heart?

BRANT. You're surely not hoping—

CHRISTINE. No. He said it was nothing serious. But I've let it be known that he has heart trouble. I went to see our old family doctor and told him about Ezra's letter. I pretended to be dreadfully worried, until I got him worried too. He's the town's worst old gossip. I'm sure everyone knows about Ezra's weak heart by this time.

BRANT. What are you driving at, Christine?

CHRISTINE. Something I've been thinking of ever since I realized he might soon come home. And now that Vinnie—but even if we didn't have to consider her, it'd be the only way! I couldn't fool him long. He's a strange, hidden man. His silence always creeps into my thoughts. Even if he never spoke, I would feel what was in his mind and some night, lying beside him, it would drive me mad and I'd have to kill his silence by screaming out the truth! (*She has been staring before her—now she suddenly turns on* BRANT—*slowly*) If he died suddenly now, no one would think it was anything but heart failure. I've been reading a book in Father's medical library. I saw it there one day a few weeks ago—it was as if some fate in me forced me to see it! (*She reaches in the sleeve of her dress and takes out the slip of paper she had written on*) I've written something here. I want you to get it for me. (*His fingers close on it mechanically. He stares at it with a strange stupid dread. She hurries on so as not to give him time for reflection*) The work on the "Flying Trades" is all finished, isn't it? You sail to Boston tomorrow, to wait for cargo?

BRANT. (*dully*) Aye.

CHRISTINE. Get this at some druggist's down by the waterfront the minute you reach there. You can make up some story about a sick dog on your ship. As soon as you get it, mail it to me here. I'll be on the lookout, so Vinnie will never know it came. Then you must wait on the "Flying Trades" until you hear from me or I come to you— afterward!

BRANT. (*dully*) But how can you do it—so no one will suspect?

CHRISTINE. He's taking medicine. I'll give him his medicine. Oh, I've planned it carefully.

BRANT. But—if he dies suddenly, won't Vinnie—

CHRISTINE. There'll be no reason for her to suspect. She's worried

40

already about his heart. Besides, she may hate me, but she would never think—

BRANT. Orin will be coming home, too.

CHRISTINE. Orin will believe anything I want him to. As for the people here, they'd never dream of such a thing in the Mannon house! And the sooner I do it, the less suspicion there'll be! They will think the excitement of coming home and the reaction were too much for his weak heart! Doctor Blake will think so. I'll see that's what he thinks.

BRANT. (*harshly*) Poison! It's a coward's trick!

CHRISTINE. (*with fierce scorn now, seeing the necessity of goading him*) Do you think you would be braver to give me up to him and let him take away your ship?

BRANT. No!

CHRISTINE. Didn't you say you wanted to kill him?

BRANT. Aye! But I'd give him his chance!

CHRISTINE. Did he give your mother her chance?

BRANT. (*aroused*) No, damn him!

CHRISTINE. Then what makes you suddenly so scrupulous about his death? (*With a sneer*) It must be the Mannon in you coming out! Are you going to prove, the first time your love is put to a real test, that you're a weak coward like your father?

BRANT. Christine! If it was any man said that to me—!

CHRISTINE. (*passionately*) Have you thought of this side of his homecoming—that he's coming back to my bed? If you love me as much as you claim, I should think that would rid you of any scruples! If it was a question of some woman taking you from me, I wouldn't have qualms about which was or wasn't the way to kill her! (*More tauntingly*) But perhaps your love has been only a lie you told me— to take the sneaking revenge on him of being a backstairs lover! Perhaps—

BRANT. (*stung, grabbing her by the shoulders—fiercely*) Stop it! I'll do anything you want! You know it! (*Then with a change to somber grimness—putting the paper in his pocket*) And you're right. I'm a damn fool to have any feeling about how Ezra Mannon dies!

CHRISTINE. (*a look of exultant satisfaction comes to her face as she sees he is definitely won over now. She throws her arms around him and kisses him passionately*) Ah! Now you're the man I love again, not a hypocritical Mannon! Promise me, no more cowardly romantic scruples! Promise me!

BRANT. I promise. (*The boom of a cannon sounds from the fort that guards the harbor. He and* CHRISTINE *start frightenedly and stand staring at each other. Another boom comes, reverberating, rattling the windows.* CHRISTINE *recovers herself.*)

CHRISTINE. You hear? That's the salute to his homecoming! (*She kisses him—with fierce insistence*) Remember your mother's death! Remember your dream of your own ship! Above all, remember you'll have me!—all your own—your wife! (*Then urgently*) And now you must go! She'll be coming back—and you're not good at hiding your thoughts. (*Urging him toward the door*) Hurry! I don't want you to meet her! (*The cannon at the fort keep booming at regular intervals until the end of the scene.* BRANT *goes out in the hall and a moment later the front door is heard closing after him.* CHRISTINE *hurries from the door to the window and watches him from behind the curtains as he goes down the drive. She is in a state of tense, exultant excitement. Then, as if an idea had suddenly come to her, she speaks to his retreating figure with a strange sinister air of elation*) You'll never dare leave me now, Adam—for your ships or your sea or your naked Island girls—when I grow old and ugly! (*She turns back from the window. Her eyes are caught by the eyes of her husband in the portrait and for a moment she stares back into them, as if fascinated. Then she jerks her glance away and, with a little shudder she cannot repress, turns and walks quickly from the room and closes the door behind her.*)

CURTAIN

ACT THREE

Scene—*The same as Act One, Scene One—exterior of the Mannon house. It is around nine o'clock of a night a week later. The light of a half moon falls on the house, giving it an unreal, detached, eerie quality. The pure white temple front seems more than ever like an incongruous mask fixed on the somber stone house. All the shutters are closed. The white columns of the portico cast black bars of shadow on the gray wall behind them. The trunk of the pine at right is an ebony pillar, its branches a mass of shade.*

Lavinia is sitting on the top of the steps to the portico. She is dressed, as before, severely in black. Her thin figure, seated stiffly upright, arms against her sides, the legs close together, the shoulders square, the head upright, is like that of an Egyptian statue. She is staring straight before her. The sound of Seth's thin, aged baritone mournfully singing the chanty "Shenandoah" is heard from down the drive, off right front. He is approaching the house and the song draws quickly nearer:

> "Oh, Shenandoah, I long to hear you
> A-way, my rolling river.
> Oh, Shenandoah, I can't get near you
> Way-ay, I'm bound away
> Across the wide Missouri.

> "Oh, Shenandoah, I love your daughter
> A-way, my rolling river."

He enters right front. He is a bit drunk but holding his liquor well. He walks up by the lilacs starting the next line "Oh, Shenandoah"— then suddenly sees Lavinia on the steps and stops abruptly, a bit sheepish.

43

LAVINIA. (*disapprovingly*) This is the second time this week I've caught you coming home like this.

SETH. (*unabashed, approaches the steps—with a grin*) I'm aimin' to do my patriotic duty, Vinnie. The first time was celebratin' Lee's surrender and this time is drownin' my sorrow for the President gittin' shot! And the third'll be when your Paw gits home!

LAVINIA. Father might arrive tonight.

SETH. Gosh, Vinnie, I never calc'lated he could git here so soon!

LAVINIA. Evidently you didn't. He'd give you fits if he caught you drunk. Oh, I don't believe he'll come, but it's possible he might.

SETH. (*is evidently trying to pull himself together. He suddenly leans over toward her and, lowering his voice, asks soberly*) Did you find out anything about that Brant?

LAVINIA. (*sharply*) Yes. There's no connection. It was just a silly idea of yours.

SETH. (*stares at her—then understandingly*) Wal, if you want it left that way. I'll leave it that way. (*A pause. He continues to stand looking at her, while she stares in front of her.*)

LAVINIA. (*in a low voice*) What was that Marie Brantôme like, Seth?

SETH. Marie? She was always laughin' and singin'—frisky and full of life—with something free and wild about her like an animile. Purty she was, too! (*Then he adds*) Hair just the color of your Maw's and yourn she had.

LAVINIA. I know.

SETH. Oh, everyone took to Marie—couldn't help it. Even your Paw. He was only a boy then, but he was crazy about her, too, like a youngster would be. His mother was stern with him, while Marie, she made a fuss over him and petted him.

LAVINIA. Father, too!

SETH. Ayeh—but he hated her worse than anyone when it got found out she was his Uncle David's fancy woman.

LAVINIA. (*in a low voice, as if to herself, staring at the house*) It's all so strange! It frightens me! (*She checks herself abruptly—turns to*

SETH, *curtly*) I don't believe that about Father. You've had too much whiskey. Go to bed and sleep it off. (*She walks up the steps again.*)

SETH. (*gazes at her with understanding*) Ayeh. (*Then warningly, making a surreptitious signal as he sees the front door opening behind her*) Ssstt! (CHRISTINE *appears outlined in the light from the hall. She is dressed in a gown of green velvet that sets off her hair. The light behind her glows along the edges of the dress and in the color of her hair. She closes the door and comes into the moonlight at the edge of the steps, standing above and a little to the right of* LAVINIA. *The moonlight, falling full on them, accentuates strangely the resemblance between their faces and at the same time the hostile dissimilarity in body and dress.* LAVINIA *does not turn or give any sign of knowing her mother is behind her. There is a second's uncomfortable silence.* SETH *moves off left*) Wal, I'll trot along! (*He disappears around the corner of the house. There is a pause. Then* CHRISTINE *speaks in a dry mocking tone.*)

CHRISTINE. What are you moongazing at? Puritan maidens shouldn't peer too inquisitively into Spring! Isn't beauty an abomination and love a vile thing? (*She laughs with bitter mockery—then tauntingly*) Why don't you marry Peter? You don't want to be left an old maid, do you?

LAVINIA. (*quietly*) You needn't hope to get rid of me that way. I'm not marrying anyone. I've got my duty to Father.

CHRISTINE. Duty! How often I've heard that word in this house! Well, you can't say I didn't do mine all these years. But there comes an end.

LAVINIA. (*grimly*) And there comes another end—and you must do your duty again!

CHRISTINE. (*starts as if to retort defiantly—then says calmly*) Yes, I realize that.

LAVINIA. (*after a pause—suspiciously*) What's going on at the bottom of your mind? I know you're plotting something!

CHRISTINE. (*controlling a start*) Don't be stupid, please!

45

LAVINIA. Are you planning how you can see Adam again? You better not!

CHRISTINE. (*calmly*) I'm not so foolish. I said good-bye once. Do you think I want to make it harder for myself?

LAVINIA. Has it been hard for you? I'd never guess it—and I've been watching you.

CHRISTINE. I warned you you would have no chance to gloat! (*After a pause*) When do you expect your father home? You want me to play my part well when he comes, don't you?—for his sake. I'd like to be forewarned.

LAVINIA. His letter said he wouldn't wait until his brigade was disbanded but would try to get leave at once. He might arrive tonight—or tomorrow—or the next day. I don't know.

CHRISTINE. You think he might come tonight? (*Then with a mocking smile*) So he's the beau you're waiting for in the spring moonlight! (*Then after a pause*) But the night train got in long ago.

LAVINIA. (*glances down the drive, left front—then starts to her feet excitedly*) Here's someone! (CHRISTINE *slowly rises. There is the sound of footsteps. A moment later Ezra Mannon enters from left, front. He stops short in the shadow for a second and stands, erect and stiff, as if at attention, staring at his house, his wife and daughter. He is a tall, spare, big-boned man of fifty, dressed in the uniform of a Brigadier-General. One is immediately struck by the mask-like look of his face in repose, more pronounced in him than in the others. He is exactly like the portrait in his study, which we have seen in Act Two, except that his face is more lined and lean and the hair and beard are grizzled. His movements are exact and wooden and he has a mannerism of standing and sitting in stiff, posed attitudes that suggest the statues of military heroes. When he speaks, his deep voice has a hollow repressed quality, as if he were continually withholding emotion from it. His air is brusque and authoritative.*)

LAVINIA. (*seeing the man's figure stop in the shadow—calls excitedly*) Who's that?

46

MANNON. (*stepping forward into the moonlight*) It's I.

LAVINIA. (*with a cry of joy*) Father! (*She runs to him and throws her arms around him and kisses him*) Oh, Father! (*She bursts into tears and hides her face against his shoulder.*)

MANNON. (*embarrassed—patting her head—gruffly*) Come! I thought I'd taught you never to cry.

LAVINIA. (*obediently forcing back her tears*) I'm sorry, Father—but I'm so happy!

MANNON. (*awkwardly moved*) Tears are queer tokens of happiness! But I appreciate your—your feeling.

CHRISTINE. (*has slowly descended the steps, her eyes fixed on him—tensely*) Is it really you, Ezra? We had just given up hope of your coming tonight.

MANNON. (*going stiffly to meet her*) Train was late. The railroad is jammed up. Everybody has got leave. (*He meets her at the foot of the steps and kisses her with a chill dignity—formally*) I am glad to see you, Christine. You are looking well. (*He steps back and stares at her—then in a voice that betrays a deep undercurrent of suppressed feeling*) You have changed, somehow. You are prettier than ever— But you always were pretty.

CHRISTINE. (*forcing a light tone*) Compliments from one's husband! How gallant you've become, Ezra! (*Then solicitously*) You must be terribly tired. Wouldn't you like to sit here on the steps for a while? The moonlight is so beautiful.

LAVINIA. (*who has been hovering about jealously, now manages to worm herself between them—sharply*) No. It's too damp out here. And Father must be hungry. (*Taking his arm*) Come inside with me and I'll get you something to eat. You poor dear! You must be starved.

MANNON. (*really revelling in his daughter's coddling but embarrassed before his wife—pulling his arm back—brusquely*) No, thanks! I would rather rest here for a spell. Sit down, Vinnie. (CHRISTINE *sits on the top step at center; he sits on the middle step at right;* LAVINIA

47

on the lowest step at left. While they are doing this he keeps on talking in his abrupt sentences, as if he were trying to cover up some hidden uneasiness) I've got leave for a few days. Then I must go back and disband my brigade. Peace ought to be signed soon. The President's assassination is a frightful calamity. But it can't change the course of events.

LAVINIA. Poor man! It's dreadful he should die just at his moment of victory.

MANNON. Yes! (*Then after a pause—somberly*) All victory ends in the defeat of death. That's sure. But does defeat end in the victory of death? That's what I wonder! (*They both stare at him,* LAVINIA *in surprise,* CHRISTINE *in uneasy wonder. A pause.*)

CHRISTINE. Where is Orin? Couldn't you get leave for him too?

MANNON. (*hesitates—then brusquely*) I've been keeping it from you. Orin was wounded.

LAVINIA. Wounded! You don't mean—badly hurt?

CHRISTINE. (*half starting to her feet impulsively—with more of angry bitterness than grief*) I knew it! I knew when you forced him into your horrible war—! (*Then sinking back—tensely*) You needn't trouble to break the news gradually, Ezra. Orin is dead, isn't he?

LAVINIA. Don't say that! It isn't true, is it, Father?

MANNON. (*curtly—a trace of jealousy in his tone*) Of course it isn't! If your mother would permit me to finish instead of jumping at conclusions about her baby—! (*With a grim, proud satisfaction*) He's no baby now. I've made a man of him. He did one of the bravest things I've seen in the war. He was wounded in the head—a close shave but it turned out only a scratch. But he got brain fever from the shock. He's all right now. He was in a rundown condition, they say at the hospital. I never guessed it. Nerves. I wouldn't notice nerves. He's always been restless. (*Half turning to* CHRISTINE) He gets that from you.

CHRISTINE. When will he be well enough to come home?

MANNON. Soon. The doctor advised a few more days' rest. He's still

48

weak. He was out of his head for a long time. Acted as if he were a little boy again. Seemed to think you were with him. That is, he kept talking to "Mother."

CHRISTINE. (*with a tense intake of breath*) Ah!

LAVINIA. (*pityingly—with a tinge of scorn in her voice*) Poor Orin!

MANNON. I don't want you to baby him when he comes home, Christine. It would be bad for him to get tied to your apron strings again.

CHRISTINE. You needn't worry. That passed—when he left me. (*Another pause. Then* LAVINIA *speaks.*)

LAVINIA. How is the trouble with your heart, Father? I've been so afraid you might be making it out less serious than it really was to keep us from worrying.

MANNON. (*gruffly*) If it was serious, I'd tell you, so you'd be prepared. If you'd seen as much of death as I have in the past four years, you wouldn't be afraid of it. (*Suddenly jumping to his feet—brusquely*) Let's change the subject! I've had my fill of death. What I want now is to forget it. (*He turns and paces up and down to the right of steps.* LAVINIA *watches him worriedly*) All I know is the pain is like a knife. It puts me out of commission while it lasts. The doctor gave me orders to avoid worry or any over-exertion or excitement.

CHRISTINE. (*staring at him*) You don't look well. But probably that's because you're so tired. You must go to bed soon, Ezra.

MANNON. (*comes to a stop in his pacing directly before her and looks into her eyes—a pause—then he says in a voice that he tries to make ordinary*) Yes, I want to—soon.

LAVINIA. (*who has been watching him jealously—suddenly pulling him by the arm—with a childish volubility*) No! Not yet! Please, Father! You've only just come! We've hardly talked at all! (*Defiantly to her mother*) How can you tell him he looks tired? He looks as well as I've ever seen him. (*Then to her father with a vindictive look at Christine*) We've so much to tell you. All about Captain Brant. (*If she had expected her mother to flinch at this, she is dis-*

49

appointed. CHRISTINE *is prepared and remains unmoved beneath the searching, suspicious glance Mannon now directs at her.*)

MANNON. Vinnie wrote me you'd had company. I never heard of him. What business had he here?

CHRISTINE. (*with an easy smile*) You had better ask Vinnie! He's her latest beau! She even went walking in the moonlight with him!

LAVINIA. (*with a gasp at being defied so brazenly*) Oh!

MANNON. (*now jealous and suspicious of his daughter*) I notice you didn't mention that in your letter, young lady!

LAVINIA. I only went walking once with him—and that was before— (*She checks herself abruptly.*)

MANNON. Before what?

LAVINIA. Before I knew he's the kind who chases after every woman he sees.

MANNON. (*angrily to* CHRISTINE) A fine guest to receive in my absence!

LAVINIA. I believe he even thought Mother was flirting with him. That's why I felt it my duty to write you. You know how folks in town gossip, Father. I thought you ought to warn Mother she was foolish to allow him to come here.

MANNON. Foolish! It was downright—!

CHRISTINE. (*coldly*) I would prefer not to discuss this until we are alone, Ezra—if you don't mind! And I think Vinnie is extremely inconsiderate the moment you're home—to annoy you with such ridiculous nonsense! (*She turns to* LAVINIA) I think you've done enough mischief. Will you kindly leave us?

LAVINIA. No.

MANNON. (*sharply*) Stop your squabbling, both of you! I hoped you had grown out of that nonsense! I won't have it in my house!

LAVINIA. (*obediently*) Yes, Father.

MANNON. It must be your bedtime, Vinnie.

LAVINIA. Yes, Father. (*She comes and kisses him—excitedly*) Oh,

I'm so happy you're here! Don't let Mother make you believe I— You're the only man I'll ever love! I'm going to stay with you!

MANNON. (*patting her hair—with gruff tenderness*) I hope so. I want you to remain my little girl—for a while longer, at least. (*Then suddenly catching* CHRISTINE's *scornful glance—pushes* LAVINIA *away—brusquely*) March now!

LAVINIA. Yes, Father. (*She goes up the steps past her mother without a look. Behind her mother, in the portico, she stops and turns*) Don't let anything worry you, Father. I'll always take care of you. (*She goes in.* MANNON *looks at his wife who stares before her. He clears his throat as if about to say something—then starts pacing self-consciously up and down at the right of steps.*)

CHRISTINE. (*forcing a gentle tone*) Sit down, Ezra. You will only make yourself more tired, keeping on your feet. (*He sits awkwardly two steps below her, on her left, turned sideways to face her. She asks with disarming simplicity*) Now please tell me just what it is you suspect me of?

MANNON. (*taken aback*) What makes you think I suspect you?

CHRISTINE. Everything! I've felt your distrust from the moment you came. Your eyes have been probing me, as if you were a judge again and I were the prisoner.

MANNON. (*guiltily*) I—?

CHRISTINE. And all on account of a stupid letter Vinnie had no business to write. It seems to me a late day, when I am an old woman with grown-up children, to accuse me of flirting with a stupid ship captain!

MANNON. (*impressed and relieved—placatingly*) There's no question of accusing you of that. I only think you've been foolish to give the gossips a chance to be malicious.

CHRISTINE. Are you sure that's all you have in your heart against me?

MANNON. Yes! Of course! What else? (*Patting her hand embarrassedly*) We'll say no more about it. (*Then he adds gruffly*) But I'd like you to explain how this Brant happened—

51

CHRISTINE. I'm only too glad to! I met him at Father's. Father has taken a fancy to him for some reason. So when he called here I couldn't be rude, could I? I hinted that his visits weren't welcome, but men of his type don't understand hints. But he's only been here four times in all, I think. And as for there having been gossip, that's nonsense! The only talk has been that he came to court Vinnie! You can ask anyone in town.

MANNON. Damn his impudence! It was your duty to tell him flatly he wasn't wanted!

CHRISTINE. (*forcing a contrite air*) Well, I must confess I didn't mind his coming as much as I might have—for one reason. He always brought me news of Father. Father's been sick for the past year, as I wrote you. (*Then with a twitch of the lips, as if she were restraining a derisive smile*) You can't realize what a strain I've been under—worrying about Father and Orin and—you.

MANNON. (*deeply moved, turns to her and takes her hand in both of his—awkwardly*) Christine—I deeply regret—having been unjust. (*He kisses her hand impulsively—then embarrassed by this show of emotion, adds in a gruff, joking tone*) Afraid old Johnny Reb would pick me off, were you?

CHRISTINE. (*controlling a wild impulse to burst into derisive laughter*) Do you need to ask that? (*A pause. He stares at her, fascinated and stirred.*)

MANNON. (*finally blurts out*) I've dreamed of coming home to you, Christine! (*Leans toward her, his voice trembling with desire and a feeling of strangeness and awe—touching her hair with an awkward caress*) You're beautiful! You look more beautiful than ever—and strange to me. I don't know you. You're younger. I feel like an old man beside you. Only your hair is the same—your strange beautiful hair I always—

CHRISTINE. (*with a start of repulsion, shrinking from his hand*) Don't! (*Then as he turns away, hurt and resentful at this rebuff—hastily*) I'm sorry, Ezra. I didn't mean—I—I'm nervous tonight.

(MANNON *paces to the right and stands looking at the trees.* CHRISTINE *stares at his back with hatred. She sighs with affected weariness and leans back and closes her eyes.*)

CHRISTINE. I'm tired, Ezra.

MANNON. (*blurts out*) I shouldn't have bothered you with that foolishness about Brant tonight. (*He forces a strained smile*) But I was jealous a mite, to tell you the truth. (*He forces himself to turn and, seeing her eyes are shut, suddenly comes and leans over her awkwardly, as if to kiss her, then is stopped by some strangeness he feels about her still face.*)

CHRISTINE. (*feeling his desire and instinctively shrinking—without opening her eyes*) Why do you look at me like that?

MANNON. (*turns away guiltily*) Like what? (*Uneasily*) How do you know? Your eyes are shut. (*Then, as if some burden of depression were on him that he had to throw off, he blurts out heavily*) I can't get used to home yet. It's so lonely. I've got used to the feel of camps with thousands of men around me at night—a sense of protection, maybe! (*Suddenly uneasy again*) Don't keep your eyes shut like that! Don't be so still! (*Then, as she opens her eyes—with an explosive appeal*) God, I want to talk to you, Christine! I've got to explain some things—inside me—to my wife—try to, anyway! (*He sits down beside her*) Shut your eyes again! I can talk better. It has always been hard for me to talk—about feelings. I never could when you looked at me. Your eyes were always so—so full of silence! That is, since we've been married. Not before, when I was courting you. They used to speak then. They made me talk—because they answered.

CHRISTINE. (*her eyes closed—tensely*) Don't talk, Ezra.

MANNON. (*as if he had determined, once started, to go on doggedly without heeding any interruption*) It was seeing death all the time in this war got me to thinking these things. Death was so common, it didn't mean anything. That freed me to think of life. Queer, isn't it? Death made me think of life. Before that life had only made me think of death!

53

CHRISTINE. (*without opening her eyes*) Why are you talking of death?

MANNON. That's always been the Mannons' way of thinking. They went to the white meeting-house on Sabbaths and meditated on death. Life was a dying. Being born was starting to die. Death was being born. (*Shaking his head with a dogged bewilderment*) How in hell people ever got such notions! That white meeting-house. It stuck in my mind—clean-scrubbed and whitewashed—a temple of death! But in this war I've seen too many white walls splattered with blood that counted no more than dirty water. I've seen dead men scattered about, no more important than rubbish to be got rid of. That made the white meeting-house seem meaningless—making so much solemn fuss over death!

CHRISTINE. (*opens her eyes and stares at him with a strange terror*) What has this talk of death to do with me?

MANNON. (*avoiding her glance—insistently*) Shut your eyes again. Listen and you'll know. (*She shuts her eyes. He plods on with a note of desperation in his voice*) I thought about my life—lying awake nights—and about your life. In the middle of battle I'd think maybe in a minute I'll be dead. But my life as just me ending, that didn't appear worth a thought one way or another. But listen, me as your husband being killed, that seemed queer and wrong—like something dying that had never lived. Then all the years we've been man and wife would rise up in my mind and I would try to look at them. But nothing was clear except that there'd always been some barrier between us—a wall hiding us from each other! I would try to make up my mind exactly what that wall was but I never could discover. (*With a clumsy appealing gesture*) Do you know?

CHRISTINE. (*tensely*) I don't know what you're talking about.

MANNON. But you've known it was there! Don't lie, Christine! (*He looks at her still face and closed eyes, imploring her to reassure him—then blunders on doggedly*) Maybe you've always known you didn't love me. I call to mind the Mexican War. I could see you wanted me

54

to go. I had a feeling you'd grown to hate me. Did you? (*She doesn't answer*) That was why I went. I was hoping I might get killed. Maybe you were hoping that too. Were you?

CHRISTINE. (*stammers*) No, no, I— What makes you say such things?

MANNON. When I came back you had turned to your new baby, Orin. I was hardly alive for you any more. I saw that. I tried not to hate Orin. I turned to Vinnie, but a daughter's not a wife. Then I made up my mind I'd do my work in the world and leave you alone in your life and not care. That's why the shipping wasn't enough— why I became a judge and a mayor and such vain truck, and why folks in town look on me as so able! Ha! Able for what? Not for what I wanted most in life! Not for your love! No! Able only to keep my mind from thinking of what I'd lost! (*He stares at her—then asks pleadingly*) For you did love me before we were married. You won't deny that, will you?

CHRISTINE. (*desperately*) I don't deny anything!

MANNON. (*drawing himself up with a stern pride and dignity and surrendering himself like a commander against hopeless odds*) All right, then. I came home to surrender to you—what's inside me. I love you. I loved you then, and all the years between, and I love you now.

CHRISTINE. (*distractedly*) Ezra! Please!

MANNON. I want that said! Maybe you have forgotten it. I wouldn't blame you. I guess I haven't said it or showed it much—ever. Something queer in me keeps me mum about the things I'd like most to say—keeps me hiding the things I'd like to show. Something keeps me sitting numb in my own heart—like a statue of a dead man in a town square. (*Suddenly he reaches over and takes her hand*) I want to find what that wall is marriage put between us! You've got to help me smash it down! We have twenty good years still before us! I've been thinking of what we could do to get back to each other. I've a notion if we'd leave the children and go off on a voyage together—to the

55

other side of the world—find some island where we could be alone a while. You'll find I have changed, Christine. I'm sick of death! I want life! Maybe you could love me now! (*In a note of final desperate pleading*) I've got to make you love me!

CHRISTINE. (*pulls her hand away from him and springs to her feet wildly*) For God's sake, stop talking. I don't know what you're saying. Leave me alone! What must be, must be! You make me weak! (*Then abruptly*) It's getting late.

MANNON. (*terribly wounded, withdrawn into his stiff soldier armor —takes out his watch mechanically*) Yes—six past eleven. Time to turn in. (*He ascends two steps, his face toward the door. He says bitterly*) You tell me to stop talking! By God, that's funny!

CHRISTINE. (*collected now and calculating—takes hold of his arm, seductively*) I meant—what is the good of words? There is no wall between us. I love you.

MANNON. (*grabs her by the shoulders and stares into her face*) Christine! I'd give my soul to believe that—but—I'm afraid! (*She kisses him. He presses her fiercely in his arms—passionately*) Christine! (*The door behind him is opened and* LAVINIA *appears at the edge of the portico behind and above him. She wears slippers over her bare feet and has a dark dressing-gown over her night dress. She shrinks back from their embrace with aversion. They separate, startled.*)

MANNON. (*embarrassed—irritably*) Thought you'd gone to bed, young lady!

LAVINIA. (*woodenly*) I didn't feel sleepy. I thought I'd walk a little. It's such a fine night.

CHRISTINE. We are just going to bed. Your father is tired. (*She moves up, past her daughter, taking* MANNON's *hand, leading him after her to the door.*)

MANNON. No time for a walk, if you ask me. See you turn in soon.

LAVINIA. Yes, Father.

MANNON. Good night. (*The door closes behind them.* LAVINIA *stands staring before her—then walks stiffly down the steps and stands again.*)

Light appears between the chinks of the shutters in the bedroom on the second floor to the left. She looks up.)

LAVINIA. (*in an anguish of jealous hatred*) I hate you! You steal even Father's love from me again! You stole all love from me when I was born! (*Then almost with a sob, hiding her face in her hands*) Oh, Mother! Why have you done this to me? What harm had I done you? (*Then looking up at the window again—with passionate disgust*) Father, how can you love that shameless harlot? (*Then frenziedly*) I can't bear it! I won't! It's my duty to tell him about her! I will (*She calls desperately*) Father! Father! (*The shutter of the bedroom is pushed open and* MANNON *leans out.*)

MANNON. (*sharply*) What is it? Don't shout like that!

LAVINIA. (*stammers lamely*) I—I remembered I forgot to say good night, Father.

MANNON. (*exasperated*) Good heavens! What— (*Then gently*) Oh—all right—good night, Vinnie. Get to bed soon, like a good girl.

LAVINIA. Yes, Father. Good night. (*He goes back in the bedroom and pulls the shutter closed. She stands staring fascinatedly up at the window, wringing her hands in a pitiful desperation.*)

CURTAIN

57

ACT FOUR

SCENE—EZRA MANNON's *bedroom. A big four-poster bed is at rear, center, the foot front, the head against the rear wall. A small stand, with a candle on it, is by the head of the bed on the left. To the left of the stand is a door leading into* CHRISTINE's *room. The door is open. In the left wall are two windows. At left, front, is a table with a lamp on it and a chair beside it. In the right wall, front, is a door leading to the hall. Further back, against the wall, is a bureau.*

None of these details can be discerned at first because the room is in darkness, except for what moonlight filters feebly through the shutters. It is around dawn of the following morning.

Christine's form can be made out, a pale ghost in the darkness, as she slips slowly and stealthily from the bed. She tiptoes to the table, left front, and picks up a light-colored dressing-gown that is flung over the chair and puts it on. She stands listening for some sound from the bed. A pause. Then MANNON's *voice comes suddenly from the bed, dull and lifeless.*

MANNON. Christine.

CHRISTINE. (*starts violently—in a strained voice*) Yes.

MANNON. Must be near daybreak, isn't it?

CHRISTINE. Yes. It is beginning to get gray.

MANNON. What made you jump when I spoke? Is my voice so strange to you?

CHRISTINE. I thought you were asleep.

MANNON. I haven't been able to sleep. I've been lying here thinking. What makes you so uneasy?

CHRISTINE. I haven't been able to sleep either.

MANNON. You slunk out of bed so quietly.

58

CHRISTINE. I didn't want to wake you.

MANNON. (*bitterly*) Couldn't you bear it—lying close to me?

CHRISTINE. I didn't want to disturb you by tossing around.

MANNON. We'd better light the light and talk a while.

CHRISTINE. (*with dread*) I don't want to talk! I prefer the dark.

MANNON. I want to see you. (*He takes matches from the stand by the bed and lights the candle on it.* CHRISTINE *hastily sits down in the chair by the table, pushing it so she sits facing left, front, with her face turned three-quarters away from him. He pushes his back up against the head of the bed in a half-sitting position. His face, with the flickering candlelight on its side, has a grim, bitter expression*) You like the dark where you can't see your old man of a husband, is that it?

CHRISTINE. I wish you wouldn't talk like that, Ezra. If you are going to say stupid things, I'll go in my own room. (*She gets to her feet but keeps her face turned away from him.*)

MANNON. Wait! (*Then a note of pleading in his voice*) Don't go. I don't want to be alone. (*She sits again in the same position as before. He goes on humbly*) I didn't mean to say those things. I guess there's bitterness inside me—my own cussedness, maybe—and sometimes it gets out before I can stop it.

CHRISTINE. You have always been bitter.

MANNON. Before we married?

CHRISTINE. I don't remember.

MANNON. You don't want to remember you ever loved me!

CHRISTINE. (*tensely*) I don't want to talk of the past! (*Abruptly changing the subject*) Did you hear Vinnie the first part of the night? She was pacing up and down before the house like a sentry guarding you. She didn't go to bed until two. I heard the clock strike.

MANNON. There is one who loves me, at least! (*Then after a pause*) I feel strange, Christine.

CHRISTINE. You mean—your heart? You don't think you are going to be—taken ill, do you?

MOURNING BECOMES ELECTRA

MANNON. (*harshly*) No! (*A pause—then accusingly*) Is that what you're waiting for? Is that why you were so willing to give yourself tonight? Were you hoping—?

CHRISTINE. (*springing up*) Ezra! Stop talking like that! I can't stand it! (*She moves as if to go into her own room.*)

MANNON. Wait! I'm sorry I said that. (*Then, as she sits down again, he goes on gloomily*) It isn't my heart. It's something uneasy troubling my mind—as if something in me was listening, watching, waiting for something to happen.

CHRISTINE. Waiting for what to happen?

MANNON. I don't know. (*A pause—then he goes on somberly*) This house is not my house. This is not my room nor my bed. They are empty—waiting for someone to move in! And you are not my wife! You are waiting for something!

CHRISTINE. (*beginning to snap under the strain—jumps to her feet again*) What would I be waiting for?

MANNON. For death—to set you free!

CHRISTINE. Leave me alone! Stop nagging at me with your crazy suspicions! (*Then anger and hatred come into her voice*) Not your wife! You acted as if I were your wife—your property—not so long ago!

MANNON. (*with bitter scorn*) Your body? What are bodies to me? I've seen too many rotting in the sun to make grass greener! Ashes to ashes, dirt to dirt! Is that your notion of love? Do you think I married a body? (*Then, as if all the bitterness and hurt in him had suddenly burst its dam*) You were lying to me tonight as you've always lied! You were only pretending love! You let me take you as if you were a nigger slave I'd bought at auction! You made me appear a lustful beast in my own eyes!—as you've always done since our first marriage night! I would feel cleaner now if I had gone to a brothel! I would feel more honor between myself and life!

CHRISTINE. (*in a stifled voice*) Look out, Ezra! I won't stand—

MANNON. (*with a harsh laugh*) And I had hoped my homecoming

60

would mark a new beginning—new love between us! I told you my secret feelings. I tore my insides out for you—thinking you'd understand! By God, I'm an old fool!

CHRISTINE. (*her voice grown strident*) Did you think you could make me weak—make me forget all the years? Oh, no, Ezra! It's too late! (*Then her voice changes, as if she had suddenly resolved on a course of action, and becomes deliberately taunting*) You want the truth? You've guessed it! You've used me, you've given me children, but I've never once been yours! I never could be! And whose fault is it? I loved you when I married you! I wanted to give myself! But you made me so I couldn't give! You filled me with disgust!

MANNON. (*furiously*) You say that to me! (*Then trying to calm himself—stammers*) No! Be quiet! We mustn't fight! I mustn't lose my temper! It will bring on—!

CHRISTINE. (*goading him with calculating cruelty*) Oh, no! You needn't adopt that pitiful tone! You wanted the truth and you're going to hear it now!

MANNON. (*frightened—almost pleading*) Be quiet, Christine!

CHRISTINE. I've lied about everything! I lied about Captain Brant! He is Marie Brantôme's son! And it was I he came to see, not Vinnie! I made him come!

MANNON. (*seized with fury*) You dared—! You—! The son of that—!

CHRISTINE. Yes, I dared! And all my trips to New York weren't to visit Father but to be with Adam! He's gentle and tender, he's everything you've never been. He's what I've longed for all these years with you—a lover! I love him! So now you know the truth!

MANNON. (*in a frenzy—struggling to get out of bed*) You—you whore—I'll kill you! (*Suddenly he falls back, groaning, doubled up on his left side, with intense pain.*)

CHRISTINE. (*with savage satisfaction*) Ah! (*She hurries through the doorway into her room and immediately returns with a small box in her hand. He is facing away from her door, and, even if the intense*

61

pain left him any perception, he could not notice her departure and return, she moves so silently.)

MANNON. (*gaspingly*) Quick—medicine!

CHRISTINE. (*turned away from him, takes a pellet from the box, asking tensely as she does so*) Where is your medicine?

MANNON. On the stand! Hurry!

CHRISTINE. Wait. I have it now. (*She pretends to take something from the stand by the head of the bed—then holds out the pellet and a glass of water which is on the stand*) Here. (*He turns to her, groaning and opens his mouth. She puts the pellet on his tongue and presses the glass of water to his lips*) Now drink.

MANNON. (*takes a swallow of water—then suddenly a wild look of terror comes over his face. He gasps*) That's not—my medicine! (*She shrinks back to the table, the hand with the box held out behind her, as if seeking a hiding place. Her fingers release the box on the table top and she brings her hand in front of her as if instinctively impelled to prove to him she has nothing. His eyes are fixed on her in a terrible accusing glare. He tries to call for help but his voice fades to a wheezy whisper*) Help! Vinnie! (*He falls back in a coma, breathing stertorously.* CHRISTINE *stares at him fascinatedly—then starts with terror as she hears a noise from the hall and frantically snatches up the box from the table and holds it behind her back, turning to face the door as it opens and* LAVINIA *appears in the doorway. She is dressed as at the end of Act Three, in nightgown, wrapper and slippers. She stands, dazed and frightened and hesitating, as if she had just awakened.*)

LAVINIA. I had a horrible dream—I thought I heard Father calling me—it woke me up—

CHRISTINE. (*trembling with guilty terror—stammers*) He just had—an attack.

LAVINIA. (*hurries to the bed*) Father! (*She puts her arms around him*) He's fainted!

CHRISTINE. No. He's all right now. Let him sleep. (*At this moment*

MANNON, *with a last dying effort, straightens up in a sitting position in* LAVINIA'S *arms, his eyes glaring at his wife, and manages to raise his arm and point an accusing finger at her.*)

MANNON. (*gasps*) She's guilty—not medicine! (*He falls back limply.*)

LAVINIA. Father! (*Frightenedly she feels for his pulse, puts her ear against his chest to listen for a heartbeat.*)

CHRISTINE. Let him alone. He's asleep.

LAVINIA. He's dead!

CHRISTINE. (*repeats mechanically*) Dead? (*Then in a strange flat tone*) I hope—he rests in peace.

LAVINIA. (*turning on her with hatred*) Don't you dare pretend—! You wanted him to die! You— (*She stops and stares at her mother with a horrified suspicion—then harshly accusing*) Why did he point at you like that? Why did he say you were guilty? Answer me!

CHRISTINE. (*stammers*) I told him—Adam was my lover.

LAVINIA. (*aghast*) You told him that—when you knew his heart—! Oh! You did it on purpose! You murdered him!

CHRISTINE. No—it was your fault—you made him suspicious—he kept talking of love and death—he forced me to tell him! (*Her voice becomes thick, as if she were drowsy and fighting off sleep. Her eyes half close*).

LAVINIA. (*grabbing her by the shoulders—fiercely*) Listen! Look at me! He said "not medicine"! What did he mean?

CHRISTINE. (*keeping the hand with the poison pressed against her back*) I—I don't know.

LAVINIA. You do know! What was it? Tell me!

CHRISTINE. (*with a last effort of will manages to draw herself up and speak with a simulation of outraged feeling*) Are you accusing your mother of—

LAVINIA. Yes! I—! (*Then distractedly*) No—you can't be that evil!

CHRISTINE. (*her strength gone—swaying weakly*) I don't know what —you're talking about. (*She edges away from* LAVINIA *toward her bed-*

*room door, the hand with the poison stretched out behind her—
weakly)* I—feel faint. I must go—and lie down. I— (*She turns as if
to run into the room, takes a tottering step—then her knees suddenly
buckle under her and she falls in a dead faint at the foot of the bed.
As her hand strikes the floor the fingers relax and the box slips out
onto one of the hooked rugs.*)

LAVINIA. (*does not notice this. Startled by* CHRISTINE's *collapse, she
automatically bends on one knee beside her and hastily feels for her
pulse. Then satisfied she has only fainted, her anguished hatred immediately returns and she speaks with strident denunciation*) You
murdered him just the same—by telling him! I suppose you think
you'll be free to marry Adam now! But you won't! Not while I'm
alive! I'll make you pay for your crime! I'll find a way to punish you!
(*She is starting to her feet when her eyes fall on the little box on the
rug. Immediately she snatches it up and stares at it, the look of suspicion changing to a dreadful, horrified certainty. Then with a shuddering cry she shrinks back along the side of the bed, the box clutched
in her hand, and sinks on her knees by the head of the bed, and flings
her arms around the dead man. With anguished beseeching*) Father!
Don't leave me alone! Come back to me! Tell me what to do!

CURTAIN

THE HUNTED

CHARACTERS

CHRISTINE, *Ezra Mannon's widow*

LAVINIA (VINNIE), *her daughter*

ORIN, *her son, First Lieutenant of Infantry*

CAPTAIN ADAM BRANT

HAZEL NILES

PETER, *her brother, Captain of Artillery*

JOSIAH BORDEN, *manager of the shipping company*

EMMA, *his wife*

EVERETT HILLS, D.D., *of the First Congregational Church*

HIS WIFE

DOCTOR JOSEPH BLAKE

THE CHANTYMAN

SCENES

ACT ONE: Exterior of the Mannon house—a moonlight night two days after the murder of EZRA MANNON.

ACT TWO: Sitting-room in the house—immediately follows Act One.

ACT THREE: EZRA MANNON's study—immediately follows Act Two.

ACT FOUR: The stern of the clipper ship "Flying Trades," at a wharf in East Boston—a night two days later.

ACT FIVE: Same as Act One—Exterior of the Mannon house the night of the following day.

THE HUNTED

ACT ONE

SCENE—*The same as Acts One and Three of "Homecoming"—Exterior of the Mannon House.*

It is a moonlight night two days after the murder of EZRA MANNON. *The house has the same strange eerie appearance, its white portico like a mask in the moonlight, as it had on that night. All the shutters are closed. A funeral wreath is fixed to the column at the right of steps. Another wreath is on the door.*

There is a sound of voices from inside the house, the front door is opened and JOSIAH BORDEN *and his wife,* EVERETT HILLS, *the Congregational minister, and his wife, and* DOCTOR JOSEPH BLAKE, *the Mannons' family physician, come out.* CHRISTINE *can be seen in the hall just inside the door. There is a chorus of "Good night, Mrs. Mannon," and then they turn to the steps and the door is closed.*

These people—the BORDENS, HILLS *and his wife and* DOCTOR BLAKE—*are, as were the Ames of Act One of "Homecoming," types of townsfolk, a chorus representing as those others had, but in a different stratum of society, the town as a human background for the drama of the Mannons.*

JOSIAH BORDEN, *the manager of the Mannon shipping company, is shrewd and competent. He is around sixty, small and wizened, white hair and beard, rasping nasal voice, and little sharp eyes. His wife, about ten years his junior, is a typical New England woman of pure English ancestry, with a horse face, buck teeth and big feet, her manner defensively sharp and assertive.* HILLS *is the type of well-fed minister of a prosperous small-town congregation—stout and unctuous, snobbish and ingratiating, conscious of godliness, but timid and*

*always feeling his way. He is in the fifties, as is his wife, a sallow,
flabby, self-effacing minister's wife.* DOCTOR BLAKE *is the old kindly
best-family physician—a stout, self-important old man with a stubborn opinionated expression.*

They come down the steps to the drive. MRS. BORDEN *and* MRS. HILLS
*walk together toward left front until they are by the bench. There
they stop to wait for the men who stand at the foot of the steps while*
BORDEN *and* BLAKE *light cigars.*

MRS. BORDEN. (*tartly*) I can't abide that woman!

MRS. HILLS. No. There's something queer about her.

MRS. BORDEN. (*grudgingly honest*) Still and all, I come nearer to
liking her now than I ever did before when I see how broken down
she is over her husband's death.

MRS. HILLS. Yes. She looks terrible, doesn't she? Doctor Blake says
she will have herself in bed sick if she doesn't look out.

MRS. BORDEN. I'd never have suspected she had that much feeling in
her. Not but what she hasn't always been a dutiful wife, as far as
anyone knows.

MRS. HILLS. Yes. She's seemed to be.

MRS. BORDEN. Well, it only goes to show how you can misjudge a
person without meaning to—especially when that person is a Mannon. They're not easy to make head or tail of. Queer, the difference
in her and Lavinia—the way they take his death. Lavinia is cold and
calm as an icicle.

MRS. HILLS. Yes. She doesn't seem to feel as much sorrow as she
ought.

MRS. BORDEN. That's where you're wrong. She feels it as much as
her mother. Only she's too Mannon to let anyone see what she feels.
But did you notice the look in her eyes?

MRS. HILLS. I noticed she never said a word to anyone. Where did
she disappear to all of a sudden?

MRS. BORDEN. Went to the train with Peter Niles to meet Orin. I

overheard her mother talking to Lavinia in the hall. She was insisting Peter should escort her to meet the train. Lavinia must have
been starting to go alone. Her mother seemed real angry about it.
(*Then glancing toward the men who have moved a little away from
the steps and are standing talking in low tones*) Whatever are those
men gossiping about? (*She calls*) Josiah! It's time we were getting
home.

BORDEN. I'm coming, Emma. (*The three men join the women by
the bench,* BORDEN *talking as they come*) It isn't for me to question
the arrangements she's made, Joe, but it does seem as if Ezra should
have been laid out in the town hall where the whole town could
have paid their respects to him, and had a big public funeral tomorrow.

HILLS. That's my opinion. He was mayor of the town and a
national war hero—

BLAKE. She says it was Ezra's wish he'd often expressed that everything should be private and quiet. That's just like Ezra. He never
was one for show. He did the work and let others do the showing-off.

HILLS. (*unctuously*) He was a great man. His death is a real loss to
everyone in this community. He was a power for good.

BORDEN. Yes. He got things done.

HILLS. What a tragedy to be taken his first night home after passing unharmed through the whole war!

BORDEN. I couldn't believe the news. Who'd ever suspect— It's
queer. It's like fate.

MRS. HILLS. (*breaks in tactlessly*) Maybe it is fate. You remember,
Everett, you've always said about the Mannons that pride goeth before a fall and that some day God would humble them in their sinful
pride. (*Everyone stares at her, shocked and irritated.*)

HILLS. (*flusteredly*) I don't remember ever saying—

BLAKE. (*huffily*) If you'll excuse me, that's darn nonsense! I've
known Ezra Mannon all my life, and to those he wanted to know
he was as plain and simple—

69

HILLS. (*hastily*) Of course, Doctor. My wife entirely misunderstood me. I was, perhaps wrongly, referring to Mrs. Mannon.

BLAKE. She's all right too—when you get to know her.

HILLS. (*dryly*) I have no doubt.

BLAKE. And it's a poor time, when this household is afflicted by sudden death, to be—

HILLS. You are quite right, Doctor. My wife should have remembered—

MRS. HILLS. (*crushed*) I didn't mean anything wrong, Doctor.

BLAKE. (*mollifiedly*) Let's forget it then. (*Turning to* BORDEN— *with a self-satisfied, knowing air*) As for your saying who'd ever expect it—well, you and Emma know I expected Ezra wouldn't last long.

BORDEN. Yes. I remember you said you were afraid his heart was bad.

MRS. BORDEN. I remember you did too.

BLAKE. From the symptoms Mrs. Mannon described from his letter to her, I was as certain as if I'd examined him he had angina. And I wasn't surprised neither. I'd often told Ezra he was attempting more than one man could handle and if he didn't rest he'd break down. The minute they sent for me I knew what'd happened. And what she told me about waking up to find him groaning and doubled with pain confirmed it. She'd given him his medicine—it was what I would have prescribed myself—but it was too late. And as for dying, his first night home—well, the war was over, he was worn out, he'd had a long, hard trip home—and angina is no respecter of time and place. It strikes when it has a mind to.

BORDEN. (*shaking his head*) Too bad. Too durned bad. The town won't find another as able as Ezra in a hurry. (*They all shake their heads and look sad. A pause.*)

MRS. BORDEN. Well, we aren't doing anyone any good standing here. We ought to get home, Josiah.

MRS. HILLS. Yes. We must, too, Everett. (*They begin moving slowly*

70

off left, HILLS *going with the two women.* DOCTOR BLAKE *nudges* BORDEN *and motions him to stay behind. After the others disappear, he whispers with a meaning grin.*)

BLAKE. I'll tell you a secret, Josiah—strictly between you and me.

BORDEN. (*sensing something from his manner—eagerly*) Of course. What is it, Joe?

BLAKE. I haven't asked Christine Mannon any embarrassing questions, but I have a strong suspicion it was love killed Ezra!

BORDEN. Love?

BLAKE. That's what! Leastways, love made angina kill him, if you take my meaning. She's a damned handsome woman and he'd been away a long time. Only natural between man and wife—but not the treatment I'd recommend for angina. He should have known better, but—well—he was human.

BORDEN. (*with a salacious smirk*) Can't say as I blame him! She's a looker! I don't like her and never did but I can imagine worse ways of dying! (*They both chuckle*) Well, let's catch up with the folks. (*They go off, left. They have hardly disappeared before the door of the house is opened and* CHRISTINE MANNON *comes out and stands at the head of the steps a moment, then descends to the drive. She is obviously in a terrible state of strained nerves. Beneath the mask-like veneer of her face there are deep lines about her mouth, and her eyes burn with a feverish light. Feeling herself free from observation for a moment she lets go, her mouth twitches, her eyes look desperately on all sides, as if she longed to fly from something.* HAZEL NILES *comes out of the house to the head of the steps. She is the same as in "Homecoming."* CHRISTINE *at once senses her presence behind her and regains her tense control of herself.*)

HAZEL. (*with a cheering, sympathetic air*) So here you are. I looked everywhere around the house and couldn't find you.

CHRISTINE. (*tensely*) I couldn't stay in. I'm so nervous. It's been a little harrowing—all these people coming to stand around and stare at the dead—and at me.

71

HAZEL. I know. But there won't be any more now. (*Then a tone of eagerness breaking through in spite of herself*) Peter and Vinnie ought to be back soon, if the train isn't late. Oh, I hope Orin will surely come!

CHRISTINE. (*strangely*) The same train! It was late that night he came! Only two days ago! It seems a lifetime! I've grown old.

HAZEL. (*gently*) Try not to think of it.

CHRISTINE. (*tensely*) As if I hadn't tried! But my brain keeps on— over and over and over!

HAZEL. I'm so afraid you will make yourself sick.

CHRISTINE. (*rallying herself and forcing a smile*) There, I'm all right. I mustn't appear too old and haggard when Orin comes, must I? He always liked me to be pretty.

HAZEL. It will be so good to see him again! (*Then quickly*) He ought to be such a comfort to you in your grief.

CHRISTINE. Yes. (*Then strangely*) He used to be my baby, you know—before he left me. (*Suddenly staring at* HAZEL, *as if struck by an idea*) You love Orin, don't you?

HAZEL. (*embarrassed—stammers shyly*) I—I—

CHRISTINE. I am glad. I want you to. I want him to marry you. (*Putting an arm around her—in a strained tone*) We'll be secret conspirators, shall we, and I'll help you and you'll help me?

HAZEL. I don't understand.

CHRISTINE. You know how possessive Vinnie is with Orin. She's always been jealous of you. I warn you she'll do everything she can to keep him from marrying you.

HAZEL. (*shocked*) Oh, Mrs. Mannon, I can't believe Vinnie—!

CHRISTINE. (*unheeding*) So you must help me. We mustn't let Orin come under her influence again. Especially now in the morbid, crazy state of grief she's in! Haven't you noticed how queer she's become? She hasn't spoken a single word since her father's death! When I talk to her she won't answer me. And yet she follows me around everywhere—she hardly leaves me alone a minute. (*Forcing a nervous laugh*) It gets on my nerves until I could scream!

HAZEL. Poor Vinnie! She was so fond of her father. I don't wonder she—

CHRISTINE. (*staring at her—strangely*) You are genuinely good and pure of heart, aren't you?

HAZEL. (*embarrassed*) Oh, no! I'm not at all—

CHRISTINE. I was like you once—long ago—before— (*Then with bitter longing*) If I could only have stayed as I was then! Why can't all of us remain innocent and loving and trusting? But God won't leave us alone. He twists and wrings and tortures our lives with others' lives until—we poison each other to death! (*Seeing* HAZEL's *look, catches herself—quickly*) Don't mind what I said! Let's go in, shall we? I would rather wait for Orin inside. I couldn't bear to wait and watch him coming up the drive—just like—he looks so much like his father at times—and like—but what nonsense I'm talking! Let's go in. I hate moonlight. It makes everything so haunted. (*She turns abruptly and goes into the house.* HAZEL *follows her and shuts the door. There is a pause. Then footsteps and voices are heard from off right front and a moment later* ORIN MANNON *enters with* PETER *and* LAVINIA. *One is at once struck by his startling family resemblance to* EZRA MANNON *and* ADAM BRANT [*whose likeness to each other we have seen in "Homecoming"*]. *There is the same lifelike mask quality of his face in repose, the same aquiline nose, heavy eyebrows, swarthy complexion, thick straight black hair, light hazel eyes. His mouth and chin have the same general characteristics as his father's had, but the expression of his mouth gives an impression of tense oversensitiveness quite foreign to the General's, and his chin is a refined, weakened version of the dead man's. He is about the same height as* MANNON *and* BRANT, *but his body is thin and his swarthy complexion sallow. He wears a bandage around his head high up on his forehead. He carries himself by turns with a marked slouchiness or with a self-conscious square-shouldered stiffness that indicates a soldierly bear-*

ing is unnatural to him. When he speaks it is jerkily, with a strange, vague, preoccupied air. But when he smiles naturally his face has a gentle boyish charm which makes women immediately want to mother him. He wears a mustache similar to BRANT'S *which serves to increase their resemblance to each other. Although he is only twenty, he looks thirty. He is dressed in a baggy, ill-fitting uniform —that of a first lieutenant of infantry in the Union Army.*)

ORIN. (*as they enter looks eagerly toward the house—then with bitter, hurt disappointment in his tone*) Where's Mother? I thought she'd surely be waiting for me. (*He stands staring at the house*) God, how I've dreamed of coming home! I thought it would never end, that we'd go on murdering and being murdered until no one was left alive! Home at last! No, by God, I must be dreaming again! (*Then in an awed tone*) But the house looks strange. Or is it something in me? I was out of my head so long, everything has seemed queer since I came back to earth. Did the house always look so ghostly and dead?

PETER. That's only the moonlight, you chump.

ORIN. Like a tomb. That's what mother used to say it reminded her of, I remember.

LAVINIA. (*reproachfully*) It is a tomb—just now, Orin.

ORIN. (*hurriedly—shamefacedly*) I—I'd forgotten. I simply can't realize he's dead yet. I suppose I'd come to expect he would live forever. (*A trace of resentment has crept into his tone*) Or, at least outlive me. I never thought his heart was weak. He told me the trouble he had wasn't serious.

LAVINIA. (*quickly*) Father told you that, too? I was hoping he had. (*Then turning to* PETER) You go ahead in, Peter. Say we're coming a little behind. I want to speak to Orin a moment.

PETER. Sure thing, Vinnie. (*He goes in the front door, closing it behind him.*)

ORIN. I'm glad you got rid of him. Peter is all right but—I want to talk to you alone. (*With a boyish brotherly air—putting an arm around her*) You certainly are a sight for sore eyes, Vinnie! How are you, anyway, you old bossy fuss-buzzer! Gosh, it seems natural to hear myself calling you that old nickname again. Aren't you glad to see me?

LAVINIA. (*affectionately*) Of course I am!

ORIN. I'd never guess it! You've hardly spoken a word since you met me. What's happened to you? (*Then, as she looks at him reproachfully, he takes away his arm—a bit impatiently*) I told you I can't get used to the idea of his being dead. Forgive me, Vinnie. I know what a shock it must be to you.

LAVINIA. Isn't it a shock to you, Orin?

ORIN. Certainly! What do you think I am? But—oh, I can't explain! You wouldn't understand, unless you'd been at the front. I hardened myself to expect my own death and everyone else's, and think nothing of it. I had to—to keep alive! It was part of my training as a soldier under him. He taught it to me, you might say! So when it's his turn he can hardly expect— (*He has talked with increasing bitterness.* LAVINIA *interrupts him sharply.*)

LAVINIA. Orin! How can you be so unfeeling?

ORIN. (*again shamefaced*) I didn't mean that. My mind is still full of ghosts. I can't grasp anything but war, in which he was so alive. He was the war to me—the war that would never end until I died. I can't understand peace—his end! (*Then with exasperation*) God damn it, Vinnie, give me a chance to get used to things!

LAVINIA. Orin!

ORIN. (*resentfully*) I'm sorry! Oh, I know what you're thinking! I used to be such a nice gentlemanly cuss, didn't I?—and now— Well, you wanted me to be a hero in blue, so you better be resigned! Murdering doesn't improve one's manners! (*Abruptly changing the subject*) But what the devil are we talking about me for? Listen, Vinnie. There's something I want to ask you before I see Mother.

LAVINIA. Hurry, then! She'll be coming right out! I've got to tell you something too!

ORIN. What was that stuff you wrote about some Captain Brant coming to see Mother? Do you mean to tell me there's actually been gossip started about her? (*Then without waiting for a reply, bursting into jealous rage*) By God, if he dares come here again, I'll make him damned sorry he did!

LAVINIA. (*grimly*) I'm glad you feel that way about him. But there's no time to talk now. All I want to do is warn you to be on your guard. Don't let her baby you the way she used to and get you under her thumb again. Don't believe the lies she'll tell you! Wait until you've talked to me! Will you promise me?

ORIN. (*staring at her bewilderedly*) You mean—Mother? (*Then angrily*) What the hell are you talking about, anyway? Are you loony? Honestly, Vinnie, I call that carrying your everlasting squabble with Mother a bit too far! You ought to be ashamed of yourself! (*Then suspiciously*) What are you being so mysterious about? Is it Brant—?

LAVINIA. (*at a sound from inside the house*) Ssshh! (*The front door of the house is opened and* CHRISTINE *hurries out.*)

CHRISTINE. (*angrily to* PETER *who is in the hall*) Why didn't you call me, Peter? You shouldn't have left him alone! (*She calls uncertainly*) Orin.

ORIN. Mother! (*She runs down the steps and flings her arms around him.*)

CHRISTINE. My boy! My baby! (*She kisses him.*)

ORIN. (*melting, all his suspicion forgotten*) Mother! God, it's good to see you! (*Then almost roughly, pushing her back and staring at her*) But you're different! What's happened to you?

CHRISTINE. (*forcing a smile*) I? Different? I don't think so, dear. Certainly I hope not—to you! (*Touching the bandage on his head tenderly*) Your head! Does it pain dreadfully? You poor darling, how you must have suffered! (*She kisses him*) But it's all over now, thank God. I've got you back again! (*Keeping her arm around him, she leads him up the steps*) Let's go in. There's someone else waiting who will be so glad to see you.

LAVINIA. (*who has come to the foot of the steps—harshly*) Remember, Orin! (CHRISTINE *turns around to look down at her. A look of hate flashes between mother and daughter.* ORIN *glances at his mother suspiciously and draws away from her.*)

CHRISTINE. (*immediately recovers her poise—to* ORIN, *as if* LAVINIA *hadn't spoken*) Come on in, dear. It's chilly. Your poor head— (*She takes his hand and leads him through the door and closes it behind them.* LAVINIA *remains by the foot of the steps, staring after them. Then the door is suddenly opened again and* CHRISTINE *comes out, closing it behind her, and walks to the head of the steps. For a moment mother and daughter stare into each other's eyes. Then* CHRISTINE *begins haltingly in a tone she vainly tries to make kindly and persuasive*) Vinnie, I—I must speak with you a moment—now Orin is here. I appreciate your grief has made you—not quite normal—and I make allowances. But I cannot understand your attitude toward me. Why do you keep following me everywhere—and stare at me like that? I had been a good wife to him for twenty-three years —until I met Adam. I was guilty then, I admit. But I repented and put him out of my life. I would have been a good wife again as long as your father had lived. After all, Vinnie, I am your mother. I brought you into the world. You ought to have some feeling for me. (*She pauses, waiting for some response, but* LAVINIA *simply stares at her, frozen and silent. Fear creeps into* CHRISTINE's *tone*) Don't stare like that! What are you thinking? Surely you can't still have that insane suspicion—that I— (*Then guiltily*) What did you do that night after I fainted? I—I've missed something—some medicine I take to put me to sleep— (*Something like a grim smile of satisfaction forms on* LAVINIA's *lips.* CHRISTINE *exclaims frightenedly*) Oh, you did—you found—and I suppose you connect that—but don't you see how insane—to suspect—when Doctor Blake knows he died of—! (*Then angrily*) I know what you've been waiting for—to tell Orin your lies and get him to go to the police! You don't dare do that on your own responsibility—but if you can make Orin— Isn't that it? Isn't that what you've been planning the last two days? Tell me! (*Then, as* LAVINIA *remains silent,* CHRISTINE *gives way to fury and rushes down the steps and grabs her by the arm and shakes her*) Answer me when I speak to you! What are you plotting? What are you going to do? Tell me! (LAVINIA *keeps her body rigid, her eyes staring into her mother's.* CHRISTINE *lets go and steps away from her. Then* LAVINIA, *turning her back, walks slowly and woodenly off left between the lilac clump and the house.* CHRISTINE *stares after her, her strength seems to leave her, she trembles with dread. From inside the house comes the sound of* ORIN'S *voice calling sharply "Mother! Where are you?"* CHRISTINE *starts and immediately by an effort of will regains control over herself. She hurries up the steps and opens the door. She speaks to* ORIN *and her voice is tensely quiet and normal*) Here I am, dear! (*She shuts the door behind her.*)

CURTAIN

ACT TWO

Scene—*The sitting-room of the Mannon house. Like the study, but much larger, it is an interior composed of straight severe lines with heavy detail. The walls are plain plastered surfaces, light gray with a white trim. It is a bleak room without intimacy, with an atmosphere of uncomfortable, stilted stateliness. The furniture is stationed about with exact precision. On the left, front, is a doorway leading to the dining-room. Farther back, on the left, are a wall table and chair and a writing desk and chair. In the rear wall, center, is the doorway giving on the main hall and the stairs. At right is a fireplace with a chimneypiece of black marble, flanked by two windows. Portraits of ancestors hang on the walls. At the rear of the fireplace, on the right, is one of a grim-visaged minister of the witch-burning era. Between fireplace and front is another of* EZRA MANNON'S *grandfather, in the uniform of an officer in Washington's army. Directly over the fireplace is the portrait of* EZRA'S *father,* ABE MANNON, *done when he was sixty. Except for the difference in ages, his face looks exactly like* EZRA'S *in the painting in the study.*

*Of the three portraits on the other walls, two are of women—*ABE MANNON'S *wife and the wife of Washington's officer. The third has the appearance of a prosperous shipowner of Colonial days. All the faces in the portraits have the same mask quality of those of the living characters in the play.*

At the left center of the room, front, is a table with two chairs. There is another chair at center, front, and a sofa at right, front, facing left.

The opening of this scene follows immediately the close of the preceding one. HAZEL *is discovered sitting on the chair at center, front.*

PETER *is sitting on the sofa at right. From the hall* ORIN *is heard calling* "Mother! Where are you?" *as at the close of the preceding act.*

HAZEL. Where can she have gone? She's worked herself into such a state of grief I don't think she knows what she's doing.

PETER. Vinnie's completely knocked out, too.

HAZEL. And poor Orin! What a terrible homecoming this is for him! How sick and changed he looks, doesn't he, Peter?

PETER. Head wounds are no joke. He's darned lucky to have come out alive. (*They stop talking self-consciously as* ORIN *and* CHRISTINE *enter from the rear.* ORIN *is questioning her suspiciously.*)

ORIN. Why did you sneak away like that? What were you doing?

CHRISTINE. (*forcing a wan smile*) The happiness of seeing you again was a little too much for me, I'm afraid, dear. I suddenly felt as if I were going to faint, so I rushed out in the fresh air.

ORIN. (*immediately ashamed of himself—tenderly, putting his arm around her*) Poor Mother! I'm sorry— Look here, then. You sit down and rest. Or maybe you better go right to bed.

HAZEL. That's right, Orin, you make her. I've been trying to get her to but she won't listen to me.

CHRISTINE. Go to bed the minute he comes home! I should say not!

ORIN. (*worried and pleased at the same time*) But you mustn't do anything to—

CHRISTINE. (*patting his cheek*) Fiddlesticks! Having you again is just the medicine I need to give me strength—to bear things. (*She turns to* HAZEL) Listen to him, Hazel! You'd think I was the invalid and not he.

HAZEL. Yes. You've got to take care of yourself, too, Orin.

ORIN. Oh, forget me. I'm all right.

CHRISTINE. We'll play nurses, Hazel and I, and have you your old self again before you know it. Won't we, Hazel?

HAZEL. (*smiling happily*) Of course we will.

CHRISTINE. Don't stand, dear. You must be worn out. Wait. We'll make you comfortable. Hazel, will you bring me a cushion? (HAZEL

80

gets a cushion and helps to place it behind his back in the chair at right of table. ORIN's *eyes light up and he grins boyishly, obviously reveling in being coddled.*)

ORIN. How's this for the comforts of home, Peter? The front was never like this, eh?

PETER. Not so you'd notice it!

ORIN. (*with a wink at* HAZEL) Peter will be getting jealous! You better call Vinnie in to put a pillow behind him!

HAZEL. (*with a smile*) I can't picture Vinnie being that soft.

ORIN. (*a jealous resentment creeping into his voice*) She can be soft—on occasion. She's always coddling Father and he likes it, although he pretends—

CHRISTINE. (*turning away and restraining a shudder*) Orin! You're talking as if he were—alive! (*There is an uncomfortable silence.* HAZEL *goes quietly back to her chair at center.* CHRISTINE *goes around the table to the chair opposite* ORIN *and sits down.*)

ORIN. (*with a wry smile*) We'd all forgotten he's dead, hadn't we? Well, I can't believe it even yet. I feel him in this house—alive!

CHRISTINE. Orin!

ORIN. (*strangely*) Everything is changed—in some queer way—this house, Vinnie, you, I—everything but Father. He's the same and always will be—here—the same! Don't you feel that, Mother? (*She shivers, looking before her but doesn't answer.*)

HAZEL. (*gently*) You mustn't make your mother think of it, Orin.

ORIN. (*staring at her—in a queer tone of gratitude*) You're the same, Hazel—sweet and good. (*He turns to his mother accusingly*) At least Hazel hasn't changed, thank God!

CHRISTINE. (*rousing herself—turns to force a smile at him*) Hazel will never change, I hope. I am glad you appreciate her. (HAZEL *looks embarrassed.* CHRISTINE *goes on—with motherly solicitude*) Wasn't the long train trip terribly hard on you, dear?

ORIN. Well, it wasn't a pleasure trip exactly. My head got aching till I thought it would explode.

81

CHRISTINE. (*leans over and puts her hand on his forehead*) Poor boy! Does it pain now?

ORIN. Not much. Not at all when your hand is there. (*Impulsively he takes her hand and kisses it—boyishly*) Gosh, Mother, it feels so darned good to be home with you! (*Then staring at her suspiciously again*) Let me have a good look at you. You're so different. I noticed it even outside. What is it?

CHRISTINE. (*avoiding his eyes—forcing a smile*) It's just that I'm getting old, I'm afraid, dear.

ORIN. No. You're more beautiful than ever! You're younger, too, somehow. But it isn't that. (*Almost pushing her hand away—bitterly*) Maybe I can guess!

CHRISTINE. (*forces a laugh*) Younger and more beautiful! Do you hear him going on, Hazel? He has learned to be very gallant, I must say! (LAVINIA *appears in the doorway at rear. She enters but remains standing just inside the doorway and keeps her eyes fixed on her mother and* ORIN.)

ORIN. (*who is again looking at* HAZEL, *breaks out harshly*) Do you remember how you waved your handkerchief, Hazel, the day I set off to become a hero? I thought you would sprain your wrist! And all the mothers and wives and sisters and girls did the same! Sometime in some war they ought to make the women take the men's place for a month or so. Give them a taste of murder!

CHRISTINE. Orin!

ORIN. Let them batter each other's brains out with rifle butts and rip each other's guts with bayonets! After that, maybe they'd stop waving handkerchiefs and gabbing about heroes! (HAZEL *gives a shocked exclamation.*)

CHRISTINE. Please!

PETER. (*gruffly*) Give it a rest, Orin! It's over. Give yourself a chance to forget it. None of us liked it any more than you did.

ORIN. (*immediately shamefaced*) You're right, Peter. I'm a damned whining fool! I'm sorry, Hazel. That was rotten of me.

82

HAZEL. It was nothing, Orin. I understand how you feel. Really I do.

ORIN. I—I let off steam when I shouldn't. (*Then suddenly*) Do you still sing, Hazel? I used to hear you singing—down there. It made me feel life might still be alive somewhere—that, and my dreams of Mother, and the memory of Vinnie bossing me around like a drill sergeant. I used to hear you singing at the queerest times—so sweet and clear and pure! It would rise about the screams of the dying—

CHRISTINE. (*tensely*) I wish you wouldn't talk of death!

LAVINIA. (*from the doorway—in a brusque commanding tone like her father's*) Orin! Come and see Father.

ORIN. (*starts up from his chair and makes an automatic motion as if to salute—mechanically*) Yes, sir. (*Then confusedly*) What the devil—? You sounded just like him. Don't do that again, for heaven's sake! (*He tries to force a laugh—then shamefacedly*) I meant to look at him the first thing—but I got talking—I'll go in right now.

CHRISTINE. (*her voice tense and strained*) No! Wait! (*Angrily to* LAVINIA) Can't you let your brother have a minute to rest? You can see how worn out he is! (*Then to* ORIN) I've hardly had a chance to say a word to you yet—and it has been so long! Stay with me a little while, won't you?

ORIN. (*touched, coming back to her*) Of course, Mother! You come before everything!

LAVINIA. (*starts to make a bitter retort, glances at* PETER *and* HAZEL, *then remarks evenly*) Very well. Only remember what I said, Orin. (*She turns her back and starts to go into the hall.*)

CHRISTINE. (*frightenedly*) Vinnie! Where are you going?

LAVINIA. (*does not answer her but calls back to her brother over her shoulder*) You'll come in a little while, won't you? (*She disappears across the hall.* ORIN *gives his mother a sidelong glance of uneasy suspicion.* CHRISTINE *is desperately trying to appear calm.* PETER *and* HAZEL *stand up, feeling uncomfortable.*)

HAZEL. Peter, we really must be getting home.

83

PETER. Yes.

CHRISTINE. It was so kind of you to come.

HAZEL. (*giving her hand to* ORIN) You must rest all you can now, Orin—and try not to think about things.

ORIN. You're darned kind, Hazel. It's fine to see you again—the same as ever!

HAZEL. (*delighted but pulling her hand away shyly*) I'm glad, too. Good night, Orin.

PETER. (*shakes his hand*) Good night. Rest up and take it easy.

ORIN. Good night, Peter. Thanks for meeting me.

CHRISTINE. (*goes with them to the hall*) I'm afraid this isn't a very cheerful house to visit just now—but please come soon again. You will do Orin more good than anyone, Hazel. (*The look of suspicion again comes to* ORIN's *eyes. He sits down in the chair at left of table and stares before him bitterly.* CHRISTINE *returns from the hall, closing the sliding doors behind her silently. She stands for a moment looking at* ORIN, *visibly bracing herself for the ordeal of the coming interview, her eyes full of tense calculating fear.*)

ORIN. (*without looking at her*) What's made you take such a fancy to Hazel all of a sudden? You never used to think much of her. You didn't want me going around with her.

CHRISTINE. (*coming forward and sitting across the table from him—in her gentle motherly tone*) I was selfish then. I was jealous, too, I'll confess. But all I want now is your happiness, dear. I know how much you used to like Hazel—

ORIN. (*blurts out*) That was only to make you jealous! (*Then bitterly*) But now you're a widow, I'm not home an hour before you're trying to marry me off! You must be damned anxious to get rid of me again! Why?

CHRISTINE. You mustn't say that! If you knew how horribly lonely I've been without you—

ORIN. So lonely you've written me exactly two letters in the last six months!

84

CHRISTINE. But I wrote you much more! They must have been lost—

ORIN. I received all of Hazel's letters—and Vinnie's. It's darned funny yours should be the only ones to get lost! (*Unable to hold back any longer, he bursts forth*) Who is this Captain Brant who's been calling on you?

CHRISTINE. (*prepared for this—with well-feigned astonishment*) On me? You mean on Vinnie, don't you? (*Then as* ORIN *looks taken aback*) Wherever did you get that silly idea? Oh, of course, I know! Vinnie must have written you the same nonsense she did your father.

ORIN. She wrote him? What did he do?

CHRISTINE. Why, he laughed at it, naturally! Your father was very fond of Vinnie but he knew how jealous she's always been of me and he realized she'd tell any lie she could to—

ORIN. Oh, come on now, Mother! Just because you're always getting on each other's nerves it doesn't mean Vinnie would ever deliberately—

CHRISTINE. Oh, doesn't it, though? I think you'll discover before you're much older that there isn't anything your sister will stop at— that she will even accuse me of the vilest, most horrible things!

ORIN. Mother! Honestly now! You oughtn't to say that!

CHRISTINE. (*reaching out and taking his hand*) I mean it, Orin. I wouldn't say it to anyone but you. You know that. But we've always been so close, you and I. I feel you are really—my flesh and blood! She isn't! She is your father's! You're a part of me!

ORIN. (*with strange eagerness*) Yes! I feel that, too, Mother!

CHRISTINE. I know I can trust you to understand now as you always used to. (*With a tender smile*) We had a secret little world of our own in the old days, didn't we?—which no one but us knew about.

ORIN. (*happily*) You bet we did! No Mannons allowed was our password, remember!

CHRISTINE. And that's what your father and Vinnie could never forgive us! But we'll make that little world of our own again, won't we?

ORIN. Yes!

CHRISTINE. I want to make up to you for all the injustice you suffered at your father's hands. It may seem a hard thing to say about the dead, but he was jealous of you. He hated you because he knew I loved you better than anything in the world!

ORIN. (*pressing her hand in both of his—intensely*) Do you, Mother? Do you honestly? (*Then he is struck by what she said about his father—woundedly*) I knew he had it in for me. But I never thought he went as far as to—hate me.

CHRISTINE. He did, just the same!

ORIN. (*with resentful bitterness*) All right, then! I'll tell you the truth, Mother! I won't pretend to you I'm sorry he's dead!

CHRISTINE. (*lowering her voice to a whisper*) Yes. I am glad, too! —that he has left us alone! Oh, how happy we'll be together, you and I, if you only won't let Vinnie poison your mind against me with her disgusting lies!

ORIN. (*immediately uneasy again*) What lies? (*He releases her hand and stares at her, morbidly suspicious*) You haven't told me about that Brant yet.

CHRISTINE. There's nothing to tell—except in Vinnie's morbid revengeful mind! I tell you, Orin, you can't realize how she's changed while you've been away! She's always been a moody and strange girl, you know that, but since you've gone she has worried and brooded until I really believe she went a little out of her head. She got so she'd say the most terrible things about everyone. You simply wouldn't believe it, if I told you some of the things. And now, with the shock of your father's death on top of everything, I'm convinced she's actually insane. Haven't you noticed how queerly she acts? You must have!

ORIN. I saw she'd changed a lot. She seemed strange. But—

CHRISTINE. And her craziness all works out in hatred for me! Take this Captain Brant affair, for example—

ORIN. Ah!

86

CHRISTINE. A stupid ship captain I happened to meet at your grand-father's who took it into his silly head to call here a few times without being asked. Vinnie thought he was coming to court her. I honestly believe she fell in love with him, Orin. But she soon discovered that he wasn't after her at all!

ORIN. Who was he after—you?

CHRISTINE. (*sharply*) Orin! I'd be very angry with you if it weren't so ridiculous! (*She forces a laugh*) You don't seem to realize I'm an old married woman with two grown-up children! No, all he was after was to insinuate himself as a family friend and use your father when he came home to get him a better ship! I soon saw through his little scheme and he'll never call here again, I promise you that! (*She laughs—then with a teasing air*) And that's the whole of the great Captain Brant scandal! Are you satisfied now, you jealous goose, you?

ORIN. (*penitent and happy*) I'm a fool! The war has got me silly, I guess! If you knew all the hell I've been through!

CHRISTINE. It was Vinnie's fault you ever went to war! I'll never forgive her for that! It broke my heart, Orin! (*Then quickly*) But I was going to give you an example of her insane suspicions from the Captain Brant incident. Would you believe it that she has worked it all out that because his name is Brant, he must be the son of that nurse girl Marie Brantôme? Isn't that crazy? And to imagine for a moment, if he were, he'd ever come here to visit!

ORIN. (*his face hardening*) By God, I'd like to see him! His mother brought disgrace enough on our family without—

CHRISTINE. (*frightened, shrinking from him*) Orin! Don't look like that! You're so like your father! (*Then hurrying on*) But I haven't told you the worst yet. Vinnie actually accuses me—your mother—of being in love with that fool and of having met him in New York and gone to his room! I am no better than a prostitute in your sister's eyes!

ORIN. (*stunned*) I don't believe it! Vinnie couldn't!

87

CHRISTINE. I told you she'd gone crazy! She even followed me to New York, when I went to see your sick grandfather, to spy on me. She saw me meet a man—and immediately to her crazy brain the man was Brant. Oh, it's too revolting, Orin! You don't know what I've had to put up with from Vinnie, or you'd pity me!

ORIN. Good God! Did she tell Father that? No wonder he's dead! (*Then harshly*) Who was this man you met in New York?

CHRISTINE. It was Mr. Lamar, your grandfather's old friend who has known me ever since I was a baby! I happened to meet him and he asked me to go with him to call on his daughter. (*Then, seeing* ORIN *wavering, pitifully*) Oh, Orin! You pretend to love me! And yet you question me as if you suspected me, too! And you haven't Vinnie's excuse! You aren't out of your mind! (*She weeps hysterically.*)

ORIN. (*overcome at once by remorse and love*) No! I swear to you! (*He throws himself on his knees beside her and puts his arm around her*) Mother! Please! Don't cry! I do love you! I do!

CHRISTINE. I haven't told you the most horrible thing of all! Vinnie suspects me of having poisoned your father!

ORIN. (*horrified*) What! No, by God, that's too much! If that's true, she ought to be put in an asylum!

CHRISTINE. She found some medicine I take to make me sleep, but she is so crazy I know she thinks— (*Then, with real terror, clinging to him*) Oh, Orin, I'm so afraid of her! God knows what she might do, in her state! She might even go to the police and— Don't let her turn you against me! Remember you're all I have to protect me! You are all I have in the world, dear!

ORIN. (*tenderly soothing her*) Turn me against you? She can't be so crazy as to try that! But listen. I honestly think you— You're a little hysterical, you know. That—about Father—is all such damned nonsense! And as for her going to the police—do you suppose I wouldn't prevent that—for a hundred reasons—the family's sake—my own sake and Vinnie's, too, as well as yours—even if I knew—

CHRISTINE. (*staring at him—in a whisper*) Knew? Orin, you don't believe—?

ORIN. No! For God's sake! I only meant that no matter what you ever did, I love you better than anything in the world and—

CHRISTINE. (*in an outburst of grateful joy—pressing him to her and kissing him*) Oh, Orin, you are my boy, my baby! I love you!

ORIN. Mother! (*Then seizing her by the shoulders and staring into her eyes—with somber intensity*) I could forgive anything—anything!—in my mother—except that other—that about Brant!

CHRISTINE. I swear to you—!

ORIN. If I thought that damned—! (*With savage vengefulness*) By God, I'd show you then I hadn't been taught to kill for nothing!

CHRISTINE. (*full of new terror now—for* BRANT's *life—distractedly*) For God's sake, don't talk like that! You're not like my Orin! You're cruel and horrible! You frighten me!

ORIN. (*immediately contrite and soothing, petting her*) There, there, Mother! We won't ever think about it again! We'll talk of something else. I want to tell you something. (*He sits on the floor at her feet and looks up into her face. A pause. Then he asks tenderly, taking her hand*) Did you really want me to come back, Mother?

CHRISTINE. (*has calmed herself, but her eyes are still terrified and her voice trembles*) What a foolish question, dear!

ORIN. But your letters got farther and farther between—and they seemed so cold! It drove me crazy! I wanted to desert and run home —or else get killed! If you only knew how I longed to be here with you—like this! (*He leans his head against her knee. His voice becomes dreamy and low and caressing*) I used to have the most wonderful dreams about you. Have you ever read a book called "Typee"—about the South Sea Islands?

CHRISTINE. (*with a start—strangely*) Islands! Where there is peace?

ORIN. Then you did read it?

CHRISTINE. No.

ORIN. Someone loaned me the book. I read it and reread it until finally those Islands came to mean everything that wasn't war, every-thing that was peace and warmth and security. I used to dream I was there. And later on all the time I was out of my head I seemed really to be there. There was no one there but you and me. And yet I never saw you, that's the funny part. I only felt you all around me. The breaking of the waves was your voice. The sky was the same color as your eyes. The warm sand was like your skin. The whole island was you. (*He smiles with a dreamy tenderness*) A strange notion, wasn't it? But you needn't be provoked at being an island because this was the most beautiful island in the world—as beautiful as you, Mother!

CHRISTINE. (*has been staring over his head, listening fascinatedly, more and more deeply moved. As he stops, an agonizing tenderness for him wells up in her—with tortured longing*) Oh, if only you had never gone away! If you only hadn't let them take you from me!

ORIN. (*uneasily*) But I've come back. Everything is all right now, isn't it?

CHRISTINE. (*hastily*) Yes! I didn't mean that. It had to be.

ORIN. And I'll never leave you again now. I don't want Hazel or anyone. (*With a tender grin*) You're my only girl!

CHRISTINE. (*again with tenderness, stroking his hair—smiling*) You're a big man now, aren't you? I can't believe it. It seems only yesterday when I used to find you in your nightshirt hiding in the hall upstairs on the chance that I'd come up and you'd get one more good-night kiss! Do you remember?

ORIN. (*with a boyish grin*) You bet I remember! And what a row there was when Father caught me! And do you remember how you used to let me brush your hair and how I loved to? He hated me doing that, too. You've still got the same beautiful hair, Mother. That hasn't changed. (*He reaches up and touches her hair caressingly. She gives a little shudder of repulsion and draws away from him but he is too happy to notice*) Oh, Mother, it's going to be wonderful from now on! We'll get Vinnie to marry Peter and there will be just you and I!

90

(*The sliding doors in rear are opened a little and* LAVINIA *slips silently in and stands looking at them.*)

CHRISTINE. (*immediately senses her presence—controlling a start, harshly*) What do you want? (ORIN *turns to look at his sister resentfully.*)

LAVINIA. (*in a flat, emotionless voice*) Aren't you coming in to see Father, Orin?

ORIN. (*scrambling to his feet—irritably*) Oh, all right, I'll come now. (*He hurries out past* LAVINIA *with the air of one with a disagreeable duty he wants to get over quickly and closes the door with a bang behind him.* LAVINIA *stares at her mother a moment—then about-faces stiffly to follow him.*)

CHRISTINE. (*springs to her feet*) Vinnie! (*As* LAVINIA *turns to face her—sharply*) Come here—please. I don't want to shout across the room. (LAVINIA *comes slowly forward until she is at arm's length. Her eyes grow bleak and her mouth tightens to a thin line. The resemblance between mother and daughter as they stand confronting each other is strikingly brought out.* CHRISTINE *begins to speak in a low voice, coolly defiant, almost triumphant*) Well, you can go ahead now and tell Orin anything you wish! I've already told him—so you might as well save yourself the trouble. He said you must be insane! I told him how you lied about my trips to New York—for revenge!—because you loved Adam yourself! (LAVINIA *makes a movement like a faint shudder but is immediately stiff and frozen again.* CHRISTINE *smiles tauntingly*) So hadn't you better leave Orin out of it? You can't get him to go to the police for you. Even if you convinced him I poisoned your father, you couldn't! He doesn't want—any more than you do, or your father, or any of the Mannon dead—such a public disgrace as a murder trial would be! For it would all come out! Everything! Who Adam is and my adultery and your knowledge of it—and your love for Adam! Oh, believe me, I'll see to it that comes out if anything ever gets to a trial! I'll show you to the world as a daughter who desired her mother's lover and then tried to get her mother hanged out of hatred and jealousy! (*She laughs taunt-ingly.* LAVINIA *is trembling but her face remains hard and emotionless. Her lips open as if to speak but she closes them again.* CHRISTINE *seems drunk with her own defiant recklessness*) Go on! Try and convince Orin of my wickedness! He loves me! He hated his father! He's glad he's dead! Even if he knew I had killed him, he'd protect me! (*Then all her defiant attitude collapses and she pleads, seized by an hysterical terror, by some fear she has kept hidden*) For God's sake, keep Orin out of this! He's still sick! He's changed! He's grown hard and cruel! All he thinks of is death! Don't tell him about Adam! He would kill him! I couldn't live then! I would kill myself! (LAVINIA *starts and her eyes light up with a cruel hatred. Again her pale lips part as if she were about to say something but she controls the impulse and about-faces abruptly and walks with jerky steps from the room like some tragic mechanical doll.* CHRISTINE *stares after her—then as she disap-pears, collapses, catching at the table for support—terrifiedly*) I've got to see Adam! I've got to warn him! (*She sinks in the chair at right of table.*)

CURTAIN

ACT THREE

Scene—*The same as Act Two of "Homecoming"*—EZRA MANNON'S *study. His body, dressed in full uniform, is laid out on a bier draped in black which is placed lengthwise directly before the portrait of him over the fireplace. His head is at right. His mask-like face is a startling reproduction of the face in the portrait above him, but grimly remote and austere in death, like the carven face of a statue.*

The table and chairs which had been at center have been moved to the left. There is a lamp on this table. Two stands of three lighted candles are at each end of the black marble chimneypiece, throwing their light above on the portrait and below on the dead man. There is a chair by the dead man's head, at front of bier.

ORIN *is standing by the head of the bier, at the rear of it, stiffly erect like a sentinel at attention. He is not looking down at his father but is staring straight before him, deep in suspicious brooding. His face in the candlelight bears a striking resemblance to that of the portrait above him and the dead man's.*

The time of the opening of this act precedes by a few moments that of the end of the previous act.

ORIN. (*ashamed and guilty—bursts out angrily at himself*) Christ, I won't have such thoughts! I am a rotten swine to— Damn Vinnie! She must be crazy! (*Then, as if to distract his mind from these reflections, he turns to gaze down at his father. At the same moment* LAVINIA *appears silently in the doorway from the hall and stands looking at him. He does not notice her entrance. He stares at his father's mask-like face and addresses it with a strange friendly mockery*) Who are you? Another corpse! You and I have seen fields and hillsides sown with them—and they meant nothing!—nothing but a dirty joke life

93

plays on life! (*Then with a dry smile*) Death sits so naturally on you! Death becomes the Mannons! You were always like a statue of an eminent dead man—sitting on a chair in a park or straddling a horse in a town square—looking over the head of life without a sign of recognition—cutting it dead for the impropriety of living! (*He chuckles to himself with a queer affectionate amusement*) You never cared to know me in life—but I really think we might be friends now you are dead!

LAVINIA. (*sternly*) Orin!

ORIN. (*turns to her startledly*) Damn it, don't sneak around like that! What are you trying to do, anyway? I'm jumpy enough without— (*Then as she turns and locks the door behind her—suspiciously*) What are you locking the door for?

LAVINIA. I've got to talk to you—and I don't want to be interrupted. (*Then sternly*) What made you say such things just then? I wouldn't believe you could have grown so callous to all feeling of respect—

ORIN. (*guilty and resentful*) You folks at home take death so solemnly! You would have soon learned at the front that it's only a joke! You don't understand, Vinnie. You have to learn to mock or go crazy, can't you see? I didn't mean it in an unkind way. It simply struck me he looks so strangely familiar—the same familiar stranger I've never known. (*Then glancing at the dead man with a kindly amused smile*) Do you know his nickname in the army? Old Stick—short for Stick-in-the-Mud. Grant himself started it—said Father was no good on an offensive but he'd trust him to stick in the mud and hold a position until hell froze over!

LAVINIA. Orin! Don't you realize he was your father and he is dead?

ORIN. (*irritably*) What Grant said was a big compliment in a way.

LAVINIA. When I think of how proud of you he was when he came home! He boasted that you had done one of the bravest things he'd seen in the war!

ORIN. (*astonished—then grins with bitter mockery*) One of the bravest things he'd seen! Oh, that's too rich! I'll tell you the joke about that heroic deed. It really began the night before when I sneaked through their lines. I was always volunteering for extra danger. I was so scared anyone would guess I was afraid! There was a thick mist and it was so still you could hear the fog seeping into the ground. I met a Reb crawling toward our lines. His face drifted out of the mist toward mine. I shortened my sword and let him have the point under the ear. He stared at me with an idiotic look as if he'd sat on a tack—and his eyes dimmed and went out— (*His voice has sunk lower and lower, as if he were talking to himself. He pauses and stares over his father's body fascinatedly at nothing.*)

LAVINIA. (*with a shudder*) Don't think of that now!

ORIN. (*goes on with the same air*) Before I'd gotten back I had to kill another in the same way. It was like murdering the same man twice. I had a queer feeling that war meant murdering the same man over and over, and that in the end I would discover the man was myself! Their faces keep coming back in dreams—and they change to Father's face—or to mine— What does that mean, Vinnie?

LAVINIA. I don't know! I've got to talk to you! For heaven's sake, forget the war! It's over now!

ORIN. Not inside us who killed! (*Then quickly—with a bitter, joking tone*) The rest is all a joke! The next morning I was in the trenches. This was at Petersburg. I hadn't slept. My head was queer. I thought what a joke it would be on the stupid Generals like Father if everyone on both sides suddenly saw the joke war was on them and laughed and shook hands! So I began to laugh and walked toward their lines with my hand out. Of course, the joke was on me and I got this wound in the head for my pains. I went mad, wanted to kill and ran on, yelling. Then a lot of our fools went crazy, too, and followed me and we captured a part of their line we hadn't dared tackle before. I had acted without orders, of course—but Father decided it was better policy to overlook that and let me be a hero! So do you wonder I laugh!

95

LAVINIA. (*soothingly, coming to him and taking his arm*) You were brave and you know it. I'm proud of you, too.

ORIN. (*helplessly*) Oh, all right! Be proud, then! (*He leaves her and sprawls in the chair at left of table. She stands by the head of the bier and faces him. He says resentfully*) Well? Fire away and let's get this over! But you're wasting your breath. I know what you're going to say. Mother warned me. (*The whole memory of what his mother had said rushes over him*) My God, how can you think such things of Mother? What the hell's got into you? (*Then humoringly*) But I realize you're not yourself. I know how hard his death has hit you. Don't you think it would be better to postpone our talk until—

LAVINIA. No! (*Bitterly*) Has she succeeded in convincing you I'm out of my mind? Oh, Orin, how can you be so stupid? (*She goes to him and, grasping him by his shoulders, brings her face close to him—compellingly*) Look at me! You know in your heart I'm the same as I always was—your sister—who loves you, Orin!

ORIN. (*moved*) I didn't mean—I only think the shock of his death—

LAVINIA. I've never lied to you, have I? Even when we were little you always knew I told you the truth, didn't you?

ORIN. Yes—but—

LAVINIA. Then you must believe I wouldn't lie to you now!

ORIN. No one is saying you'd deliberately lie. It's a question of—

LAVINIA. And even if she's got you so under her thumb again that you doubt my word, you can't doubt the absolute proof!

ORIN. (*roughly*) Never mind what you call proofs! I know all about them already! (*Then excitedly*) Now, listen here, if you think you're going to tell me a lot of crazy stuff about Mother, I warn you I won't listen! So shut up before you start!

LAVINIA. (*threateningly now*) If you don't, I'll go to the police!

ORIN. Don't be a damn fool!

LAVINIA. As a last resort I will—if you force me to!

ORIN. By God, you must be crazy even to talk of—!

LAVINIA. They won't think so!

ORIN. Vinnie! Do you realize what it would mean—?

LAVINIA. I realize only too well! You and I, who are innocent, would suffer a worse punishment than the guilty—for we'd have to live on! It would mean that Father's memory and that of all the honorable Mannon dead would be dragged through the horror of a murder trial! But I'd rather suffer that than let the murder of our father go unpunished!

ORIN. Good God, do you actually believe—?

LAVINIA. Yes! I accuse her of murder! (*She takes the little box she has found in* CHRISTINE's *room right after the murder* [*Act Four "Homecoming"*] *from the bosom of her dress and holds it out to him*) You see this? I found it right after Father died!

ORIN. Don't be a damned lunatic! She told me all about that! It's only some stuff she takes to make her sleep!

LAVINIA. (*goes on implacably, ignoring his interruptions*) And Father knew she'd poisoned him! He said to me, "She's guilty!"

ORIN. That's all your crazy imagination! God, how can you think—? Do you realize you're deliberately accusing your own mother— It's too horrible and mad! I'll have you declared insane by Doctor Blake and put away in an asylum!

LAVINIA. I swear by our dead father I am telling you the truth! (*She puts her hand on the dead man and addresses him*) Make Orin believe me, Father!

ORIN. (*harshly*) Don't drag him in! He always sided with you against Mother and me! (*He grabs her arm and forces the box from her hand*) Here! Give me that! (*He slips it into his coat pocket.*)

LAVINIA. Ah! So you are afraid it's true!

ORIN. No! But I'm going to stop your damned— But I'm a fool to pay any attention to you! The whole thing is too insane! I won't talk to a crazy woman! But, by God, you look out, Vinnie! You leave Mother alone or—!

LAVINIA. (*regarding him bitterly*) Poor Father! He thought the war had made a man of you! But you're not! You're still the spoiled crybaby that she can make a fool of whenever she pleases!

ORIN. (*stung*) That's enough from you!

LAVINIA. Oh, she warned me just now what to expect! She boasted that you wouldn't believe me, and that even if you knew she'd murdered Father you would be glad because you hated him! (*Then a note of entreaty in her voice*) Orin! For God's sake—here, before him!—tell me that isn't true, at least!

ORIN. (*overcome by a sense of guilt—violently defensive*) Of course, I never said that—and I don't believe she did. But Mother means a thousand times more to me than he ever did! I say that before him now as I would if he could hear me!

LAVINIA. (*with a calculated scornful contempt now*) Then if I can't make you see your duty one way, I will another! If you won't help me punish her, I hope you're not such a coward that you're willing to let her lover escape!

ORIN. (*in a tone of awakening suspicion*) Lover? Who do you mean?

LAVINIA. I mean the man who plotted Father's murder with her, who must have got the poison for her! I mean the Captain Brant I wrote you about!

ORIN. (*thickly, trying to fight back his jealous suspicion*) You lie! She told me your rotten lies—about him—about following her to New York. That was Mr. Lamar she met.

LAVINIA. So that's what she told you! As if I could mistake Lamar for Adam Brant! What a fool you are, Orin! She kisses you and pretends she loves you—when she'd forgotten you were ever alive, when all she's thought of is this low lover of hers—!

ORIN. (*wildly*) Stop! I won't stand—!

LAVINIA. When all she is thinking of right now is how she can use you to keep me from doing anything, so she'll get a chance to run off and marry him!

ORIN. You lie!

98

LAVINIA. She pets you and plays the loving mother and you're so blind you can't see through her! I tell you she went to his room! I followed them upstairs. I heard her telling him, "I love you, Adam." She was kissing him!

ORIN. (*grabs her by the shoulder and shakes her, forcing her to her knees—frenziedly*) Damn you! Tell me you're lying or—!

LAVINIA. (*unafraid—looking up into his eyes—coldly*) You know I'm not lying! She's been going to New York on the excuse of visiting Grandfather Hamel, but really to give herself to—!

ORIN. (*in anguish*) You lie, damn you! (*Threateningly*) You dare say that about Mother! Now you've got to prove it or else—! You're not insane! You know what you're saying! So you prove it—or by God, I'll—!

LAVINIA. (*taking his hands off her shoulders and rising*) All I ask is a chance to prove it! (*Then intensely*) But when I do, will you help me punish Father's murderers?

ORIN. (*in a burst of murderous rage*) I'll kill that bastard! (*In anguished uncertainty again*) But you haven't proved anything yet! It's only your word against hers! I don't believe you! You say Brant is her lover! If that's true, I'll hate her! I'll know she murdered Father then! I'll help you punish her! But you've got to prove it!

LAVINIA. (*coldly*) I can do that very soon. She's frightened out of her wits! She'll go to see Brant the first chance she gets. We must give her that chance. Will you believe me when you find them together?

ORIN. (*torturedly*) Yes. (*Then in a burst of rage*) God damn him, I'll—!

LAVINIA. (*sharply*) Ssshh! Be quiet. There's someone in the hall! (*They wait, staring at the door. Then someone knocks loudly.*)

CHRISTINE. (*her voice comes through the door, frightened and strained*) Orin!

ORIN. (*stammers*) God! I can't face her now!

99

LAVINIA. (*in a quick whisper*) Don't let her know you suspect her. Pretend you think I'm out of my mind, as she wanted you to.

CHRISTINE. Orin! Why don't you answer me? (*She tries the door-knob, and finding the door locked, her voice becomes terrified*) Why have you locked me out? Let me in! (*She pounds on the door violently.*)

LAVINIA. (*in a whisper*) Answer her. Let her in.

ORIN. (*obeying mechanically—calls in a choked voice*) All right. I'm coming. (*He moves reluctantly toward the door.*)

LAVINIA. (*struck by a sudden idea—grasps his arm*) Wait! (*Before he can prevent it, she reaches in his pocket and gets possession of the box and puts it conspicuously on the body over the dead man's heart*) Watch her when she sees that—if you want proof!

CHRISTINE. Open the door! (*He forces himself to open the door and steps aside.* CHRISTINE *almost falls in. She is in a state bordering on collapse. She throws her arms around* ORIN *as if seeking protection from him*) Orin! I got so afraid—when I found the door locked!

ORIN. (*controls a furious jealous impulse to push her violently away from him—harshly*) What made you afraid, Mother?

CHRISTINE. (*stammers*) Why do you look at me—like that? You look—so like—your father!

ORIN. I am his son, too, remember that!

LAVINIA. (*warningly*) Orin!

CHRISTINE. (*turning on* LAVINIA *who stands by the head of the bier*) I suppose you've been telling him your vile lies, you—

ORIN. (*remembering his instructions, forces himself to blurt out*) She—she's out of her head, Mother.

CHRISTINE. Didn't I tell you! I knew you'd see that! (*Then anxiously, keeping her eyes on* LAVINIA) Did she tell you what she's going to do, Orin? I know she's plotting something—crazy! Did she threaten to go to the police? They might not believe she's crazy—(*Pleading desperately, her eyes still on* LAVINIA) You won't let her do anything dreadful like that, will you?

ORIN. (*feeling her guilt, stammers*) No, Mother.

CHRISTINE. (*her eyes, which have been avoiding the corpse, now fasten on the dead man's face with fascinated horror*) No—remember your father wouldn't want—any scandal—he mustn't be worried, he said—he needs rest and peace— (*She addresses the dead man directly in a strange tone of defiant scorn*) You seem the same to me in death, Ezra! You were always dead to me! I hate the sight of death! I hate the thought of it! (*Her eyes shift from his face and she sees the box of poison. She starts back with a stifled scream and stares at it with guilty fear.*)

ORIN. Mother! For God's sake, be quiet! (*The strain snaps for him and he laughs with savage irony*) God! To think I hoped home would be an escape from death! I should never have come back to life—from my island of peace! (*Then staring at his mother strangely*) But that's lost now! You're my lost island, aren't you, Mother? (*He turns and stumbles blindly from the room.* LAVINIA *reaches out stealthily and snatches up the box. This breaks the spell for* CHRISTINE *whose eyes have been fixed on it hypnotically. She looks wildly at* LAVINIA's *frozen accusing face.*)

LAVINIA. (*in a cold, grim voice*) It was Brant who got you this—medicine to make you sleep—wasn't it?

CHRISTINE. (*distractedly*) No! No! No!

LAVINIA. You're telling me it was. I knew it—but I wanted to make sure. (*She puts the box back in the bosom of her dress—turns, rigid and square-shouldered, and walks woodenly from the room.*)

CHRISTINE. (*stares after her wildly, then her eyes fasten again on the dead man's face. Suddenly she appeals to him distractedly*) Ezra! Don't let her harm Adam! I am the only guilty one! Don't let Orin—! (*Then, as if she read some answer in the dead man's face, she stops in terror and, her eyes still fixed on his face, backs to the door and rushes out.*)

CURTAIN

ACT FOUR

T HE *stern section of a clipper ship moored alongside a wharf in East Boston, with the floor of the wharf in the foreground. The vessel lies with her bow and amidships off left and only the part aft of the mizzenmast is visible with the curve of the stern at right. The ship is unloaded and her black side rises nine or ten feet above the level of the wharf. On the poop deck above, at right, is the wheel. At left is the chart room and the entrance to the companionway stairs leading below to the cabin. At extreme left is the mizzenmast, the lowest yard just visible above, the boom of the spanker extending out above the deck to the right. Below the deck the portholes show a faint light from the interior of the cabin. On the wharf the end of a warehouse is at left front.*

It is a night two days after Act Two—the day following EZRA MANNON's *funeral. The moon is rising above the horizon off left rear, its light accentuating the black outlines of the ship.*

Borne on the wind the melancholy refrain of the capstan chanty "Shenandoah," sung by a chantyman with the crew coming in on the chorus, drifts over the water from a ship that is weighing anchor in the harbor. Half in and half out of the shadow of the warehouse, the CHANTYMAN *lies sprawled on his back, snoring in a drunken slumber. The sound of the singing seems to strike a responsive chord in his brain, for he stirs, grunts, and with difficulty raises himself to a sitting position in the moonlight beyond the shadow.*

He is a thin, wiry man of sixty-five or so, with a tousled mop of black hair, unkempt black beard and mustache. His weather-beaten face is dissipated, he has a weak mouth, his big round blue eyes are bloodshot, dreamy and drunken. But there is something romantic, a queer troubadour-of-the-sea quality about him.

102

CHANTYMAN. (*listens to the singing with critical disapproval*) A
hell of a chantyman that feller be! Screech owls is op'ry singers compared to him! I'll give him a taste of how "Shenandoah" ought t' be
sung! (*He begins to sing in a surprisingly good tenor voice, a bit
blurry with booze now and sentimentally mournful to a degree, but
still managing to get full value out of the chanty.*)

> "Oh, Shenandoah, I long to hear you—
> A-way, my rolling river!
> Oh, Shenandoah, I can't get near you—
> Way—ay, I'm bound away
> Across the wide Missouri!
>
> "Oh, Shenandoah, I love your daughter
> A-way, my rolling river!

(*He stops abruptly, shaking his head—mournfully*) No good! Too
drunk to do myself jestice! Pipe down, my John! Sleep it off! (*He
sprawls back on his elbows—confusedly*) Where am I? What the hell
difference is it? There's plenty o' fresh air and the moon fur a glim.
Don't be so damn pertic'lar! What ye want anyways? Featherbed
an' a grand piany? (*He sings with a maudlin zest.*)

> "A bottle o' wine and a bottle o' beer
> And a bottle of Irish whiskey oh!
> So early in the morning
> The sailor likes his bottle oh!"

(*He stops and mutters*) Who'll buy a drink fur the slickest chantyman on the Western or any other damn ocean? Go to hell then! I
kin buy it myself! (*He fumbles in his pants pocket*) I had it in
this pocket—I remember I put it there pertic'lar—ten dollars in this
pocket—(*He pulls the pocket inside out—with bewildered drunken
anger*) By Christ, it's gone! I'm plucked clean! (*He struggles to a
sitting position*) Where was I last? Aye, I remember! That yaller-

haired pig with the pink dress on! Put her arm around me so lovin'! Told me how fine I could sing! (*He scrambles unsteadily to his feet*) By Christ, I'll go back an' give her a seaboot in her fat tail that'll learn her—! (*He takes a step but lurches into the shadow and leans against the warehouse*) Hard down! Heavy gales around Cape Stiff! All is sunk but honor, as the feller says, an' there's damn little o' that afloat! (*He stands against the warehouse, waiting for the swaying world to subside. The companionway door on the poop deck of the vessel is opened and* ADAM BRANT *comes cautiously out. He looks around him quickly with an uneasy suspicious air. He is dressed in a merchant captain's blue uniform. Satisfied that there is no one on the deck, he comes to the rail and stares expectantly up the wharf, off left. His attitude is tense and nervous and he keeps one hand in his coat pocket. The* CHANTYMAN *loses his balance, lurches forward, then back against the warehouse with a thump.* BRANT *leaps back from the rail startledly, jerking a revolver from his coat pocket—then leans over the rail again and calls threateningly.*)

BRANT. Who's there? Come out and let me have a look at you or by God I'll shoot!

CHANTYMAN. (*stares up, startled in his turn and momentarily sobered—hastily*) Easy goes, shipmate! Stow that pistol! I'm doin' you no harm. (*He lurches out into the moonlight—suddenly pugnacious*) Not that I'm skeered o' you or your shooter! Who the hell are you to be threatenin' the life of an honest chantyman? Tryin' to hold me up, air ye? I been robbed once tonight! I'll go to the police station and tell 'em there's a robber here—

BRANT. (*hastily, with a placating air*) No harm meant. I'm skipper of this vessel and there have been a lot of waterfront thieves around here lately. I'm lacking a watchman and I've got to keep my weather eye open.

CHANTYMAN. (*again momentarily sobered—touching his forehead*) Aye—aye, sir. Mind your eye. I heer'd tell robbers broke in the

"Annie Lodge's" cabin two nights back. Smashed everything and stole two hundred dollars off her skipper. Murderous, too, they be! Near beat the watchman's brains out! (*Then drunken pugnaciousness comes over him again*) Think I'm one o' that gang, do ye? Come down out o' that and I'll show ye who's a thief! I don't give a damn if ye air a skipper! Ye could be Bully Watermann himself an' I'd not let you insult me! I ain't signed on your old hooker! You've got no rights over me! I'm on dry land, by Christ, and this is a free country and— (*His voice has risen to a shout.* BRANT *is alarmed that this uproar will attract someone. He puts the pistol back in his pocket hastily and peers anxiously down the wharf. Then he interrupts the* CHANTY-MAN's *tirade by a sharp command.*)

BRANT. Stow your damned jaw! Or, by the Eternal, I'll come down and pound some sense in your head!

CHANTYMAN. (*automatically reacts to the voice of authority—quietly*) Aye—aye, sir. (*Then inconsequentially*) You ain't needin' a chantyman fur your next vi'ge, are ye, sir?

BRANT. I'm not sailing for a month yet. If you're still out of a job then—

CHANTYMAN. (*proudly*) You don't know me, that's plain! I'm the finest damn chantyman that ever put a tune to his lip! I ain't lookin' fur berths—they're lookin' fur me! Aye! Skippers are on'y too glad to git me! Many's a time I've seed a skipper an' mates sweatin' blood to beat work out of a crew but nary a lick could they git into 'em till I raised a tune—and then there'd be full sail on her afore ye knowed it!

BRANT. (*impatiently*) I'm not doubting your ability. But I'd advise you to turn in and sleep it off.

CHANTYMAN. (*not heeding this—sadly*) Aye, but it ain't fur long, steam is comin' in, the sea is full o' smoky tea-kettles, the old days is dyin', and where'll you an' me be then? (*Lugubriously drunken again*) Everything is dyin'! Abe Lincoln is dead. I used to ship on

105

the Mannon packets an' I seed in the paper where Ezra Mannon was dead! (BRANT *starts guiltily. The* CHANTYMAN *goes on maudlinly*) Heart failure killed him, it said, but I know better! I've sailed on Mannon hookers an' been worked t' death and gotten swill fur grub, an' I know he didn't have no heart in him! Open him up an' you'd find a dried turnip! The old skinflint must have left a pile o' money. Who gits it, I wonder? Leave a widder, did he?

BRANT. (*harshly*) How would I know? (*Changing the subject calculatingly*) What are you doing here, Chantyman? I'd expect a man with your voice would be in a saloon, singing and making merry!

CHANTYMAN. So I would! So I would! But I was robbed, sir—aye —an' I know who done it—a yaller-haired wench had her arm around me. Steer clear o' gals or they'll skin your hide off an' use it fur a carpet! I warn ye, skipper! They're not fur sailormen like you an' me, 'less we're lookin' fur sorrow! (*Then insinuatingly*) I ain't got the price of a drink, that's why I'm here, sir.

BRANT. (*reaches in his pocket and tosses him down a silver dollar*) Here!

CHANTYMAN. (*fumbles around and finds the dollar*) Thank ye, sir. (*Then flatteringly*) It's a fine ship you've got there, sir. Crack sail on her and she'll beat most of 'em—an' you're the kind to crack sail on, I kin tell by your cut.

BRANT. (*pleased, glancing up at his ship's lofty rig*) Aye! I'll make her go right enough!

CHANTYMAN. All you need is a good chantyman to help ye. Here's "Hanging Johnny" fur ye! (BRANT *starts at this. The* CHANTYMAN *suddenly begins to sing the chanty "Hanging Johnny" with sentimental mournfulness.*)

> "Oh, they call me Hanging Johnny
> Away—ay—i—oh!
> They says I hangs for money
> Oh, hang, boys, hang!"

BRANT (*harshly*) Stop that damned dirge! And get out of here!
Look lively now!

CHANTYMAN. (*starting to go*) Aye—aye, sir. (*Then resentfully*) I
see ye ain't got much ear fur music. Good night.

BRANT. (*with exasperated relief*) Good night. (*The* CHANTYMAN
*goes unsteadily off left, between the warehouse and the ship. He
bursts again into his mournful dirge, his voice receding*)

> "*They say I hanged my mother*
> *Away—ay—i—oh!*
> *They say I hanged my mother*
> *Oh, hang, boys, hang!*"

(BRANT, *standing by the rail looking after him, mutters a curse and
starts pacing up and down the deck*) Damn that chanty! It's sad as
death! I've a foreboding I'll never take this ship to sea. She doesn't
want me now—a coward hiding behind a woman's skirts! The sea
hates a coward! (*A woman's figure dressed in black, heavily veiled,
moves stealthily out from the darkness between the ship and the
warehouse, left. She sees the figure on the deck above her and shrinks
back with a stifled gasp of fear.* BRANT *hears the noise. Immediately
his revolver is in his hand and he peers down into the shadows of the
warehouse*) Who's there?

CHRISTINE. (*with a cry of relief*) Adam!

BRANT. Christine! (*Then quickly*) Go back to the gangplank. I'll
meet you there. (*She goes back. He hurries along the deck and disappears off left to meet her. Their voices are heard and a moment
later they enter on the poop deck, from left. She leans against him
weakly and he supports her with his arm around her*) I have to bring
you this way. I bolted the door to the main deck.

CHRISTINE. I was so frightened. I wasn't sure which ship! Some
drunken man came along singing—

BRANT. Aye. I just got rid of him. I fired the watchman this morning so I'd be alone at night. I was hoping you'd come soon. Did that drunk see you?

CHRISTINE. No. I hid behind some boxes. (*Then frightenedly*) Why have you got that pistol?

BRANT. (*grimly*) I was going to give them a fight for it—if things went wrong.

CHRISTINE. Adam!

BRANT. By God, you don't think I'll ever let them take me alive, do you?

CHRISTINE. Please, please! Don't talk of that for a moment! Only hold me close to you! Tell me you love me!

BRANT. (*harshly*) It's no time! I want to know what's happened! (*Then immediately repentant he kisses her—with rough tenderness*) Don't mind me! My nerves are gone from waiting alone here not knowing anything but what I read in the papers—that he was dead. These last days have been hell!

CHRISTINE. If you knew what they have been for me!

BRANT. There's something gone wrong! I can read that in your face! What is it, Christine?

CHRISTINE. (*falteringly*) Vinnie knows—! She came into the room when he was dying! He told her—

BRANT. (*harshly*) God! What is she going to do? (*Then, without giving her time to answer his question, he suddenly looks around uneasily*) Christine! How did you get away? She'd suspect you weren't going to your father's now. She followed you once before—

CHRISTINE. No. It's all right. This morning Orin said his cousins, the Bradfords, had invited him and Vinnie to visit them overnight at Blackridge and he was taking Vinnie with him because he thought a change would bring her back to her senses. I've made him think she's out of her head with grief—so he wouldn't listen to her—

BRANT. (*eagerly*) And he believes that?

CHRISTINE. (*weakly*) Yes—he does—now—but I don't know how long—

BRANT. Ah!

CHRISTINE. So I told him by all means to go. It gave me the chance I wanted to come to you. They went this morning. They don't know I've gone and even after they've found out they can't prove where I went. I can only stay a little while, Adam—we've got to plan—so many things have happened I couldn't foresee—I came to warn you—

BRANT. Ssshh! Come below in the cabin! We're fools to be talking out here. (*He guides her with his arm around her through the door to the companionway stairs and closes it quietly behind them. A pause in which the singing of the crew on the ship in the harbor comes mournfully over the water. Then* ORIN *and* LAVINIA *come in stealthily along the deck from the left. She is dressed in black as before. He wears a long cloak over his uniform and has a slouch hat pulled down over his eyes. Her manner is cold and grim.* ORIN *is holding in a savage, revengeful rage. They approach the cabin skylight silently.* ORIN *bends down by it to listen. His face, in the light from the skylight, becomes distorted with jealous fury.* LAVINIA *puts a restraining hand on his arm.*

The scene fades out into darkness. Several minutes are supposed to elapse. When the light comes on again, a section of the ship has been removed to reveal the interior of the cabin, a small compartment, the walls newly painted a light brown. The skylight giving on the deck above is in the middle of the ceiling. Suspended in the skylight is a ship's compass. Beneath it is a pine table with three chairs, one at rear, the other two at the table ends, left and right. On the table is a bottle of whiskey, half full, with a glass and a pitcher of water.

Built against the right wall of the cabin is a long narrow couch, like a bunk, with leather cushions. In the rear wall, at right, is a door leading into the captain's stateroom. A big sideboard stands against the left wall, center. Above it, a ship's clock. Farther back is a door opening on the alleyway leading to the main deck. The companionway stairs lead down to this alleyway.

There is a lighted lamp on the sideboard and a ship's lantern, also lighted, at the right end of the table.

In the cabin, BRANT *is seated at the right of table,* CHRISTINE *to the rear of it. Her face looks haggard and aging, the mouth pinched and drawn down at the corners, and her general appearance, the arrangement of her hair and clothes, has the disheveled touch of the fugitive. She is just finishing her story of the murder and the events following it. He is listening tensely.*

On the deck above, ORIN *and* LAVINIA *are discovered as before, with* ORIN *bending down by the transom, listening.*)

CHRISTINE. When he was dying he pointed at me and told her I was guilty! And afterwards she found the poison—

BRANT. (*springing to his feet*) For God's sake, why didn't you—

CHRISTINE. (*pitifully*) I fainted before I could hide it! And I had planned it all so carefully. But how could I foresee that she would come in just at that moment? And how could I know he would talk to me the way he did? He drove me crazy! He kept talking of death! He was torturing me! I only wanted him to die and leave me alone!

BRANT. (*his eyes lighting up with savage satisfaction*) He knew before he died whose son I was, you said? By God, I'll bet that maddened him!

CHRISTINE. (*repeats pitifully*) I'd planned it so carefully—but something made things happen!

BRANT. (*overcome by gloomy dejection, sinks down on his chair again*) I knew it! I've had a feeling in my bones! It serves me right, what has happened and is to happen! It wasn't that kind of revenge I had sworn on my mother's body! I should have done as I wanted—fought with Ezra Mannon as two men fight for love of a woman! (*With bitter self-contempt*) I have my father's rotten coward blood in me, I think! Aye!

CHRISTINE. Adam! You make me feel so guilty!

BRANT. (*rousing himself—shamefacedly*) I didn't mean to blame you, Christine. (*Then harshly*) It's too late for regrets now, anyway. We've got to think what to do.

CHRISTINE. Yes! I'm so terrified of Vinnie! Oh, Adam, you must promise me to be on your guard every minute! If she convinces Orin you are my lover— Oh, why can't we go away, Adam? Once we're out of her reach, she can't do anything.

BRANT. The "Flying Trades" won't be sailing for a month or more. We can't get cargo as soon as the owners thought.

CHRISTINE. Can't we go on another ship—as passengers—to the East —we could be married out there—

BRANT (*gloomily*) But everyone in the town would know you were gone. It would start suspicion—

CHRISTINE. No. Orin and Vinnie would lie to people. They'd have to for their own sakes. They'd say I was in New York with my father. Oh, Adam, it's the only thing we can do! If we don't get out of Vinnie's reach right away I know something horrible will happen!

BRANT. (*dejectedly*) Aye. I suppose it's the only way out for us now. The "Atlantis" is sailing on Friday for China. I'll arrange with her skipper to give us passage—and keep his mouth shut. She sails at daybreak Friday. You'd better meet me here Thursday night. (*Then with an effort*) I'll write Clark and Dawson tonight they'll have to find another skipper for the "Flying Trades."

CHRISTINE. (*noticing the hurt in his tone—miserably*) Poor Adam! I know how it hurts you to give up your ship.

BRANT. (*rousing himself guiltily—pats her hand—with gruff tenderness*) There are plenty of ships—but there is only one you, Christine!

CHRISTINE. I feel so guilty! I've brought you nothing but misfortune!

BRANT. You've brought love—and the rest is only the price. It's worth it a million times! You're all mine now, anyway! (*He hugs her to him, staring over her head with sad blank eyes.*)

CHRISTINE. (*her voice trembling*) But I'm afraid I'm not much to boast about having—now. I've grown old in the past few days. I'm ugly. But I'll make myself beautiful again—for you—! I'll make up to you for everything! Try not to regret your ship too much, Adam!

BRANT. (*gruffly*) Let's not talk of her any more. (*Then forcing a wry smile*) I'll give up the sea. I think it's through with me now, anyway! The sea hates a coward.

CHRISTINE. (*trying pitifully to cheer him*) Don't talk like that! You have me, Adam! You have me! And we will be happy—once we're safe on your Blessed Islands! (*Then suddenly, with a little shudder*) It's strange. Orin was telling me of an island— (*On the deck above,* ORIN, *who has bent closer to the transom, straightens up with a threatening movement.* LAVINIA *grips his arm, restraining him.*)

BRANT. (*with a bitter, hopeless yearning*) Aye—the Blessed Isles— Maybe we can still find happiness and forget! (*Then strangely, as if to himself*) I can see them now—so close—and a million miles away! The warm earth in the moonlight, the trade winds rustling the coco palms, the surf on the barrier reef singing a croon in your ears like a lullaby! Aye! There's peace, and forgetfulness for us there —if we can ever find those islands now!

CHRISTINE. (*desperately*) We will find them! We will! (*She kisses him. A pause. Suddenly she glances frightenedly at the clock*) Look at the time! I've got to go, Adam!

BRANT. For the love of God, watch out for Vinnie. If anything happened to you now—!

CHRISTINE. Nothing will happen to me. But you must be on your guard in case Orin— Good-bye, my lover! I must go! I must! (*She tears herself from his arms but immediately throws herself in them again—terrifiedly*) Oh! I feel so strange—so sad—as if I'd never see you again! (*She begins to sob hysterically*) Oh, Adam, tell me you don't regret! Tell me we're going to be happy! I can't bear this horrible feeling of despair!

BRANT. Of course we'll be happy! Come now! It's only a couple of days. (*They start for the door*) We'll go by the main deck. It's shorter. I'll walk to the end of the wharf with you. I won't go further. We might be seen.

CHRISTINE. Then we don't have to say good-bye for a few minutes yet! Oh, thank God! (*They go out to the alleyway,* BRANT *closing the door behind him. A pause. On the deck above* ORIN *pulls a revolver from under his cloak and makes a move, as if to rush off left down to the main deck after them.* LAVINIA *has been dreading this and throws herself in his way, grasping his arm.*)

ORIN. (*in a furious whisper*) Let me go!

LAVINIA. (*struggling with him*) No! Be quiet! Ssshh! I hear them on the main deck! Quick! Come to his cabin! (*She urges him to the companionway door, gets him inside and shuts the door behind them. A moment later the door on the left of the cabin below is opened and they enter.*)

LAVINIA. He's going to the end of the wharf. That gives us a few minutes. (*Grimly*) You wanted proof! Well, are you satisfied now?

ORIN. Yes! God damn him! Death is too good for him! He ought to be—

LAVINIA. (*sharply commanding*) Orin! Remember you promised not to lose your head. You've got to do everything exactly as we planned it, so there'll be no suspicion about us. There would be no justice if we let ourselves—

ORIN. (*impatiently*) You've said all that before! Do you think I'm a fool? I'm not anxious to be hanged—for that skunk! (*Then with bitter anguish*) I heard her asking him to kiss her! I heard her warn him against me! (*He gives a horrible chuckle*) And my island I told her about—which was she and I—she wants to go there—with him! (*Then furiously*) Damn you! Why did you stop me? I'd have shot his guts out in front of her!

LAVINIA. (*scornfully*) Outside on deck where the shot would be sure to be heard? We'd have been arrested—and then I'd have to tell the truth to save us. She'd be hanged, and even if we managed to get off, our lives would be ruined! The only person to come off lucky would be Brant! He could die happy, knowing he'd revenged himself on us more than he ever dared hope! Is that what you want?

ORIN. (*sullenly*) No.

LAVINIA. Then don't act like a fool again. (*Looks around the cabin calculatingly—then in a tone of command*) Go and hide outside. He won't see you when he passes along the alleyway in the dark. He'll come straight in here. That's the time for you—

ORIN. (*grimly*) You needn't tell me what to do. I've had a thorough training at this game—thanks to you and Father.

LAVINIA. Quick! Go out now! He won't be long!

ORIN. (*goes to the door—then quickly*) I hear him coming. (*He slips out silently. She hurriedly hides herself by the sideboard at left, front. A moment later* BRANT *appears in the doorway and stands just inside it blinking in the light. He looks around the cabin sadly.*)

BRANT. (*huskily*) So it's good-bye to you, "Flying Trades"! And you're right! I wasn't man enough for you! (ORIN *steps through the door and with the pistol almost against* BRANT's *body fires twice.* BRANT *pitches forward to the floor by the table, rolls over, twitches a moment on his back and lies still.* ORIN *springs forward and stands over the body, his pistol aimed down at it, ready to fire again.*)

LAVINIA. (*stares fascinatedly at* BRANT's *still face*) Is he—dead?

ORIN. Yes.

LAVINIA. (*sharply*) Don't stand there! Where's the chisel you brought? Smash open everything in his stateroom. We must make it look as if thieves killed him, remember! Take anything valuable! We can sink it overboard afterwards! Hurry! (ORIN *puts his revolver on the table and takes a chisel that is stuck in his belt under his cloak and goes into the stateroom. A moment later there is the sound of splintering wood as he pries open a drawer.*)

LAVINIA. (*goes slowly to the body and stands looking down into* BRANT's *face. Her own is frozen and expressionless. A pause.* ORIN *can be heard in the stateroom prying open* BRANT's *desk and scattering the contents of drawers around. Finally* LAVINIA *speaks to the corpse in a grim bitter tone*) How could you love that vile old woman so? (*She throws off this thought—harshly*) But you're dead! It's ended! (*She turns away from him resolutely—then suddenly turns back and stands stiffly upright and grim beside the body and prays coldly, as if carrying out a duty*) May God find forgiveness for your sins! May the soul of our cousin, Adam Mannon, rest in peace! (ORIN *comes in from the stateroom and overhears the last of her prayer.*)

ORIN. (*harshly*) Rest in hell, you mean! (*He comes to her*) I've pried open everything I could find.

LAVINIA. Then come along. Quick. There's your pistol. Don't forget that. (*She goes to the door.*)

ORIN. (*putting it in his pocket*) We've got to go through his pockets to make everything look like a burglary. (*He quickly turns* BRANT'S *pockets inside out and puts the revolver he finds, along with bills and coins, watch and chain, knife, etc., into his own*) I'll sink these overboard from the dock, along with what was in his stateroom. (*Having finished this, he still remains stooping over the body and stares into* BRANT'S *face, a queer fascinated expression in his eyes.*)

LAVINIA. (*uneasily*) Orin!

ORIN. By God, he does look like Father!

LAVINIA. No! Come along!

ORIN. (*as if talking to himself*) This is like my dream. I've killed him before—over and over.

LAVINIA. Orin!

ORIN. Do you remember me telling you how the faces of the men I killed came back and changed to Father's face and finally became my own? (*He smiles grimly*) He looks like me, too! Maybe I've committed suicide!

LAVINIA. (*frightenedly—grabbing his arm*) Hurry! Someone may come!

ORIN. (*not heeding her, still staring at* BRANT—*strangely*) If I had been he I would have done what he did! I would have loved her as he loved her—and killed Father too—for her sake!

LAVINIA. (*tensely—shaking him by the arm*) Orin, for God's sake, will you stop talking crazy and come along? Do you want us to be found here? (*She pulls him away forcibly.*)

ORIN. (*with a last look at the dead man*) It's queer! It's a rotten dirty joke on someone! (*He lets her hustle him out to the alleyway.*)

CURTAIN

ACT FIVE

SCENE—*The same as Act Three of "Homecoming"—exterior of the Mannon house. It is the following night. The moon has just risen. The right half of the house is in the black shadow cast by the pine trees but the moonlight falls full on the part to the left of the doorway. The door at center is open and there is a light in the hall behind. All the shutters of the windows are closed.*

CHRISTINE *is discovered walking back and forth on the drive before the portico, passing from moonlight into the shadow of the pines and back again. She is in a frightful state of tension, unable to keep still.*

She sees someone she is evidently expecting approaching the house from up the drive, off left, and she hurries down as far as the bench to meet her.

HAZEL. (*enters from left—with a kindly smile*) Here I am! Seth brought your note and I hurried right over.

CHRISTINE. (*kissing her—with unnatural effusiveness*) I'm so glad you've come! I know I shouldn't have bothered you.

HAZEL. It's no bother at all, Mrs. Mannon. I'm only too happy to keep you company.

CHRISTINE. I was feeling so terribly sad—and nervous here. I had let Hannah and Annie have the night off. I'm all alone. (*She sits on the bench*) Let's sit out here. I can't bear it in the house. (HAZEL *sits beside her.*)

HAZEL. (*pityingly*) I know. It must be terribly lonely for you. You must miss him so much.

CHRISTINE. (*with a shudder*) Please don't talk about— He is buried! He is gone!

HAZEL. (*gently*) He is at peace, Mrs. Mannon.

CHRISTINE. (*with bitter mockery*) I was like you once! I believed in heaven! Now I know there is only hell!

HAZEL. Ssshh! You mustn't say that.

CHRISTINE. (*rousing herself—forcing a smile*) I'm not fit company for a young girl, I'm afraid. You should have youth and beauty and freedom around you. I'm old and ugly and haunted by death! (*Then, as if to herself—in a low desperate tone*) I can't let myself get ugly! I can't!

HAZEL. You're only terribly worn out. You ought to try and sleep.

CHRISTINE. I don't believe there's such a thing on this earth as sleep! It's only in the earth one sleeps! One must feel so at peace—at last—with all one's fears ended! (*Then forcing a laugh*) Good heavens, what a bore it must be for you, listening to my gloomy thoughts! I honestly didn't send for you to— I wanted to ask if you or Peter had heard anything from Orin and Vinnie.

HAZEL. (*surprised*) Why, no. We haven't seen them since the funeral.

CHRISTINE. (*forcing a smile*) They seem to have deserted me. (*Then quickly*) I mean they should have been home before this. I can't imagine what's keeping them. They went to Blackridge to stay overnight at the Bradfords'.

HAZEL. Then there's nothing to worry about. But I don't see how they could leave you alone—just now.

CHRISTINE. Oh, that part is all right. I urged them to go. They left soon after the funeral, and afterwards I thought it would be a good opportunity for me to go to New York and see my father. He's sick, you know, but I found him so much better I decided to come home again last night. I expected Vinnie and Orin back this noon, but here it's night and no sign of them. I—I must confess I'm worried—and frightened. You can't know the horror of being all night

—alone in that house! (*She glances at the house behind her with a shudder.*)

HAZEL. Would it help you if I stayed with you tonight—I mean if they don't come?

CHRISTINE. (*eagerly*) Oh, would you? (*Hysterical tears come to her eyes. She kisses* HAZEL *with impulsive gratitude*) I can't tell you how grateful I'd be! You're so good! (*Then forcing a laugh*) But it's an imposition to ask you to face such an ordeal. I can't stay still. I'm terrified at every sound. You would have to sit up.

HAZEL. Losing a little sleep won't hurt me any.

CHRISTINE. I mustn't sleep! If you see me falling asleep you must promise to wake me!

HAZEL. But it's just what you need.

CHRISTINE. Yes—afterwards—but not now. I must keep awake. (*In tense desperation*) I wish Orin and Vinnie would come!

HAZEL. (*worriedly*) Perhaps Orin got so sick he wasn't able to. Oh, I hope that isn't it! (*Then getting up*) If I'm going to stay all night I'll have to run home and tell Mother, so she won't worry.

CHRISTINE. Yes—do. (*Then frightenedly*) You won't be long, will you? I'm afraid—to be alone.

HAZEL. (*kisses her—pityingly*) I'll be as quick as I possibly can. (*She walks down the drive, off left, waving her hand as she disappears.* CHRISTINE *stands by the bench—then begins to pace back and forth again.*)

CHRISTINE. (*her eyes caught by something down the drive—in a tense whisper*) She's met someone by the gate! Oh, why am I so afraid! (*She turns, seized by panic, and runs to the house—then stops at the top of the steps and faces around, leaning against a column for support*) Oh, God, I'm afraid to know! (*A moment later* ORIN *and* LAVINIA *come up the drive from the left.* LAVINIA *is stiffly square-shouldered, her eyes hard, her mouth grim and set.* ORIN *is in a state of morbid excitement. He carries a newspaper in his hand.*)

ORIN. (*speaking to* VINNIE *as they enter—harshly*) You let me do the talking! I want to be the one— (*He sees his mother—startledly*) Mother! (*Then with vindictive mockery*) Ah! So this time at last you are waiting to meet me when I come home!

CHRISTINE. (*stammers*) Orin! What kept you—?

ORIN. We just met Hazel. She said you were terribly frightened at being alone here. That is strange—when you have the memory of Father for company!

CHRISTINE. You—you stayed all this time—at the Bradfords'?

ORIN. We didn't go to the Bradfords'.

CHRISTINE. (*stupidly*) You didn't go—to Blackridge?

ORIN. We took the train there but we decided to stay right on and go to Boston instead.

CHRISTINE. (*terrifiedly*) To—Boston—?

ORIN. And in Boston we waited until the evening train got in. We met that train.

CHRISTINE. Ah!

ORIN. We had an idea you would take advantage of our being in Blackridge to be on it—and you were! And we followed you when you called on your lover in his cabin!

CHRISTINE. (*with a pitiful effort at indignation*) Orin! How dare you talk—! (*Then brokenly*) Orin! Don't look at me like that! Tell me—

ORIN. Your lover! Don't lie! You've lied enough, Mother! I was on deck, listening! What would you have done if you had discovered me? Would you have gotten your lover to murder me, Mother? I heard you warning him against me! But your warning was no use!

CHRISTINE. (*chokingly*) What—? Tell me—!

ORIN. I killed him!

CHRISTINE. (*with a cry of terror*) Oh—oh! I knew! (*Then clutching at* ORIN) No—Orin! You—you're just telling me that—to punish

120

me, aren't you? You said you loved me—you'd protect me—protect your mother—you couldn't murder—!

ORIN. (*harshly, pushing her away*) You could murder Father, couldn't you? (*He thrusts the newspaper into her hands, pointing to the story*) Here! Read that, if you don't believe me! We got it in Boston to see whom the police would suspect. It's only a few lines. Brant wasn't important—except to you! (*She looks at the paper with fascinated horror. Then she lets it slip through her fingers, sinks down on the lowest step and begins to moan to herself, wringing her hands together in stricken anguish.* ORIN *turns from her and starts to pace up and down by the steps.* LAVINIA *stands at the left of the steps, rigid and erect, her face mask-like.*)

ORIN. (*harshly*) They think exactly what we planned they should think—that he was killed by waterfront thieves. There's nothing to connect us with his death! (*He stops by her. She stares before her, wringing her hands and moaning. He blurts out*) Mother! Don't moan like that! (*She gives no sign of having heard him. He starts to pace up and down again—with savage resentment*) Why do you grieve for that servant's bastard? I know he was the one who planned Father's murder! You couldn't have done that! He got you under his influence to revenge himself! He hypnotized you! I saw you weren't yourself the minute I got home, remember? How else could you ever have imagined you loved that low swine! How else could you ever have said the things— (*He stops before her*) I heard you planning to go with him to the island I had told you about—our island—that was you and I! (*He starts to pace up and down again distractedly. She remains as before except that her moaning has begun to exhaust itself.* ORIN *stops before her again and grasps her by the shoulders, kneeling on the steps beside her—desperately pleading now*) Mother! Don't moan like that! You're still under his influence! But you'll forget him! I'll make you forget him! I'll make you happy! We'll

121

leave Vinnie here and go away on a long voyage—to the South
Seas—

LAVINIA. (*sharply*) Orin!

ORIN. (*not heeding her, stares into his mother's face. She has stopped
moaning, the horror in her eyes is dying into blankness, the expression
of her mouth congealing to one of numbed grief. She gives no sign
of having heard him.* ORIN *shakes her—desperately*) Mother! Don't
you hear me? Why won't you speak to me? Will you always love
him? Do you hate me now? (*He sinks on his knees before her*)
Mother! Answer me! Say you forgive me!

LAVINIA. (*with bitter scorn*) Orin! After all that's happened, are
you becoming her crybaby again? (ORIN *starts and gets to his feet,
staring at her confusedly, as if he had forgotten her existence.* LAVINIA
speaks again in curt commanding tone that recalls her father) Leave
her alone! Go in the house! (*As he hesitates—more sharply*) Do you
hear me? March!

ORIN. (*automatically makes a confused motion of military salute
—vaguely*) Yes, sir. (*He walks mechanically up the steps—gazing
up at the house—strangely*) Why are the shutters still closed? Father
has gone. We ought to let in the moonlight. (*He goes into the house.*
LAVINIA *comes and stands beside her mother.* CHRISTINE *continues to
stare blankly in front of her. Her face has become a tragic death
mask. She gives no sign of being aware of her daughter's presence.*
LAVINIA *regards her with bleak, condemning eyes.*)

LAVINIA. (*finally speaks sternly*) He paid the just penalty for his
crime. You know it was justice. It was the only way true justice could
be done. (*Her mother starts. The words shatter her merciful numbness and awaken her to agony again. She springs to her feet and stands
glaring at her daughter with a terrible look in which a savage hatred
fights with horror and fear. In spite of her frozen self-control,* LAVINIA
recoils before this. Keeping her eyes on her, CHRISTINE *shrinks back-*

ward up the steps until she stands at the top between the two columns of the portico before the front door. LAVINIA *suddenly makes a motion, as if to hold her back. She calls shakenly as if the words were wrung out of her against her will)* Mother! What are you going to do? You can live!

CHRISTINE. (*glares at her as if this were the last insult—with strident mockery*) Live! (*She bursts into shrill laughter, stops it abruptly, raises her hands between her face and her daughter and pushes them out in a gesture of blotting* LAVINIA *forever from her sight. Then she turns and rushes into the house.* LAVINIA *again makes a movement to follow her. But she immediately fights down this impulse and turns her back on the house determinedly, standing square-shouldered and stiff like a grim sentinel in black.*)

LAVINIA. (*implacably to herself*) It is justice! (*From the street, away off right front,* SETH's *thin wraith of a baritone is raised in his favorite mournful "Shenandoah," as he nears the gateway to the drive, returning from his nightly visit to the saloon.*)

> "Oh, Shenandoah, I long to hear you
> A-way, my rolling river!
> Oh, Shenandoah, I can't get near you
> Way—ay, I'm bound away
> Across the wide—"

(*There is the sharp report of a pistol from the left ground floor of the house where* EZRA MANNON's *study is.* LAVINIA *gives a shuddering gasp, turns back to the steps, starts to go up them, stops again and stammers shakenly*) It is justice! It is your justice, Father! (ORIN's *voice is heard calling from the sitting-room at right* "What's that!" *A door slams. Then* ORIN's *horrified cry comes from the study as he finds his mother's body, and a moment later he rushes out frantically to* LAVINIA.)

ORIN. Vinnie! (*He grabs her arm and stammers distractedly*) Mother—shot herself—Father's pistol—get a doctor— (*Then with hopeless anguish*) No—it's too late—she's dead! (*Then wildly*) Why —why did she, Vinnie? (*With tortured self-accusation*) I drove her to it! I wanted to torture her! She couldn't forgive me! Why did I have to boast about killing him? Why—?

LAVINIA. (*frightenedly, puts her hands over his mouth*) Be quiet!

ORIN. (*tears her hand away—violently*) Why didn't I let her believe burglars killed him! She wouldn't have hated me then! She would have forgotten him! She would have turned to me! (*In a final frenzy of self-denunciation*) I murdered her!

LAVINIA. (*grabbing him by the shoulders*) For God's sake, will you be quiet?

ORIN. (*frantically—trying to break away from her*) Let me go! I've got to find her! I've got to make her forgive me! I—! (*He suddenly breaks down and weeps in hysterical anguish.* LAVINIA *puts her arm around him soothingly. He sobs despairingly*) But she's dead— She's gone—How can I ever get her to forgive me now?

LAVINIA. (*soothingly*) Ssshh! Ssshh! You have me, haven't you? I love you. I'll help you to forget. (*He turns to go back into the house, still sobbing helplessly.* SETH's *voice comes from the drive, right, close at hand:*

> "She's far across the stormy water
> Way-ay, I'm bound away—"

He enters right, front. LAVINIA *turns to face him.*)

SETH. (*approaching*) Say, Vinnie, did you hear a shot—?

LAVINIA. (*sharply*) I want you to go for Doctor Blake. Tell him Mother has killed herself in a fit of insane grief over Father's death. (*Then as he stares, dumbfounded and wondering, but keeping his face expressionless—more sharply*) Will you remember to tell him that?

SETH. (*slowly*) Ayeh. I'll tell him, Vinnie—anything you say. (*His face set grimly, he goes off right front.* LAVINIA *turns and, stiffly erect, her face stern and mask-like, follows* ORIN *into the house.*)

CURTAIN

THE HAUNTED

CHARACTERS

LAVINIA MANNON

ORIN, *her brother*

PETER NILES

HAZEL, *his sister*

SETH

AMOS AMES

IRA MACKEL

JOE SILVA

ABNER SMALL

SCENES

ACT ONE—*Scene* I: Exterior of the Mannon house—an evening in the summer of 1866.

ACT ONE—*Scene* II: Sitting-room in the house—immediately follows Scene One.

ACT TWO: The study—an evening a month later.

ACT THREE: The sitting-room—immediately follows Act Two.

ACT FOUR: Same as Act One, Scene One—Exterior of the Mannon house—a late afternoon three days later.

THE HAUNTED

ACT ONE—SCENE ONE

EXTERIOR *of the Mannon house* (*as in the two preceding plays*) *on the evening of a clear day in summer a year later. It is shortly after sunset but the afterglow in the sky still bathes the white temple portico in a crimson light. The columns cast black bars of shadow on the wall behind them. All the shutters are closed and the front door is boarded up, showing that the house is unoccupied.*

A group of five men is standing on the drive by the bench at left, front. SETH BECKWITH *is there and* AMOS AMES, *who appeared in the first act of* "Homecoming." *The others are* ABNER SMALL, JOE SILVA *and* IRA MACKEL.

These four—AMES, SMALL, SILVA *and* MACKEL—*are, as were the townsfolk of the first acts of* "Homecoming" *and* "The Hunted," *a chorus of types representing the town as a human background for the drama of the Mannons.*

SMALL *is a wiry old man of sixty-five, a clerk in a hardware store. He has white hair and a wispy goat's beard, bright inquisitive eyes, ruddy complexion, and a shrill rasping voice.* SILVA *is a Portuguese fishing captain—a fat, boisterous man, with a hoarse bass voice. He has matted gray hair and a big grizzled mustache. He is sixty.* MACKEL, *who is a farmer, hobbles along with the aid of a cane. His shiny wrinkled face is oblong with a square white chin whisker. He is bald. His yellowish brown eyes are sly. He talks in a drawling wheezy cackle.*

All five are drunk. SETH *has a stone jug in his hand. There is a grotesque atmosphere of boys out on a forbidden lark about these old men.*

SMALL. God A'mighty, Seth, be you glued to that jug?

MACKEL. Gol durn him, he's gittin' stingy in his old age!

SILVA. (*bursts into song*)

"*A bottle of beer and a bottle of gin*
And a bottle of Irish whiskey oh!
So early in the morning
A sailor likes his bottle oh!"

AMES. (*derisively*) You like your bottle 'ceptin' when your old woman's got her eye on ye!

SILVA. She's visitin' her folks to New Bedford. What the hell I care! (*Bursts into song again*)

"*Hurrah! Hurrah! I sing the jubilee*
Hurrah! Hurrah! Her folks has set me free!"

AMES. (*slapping him on the back*) God damn you, Joe, you're gittin' to be a poet! (*They all laugh.*)

SMALL. God A'mighty, Seth, ain't ye got no heart in ye? Watch me perishin' fur lack o' whiskey and ye keep froze to that jug! (*He reaches out for it.*)

SETH. No, ye don't! I'm onto your game! (*With a wink at the others*) He's aimin' to git so full of Injun courage he wouldn't mind if a ghost sot on his lap! Purty slick you be, Abner! Swill my licker so's you kin skin me out o' my bet!

MACKEL. That's it, Seth! Don't let him play no skin games!

JOE. By God, if ghosts look like the livin', I'd let Ezra's woman's ghost set on my lap! M'm! (*He smacks his lips lasciviously.*)

AMES. Me, too! She was a looker!

SMALL. (*with an uneasy glance at the house*) It's her ghost folks is sayin' haunts the place, ain't it?

SETH. (*with a wink at the others*) Oh, hers and a hull passel of others. The graveyard's full of Mannons and they all spend their nights to hum here. You needn't worry but you'll have plenty o' company,

Abner! (*The others laugh, their mirth a bit forced, but* SMALL *looks rather sick*.)

SMALL. It ain't in our bet for you to put sech notions in my head afore I go in, be it? (*Then forcing a perky bravado*) Think you kin scare me? There ain't no sech thing as ghosts!

SETH. An' I'm sayin' you're scared to prove there ain't! Let's git our bet set out plain afore witnesses. I'm lettin' you in the Mannon house and I'm bettin' you ten dollars and a gallon of licker you dasn't stay there till moonrise at ten o'clock. If you come out afore then, you lose. An' you're to stay in the dark and not even strike a match! Is that agreed?

SMALL. (*trying to put a brave face on it*) That's agreed—an' it's like stealin' ten dollars off you!

SETH. We'll see! (*Then with a grin*) An' you're supposed to go in sober! But I won't make it too dead sober! I ain't that hard-hearted. I wouldn't face what you'll face with a gallon under my belt! (*Handing him the jug*) Here! Take a good swig! You're lookin' a mite pale about the gills a'ready!

SMALL. No sech thing! (*But he puts the jug to his lips and takes an enormous swallow*.)

MACKEL. Whoa thar! Ye ain't drinkin' fur all on us! (SMALL *hands the jug to him and he drinks and passes it around until it finally reaches* SETH *again. In the meantime* SMALL *talks to* SETH.)

SMALL. Be it all right fur me to go in afore dark? I'd like to know where I'm at while I kin see.

SETH. Wal, I calc'late you kin. Don't want you runnin' into furniture an' breakin' things when them ghosts git chasin' you! Vinnie an' Orin's liable to be back from Chiny afore long an' she'd give me hell if anythin' was broke. (*The jug reaches him. He takes a drink—then sets it down on the drive*) Come along! I've took the screws out o' that door. I kin let you right in. (*He goes toward the portico,* SMALL *following him, whistling with elaborate nonchalance*.)

131

SMALL. (*to the others who remain where they are*) So long, fellers. We'll have a good spree on that ten dollars.

MACKEL. (*with a malicious cackle*) Mebbe! Would you like me fur one o' your pallbearers, Abner?

AMES. I'll comfort your old woman—providin' she'll want comfortin', which ain't likely!

SILVA. And I'll water your grave every Sunday after church! That's the kind of man I be, by God. I don't forget my friends when they're gone!

SETH. (*from the portico*) We'll all jine in, Joe! If he ain't dead, by God, we'll drown him! (*They all roar with laughter.* SMALL *looks bitter. The jest strikes him as being unfeeling— All glow has faded from the sky and it is getting dark.*)

SMALL. To hell with ye! (SETH *pries off the board door and unlocks the inner door.*)

SETH. Come on. I'll show you the handiest place to say your prayers. (*They go in. The group outside becomes serious.*)

AMES. (*voicing the opinion of all of them*) Wal, all the same, I wouldn't be in Abner's boots. It don't do to monkey with them thin's.

MACKEL. You believe in ghosts, Amos?

AMES. Mebbe. Who knows there ain't?

MACKEL. Wal, I believe in 'em. Take the Nims' place out my way. Asa Nims killed his wife with a hatchet—she'd nagged him—then hung himself in the attic. I knew Ben Willett that bought the place. He couldn't live thar—had to move away. It's fallen to ruins now. Ben used to hear things clawin' at the walls an' winders and see the chairs move about. He wasn't a liar nor chicken-hearted neither.

SILVA. There is ghosts, by God! My cousin, Manuel, he seen one! Off on a whaler in the Injun Ocean, that was. A man got knifed and pushed overboard. After that, on moonlight nights, they'd see him a-settin' on the yards and hear him moanin' to himself. Yes, sir, my cousin Manuel, he ain't no liar neither—'ceptin' when he's drunk— and he seen him with his own eyes!

132

AMES. (*with an uneasy glance around, reaching for the jug*) Wal, let's have a drink. (*He takes a swig just as* SETH *comes out of the house, shutting the door behind him.*)

MACKEL. That's Seth. He ain't anxious to stay in thar long, I notice! (SETH *hurries down to them, trying to appear to saunter.*)

SETH. (*with a forced note to his joking*) God A'mighty, ye'd ought to see Abner! He's shyin' at the furniture covers an' his teeth are clickin' a'ready. He'll come runnin' out hell fur leather afore long. All I'm wonderin' is, has he got ten dollars?

MACKEL. (*slyly*) You seem a mite shaky.

SETH. (*with a scowl*) You're a liar. What're ye all lookin' glum as owls about?

MACKEL. Been talkin' of ghosts. Do you really believe that there house is haunted, Seth, or are ye only jokin' Abner?

SETH. (*sharply*) Don't be a durned fool! I'm on'y jokin' him, of course!

MACKEL. (*insistently*) Still, it'd be only natural if it was haunted. She shot herself there. Do you think she done it fur grief over Ezra's death, like the daughter let on to folks?

SETH. 'Course she did!

MACKEL. Ezra dyin' sudden his first night to hum—that was durned queer!

SETH. (*angrily*) It's durned queer old fools like you with one foot in the grave can't mind their own business in the little time left to 'em. That's what's queer!

MACKEL. (*angry in his turn*) Wal, all I say is if they hadn't been Mannons with the town lickin' their boots, there'd have been queer doin's come out! And as fur me bein' an old fool, you're older an' a worse fool! An' your foot's deeper in the grave than mine be!

SETH. (*shaking his fist in* MACKEL's *face*) It ain't so deep but what I kin whale the stuffin' out o' you any day in the week!

SILVA. (*comes between them*) Here, you old roosters! No fightin' allowed!

133

MACKEL. (*subsiding grumpily*) This is a free country, ain't it? I got a right to my opinions!

AMES. (*suddenly looking off down left*) Ssshh! Look, Seth! There's someone comin' up the drive.

SETH. (*peering*) Ayeh! Who the hell—? It's Peter 'n' Hazel. Hide that jug, durn ye! (*The jug is hidden under the lilacs. A moment later,* HAZEL *and* PETER *enter. They stop in surprise on seeing* SETH *and his friends.* SETH *greets them self-consciously*) Good evenin'. I was just showin' some friends around—

PETER. Hello, Seth. Just the man we're looking for. We've just had a telegram. Vinnie and Orin have landed in New York and— (*He is interrupted by a muffled yell of terror from the house. As they all turn to look, the front door is flung open and* SMALL *comes tearing out and down the portico steps, his face chalky white and his eyes popping.*)

SMALL. (*as he reaches them—terrifiedly*) God A'mighty! I heard 'em comin' after me, and I run in the room opposite, an' I seed Ezra's ghost dressed like a judge comin' through the wall—and, by God, I run! (*He jerks a bill out of his pocket and thrusts it on* SETH) Here's your money, durn ye! I wouldn't stay in there fur a million! (*This breaks the tension, and the old men give way to an hysterical, boisterous, drunken mirth, roaring with laughter, pounding each other on the back.*)

PETER. (*sharply*) What's this all about? What was he doing in there?

SETH. (*controlling his laughter—embarrassedly*) Only a joke, Peter. (*Then turning on* SMALL—*scornfully*) That was Ezra's picture hangin' on the wall, not a ghost, ye durned idjut!

SMALL. (*indignantly*) I know pictures when I see 'em an' I knowed him. This was him! Let's get out o' here. I've had enough of this durned place!

SETH. You fellers trot along. I'll jine you later. (*They all mutter good evenings to* PETER *and* HAZEL *and go off, left front.* SMALL's *excited voice can be heard receding as he begins to embroider on the horrors of his adventure.* SETH *turns to* PETER *apologetically*) Abner Small's always braggin' how brave he is—so I bet him he dasn't stay in there—

HAZEL. (*indignantly*) Seth! What would Vinnie say if she knew you did such things?

SETH. There ain't no harm done. I calc'late Abner didn't break nothin'. And Vinnie wouldn't mind when she knew why I done it. I was aimin' to stop the durned gabbin' that's been goin' round town about this house bein' haunted. You've heard it, ain't ye?

PETER. I heard some silly talk but didn't pay any attention—

SETH. That durned idjut female I got in to clean a month after Vinnie and Orin sailed started it. Said she'd felt ghosts around. You know how them things grow. Seemed to me Abner's braggin' gave me a good chance to stop it by turnin' it all into a joke on him folks'd laugh at. An' when I git through tellin' my story of it round town tomorrow you'll find folks'll shet up and not take it serious no more.

PETER. (*appreciatively*) You're right, Seth. That was a darned slick notion! Nothing like a joke to lay a ghost!

SETH. Ayeh. But— (*He hesitates—then decides to say it*) Between you 'n' me 'n' the lamp post, it ain't all sech a joke as it sounds—that about the hauntin', I mean.

PETER. (*incredulously*) You aren't going to tell me you think the house is haunted too!

SETH. (*grimly*) Mebbe, and mebbe not. All I know is I wouldn't stay in there all night if you was to give me the town!

HAZEL. (*impressed but forcing a teasing tone*) Seth! I'm ashamed of you!

PETER. First time I ever heard you say you were afraid of anything!

SETH. There's times when a man's a darn fool not to be scared! Oh, don't git it in your heads I take stock in spirits trespassin' round in windin' sheets or no sech lunatic doin's. But there is sech a thing as evil spirit. An' I've felt it, goin' in there daytimes to see to things—like somethin' rottin' in the walls!

PETER. Bosh!

SETH. (*quietly*) 'Tain't bosh, Peter. There's been evil in that house since it was first built in hate—and it's kept growin' there ever since, as what's happened there has proved. You understand I ain't sayin' this to no one but you two. An' I'm only tellin' you fur one reason—because you're closer to Vinnie and Orin than anyone and you'd ought to persuade them, now they're back, not to live in it. (*He adds impressively*) Fur their own good! (*Then with a change of tone*) An' now I've got that off my chest, tell me about 'em. When are they comin'?

PETER. Tomorrow. Vinnie asked us to open the house. So let's start right in.

SETH. (*with evident reluctance*) You want to do it tonight?

HAZEL. We must, Seth. We've got so little time. We can at least tidy up the rooms a little and get the furniture covers off.

SETH. Wal, I'll go to the barn and git lanterns. There's candles in the house. (*He turns abruptly and goes off left between the lilacs and the house.*)

HAZEL. (*looking after him—uneasily*) I can't get over Seth acting so strangely.

PETER. Don't mind him. It's rum and old age.

HAZEL. (*shaking her head—slowly*) No. There is something queer about this house. I've always felt it, even before the General's death and her suicide. (*She shudders*) I can still see her sitting on that bench as she was that last night. She was so frightened of being alone. But I thought when Vinnie and Orin came back she would be all right. (*Then sadly*) Poor Orin! I'll never forget to my dying day the way he looked when we saw him at the funeral. I hardly recognized him, did you?

PETER. No. He certainly was broken up.

HAZEL. And the way he acted—like someone in a trance! I don't believe when Vinnie rushed him off on this trip to the East he knew what he was doing or where he was going or anything.

136

PETER. A long voyage like that was the best thing to help them both forget.

HAZEL. (*without conviction*) Yes. I suppose it was—but— (*She stops and sighs—then worriedly*) I wonder how Orin is. Vinnie's letters haven't said much about him, or herself, for that matter—only about the trip. (*She sees* SETH *approaching, whistling loudly, from left, rear, with two lighted lanterns*) Here's Seth. (*She walks up the steps to the portico.* PETER *follows her. She hesitates and stands looking at the house—in a low tone, almost of dread*) Seth was right. You feel something cold grip you the moment you set foot—

PETER. Oh, nonsense! He's got you going, too! (*Then with a chuckle*) Listen to him whistling to keep his courage up! (SETH *comes in from the left. He hands one of the lanterns to* PETER.)

SETH. Here you be, Peter.

HAZEL. Well, let's go in. You better come out to the kitchen and help me first, Peter. We ought to start a fire. (*They go in. There is a pause in which* PETER *can be heard opening windows behind the shutters in the downstairs rooms. Then silence. Then* LAVINIA *enters, coming up the drive from left, front, and stands regarding the house. One is at once aware of an extraordinary change in her. Her body, formerly so thin and undeveloped, has filled out. Her movements have lost their square-shouldered stiffness. She now bears a striking resemblance to her mother in every respect, even to being dressed in the green her mother had affected. She walks to the clump of lilacs and stands there staring at the house.*)

LAVINIA. (*turns back and calls coaxingly in the tone one would use to a child*) Don't stop there, Orin! What are you afraid of? Come on! (*He comes slowly and hesitatingly in from left, front. He carries himself woodenly erect now, like a soldier. His movements and attitudes have the statue-like quality that was so marked in his father. He now wears a close-cropped beard in addition to his mustache, and this accentuates his resemblance to his father. The Mannon semblance of his face in repose to a mask is more pronounced than ever. He has*

137

grown dreadfully thin and his black suit hangs loosely on his body. His haggard swarthy face is set in a blank lifeless expression.)

LAVINIA. (*glances at him uneasily—concealing her apprehension under a coaxing motherly tone*) You must be brave! This is the test! You have got to face it! (*Then anxiously as he makes no reply*) Do you feel you can—now we're here?

ORIN. (*dully*) I'll be all right—with you.

LAVINIA. (*takes his hand and pats it encouragingly*) That's all I wanted—to hear you say that. (*Turning to the house*) Look, I see a light through the shutters of the sitting-room. That must be Peter and Hazel. (*Then as she sees he still keeps his eyes averted from the house*) Why don't you look at the house? Are you afraid? (*Then sharply commanding*) Orin! I want you to look now! Do you hear me?

ORIN. (*dully obedient*) Yes, Vinnie. (*He jerks his head around and stares at the house and draws a deep shuddering breath.*)

LAVINIA. (*her eyes on his face—as if she were willing her strength into him*) Well? You don't see any ghosts, do you? Tell me!

ORIN. (*obediently*) No.

LAVINIA. Because there are none! Tell me you know there are none, Orin!

ORIN. (*as before*) Yes.

LAVINIA. (*searches his face uneasily—then is apparently satisfied*) Come. Let's go in. We'll find Hazel and Peter and surprise them— (*She takes his arm and leads him to the steps. He walks like an automaton. When they reach the spot where his mother had sat moaning, the last time he had seen her alive* [*Act Five of "The Hunted"*] *he stops with a shudder.*)

ORIN. (*stammers—pointing*) It was here—she—the last time I saw her alive—

LAVINIA. (*quickly, urging him on commandingly*) That is all past and finished! The dead have forgotten us! We've forgotten them! Come! (*He obeys woodenly. She gets him up the steps and they pass into the house.*)   **CURTAIN**

138

ACT ONE—SCENE TWO

S AME *as Act Two of "The Hunted"—The sitting-room in the Man-*
non house. PETER *has lighted two candles on the mantel and put*
the lantern on the table at front. In this dim, spotty light the room is
full of shadows. It has the dead appearance of a room long shut up,
and the covered furniture has a ghostly look. In the flickering candle-
light the eyes of the Mannon portraits stare with a grim forbiddingness.

LAVINIA *appears in the doorway at rear. In the lighted room, the*
change in her is strikingly apparent. At a first glance, one would
mistake her for her mother as she appeared in the first act of "Home-
coming." She seems a mature woman, sure of her feminine attractive-
ness. Her brown-gold hair is arranged as her mother's had been. Her
green dress is like a copy of her mother's in Act One of "Homecom-
ing." She comes forward slowly. The movements of her body now
have the feminine grace her mother's had possessed. Her eyes are
caught by the eyes of the Mannons in the portraits and she approaches
as if compelled in spite of herself until she stands directly under them
in front of the fireplace. She suddenly addresses them in a harsh re-
sentful voice.)

LAVINIA. Why do you look at me like that? I've done my duty by
you! That's finished and forgotten! (*She tears her eyes from theirs*
and, turning away, becomes aware that ORIN *has not followed her into*
the room, and is immediately frightened and uneasy and hurries to-
ward the door, calling) Orin!

ORIN. (*his voice comes from the dark hall*) I'm here.

LAVINIA. What are you doing out there? Come here! (ORIN *appears*
in the doorway. His face wears a dazed expression and his eyes have
a wild, stricken look. He hurries to her as if seeking protection. She
exclaims frightenedly) Orin! What is it?

ORIN. (*strangely*) I've just been in the study. I was sure she'd be waiting for me in there, where— (*Torturedly*) But she wasn't! She isn't anywhere. It's only they— (*He points to the portraits*) They're everywhere! But she's gone forever. She'll never forgive me now!

LAVINIA. (*harshly*) Orin! Will you be quiet!

ORIN. (*unheeding—with a sudden turn to bitter resentful defiance*) Well, let her go! What is she to me? I'm not her son any more! I'm Father's! I'm a Mannon! And they'll welcome me home!

LAVINIA. (*angrily commanding*) Stop it, do you hear me!

ORIN. (*shocked back to awareness by her tone—pitifully confused*) I—I didn't—don't be angry, Vinnie!

LAVINIA. (*soothing him now*) I'm not angry, dear—only do get hold of yourself and be brave. (*Leading him to the sofa*) Here. Come. Let's sit down for a moment, shall we, and get used to being home? (*They sit down. She puts an arm around him reproachfully*) Don't you know how terribly you frighten me when you act so strangely? You don't mean to hurt me, do you?

ORIN. (*deeply moved*) God knows I don't, Vinnie! You're all I have in the world! (*He takes her hand and kisses it humbly.*)

LAVINIA. (*soothingly*) That's a good boy. (*Then with a cheerful matter-of-fact note*) Hazel and Peter must be back in the kitchen. Won't you be glad to see Hazel again?

ORIN. (*dully now*) You've kept talking about them all the voyage home. Why? What can they have to do with us—now?

LAVINIA. A lot. What we need most is to get back to simple normal things and begin a new life. And their friendship and love will help us more than anything to forget.

ORIN. (*with sudden harshness*) Forget? I thought you'd forgotten long ago—if you ever remembered, which you never seemed to! (*Then with somber bitterness*) Love! What right have I—or you—to love?

LAVINIA. (*defiantly*) Every right!

ORIN. (*grimly*) Mother felt the same about— (*Then with a strange, searching glance at her*) You don't know how like Mother you've become, Vinnie. I don't mean only how pretty you've gotten—

LAVINIA. (*with a strange shy eagerness*) Do you really think I'm as pretty now as she was, Orin?

ORIN. (*as if she hadn't interrupted*) I mean the change in your soul, too. I've watched it ever since we sailed for the East. Little by little it grew like Mother's soul—as if you were stealing hers—as if her death had set you free—to become her!

LAVINIA. (*uneasily*) Now don't begin talking nonsense again, please!

ORIN. (*grimly*) Don't you believe in souls any more? I think you will after we've lived in this house awhile! The Mannon dead will convert you. (*He turns to the portraits mockingly*) Ask them if I'm not right!

LAVINIA. (*sharply*) Orin! What's come over you? You haven't had one of these morbid spells since we left the Islands. You swore to me you were all over them, or I'd never have agreed to come home.

ORIN. (*with a strange malicious air*) I had to get you away from the Islands. My brotherly duty! If you'd stayed there much longer— (*He chuckles disagreeably.*)

LAVINIA. (*with a trace of confusion*) I don't know what you're talking about. I only went there for your sake.

ORIN. (*with another chuckle*) Yes—but afterwards—

LAVINIA. (*sharply*) You promised you weren't going to talk any more morbid nonsense. (*He subsides meekly. She goes on reproachfully*) Remember all I've gone through on your account. For months after we sailed you didn't know what you were doing. I had to live in constant fear of what you might say. I wouldn't live through those horrible days again for anything on earth. And remember this homecoming is what you wanted. You told me that if you could come home and face your ghosts, you knew you could rid yourself forever of your silly guilt about the past.

ORIN. (*dully*) I know, Vinnie.

LAVINIA. And I believed you, you seemed so certain of yourself. But now you've suddenly become strange again. You frighten me. So much depends on how you start in, now we're home. (*Then sharply commanding*) Listen, Orin! I want you to start again—by facing all your ghosts right now! (*He turns and his eyes remain fixed on hers from now on. She asks sternly*) Who murdered Father?

ORIN. (*falteringly*) Brant did—for revenge because—

LAVINIA. (*more sternly*) Who murdered Father? Answer me!

ORIN. (*with a shudder*) Mother was under his influence—

LAVINIA. That's a lie! It was he who was under hers. You know the truth!

ORIN. Yes.

LAVINIA. She was an adulteress and a murderess, wasn't she?

ORIN. Yes.

LAVINIA. If we'd done our duty under the law, she would have been hanged, wouldn't she?

ORIN. Yes.

LAVINIA. But we protected her. She could have lived, couldn't she? But she chose to kill herself as a punishment for her crime—of her own free will! It was an act of justice! You had nothing to do with it! You see that now, don't you? (*As he hesitates, trembling violently, she grabs his arm fiercely*) Tell me!

ORIN. (*hardly above a whisper*) Yes.

LAVINIA. And your feeling of being responsible for her death was only your morbid imagination! You don't feel it now! You'll never feel it again!

ORIN. No.

LAVINIA. (*gratefully—and weakly because the strength she has willed into him has left her exhausted*) There! You see! You can do it when you will to! (*She kisses him. He breaks down, sobbing weakly against her breast. She soothes him*) There! Don't cry! You ought to feel proud. You've proven you can laugh at your ghosts from now on. (*Then briskly, to distract his mind*) Come now. Help me to take off these furniture covers. We might as well start making ourselves useful. (*She starts to work. For a moment he helps. Then he goes to one of the windows and pushes back a shutter and stands staring out.*

PETER *comes in the door from rear. At the sight of* LAVINIA *he stops startledly, thinks for a second it is her mother's ghost and gives an exclamation of dread. At the same moment she sees him. She stares at him with a strange eager possessiveness. She calls softly.*)

LAVINIA. Peter! (*She goes toward him, smiling as her mother might have smiled*) Don't you know me any more, Peter?

PETER. (*stammers*) Vinnie! I—I thought you were—! I can't realize it's you! You've grown so like your— (*Checking himself awkwardly*) I mean you've changed so—and we weren't looking for you until— (*He takes her hand automatically, staring at her stupidly.*)

LAVINIA. I know. We had intended to stay in New York tonight but we decided later we'd better come right home. (*Then taking him in with a smiling appreciative possessiveness*) Let me look at you, Peter. You haven't gone and changed, have you? No, you're the same, thank goodness! I've been thinking of you all the way home and wondering—I was so afraid you might have.

PETER. (*plucking up his courage—blurts out*) You—you ought to know I'd never change—with you! (*Then, alarmed by his own boldness, he hastily looks away from her.*)

LAVINIA. (*teasingly*) But you haven't said yet you're glad to see me!

PETER. (*has turned back and is staring fascinatedly at her. A surge of love and desire overcomes his timidity and he bursts out*) I—you know how much I—! (*Then he turns away again in confusion and takes refuge in a burst of talk*) Gosh, Vinnie, you ought to have given us more warning. We've only just started to open the place up. I was with Hazel, in the kitchen, starting a fire—

LAVINIA. (*laughing softly*) Yes. You're the same old Peter! You're still afraid of me. But you mustn't be now. I know I used to be an awful old stick, but—

PETER. Who said so? You were not! (*Then with enthusiasm*) Gosh, you look so darned pretty—and healthy. Your trip certainly did you good! (*Staring at her again, drinking her in*) I can't get over seeing you dressed in color. You always used to wear black.

LAVINIA. (*with a strange smile*) I was dead then.

PETER. You ought always to wear color.

LAVINIA. (*immensely pleased*) Do you think so?

PETER. Yes. It certainly is becoming. I— (*Then embarrassedly changing the subject*) But where's Orin?

LAVINIA. (*turning to look around*) Why, he was right here. (*She sees him at the window*) Orin, what are you doing there? Here's Peter. (ORIN *closes the shutter he has pushed open and turns back from the window. He comes forward, his eyes fixed in a strange preoccupation, as if he were unaware of their presence.* LAVINIA *watches him uneasily and speaks sharply*) Don't you see Peter? Why don't you speak to him? You mustn't be so rude.

PETER. (*good-naturedly*) Give him a chance. Hello, Orin. Darned glad to see you back. (*They shake hands.* PETER *has difficulty in hiding his pained surprise at* ORIN's *sickly appearance.*)

ORIN. (*rousing himself, forces a smile and makes an effort at his old friendly manner with* PETER) Hello, Peter. You know I'm glad to see you without any polite palaver. Vinnie is the same old bossy fuss-buzzer—you remember—always trying to teach me manners!

PETER. You bet I remember! But say, hasn't she changed, though? I didn't know her, she's grown so fat! And I was just telling her how well she looked in color. Don't you agree?

ORIN. (*in a sudden strange tone of jeering malice*) Did you ask her why she stole Mother's colors? I can't see why—yet—and I don't think she knows herself. But it will prove a strange reason, I'm certain of that, when I do discover it!

LAVINIA. (*making a warning sign to* PETER *not to take this seriously—forcing a smile*) Don't mind him, Peter.

ORIN. (*his tone becoming sly, insinuating and mocking*) And she's become romantic! Imagine that! Influence of the "dark and deep blue ocean"—and of the Islands, eh, Vinnie?

PETER. (*surprised*) You stopped at the Islands?

ORIN. Yes. We took advantage of our being on a Mannon ship to make the captain touch there on the way back. We stopped a month. (*With resentful bitterness*) But they turned out to be Vinnie's islands, not mine. They only made me sick—and the naked women disgusted me. I guess I'm too much of a Mannon, after all, to turn into a pagan. But you should have seen Vinnie with the men—!

LAVINIA. (*indignantly but with a certain guiltiness*) How can you—!

ORIN. (*jeeringly*) Handsome and romantic-looking, weren't they, Vinnie?—with colored rags around their middles and flowers stuck over their ears! Oh, she was a bit shocked at first by their dances, but afterwards she fell in love with the Islanders. If we'd stayed another month, I know I'd have found her some moonlight night dancing under the palm trees—as naked as the rest!

LAVINIA. Orin! Don't be disgusting!

ORIN. (*points to the portraits mockingly*) Picture, if you can, the feelings of the God-fearing Mannon dead at that spectacle!

LAVINIA. (*with an anxious glance at* PETER) How can you make up such disgusting fibs?

ORIN. (*with a malicious chuckle*) Oh, I wasn't as blind as I pretended to be! Do you remember Avahanni?

LAVINIA. (*angrily*) Stop talking like a fool! (*He subsides meekly again. She forces a smile and a motherly tone*) You're a naughty boy, do you know it? What will Peter think? Of course, he knows you're only teasing me—but you shouldn't go on like that. It isn't nice. (*Then changing the subject abruptly*) Why don't you go and find Hazel? Here. Let me look at you. I want you to look your best when she sees you. (*She arranges him as a mother would a boy, pulling down his coat, giving a touch to his shirt and tie.* ORIN *straightens woodenly to a soldierly attention. She is vexed by this*) Don't stand like a ramrod. You'd be so handsome if you'd only shave off that silly beard and not carry yourself like a tin soldier!

ORIN. (*with a sly cunning air*) Not look so much like Father, eh? More like a romantic clipper captain, is that it? (*As she starts and stares at him frightenedly, he smiles an ugly taunting smile*) Don't look so frightened, Vinnie!

LAVINIA. (*with an apprehensive glance at* PETER—*pleading and at the same time warning*) Ssshh! You weren't to talk nonsense, remember! (*Giving him a final pat*) There! Now run along to Hazel.

ORIN. (*looks from her to* PETER *suspiciously*) You seem damned anxious to get rid of me. (*He turns and stalks stiffly with hurt dignity from the room.* LAVINIA *turns to* PETER. *The strain of* ORIN's *conduct has told on her. She seems suddenly weak and frightened.*)

PETER. (*in shocked amazement*) What's come over him?

LAVINIA. (*in a strained voice*) It's the same thing—what the war did to him—and on top of that Father's death—and the shock of Mother's suicide.

PETER. (*puts his arm around her impulsively—comfortingly*) It'll be all right! Don't worry, Vinnie!

LAVINIA. (*nestling against him gratefully*) Thank you, Peter. You're so good. (*Then looking into his eyes*) Do you still love me, Peter?

PETER. Don't have to ask that, do you? (*He squeezes her awkwardly —then stammers*) But do you—think now—you maybe—can love me?

LAVINIA. Yes.

PETER. You really mean that!

LAVINIA. Yes! I do! I've thought of you so much! Things were always reminding me of you—the ship and the sea—everything that was honest and clean! And the natives on the Islands reminded me of you too. They were so simple and fine— (*Then hastily*) You mustn't mind what Orin was saying about the Islands. He's become a regular bigoted Mannon.

PETER. (*amazed*) But, Vinnie—!

LAVINIA. Oh, I know it must sound funny hearing me talk like that. But remember I'm only half Mannon. (*She looks at the portraits defiantly*) And I've done my duty by them. They can't say I haven't!

PETER. (*mystified but happy*) Gosh, you certainly have changed! But I'm darned glad!

146

LAVINIA. Orin keeps teasing that I was flirting with that native he spoke about, simply because he used to smile at me and I smiled back.

PETER. (*teasingly*) Now, I'm beginning to get jealous, too.

LAVINIA. You mustn't. He made me think of you. He made me dream of marrying you—and everything.

PETER. Oh, well then, I take it all back! I owe him a vote of thanks! (*He hugs her.*)

LAVINIA. (*dreamily*) I loved those Islands. They finished setting me free. There was something there mysterious and beautiful—a good spirit—of love—coming out of the land and sea. It made me forget death. There was no hereafter. There was only this world— the warm earth in the moonlight—the trade wind in the coco palms —the surf on the reef—the fires at night and the drum throbbing in my heart—the natives dancing naked and innocent—without knowledge of sin! (*She checks herself abruptly and frightenedly*) But what in the world! I'm gabbing on like a regular chatterbox. You must think I've become awfully scatterbrained!

PETER. (*with a chuckle*) Gosh no! I'm glad you've grown that way! You never used to say a word unless you had to!

LAVINIA. (*suddenly filled with grateful love for him, lets herself go and throws her arms around him*) Oh, Peter, hold me close to you! I want to feel love! Love is all beautiful! I never used to know that! I was a fool! (*She kisses him passionately. He returns it, aroused and at the same time a little shocked by her boldness. She goes on longingly*) We'll be married soon, won't we, and settle out in the country away from folks and their evil talk. We'll make an island for ourselves on land, and we'll have children and love them and teach them to love life so that they can never be possessed by hate and death! (*She gives a start—in a whisper as if to herself*) But I'm forgetting Orin!

PETER. What's Orin got to do with us marrying?

LAVINIA. I can't leave him—until he's all well again. I'd be afraid—.

PETER. Let him live with us.

147

LAVINIA. (*with sudden intensity*) No! I want to be rid of the past. (*Then after a quick look at him—in a confiding tone*) I want to tell you what's wrong with Orin—so you and Hazel can help me. He feels guilty about Mother killing herself. You see, he'd had a quarrel with her that last night. He was jealous and mad and said things he was sorry for after and it preyed on his mind until he blames himself for her death.

PETER. But that's crazy!

LAVINIA. I know it is, Peter, but you can't do anything with him when he gets his morbid spells. Oh, I don't mean he's the way he is tonight most of the time. Usually he's like himself, only quiet and sad—so sad it breaks my heart to see him—like a little boy who's been punished for something he didn't do. Please tell Hazel what I've told you, so she'll make allowances for any crazy thing he might say.

PETER. I'll warn her. And now don't you worry any more about him. We'll get him all right again one way or another.

LAVINIA. (*again grateful for his simple goodness—lovingly*) Bless you, Peter! (*She kisses him. As she does so,* HAZEL *and* ORIN *appear in the doorway at rear.* HAZEL *is a bit shocked, then smiles happily.* ORIN *starts as if he'd been struck. He glares at them with jealous rage and clenches his fists as if he were going to attack them.*)

HAZEL. (*with a teasing laugh*) I'm afraid we're interrupting, Orin. (PETER *and* VINNIE *jump apart in confusion.*)

ORIN. (*threateningly*) So that's it! By God—!

LAVINIA. (*frightened but managing to be stern*) Orin!

ORIN. (*pulls himself up sharply—confusedly, forcing a sickly smile*) Don't be so solemn—Fuss Buzzer! I was only trying to scare you— for a joke! (*Turning to* PETER *and holding out his hand, his smile becoming ghastly*) I suppose congratulations are in order. I—I'm glad. (PETER *takes his hand awkwardly.* HAZEL *moves toward* LAVINIA *to greet her, her face full of an uneasy bewilderment.* LAVINIA *stares at* ORIN *with eyes full of dread.*)

CURTAIN

148

ACT TWO

Scene—*Same as Act Three of "The Hunted"—*ezra mannon's *study—on an evening a month later. The shutters of the windows are closed. Candles on the mantel above the fireplace light up the portrait of* ezra mannon *in his judge's robes.* orin *is sitting in his father's chair at left of table, writing by the light of a lamp. A small pile of manuscript is stacked by his right hand. He is intent on his work. He has aged in the intervening month. He looks almost as old now as his father in the portrait. He is dressed in black and the resemblance between the two is uncanny. A grim smile of satisfaction twitches his lips as he stops writing and reads over the paragraph he has just finished. Then he puts the sheet down and stares up at the portrait, sitting back in his chair.*

orin. (*sardonically, addressing the portrait*) The truth, the whole truth and nothing but the truth! Is that what you're demanding, Father? Are you sure you want the whole truth? What will the neighbors say if this whole truth is ever known? (*He chuckles grimly*) A ticklish decision for you, Your Honor! (*There is a knock on the door. He hastily grabs the script and puts it in the drawer of the desk*) Who's there?

lavinia. It's I.

orin. (*hastily locking the drawer and putting the key in his pocket*) What do you want?

lavinia. (*sharply*) Please open the door!

orin. All right. In a minute. (*He hurriedly straightens up the table and grabs a book at random from the bookcase and lays it open on the table as if he had been reading. Then he unlocks the door and comes back to his chair as* lavinia *enters. She wears a green velvet*

149

gown similar to that worn by CHRISTINE *in Act Three of "Homecoming." It sets off her hair and eyes. She is obviously concealing beneath a surface calm a sense of dread and desperation.*)

LAVINIA. (*glances at him suspiciously, but forces a casual air*) Why did you lock yourself in? (*She comes over to the table*) What are you doing?

ORIN. Reading.

LAVINIA. (*picks up the book*) Father's law books?

ORIN. (*mockingly*) Why not? I'm considering studying law. He wanted me to, if you remember.

LAVINIA. Do you expect me to believe that, Orin? What is it you're really doing?

ORIN. Curious, aren't you?

LAVINIA. (*forcing a smile*) Good gracious, why wouldn't I be? You've acted so funny lately, locking yourself in here with the blinds closed and the lamp burning even in the daytime. It isn't good for you staying in this stuffy room in this weather. You ought to get out in the fresh air.

ORIN. (*harshly*) I hate the daylight. It's like an accusing eye! No, we've renounced the day, in which normal people live—or rather it has renounced us. Perpetual night—darkness of death in life—that's the fitting habitat for guilt! You believe you can escape that, but I'm not so foolish!

LAVINIA. Now you're being stupid again!

ORIN. And I find artificial light more appropriate for my work—man's light, not God's—man's feeble striving to understand himself, to exist for himself in the darkness! It's a symbol of his life—a lamp burning out in a room of waiting shadows!

LAVINIA. (*sharply*) Your work? What work?

ORIN. (*mockingly*) Studying the law of crime and punishment, as you saw.

LAVINIA. (*forcing a smile again and turning away from him*) All right, if you won't tell me. Go on being mysterious, if you like. (*In*

150

a tense voice) It's so close in here! It's suffocating! It's bad for you! (*She goes to the window and throws the shutters open and looks out*) It's black as pitch tonight. There isn't a star.

ORIN. (*somberly*) Darkness without a star to guide us! Where are we going, Vinnie? (*Then with a mocking chuckle*) Oh, I know you think you know where you're going, but there's many a slip, remember!

LAVINIA. (*her voice strident, as if her will were snapping*) Be quiet! Can't you think of anything but— (*Then controlling herself, comes to him—gently*) I'm sorry. I'm terribly nervous tonight. It's the heat, I guess. And you get me so worried with your incessant brooding over the past. It's the worst thing for your health. (*She pats him on the arm—soothingly*) That's all I'm thinking about, dear.

ORIN. Thank you for your anxiety about my health! But I'm afraid there isn't much hope for you there! I happen to feel quite well!

LAVINIA. (*whirling on him—distractedly*) How can you insinuate such horrible—! (*Again controlling herself with a great effort, forcing a smile*) But you're only trying to rile me—and I'm not going to let you. I'm so glad you're feeling better. You ate a good supper tonight—for you. The long walk we took with Hazel did you good.

ORIN. (*dully*) Yes. (*He slumps down in his chair at left of table*) Why is it you never leave me alone with her more than a minute? You approved of my asking her to marry me—and now we're engaged you never leave us alone! (*Then with a bitter smile*) But I know the reason well enough. You're afraid I'll let something slip.

LAVINIA. (*sits in the chair opposite him—wearily*) Can you blame me, the way you've been acting?

ORIN. (*somberly*) No. I'm afraid myself of being too long alone with her—afraid of myself. I have no right in the same world with her. And yet I feel so drawn to her purity! Her love for me makes me appear less vile to myself! (*Then with a harsh laugh*) And, at the same time, a million times more vile, that's the hell of it! So I'm afraid you can't hope to get rid of me through Hazel. She's another lost island! It's wiser for you to keep Hazel away from me, I warn you. Because when I see love for a murderer in her eyes my guilt crowds up in my throat like poisonous vomit and I long to spit it out—and confess!

LAVINIA. (*in a low voice*) Yes, that is what I live in terror of— that in one of your fits you'll say something before someone—now after it's all past and forgotten—when there isn't the slightest suspicion—

ORIN. (*harshly*) Were you hoping you could escape retribution? You can't! Confess and atone to the full extent of the law! That's the only way to wash the guilt of our mother's blood from our souls!

LAVINIA. (*distractedly*) Ssshh! Will you stop!

ORIN. Ask our father, the Judge, if it isn't! He knows! He keeps telling me!

LAVINIA. Oh, God! Over and over and over! Will you never lose your stupid guilty conscience! Don't you see how you torture me? You're becoming my guilty conscience, too! (*With an instinctive flare-up of her old jealousy*) How can you still love that vile woman so—when you know all she wanted was to leave you without a thought and marry that—

ORIN. (*with fierce accusation*) Yes! Exactly as you're scheming now to leave me and marry Peter! But, by God, you won't! You'll damn soon stop your tricks when you know what I've been writing!

LAVINIA. (*tensely*) What have you written?

ORIN. (*his anger turned to gloating satisfaction*) Ah! That frightens you, does it? Well, you better be frightened!

LAVINIA. Tell me what you've written!

ORIN. None of your damned business.

LAVINIA. I've got to know!

ORIN. Well, as I've practically finished it—I suppose I might as well tell you. At his earnest solicitation— (*He waves a hand to the portrait mockingly*) as the last male Mannon—thank God for that, eh!—I've been writing the history of our family! (*He adds, with a glance at the portrait and a malicious chuckle*) But I don't wish to convey that he approves of all I've set down—not by a damned sight!

LAVINIA. (*trying to keep calm—tensely*) What kind of history do you mean?

ORIN. A true history of all the family crimes, beginning with Grandfather Abe's—all of the crimes, including ours, do you understand?

LAVINIA. (*aghast*) Do you mean to tell me you've actually written—

ORIN. Yes! I've tried to trace to its secret hiding place in the Mannon past the evil destiny behind our lives! I thought if I could see it clearly in the past I might be able to foretell what fate is in store for us, Vinnie—but I haven't dared predict that—not yet—although I can guess— (*He gives a sinister chuckle.*)

LAVINIA. Orin!

ORIN. Most of what I've written is about you! I found you the most interesting criminal of us all!

LAVINIA. (*breaking*) How can you say such dreadful things to me, after all I—

ORIN. (*as if he hadn't heard—inexorably*) So many strange hidden things out of the Mannon past combine in you! For one example, do you remember the first mate, Wilkins, on the voyage to Frisco? Oh, I know you thought I was in a stupor of grief—but I wasn't blind! I saw how you wanted him!

LAVINIA. (*angrily, but with a trace of guilty confusion*) I never gave him a thought! He was an officer of the ship to me, and nothing more!

ORIN. (*mockingly*) Adam Brant was a ship's officer, too, wasn't he? Wilkins reminded you of Brant—

LAVINIA. No!

ORIN. And that's why you suddenly discarded mourning in Frisco and bought new clothes—in Mother's colors!

LAVINIA. (*furiously*) Stop talking about her! You'd think, to hear you, I had no life of my own!

ORIN. You wanted Wilkins just as you'd wanted Brant!

153

LAVINIA. That's a lie!

ORIN. You're doing the lying! You know damned well that behind all your pretense about Mother's murder being an act of justice was your jealous hatred! She warned me of that and I see it clearly now! You wanted Brant for yourself!

LAVINIA. (*fiercely*) It's a lie! I hated him!

ORIN. Yes, after you knew he was her lover! (*He chuckles with a sinister mockery*) But we'll let that pass for the present—I know it's the last thing you could ever admit to yourself!—and come to what I've written about your adventures on my lost islands. Or should I say, Adam Brant's islands! He had been there too, if you'll remember! Probably he'd lived with one of the native women! He was that kind! Were you thinking of that when we were there?

LAVINIA. (*chokingly*) Stop it! I—I warn you—I won't bear it much longer!

ORIN. (*as if he hadn't heard—in the same sinister mocking tone*) What a paradise the Islands were for you, eh? All those handsome men staring at you and your strange beautiful hair! It was then you finally became pretty—like Mother! You knew they all desired you, didn't you? It filled you with pride! Especially Avahanni! You watched him stare at your body through your clothes, stripping you naked! And you wanted him!

LAVINIA. No!

ORIN. Don't lie! (*He accuses her with fierce jealousy*) What did you do with him the night I was sick and you went to watch their shameless dance? Something happened between you! I saw your face when you came back and stood with him in front of our hut!

LAVINIA. (*quietly—with simple dignity now*) I had kissed him good night, that was all—in gratitude! He was innocent and good. He had made me feel for the first time in my life that everything about love could be sweet and natural.

ORIN. So you kissed him, did you? And that was all?

LAVINIA. (*with a sudden flare of deliberately evil taunting that re-*

calls her mother in the last act of "Homecoming," when she was goading EZRA MANNON *to fury just before his murder*) And what if it wasn't? I'm not your property! I have a right to love!

ORIN. (*reacting as his father had—his face grown livid—with a hoarse cry of fury grabs her by the throat*) You—you whore! I'll kill you! (*Then suddenly he breaks down and becomes weak and pitiful*) No! You're lying about him, aren't you? For God's sake, tell me you're lying, Vinnie!

LAVINIA. (*strangely shaken and trembling—stammers*) Yes—it was a lie—how could you believe I—Oh, Orin, something made me say that to you—against my will—something rose up in me—like an evil spirit!

ORIN. (*laughs wildly*) Ghosts! You never seemed so much like Mother as you did just then!

LAVINIA. (*pleading distractedly*) Don't talk about it! Let's forget it ever happened! Forgive me! Please forget it!

ORIN. All right—if the ghosts will let us forget! (*He stares at her fixedly for a moment—then satisfied*) I believe you about Avahanni. I never really suspected, or I'd have killed him—and you, too! I hope you know that! (*Then with his old obsessed insistence*) But you were guilty in your mind just the same!

LAVINIA. (*in a flash of distracted anger*) Stop harping on that! Stop torturing me or I—! I've warned you! I warn you again! I can't bear any more! I won't!

ORIN. (*with a mocking diabolical sneer—quietly*) Then why don't you murder me? I'll help you plan it, as we planned Brant's, so there will be no suspicion on you! And I'll be grateful! I loathe my life!

LAVINIA. (*speechless with horror—can only gasp*) Oh!

ORIN. (*with a quiet mad insistence*) Can't you see I'm now in Father's place and you're Mother? That's the evil destiny out of the past I haven't dared predict! I'm the Mannon you're chained to! So isn't it plain—

LAVINIA. (*putting her hands over her ears*) For God's sake, won't

155

you be quiet! (*Then suddenly her horror turning into a violent rage —unconsciously repeating the exact threat she had goaded her mother to make to her in Act Two of "Homecoming"*) Take care, Orin! You'll be responsible if—! (*She stops abruptly, terrified by her own words.*)

ORIN. (*with a diabolical mockery*) If what? If I should die mysteriously of heart failure?

LAVINIA. Leave me alone! Leave me alone! Don't keep saying that! How can you be so horrible? Don't you know I'm your sister, who loves you, who would give her life to bring you peace?

ORIN. (*with a change to a harsh threatening tone*) I don't believe you! I know you're plotting something! But you look out! I'll be watching you! And I warn you I won't stand your leaving me for Peter! I'm going to put this confession I've written in safe hands—to be read in case you try to marry him—or if I should die—

LAVINIA. (*frantically grabbing his arm and shaking him fiercely*) Stop having such thoughts! Stop making me have them! You're like a devil torturing me! I won't listen! (*She breaks down and sobs brokenly.* ORIN *stares at her dazedly—seems half to come back to his natural self and the wild look fades from his eyes leaving them glazed and lifeless.*)

ORIN. (*strangely*) Don't cry. The damned don't cry. (*He slumps down heavily in his father's chair and stares at the floor. Suddenly he says harshly again*) Go away, will you? I want to be alone—to finish my work. (*Still sobbing, her hand over her eyes,* LAVINIA *feels blindly for the door and goes out closing it after her.* ORIN *unlocks the table drawer, pulls out his manuscript, and takes up his pen.*)

CURTAIN

ACT THREE

SCENE—*Same as Act One, Scene Two—the sitting-room. The lamp on the table is lighted but turned low. Two candles are burning on the mantel over the fireplace at right, shedding their flickering light on the portrait of* ABE MANNON *above, and of the other Mannons on the walls on each side of him. The eyes of the portraits seem to possess an intense bitter life, with their frozen stare "looking over the head of life, cutting it dead for the impropriety of living," as* ORIN *had said of his father in Act Two of "The Hunted."*

No time has elapsed since the preceding act. LAVINIA *enters from the hall in the rear, having just come from the study. She comes to the table and turns up the lamp. She is in a terrific state of tension. The corners of her mouth twitch, she twines and untwines the fingers of her clasped hands with a slow wringing movement which recalls her mother in the last act of "The Hunted."*

LAVINIA. (*torturedly—begins to pace up and down, muttering her thoughts aloud*) I can't bear it! Why does he keep putting his death in my head? He would be better off if— Why hasn't he the courage—? (*Then in a frenzy of remorseful anguish, her eyes unconsciously seeking the Mannon portraits on the right wall, as if they were the visible symbol of her God*) Oh, God, don't let me have such thoughts! You know I love Orin! Show me the way to save him! Don't let me think of death! I couldn't bear another death! Please! Please! (*At a noise from the hall she controls herself and pretends to be glancing through a book on the table.* SETH *appears in the doorway.*)

SETH. Vinnie!

LAVINIA. What is it, Seth?

SETH. That durned idjut, Hannah, is throwin' fits agin. Went down cellar and says she felt ha'nts crawlin' behind her. You'd better come and git her calmed down—or she'll be leavin'. (*Then he adds disgustedly*) That's what we git fur freein' 'em!

LAVINIA. (*wearily*) All right. I'll talk to her. (*She goes out with* SETH. *A pause. Then a ring from the front-door bell. A moment later* SETH *can be seen coming back along the hall. He opens the front door and is heard greeting* HAZEL *and* PETER *and follows them in as they enter the room.*)

SETH. Vinnie's back seein' to somethin'. You set down and she'll be here soon as she kin.

PETER. All right, Seth. (SETH *goes out again. They come forward and sit down,* PETER *looks hearty and good-natured, the same as ever, but* HAZEL'S *face wears a nervous, uneasy look although her air is determined.*)

PETER. I'll have to run along soon and drop in at the Council meeting. I can't get out of it. I'll be back in half an hour—maybe sooner.

HAZEL. (*suddenly with a little shiver*) I hate this house now. I hate coming here. If it wasn't for Orin— He's getting worse. Keeping him shut up here is the worst thing Vinnie could do.

PETER. He won't go out. You know very well she has to force him to walk with you.

HAZEL. And comes along herself! Never leaves him alone hardly a second!

PETER. (*with a grin*) Oh, that's what you've got against her, eh?

HAZEL. (*sharply*) Don't be silly, Peter! I simply think, and I'd say it to her face, that she's a bad influence for Orin. I feel there's something awfully wrong—somehow. He scares me at times—and Vinnie —I've watched her looking at you. She's changed so. There's something bold about her.

PETER. (*getting up*) If you're going to talk like that—! You ought to be ashamed, Hazel!

HAZEL. Well, I'm not! I've got some right to say something about

158

how he's cared for! And I'm going to from now on! I'm going to make her let him visit us for a spell. I've asked Mother and she'll be glad to have him.

PETER. Say, I think that's a darned good notion for both of them. She needs a rest from him, too.

HAZEL. Vinnie doesn't think it's a good notion! I mentioned it yesterday and she gave me such a look! (*Determinedly*) But I'm going to make him promise to come over tomorrow, no matter what she says!

PETER. (*soothingly, patting her shoulder*) Don't get angry now—about nothing. I'll help you persuade her to let him come. (*Then with a grin*) I'll help you do anything to help Orin get well—if only for selfish reasons. As long as Vinnie's tied down to him we can't get married.

HAZEL. (*stares at him—slowly*) Do you really want to marry her —now?

PETER. Why do you ask such a fool question? What do you mean, do I want to now?

HAZEL. (*her voice trembles and she seems about to burst into tears*) Oh, I don't know, Peter! I don't know!

PETER. (*sympathetic and at the same time exasperated*) What in the dickens is the matter with you?

HAZEL. (*hears a noise from the hall and collects herself—warningly*) Ssshh! (ORIN *appears in the doorway at rear. He glances at them, then quickly around the room to see if* LAVINIA *is there. They both greet him with* "Hello, Orin.")

ORIN. Hello! (*Then in an excited whisper, coming to them*) Where's Vinnie?

HAZEL. She's gone to see to something, Seth said.

PETER. (*glancing at his watch*) Gosh, I've got to hurry to that darned Council meeting.

ORIN. (*eagerly*) You're going?

PETER. (*jokingly*) You needn't look so darned tickled about it! It isn't polite!

ORIN. I've got to see Hazel alone!

PETER. All right! You don't have to put me out! (*He grins, slapping* ORIN *on the back and goes out.* ORIN *follows him with his eyes until he hears the front door close behind him.*)

ORIN. (*turning to* HAZEL—*with queer furtive excitement*) Listen, Hazel! I want you to do something! But wait! I've got to get— (*He rushes out and can be heard going across the hall to the study.* HAZEL *looks after him worriedly. A moment later he hurries back with a big sealed envelope in his hand which he gives to* HAZEL, *talking breathlessly, with nervous jerks of his head, as he glances apprehensively at the door*) Here! Take this! Quick! Don't let her see it! I want you to keep it in a safe place and never let anyone know you have it! It will be stolen if I keep it here! I know her! Will you promise?

HAZEL. But—what is it, Orin?

ORIN. I can't tell you. You mustn't ask me. And you must promise never to open it—unless something happens to me.

HAZEL. (*frightened by his tone*) What do you mean?

ORIN. I mean if I should die—or—but this is the most important, if she tries to marry Peter—the day before the wedding—I want you to make Peter read what's inside.

HAZEL. You don't want her to marry Peter?

ORIN. No! She can't have happiness! She's got to be punished! (*Suddenly taking her hand—excitedly*) And listen, Hazel! You mustn't love me any more. The only love I can know now is the love of guilt for guilt which breeds more guilt—until you get so deep at the bottom of hell there is no lower you can sink and you rest there in peace! (*He laughs harshly and turns away from her.*)

HAZEL. Orin! Don't talk like that! (*Then conquering her horror —resolutely tender and soothing*) Ssshh! Poor boy! Come here to me. (*He comes to her. She puts an arm around him*) Listen. I know something is worrying you—and I don't want to seem prying—but

160

I've had such a strong feeling at times that it would relieve your mind if you could tell me what it is. Haven't you thought that, Orin?

ORIN. (*longingly*) Yes! Yes! I want to confess to your purity! I want to be forgiven! (*Then checking himself abruptly as he is about to speak—dully*) No. I can't. Don't ask me. I love her.

HAZEL. But, you silly boy, Vinnie told Peter herself what it is and told him to tell me.

ORIN. (*staring at her wildly*) What did she tell?

HAZEL. About your having a quarrel with your poor mother that night before she—and how you've brooded over it until you blame yourself for her death.

ORIN. (*harshly*) I see! So in case I did tell you—oh, she's cunning! But not cunning enough this time! (*Vindictively*) You remember what I've given you, Hazel, and you do exactly what I said with it. (*Then with desperate pleading*) For God's sake, Hazel, if you love me help me to get away from here—or something terrible will happen!

HAZEL. That's just what I want to do! You come over tomorrow and stay with us.

ORIN. (*bitterly*) Do you suppose for a moment she'll ever let me go?

HAZEL. But haven't you a right to do as you want to?

ORIN. (*furtively*) I could sneak out when she wasn't looking—and then you could hide me and when she came for me tell her I wasn't there.

HAZEL. (*indignantly*) I won't do any such thing! I don't tell lies, Orin! (*Then scornfully*) How can you be so scared of Vinnie?

ORIN. (*hearing a noise from the hall—hastily*) Ssshh! She's coming! Don't let her see what I gave you. And go home right away and lock it up! (*He tiptoes away as if he were afraid of being found close to her and sits on the sofa at right, adopting a suspiciously careless attitude.* HAZEL *looks self-conscious and stiff.* LAVINIA *appears in the doorway and gives a start as she sees* HAZEL *and* ORIN *are alone.*

*She quickly senses something in the atmosphere and glances sharply
from one to the other as she comes into the room.)*

LAVINIA. (*to* HAZEL, *forcing a casual air*) I'm sorry being so long.

HAZEL. I didn't mind waiting.

LAVINIA. (*sitting down on the chair at center*) Where's Peter?

HAZEL. He had to go to a Council meeting. He's coming back.

LAVINIA. (*uneasiness creeping into her tone*) Has he been gone
long?

HAZEL. Not very long.

LAVINIA. (*turning to* ORIN—*sharply*) I thought you were in the
study.

ORIN. (*sensing her uneasiness—mockingly*) I finished what I was
working on.

LAVINIA. You finished—? (*She glances sharply at* HAZEL—*forcing
a joking tone*) My, but you two look mysterious! What have you been
up to?

HAZEL. (*trying to force a laugh*) Why, Vinnie? What makes you
think—?

LAVINIA. You're hiding something. (HAZEL *gives a start and instinctively moves the hand with the envelope farther behind her
back.* LAVINIA *notices this. So does* ORIN *who uneasily comes to* HAZEL's
rescue.)

ORIN. We're not hiding anything. Hazel has invited me over to their
house to stay for a while—and I'm going.

HAZEL. (*backing him up resolutely*) Yes. Orin is coming tomorrow.

LAVINIA. (*alarmed and resentful—coldly*) It's kind of you. I know
you mean it for the best. But he can't go.

HAZEL. (*sharply*) Why not?

LAVINIA. I don't care to discuss it, Hazel. You ought to know—

HAZEL. (*angrily*) I don't know! Orin is of age and can go where
he pleases!

ORIN. Let her talk all she likes, Hazel. I'll have the upper hand for a change, from now on! (LAVINIA *looks at him, frightened by the triumphant satisfaction in his voice.*)

HAZEL. (*anxious to score her point and keep* ORIN's *mind on it*) I should think you'd be glad. It will be the best thing in the world for him.

LAVINIA. (*turns on her—angrily*) I'll ask you to please mind your own business, Hazel!

HAZEL. (*springs to her feet, in her anger forgetting* **to** *hide the envelope which she now holds openly in her hand*) It is my business! I love Orin better than you! I don't think you love him at all, the way you've been acting!

ORIN. (*sees the envelope in plain sight and calls to her warningly*) Hazel! (*She catches his eye and hastily puts her hand behind her.* LAVINIA *sees the movement but doesn't for a moment realize the meaning of it.* ORIN *goes on warningly*) You said you had to go home early. I don't want to remind you but—

HAZEL. (*hastily*) Yes, I really must. (*Starting to go, trying to keep the envelope hidden, aware that* LAVINIA *is watching her suspiciously—defiantly to* ORIN) We'll expect you tomorrow, and have your room ready. (*Then to* LAVINIA—*coldly*) After the way you've insulted me, Vinnie, I hope you realize there's no more question of any friendship between us. (*She tries awkwardly to sidle toward the door.*)

LAVINIA. (*suddenly gets between her and the door—with angry accusation*) What are you hiding behind your back? (HAZEL *flushes guiltily, but refusing to lie, says nothing.* LAVINIA *turns on* ORIN) Have you given her what you've written? (*As he hesitates—violently*) Answer me!

ORIN. That's my business! What if I have?

LAVINIA. You—you traitor! You coward! (*Fiercely to* HAZEL) Give it to me! Do you hear?

HAZEL. Vinnie! How dare you talk that way to me! (*She tries to go but* LAVINIA *keeps directly between her and the door.*)

LAVINIA. You shan't leave here until—! (*Then breaking down and pleading*) Orin! Think what you're doing! Tell her to give it to me!

ORIN. No!

LAVINIA. (*goes and puts her arms around him—beseechingly as he avoids her eyes*) Think sanely for a moment! You can't do this! You're a Mannon!

ORIN. (*harshly*) It's because I'm one!

LAVINIA. For Mother's sake, you can't! You loved her!

ORIN. A lot she cared! Don't call on her!

LAVINIA. (*desperately*) For my sake, then! You know I love you! Make Hazel give that up and I'll do anything—anything you want me to!

ORIN. (*stares into her eyes, bending his head until his face is close to hers—with morbid intensity*) You mean that?

LAVINIA. (*shrinking back from him—falteringly*) Yes.

ORIN. (*laughs with a crazy triumph—checks this abruptly—and goes to* HAZEL *who has been standing bewilderedly, not understanding what is behind their talk but sensing something sinister, and terribly frightened.* ORIN *speaks curtly, his eyes fixed on* LAVINIA) Let me have it, Hazel.

HAZEL. (*hands him the envelope—in a trembling voice*) I'll go home. I suppose—we can't expect you tomorrow—now.

ORIN. No. Forget me. The Orin you loved was killed in the war. (*With a twisted smile*) Remember only that dead hero and not his rotting ghost! Good-bye! (*Then harshly*) Please go! (HAZEL *begins to sob and hurries blindly from the room.* ORIN *comes back to* LAVINIA *who remains kneeling by the chair. He puts the envelope in her hand—harshly*) Here! You realize the promise you made means giving up Peter? And never seeing him again?

LAVINIA. (*tensely*) Yes.

ORIN. And I suppose you think that's all it means, that I'll be content with a promise I've forced out of you, which you'll always be plotting to break? Oh, no! I'm not such a fool! I've got to be sure—- (*She doesn't reply or look at him. He stares at her and slowly a dis-*

torted look of desire comes over his face) You said you would do anything for me. That's a large promise, Vinnie—anything!

LAVINIA. (*shrinking from him*) What do you mean? What terrible thing have you been thinking lately—behind all your crazy talk? No, I don't want to know! Orin! Why do you look at me like that?

ORIN. You don't seem to feel all you mean to me now—all you have made yourself mean—since we murdered Mother!

LAVINIA. Orin!

ORIN. I love you now with all the guilt in me—the guilt we share! Perhaps I love you too much, Vinnie!

LAVINIA. You don't know what you're saying!

ORIN. There are times now when you don't seem to be my sister, nor Mother, but some stranger with the same beautiful hair— (*He touches her hair caressingly. She pulls violently away. He laughs wildly*) Perhaps you're Marie Brantôme, eh? And you say there are no ghosts in this house?

LAVINIA. (*staring at him with fascinated horror*) For God's sake—! No! You're insane! You can't mean—!

ORIN. How else can I be sure you won't leave me? You would never dare leave me—then! You would feel as guilty then as I do! You would be as damned as I am! (*Then with sudden anger as he sees the growing horrified repulsion on her face*) Damn you, don't you see I must find some certainty some way or go mad? You don't want me to go mad, do you? I would talk too much! I would confess! (*Then as if the words stirred something within him his tone instantly changes to one of passionate pleading*) Vinnie! For the love of God, let's go now and confess and pay the penalty for Mother's murder, and find peace together!

LAVINIA. (*tempted and tortured, in a longing whisper*) Peace! (*Then summoning her will, springs to her feet wildly*) No! You coward! There is nothing to confess! There was only justice!

ORIN. (*turns and addresses the portraits on the wall with a crazy mockery*) You hear her? You'll find Lavinia Mannon harder to break than me! You'll have to haunt and hound her for a lifetime!

LAVINIA. (*her control snapping—turning on him now in a burst of frantic hatred and rage*) I hate you! I wish you were dead! You're too vile to live! You'd kill yourself if you weren't a coward!

ORIN. (*starts back as if he'd been struck, the tortured mad look on his face changing to a stricken terrified expression*) Vinnie!

LAVINIA. I mean it! I mean it! (*She breaks down and sobs hysterically.*)

ORIN. (*in a pitiful pleading whisper*) Vinnie! (*He stares at her with the lost stricken expression for a moment more—then the obsessed wild look returns to his eyes—with harsh mockery*) Another act of justice, eh? You want to drive me to suicide as I drove Mother! An eye for an eye, is that it? But— (*He stops abruptly and stares before him, as if this idea were suddenly taking hold of his tortured imagination and speaks fascinatedly to himself*) Yes! That would be justice— now you are Mother! She is speaking now through you! (*More and more hypnotized by this train of thought*) Yes! It's the way to peace— to find her again—my lost island—Death is an Island of Peace, too— Mother will be waiting for me there— (*With excited eagerness now, speaking to the dead*) Mother! Do you know what I'll do then? I'll get on my knees and ask your forgiveness—and say— (*His mouth grows convulsed, as if he were retching up poison*) I'll say, I'm glad you found love, Mother! I'll wish you happiness—you and Adam! (*He laughs exultantly*) You've heard me! You're here in the house now! You're calling me! You're waiting to take me home! (*He turns and strides toward the door.*)

LAVINIA. (*who has raised her head and has been staring at him with dread during the latter part of his talk—torn by remorse, runs after him and throws her arms around him*) No, Orin! No!

ORIN. (*pushes her away—with a rough brotherly irritation*) Get out of my way, can't you? Mother's waiting! (*He gets to the door. Then he turns back and says sharply*) Ssshh! Here's Peter! Shut up, now! (*He steps back in the room as* PETER *appears in the doorway.*)

PETER. Excuse my coming right in. The door was open. Where's Hazel?

ORIN. (*with unnatural casualness*) Gone home. (*Then with a quick, meaning, mocking glance at* LAVINIA) I'm just going in the study to clean my pistol. Darn thing's gotten so rusty. Glad you came now, Peter. You can keep Vinnie company. (*He turns and goes out the door.* PETER *stares after him puzzledly.*)

LAVINIA. (*with a stifled cry*) Orin! (*There is no answer but the sound of the study door being shut. She starts to run after him, stops herself, then throws herself into* PETER's *arms, as if for protection against herself and begins to talk volubly to drown out thought*) Hold me close, Peter! Nothing matters but love, does it? That must come first! No price is too great, is it? Or for peace! One must have peace— one is too weak to forget—no one has the right to keep anyone from peace! (*She makes a motion to cover her ears with her hands.*)

PETER. (*alarmed by her hectic excitement*) He's a darned fool to monkey with a pistol—in his state. Shall I get it away from him?

LAVINIA. (*holding him tighter—volubly*) Oh, won't it be wonderful, Peter—once we're married and have a home with a garden and trees! We'll be so happy! I love everything that grows simply—up toward the sun—everything that's straight and strong! I hate what's warped and twists and eats into itself and dies for a lifetime in shadow. (*Then her voice rising as if it were about to break hysterically—again with the instinctive movement to cover her ears*) I can't bear waiting— waiting and waiting and waiting—! (*There is a muffled shot from the study across the hall.*)

PETER. (*breaking from her and running for the door*) Good God! What's that? (*He rushes into the hall.*)

LAVINIA. (*sags weakly and supports herself against the table—in a faint, trembling voice*) Orin! Forgive me! (*She controls herself with a terrible effort of will. Her mouth congeals into a frozen line. Mechanically she hides the sealed envelope in a drawer of the table and*

167

locks the drawer) I've got to go in— (*She turns to go and her eyes catch the eyes of the Mannons in the portraits fixed accusingly on her —defiantly*) Why do you look at me like that? Wasn't it the only way to keep your secret, too? But I'm through with you forever now, do you hear? I'm Mother's daughter—not one of you! I'll live in spite of you! (*She squares her shoulders, with a return of the abrupt military movement copied from her father which she had of old—as if by the very act of disowning the Mannons she had returned to the fold— and marches stiffly from the room.*)

CURTAIN

ACT FOUR

SCENE—*Same as Act One, Scene One—exterior of the house. It is in the late afternoon of a day three days later. The Mannon house has much the same appearance as it had in the first act of "Homecoming." Soft golden sunlight shimmers in a luminous mist on the Greek temple portico, intensifying the whiteness of the columns, the deep green of the shutters, the green of the shrubbery, the black and green of the pines. The columns cast black bars of shadow on the gray stone wall behind them. The shutters are all fastened back, the windows open. On the ground floor, the upper part of the windows, raised from the bottom, reflect the sun in a smouldering stare, as of brooding revengeful eyes.*

SETH *appears walking slowly up the drive from right, front. He has a pair of grass clippers and potters along pretending to trim the edge of the lawn along the drive. But in reality he is merely killing time, chewing tobacco, and singing mournfully to himself, in his aged, plaintive wraith of a once-good baritone, the chanty "Shenandoah":*

> "Oh, Shenandoah, I long to hear you
>   A-way, my rolling river,
>   Oh, Shenandoah, I can't get near you
>   Way-ay, I'm bound away
>   Across the wide Missouri.

> "Oh, Shenandoah, I love your daughter
>   A-way, you rolling river."

SETH. (*stops singing and stands peering off left toward the flower garden—shakes his head and mutters to himself*) There she be pickin' my flowers agin. Like her Maw used to—on'y wuss. She's got every

169

room in the house full of 'em a'ready. Durn it, I hoped she'd stop that once the funeral was over. There won't be a one left in my garden! (*He looks away and begins pottering about again, and mutters grimly*) A durn queer thin' fur a sodger to kill himself cleanin' his gun, folks is sayin'. They'll fight purty shy of her now. A Mannon has come to mean sudden death to 'em. (*Then with a grim pride*) But Vinnie's able fur 'em. They'll never git her to show nothin'. Clean Mannon strain!

(LAVINIA *enters from the left. The three days that have intervened have effected a remarkable change in her. Her body, dressed in deep mourning, again appears flat-chested and thin. The Mannon mask-semblance of her face appears intensified now. It is deeply lined, haggard with sleeplessness and strain, congealed into a stony emotionless expression. Her lips are bloodless, drawn taut in a grim line. She is carrying a large bunch of flowers. She holds them out to* SETH *and speaks in a strange, empty voice.*)

LAVINIA. Take these, Seth, and give them to Hannah. Tell her to set them around inside. I want the house to be full of flowers. Peter is coming, and I want everything to be pretty and cheerful. (*She goes and sits at the top of the steps, bolt upright, her arms held stiffly to her sides, her legs and feet pressed together, and stares back into the sun-glare with unblinking, frozen, defiant eyes.*)

SETH. (*stands holding the flowers and regarding her worriedly*) I seed you settin' out here on the steps when I got up at five this mornin'—and every mornin' since Orin— Ain't you been gittin' no sleep? (*She stares before her as if she had not heard him. He goes on coaxingly*) How'd you like if I hauled one of them sofas out fur you to lie on, Vinnie? Mebbe you could take a couple o' winks an' it'd do you good.

LAVINIA. No, thank you, Seth. I'm waiting for Peter. (*Then after a pause, curiously*) Why didn't you tell me to go in the house and lie down? (SETH *pretends not to hear the question, avoiding her eyes*)

You understand, don't you? You've been with us Mannons so long! You know there's no rest in this house which Grandfather built as a temple of Hate and Death!

SETH. (*blurts out*) Don't you try to live here, Vinnie! You marry Peter and git clear!

LAVINIA. I'm going to marry him! And I'm going away with him and forget this house and all that ever happened in it!

SETH. That's talkin', Vinnie!

LAVINIA. I'll close it up and leave it in the sun and rain to die. The portraits of the Mannons will rot on the walls and the ghosts will fade back into death. And the Mannons will be forgotten. I'm the last and I won't be one long. I'll be Mrs. Peter Niles. Then they're finished! Thank God! (*She leans back in the sunlight and closes her eyes.* SETH *stares at her worriedly, shakes his head and spits. Then he hears something and peers down the drive, off left.*)

SETH. Vinnie. Here's Hazel comin'.

LAVINIA. (*jerks up stiffly with a look of alarm*) Hazel? What does she want? (*She springs up as if she were going to run in the house, then stands her ground on the top of the steps, her voice hardening*) Seth, you go work in back, please!

SETH. Ayeh. (*He moves slowly off behind the lilacs as* HAZEL *enters from left, front—calling back*) Evenin', Hazel.

HAZEL. Good evening, Seth. (*She stops short and stares at* LAVINIA. LAVINIA's *eyes are hard and defiant as she stares back.* HAZEL *is dressed in mourning. Her face is sad and pale, her eyes show evidence of much weeping, but there is an air of stubborn resolution about her as she makes up her mind and walks to the foot of the steps.*)

LAVINIA. What do you want? I've got a lot to attend to.

HAZEL. (*quietly*) It won't take me long to say what I've come to say, Vinnie. (*Suddenly she bursts out*) It's a lie about Orin killing himself by accident! I know it is! He meant to!

LAVINIA. You better be careful what you say. I can prove what happened. Peter was here—

171

HAZEL. I don't care what anyone says!

LAVINIA. I should think you'd be the last one to accuse Orin—

HAZEL. I'm not accusing him! Don't you dare say that! I'm accusing you! You drove him to it! Oh, I know I can't prove it—any more than I can prove a lot of things Orin hinted at! But I know terrible things must have happened—and that you're to blame for them, somehow!

LAVINIA. (*concealing a start of fear—changing to a forced reproachful tone*) What would Orin think of you coming here the day of his funeral to accuse me of the sorrow that's afflicted our family?

HAZEL. (*feeling guilty and at the same time defiant and sure she is right*) All right, Vinnie. I won't say anything more. But I know there's something—and so do you—something that was driving Orin crazy— (*She breaks down and sobs*) Poor Orin!

LAVINIA. (*stares straight before her. Her lips twitch. In a stifled voice between her clenched teeth*) Don't—do that!

HAZEL. (*controlling herself—after a pause*) I'm sorry. I didn't come to talk about Orin.

LAVINIA. (*uneasily*) What did you come for?

HAZEL. About Peter.

LAVINIA. (*as if this were something she had been dreading—harshly*) You leave Peter and me alone!

HAZEL. I won't! You're not going to marry Peter and ruin his life! (*Pleading now*) You can't! Don't you see he could never be happy with you, that you'll only drag him into this terrible thing—whatever it is—and make him share it?

LAVINIA. There is no terrible thing!

HAZEL. I know Peter can't believe evil of anyone, but living alone with you, married, you couldn't hide it, he'd get to feel what I feel. You could never be happy because it would come between you! (*Pleading again*) Oh, Vinnie, you've got to be fair to Peter! You've got to consider his happiness—if you really love him!

LAVINIA. (*hoarsely*) I do love him!

HAZEL. It has started already—his being made unhappy through you!

LAVINIA. You're lying!

HAZEL. He fought with Mother last night when she tried to talk to him—the first time he ever did such a thing! It isn't like Peter. You've changed him. He left home and went to the hotel to stay. He said he'd never speak to Mother or me again. He's always been such a wonderful son before—and brother. We three have been so happy. It's broken Mother's heart. All she does is sit and cry. (*Desperately*) Oh, Vinnie, you can't do it! You will be punished if you do! Peter would get to hate you in the end!

LAVINIA. No!

HAZEL. Do you want to take the risk of driving Peter to do what Orin did? He might—if he ever discovered the truth!

LAVINIA. (*violently*) What truth, you little fool! Discover what?

HAZEL. (*accusingly*) I don't know—but you know! Look in your heart and ask your conscience before God if you ought to marry Peter!

LAVINIA. (*desperately—at the end of her tether*) Yes! Before God! Before anything! (*Then glaring at her—with a burst of rage*) You leave me alone—go away—or I'll get Orin's pistol and kill you! (*Her rage passes, leaving her weak and shaken. She goes to her chair and sinks on it.*)

HAZEL. (*recoiling*) Oh! You are wicked! I believe you would—! Vinnie! What's made you like this?

LAVINIA. Go away!

HAZEL. Vinnie! (LAVINIA *closes her eyes.* HAZEL *stands staring at her. After a pause—in a trembling voice*) All right. I'll go. All I can do is trust you. I know in your heart you can't be dead to all honor and justice—you, a Mannon! (LAVINIA *gives a little bitter laugh without opening her eyes*) At least you owe it to Peter to let him read what Orin had in that envelope. Orin asked me to make him read it before he married you. I've told Peter about that, Vinnie.

LAVINIA. (*without opening her eyes—strangely, as if to herself*) The dead! Why can't the dead die!

HAZEL. (*stares at her frightenedly, not knowing what to do—looks around her uncertainly and sees someone coming from off left, front —quickly*) Here he comes now. I'll go by the back. I don't want him to meet me. (*She starts to go but stops by the clump of lilacs—pityingly*) I know you're suffering, Vinnie—and I know your conscience will make you do what's right—and God will forgive you. (*She goes quickly behind the lilacs and around the house to the rear.*)

LAVINIA. (*looks after her and calls defiantly*) I'm not asking God or anybody for forgiveness. I forgive myself! (*She leans back and closes her eyes again—bitterly*) I hope there is a hell for the good somewhere! (PETER *enters from the left, front. He looks haggard and tormented. He walks slowly, his eyes on the ground—then sees* LAVINIA *and immediately makes an effort to pull himself together and appear cheerful.*)

PETER. Hello, Vinnie. (*He sits on the edge of the portico beside her. She still keeps her eyes closed, as if afraid to open them. He looks at her worriedly*) You look terribly worn out. Haven't you slept? (*He pats her hand with awkward tenderness. Her mouth twitches and draws down at the corners as she stifles a sob. He goes on comfortingly*) You've had an awfully hard time of it, but never mind, we'll be married soon.

LAVINIA. (*without opening her eyes—longingly*) You'll love me and keep me from remembering?

PETER. You bet I will! And the first thing is to get you away from this darned house! I may be a fool but I'm beginning to feel superstitious about it myself.

LAVINIA. (*without opening her eyes—strangely*) Yes. Love can't live in it. We'll go away and leave it alone to die—and we'll forget the dead.

PETER. (*a bitter resentful note coming into his voice*) We can't move too far away to suit me! I hate this damned town now and everyone in it!

LAVINIA. (*opens her eyes and looks at him startledly*) I never heard you talk that way before, Peter—bitter!

PETER. (*avoiding her eyes*) Some things would make anyone bitter!

LAVINIA. You've quarreled with your mother and Hazel—on account of me—is that it?

PETER. How did you know?

LAVINIA. Hazel was just here.

PETER. She told you? The darned fool! What did she do that for?

LAVINIA. She doesn't want me to marry you.

PETER. (*angrily*) The little sneak! What right has she—? (*Then a bit uneasily—forcing a smile*) Well, you won't pay any attention to her, I hope.

LAVINIA. (*more as if she were answering some voice in herself than him—stiffening in her chair—defiantly*) No!

PETER. She and Mother suddenly got a lot of crazy notions in their heads. But they'll get over them.

LAVINIA. (*staring at him searchingly—uneasily*) Supposing they don't?

PETER. They will after we are married—or I'm through with them!

LAVINIA. (*a pause. Then she takes his face in her hands and turns it to hers*) Peter! Let me look at you! You're suffering! Your eyes have a hurt look! They've always been so trustful! They look suspicious and afraid of life now! Have I done this to you already, Peter? Are you beginning to suspect me? Are you wondering what it was Orin wrote?

PETER. (*protesting violently*) No! Of course I'm not! Don't I know Orin was out of his mind? Why would I pay any attention—?

LAVINIA. You swear you'll never suspect me—of anything?

PETER. What do you think I am?

LAVINIA. And you'll never let anyone come between us? Nothing can keep us from being happy, can it? You won't let anything, will you?

PETER. Of course I won't!

LAVINIA. (*more and more desperately*) I want to get married right away, Peter! I'm afraid! Would you marry me now—this evening? We can find a minister to do it. I can change my clothes in a second and put on the color you like! Marry me today, Peter! I'm afraid to wait!

PETER. (*bewildered and a bit shocked*) But—you don't mean that, do you? We couldn't. It wouldn't look right the day Orin—out of respect for him. (*Then suspicious in spite of himself*) I can't see why you're so afraid of waiting. Nothing can happen, can it? Was there anything in what Orin wrote that would stop us from—

LAVINIA. (*with a wild beaten laugh*) The dead coming between! They always would, Peter! You trust me with your happiness! But that means trusting the Mannon dead—and they're not to be trusted with love! I know them too well! And I couldn't bear to watch your eyes grow bitter and hidden from me and wounded in their trust of life! I love you too much!

PETER. (*made more uneasy and suspicious by this*) What are you talking about, Vinnie? You make me think there was something—

LAVINIA. (*desperately*) No—nothing! (*Then suddenly throwing her arms around him*) No! Don't think of that—not yet! I want a little while of happiness—in spite of all the dead! I've earned it! I've done enough—! (*Growing more desperate—pleading wildly*) Listen, Peter! Why must we wait for marriage? I want a moment of joy— of love—to make up for what's coming! I want it now! Can't you be strong, Peter? Can't you be simple and pure? Can't you forget sin and see that all love is beautiful? (*She kisses him with desperate passion*) Kiss me! Hold me close! Want me! Want me so much you'd murder anyone to have me! I did that—for you! Take me in this house of the dead and love me! Our love will drive the dead away! It will shame them back into death! (*At the topmost pitch of des-*

176

perate, frantic abandonment) Want me! Take me, Adam! (*She is brought back to herself with a start by this name escaping her—bewilderedly, laughing idiotically*) Adam? Why did I call you Adam? I never even heard that name before—outside of the Bible! (*Then suddenly with a hopeless, dead finality*) Always the dead between! It's no good trying any more!

PETER. (*convinced she is hysterical and yet shocked and repelled by her display of passion*) Vinnie! You're talking crazy! You don't know what you're saying! You're not—like that!

LAVINIA. (*in a dead voice*) I can't marry you, Peter. You mustn't ever see me again. (*He stares at her, stunned and stupid*) Go home. Make it up with your mother and Hazel. Marry someone else. Love isn't permitted to me. The dead are too strong!

PETER. (*his mind in a turmoil*) Vinnie! You can't—! You've gone crazy—! What's changed you like this? (*Then suspiciously*) Is it—what Orin wrote? What was it? I've got a right to know, haven't I? (*Then as she doesn't answer—more suspiciously*) He acted so queer about—what happened to you on the Islands. Was it something there—something to do with that native—?

LAVINIA. (*her first instinctive reaction one of hurt insult*) Peter! Don't you dare—! (*Then suddenly seizing on this as a way out—with calculated coarseness*) All right! Yes, if you must know! I won't lie any more! Orin suspected I'd lusted with him! And I had!

PETER. (*shrinking from her aghast—brokenly*) Vinnie! You've gone crazy! I don't believe— You—you couldn't!

LAVINIA. (*stridently*) Why shouldn't I? I wanted him! I wanted to learn love from him—love that wasn't a sin! And I did, I tell you! He had me! I was his fancy woman!

PETER. (*wincing as if she had struck him in the face, stares at her with a stricken look of horrified repulsion—with bitter, broken anger*) Then—Mother and Hazel were right about you—you are bad at heart—no wonder Orin killed himself—God, I—I hope you'll be punished—I—! (*He hurries blindly off down the drive to the left.*)

LAVINIA. (*watches him go—then with a little desperate cry starts after him*) Peter! It's a lie! I didn't—! (*She stops abruptly and stiffens into her old, square-shouldered attitude. She looks down the drive after him—then turns away, saying in a lost, empty tone*) Goodbye, Peter. (SETH *enters from the left rear, coming around the corner of the house. He stands for a moment watching her, grimly wondering. Then to call her attention to his presence, he begins singing half under his breath his melancholy "Shenandoah" chanty, at the same time looking at the ground around him as if searching for something.*)

> *"Oh, Shenandoah, I can't get near you*
> *Way-ay, I'm bound away—"*

LAVINIA. (*without looking at him, picking up the words of the chanty—with a grim writhen smile*) I'm not bound away—not now, Seth. I'm bound here—to the Mannon dead! (*She gives a dry little cackle of laughter and turns as if to enter the house.*)

SETH. (*frightened by the look on her face, grabs her by the arm*) Don't go in there, Vinnie!

LAVINIA. (*grimly*) Don't be afraid. I'm not going the way Mother and Orin went. That's escaping punishment. And there's no one left to punish me. I'm the last Mannon. I've got to punish myself! Living alone here with the dead is a worse act of justice than death or prison! I'll never go out or see anyone! I'll have the shutters nailed closed so no sunlight can ever get in. I'll live alone with the dead, and keep their secrets, and let them hound me, until the curse is paid out and the last Mannon is let die! (*With a strange cruel smile of gloating over the years of self-torture*) I know they will see to it I live for a long time! It takes the Mannons to punish themselves for being born!

SETH. (*with grim understanding*) Ayeh. And I ain't heard a word you've been sayin', Vinnie. (*Pretending to search the ground again*) Left my clippers around somewheres.

LAVINIA. (*turns to him sharply*) You go now and close the shutters and nail them tight.

SETH. Ayeh.

LAVINIA. And tell Hannah to throw out all the flowers.

SETH. Ayeh. (*He goes past her up the steps and into the house. She ascends to the portico—and then turns and stands for a while, stiff and square-shouldered, staring into the sunlight with frozen eyes.* SETH *leans out of the window at the right of the door and pulls the shutters closed with a decisive bang. As if this were a word of command,* LAVINIA *pivots sharply on her heel and marches woodenly into the house, closing the door behind her.*)

CURTAIN

AH, WILDERNESS!

TO GEORGE JEAN NATHAN

*Who also, once upon a time, in peg-top trousers
went the pace that kills along the road to ruin*

CHARACTERS

NAT MILLER, *owner of the* EVENING GLOBE

ESSIE, *his wife*

ARTHUR

RICHARD

MILDRED *their children*

TOMMY

SID DAVIS, *Essie's brother*

LILY MILLER, *Nat's sister*

DAVID MC COMBER

MURIEL MC COMBER, *his daughter*

WINT SELBY, *a classmate of Arthur's at Yale*

BELLE

NORAH

BARTENDER

SALESMAN

SCENES

AH, WILDERNESS!

ACT ONE

SCENE—*Sitting-room of the Miller home in a large small-town in Connecticut—about 7:30 in the morning of July 4th, 1906.*

The room is fairly large, homely looking and cheerful in the morning sunlight, furnished with scrupulous medium-priced tastelessness of the period. Beneath the two windows at left, front, a sofa with silk and satin cushions stands against the wall. At rear of sofa, a bookcase with glass doors, filled with cheap sets, extends along the remaining length of wall. In the rear wall, left, is a double doorway with sliding doors and portières, leading into a dark, windowless, back parlor. At right of this doorway, another bookcase, this time a small, open one, crammed with boys' and girls' books and the best-selling novels of many past years—books the family really have read. To the right of this bookcase is the mate of the double doorway at its left, with sliding doors and portières, this one leading to a well-lighted front parlor. In the right wall, rear, a screen door opens on a porch. Farther forward in this wall are two windows, with a writing desk and a chair between them. At center is a big, round table with a green-shaded reading lamp, the cord of the lamp running up to one of five sockets in the chandelier above. Five chairs are grouped about the table—three rockers at left, right, and right rear of it, two armchairs at rear and left rear. A medium-priced, inoffensive rug covers most of the floor. The walls are papered white with a cheerful, ugly blue design.

Voices are heard in a conversational tone from the dining-room beyond the back parlor, where the family are just finishing breakfast.

Then MRS. MILLER'S *voice, raised commandingly,* "Tommy! Come back here and finish your milk!" *At the same moment* TOMMY *appears in the doorway from the back parlor—a chubby, sun-burnt boy of eleven with dark eyes, blond hair wetted and plastered down in a part, and a shiny, good-natured face, a rim of milk visible about his lips. Bursting with bottled-up energy and a longing to get started on the Fourth, he nevertheless has hesitated obediently at his mother's call.*

TOMMY. (*calls back pleadingly*) Aw, I'm full, Ma. And I said excuse me and you said all right. (*His* FATHER'S *voice is heard speaking to his mother. Then she calls:* "All right, Tommy," *and* TOMMY *asks eagerly*) Can I go out now?

MOTHER'S VOICE. (*correctingly*) May I!

TOMMY. (*fidgeting, but obediently*) May I, Ma?

MOTHER'S VOICE. Yes. (TOMMY *jumps for the screen door to the porch at right like a sprinter released by the starting shot.*)

FATHER'S VOICE. (*shouts after him*) But you set off your crackers away from the house, remember! (*But* TOMMY *is already through the screen door, which he leaves open behind him.*)

(*A moment later the family appear from the back parlor, coming from the dining-room. First are* MILDRED *and* ARTHUR. MILDRED *is fifteen, tall and slender, with big, irregular features, resembling her father to the complete effacing of any pretense at prettiness. But her big, gray eyes are beautiful; she has vivacity and a fetching smile, and everyone thinks of her as an attractive girl. She is dressed in shirtwaist and skirt in the fashion of the period.*

(ARTHUR, *the eldest of the Miller children who are still living home, is nineteen. He is tall, heavy, barrel-chested and muscular, the type of football linesman of that period, with a square, stolid face, small blue eyes and thick sandy hair. His manner is solemnly collegiate. He is dressed in the latest college fashion of that day, which has receded a bit from the extreme of preceding years, but still runs to padded shoulders and pants half-pegged at the top, and so small at their wide-cuffed bottoms that they cannot be taken off with shoes on.*)

MILDRED. (*as they appear—inquisitively*) Where are you going to-day, Art?

ARTHUR. (*with superior dignity*) That's my business. (*He ostentatiously takes from his pocket a tobacco pouch with a big Y and class numerals stamped on it, and a heavy bulldog briar pipe with silver Y and numerals, and starts filling the pipe.*)

MILDRED. (*teasingly*) Bet I know, just the same! Want me to tell you her initials? E.R.! (*She laughs.* ARTHUR, *pleased by this insinuation at his lady-killing activities, yet finds it beneath his dignity to reply. He goes to the table, lights his pipe and picks up the local morning paper, and slouches back into the armchair at left rear of table, beginning to whistle "Oh, Waltz Me Around Again, Willie" as he scans the headlines.* MILDRED *sits on the sofa at left, front.*)

(*Meanwhile, their mother and their* AUNT LILY, *their father's sister, have appeared, following them from the back parlor.* MRS. MILLER *is around fifty, a short, stout woman with fading light-brown hair sprinkled with gray, who must have been decidedly pretty as a girl in a round-faced, cute, small-featured, wide-eyed fashion. She has big brown eyes, soft and maternal—a bustling, mother-of-a-family manner. She is dressed in shirtwaist and skirt.*

(LILY MILLER, *her sister-in-law, is forty-two, tall, dark and thin. She conforms outwardly to the conventional type of old-maid school teacher, even to wearing glasses. But behind the glasses her gray eyes are gentle and tired, and her whole atmosphere is one of shy kindliness. Her voice presents the greatest contrast to her appearance —soft and full of sweetness. She, also, is dressed in a shirtwaist and skirt.*)

MRS. MILLER. (*as they appear*) Getting milk down him is like— (*Suddenly she is aware of the screen door standing half open*) Goodness, look at that door he's left open! The house will be alive with flies! (*Rushing out to shut it*) I've told him again and again—and that's all the good it does! It's just a waste of breath! (*She slams the door shut.*)

LILY. (*smiling*) Well, you can't expect a boy to remember to shut doors—on the Fourth of July. (*She goes diffidently to the straight-backed chair before the desk at right, front, leaving the comfortable chairs to the others.*)

MRS. MILLER. That's you all over, Lily—always making excuses for him. You'll have him spoiled to death in spite of me. (*She sinks in rocker at right of table*) Phew, I'm hot, aren't you? This is going to be a scorcher. (*She picks up a magazine from the table and begins to rock, fanning herself.*)

(*Meanwhile, her husband and her brother have appeared from the back parlor, both smoking cigars.* NAT MILLER *is in his late fifties, a tall, dark, spare man, a little stoop-shouldered, more than a little bald, dressed with an awkward attempt at sober respectability imposed upon an innate heedlessness of clothes. His long face has large, irregular, undistinguished features, but he has fine, shrewd, humorous gray eyes.*

(SID DAVIS, *his brother-in-law, is forty-five, short and fat, bald-headed, with the Puckish face of a Peck's Bad Boy who has never grown up. He is dressed in what had once been a very natty loud light suit but is now a shapeless and faded nondescript in cut and color.*)

SID. (*as they appear*) Oh, I like the job first rate, Nat. Waterbury's a nifty old town with the lid off, when you get to know the ropes. I rang in a joke in one of my stories that tickled the folks there pink. Waterwagon—Waterbury—Waterloo!

MILLER. (*grinning*) Darn good!

SID. (*pleased*) I thought it was pretty fair myself. (*Goes on a bit ruefully, as if oppressed by a secret sorrow*) Yes, you can see life in Waterbury, all right—that is, if you're looking for life in Waterbury!

MRS. MILLER. What's that about Waterbury, Sid?

188

SID. I was saying it's all right in its way—but there's no place like home. (*As if to punctuate this remark, there begins a series of bangs from just beyond the porch outside, as* TOMMY *inaugurates his celebration by setting off a package of firecrackers. The assembled family jump in their chairs.*)

MRS. MILLER. That boy! (*She rushes to the screen door and out on the porch, calling*) Tommy! You mind what your Pa told you! You take your crackers out in the back yard, you hear me!

ARTHUR. (*frowning scornfully*) Fresh kid! He did it on purpose to scare us.

MILLER. (*grinning through his annoyance*) Darned youngster! He'll have the house afire before the day's out.

SID. (*grins and sings*)

> "*Dunno what ter call 'im*
> *But he's mighty like a Rose—velt.*"

(*They all laugh.*)

LILY. Sid, you Crazy! (SID *beams at her.* MRS. MILLER *comes back from the porch, still fuming.*)

MRS. MILLER. Well, I've made him go out back at last. Now we'll have a little peace. (*As if to contradict this, the bang of firecrackers and torpedoes begins from the rear of the house, left, and continues at intervals throughout the scene, not nearly so loud as the first explosion, but sufficiently emphatic to form a disturbing punctuation to the conversation.*)

MILLER. Well, what's on the tappee for all of you today? Sid, you're coming to the Sachem Club picnic with me, of course.

SID. (*a bit embarrassedly*) You bet. I mean I'd like to, Nat—that is, if—

MRS. MILLER. (*regarding her brother with smiling suspicion*) Hmm! I know what that Sachem Club picnic's always meant!

LILY. (*breaks in in a forced joking tone that conceals a deep earnest-*

ness) No, not this time, Essie. Sid's a reformed character since he's been on the paper in Waterbury. At least, that's what he swore to me last night.

SID. (*avoiding her eyes, humiliated—joking it off*) Pure as the driven snow, that's me. They're running me for president of the W.C.T.U. (*They all laugh.*)

MRS. MILLER. Sid, you're a caution. You turn everything into a joke. But you be careful, you hear? We're going to have dinner in the evening tonight, you know—the best shore dinner you ever tasted and I don't want you coming home—well, not able to appreciate it.

LILY. Oh, I know he'll be careful today. Won't you, Sid?

SID. (*more embarrassed than ever—joking it off melodramatically*) Lily, I swear to you if any man offers me a drink, I'll kill him—that is, if he changes his mind! (*They all laugh except* LILY, *who bites her lip and stiffens.*)

MRS. MILLER. No use talking to him, Lily. You ought to know better by this time. We can only hope for the best.

MILLER. Now, you women stop picking on Sid. It's the Fourth of July and even a downtrodden newspaperman has a right to enjoy himself when he's on his holiday.

MRS. MILLER. I wasn't thinking only of Sid.

MILLER. (*with a wink at the others*) What, are you insinuating I ever—?

MRS. MILLER. Well, to do you justice, no, not what you'd really call— But I've known you to come back from this darned Sachem Club picnic— Well, I didn't need any little bird to whisper that you'd been some place besides to the well! (*She smiles good-naturedly.* MILLER *chuckles.*)

SID. (*after a furtive glance at the stiff and silent* LILY—*changes the subject abruptly by turning to* ARTHUR) How are you spending the festive Fourth, Boola-Boola? (ARTHUR *stiffens dignifiedly.*)

MILDRED. (*teasingly*) I can tell you, if he won't.

MRS. MILLER. (*smiling*) Off to the Rands', I suppose.

190

ARTHUR. (*with dignity*) I and Bert Turner are taking Elsie and Ethel Rand canoeing. We're going to have a picnic lunch on Strawberry Island. And this evening I'm staying at the Rands' for dinner.

MILLER. You're accounted for, then. How about you, Mid?

MILDRED. I'm going to the beach to Anne Culver's.

ARTHUR. (*sarcastically*) Of course, there won't be any boys present! Johnny Dodd, for example?

MILDRED. (*giggles—then with a coquettish toss of her head*) Pooh! What do I care for him? He's not the only pebble on the beach.

MILLER. Stop your everlasting teasing, you two. How about you and Lily, Essie?

MRS. MILLER. I don't know. I haven't made any plans. Have you, Lily?

LILY. (*quietly*) No. Anything you want to do.

MRS. MILLER. Well, I thought we'd just sit around and rest and talk.

MILLER. You can gossip any day. This is the Fourth. Now, I've got a better suggestion than that. What do you say to an automobile ride? I'll get out the Buick and we'll drive around town and out to the lighthouse and back. Then Sid and I will let you off here, or anywhere you say, and we'll go on to the picnic.

MRS. MILLER. I'd love it. Wouldn't you, Lily?

LILY. It would be nice.

MILLER. Then, that's all settled.

SID. (*embarrassedly*) Lily, want to come with me to the fireworks display at the beach tonight?

MRS. MILLER. That's right, Sid. You take her out. Poor Lily never has any fun, always sitting home with me.

LILY. (*flustered and grateful*) I—I'd like to, Sid, thank you. (*Then an apprehensive look comes over her face*) Only not if you come home —you know.

SID. (*again embarrassed and humiliated—again joking it off, solemnly*) Evil-minded, I'm afraid, Nat. I hate to say it of your sister. (*They all laugh. Even* LILY *cannot suppress a smile.*)

ARTHUR. (*with heavy jocularity*) Listen, Uncle Sid. Don't let me catch you and Aunt Lily spooning on a bench tonight—or it'll be my duty to call a cop! (SID *and* LILY *both look painfully embarrassed at this, and the joke falls flat, except for* MILDRED *who can't restrain a giggle at the thought of these two ancients spooning.*)

MRS. MILLER. (*rebukingly*) Arthur!

MILLER. (*dryly*) That'll do you. Your education in kicking a football around Yale seems to have blunted your sense of humor.

MRS. MILLER. (*suddenly—startledly*) But where's Richard? We're forgetting all about him. Why, where is that boy? I thought he came in with us from breakfast.

MILDRED. I'll bet he's off somewhere writing a poem to Muriel McComber, the silly! Or pretending to write one. I think he just copies—

ARTHUR. (*looking back toward the dining-room*) He's still in the dining-room, reading a book. (*Turning back—scornfully*) Gosh, he's always reading now. It's not my idea of having a good time in vacation.

MILLER. (*caustically*) He read his school books, too, strange as that may seem to you. That's why he came out top of his class. I'm hoping before you leave New Haven they'll find time to teach you reading is a good habit.

MRS. MILLER. (*sharply*) That reminds me, Nat. I've been meaning to speak to you about those awful books Richard is reading. You've got to give him a good talking to— (*She gets up from her chair*) I'll go up and get them right now. I found them where he'd hid them on the shelf in his wardrobe. You just wait till you see what— (*She bustles off, rear right, through the front parlor.*)

MILLER. (*plainly not relishing whatever is coming—to* SID, *grumblingly*) Seems to me she might wait until the Fourth is over before bringing up— (*Then with a grin*) I know there's nothing to it, anyway. When I think of the books I used to sneak off and read when I was a kid.

SID. Me, too. I suppose Dick is deep in Nick Carter or Old Cap Collier.

MILLER. No, he passed that period long ago. Poetry's his red meat nowadays, I think—love poetry—and socialism, too, I suspect, from some dire declarations he's made. (*Then briskly*) Well, might as well get him on the carpet. (*He calls*) Richard. (*No answer—louder*) Richard. (*No answer—then in a bellow*) Richard!

ARTHUR. (*shouting*) Hey, Dick, wake up! Pa's calling you.

RICHARD'S VOICE. (*from the dining-room*) All right. I'm coming.

MILLER. Darn him! When he gets his nose in a book, the house could fall down and he'd never—

(RICHARD *appears in the doorway from the back parlor, the book he has been reading in one hand, a finger marking his place. He looks a bit startled still, reluctantly called back to earth from another world.*

(*He is going on seventeen, just out of high school. In appearance he is a perfect blend of father and mother, so much so that each is convinced he is the image of the other. He has his mother's light-brown hair, his father's gray eyes; his features are neither large nor small; he is of medium height, neither fat nor thin. One would not call him a handsome boy; neither is he homely. But he is definitely different from both of his parents, too. There is something of extreme sensitiveness added—a restless, apprehensive, defiant, shy, dreamy, self-conscious intelligence about him. In manner he is alternately plain simple boy and a posey actor solemnly playing a role. He is dressed in prep school reflection of the college style of* ARTHUR.)

RICHARD. Did you want me, Pa?

MILLER. I'd hoped I'd made that plain. Come and sit down a while. (*He points to the rocking chair at the right of table near his.*)

RICHARD. (*coming forward—seizing on the opportunity to play up his preoccupation—with apologetic superiority*) I didn't hear you, Pa. I was off in another world. (MILDRED *slyly shoves her foot out so that he trips over it, almost falling. She laughs gleefully. So does* ARTHUR.)

ARTHUR. Good for you, Mid! That'll wake him up!

RICHARD. (*grins sheepishly—all boy now*) Darn you, Mid! I'll show you! (*He pushes her back on the sofa and tickles her with his free hand, still holding the book in the other. She shrieks.*)

ARTHUR. Give it to her, Dick!

MILLER. That's enough, now. No more roughhouse. You sit down here, Richard. (RICHARD *obediently takes the chair at right of table, opposite his father*) What were you planning to do with yourself today? Going out to the beach with Mildred?

RICHARD. (*scornfully superior*) That silly skirt party! I should say not!

MILDRED. He's not coming because Muriel isn't. I'll bet he's got a date with her somewheres.

RICHARD. (*flushing bashfully*) You shut up! (*Then to his father*) I thought I'd just stay home, Pa—this morning, anyway.

MILLER. Help Tommy set off firecrackers, eh?

RICHARD. (*drawing himself up—with dignity*) I should say not. (*Then frowning portentously*) I don't believe in this silly celebrating the Fourth of July—all this lying talk about liberty—when there is no liberty!

MILLER. (*a twinkle in his eye*) Hmm.

RICHARD. (*getting warmed up*) The land of the free and the home of the brave! Home of the slave is what they ought to call it—the wage slave ground under the heel of the capitalist class, starving, crying for bread for his children, and all he gets is a stone! The Fourth of July is a stupid farce!

MILLER. (*putting a hand to his mouth to conceal a grin*) Hmm. Them are mighty strong words. You'd better not repeat such sentiments outside the bosom of the family or they'll have you in jail.

SID. And throw away the key.

RICHARD. (*darkly*) Let them put me in jail. But how about the freedom of speech in the Constitution, then? That must be a farce, too. (*Then he adds grimly*) No, you can celebrate your Fourth of July. I'll celebrate the day the people bring out the guillotine again

194

and I see Pierpont Morgan being driven by in a tumbril! (*His father and* SID *are greatly amused;* LILY *is shocked but, taking her cue from them, smiles.* MILDRED *stares at him in puzzled wonderment, never having heard this particular line before. Only* ARTHUR *betrays the outraged reaction of a patriot.*)

ARTHUR. Aw say, you fresh kid, tie that bull outside! You ought to get a punch in the nose for talking that way on the Fourth!

MILLER. (*solemnly*) Son, if I didn't know it was you talking, I'd think we had Emma Goldman with us.

ARTHUR. Never mind, Pa. Wait till we get him down to Yale. We'll take that out of him!

RICHARD. (*with high scorn*) Oh, Yale! You think there's nothing in the world besides Yale. After all, what is Yale?

ARTHUR. You'll find out what!

SID. (*provocatively*) Don't let them scare you, Dick. Give 'em hell!

LILY. (*shocked*) Sid! You shouldn't swear before—

RICHARD. What do you think I am, Aunt Lily—a baby? I've heard worse than anything Uncle Sid says.

MILDRED. And said worse himself, I bet!

MILLER. (*with a comic air of resignation*) Well, Richard, I've always found I've had to listen to at least one stump speech every Fourth. I only hope getting your extra strong one right after breakfast will let me off for the rest of the day. (*They all laugh now, taking this as a cue.*)

RICHARD. (*somberly*) That's right, laugh! After you, the deluge, you think! But look out! Supposing it comes before? Why shouldn't the workers of the world unite and rise? They have nothing to lose but their chains! (*He recites threateningly*) "The days grow hot, O Babylon! 'Tis cool beneath thy willow trees!"

MILLER. Hmm. That's good. But where's the connection, exactly? Something from that book you're reading?

RICHARD. (*superior*) No. That's poetry. This is prose.

MILLER. I've heard there was a difference between 'em. What is the book?

RICHARD. (*importantly*) Carlyle's "French Revolution."

MILLER. Hmm. So that's where you drove the tumbril from and piled poor old Pierpont in it. (*Then seriously*) Glad you're reading it, Richard. It's a darn fine book.

RICHARD. (*with unflattering astonishment*) What, have you read it?

MILLER. Well, you see, even a newspaper owner can't get out of reading a book every now and again.

RICHARD. (*abashed*) I—I didn't mean—I know you— (*Then enthusiastically*) Say, isn't it a great book, though—that part about Mirabeau—and about Marat and Robespierre—

MRS. MILLER. (*appears from the front parlor in a great state of flushed annoyance*) Never you mind Robespierre, young man! You tell me this minute where you've hidden those books! They were on the shelf in your wardrobe and now you've gone and hid them somewheres else. You go right up and bring them to your father! (RICHARD, *for a second, looks suddenly guilty and crushed. Then he bristles defensively.*)

MILLER. (*after a quick understanding glance at him*) Never mind his getting them now. We'll waste the whole morning over those darned books. And anyway, he has a right to keep his library to himself—that is, if they're not too— What books are they, Richard?

RICHARD. (*self-consciously*) Well—there's—

MRS. MILLER. I'll tell you, if he won't—and you give him a good talking to. (*Then, after a glance at* RICHARD, *mollifiedly*) Not that I blame Richard. There must be some boy he knows who's trying to show off as advanced and wicked, and he told him about—

RICHARD. No! I read about them myself, in the papers and in other books.

MRS. MILLER. Well, no matter how, there they were on his shelf. Two by that awful Oscar Wilde they put in jail for heaven knows what wickedness.

ARTHUR. (*suddenly—solemnly authoritative*) He committed big-amy. (*Then as* SID *smothers a burst of ribald laughter*) What are you laughing at? I guess I ought to know. A fellow at college told me. His father was in England when this Wilde was pinched—and he said he remembered once his mother asked his father about it and he told her he'd committed bigamy.

MILLER. (*hiding a smile behind his hand*) Well then, that must be right, Arthur.

MRS. MILLER. I wouldn't put it past him, nor anything else. One book was called the Picture of something or other.

RICHARD. "The Picture of Dorian Gray." It's one of the greatest novels ever written!

MRS. MILLER. Looked to me like cheap trash. And the second book was poetry. The Ballad of I forget what.

RICHARD. "The Ballad of Reading Gaol," one of the greatest poems ever written. (*He pronounces it Reading Goal* [*as in goalpost*].)

MRS. MILLER. All about someone who murdered his wife and got hung, as he richly deserved, as far as I could make out. And then there were two books by that Bernard Shaw—

RICHARD. The greatest playwright alive today!

MRS. MILLER. To hear him tell it, maybe! You know, Nat, the one who wrote a play about—well, never mind—that was so vile they wouldn't even let it play in New York!

MILLER. Hmm. I remember.

MRS. MILLER. One was a book of his plays and the other had a long title I couldn't make head or tail of, only it wasn't a play.

RICHARD. (*proudly*) "The Quintessence of Ibsenism."

MILDRED. Phew! Good gracious, what a name! What does it mean, Dick? I'll bet he doesn't know.

RICHARD. (*outraged*) I do, too, know! It's about Ibsen, the greatest playwright since Shakespeare!

MRS. MILLER. Yes, there was a book of plays by that Ibsen there, too! And poems by Swin something—

RICHARD. "Poems and Ballads" by Swinburne, Ma. The greatest poet since Shelley! He tells the truth about real love!

MRS. MILLER. Love! Well, all I can say is, from reading here and there, that if he wasn't flung in jail along with Wilde, he should have been. Some of the things I simply couldn't read, they were so indecent— All about—well, I can't tell you before Lily and Mildred.

SID. (*with a wink at* RICHARD—*jokingly*) Remember, I'm next on that one, Dick. I feel the need of a little poetical education.

LILY. (*scandalized, but laughing*) Sid! Aren't you ashamed?

MRS. MILLER. This is no laughing matter. And then there was Kipling—but I suppose he's not so bad. And last there was a poem—a long one—the Rubay— What is it, Richard?

RICHARD. "The Rubaiyat of Omar Khayyam." That's the best of all!

MILLER. Oh, I've read that, Essie—got a copy down at the office.

SID. (*enthusiastically*) So have I. It's a pippin!

LILY. (*with shy excitement*) I—I've read it, too—at the library. I like—some parts of it.

MRS. MILLER. (*scandalized*) Why, Lily!

MILLER. Everybody's reading that now, Essie—and it don't seem to do them any harm. There's fine things in it, seems to me— true things.

MRS. MILLER. (*a bit bewildered and uncertain now*) Why, Nat, I don't see how you— It looked terrible blasphemous—parts I read.

SID. Remember this one: (*He quotes rhetorically*) "Oh Thou, who didst with pitfall and gin beset the path I was to wander in—" Now, I've always noticed how beset my path was with gin—in the past, you understand! (*He casts a joking side glance at* LILY. *The others laugh. But* LILY *is in a melancholy dream and hasn't heard him.*)

MRS. MILLER. (*tartly, but evidently suppressing her usual smile where he is concerned*) You would pick out the ones with liquor in them!

LILY. (*suddenly—with a sad pathos, quotes awkwardly and shyly*) I like—because it's true:

198

> *"The Moving Finger writes, and having writ,*
> *Moves on: nor all your Piety nor Wit*
> *Shall lure it back to cancel half a Line,*
> *Nor all your Tears wash out a Word of it."*

MRS. MILLER. (*astonished, as are all the others*) Why, Lily, I never knew you to recite poetry before!

LILY. (*immediately guilty and apologetic*) I—it just stuck in my memory somehow.

RICHARD. (*looking at her as if he had never seen her before*) Good for you, Aunt Lily! (*Then enthusiastically*) But that isn't the best. The best is:

> *"A Book of Verses underneath the Bough,*
> *A Jug of Wine, A Loaf of Bread—and Thou*
> *Beside me singing in the Wilderness—"*

ARTHUR. (*who, bored to death by all this poetry quoting, has wandered over to the window at rear of desk, right*) Hey! Look who's coming up the walk— Old Man McComber!

MILLER. (*irritably*) Dave? Now what in thunder does that damned old— Sid, I can see where we never are going to get to that picnic.

MRS. MILLER. (*vexatiously*) He'll know we're in this early, too. No use lying. (*Then appalled by another thought*) That Norah—she's that thick, she never can answer the front door right unless I tell her each time. Nat, you've got to talk to Dave. I'll have her show him in here. Lily, you run up the back stairs and get your things on. I'll be up in a second. Nat, you get rid of him the first second you can! Whatever can the old fool want— (*She and* LILY *hurry out through the back parlor.*)

ARTHUR. I'm going to beat it—just time to catch the eight-twenty trolley.

MILDRED. I've got to catch that, too. Wait till I get my hat, Art! (*She rushes into the back parlor.*)

ARTHUR. (*shouts after her*) I can't wait. You can catch up with me if you hurry. (*He turns at the back-parlor door—with a grin*) Mc-Comber may be coming to see if your intentions toward his daughter are dishonorable, Dick! You'd better beat it while your shoes are good! (*He disappears through the back-parlor door, laughing.*)

RICHARD. (*a bit shaken, but putting on a brave front*) Think I'm scared of him?

MILLER. (*gazing at him—frowning*) Can't imagine what— But it's to complain about something, I know that. I only wish I didn't have to be pleasant with the old buzzard—but he's about the most valuable advertiser I've got.

SID. (*sympathetically*) I know. But tell him to go to hell, anyway. He needs that ad more than you.

(*The sound of the bell comes from the rear of the house, off left from back parlor.*)

MILLER. There he is. You clear out, Dick—but come right back as soon as he's gone, you hear? I'm not through with you, yet.

RICHARD. Yes, Pa.

MILLER. You better clear out, too, Sid. You know Dave doesn't approve jokes.

SID. And loves me like poison! Come on, Dick, we'll go out and help Tommy celebrate. (*He takes* RICHARD's *arm and they also disappear through the back-parlor door.* MILLER *glances through the front parlor toward the front door, then calls in a tone of strained heartiness.*)

MILLER. Hello, Dave. Come right in here. What good wind blows you around on this glorious Fourth?

(*A flat, brittle voice answers him:* "Good morning," *and a moment later* DAVID MC COMBER *appears in the doorway from the front parlor. He is a thin, dried-up little man with a head too large for his body perched on a scrawny neck, and a long solemn horse face with deep-set little black eyes, a blunt formless nose and a tiny slit of a mouth. He is about the same age as* MILLER *but is entirely bald, and looks ten years older. He is dressed with a prim neatness in shiny old black clothes.*)

MILLER. Here, sit down and make yourself comfortable. (*Holding out the cigar box*) Have a cigar?

MC COMBER. (*sitting down in the chair at the right of table—acidly*) You're forgetting. I never smoke.

MILLER. (*forcing a laugh at himself*) That's so. So I was. Well, I'll smoke alone then. (*He bites off the end of the cigar viciously, as if he wished it were* MC COMBER's *head, and sits down opposite him.*)

MC COMBER. You asked me what brings me here, so I'll come to the point at once. I regret to say it's something disagreeable—disgraceful would be nearer the truth—and it concerns your son, Richard!

MILLER. (*beginning to bristle—but calmly*) Oh, come now, Dave, I'm sure Richard hasn't—

MC COMBER. (*sharply*) And I'm positive he has. You're not accusing me of being a liar, I hope.

MILLER. No one said anything about liar. I only meant you're surely mistaken if you think—

MC COMBER. I'm not mistaken. I have proof of everything in his own handwriting!

MILLER. (*sharply*) Let's get down to brass tacks. Just what is it you're charging him with?

MC COMBER. With being dissolute and blasphemous—with deliberately attempting to corrupt the morals of my young daughter, Muriel.

MILLER. Then I'm afraid I will have to call you a liar, Dave!

MC COMBER. (*without taking offense—in the same flat, brittle voice*) I thought you'd get around to that, so I brought some of the proofs with me. I've a lot more of 'em at home. (*He takes a wallet from his inside coat pocket, selects five or six slips of paper, and holds them out to* MILLER) These are good samples of the rest. My wife discovered them in one of Muriel's bureau drawers hidden under the underwear.

They're all in his handwriting, you can't deny it. Anyway, Muriel's confessed to me he wrote them. You read them and then say I'm a liar. (MILLER *has taken the slips and is reading them frowningly*. MC COMBER *talks on*) Evidently you've been too busy to take the right care about Richard's bringing up or what he's allowed to read—though I can't see why his mother failed in her duty. But that's your misfortune, and none of my business. But Muriel is my business and I can't and I won't have her innocence exposed to the contamination of a young man whose mind, judging from his choice of reading matter, is as foul—

MILLER. (*making a tremendous effort to control his temper*) Why, you damned old fool! Can't you see Richard's only a fool kid who's just at the stage when he's out to rebel against all authority, and so he grabs at everything radical to read and wants to pass it on to his elders and his girl and boy friends to show off what a young hellion he is! Why, at heart you'd find Richard is just as innocent and as big a kid as Muriel is! (*He pushes the slips of paper across the table contemptuously*) This stuff doesn't mean anything to me—that is, nothing of what you think it means. If you believe this would corrupt Muriel, then you must believe she's easily corrupted! But I'll bet you'd find she knows a lot more about life than you give her credit for— and can guess a stork didn't bring her down your chimney!

MC COMBER. Now you're insulting my daughter. I won't forget that.

MILLER. I'm not insulting her. I think Muriel is a darn nice girl. That's why I'm giving her credit for ordinary good sense. I'd say the same about my own Mildred, who's the same age.

MC COMBER. I know nothing about your Mildred except that she's known all over as a flirt. (*Then more sharply*) Well, I knew you'd prove obstinate, but I certainly never dreamed you'd have the impudence, after reading those papers, to claim your son was innocent of all wrongdoing!

MILLER. And what did you dream I'd do?

MC COMBER. Do what it's your plain duty to do as a citizen to protect other people's children! Take and give him a hiding he'd remember to the last day of his life! You'd ought to do it for his sake, if you had any sense—unless you want him to end up in jail!

MILLER. (*his fists clenched, leans across the table*) Dave, I've stood all I can stand from you! You get out! And get out quick, if you don't want a kick in the rear to help you!

MC COMBER. (*again in his flat, brittle voice, slowly getting to his feet*) You needn't lose your temper. I'm only demanding you do your duty by your own as I've already done by mine. I'm punishing Muriel. She's not to be allowed out of the house for a month and she's to be in bed every night by eight sharp. And yet she's blameless, compared to that—

MILLER. I said I'd had enough out of you, Dave! (*He makes a threatening movement.*)

MC COMBER. You needn't lay hands on me. I'm going. But there's one thing more. (*He takes a letter from his wallet*) Here's a letter from Muriel for your son. (*Puts it on the table*) It makes clear, I think, how she's come to think about him, now that her eyes have been opened. I hope he heeds what's inside—for his own good and yours—because if I ever catch him hanging about my place again I'll have him arrested! And don't think I'm not going to make you regret the insults you've heaped on me. I'm taking the advertisement for my store out of your paper—and it won't go in again, I tell you, not unless you apologize in writing and promise to punish—

MILLER. I'll see you in hell first! As for your damned old ad, take it out and go to hell!

MC COMBER. That's plain bluff. You know how badly you need it. So do I. (*He starts stiffly for the door.*)

MILLER. Here! Listen a minute! I'm just going to call *your* bluff and tell you that, whether you want to reconsider your decision or not, I'm going to refuse to print your damned ad after tomorrow! Put that in your pipe and smoke it! Furthermore, I'll start a campaign to encourage outside capital to open a dry-goods store in opposition to you that won't be the public swindle I can prove yours is!

MC COMBER. (*a bit shaken by this threat—but in the same flat tone*) I'll sue you for libel.

MILLER. When I get through, there won't be a person in town will buy a dishrag in your place!

MC COMBER. (*more shaken, his eyes shifting about furtively*) That's all bluff. You wouldn't dare— (*Then finally he says uncertainly*) Well, good day. (*And turns and goes out. NAT stands looking after him. Slowly the anger drains from his face and leaves him looking a bit sick and disgusted. SID appears from the back parlor. He is nursing a burn on his right hand, but his face is one broad grin of satisfaction.*)

SID. I burned my hand with one of Tommy's damned firecrackers and came in to get some vaseline. I was listening to the last of your scrap. Good for you, Nat! You sure gave him hell!

MILLER. (*dully*) Much good it'll do. He knows it was all talk.

SID. That's just what he don't know, Nat. The old skinflint has a guilty conscience.

MILLER. Well, anyone who knows me knows I wouldn't use my paper for a dirty, spiteful trick like that—no matter what he did to me.

SID. Yes, everyone knows you're an old sucker, Nat, too decent for your own good. But McComber never saw you like this before. I tell you you scared the pants off him. (*He chuckles.*)

MILLER. (*still dejectedly*) I don't know what made me let go like that. The hell of skunks like McComber is that after being with them ten minutes you become as big skunks as they are.

SID. (*notices the slips of paper on the table*) What's this? Something he brought? (*He picks them up and starts to read.*)

MILLER. (*grimly*) Samples of the new freedom—from those books Essie found—that Richard's been passing on to Muriel to educate her. They're what started the rumpus. (*Then frowning*) I've got to do something about that young anarchist or he'll be getting me, and himself, in a peck of trouble. (*Then pathetically helpless*) But what can I do? Putting the curb bit on would make him worse. Then he'd have a harsh tyrant to defy. He'd love that, darn him!

SID. (*has been reading the slips, a broad grin on his face—suddenly he whistles*) Phew! This is a warm lulu for fair! (*He recites with a joking intensity*)

> "*My life is bitter with thy love; thine eyes*
> *Blind me, thy tresses burn me, thy sharp sighs*
> *Divide my flesh and spirit with soft sound—*"

MILLER. (*with a grim smile*) Hmm. I missed that one. That must be Mr. Swinburne's copy. I've never read him, but I've heard something like that was the matter with him.

SID. Yes, it's labelled Swinburne—"Anactoria." Whatever that is. But wait, watch and listen! The worst is yet to come! (*He recites with added comic intensity*)

> "*That I could drink thy veins as wine, and eat*
> *Thy breasts like honey, that from face to feet*
> *Thy body were abolished and consumed,*
> *And in my flesh thy very flesh entombed!*"

MILLER. (*an irrepressible boyish grin coming to his face*) Hell and hallelujah! Just picture old Dave digesting that for the first time! Gosh, I'd give a lot to have seen his face! (*Then a trace of shocked reproof showing in his voice*) But it's no joking matter. That stuff *is* warm—too damned warm, if you ask me! I don't like this a damned bit, Sid. That's no kind of thing to be sending a decent girl. (*More worriedly*) I thought he was really stuck on her—as one gets stuck on a decent girl at his age—all moonshine and holding hands and a kiss now and again. But this looks—I wonder if he is hanging around her to see what he can get? (*Angrily*) By God, if that's true, he deserves that licking McComber says it's my duty to give him! I've got to draw the line somewhere!

205

SID. Yes, it won't do to have him getting any decent girl in trouble.

MILLER. The only thing I can do is put it up to him straight. (*With pride*) Richard'll stand up to his guns, no matter what. I've never known him to lie to me.

SID. (*at a noise from the back parlor, looks that way—in a whisper*) Then now's your chance. I'll beat it and leave you alone—see if the women folks are ready upstairs. We ought to get started soon—if we're ever going to make that picnic. (*He is halfway to the entrance to the front parlor as* RICHARD *enters from the back parlor, very evidently nervous about* MC COMBER'S *call.*)

RICHARD. (*adopting a forced, innocent tone*) How's your hand, Uncle Sid?

SID. All right, Dick, thanks—only hurts a little. (*He disappears.* MILLER *watches his son frowningly.* RICHARD *gives him a quick side glance and grows more guiltily self-conscious.*)

RICHARD. (*forcing a snicker*) Gee, Pa, Uncle Sid's a bigger kid than Tommy is. He was throwing firecrackers in the air and catching them on the back of his hand and throwing 'em off again just before they went off—and one came and he wasn't quick enough, and it went off almost on top of—

MILLER. Never mind that. I've got something else to talk to you about besides firecrackers.

RICHARD. (*apprehensively*) What, Pa?

MILLER. (*suddenly puts both hands on his shoulders—quietly*) Look here, Son. I'm going to ask you a question, and I want an honest answer. I warn you beforehand if the answer is "yes" I'm going to punish you and punish you hard because you'll have done something no boy of mine ought to do. But you've never lied to me before, I know, and I don't believe, even to save yourself punishment, you'd lie to me now, would you?

RICHARD. (*impressed—with dignity*) I won't lie, Pa.

MILLER. Have you been trying to have something to do with Muriel --something you shouldn't—you know what I mean.

RICHARD. (*stares at him for a moment, as if he couldn't comprehend —then, as he does, a look of shocked indignation comes over his face*) No! What do you think I am, Pa? I never would! She's not that kind! Why, I—I love her! I'm going to marry her—after I get out of college! She's said she would! We're engaged!

MILLER. (*with great relief*) All right. That's all I wanted to know. We won't talk any more about it. (*He gives him an approving pat on the back.*)

RICHARD. I don't see how you could think— Did that old idiot Mc-Comber say that about me?

MILLER. (*joking now*) Shouldn't call your future father-in-law names, should you? 'Tain't respectful. (*Then after a glance at* RICH-ARD's *indignant face—points to the slips of paper on the table*) Well, you can't exactly blame old Dave, can you, when you read through that literature you wished on his innocent daughter?

RICHARD. (*sees the slips for the first time and is overcome by embarrassment, which he immediately tries to cover up with a superior carelessness*) Oh, so that's why. He found those, did he? I told her to be careful— Well, it'll do him good to read the truth about life for once and get rid of his old-fogy ideas.

MILLER. I'm afraid I've got to agree with him, though, that they're hardly fit reading for a young girl. (*Then with subtle flattery*) They're all well enough, in their way, for you who're a man, but— Think it over, and see if you don't agree with me.

RICHARD. (*embarrassedly*) Aw, I only did it because I liked them—and I wanted her to face life as it is. She's so darned afraid of life—afraid of her Old Man—afraid of people saying this or that about her —afraid of being in love—afraid of everything. She's even afraid to let me kiss her. I thought, maybe, reading those things—they're beautiful, aren't they, Pa?— I thought they would give her the spunk to lead her own life, and not be—always thinking of being afraid.

MILLER. I see. Well, I'm afraid she's still afraid. (*He takes the letter from the table*) Here's a letter from her he said to give you. (RICHARD *takes the letter from him uncertainly, his expression changing to one of apprehension.* MILLER *adds with a kindly smile*) You better be prepared for a bit of a blow. But never mind. There's lots of other fish in the sea. (RICHARD *is not listening to him, but staring at the letter with a sort of fascinated dread.* MILLER *looks into his son's face a second, then turns away, troubled and embarrassed*) Darn it! I better go upstairs and get rigged out or I never will get to that picnic. (*He moves awkwardly and self-consciously off through the front parlor.* RICHARD *continues to stare at the letter for a moment—then girds up his courage and tears it open and begins to read swiftly. As he reads his face grows more and more wounded and tragic, until at the end his mouth draws down at the corners, as if he were about to break into tears. With an effort he forces them back and his face grows flushed with humiliation and wronged anger.*)

RICHARD. (*blurts out to himself*) The little coward! I hate her! She can't treat me like that! I'll show her! (*At the sound of voices from the front parlor, he quickly shoves the letter into the inside pocket of his coat and does his best to appear calm and indifferent, even attempting to whistle "Waiting at the Church." But the whistle peters out miserably as his mother,* LILY *and* SID *enter from the front parlor. They are dressed in all the elaborate paraphernalia of motoring at that period—linen dusters, veils, goggles,* SID *in a snappy cap.*)

MRS. MILLER. Well, we're about ready to start at last, thank goodness! Let's hope no more callers are on the way. What did that McComber want, Richard, do you know? Sid couldn't tell us.

RICHARD. You can search me. Ask Pa.

MRS. MILLER. (*immediately sensing something "down" in his manner—going to him worriedly*) Why, whatever's the matter with you, Richard? You sound as if you'd lost your last friend! What is it?

RICHARD. (*desperately*) I— I don't feel so well—my stomach's sick.

MRS. MILLER. (*immediately all sympathy—smoothing his hair back from his forehead*) You poor boy! What a shame—on the Fourth, too, of all days! (*Turning to the others*) Maybe I better stay home with him, if he's sick.

LILY. Yes, I'll stay, too.

RICHARD. (*more desperately*) No! You go, Ma! I'm not really sick. I'll be all right. You go. I want to be alone! (*Then, as a louder bang comes from in back as* TOMMY *sets off a cannon cracker, he jumps to his feet*) Darn Tommy and his darned firecrackers! You can't get any peace in this house with that darned kid around! Darn the Fourth of July, anyway! I wish we still belonged to England! (*He strides off in an indignant fury of misery through the front parlor.*)

MRS. MILLER. (*stares after him worriedly—then sighs philosophically*) Well, I guess he can't be so very sick—after that. (*She shakes her head*) He's a queer boy. Sometimes I can't make head or tail of him.

MILLER. (*calls from the front door beyond the back parlor*) Come along folks. Let's get started.

SID. We're coming, Nat. (*He and the two women move off through the front parlor.*)

CURTAIN

ACT TWO

SCENE—*Dining-room of the* MILLER *home—a little after 6 o'clock in the evening of the same day.*

The room is much too small for the medium-priced, formidable dining-room set, especially now when all the leaves of the table are in. At left, toward rear, is a double doorway with sliding doors and portières leading into the back parlor. In the rear wall, left, is the door to the pantry. At the right of door is the china closet with its display of the family cut glass and fancy china. In the right wall are two windows looking out on a side lawn. In front of the windows is a heavy, ugly sideboard with three pieces of old silver on its top. In the left wall, extreme front, is a screen door opening on a side porch. A dark rug covers most of the floor. The table, with a chair at each end, left and right, three chairs on the far side, facing front, and two on the near side, their backs to front, takes up most of the available space. The walls are papered in a somber brown and dark-red design.

MRS. MILLER *is supervising and helping the Second Girl,* NORAH, *in the setting of the table.* NORAH *is a clumsy, heavy-handed, heavy-footed, long-jawed, beamingly good-natured young Irish girl—a "greenhorn."*

MRS. MILLER. I really think you better put on the lights, Norah. It's getting so cloudy out, and this pesky room is so dark, anyway.

NORAH. Yes, Mum. (*She stretches awkwardly over the table to reach the chandelier that is suspended from the middle of the ceiling and manages to turn one light on—scornfully*) Arrah, the contraption!

MRS. MILLER. (*worriedly*) Careful!

NORAH. Careful as can be, Mum. (*But in moving around to reach the next bulb she jars heavily against the table.*)

210

MRS. MILLER. There! I knew it! I do wish you'd watch—!

NORAH. (*a flustered appeal in her voice*) Arrah, what have I done wrong now?

MRS. MILLER. (*draws a deep breath—then sighs helplessly*) Oh, nothing. Never mind the rest of the lights. You might as well go out in the kitchen and wait until I ring.

NORAH. (*relieved and cheerful again*) Yes, Mum. (*She starts for the pantry.*)

MRS. MILLER. But there's one thing— (NORAH *turns apprehensively*) No, two things—things I've told you over and over, but you always forget. Don't pass the plates on the wrong side at dinner tonight, and do be careful not to let that pantry door slam behind you. Now you will try to remember, won't you?

NORAH. Yes, Mum. (*She goes into the pantry and shuts the door behind her with exaggerated care as* MRS. MILLER *watches her apprehensively.* MRS. MILLER *sighs and reaches up with difficulty and turns on another of the four lights in the chandelier. As she is doing so,* LILY *enters from the back parlor.*)

LILY. Here, let me do that, Essie. I'm taller. You'll only strain yourself. (*She quickly lights the other two bulbs.*)

MRS. MILLER. (*gratefully*) Thank you, Lily. It's a stretch for me, I'm getting so fat.

LILY. But where's Norah? Why didn't she—?

MRS. MILLER. (*exasperatedly*) Oh, that girl! Don't talk about her! She'll be the death of me! She's that thick, you honestly wouldn't believe it possible.

LILY. (*smiling*) Why, what did she do now?

MRS. MILLER. Oh, nothing. She means all right.

LILY. Anything else I can do, Essie?

MRS. MILLER. Well, she's got the table all wrong. We'll have to reset it. But you're always helping me. It isn't fair to ask you—in your vacation. You need your rest after teaching a pack of wild Indians of kids all year.

LILY. (*beginning to help with the table*) You know I love to help. It makes me feel I'm some use in this house instead of just sponging—

MRS. MILLER. (*indignantly*) Sponging! You pay, don't you?

LILY. Almost nothing. And you and Nat only take that little to make me feel better about living with you. (*Forcing a smile*) I don't see how you stand me—having a cranky old maid around all the time.

MRS. MILLER. What nonsense you talk! As if Nat and I weren't only too tickled to death to have you! Lily Miller, I've no patience with you when you go on like that. We've been over this a thousand times before, and still you go on! Crazy, that's what it is! (*She changes the subject abruptly*) What time's it getting to be?

LILY. (*looking at her watch*) Quarter past six.

MRS. MILLER. I do hope those men folks aren't going to be late for dinner. (*She sighs*) But I suppose with that darned Sachem Club picnic it's more likely than not. (LILY *looks worried, and sighs.* MRS. MILLER *gives her a quick side glance*) I see you've got your new dress on.

LILY. (*embarrassedly*) Yes, I thought—if Sid's taking me to the fireworks—I ought to spruce up a little.

MRS. MILLER. (*looking away*) Hmm. (*A pause—then she says with an effort to be casual*) You mustn't mind if Sid comes home feeling a bit—gay. I expect Nat to—and we'll have to listen to all those old stories of his about when he was a boy. You know what those picnics are, and Sid'd be running into all his old friends.

LILY. (*agitatedly*) I don't think he will—this time—not after his promise.

MRS. MILLER. (*avoiding looking at her*) I know. But men are weak. (*Then quickly*) That was a good notion of Nat's, getting Sid the job on the Waterbury *Standard*. All he ever needed was to get away from the rut he was in here. He's the kind that's the victim of his friends. He's easily led—but there's no real harm in him, you know that. (LILY *keeps silent, her eyes downcast.* MRS. MILLER *goes on meaningly*) He's

212

making good money in Waterbury, too—thirty-five a week. He's in a better position to get married than he ever was.

LILY. (*stiffly*) Well, I hope he finds a woman who's willing—though after he's through with his betting on horse races, and dice, and playing Kelly pool, there won't be much left for a wife—even if there was nothing else he spent his money on.

MRS. MILLER. Oh, he'd give up all that—for the right woman. (*Suddenly she comes directly to the point*) Lily, why don't you change your mind and marry Sid and reform him? You love him and always have—

LILY. (*stiffly*) I can't love a man who drinks.

MRS. MILLER. You can't fool me. I know darned well you love him. And he loves you and always has.

LILY. Never enough to stop drinking for. (*Cutting off* MRS. MILLER's *reply*) No, it's no good in your talking, Essie. We've been over this a thousand times before and I'll always feel the same as long as Sid's the same. If he gave me proof he'd—but even then I don't believe I could. It's sixteen years since I broke off our engagement, but what made me break it off is as clear to me today as it was then. It was what he'd be liable to do now to anyone who married him—his taking up with bad women.

MRS. MILLER. (*protests half-heartedly*) But he's always sworn he got raked into that party and never had anything to do with those harlots.

LILY. Well, I don't believe him—didn't then and don't now. I do believe he didn't deliberately plan to, but— Oh, it's no good talking, Essie. What's done is done. But you know how much I like Sid—in spite of everything. I know he was just born to be what he is—irresponsible, never meaning to harm but harming in spite of himself. But don't talk to me about marrying him—because I never could.

MRS. MILLER. (*angrily*) He's a dumb fool—a stupid dumb fool, that's what he is!

LILY. (*quietly*) No. He's just Sid.

MRS. MILLER. It's a shame for you—a measly shame—you that would have made such a wonderful wife for any man—that ought to have your own home and children!

LILY. (*winces but puts her arm around her affectionately—gently*) Now don't you go feeling sorry for me. I won't have that. Here I am, thanks to your and Nat's kindness, with the best home in the world; and as for the children, I feel the same love for yours as if they were mine, and I didn't have the pain of bearing them. And then there are all the boys and girls I teach every year. I like to feel I'm a sort of second mother to them and helping them to grow up to be good men and women. So I don't feel such a useless old maid, after all.

MRS. MILLER. (*kisses her impulsively—her voice husky*) You're a good woman, Lily—too good for the rest of us. (*She turns away, wiping a tear furtively—then abruptly changing the subject*) Good gracious, if I'm not forgetting one of the most important things! I've got to warn that Tommy against giving me away to Nat about the fish. He knows, because I had to send him to market for it, and he's liable to burst out laughing—

LILY. Laughing about what?

MRS. MILLER. (*guiltily*) Well, I've never told you, because it seemed sort of a sneaking trick, but you know how Nat carries on about not being able to eat bluefish.

LILY. I know he says there's a certain oil in it that poisons him.

MRS. MILLER. (*chuckling*) Poisons him, nothing! He's been eating bluefish for years—only I tell him each time it's weakfish. We're having it tonight—and I've got to warn that young imp to keep his face straight.

LILY. (*laughing*) Aren't you ashamed, Essie!

MRS. MILLER. Not much, I'm not! I like bluefish! (*She laughs*) Where is Tommy? In the sitting-room?

LILY. No, Richard's there alone. I think Tommy's out on the piazza with Mildred. (MRS. MILLER *bustles out through the back parlor. As soon as she is gone, the smile fades from* LILY's *lips. Her face grows sad and she again glances nervously at her watch.* RICHARD *appears*

214

from the back parlor, moving in an aimless way. His face wears a set expression of bitter gloom; he exudes tragedy. For RICHARD, *after his first outburst of grief and humiliation, has begun to take a masochistic satisfaction in his great sorrow, especially in the concern which it arouses in the family circle. On seeing his aunt, he gives her a dark look and turns and is about to stalk back toward the sitting-room when she speaks to him pityingly*) Feel any better, Richard?

RICHARD. (*somberly*) I'm all right, Aunt Lily. You mustn't worry about me.

LILY. (*going to him*) But I do worry about you. I hate to see you so upset.

RICHARD. It doesn't matter. Nothing matters.

LILY. (*puts her around him sympathetically*) You really mustn't let yourself take it so seriously. You know, something happens and things like that come up, and we think there's no hope—

RICHARD. Things like what come up?

LILY. What's happened between you and Muriel.

RICHARD. (*with disdain*) Oh, her! I wasn't even thinking about her. I was thinking about life.

LILY. But then—if we really, *really* love—why, then something else is bound to happen soon that changes everything again, and it's all as it was before the misunderstanding, and everything works out all right in the end. That's the way it is with life.

RICHARD. (*with a tragic sneer*) Life! Life is a joke! And everything comes out all wrong in the end!

LILY. (*a little shocked*) You mustn't talk that way. But I know you don't mean it.

RICHARD. I do too mean it! You can have your silly optimism, if you like, Aunt Lily. But don't ask me to be so blind. I'm a pessimist! (*Then with an air of cruel cynicism*) As for Muriel, that's all dead and past. I was only kidding her, anyway, just to have a little fun, and she took it seriously, like a fool. (*He forces a cruel smile to his lips*) You know what they say about women and trolley cars, Aunt Lily: there's always another one along in a minute.

LILY. (*really shocked this time*) I don't like you when you say such horrible, cynical things. It isn't nice.

RICHARD. Nice! that's all you women think of! I'm proud to be a cynic. It's the only thing you can be when you really face life. I suppose you think I ought to be heartbroken about Muriel—a little coward that's afraid to say her soul's her own, and keeps tied to her father's apron strings! Well, not for mine! There's plenty of other fish in the sea! (*As he is finishing, his mother comes back through the back parlor.*)

MRS. MILLER. Why, hello. You here, Richard? Getting hungry, I suppose?

RICHARD. (*indignantly*) I'm not hungry a bit! That's all you think of, Ma—food!

MRS. MILLER. Well, I must say I've never noticed you to hang back at meal times. (*To* LILY) What's that he was saying about fish in the sea?

LILY. (*smiling*) He says he's through with Muriel now.

MRS. MILLER. (*tartly—giving her son a rebuking look*) She's through with him, he means! The idea of your sending a nice girl like her things out of those indecent books! (*Deeply offended,* RICHARD *disdains to reply but stalks woundedly to the screen door at left, front, and puts a hand on the knob*) Where are you going?

RICHARD. (*quotes from "Candida" in a hollow voice*) "Out, then, into the night with me!" (*He stalks out, slamming the door behind him.*)

MRS. MILLER. (*calls*) Well, don't you go far, 'cause dinner'll be ready in a minute, and I'm not coming running after you! (*She turns to* LILY *with a chuckle*) Goodness, that boy! He ought to be on the stage! (*She mimics*) "Out—into the night"—and it isn't even dark yet! He got that out of one of those books, I suppose. Do you know, I'm actually grateful to old Dave McComber for putting an end to his non-

216

sense with Muriel. I never did approve of Richard getting so interested in girls. He's not old enough for such silliness. Why, seems to
me it was only yesterday he was still a baby. (*She sighs—then matter-
of-factly*) Well, nothing to do now till those men turn up. No use
standing here like gawks. We might as well go in the sitting-room
and be comfortable.

LILY. (*the nervous, worried note in her voice again*) Yes, we might
as well. (*They go out through the back parlor. They have no sooner
disappeared than the screen door is opened cautiously and* RICHARD
comes back in the room.)

RICHARD. (*stands inside the door, looking after them—quotes bitterly*) "They do not know the secret in the poet's heart." (*He comes
nearer the table and surveys it, especially the cut-glass dish containing
olives, with contempt and mutters disdainfully*) Food! (*But the dish
of olives seems to fascinate him and presently he has approached
nearer, and stealthily lifts a couple and crams them into his mouth.
He is just reaching out for more when the pantry door is opened
slightly and* NORAH *peers in.*)

NORAH. Mister Dick, you thief, lave them olives alone, or the
missus'll be swearing it was me at them!

RICHARD. (*draws back his hand as if he had been stung—too flustered to be anything but guilty boy for a second*) I—I wasn't eating—

NORAH. Oho, no, of course not, divil fear you, you was only feeling
their pulse! (*Then warningly*) Mind what I'm saying now, or I'll
have to tell on you to protect me good name! (*She draws back into
the pantry, closing the door.* RICHARD *stands, a prey to feelings of
bitterest humiliation and seething revolt against everyone and everything. A low whistle comes from just outside the porch door. He starts.
Then a masculine voice calls: "Hey, Dick." He goes over to the
screen door grumpily—then as he recognizes the owner of the voice,
his own as he answers becomes respectful and admiring.*)

RICHARD. Oh, hello, Wint. Come on in. (*He opens the door and*
WINT SELBY *enters and stands just inside the door.* SELBY *is nineteen,*

a classmate of ARTHUR'S *at Yale. He's a typical, good-looking college boy of the period, not the athletic but the hell-raising sport type. He is tall, blond, dressed in extreme collegiate cut.*)

WINT. (*as he enters—warningly, in a low tone*) Keep it quiet, Kid. I don't want the folks to know I'm here. Tell Art I want to see him a second—on the Q.T.

RICHARD. Can't. He's up at the Rands'—won't be home before ten, anyway.

WINT. (*irritably*) Damn, I thought he'd be here for dinner. (*More irritably*) Hell, that gums the works for fair!

RICHARD. (*ingratiatingly*) What is it, Wint? Can't I help?

WINT. (*gives him an appraising glance*) I might tell you, if you can keep your face shut.

RICHARD. I can.

WINT. Well, I ran into a couple of swift babies from New Haven this after. and I dated them up for tonight, thinking I could catch Art. But now it's too late to get anyone else and I'll have to pass it up. I'm nearly broke and I can't afford to blow them both to drinks.

RICHARD. (*with shy eagerness*) I've got eleven dollars saved up. I could loan you some.

WINT. (*surveys him appreciatively*) Say, you're a good sport. (*Then shaking his head*) Nix, Kid, I don't want to borrow your money. (*Then getting an idea*) But say, have you got anything on for tonight?

RICHARD. No.

WINT. Want to come along with me? (*Then quickly*) I'm not try-ing to lead you astray, understand. But it'll be a help if you would just sit around with Belle and feed her a few drinks while I'm off with Edith. (*He winks*) See what I mean? You don't have to do anything, not even take a glass of beer—unless you want to.

RICHARD. (*boastfully*) Aw, what do you think I am—a rube?

WINT. You mean you're game for anything that's doing?

RICHARD. Sure I am!

218

WINT. Ever been out with any girls—I mean, real swift ones that there's something doing with, not these dead Janes around here?

RICHARD. (*lies boldly*) Aw, what do you think? Sure I have!

WINT. Ever drink anything besides sodas?

RICHARD. Sure. Lots of times. Beer and sloe-gin fizz and—Manhattans.

WINT. (*impressed*) Hell, you know more than I thought. (*Then considering*) Can you fix it so your folks won't get wise? I don't want your old man coming after me. You can get back by half-past ten or eleven, though, all right. Think you can cook up some lie to cover that? (*As* RICHARD *hesitates—encouraging him*) Ought to be easy—on the Fourth.

RICHARD. Sure. Don't worry about that.

WINT. But you've got to keep your face closed about this, you hear? —to Art and everybody else. I tell you straight, I wouldn't ask you to come if I wasn't in a hole—and if I didn't know you were coming down to Yale next year, and didn't think you're giving me the straight goods about having been around before. I don't want to lead you astray.

RICHARD. (*scornfully*) Aw, I told you that was silly.

WINT. Well, you be at the Pleasant Beach House at half-past nine then. Come in the back room. And don't forget to grab some cloves to take the booze off your breath.

RICHARD. Aw, I know what to do.

WINT. See you later, then. (*He starts out and is just about to close the door when he thinks of something*) And say, I'll say you're a Harvard freshman, and you back me up. They don't know a damn thing about Harvard. I don't want them thinking I'm travelling around with any high-school kid.

RICHARD. Sure. That's easy.

WINT. So long, then. You better beat it right after your dinner while you've got a chance, and hang around until it's time. Watch your step, Kid.

RICHARD. So long. (*The door closes behind* WINT. RICHARD *stands for a moment, a look of bitter, defiant rebellion coming over his face, and mutters to himself)* I'll show her she can't treat me the way she's done! I'll show them all! (*Then the front door is heard slamming, and a moment later* TOMMY *rushes in from the back parlor.*)

TOMMY. Where's Ma?

RICHARD. (*surlily*) In the sitting-room. Where did you think, Bonehead?

TOMMY. Pa and Uncle Sid are coming. Mid and I saw them from the front piazza. Gee, I'm glad. I'm awful hungry, ain't you? (*He rushes out through the back parlor, calling*) Ma! They're coming! Let's have dinner quick! (*A moment later* MRS. MILLER *appears from the back parlor accompanied by* TOMMY, *who keeps insisting urgently*) Gee, but I'm awful hungry, Ma!

MRS. MILLER. I know. You always are. You've got a tapeworm, that's what I think.

TOMMY. Have we got lobsters, Ma? Gee, I love lobsters.

MRS. MILLER. Yes, we've got lobsters. And fish. You remember what I told you about that fish. (*He snickers*) Now, do be quiet, Tommy! (*Then with a teasing smile at* RICHARD) Well, I'm glad to see you've got back out of the night, Richard. (*He scowls and turns his back on her.* LILY *appears through the back parlor, nervous and apprehensive. As she does so, from the front yard* SID's *voice is heard singing "Poor John!"* MRS. MILLER *shakes her head forebodingly—but, so great is the comic spell for her even in her brother's voice, a humorous smile hovers at the corners of her lips*) Mmm! Mmm! Lily, I'm afraid—

LILY. (*bitterly*) Yes, I might have known. (MILDRED *runs in through the back parlor. She is laughing to herself a bit shamefacedly. She rushes to her mother.*)

MILDRED. Ma, Uncle Sid's— (*She whispers in her ear.*)

MRS. MILLER. Never mind! You shouldn't notice such things—at your age! And don't you encourage him by laughing at his foolishness, you hear!

TOMMY. You needn't whisper, Mid. Think I don't know? Uncle Sid's soused again.

MRS. MILLER. (*shakes him by the arm indignantly*) You be quiet! Did I ever! You're getting too smart! (*Gives him a push*) Go to your place and sit right down and not another word out of you!

TOMMY. (*aggrieved—rubbing his arm as he goes to his place*) Aw, Ma!

MRS. MILLER. And you sit down, Richard and Mildred. You better, too, Lily. We'll get him right in here and get some food in him. He'll be all right then. (RICHARD, *preserving the pose of the bitter, disillusioned pessimist, sits down in his place in the chair at right of the two whose backs face front.* MILDRED *takes the other chair facing back, at his left.* TOMMY *has already slid into the end chair at right of those at the rear of table facing front.* LILY *sits in the one of those at left, by the head of the table, leaving the middle one* [SID's] *vacant. While they are doing this, the front screen door is heard slamming and* NAT's *and* SID's *laughing voices, raised as they come in and for a moment after, then suddenly cautiously lowered.* MRS. MILLER *goes to the entrance to the back parlor and calls peremptorily*) You come right in here! Don't stop to wash up or anything. Dinner's coming right on the table.

MILLER'S VOICE. (*jovially*) All right, Essie. Here we are! Here we are!

MRS. MILLER. (*goes to pantry door, opens it and calls*) All right, Norah. You can bring in the soup. (*She comes back to the back-parlor entrance just as* MILLER *enters. He isn't drunk by any means. He is just mellow and benignly ripened. His face is one large, smiling, happy beam of utter appreciation of life. All's right with the world, so satisfyingly right that he becomes sentimentally moved even to think of it.*)

MILLER. Here we are, Essie! Right on the dot! Here we are! (*He pulls her to him and gives her a smacking kiss on the ear as she jerks her head away.* MILDRED *and* TOMMY *giggle.* RICHARD *holds rigidly aloof and disdainful, his brooding gaze fixed on his plate.* LILY *forces a smile.*)

MRS. MILLER. (*pulling away—embarrassedly, almost blushing*) Don't, you Crazy! (*Then recovering herself—tartly*) So I see, you're here! And if I didn't, you've told me four times already!

MILLER. (*beamingly*) Now, Essie, don't be critical. Don't be carpingly critical. Good news can stand repeating, can't it? 'Course it can! (*He slaps her jovially on her fat buttocks.* TOMMY *and* MILDRED *roar with glee. And* NORAH, *who has just entered from the pantry with a huge tureen of soup in her hands, almost drops it as she explodes in a merry guffaw.*)

MRS. MILLER. (*scandalized*) Nat! Aren't you ashamed!

MILLER. Couldn't resist it! Just simply couldn't resist it! (NORAH, *still standing with the soup tureen held out stiffly in front of her, again guffaws.*)

MRS. MILLER. (*turns on her with outraged indignation*) Norah! Bring that soup here this minute! (*She stalks with stiff dignity toward her place at the foot of the table, right.*)

NORAH. (*guiltily*) Yes, Mum. (*She brings the soup around the head of the table, passing* MILLER.)

MILLER. (*jovially*) Why, hello, Norah!

MRS. MILLER. Nat! (*She sits down stiffly at the foot of the table.*)

NORAH. (*rebuking him familiarly*) Arrah now, don't be making me laugh and getting me into trouble!

MRS. MILLER. Norah!

NORAH. (*a bit resentfully*) Yes, Mum. Here I am. (*She sets the soup tureen down with a thud in front of* MRS. MILLER *and passes around the other side, squeezing with difficulty between the china closet and the backs of chairs at the rear of the table.*)

MRS. MILLER. Tommy! Stop spinning your napkin ring! How often have I got to tell you? Mildred! Sit up straight in your chair! Do you want to grow up a humpback? Richard! Take your elbows off the table!

MILLER. (*coming to his place at the head of the table, rubbing his hands together genially*) Well, well, well. Well, well, well. It's good to be home again. (NORAH *exits into the pantry and lets the door slam with a bang behind her.*)

MRS. MILLER. (*jumps*) Oh! (*Then exasperatedly*) Nat, I do wish you wouldn't encourage that stupid girl by talking to her, when I'm doing my best to train—

MILLER. (*beamingly*) All right, Essie. Your word is law! (*Then laughingly*) We did have the darndest fun today! And Sid was the life of that picnic! You ought to have heard him! Honestly, he had that crowd just rolling on the ground and splitting their sides! He ought to be on the stage.

MRS. MILLER. (*as* NORAH *comes back with a dish of saltines—begins ladling soup into the stack of plates before her*) He ought to be at this table eating something to sober him up, that's what he ought to be! (*She calls*) Sid! You come right in here! (*Then to* NORAH, *handing her a soup plate*) Here, Norah. (NORAH *begins passing soup*) Sit down, Nat, for goodness sakes. Start eating, everybody. Don't wait for me. You know I've given up soup.

MILLER. (*sits down but bends forward to call to his wife in a confidential tone*) Essie—Sid's sort of embarrassed about coming—I mean I'm afraid he's a little bit—not too much, you understand—but he met such a lot of friends and—well, you know, don't be hard on him. Fourth of July is like Christmas—comes but once a year. Don't pretend to notice, eh? And don't you kids, you hear! And don't you, Lily. He's scared of you.

LILY. (*with stiff meekness*) Very well, Nat.

MILLER. (*beaming again—calls*) All right, Sid. The coast's clear. (*He begins to absorb his soup ravenously*) Good soup, Essie! Good soup! (*A moment later* SID *makes his entrance from the back parlor. He is in a condition that can best be described as blurry. His movements have a hazy uncertainty about them. His shiny fat face is one broad, blurred, Puckish, naughty-boy grin; his eyes have a blurred,*

223

wondering vagueness. As he enters he makes a solemnly intense effort to appear casual and dead, cold sober. He waves his hand aimlessly and speaks with a silly gravity.)

SID. Good evening. (*They all answer "Good evening," their eyes on their plates. He makes his way vaguely toward his place, continuing his grave effort at conversation*) Beautiful evening. I never remember seeing—more beautiful sunset. (*He bumps vaguely into* LILY's *chair as he attempts to pass behind her—immediately he is all grave politeness*) Sorry—sorry, Lily—deeply sorry.

LILY. (*her eyes on her plate—stiffly*) It's all right.

SID. (*manages to get into his chair at last—mutters to himself*) Wha' was I sayin'? Oh, sunsets. But why butt in? Hasn't sun—perfect right to set? Mind y'r own business. (*He pauses thoughtfully, considering this—then looks around from face to face, fixing each with a vague, blurred, wondering look, as if some deep puzzle were confronting him. Then suddenly he grins mistily and nods with satisfaction*) And there you are! Am I right?

MILLER. (*humoring him*) Right.

SID. Right! (*He is silent, studying his soup plate, as if it were some strange enigma. Finally he looks up and regards his sister and asks with wondering amazement*) Soup?

MRS. MILLER. Of course, it's soup. What did you think it was? And you hurry up and eat it.

SID. (*again regards his soup with astonishment*) Well! (*Then suddenly*) Well, all right then! Soup be it! (*He picks up his spoon and begins to eat, but after two tries in which he finds it difficult to locate his mouth, he addresses the spoon plaintively*) Spoon, is this any way to treat a pal? (*Then suddenly comically angry, putting the spoon down with a bang*) Down with spoons! (*He raises his soup plate and declaims*) "We'll drink to the dead already, and hurrah for the next who dies." (*Bowing solemnly to right and left*) Your good health, ladies *and* gents. (*He starts drinking the soup.* MILLER *guffaws and* MILDRED *and* TOMMY *giggle. Even* RICHARD *forgets his melancholy and snickers, and* MRS. MILLER *conceals a smile. Only* LILY *remains stiff and silent.*)

MRS. MILLER. (*with forced severity*) Sid!

SID. (*peers at her muzzily, lowering the soup plate a little from his lips*) Eh?

MRS. MILLER. Oh, nothing. Never mind.

SID. (*solemnly offended*) Are you—publicly rebuking me before assembled—? Isn't soup liquid? Aren't liquids drunk? (*Then considering this to himself*) What if they are drunk? It's a good man's failing. (*He again peers mistily about at the company*) Am I right or wrong?

MRS. MILLER. Hurry up and finish your soup, and stop talking nonsense!

SID. (*turning to her—again offendedly*) Oh, no, Essie, if I ever so far forget myself as to drink a leg of lamb, then you might have some —excuse for— Just think of waste effort eating soup with spoons— fifty gruelling lifts per plate—billions of soup-eaters on globe—why, it's simply staggering! (*Then darkly to himself*) No more spoons for me! If I want to develop my biceps, I'll buy Sandow Exerciser! (*He drinks the rest of his soup in a gulp and beams around at the company, suddenly all happiness again*) Am I right, folks?

MILLER. (*who has been choking with laughter*) Haw, haw! You're right, Sid.

SID. (*peers at him blurredly and shakes his head sadly*) Poor old Nat! Always wrong—but heart of gold, heart of purest gold. And drunk again, I regret to note. Sister, my heart bleeds for you and your poor fatherless chicks!

MRS. MILLER. (*restraining a giggle—severely*) Sid! Do shut up for a minute! Pass me your soup plates, everybody. If we wait for that girl to take them, we'll be here all night. (*They all pass their plates, which* MRS. MILLER *stacks up and then puts on the sideboard. As she is doing this,* NORAH *appears from the pantry with a platter of broiled fish. She is just about to place these before* MILLER *when* SID *catches her eye mistily and rises to his feet, making her a deep, uncertain bow.*)

SID. (*raptly*) Ah, Sight for Sore Eyes, my beautiful Macushla, my star-eyed Mavourneen—

MRS. MILLER. Sid!

NORAH. (*immensely pleased—gives him an arch, flirtatious glance*) Ah sure, Mister Sid, it's you that have kissed the Blarney Stone, when you've a drop taken!

MRS. MILLER. (*outraged*) Norah! Put down that fish!

NORAH. (*flusteredly*) Yes, Mum. (*She attempts to put the fish down hastily before* MILLER, *but her eyes are fixed nervously on* MRS. MILLER *and she gives* MILLER *a nasty swipe on the side of the head with the edge of the dish.*)

MILLER. Ouch! (*The children, even* RICHARD, *explode into laughter.*)

NORAH. (*almost lets the dish fall*) Oh, glory be to God! Is it hurted you are?

MILLER. (*rubbing his head—good-naturedly*) No, no harm done. Only careful, Norah, careful.

NORAH. (*gratefully*) Yes, sorr. (*She thumps down the dish in front of him with a sigh of relief.*)

SID. (*who is still standing—with drunken gravity*) Careful, Mavourneen, careful! You might have hit him some place besides the head. Always aim at his head, remember—so as not to worry us. (*Again the children explode. Also* NORAH. *Even* LILY *suddenly lets out an hysterical giggle and is furious with herself for doing so.*)

LILY. I'm so sorry, Nat. I didn't mean to laugh. (*Turning on* SID *furiously*) Will you please sit down and stop making a fool of yourself? (SID *gives her a hurt, mournful look and then sinks meekly down on his chair.*)

NORAH. (*grinning cheerfully, gives* LILY *a reassuring pat on the back*) Ah, Miss Lily, don't mind him. He's only under the influence. Sure, there's no harm in him at all.

MRS. MILLER. Norah! (NORAH *exits hastily into the pantry, letting the door slam with a crash behind her. There is silence for a moment as* MILLER *serves the fish and it is passed around.* NORAH *comes back with the vegetables and disappears again, and these are dished out.*)

MILLER. (*is about to take his first bite—stops suddenly and asks his wife*) This isn't, by any chance, bluefish, is it, my dear?

MRS. MILLER. (*with a warning glance at* TOMMY) Of course not. You know we never have bluefish, on account of you.

MILLER. (*addressing the table now with the gravity of a man confessing his strange peculiarities*) Yes, I regret to say, there's a certain peculiar oil in bluefish that invariably poisons me. (*At this,* TOMMY *cannot stand it any more but explodes into laughter.* MRS. MILLER, *after a helpless glance at him, follows suit; then* LILY *goes off into uncontrollable, hysterical laughter, and* RICHARD *and* MILDRED *are caught in the contagion.* MILLER *looks around at them with a weak smile, his dignity now ruffled a bit*) Well, I must say I don't see what's so darned funny about my being poisoned.

SID. (*peers around him—then with drunken cunning*) Aha! Nat, I suspect—plot! This fish looks blue to me—very blue—in fact despondent, desperate, and— (*He points his fork dramatically at* MRS. MILLER) See how guilty she looks—a ver—veritable Lucretia Georgia! Can it be this woman has been slowly poisoning you all these years? And how well—you've stood it! What iron constitution! Even now, when you are invariably at death's door, I can't believe— (*Everyone goes off into uncontrollable laughter.*)

MILLER. (*grumpily*) Oh, give us a rest, you darned fool! A joke's a joke, but— (*He addresses his wife in a wounded tone*) Is this true, Essie?

MRS. MILLER. (*wiping the tears from her eyes—defiantly*) Yes, it is true, if you must know, and you'd never have suspected it, if it weren't for that darned Tommy, and Sid poking his nose in. You've eaten bluefish for years and thrived on it and it's all nonsense about that peculiar oil.

MILLER. (*deeply offended*) Kindly allow me to know my own con-

---

AH, WILDERNESS!

stitution! Now I think of it, I've felt upset afterwards every damned time we've had fish! (*He pushes his plate away from him with proud renunciation*) I can't eat this.

MRS. MILLER. (*insultingly matter-of-fact*) Well, don't then. There's lots of lobster coming and you can fill up on that. (RICHARD *suddenly bursts out laughing again.*)

MILLER. (*turns to him caustically*) You seem in a merry mood, Richard. I thought you were the original of the Heart Bowed Down today.

SID. (*with mock condolence*) Never mind, Dick. Let them—scoff! What can they understand about girls whose hair sizzchels, whose lips are fireworks, whose eyes are red-hot sparks—

MILDRED. (*laughing*) Is that what he wrote to Muriel? (*Turning to her brother*) You silly goat, you!

RICHARD. (*surlily*) Aw, shut up, Mid. What do I care about her? I'll show all of you how much I care!

MRS. MILLER. Pass your plates as soon as you're through, everybody. I've rung for the lobster. And that's all. You don't get any dessert or tea after lobster, you know. (NORAH *appears bearing a platter of cold boiled lobsters which she sets before* MILLER, *and disappears.*)

TOMMY. Gee, I love lobster! (MILLER *puts one on each plate, and they are passed around and everyone starts in pulling the cracked shells apart.*)

MILLER. (*feeling more cheerful after a couple of mouthfuls—determining to give the conversation another turn, says to his daughter*) Have a good time at the beach, Mildred?

MILDRED. Oh, fine, Pa, thanks. The water was wonderful and warm.

MILLER. Swim far?

MILDRED. Yes, for me. But that isn't so awful far.

MILLER. Well, you ought to be a good swimmer, if you take after me. I used to be a regular water rat when I was a boy. I'll have to go down to the beach with you one of these days—though I'd be rusty, not having been in in all these years. (*The reminiscent look comes*

228

into his eyes of one about to embark on an oft-told tale of childhood *adventure*) You know, speaking of swimming, I never go down to that beach but what it calls to mind the day I and Red Sisk went in swimming there and I saved his life. (*By this time the family are beginning to exchange amused, guilty glances. They all know what is coming.*)

SID. (*with a sly, blurry wink around*) Ha! Now we—have it again!

MILLER. (*turning on him*) Have what?

SID. Nothing—go on with your swimming—don't mind me.

MILLER. (*glares at him—but immediately is overcome by the reminiscent mood again*) Red Sisk—his father kept a blacksmith shop where the Union Market is now—we kids called him Red because he had the darndest reddest crop of hair—

SID. (*as if he were talking to his plate*) Remarkable!—the curious imagination—of little children.

MRS. MILLER. (*as she sees MILLER about to explode—interposes tactfully*) Sid! Eat your lobster and shut up! Go on, Nat.

MILLER. (*gives SID a withering look—then is off again*) Well, as I was saying, Red and I went swimming that day. Must have been— let me see—Red was fourteen, bigger and older than me, I was only twelve—forty-five years ago—wasn't a single house down there then —but there was a stake out where the whistling buoy is now, about a mile out. (TOMMY, *who has been having difficulty restraining himself, lets out a stifled giggle.* MILLER *bends a frowning gaze on him*) One more sound out of you, young man, and you'll leave the table!

MRS. MILLER. (*quickly interposing, trying to stave off the story*) Do eat your lobster, Nat. You didn't have any fish, you know.

MILLER. (*not liking the reminder—pettishly*) Well, if I'm going to be interrupted every second anyway— (*He turns to his lobster and chews in silence for a moment.*)

MRS. MILLER. (*trying to switch the subject*) How's Anne's mother's rheumatism, Mildred?

229

MILDRED. Oh, she's much better, Ma. She was in wading today. She says salt water's the only thing that really helps her bunion.

MRS. MILLER. Mildred! Where are your manners? At the table's no place to speak of—

MILLER. (*fallen into the reminiscent obsession again*) Well, as I was saying, there was I and Red, and he dared me to race him out to the stake and back. Well, I didn't let anyone dare me in those days. I was a spunky kid. So I said all right and we started out. We swam and swam and were pretty evenly matched; though, as I've said, he was bigger and older than me, but finally I drew ahead. I was going along easy, with lots in reserve, not a bit tired, when suddenly I heard a sort of gasp from behind me—like this—"help." (*He imitates. Everyone's eyes are firmly fixed on his plate, except* SID's) And I turned and there was Red, his face all pinched and white, and he says weakly: "Help, Nat! I got a cramp in my leg!" Well, I don't mind telling you I got mighty scared. I didn't know what to do. Then suddenly I thought of the pile. If I could pull him to that, I could hang on to him till someone'd notice us. But the pile was still—well, I calculate it must have been two hundred feet away.

SID. Two hundred and fifty!

MILLER. (*in confusion*) What's that?

SID. Two hundred *and* fifty! I've taken down the distance every time you've saved Red's life for thirty years and the mean average to that pile is two hundred and fifty feet! (*There is a burst of laughter from around the table.* SID *continues complainingly*) Why didn't you let that Red drown, anyway, Nat? I never knew him but I know I'd never have liked him.

MILLER. (*really hurt, forces a feeble smile to his lips and pretends to be a good sport about it*) Well, guess you're right, Sid. Guess I have told that one too many times and bored everyone. But it's a good true story for kids because it illustrates the danger of being foolhardy in the water—

MRS. MILLER. (*sensing the hurt in his tone, comes to his rescue*) Of course it's a good story—and you tell it whenever you've a mind to. And you, Sid, if you were in any responsible state, I'd give you a good piece of my mind for teasing Nat like that.

MILLER. (*with a sad, self-pitying smile at his wife*) Getting old, I guess, Mother—getting to repeat myself. Someone ought to stop me.

MRS. MILLER. No such thing! You're as young as you ever were. (*She turns on* SID *again angrily*) You eat your lobster and maybe it'll keep your mouth shut!

SID. (*after a few chews—irrepressibly*) Lobster! Did you know, Tommy, your Uncle Sid is the man invented lobster? Fact! One day —when I was building the Pyramids—took a day off and just dashed off lobster. He was bigger'n' older than me and he had the darndest reddest crop of hair but I dashed him off just the same! Am I right, Nat? (*Then suddenly in the tones of a side-show barker*) Ladies *and* Gents—

MRS. MILLER. Mercy sakes! Can't you shut up?

SID. In this cage you see the lobster. You will not believe me, ladies *and* gents, but it's a fact that this interesting bivalve only makes love to his mate once in every thousand years—but, dearie me, how he does enjoy it! (*The children roar.* LILY *and* MRS. MILLER *laugh in spite of themselves—then look embarrassed.* MILLER *guffaws—then suddenly grows shocked.*)

MILLER. Careful, Sid, careful. Remember you're at home.

TOMMY. (*suddenly in a hoarse whisper to his mother, with an awed glance of admiration at his uncle*) Ma! Look at him! He's eating that claw, shells and all!

MRS. MILLER. (*horrified*) Sid, do you want to kill yourself? Take it away from him, Lily!

SID. (*with great dignity*) But I prefer the shells. All famous epicures prefer the shells—to the less delicate, coarser meat. It's the same with clams. Unless I eat the shells there is a certain, peculiar oil that invariably poisons— Am I right, Nat?

MILLER. (*good-naturedly*) You seem to be getting a lot of fun kidding me. Go ahead, then. I don't mind.

MRS. MILLER. He better go right up to bed for a while, that's what he better do.

SID. (*considering this owlishly*) Bed? Yes, maybe you're right. (*He gets to his feet*) I am not at all well—in very delicate condition—we are praying for a boy. Am I right, Nat? Nat, I kept telling you all day I was in delicate condition and yet you kept forcing demon chowder on me, although you knew full well—even if you were full—that there is a certain, peculiar oil in chowder that invariably— (*They are again all laughing—*LILY, *hysterically.*)

MRS. MILLER. *Will* you get to bed, you idiot!

SID. (*mutters graciously*) Immediately—if not sooner. (*He turns to pass behind* LILY, *then stops, staring down at her*) But wait. There is still a duty I must perform. No day is complete without it. Lily, answer once and for all, will you marry me?

LILY. (*with an hysterical giggle*) No, I won't—never!

SID. (*nodding his head*) Right! And perhaps it's all for the best. For how could I forget the pre—precepts taught me at mother's dying knee. "Sidney," she said, "never marry a woman who drinks! Lips that touch liquor shall never touch yours!" (*Gazing at her mournfully*) Too bad! So fine a woman once—and now such a slave to rum! (*Turning to* NAT) What can we do to save her, Nat? (*In a hoarse, confidential whisper*) Better put her in institution where she'll be removed from temptation! The mere smell of it seems to drive her frantic!

MRS. MILLER. (*struggling with her laughter*) You leave Lily alone, and go to bed!

SID. Right! (*He comes around behind* LILY's *chair and moves toward the entrance to the back parlor—then suddenly turns and says with a bow*) Good night, ladies—and gents. We will meet—bye and bye! (*He gives an imitation of a Salvation Army drum*) Boom! Boom!

Boom! Come and be saved, Brothers! (*He starts to sing the old Army hymn*)

> *"In the sweet*
> *Bye and bye*
> *We will meet on that beautiful shore."*

(*He turns and marches solemnly out through the back parlor, singing*)

> *"Work and pray*
> *While you may.*
> *We will meet in the sky bye and bye."*

(MILLER *and his wife and the children are all roaring with laughter.* LILY *giggles hysterically.*)

MILLER. (*subsiding at last*) Haw, haw. He's a case, if ever there was one! Darned if you can help laughing at him—even when he's poking fun at you!

MRS. MILLER. Goodness, but he's a caution! Oh, my sides ache, I declare! I was trying so hard not to—but you can't help it, he's so silly! But I suppose we really shouldn't. It only encourages him. But, my lands—!

LILY. (*suddenly gets up from her chair and stands rigidly, her face working—jerkily*) That's just it—you shouldn't—even I laughed— it does encourage—that's been his downfall—everyone always laughing, everyone always saying what a card he is, what a case, what a caution, so funny—and he's gone on—and we're all responsible— making it easy for him—we're all to blame—and all we do is laugh!

MILLER. (*worriedly*) Now, Lily, now, you mustn't take on so. It isn't as serious as all that.

LILY. (*bitterly*) Maybe—it is—to me. Or was—once. (*Then contritely*) I'm sorry, Nat. I'm sorry, Essie. I didn't mean to—I'm not feeling myself tonight. If you'll excuse me, I'll go in the front parlor and lie down on the sofa awhile.

233

MRS. MILLER. Of course, Lily. You do whatever you've a mind to. (LILY *goes out.*)

MILLER. (*frowning—a little shamefaced*) Hmm. I suppose she's right. Never knew Lily to come out with things that way before. Anything special happened, Essie?

MRS. MILLER. Nothing I know—except he'd promised to take her to the fireworks.

MILLER. That's so. Well, supposing I take her? I don't want her to feel disappointed.

MRS. MILLER. (*shaking her head*) Wild horses couldn't drag her there now.

MILLER. Hmm. I thought she'd got completely over her foolishness about him long ago.

MRS. MILLER. She never will.

MILLER. She'd better. He's got fired out of that Waterbury job—told me at the picnic after he'd got enough Dutch courage in him.

MRS. MILLER. Oh, dear! Isn't he the fool!

MILLER. I knew something was wrong when he came home. Well, I'll find a place for him on my paper again, of course. He always was the best news-getter this town ever had. But I'll tell him he's got to stop his damn nonsense.

MRS. MILLER. (*doubtfully*) Yes.

MILLER. Well, no use sitting here mourning over spilt milk. (*He gets up, and* RICHARD, MILDRED, TOMMY *and* MRS. MILLER *follow his example, the children quiet and a bit awed*) You kids go out in the yard and try to keep quiet for a while, so's your Uncle Sid'll get to sleep and your Aunt Lily can rest.

TOMMY. (*mournfully*) Ain't we going to set off the skyrockets and Roman candles, Pa?

MILLER. Later, Son, later. It isn't dark enough for them yet anyway.

MILDRED. Come on, Tommy. I'll see he keeps quiet, Pa.

MILLER. That's a good girl. (MILDRED *and* TOMMY *go out through the screen door.* RICHARD *remains standing, sunk in bitter, gloomy*

234

thoughts. MILLER *glances at him—then irritably*) Well, Melancholy Dane, what are you doing?

RICHARD. (*darkly*) I'm going out—for a while. (*Then suddenly*) Do you know what I think? It's Aunt Lily's fault, Uncle Sid's going to ruin. It's all because he loves her, and she keeps him dangling after her, and eggs him on and ruins his life—like all women love to ruin men's lives! I don't blame him for drinking himself to death! What does he care if he dies, after the way she's treated him! I'd do the same thing myself if I were in his boots!

MRS. MILLER. (*indignantly*) Richard! You stop that talk!

RICHARD. (*quotes bitterly*)

"*Drink! for you know not whence you come nor why.*
Drink! for you know not why you go nor where!"

MILLER. (*losing his temper—harshly*) Listen here, young man! I've had about all I can stand of your nonsense for one day! You're growing a lot too big for your size, seems to me! You keep that damn fool talk to yourself, you hear me—or you're going to regret it! Mind now! (*He strides angrily away through the back parlor.*)

MRS. MILLER. (*still indignant*) Richard, I'm ashamed of you, that's what I am. (*She follows her husband.* RICHARD *stands for a second, bitter, humiliated, wronged, even his father turned enemy, his face growing more and more rebellious. Then he forces a scornful smile to his lips.*)

RICHARD. Aw, what the hell do I care? I'll show them! (*He turns and goes out the screen door.*)

CURTAIN

ACT THREE—SCENE ONE

SCENE—*The back room of a bar in a small hotel—a small, dingy room, dimly lighted by two fly-specked globes in a fly-specked gilt chandelier suspended from the middle of the ceiling. At left, front, is the swinging door leading to the bar. At rear of door, against the wall, is a nickel-in-the-slot player-piano. In the rear wall, right, is a door leading to the "Family Entrance" and the stairway to the up-stairs rooms. In the middle of the right wall is a window with closed shutters. Three tables with stained tops, four chairs around each table, are placed at center, front, at right, toward rear, and at rear, center. A brass cuspidor is on the floor by each table. The floor is unswept, littered with cigarette and cigar butts. The hideous saffron-colored wall-paper is blotched and spotted.*

It is about 10 o'clock the same night. RICHARD *and* BELLE *are discovered sitting at the table at center,* BELLE *at left of it,* RICHARD *in the next chair at the middle of table, rear, facing front.*

BELLE *is twenty, a rather pretty peroxide blonde, a typical college "tart" of the period, and of the cheaper variety, dressed with tawdry flashiness. But she is a fairly recent recruit to the ranks, and is still a bit remorseful behind her make-up and defiantly careless manner.*

BELLE *has an empty gin-rickey glass before her,* RICHARD *a half-empty glass of beer. He looks horribly timid, embarrassed and guilty, but at the same time thrilled and proud of at last mingling with the pace that kills.*

The player-piano is grinding out "Bedelia." The BARTENDER, *a stocky young Irishman with a foxily cunning, stupid face and a cynically wise grin, stands just inside the bar entrance, watching them over the swinging door.*

BELLE. (*with an impatient glance at her escort—rattling the ice in her empty glass*) Drink up your beer, why don't you? It's getting flat.

RICHARD. (*embarrassedly*) I let it get that way on purpose. I like it better when it's flat. (*But he hastily gulps down the rest of his glass, as if it were some nasty-tasting medicine. The* BARTENDER *chuckles audibly.* BELLE *glances at him.*)

BELLE. (*nodding at the player-piano scornfully*) Say, George, is "Bedelia" the latest to hit this hick burg? Well, it's only a couple of years old! You'll catch up in time! Why don't you get a new roll for that old box?

BARTENDER. (*with a grin*) Complain to the boss, not me. We're not used to having Candy Kiddoes like you around—or maybe we'd get up to date.

BELLE. (*with a professionally arch grin at him*) Don't kid me, please. I can't bear it. (*Then she sings to the music from the piano, her eyes now on* RICHARD) "Bedelia, I'd like to feel yer." (*The* BARTENDER *laughs. She smirks at* RICHARD) Ever hear those words to it, Kid?

RICHARD. (*who has heard them but is shocked at hearing a girl say them—putting on a blasé air*) Sure, lots of times. That's old.

BELLE. (*edging her chair closer and putting a hand over one of his*) Then why don't you act as if you knew what they were all about?

RICHARD. (*terribly flustered*) Sure, I've heard that old parody lots of times. What do you think I am?

BELLE. I don't know, Kid. Honest to God, you've got me guessing.

BARTENDER. (*with a mocking chuckle*) He's a hot sport, can't you tell it? I never seen such a spender. My head's dizzy bringing you in drinks!

BELLE. (*laughs irritably—to* RICHARD) Don't let him kid you. You show him. Loosen up and buy another drink, what say?

RICHARD. (*humiliated—manfully*) Sure. Excuse me. I was thinking of something else. Have anything you like. (*He turns to the* BARTENDER *who has entered from the bar*) See what the lady will have—and have one on me yourself.

BARTENDER. (*coming to the table—with a wink at* BELLE) That's talking! Didn't I say you were a sport? I'll take a cigar on you. (*To* BELLE) What's yours, Kiddo—the same?

BELLE. Yes. And forget the house rules this time and remember a rickey is supposed to have gin in it.

BARTENDER. (*grinning*) I'll try to—seeing it's you. (*Then to* RICHARD) What's yours—another beer?

RICHARD. (*shyly*) A small one, please. I'm not thirsty.

BELLE. (*calculatedly taunting*) Say, honest, are things that slow up at Harvard? If they had you down at New Haven, they'd put you in a kindergarten! Don't be such a dead one! Filling up on beer will only make you sleepy. Have a man's drink!

RICHARD. (*shamefacedly*) All right. I was going to. Bring me a sloe-gin fizz.

BELLE. (*to* BARTENDER) And make it a real one.

BARTENDER. (*with a wink*) I get you. Something that'll warm him up, eh? (*He goes into the bar, chuckling.*)

BELLE. (*looks around the room—irritably*) Christ, what a dump! (RICHARD *is startled and shocked by this curse and looks down at the table*) If this isn't the deadest burg I ever struck! Bet they take the sidewalks in after nine o'clock! (*Then turning on him*) Say, honestly, Kid, does your mother know you're out?

RICHARD. (*defensively*) Aw, cut it out, why don't you—trying to kid me!

BELLE. (*glances at him—then resolves on a new tack—patting his hand*) All right. I didn't mean to, Dearie. Please don't get sore at me.

RICHARD. I'm not sore.

BELLE. (*seductively*) You see, it's this way with me. I think you're one of the sweetest kids I've ever met—and I could like you such a lot if you'd give me half a chance—instead of acting so cold and indifferent.

RICHARD. I'm not cold and indifferent. (*Then solemnly tragic*) It's only that I've got—a weight on my mind.

BELLE. (*impatiently*) Well, get it off your mind and give something else a chance to work. (*The* BARTENDER *comes in, bringing the drinks.*)

BARTENDER. (*setting them down—with a wink at* BELLE) This'll warm him for you. Forty cents, that is—with the cigar.

RICHARD. (*pulls out his roll and hands a dollar bill over—with exaggerated carelessness*) Keep the change. (BELLE *emits a gasp and seems about to protest, then thinks better of it. The* BARTENDER *cannot believe his luck for a moment—then pockets the bill hastily, as if afraid* RICHARD *will change his mind.*)

BARTENDER. (*respect in his voice*) Thank you, sir.

RICHARD. (*grandly*) Don't mention it.

BARTENDER. I hope you like the drink. I took special pains with it. (*The voice of the* SALESMAN, *who has just come in the bar, calls* "Hey! Anybody here?" *and a coin is rapped on the bar*) I'm coming. (*The* BARTENDER *goes out.*)

BELLE. (*remonstrating gently, a new appreciation for her escort's possibilities in her voice*) You shouldn't be so generous, Dearie. Gets him in bad habits. A dime would have been plenty.

RICHARD. Ah, that's all right. I'm no tightwad.

BELLE. That's the talk I like to hear. (*With a quick look toward the bar, she stealthily pulls up her dress—to* RICHARD's *shocked fascination —and takes a package of cheap cigarettes from her stocking*) Keep an eye out for that bartender, Kid, and tell me if you see him coming. Girls are only allowed to smoke upstairs in the rooms, he said.

RICHARD. (*embarrassedly*) All right. I'll watch.

BELLE. (*having lighted her cigarette and inhaled deeply, holds the package out to him*) Have a Sweet? You smoke, don't you?

RICHARD. (*taking one*) Sure! I've been smoking for the last two years —on the sly. But next year I'll be allowed—that is, pipes and cigars. (*He lights his cigarette with elaborate nonchalance, puffs, but does not inhale—then, watching her, with shocked concern*) Say, you oughtn't to inhale like that! Smoking's awful bad for girls, anyway, even if they don't—

BELLE. (*cynically amused*) Afraid it will stunt my growth? Gee, Kid, you are a scream! You'll grow up to be a minister yet! (RICHARD *looks shamefaced. She scans him impatiently—then holds up her drink*) Well, here's how! Bottoms up, now! Show me you really know how to drink. It'll take that load off your mind. (RICHARD *follows her example and they both drink the whole contents of their glasses before setting them down*) There! That's something like! Feel better?

RICHARD. (*proud of himself—with a shy smile*) You bet.

BELLE. Well, you'll feel still better in a minute—and then maybe you won't be so distant and unfriendly, eh?

RICHARD. I'm not.

BELLE. Yes, you are. I think you just don't like me.

RICHARD. (*more manfully*) I do too like you.

BELLE. How much? A lot?

RICHARD. Yes, a lot.

BELLE. Show me how much! (*Then as he fidgets embarrassedly*) Want me to come sit on your lap?

RICHARD. Yes—I— (*She comes and sits on his lap. He looks desperately uncomfortable, but the gin is rising to his head and he feels proud of himself and devilish, too.*)

BELLE. Why don't you put your arm around me? (*He does so awkwardly*) No, not that dead way. Hold me tight. You needn't be afraid of hurting me. I like to be held tight, don't you?

RICHARD. Sure I do.

BELLE. 'Specially when it's by a nice handsome kid like you. (*Ruffling his hair*) Gee, you've got pretty hair, do you know it? Honest, I'm awfully strong for you! Why can't you be about me? I'm not so awfully ugly, am I?

RICHARD. No, you're—you're pretty.

BELLE. You don't say it as if you meant it.

RICHARD. I do mean it—honest.

BELLE. Then why don't you kiss me? (*She bends down her lips toward his. He hesitates, then kisses her and at once shrinks back*)

Call that kissing? Here. (*She holds his head and fastens her lips on his and holds them there. He starts and struggles. She laughs*) What's the matter, Honey Boy? Haven't you ever kissed like that before?

RICHARD. Sure. Lots of times.

BELLE. Then why did you jump as if I'd bitten you? (*Squirming around on his lap*) Gee, I'm getting just crazy about you! What shall we do about it, eh? Tell me.

RICHARD. I—don't know. (*Then boldly*) I—I'm crazy about you, too.

BELLE. (*kissing him again*) Just think of the wonderful time Edith and your friend, Wint, are having upstairs—while we sit down here like two dead ones. A room only costs two dollars. And, seeing I like you so much, I'd only take five dollars—from you. I'd do it for nothing—for you—only I've got to live and I owe my room rent in New Haven—and you know how it is. I get ten dollars from everyone else. Honest! (*She kisses him again, then gets up from his lap—briskly*) Come on. Go out and tell the bartender you want a room. And hurry. Honest, I'm so strong for you I can hardly wait to get you upstairs!

RICHARD. (*starts automatically for the door to the bar—then hesitates, a great struggle going on in his mind—timidity, disgust at the money element, shocked modesty, and the guilty thought of* MURIEL, *fighting it out with the growing tipsiness that makes him want to be a hell of a fellow and go in for all forbidden fruit, and makes this tart a romantic, evil vampire in his eyes. Finally, he stops and mutters in confusion*) I can't.

BELLE. What, are you too bashful to ask for a room? Let me do it, then. (*She starts for the door.*)

RICHARD. (*desperately*) No—I don't want you to—I don't want to.

BELLE. (*surveying him, anger coming into her eyes*) Well, if you aren't the lousiest cheap skate!

RICHARD. I'm not a cheap skate!

BELLE. Keep me around here all night fooling with you when I might be out with some real live one—if there is such a thing in this burg!—

and now you quit on me! Don't be such a piker! You've got five dollars! I seen it when you paid for the drinks, so don't hand me any lies!

RICHARD. I— Who said I hadn't? And I'm not a piker. If you need the five dollars so bad—for your room rent—you can have it without —I mean, I'll be glad to give— (*He has been fumbling in his pocket and pulls out his nine-dollar roll and holds out the five to her.*)

BELLE. (*hardly able to believe her eyes, almost snatches it from his hand—then laughs and immediately becomes sentimentally grateful*) Thanks, Kid. Gee—oh, thanks— Gee, forgive me for losing my temper and bawling you out, will you? Gee, you're a regular peach! You're the nicest kid I've ever met! (*She kisses him and he grins proudly, a hero to himself now on many counts*) Gee, you're a peach! Thanks, again!

RICHARD. (*grandly—and quite tipsily*) It's—nothing—only too glad. (*Then boldly*) Here—give me another kiss, and that'll pay me back.

BELLE. (*kissing him*) I'll give you a thousand, if you want 'em. Come on, let's sit down, and we'll have another drink—and this time I'll blow you just to show my appreciation. (*She calls*) Hey, George! bring us another round—the same!

RICHARD. (*a remnant of caution coming to him*) I don't know as I ought to—

BELLE. Oh, another won't hurt you. And I want to blow you, see. (*They sit down in their former places.*)

RICHARD. (*boldly draws his chair closer and puts an arm around her —tipsily*) I like you a lot—now I'm getting to know you. You're a darned nice girl.

BELLE. Nice is good! Tell me another! Well, if I'm so nice, why didn't you want to take me upstairs? That's what I don't get.

RICHARD. (*lying boldly*) I did want to—only I— (*Then he adds solemnly*) I've sworn off. (*The* BARTENDER *enters with the drinks.*)

BARTENDER. (*setting them on the table*) Here's your pleasure. (*Then regarding* RICHARD'S *arm about her waist*) Ho-ho, we're coming on, I see. (RICHARD *grins at him muzzily.*)

242

BELLE. (*digs into her stocking and gives him a dollar*) Here. This is mine. (*He gives her change and she tips him a dime, and he goes out. She puts the five* RICHARD *had given her in her stocking and picks up her glass*) Here's how—and thanks again. (*She sips.*)

RICHARD. (*boisterously*) Bottoms up! Bottoms up! (*He drinks all of his down and sighs with exaggerated satisfaction*) Gee, that's good stuff, all right. (*Hugging her*) Give me another kiss, Belle.

BELLE. (*kisses him*) What did you mean a minute ago when you said you'd sworn off?

RICHARD. (*solemnly*) I took an oath I'd be faithful.

BELLE. (*cynically*) Till death do us part, eh? Who's the girl?

RICHARD. (*shortly*) Never mind.

BELLE. (*bristling*) I'm not good enough to talk about her, I suppose?

RICHARD. I didn't—mean that. You're all right. (*Then with tipsy gravity*) Only you oughtn't to lead this kind of life. It isn't right— for a nice girl like you. Why don't you reform?

BELLE. (*sharply*) Nix on that line of talk! Can it, you hear! You can do a lot with me for five dollars—but you can't reform me, see. Mind your own business, Kid, and don't butt in where you're not wanted!

RICHARD. I—I didn't mean to hurt your feelings.

BELLE. I know you didn't mean. You're only like a lot of people who mean well, to hear them tell it. (*Changing the subject*) So you're faithful to your one love, eh? (*With an ugly sneer*) And how about her? Bet you she's out with a guy under some bush this minute, giving him all he wants. Don't be a sucker, Kid! Even the little flies do it!

RICHARD. (*starting up his chair again—angrily*) Don't you say that! Don't you dare!

BELLE. (*unimpressed—with a cynical shrug of her shoulders*) All right. Have it your own way and be a sucker! It cuts no ice with me.

RICHARD. You don't know her or—

BELLE. And don't want to. Shut up about her, can't you? (*She stares before her bitterly.* RICHARD *subsides into scowling gloom. He is becoming perceptibly more intoxicated with each moment now. The*

BARTENDER *and the* SALESMAN *appear just inside the swinging door. The* BARTENDER *nods toward* BELLE, *giving the* SALESMAN *a wink. The* SALESMAN *grins and comes into the room, carrying his highball in his hand. He is a stout, jowly-faced man in his late thirties, dressed with cheap nattiness, with the professional breeziness and jocular, kid-'em-along manner of his kind.* BELLE *looks up as he enters and he and she exchange a glance of complete recognition. She knows his type by heart and he knows hers.*)

SALESMAN. (*passes by her to the table at right—grinning genially*) Good evening.

BELLE. Good evening.

SALESMAN. (*sitting down*) Hope I'm not butting in on your party— but my dogs were giving out standing at that bar.

BELLE. All right with me. (*Giving* RICHARD *a rather contemptuous look*) I've got no party on.

SALESMAN. That sounds hopeful.

RICHARD. (*suddenly recites sentimentally*)

"But I wouldn't do such,'cause I loved her too much,
But I learned about women from her."

(*Turns to scowl at the* SALESMAN—*then to* BELLE) Let's have 'nother drink!

BELLE. You've had enough. (RICHARD *subsides, muttering to himself.*)

SALESMAN. What is it—a child poet or a child actor?

BELLE. Don't know. Got me guessing.

SALESMAN. Well, if you could shake the cradle-robbing act, maybe we could do a little business.

BELLE. That's easy. I just pull my freight. (*She shakes* RICHARD *by the arm*) Listen, Kid. Here's an old friend of mine, Mr. Smith of New Haven, just come in. I'm going over and sit at his table for a while, see. And you better go home.

RICHARD. (*blinking at her and scowling*) I'm never going home! I'll show them!

BELLE. Have it your own way—only let me up. (*She takes his arm from around her and goes to sit by the* SALESMAN. RICHARD *stares after her offendedly.*)

RICHARD. Go on. What do I care what you do? (*He recites scornfully*) "For a woman's only a woman, but a good cigar's a smoke."

SALESMAN. (*as* BELLE *sits beside him*) Well, what kind of beer will you have, Sister?

BELLE. Mine's a gin rickey.

SALESMAN. You've got extravagant tastes, I'm sorry to see.

RICHARD. (*begins to recite sepulchrally*)

> "Yet each man kills the thing he loves,
> By each let this be heard."

SALESMAN. (*grinning*) Say, this is rich! (*He calls encouragement*) That's swell dope, young feller. Give us some more.

RICHARD. (*ignoring him—goes on more rhetorically*)

> "Some do it with a bitter look,
> Some with a flattering word,
> The coward does it with a kiss,
> The brave man with a sword!"

(*He stares at* BELLE *gloomily and mutters tragically*) I did it with a kiss! I'm a coward.

SALESMAN. That's the old stuff, Kid. You've got something on the ball, all right, all right! Give us another—right over the old pan, now!

BELLE. (*with a laugh*) Get the hook!

RICHARD. (*glowering at her—tragically*)

> "'Oho,' they cried, 'the world is wide,
> But fettered limbs go lame!
> And once, or twice, to throw the dice
> Is a gentlemanly game,
> But he does not win who plays with Sin
> In the secret House of Shame!'"

BELLE. (*angrily*) Aw, can it! Give us a rest from that bunk!

SALESMAN. (*mockingly*) This gal of yours don't appreciate poetry. She's a lowbrow. But I'm the kid that eats it up. My middle name is Kelly and Sheets! Give us some more of the same! Do you know "The Lobster and the Wise Guy"? (*Turns to* BELLE *seriously*) No kidding, that's a peacherino. I heard a guy recite it at Poli's. Maybe this nut knows it. Do you, Kid? (*But* RICHARD *only glowers at him gloomily without answering.*)

BELLE. (*surveying* RICHARD *contemptuously*) He's copped a fine skinful—and gee, he's hardly had anything.

RICHARD. (*suddenly—with a dire emphasis*) "And then—at ten o'clock—Eilert Lovborg will come—with vine leaves in his hair!"

BELLE. And bats in his belfry, if he's you!

RICHARD. (*regards her bitterly—then starts to his feet bellicosely—to the* SALESMAN) I don't believe you ever knew her in New Haven at all! You just picked her up now! You leave her alone, you hear! You won't do anything to her—not while I'm here to protect her!

BELLE. (*laughing*) Oh, my God! Listen to it!

SALESMAN. Ssshh! This is a scream! Wait! (*He addresses* RICHARD *in tones of exaggerated melodrama*) Curse you, Jack Dalton, if I won't unhand her, what then?

RICHARD. (*threateningly*) I'll give you a good punch in the snoot, that's what! (*He moves toward their table.*)

SALESMAN. (*with mock terror—screams in falsetto*) Help! Help! (*The* BARTENDER *comes in irritably.*)

BARTENDER. Hey. Cut out the noise. What the hell's up with you?

RICHARD. (*tipsily*) He's too—damn fresh!

SALESMAN. (*with a wink*) He's going to murder me. (*Then gets a bright idea for eliminating* RICHARD—*seriously to the* BARTENDER) It's none of my business, Brother, but if I were in your boots I'd give this young souse the gate. He's under age; any fool can see that.

BARTENDER. (*guiltily*) He told me he was over eighteen.

SALESMAN. Yes, and I tell you I'm the Pope—but you don't have to believe me. If you're not looking for trouble, I'd advise you to get him started for some other gin mill and let them do the lying, if anything comes up.

BARTENDER. Hmm. (*He turns to* RICHARD *angrily and gives him a push*) Come on, now. On your way! You'll start no trouble in here! Beat it now!

RICHARD. I will not beat it!

BARTENDER. Oho, won't you? (*He gives him another push that almost sends him sprawling.*)

BELLE. (*callously*) Give him the bum's rush! I'm sick of his bull! (RICHARD *turns furiously and tries to punch the* BARTENDER.)

BARTENDER. (*avoids the punch*) Oho, you would, would you! (*He grabs* RICHARD *by the back of the neck and the seat of the pants and marches him ignominiously toward the swinging door.*)

RICHARD. Leggo of me, you dirty coward!

BARTENDER. Quiet now—or I'll pin a Mary Ann on your jaw that'll quiet you! (*He rushes him through the screen door and a moment later the outer doors are heard swinging back and forth.*)

SALESMAN. (*with a chuckle*) Hand it to me, Kid. How was that for a slick way of getting rid of him?

BELLE. (*suddenly sentimental*) Poor kid. I hope he makes home all right. I liked him—before he got soused.

SALESMAN. Who is he?

BELLE. The boy who's upstairs with my friend told me, but I didn't pay much attention. Name's Miller. His old man runs a paper in this one-horse burg, I think he said.

SALESMAN. (*with a whistle*) Phew! He must be Nat Miller's kid, then.

BARTENDER. (*coming back from the bar*) Well, he's on his way—with a good boot in the tail to help him!

SALESMAN. (*with a malicious chuckle*) Yes? Well, maybe that boot will cost you a job, Brother. Know Nat Miller who runs the *Globe?* That's his kid.

BARTENDER. (*his face falling*) The hell he is! Who said so?

SALESMAN. This baby doll. (*Getting up*) Say, I'll go keep cases on him—see he gets on the trolley all right, anyway. Nat Miller's a good scout. (*He hurries out.*)

BARTENDER. (*viciously*) God damn the luck! If he ever finds out I served his kid, he'll run me out of town. (*He turns on* BELLE *furiously*) Why didn't you put me wise, you lousy tramp, you!

BELLE. Hey! I don't stand for that kind of talk—not from no hick beer-squirter like you, see!

BARTENDER. (*furiously*) You don't, don't you? Who was it but you told me to hand him dynamite in that fizz? (*He gives her chair a push that almost throws her to the floor*) Beat it, you—and beat it quick—or I'll call Sullivan from the corner and have you run in for street-walking! (*He gives her a push that lands her against the family-entrance door*) Get the hell out of here—and no long waits!

BELLE. (*opens the door and goes out—turns and calls back viciously*) I'll fix you for this, you thick Mick, if I have to go to jail for it. (*She goes out and slams the door.*)

BARTENDER. (*looks after her worriedly for a second—then shrugs his shoulders*) That's only her bull. (*Then with a sigh as he returns to the bar*) Them lousy tramps is always getting this dump in Dutch!

CURTAIN

248

ACT THREE—SCENE TWO

S CENE—*Same as Act One—Sitting-room of the Miller home—about 11 o'clock the same night.*

MILLER *is sitting in his favorite rocking-chair at left of table, front. He has discarded collar and tie, coat and shoes, and wears an old, worn, brown dressing-gown and disreputable-looking carpet slippers. He has his reading specs on and is running over items in a newspaper. But his mind is plainly preoccupied and worried, and he is not paying much attention to what he reads.*

MRS. MILLER *sits by the table at right, front. She also has on her specs. A sewing basket is on her lap and she is trying hard to keep her attention fixed on the doily she is doing. But, as in the case of her husband, but much more apparently, her mind is preoccupied, and she is obviously on tenterhooks of nervous uneasiness.*

LILY *is sitting in the armchair by the table at rear, facing right. She is pretending to read a novel, but her attention wanders, too, and her expression is sad, although now it has lost all its bitterness and become submissive and resigned again.*

MILDRED *sits at the desk at right, front, writing two words over and over again, stopping each time to survey the result critically, biting her tongue, intensely concentrated on her work.*

TOMMY *sits on the sofa at left, front. He has had a hard day and is terribly sleepy but will not acknowledge it. His eyes blink shut on him, his head begins to nod, but he isn't giving up, and every time he senses any of the family glancing in his direction, he goads himself into a bright-eyed wakefulness.*

MILDRED. (*finally surveys the two words she has been writing and is satisfied with them*) There. (*She takes the paper over to her mother*)

249

Look, Ma. I've been practising a new way of writing my name. Don't look at the others, only the last one. Don't you think it's the real goods?

MRS. MILLER. (*pulled out of her preoccupation*) Don't talk that horrible slang. It's bad enough for boys, but for a young girl supposed to have manners—my goodness, when I was your age, if my mother'd ever heard me—

MILDRED. Well, don't you think it's nice, then?

MRS. MILLER. (*sinks back into preoccupation—scanning the paper— vaguely*) Yes, very nice, Mildred—very nice, indeed. (*Hands the paper back mechanically.*)

MILDRED. (*is a little piqued, but smiles*) Absent-minded! I don't believe you even saw it. (*She passes around the table to show her* AUNT LILY. MILLER *gives an uneasy glance at his wife and then, as if afraid of meeting her eye, looks quickly back at his paper again.*)

MRS. MILLER. (*staring before her—sighs worriedly*) Oh, I do wish Richard would come home!

MILLER. There now, Essie. He'll be in any minute now. Don't you worry about him.

MRS. MILLER. But I do worry about him!

LILY. (*surveying* MILDRED's *handiwork—smiling*) This is fine, Mildred. Your penmanship is improving wonderfully. But don't you think that maybe you've got a little too many flourishes?

MILDRED. (*disappointedly*) But, Aunt Lily, that's just what I was practising hardest on.

MRS. MILLER. (*with another sigh*) What time is it now, Nat?

MILLER. (*adopting a joking tone*) I'm going to buy a clock for in here. You have me reaching for my watch every couple of minutes. (*He has pulled his watch out of his vest pocket—with forced carelessness*) Only a little past ten.

MRS. MILLER. Why, you said it was that an hour ago! Nat Miller, you're telling me a fib, so's not to worry me. You let me see that watch!

250

MILLER. (*guiltily*) Well, it's quarter to eleven—but that's not so late—when you remember it's Fourth of July.

MRS. MILLER. If you don't stop talking Fourth of July—! To hear you go on, you'd think that was an excuse for anything from murder to picking pockets!

MILDRED. (*has brought her paper around to her father and now shoves it under his nose*) Look, Pa.

MILLER. (*seizes on this interruption with relief*) Let's see. Hmm. Seems to me you've been inventing a new signature every week lately. What are you in training for—writing checks? You must be planning to catch a rich husband.

MILDRED. (*with an arch toss of her head*) No wedding bells for me! But how do you like it, Pa?

MILLER. It's overpowering—no other word for it, overpowering! You could put it on the Declaration of Independence and not feel ashamed.

MRS. MILLER. (*desolately, almost on the verge of tears*) It's all right for you to laugh and joke with Mildred! I'm the only one in this house seems to care— (*Her lips tremble.*)

MILDRED. (*a bit disgustedly*) Ah, Ma, Dick only sneaked off to the fireworks at the beach, you wait and see.

MRS. MILLER. Those fireworks were over long ago. If he had, he'd be home.

LILY. (*soothingly*) He probably couldn't get a seat, the trolleys are so jammed, and he had to walk home.

MILLER. (*seizing on this with relief*) Yes, I never thought of that, but I'll bet that's it.

MILDRED. Ah, don't let him worry you, Ma. He just wants to show off he's heartbroken about that silly Muriel—and get everyone fussing over him and wondering if he hasn't drowned himself or something.

MRS. MILLER. (*snappily*) You be quiet! The way you talk at times, I really believe you're that hard-hearted you haven't got a heart in you! (*With an accusing glance at her husband*) One thing I know, you don't get that from me! (*He meets her eye and avoids it guiltily. She sniffs and looks away from him around the room.* TOMMY, *who is nodding and blinking, is afraid her eye is on him. He straightens alertly and speaks in a voice that, in spite of his effort, is dripping with drowsiness.*)

TOMMY. Let me see what you wrote, Mid.

MILDRED. (*cruelly mocking*) You? You're so sleepy you couldn't see it?

TOMMY. (*valiantly*) I am not sleepy!

MRS. MILLER. (*has fixed her eye on him*) My gracious, I was forgetting you were still up! You run up to bed this minute! It's hours past your bedtime!

TOMMY. But it's the Fourth of July. Ain't it, Pa?

MRS. MILLER. (*gives her husband an accusing stare*) There! You see what you've done? You might know he'd copy your excuses! (*Then sharply to* TOMMY) You heard what I said, Young Man!

TOMMY. Aw, Ma, can't I stay up a *little* longer?

MRS. MILLER. I said, no! You obey me and no more arguing about it!

TOMMY. (*drags himself to his feet*) Aw! I should think I could stay up till Dick—

MILLER. (*kindly but firmly*) You heard your ma say no more arguing. When she says git, you better git. (TOMMY *accepts his fate resignedly and starts around kissing them all good night.*)

TOMMY. (*kissing her*) Good night, Aunt Lily.

LILY. Good night, dear. Sleep well.

TOMMY. (*pecking at* MILDRED) Good night, you.

MILDRED. Good night, you.

TOMMY. (*kissing him*) Good night, Pa.

MILLER. Good night, Son. Sleep tight.

TOMMY. (*kissing her*) Good night, Ma.

MRS. MILLER. Good night. Here! You look feverish. Let me feel of your head. No, you're all right. Hurry up, now. And don't forget your prayers.

(TOMMY *goes slowly to the doorway—then turns suddenly, the discovery of another excuse lighting up his face.*)

TOMMY. Here's another thing, Ma. When I was up to the water closet last—

MRS. MILLER. (*sharply*) When you were *where?*

TOMMY. The bathroom.

MRS. MILLER. That's better.

TOMMY. Uncle Sid was snoring like a fog horn—and he's right next to my room. How can I ever get to sleep while he's— (*He is overcome by a jaw-cracking yawn.*)

MRS. MILLER. I guess you'd get to sleep all right if you were inside a fog horn. You run along now. (TOMMY *gives up, grins sleepily, and moves off to bed. As soon as he is off her mind, all her former uneasiness comes back on* MRS. MILLER *tenfold. She sighs, moves restlessly, then finally asks*) What time is it now, Nat?

MILLER. Now, Essie, I just told you a minute ago.

MRS. MILLER. (*resentfully*) I don't see how you can take it so calm! Here it's midnight, you might say, and our Richard still out, and we don't even know where he is.

MILDRED. I hear someone on the piazza. Bet that's him now, Ma.

MRS. MILLER. (*her anxiety immediately turning to relieved anger*) You give him a good piece of your mind, Nat, you hear me! You're too easy with him, that's the whole trouble! The idea of him daring to stay out like this! (*The front door is heard being opened and shut, and someone whistling "Waltz Me Around Again, Willie."*)

MILDRED. No, that isn't Dick. It's Art.

MRS. MILLER. (*her face falling*) Oh. (*A moment later* ARTHUR *enters through the front parlor, whistling softly, half under his breath, looking complacently pleased with himself.*)

MILLER. (*surveys him over his glasses, not with enthusiasm— shortly*) So you're back, eh? We thought it was Richard.

ARTHUR. Is he still out? Where'd he go to?

MILLER. That's just what we'd like to know. You didn't run into him anywhere, did you?

ARTHUR. No. I've been at the Rands' ever since dinner. (*He sits down in the armchair at left of table, rear*) I suppose he sneaked off to the beach to watch the fireworks.

MILLER. (*pretending an assurance he is far from feeling*) Of course. That's what we've been trying to tell your mother, but she insists on worrying her head off.

MRS. MILLER. But if he was going to the fireworks, why wouldn't he say so? He knew we'd let him.

ARTHUR. (*with calm wisdom*) That's easy, Ma. (*He grins superiorly*) Didn't you hear him this morning showing off bawling out the Fourth like an anarchist? He wouldn't want to reneg on that to you—but he'd want to see the old fireworks just the same. (*He adds complacently*) I know. He's at the foolish age.

MILLER. (*stares at* ARTHUR *with ill-concealed astonishment, then grins*) Well, Arthur, by gosh, you make me feel as if I owed you an apology when you talk horse sense like that. (*He turns to his wife, greatly relieved*) Arthur's hit the nail right on the head, I think, Essie. That was what I couldn't figure out—why he—but now it's clear as day.

MRS. MILLER. (*with a sigh*) Well, I hope you're right. But I wish he was home.

ARTHUR. (*takes out his pipe and fills and lights it with solemn gravity*) He oughtn't to be allowed out this late at his age. I wasn't, Fourth or no Fourth—if I remember.

MILLER. (*a twinkle in his eyes*) Don't tax your memory trying to recall those ancient days of your youth. (MILDRED *laughs and* ARTHUR *looks sheepish. But he soon regains his aplomb.*)

ARTHUR. (*importantly*) We had a corking dinner at the Rands'. We had sweetbreads on toast.

MRS. MILLER. (*arising momentarily from her depression*) Just like the Rands to put on airs before you! I never could see anything to sweetbreads. Always taste like soap to me. And no real nourishment to them. I wouldn't have the pesky things on my table! (ARTHUR *again feels sat upon.*)

MILDRED. (*teasingly*) Did you kiss Elsie good night?

ARTHUR. Stop trying to be so darn funny all the time! You give me a pain in the ear!

MILDRED. And that's where she gives me a pain, the stuck-up thing! —thinks she's the whole cheese!

MILLER. (*irritably*) And it's where your everlasting wrangling gives me a pain, you two! Give us a rest! (*There is silence for a moment.*)

MRS. MILLER. (*sighs worriedly again*) I do wish that boy would get home!

MILLER. (*glances at her uneasily, peeks surreptitiously at his watch —then has an inspiration and turns to* ARTHUR) Arthur, what's this I hear about your having such a good singing voice? Rand was telling me he liked nothing better than to hear you sing—said you did every night you were up there. Why don't you ever give us folks at home here a treat?

ARTHUR. (*pleased, but still nursing wounded dignity*) I thought you'd only sit on me.

MRS. MILLER. (*perking up—proudly*) Arthur has a real nice voice. He practises when you're not at home. I didn't know you cared for singing, Nat.

MILLER. Well, I do—nothing better—and when I was a boy I had a fine voice myself and folks used to say I'd ought— (*Then abruptly, mindful of his painful experience with reminiscence at dinner, looking about him guiltily*) Hmm. But don't hide your light under a bushel, Arthur. Why not give us a song or two now? You can play for him, can't you, Mildred?

MILDRED. (*with a toss of her head*) I can play as well as Elsie Rand, at least!

255

ARTHUR. (*ignoring her—clearing his throat importantly*) I've been singing a lot tonight. I don't know if my voice—

MILDRED. (*forgetting her grudge, grabs her brother's hand and tugs at it*) Come on. Don't play modest. You know you're just dying to show off. (*This puts* ARTHUR *off it at once. He snatches his hand away from her angrily.*)

ARTHUR. Let go of me, you! (*Then with surly dignity*) I don't feel like singing tonight, Pa. I will some other time.

MILLER. You let him alone, Mildred! (*He winks at* ARTHUR, *indicating with his eyes and a nod of his head* MRS. MILLER, *who has again sunk into worried brooding. He makes it plain by this pantomime that he wants him to sing to distract his mother's mind.*)

ARTHUR. (*puts aside his pipe and gets up promptly*) Oh—sure, I'll do the best I can. (*He follows* MILDRED *into the front parlor, where he switches on the lights.*)

MILLER. (*to his wife*) It won't keep Tommy awake. Nothing could. And Sid, he'd sleep through an earthquake. (*Then suddenly, looking through the front parlor—grumpily*) Darn it, speak of the devil, here he comes. Well, he's had a good sleep and he'd ought to be sobered up. (LILY *gets up from her chair and looks around her huntedly, as if for a place to hide.* MILLER *says soothingly*) Lily, you just sit down and read your book and don't pay any attention to him. (*She sits down again and bends over her book tensely. From the front parlor comes the tinkling of a piano as* MILDRED *runs over the scales. In the midst of this,* SID *enters through the front parlor. All the effervescence of his jag has worn off and he is now suffering from a bad case of hangover—nervous, sick, a prey to gloomy remorse and bitter feelings of self-loathing and self-pity. His eyes are bloodshot and puffed, his face bloated, the fringe of hair around his baldness tousled and tufty. He sidles into the room guiltily, his eyes shifting about, avoiding looking at anyone.*)

SID. (*forcing a sickly, twitching smile*) Hello.

MILLER. (*considerately casual*) Hello, Sid. Had a good nap? (*Then, as* SID *swallows hard and is about to break into further speech,* MIL-DRED'S *voice comes from the front parlor,* "I haven't played that in ever so long, but I'll try," *and she starts an accompaniment.* MILLER *motions* SID *to be quiet*) Ssshh! Arthur's going to sing for us. (SID *flattens himself against the edge of the bookcase at center, rear, miserably self-conscious and ill-at-ease there but nervously afraid to move anywhere else.* ARTHUR *begins to sing. He has a fairly decent voice but his method is untrained sentimentality to a dripping degree. He sings that old sentimental favorite,* "Then You'll Remember Me." *The effect on his audience is instant.* MILLER *gazes before him with a ruminating melancholy, his face seeming to become gently sorrowful and old.* MRS. MILLER *stares before her, her expression becoming more and more doleful.* LILY *forgets to pretend to read her book but looks over it, her face growing tragically sad. As for* SID, *he is moved to his remorseful, guilt-stricken depths. His mouth pulls down at the corners and he seems about to cry. The song comes to an end.* MILLER *starts, then claps his hands enthusiastically and calls*) Well done, Arthur—well done! Why, you've got a splendid voice! Give us some more! You liked that, didn't you, Essie?

MRS. MILLER. (*dolefully*) Yes—but it's sad—terrible sad.

SID. (*after swallowing hard, suddenly blurts out*) Nat and Essie—and Lily—I—I want to apologize—for coming home—the way I did—there's no excuse—but I didn't mean—

MILLER. (*sympathetically*) Of course, Sid. It's all forgotten.

MRS. MILLER. (*rousing herself—affectionately pitying*) Don't be a goose, Sid. We know how it is with picnics. You forget it. (*His face lights up a bit but his gaze shifts to* LILY *with a mute appeal, hoping for a word from her which is not forthcoming. Her eyes are fixed on her book, her body tense and rigid.*)

SID. (*finally blurts out desperately*) Lily—I'm sorry—about the fireworks. Can you—forgive me? (*But* LILY *remains implacably silent. A stricken look comes over* SID'S *face. In the front parlor* MILDRED *is*

257

heard saying "But I only know the chorus"—and she starts another accompaniment.)

MILLER. (*comes to* SID'S *rescue*) Ssshh! We're going to have another song. Sit down, Sid. (SID, *hanging his head, flees to the farthest corner, left, front, and sits at the end of the sofa, facing front, hunched up, elbows on knees, face in hands, his round eyes childishly wounded and woe-begone.* ARTHUR *sings the popular "Dearie," playing up its sentimental values for all he is worth. The effect on his audience is that of the previous song, intensified—especially upon* SID. *As he finishes,* MILLER *again starts and applauds*) Mighty fine, Arthur! You sang that darned well! Didn't he, Essie?

MRS. MILLER. (*dolefully*) Yes—but I wish he wouldn't sing such sad songs. (*Then, her lips trembling*) Richard's always whistling that.

MILLER. (*hastily—calls*) Give us something cheery, next one, Arthur. You know, just for variety's sake.

SID. (*suddenly turns toward* LILY—*his voice choked with tears—in a passion of self-denunciation*) You're right, Lily!—right not to forgive me!—I'm no good and never will be!—I'm a no-good drunken bum! —you shouldn't even wipe your feet on me!—I'm a dirty, rotten drunk!—no good to myself or anybody else!—if I had any guts I'd kill myself, and good riddance!—but I haven't!—I'm yellow, too!— a yellow, drunken bum! (*He hides his face in his hands and begins to sob like a sick little boy. This is too much for* LILY. *All her bitter hurt and steely resolve to ignore and punish him vanish in a flash, swamped by a pitying love for him. She runs and puts her arm around him—even kisses him tenderly and impulsively on his bald head, and soothes him as if he were a little boy.* MRS. MILLER, *almost equally moved, has half risen to go to her brother, too, but* MILLER *winks and shakes his head vigorously and motions her to sit down.*)

LILY. There! Don't cry, Sid! I can't bear it! Of course, I forgive you! Haven't I always forgiven you? I know you're not to blame— So don't, Sid!

SID. (*lifts a tearful, humbly grateful, pathetic face to her—but a face that the dawn of a cleansed conscience is already beginning to restore to its natural Puckish expression*) Do you really forgive me— I know I don't deserve it—can you really—?

LILY. (*gently*) I told you I did, Sid—and I do.

SID. (*kisses her hand humbly, like a big puppy licking it*) Thanks, Lily. I can't tell you— (*In the front parlor,* ARTHUR *begins to sing rollickingly "Waiting at the Church," and after the first line or two* MILDRED *joins in.* SID's *face lights up with appreciation and, automatically, he begins to tap one foot in time, still holding fast to* LILY's *hand. When they come to "sent around a note, this is what she wrote,"* he can no longer resist, but joins in a shaky bawl*) "Can't get away to marry you today, My wife won't let me!" (*As the song finishes, the two in the other room laugh.* MILLER *and* SID *laugh.* LILY *smiles at* SID's *laughter. Only* MRS. MILLER *remains dolefully preoccupied, as if she hadn't heard.*)

MILLER. That's fine, Arthur and Mildred. That's darned good.

SID. (*turning to* LILY *enthusiastically*) You ought to hear Vesta Victoria sing that! Gosh, she's great! I heard her at Hammerstein's Victoria—you remember, that trip I made to New York.

LILY. (*her face suddenly tired and sad again—for her memory of certain aspects of that trip is the opposite from what he would like her to recall at this moment—gently disengaging her hand from his— with a hopeless sigh*) Yes, I remember, Sid. (*He is overcome momentarily by guilty confusion. She goes quietly and sits down in her chair again. In the front parlor, from now on,* MILDRED *keeps starting to run over popular tunes but always gets stuck and turns to another.*)

MRS. MILLER. (*suddenly*) What time is it now, Nat? (*Then without giving him a chance to answer*) Oh, I'm getting worried something dreadful, Nat! You don't know what might have happened to Richard! You read in the papers every day about boys getting run over by automobiles.

LILY. Oh, don't say that, Essie!

MILLER. (*sharply, to conceal his own reawakened apprehension*)
Don't get to imagining things, now!

MRS. MILLER. Well, why couldn't it happen, with everyone that owns
one out tonight, and lots of those driving, drunk? Or he might have
gone down to the beach dock and fallen overboard! (*On the verge of
hysteria*) Oh, I know something dreadful's happened! And you can
sit there listening to songs and laughing as if— Why don't you do
something? Why don't you go out and find him? (*She bursts into
tears.*)

LILY. (*comes to her quickly and puts her arm around her*) Essie,
you mustn't worry so! You'll make yourself sick! Richard's all right.
I've got a feeling in my bones he's all right.

MILDRED. (*comes hurrying in from the front parlor*) What's the
trouble? (ARTHUR *appears in the doorway beside her. She goes to her
mother and also puts an arm around her*) Ah, don't cry, Ma! Dick'll
turn up in a minute or two, wait and see!

ARTHUR. Sure, he will!

MILLER. (*has gotten to his feet, frowning—soberly*) I was going out
to look—if he wasn't back by twelve sharp. That'd be the time it'd
take him to walk from the beach if he left after the last car. But I'll
go now, if it'll ease your mind. I'll take the auto and drive out the
beach road—and likely pick him up on the way. (*He has taken his
collar and tie from where they hang from one corner of the bookcase
at rear, center, and is starting to put them on*) You better come with
me, Arthur.

ARTHUR. Sure thing, Pa. (*Suddenly he listens and says*) Ssshh!
There's someone on the piazza now—coming around to this door,
too. That must be him. No one else would—

MRS. MILLER. Oh, thank God, thank God!

MILLER. (*with a sheepish smile*) Darn him! I've a notion to give
him hell for worrying us all like this. (*The screen door is pushed violently open and* RICHARD *lurches in and stands swaying a little, blinking his eyes in the light. His face is a pasty pallor, shining with*

perspiration, and his eyes are glassy. The knees of his trousers are dirty, one of them torn from the sprawl on the sidewalk he had taken, following the BARTENDER's *kick. They all gape at him, too paralyzed for a moment to say anything.*)

MRS. MILLER. Oh, God, what's happened to him! He's gone crazy! Richard!

SID. (*the first to regain presence of mind—with a grin*) Crazy, nothing. He's only soused!

ARTHUR. He's drunk, that's what! (*Then shocked and condemning*) You've got your nerve! You fresh kid! We'll take that out of you when we get you down to Yale!

RICHARD. (*with a wild gesture of defiance—maudlinly dramatic*)

> "Yesterday this Day's Madness did prepare
> Tomorrow's Silence, Triumph, or Despair.
> Drink! for—"

MILLER. (*his face grown stern and angry, takes a threatening step toward him*) Richard! How dare—!

MRS. MILLER. (*hysterically*) Don't you strike him, Nat! Don't you—!

SID. (*grabbing his arm*) Steady, Nat! Keep your temper! No good bawling him out now! He don't know what he's doing!

MILLER. (*controlling himself and looking a bit ashamed*) All right —you're right, Sid.

RICHARD. (*drunkenly glorying in the sensation he is creating—recites with dramatic emphasis*) "And then—I will come—with vine leaves in my hair!" (*He laughs with a double-dyed sardonicism.*)

MRS. MILLER. (*staring at him as if she couldn't believe her eyes*) Richard! You're intoxicated!—you bad, wicked boy, you!

RICHARD. (*forces a wicked leer to his lips and quotes with ponderous mockery*) "Fancy that, Hedda!" (*Then suddenly his whole expression changes, his pallor takes on a greenish, sea-sick tinge, his eyes seem to be turned inward uneasily—and, all pose gone, he calls to his mother appealingly, like a sick little boy*) Ma! I feel—rotten! (MRS. MILLER *gives a cry and starts to go to him, but* SID *steps in her way.*)

SID. You let me take care of him, Essie. I know this game backwards.

MILLER. (*putting his arm around his wife*) Yes, you leave him to Sid.

SID. (*his arm around* RICHARD—*leading him off through the front parlor*) Come on, Old Sport! Upstairs we go! Your old Uncle Sid'll fix you up. He's the kid that wrote the book!

MRS. MILLER. (*staring after them—still aghast*) Oh, it's too terrible! Imagine our Richard! And did you hear him talking about some Hedda? Oh, I know he's been with one of those bad women, I know he has—my Richard! (*She hides her face on* MILLER's *shoulder and sobs heartbrokenly.*)

MILLER. (*a tired, harassed, deeply worried look on his face—soothing her*) Now, now, you mustn't get to imagining such things! You mustn't, Essie! (LILY *and* MILDRED *and* ARTHUR *are standing about awkwardly with awed, shocked faces.*)

CURTAIN

ACT FOUR—SCENE ONE

SCENE—*The same—Sitting-room of the Miller house—about* **one** *o'clock in the afternoon of the following day.*

As the curtain rises, the family, with the exception of RICHARD, *are discovered coming in through the back parlor from dinner in the dining-room.* MILLER *and his wife come first. His face is set in an expression of frowning severity.* MRS. MILLER'S *face is drawn and worried. She has evidently had no rest yet from a sleepless, tearful night.* SID *is himself again, his expression as innocent as if nothing had occurred the previous day that remotely concerned him. And, outside of eyes that are bloodshot and nerves that are shaky, he shows no aftereffects except that he is terribly sleepy.* LILY *is gently sad and depressed.* ARTHUR *is self-consciously a virtuous young man against whom nothing can be said.* MILDRED *and* TOMMY *are subdued, covertly watching their father.*

They file into the sitting-room in silence and then stand around uncertainly, as if each were afraid to be the first to sit down. The atmosphere is as stiltedly grave as if they were attending a funeral service. Their eyes keep fixed on the head of the house, who has gone to the window at right and is staring out frowningly, savagely chewing a toothpick.

MILLER. (*finally—irritably*) Damn it, I'd ought to be back at the office putting in some good licks! I've a whole pile of things that have got to be done today!

MRS. MILLER. (*accusingly*) You don't mean to tell me you're going back without seeing him? It's your duty—!

MILLER. (*exasperatedly*) 'Course I'm not! I wish you'd stop jumping to conclusions! What else did I come home for, I'd like to know?

Do I usually come way back here for dinner on a busy day? I was only wishing this hadn't come up—just at this particular time. (*He ends up very lamely and is irritably conscious of the fact.*)

TOMMY. (*who has been fidgeting restlessly—unable to bear the suspense a moment longer*) What is it Dick done? Why is everyone scared to tell me?

MILLER. (*seizes this as an escape valve—turns and fixes his youngest son with a stern forbidding eye*) Young man, I've never spanked you yet, but that don't mean I never will! Seems to me that you've been just itching for it lately! You keep your mouth shut till you're spoken to—or I warn you something's going to happen!

MRS. MILLER. Yes, Tommy, you keep still and don't bother your pa. (*Then warningly to her husband*) Careful what you say, Nat. Little pitchers have big ears.

MILLER. (*peremptorily*) You kids skedaddle—all of you. Why are you always hanging around the house? Go out and play in the yard, or take a walk, and get some fresh air. (MILDRED *takes* TOMMY's *hand and leads him out through the front parlor.* ARTHUR *hangs back, as if the designation "kids" couldn't possibly apply to him. His father notices this—impatiently*) You, too, Arthur. (ARTHUR *goes out with a stiff, wounded dignity.*)

LILY. (*tactfully*) I think I'll go for a walk, too. (*She goes out through the front parlor.* SID *makes a movement as if to follow her.*)

MILLER. I'd like you to stay, Sid—for a while, anyway.

SID. Sure. (*He sits down in the rocking-chair at right, rear, of table and immediately yawns*) Gosh, I'm dead. Don't know what's the matter with me today. Can't seem to keep awake.

MILLER. (*with caustic sarcasm*) Maybe that demon chowder you drank at the picnic poisoned you! (SID *looks sheepish and forces a grin. Then* MILLER *turns to his wife with the air of one who determinedly faces the unpleasant*) Where is Richard?

MRS. MILLER. (*flusteredly*) He's still in bed. I made him stay in bed to punish him—and I thought he ought to, anyway, after being so sick. But he says he feels all right.

SID. (*with another yawn*) 'Course he does. When you're young you can stand anything without it feazing you. Why, I remember when I could come down on the morning after, fresh as a daisy, and eat a breakfast of pork chops and fried onions and— (*He stops guiltily.*)

MILLER. (*bitingly*) I suppose that was before eating lobster shells had ruined your iron constitution!

MRS. MILLER. (*regards her brother severely*) If I was in your shoes, I'd keep still! (*Then turning to her husband*) Richard must be feeling better. He ate all the dinner I sent up, Norah says.

MILLER. I thought you weren't going to give him any dinner—to punish him.

MRS. MILLER. (*guiltily*) Well—in his weakened condition—I thought it best— (*Then defensively*) But you needn't think I haven't punished him. I've given him pieces of my mind he won't forget in a hurry. And I've kept reminding him his real punishment was still to come—that you were coming home to dinner on purpose—and then he'd learn that you could be terrible stern when he did such awful things.

MILLER. (*stirs uncomfortably*) Hmm!

MRS. MILLER. And that's just what it's your duty to do—punish him good and hard! The idea of him daring— (*Then hastily*) But you be careful how you go about it, Nat. Remember he's like you inside— too sensitive for his own good. And he never would have done it, I know, if it hadn't been for that darned little dunce, Muriel, and her numbskull father—and then all of us teasing him and hurting his feelings all day—and then you lost your temper and were so sharp with him right after dinner before he went out.

MILLER. (*resentfully*) I see this is going to work round to where it's all my fault!

MRS. MILLER. Now, I didn't say that, did I? Don't go losing your temper again. And here's another thing. You know as well as I,

265

Richard would never have done such a thing alone. Why, he wouldn't know how! He must have been influenced and led by someone.

MILLER. Yes, I believe that. Did you worm out of him who it was? (*Then angrily*) By God, I'll make whoever it was regret it!

MRS. MILLER. No, he wouldn't admit there was anyone. (*Then triumphantly*) But there is one thing I did worm out of him—and I can tell you it relieved my mind more'n anything. You know, I was afraid he'd been with one of those bad women. Well, turns out there wasn't any Hedda. She was just out of those books he's been reading. He swears he's never known a Hedda in his life. And I believe him. Why, he seemed disgusted with me for having such a notion. (*Then lamely*) So somehow—I can't kind of feel it's all as bad as I thought it was. (*Then quickly and indignantly*) But it's bad enough, goodness knows—and you punish him good just the same. The idea of a boy his age—! Shall I go up now and tell him to get dressed, you want to see him?

MILLER. (*helplessly—and irritably*) Yes! I can't waste all day listening to you!

MRS. MILLER. (*worriedly*) Now you keep your temper, Nat, remember! (*She goes out through the front parlor.*)

MILLER. Darn women, anyway! They always get you mixed up. Their minds simply don't know what logic is! (*Then he notices that* SID *is dozing—sharply*) Sid!

SID. (*blinking—mechanically*) I'll take the same. (*Then hurriedly*) What'd you say, Nat?

MILLER. (*caustically*) What I didn't say was what'll you have. (*Irritably*) Do you want to be of some help, or don't you? Then keep awake and try and use your brains! This is a damned sight more serious than Essie has any idea! She thinks there weren't any girls mixed up with Richard's spree last night—but I happen to know there were! (*He takes a letter from his pocket*) Here's a note a woman left with one of the boys downstairs at the office this morning—didn't ask to see me, just said give me this. He'd never seen her before—

266

said she looked like a tart. (*He has opened the letter and reads*) "Your son got the booze he drank last night at the Pleasant Beach House. The bartender there knew he was under age but served him just the same. He thought it was a good joke to get him soused. If you have any guts you will run that bastard out of town." Well, what do you think of that? It's a woman's handwriting—not signed, of course.

SID. She's one of the babies, all right—judging from her elegant language.

MILLER. See if you recognize the handwriting.

SID. (*with a reproachful look*) Nat, I resent the implication that I correspond with all the tramps around this town. (*Looking at the letter*) No, I don't know who this one could be. (*Handing the letter back*) But I deduce that the lady had a run-in with the barkeep and wants revenge.

MILLER. (*grimly*) And I deduce that before that she must have picked up Richard—or how would she know who he was?—and took him to this dive.

SID. Maybe. The Pleasant Beach House is nothing but a bed house— (*Quickly*) At least, so I've been told.

MILLER. That's just the sort of damned fool thing he might do to spite Muriel, in the state of mind he was in—pick up some tart. And she'd try to get him drunk so—

SID. Yes, it might have happened like that—and it might not. How're we ever going to prove it? Everyone at the Pleasant Beach will lie their heads off.

MILLER. (*simply and proudly*) Richard won't lie.

SID. Well, don't blame him if he don't remember everything that happened last night. (*Then sincerely concerned*) I hope you're wrong, Nat. That kind of baby is dangerous for a kid like Dick—in more ways than one. You know what I mean.

MILLER. (*frowningly*) Yep—and that's just what's got me worried. Damn it, I've got to have a straight talk with him—about women and all those things. I ought to have long ago.

sid. Yes. You ought.

miller. I've tried to a couple of times. I did it all right with Wilbur and Lawrence and Arthur, when it came time—but, hell, with Richard I always get sort of ashamed of myself and can't get started right. You feel, in spite of all his bold talk out of books, that he's so darned innocent inside.

sid. I know. I wouldn't like the job. (*Then after a pause—curiously*) How were you figuring to punish him for his sins?

miller. (*frowning*) To be honest with you, Sid, I'm damned if I know. All depends on what I feel about what he feels when I first size him up—and then it'll be like shooting in the dark.

sid. If I didn't know you so well, I'd say don't be too hard on him. (*He smiles a little bitterly*) If you remember, I was always getting punished—and see what a lot of good it did me!

miller. (*kindly*) Oh, there's lots worse than you around, so don't take to boasting. (*Then, at a sound from the front parlor—with a sigh*) Well, here comes the Bad Man, I guess.

sid. (*getting up*) I'll beat it. (*But it is* mrs. miller *who appears in the doorway, looking guilty and defensive.* sid *sits down again.*)

mrs. miller. I'm sorry, Nat—but he was sound asleep and I didn't have the heart to wake him. I waited for him to wake up but he didn't.

miller. (*concealing a relief of which he is ashamed—exasperatedly*) Well, I'll be double damned! If you're not the—

mrs. miller. (*defensively aggressive*) Now don't lose your temper at me, Nat Miller! You know as well as I do he needs all the sleep he can get today—after last night's ructions! Do you want him to be taken down sick? And what difference does it make to you anyway? You can see him when you come home for supper, can't you? My goodness, I never saw you so savage-tempered! You'd think you couldn't bear waiting to punish him!

miller. (*outraged*) Well, I'll be eternally— (*Then suddenly he laughs*) No use talking, you certainly take the cake! But you know darned well I told you I'm not coming home to supper tonight. I've got a date with Jack Lawson that may mean a lot of new advertising and it's important.

MRS. MILLER. Then you can see him when you do come home.

MILLER. (*covering his evident relief at this respite with a fuming manner*) All right! All right! I give up! I'm going back to the office. (*He starts for the front parlor*) Bring a man all the way back here on a busy day and then you— No consideration— (*He disappears, and a moment later the front door is heard shutting behind him.*)

MRS. MILLER. Well! I never saw Nat so bad-tempered.

SID. (*with a chuckle*) Bad temper, nothing. He's so tickled to get out of it for a while he can't see straight!

MRS. MILLER. (*with a sniff*) I hope I know him better than you. (*Then fussing about the room, setting this and that in place, while* SID *yawns drowsily and blinks his eyes*) Sleeping like a baby—so innocent-looking. You'd think butter wouldn't melt in his mouth. It all goes to show you never can tell by appearances—not even when it's your own child. The idea!

SID. (*drowsily*) Oh, Dick's all right, Essie. Stop worrying.

MRS. MILLER. (*with a sniff*) Of course, you'd say that. I suppose you'll have him out with you painting the town red the next thing! (*As she is talking,* RICHARD *appears in the doorway from the sitting-room. He shows no ill effects from his experience the night before. In fact, he looks surprisingly healthy. He is dressed in old clothes that look as if they had been hurriedly flung on. His expression is one of hang-dog guilt mingled with a defensive defiance.*)

RICHARD. (*with self-conscious unconcern, ignoring his mother*) Hello, Sid.

MRS. MILLER. (*whirls on him*) What are you doing here, Young Man? I thought you were asleep! Seems to me you woke up pretty quick—just after your pa left the house!

RICHARD. (*sulkily*) I wasn't asleep. I heard you in the room.

MRS. MILLER. (*outraged*) Do you mean to say you were deliberately deceiving—

RICHARD. I wasn't deceiving. You didn't ask if I was asleep.

MRS. MILLER. It amounts to the same thing and you know it! It isn't enough your wickedness last night, but now you have to take to lying!

RICHARD. I wasn't lying, Ma. If you'd asked if I was asleep I'd have said no.

MRS. MILLER. I've a good mind to send you straight back to bed and make you stay there!

RICHARD. Ah, what for, Ma? It was only giving me a headache, lying there.

MRS. MILLER. If you've got a headache, I guess you know it doesn't come from that! And imagine me standing there, and feeling sorry for you, like a fool—even having a run-in with your pa because— But you wait till he comes back tonight! If you don't catch it!

RICHARD. (*sulkily*) I don't care.

MRS. MILLER. You don't care? You talk as if you weren't sorry for what you did last night!

RICHARD. (*defiantly*) I'm not sorry.

MRS. MILLER. Richard! You ought to be ashamed! I'm beginning to think you're hardened in wickedness, that's what!

RICHARD. (*with bitter despondency*) I'm not sorry because I don't care a darn what I did, or what's done to me, or anything about anything! I won't do it again—

MRS. MILLER. (*seizing on this to relent a bit*) Well, I'm glad to hear you say that, anyway!

RICHARD. But that's not because I think it was wicked or any such old-fogy moral notion, but because it wasn't any fun. It didn't make me happy and funny like it does Uncle Sid—

SID. (*drowsily*) What's that? Who's funny?

RICHARD. (*ignoring him*) It only made me sadder—and sick—so I don't see any sense in it.

MRS. MILLER. Now you're talking sense! That's a good boy.

RICHARD. But I'm not sorry I tried it once—curing the soul by means of the senses, as Oscar Wilde says. (*Then with despairing pessimism*) But what does it matter what I do or don't do? Life is all a stupid farce! I'm through with it! (*With a sinister smile*) It's lucky there aren't any of General Gabler's pistols around—or you'd see if I'd stand it much longer!

MRS. MILLER. (*worriedly impressed by this threat—but pretending scorn*) I don't know anything about General Gabler—I suppose that's more of those darned books—but you're a silly gabbler yourself when you talk that way!

RICHARD. (*darkly*) That's how little you know about me.

MRS. MILLER. (*giving in to her worry*) I wish you wouldn't say those terrible things—about life and pistols! You don't want to worry me to death, do you?

RICHARD. (*reassuringly stoical now*) You needn't worry, Ma. It was only my despair talking. But I'm not a coward. I'll face—my fate.

MRS. MILLER. (*stands looking at him puzzledly—then gives it up with a sigh*) Well, all I can say is you're the queerest boy I ever did hear of! (*Then solicitously, putting her hand on his forehead*) How's your headache? Do you want me to get you some Bromo Seltzer?

RICHARD. (*taken down—disgustedly*) No, I don't! Aw, Ma, you don't understand anything!

MRS. MILLER. Well, I understand this much: It's your liver, that's what! You'll take a good dose of salts tomorrow morning, and no nonsense about it! (*Then suddenly*) My goodness, I wonder what time it's getting to be. I've got to go upstreet. (*She goes to the front-parlor doorway—then turns*) You stay here, Richard, you hear? Remember, you're not allowed out today—for a punishment. (*She hurries away.* RICHARD *sits in tragic gloom.* SID, *without opening his eyes, speaks to him drowsily.*)

SID. Well, how's my fellow Rum Pot, as good old Dowie calls us? Got a head?

RICHARD. (*startled—sheepishly*) Aw, don't go dragging that up, Uncle Sid. I'm never going to be such a fool again, I tell you.

SID. (*with drowsy cynicism—not unmixed with bitterness at the end*) Seems to me I've heard someone say that before. Who could it have been, I wonder? Why, if it wasn't Sid Davis! Yes, sir, I've heard him say that very thing a thousand times, must be. But then he's always fooling; you can't take a word he says seriously; he's a card, that Sid is!

RICHARD. (*darkly*) I was desperate, Uncle—even if she wasn't worth it. I was wounded to the heart.

SID. I like to the quick better myself—more stylish. (*Then sadly*) But you're right. Love is hell on a poor sucker. Don't I know it? (RICHARD *is disgusted and disdains to reply.* SID's *chin sinks on his chest and he begins to breathe noisily, fast asleep.* RICHARD *glances at him with aversion. There is a sound of someone on the porch and the screen door is opened and* MILDRED *enters. She smiles on seeing her uncle, then gives a start on seeing* RICHARD.)

MILDRED. Hello! Are you allowed up?

RICHARD. Of course, I'm allowed up.

MILDRED. (*comes and sits in her father's chair at right, front, of table*) How did Pa punish you?

RICHARD. He didn't. He went back to the office without seeing me.

MILDRED. Well, you'll catch it later. (*Then rebukingly*) And you ought to. If you'd ever seen how awful you looked last night!

RICHARD. Ah, forget it, can't you?

MILDRED. Well, are you ever going to do it again, that's what I want to know.

RICHARD. What's that to you?

MILDRED. (*with suppressed excitement*) Well, if you don't solemnly swear you won't—then I won't give you something I've got for you.

RICHARD. Don't try to kid me. You haven't got anything.

MILDRED. I have, too.

RICHARD. What?

272

MILDRED. Wouldn't you like to know! I'll give you three guesses.

RICHARD. (*with disdainful dignity*) Don't bother me. I'm in no mood to play riddles with kids!

MILDRED. Oh, well, if you're going to get snippy! Anyway you haven't promised yet.

RICHARD. (*a prey to keen curiosity now*) I promise. What is it?

MILDRED. What would you like best in the world?

RICHARD. I don't know. What?

MILDRED. And you pretend to be in love! If I told Muriel that!

RICHARD. (*breathlessly*) Is it—from her?

MILDRED. (*laughing*) Well, I guess it's a shame to keep you guessing. Yes. It is from her. I was walking past her place just now when I saw her waving from their parlor window, and I went up and she said give this to Dick, and she didn't have a chance to say anything else because her mother called her and said she wasn't allowed to have company. So I took it—and here it is. (*She gives him a letter folded many times into a tiny square.* RICHARD *opens it with a trembling eagerness and reads.* MILDRED *watches him curiously—then sighs affectedly*) Gee, it must be nice to be in love like you are—all with one person.

RICHARD. (*his eyes shining*) Gee, Mid, do you know what she says —that she didn't mean a word in that other letter. Her old man made her write it. And she loves me and only me and always will, no matter how they punish her!

MILDRED. My! I'd never think she had that much spunk.

RICHARD. Huh! You don't know her! Think I could fall in love with a girl that was afraid to say her soul's her own? I should say not! (*Then more gleefully still*) And she's going to try and sneak out and meet me tonight. She says she thinks she can do it. (*Then suddenly feeling this enthusiasm before* MILDRED *is entirely the wrong note for a cynical pessimist—with an affected bitter laugh*) Ha! I knew darned well she couldn't hold out—that she'd ask to see me again. (*He misquotes cynically*) "Women never know when the curtain has fallen. They always want another act."

MILDRED. Is that so, Smarty?

RICHARD. (*as if he were weighing the matter*) I don't know whether I'll consent to keep this date or not.

MILDRED. Well, I know! You're not allowed out, you silly! So you can't!

RICHARD. (*dropping all pretense—defiantly*) Can't I, though! You wait and see if I can't! I'll see her tonight if it's the last thing I ever do! I don't care how I'm punished after!

MILDRED. (*admiringly*) Goodness! I never thought you had such nerve!

RICHARD. You promise to keep your face shut, Mid—until after I've left—then you can tell Pa and Ma where I've gone—I mean, if they're worrying I'm off like last night.

MILDRED. All right. Only you've got to do something for me when I ask.

RICHARD. 'Course I will. (*Then excitedly*) And say, Mid! Right now's the best chance for me to get away—while everyone's out! Ma'll be coming back soon and she'll keep watching me like a cat— (*He starts for the back parlor*) I'm going. I'll sneak out the back.

MILDRED. (*excitedly*) But what'll you do till nighttime? It's ages to wait.

RICHARD. What do I care how long I wait! (*Intensely sincere now*) I'll think of her—and dream! I'd wait a million years and never mind it—for her! (*He gives his sister a superior scornful glance*) The trouble with you is, you don't understand what love means! (*He disappears through the back parlor.* MILDRED *looks after him admiringly.* SID *puffs and begins to snore peacefully.*)

CURTAIN

ACT FOUR—SCENE TWO

Scene—*A strip of beach along the harbor. At left, a bank of dark earth, running half-diagonally back along the beach, marking the line where the sand of the beach ends and fertile land begins. The top of the bank is grassy and the trailing boughs of willow trees extend out over it and over a part of the beach. At left, front, is a path leading up the bank, between the willows. On the beach, at center, front, a white, flat-bottomed rowboat is drawn up, its bow about touching the bank, the painter trailing up the bank, evidently made fast to the trunk of a willow. Halfway down the sky, at rear, left, the crescent of the new moon casts a soft, mysterious, caressing light over everything. The sand of the beach shimmers palely. The forward half (left of center) of the rowboat is in the deep shadow cast by the willow, the stern section is in moonlight. In the distance, the orchestra of a summer hotel can be heard very faintly at intervals.*

RICHARD *is discovered sitting sideways on the gunwale of the rowboat near the stern. He is facing left, watching the path. He is in a great state of anxious expectancy, squirming about uncomfortably on the narrow gunwale, kicking at the sand restlessly, twirling his straw hat, with a bright-colored band in stripes, around on his finger.*

RICHARD. (*thinking aloud*) Must be nearly nine. . . . I can hear the Town Hall clock strike, it's so still tonight . . . Gee, I'll bet Ma had a fit when she found out I'd sneaked out . . . I'll catch hell when I get back, but it'll be worth it . . . if only Muriel turns up . . . she didn't say for certain she could . . . gosh, I wish she'd come! . . . am I sure she wrote nine? . . . (*He puts the straw hat on the seat amidships and pulls the folded letter out of his pocket and peers at it in the moonlight*) Yes, it's nine, all right. (*He starts to put the note back in his pocket, then stops and kisses it—then shoves it away*

275

hastily, sheepish, looking around him shamefacedly, as if afraid he were being observed) Aw, that's silly . . . no, it isn't either . . . not when you're really in love. . . . (*He jumps to his feet restlessly*) Darn it, I wish she'd show up! . . . think of something else . . . that'll make the time pass quicker . . . where was I this time last night? . . . waiting outside the Pleasant Beach House . . . Belle . . . ah, forget her! . . . now, when Muriel's coming . . . that's a fine time to think of—! . . . but you hugged and kissed her . . . not until I was drunk, I didn't . . . and then it was all showing off . . . darned fool! . . . and I didn't go upstairs with her . . . even if she was pretty . . . aw, she wasn't pretty . . . she was all painted up . . . she was just a whore . . . she was everything dirty . . . Muriel's a million times prettier anyway . . . Muriel and I will go upstairs . . . when we're married . . . but that will be beautiful . . . but I oughtn't even to think of that yet . . . it's not right . . . I'd never— now . . . and she'd never . . . she's a decent girl . . . I couldn't love her if she wasn't . . . but after we're married. . . . (*He gives a little shiver of passionate longing—then resolutely turns his mind away from these improper, almost desecrating thoughts*) That damned barkeep kicking me . . . I'll bet you if I hadn't been drunk I'd have given him one good punch in the nose, even if he could have licked me after! . . . (*Then with a shiver of shamefaced revulsion and self-disgust*) Aw, you deserved a kick in the pants . . . making such a darned slob of yourself . . . reciting the Ballad of Reading Gaol to those lowbrows! . . . you must have been a fine sight when you got home . . . having to be put to bed and getting sick! . . . Phaw! . . . (*He squirms disgustedly*) Think of something else, can't you? . . . recite something . . . see if you remember . . .

> "Nay, let us walk from fire unto fire
> From passionate pain to deadlier delight—
> I am too young to live without desire,
> Too young art thou to waste this summernight—"

. . . gee, that's a peach! . . . I'll have to memorize the rest and recite it to Muriel the next time. . . . I wish I could write poetry . . . about her and me. . . . (*He sighs and stares around him at the night*) Gee, it's beautiful tonight . . . as if it was a special night . . . for me and Muriel. . . . Gee, I love tonight. . . . I love the sand, and the trees, and the grass, and the water and the sky, and the moon . . . it's all in me and I'm in it . . . God, it's so beautiful! (*He stands staring at the moon with a rapt face. From the distance the Town Hall clock begins to strike. This brings him back to earth with a start*) There's nine now. . . . (*He peers at the path apprehensively*) I don't see her . . . she must have got caught. . . . (*Almost tearfully*) Gee, I hate to go home and catch hell . . . without having seen her! . . . (*Then calling a manly cynicism to his aid*) Aw, who ever heard of a woman ever being on time. . . . I ought to know enough about life by this time not to expect . . . (*Then with sudden excitement*) There she comes now. . . . Gosh! (*He heaves a huge sigh of relief—then recites dramatically to himself, his eyes on the approaching figure*)

"*And lo my love, mine own soul's heart, more dear
Than mine own soul, more beautiful than God,
Who hath my being between the hands of her—*'

(*Then hastily*) Mustn't let her know I'm so tickled. . . . I ought to be mad about that first letter, anyway . . . if women are too sure of you, they treat you like slaves . . . let her suffer, for a change. . . . (*He starts to stroll around with exaggerated carelessness, turning his back on the path, hands in pockets, whistling with insouciance "Waiting at the Church."*

(MURIEL MC COMBER *enters from down the path, left front. She is fifteen, going on sixteen. She is a pretty girl with a plump, graceful little figure, fluffy, light-brown hair, big naïve wondering dark eyes, a round dimpled face, a melting drawly voice. Just now she is in a great thrilled state of timid adventurousness. She hesitates in the*

277

AH, WILDERNESS!

shadow at the foot of the path, waiting for RICHARD *to see her; but he resolutely goes on whistling with back turned, and she has to call him.*)

MURIEL. Oh, Dick.

RICHARD. (*turns around with an elaborate simulation of being disturbed in the midst of profound meditation*) Oh, hello. Is it nine already? Gosh, time passes—when you're thinking.

MURIEL. (*coming toward him as far as the edge of the shadow—disappointedly*) I thought you'd be waiting right here at the end of the path. I'll bet you'd forgotten I was even coming.

RICHARD. (*strolling a little toward her but not too far—carelessly*) No, I hadn't forgotten, honest. But I got to thinking about life.

MURIEL. You might think of me for a change, after all the risk I've run to see you! (*Hesitating timidly on the edge of the shadow*) Dick! You come here to me. I'm afraid to go out in that bright moonlight where anyone might see me.

RICHARD. (*coming toward her—scornfully*) Aw, there you go again—always scared of life!

MURIEL. (*indignantly*) Dick Miller, I do think you've got an awful nerve to say that after all the risks I've run making this date and then sneaking out! You didn't take the trouble to sneak any letter to me, I notice!

RICHARD. No, because after your first letter, I thought everything was dead and past between us.

MURIEL. And I'll bet you didn't care one little bit! (*On the verge of humiliated tears*) Oh, I was a fool ever to come here! I've got a good notion to go right home and never speak to you again! (*She half turns back toward the path.*)

RICHARD. (*frightened—immediately becomes terribly sincere—grabbing her hand*) Aw, don't go, Muriel! Please! I didn't mean anything like that, honest, I didn't! Gee, if you knew how broken-hearted I was by that first letter, and how darned happy your second letter made me—!

278

MURIEL. (*happily relieved—but appreciates she has the upper hand now and doesn't relent at once*) I don't believe you.

RICHARD. You ask Mid how happy I was. She can prove it.

MURIEL. She'd say anything you told her to. I don't care anything about what she'd say. It's you. You've got to swear to me—

RICHARD. I swear!

MURIEL. (*demurely*) Well then, all right, I'll believe you.

RICHARD. (*his eyes on her face lovingly—genuine adoration in his voice*) Gosh, you're pretty tonight, Muriel! It seems ages since we've been together! If you knew how I've suffered—!

MURIEL. I did, too.

RICHARD. (*unable to resist falling into his tragic literary pose for a moment*) The despair in my soul— (*He recites dramatically*) "Something was dead in each of us, And what was dead was Hope!" That was me! My hope of happiness was dead! (*Then with sincere boyish fervor*) Gosh, Muriel, it sure is wonderful to be with you again! (*He puts a timid arm around her awkwardly.*)

MURIEL. (*shyly*) I'm glad—it makes you happy. I'm happy, too.

RICHARD. Can't I—won't you let me kiss you—now? Please! (*He bends his face toward hers.*)

MURIEL. (*ducking her head away—timidly*) No. You mustn't. Don't—

RICHARD. Aw, why can't I?

MURIEL. Because—I'm afraid.

RICHARD. (*discomfited—taking his arm from around her—a bit sulky and impatient with her*) Aw, that's what you always say! You're always so afraid! Aren't you ever going to let me?

MURIEL. I will—sometime.

RICHARD. When?

MURIEL. Soon, maybe.

RICHARD. Tonight, will you?

MURIEL. (*coyly*) I'll see.

RICHARD. Promise?

MURIEL. I promise—maybe.

RICHARD. All right. You remember you've promised. (*Then coaxingly*) Aw, don't let's stand here. Come on out and we can sit down in the boat.

MURIEL. (*hesitantly*) It's so bright out there.

RICHARD. No one'll see. You know there's never anyone around here at night.

MURIEL. (*illogically*) I know there isn't. That's why I thought it would be the best place. But there might be someone.

RICHARD. (*taking her hand and tugging at it gently*) There isn't a soul. (MURIEL *steps out a little and looks up and down fearfully*. RICHARD *goes on insistently*) Aw, what's the use of a moon if you can't see it!

MURIEL. But it's only a new moon. That's not much to look at.

RICHARD. But I want to see you. I can't here in the shadow. I want to—drink in—all your beauty.

MURIEL. (*can't resist this*) Well, all right—only I can't stay only a few minutes. (*She lets him lead her toward the stern of the boat.*)

RICHARD. (*pleadingly*) Aw, you can stay a little while, can't you? Please! (*He helps her in and she settles herself in the stern seat of the boat, facing diagonally left front.*)

MURIEL. A little while. (*He sits beside her*) But I've got to be home in bed again pretending to be asleep by ten o'clock. That's the time Pa and Ma come up to bed, as regular as clock work, and Ma always looks into my room.

RICHARD. But you'll have oodles of time to do that.

MURIEL. (*excitedly*) Dick, you have no idea what I went through to get here tonight! My, but it was exciting! You know Pa's punishing me by sending me to bed at eight sharp, and I had to get all undressed and into bed 'cause at half-past he sends Ma up to make sure I've obeyed, and she came up, and I pretended to be asleep, and she went down again, and I got up and dressed in such a hurry—I must look a sight, don't I?

280

AH, WILDERNESS!

RICHARD. You do not! You look wonderful!

MURIEL. And then I sneaked down the back stairs. And the pesky old stairs squeaked, and my heart was in my mouth, I was so scared, and then I sneaked out through the back yard, keeping in the dark under the trees, and— My, but it was exciting! Dick, you don't realize how I've been punished for your sake. Pa's been so mean and nasty, I've almost hated him!

RICHARD. And you don't realize what I've been through for you— and what I'm in for—for sneaking out— (*Then darkly*) And for what I did last night—what your letter made me do!

MURIEL. (*made terribly curious by his ominous tone*) What did my letter make you do?

RICHARD. (*beginning to glory in this*) It's too long a story—and let the dead past bury its dead. (*Then with real feeling*) Only it isn't past, I can tell you! What I'll catch when Pa gets hold of me!

MURIEL. Tell me, Dick! Begin at the beginning and tell me!

RICHARD. (*tragically*) Well, after your old—your father left our place I caught holy hell from Pa.

MURIEL. Dick! You mustn't swear!

RICHARD. (*somberly*) Hell is the only word that can describe it. And on top of that, to torture me more, he gave me your letter. After I'd read that I didn't want to live any more. Life seemed like a tragic farce.

MURIEL. I'm so awful sorry, Dick—honest I am! But you might have known I'd never write that unless—

RICHARD. I thought your love for me was dead. I thought you'd never loved me, that you'd only been cruelly mocking me—to torture me!

MURIEL. Dick! I'd never! You know I'd never!

RICHARD. I wanted to die. I sat and brooded about death. Finally I made up my mind I'd kill myself.

MURIEL. (*excitedly*) Dick! You didn't!

RICHARD. I did, too! If there'd been one of Hedda Gabler's pistols

281

around, you'd have seen if I wouldn't have done it beautifully! I thought, when I'm dead, she'll be sorry she ruined my life!

MURIEL. (*cuddling up a little to him*) If you ever had! I'd have died, too! Honest, I would!

RICHARD. But suicide is the act of a coward. That's what stopped me. (*Then with a bitter change of tone*) And anyway, I thought to myself, she isn't worth it.

MURIEL. (*huffily*) That's a nice thing to say!

RICHARD. Well, if you meant what was in the letter, you wouldn't have been worth it, would you?

MURIEL. But I've told you Pa—

RICHARD. So I said to myself, I'm through with women; they're all alike!

MURIEL. I'm not.

RICHARD. And I thought, what difference does it make what I do now? I might as well forget her and lead the pace that kills, and drown my sorrows! You know I had eleven dollars saved up to buy you something for your birthday, but I thought, she's dead to me now and why shouldn't I throw it away? (*Then hastily*) I've still got almost five left, Muriel, and I can get you something nice with that.

MURIEL. (*excitedly*) What do I care about your old presents? You tell me what you did!

RICHARD. (*darkly again*) After it was dark, I sneaked out and went to a low dive I know about.

MURIEL. Dick Miller, I don't believe you ever!

RICHARD. You ask them at the Pleasant Beach House if I didn't! They won't forget me in a hurry!

MURIEL. (*impressed and horrified*) You went there? Why, that's a terrible place! Pa says it ought to be closed by the police!

RICHARD. (*darkly*) I said it was a dive, didn't I? It's a "secret house of shame." And they let me into a secret room behind the barroom. There wasn't anyone there but a Princeton Senior I know—he belongs to Tiger Inn and he's fullback on the football team—and he had two chorus girls from New York with him, and they were all drinking champagne.

MURIEL. (*disturbed by the entrance of the chorus girls*) Dick Miller! I hope you didn't notice—

RICHARD. (*carelessly*) I had a highball by myself and then I noticed one of the girls—the one that wasn't with the fullback—looking at me. She had strange-looking eyes. And then she asked me if I wouldn't drink champagne with them and come and sit with her.

MURIEL. She must have been a nice thing! (*Then a bit falteringly*) And did—you?

RICHARD. (*with tragic bitterness*) Why shouldn't I, when you'd told me in that letter you'd never see me again?

MURIEL. (*almost tearfully*) But you ought to have known Pa made me—

RICHARD. I didn't know that then. (*Then rubbing it in*) Her name was Belle. She had yellow hair—the kind that burns and stings you!

MURIEL. I'll bet it was dyed!

RICHARD. She kept smoking one cigarette after another—but that's nothing for a chorus girl.

MURIEL. (*indignantly*) She was low and bad, that's what she was or she couldn't be a chorus girl, and her smoking cigarettes proves it! (*Then falteringly again*) And then what happened?

RICHARD. (*carelessly*) Oh, we just kept drinking champagne—I bought a round—and then I had a fight with the barkeep and knocked him down because he'd insulted her. He was a great big thug but—

MURIEL. (*huffily*) I don't see how he could—insult that kind! And why did you fight for her? Why didn't the Princeton fullback who'd brought them there? He must have been bigger than you.

RICHARD. (*stopped for a moment—then quickly*) He was too drunk by that time.

MURIEL. And were you drunk?

RICHARD. Only a little then. I was worse later. (*Proudly*) You ought to have seen me when I got home! I was on the verge of delirium tremens!

MURIEL. I'm glad I didn't see you. You must have been awful. I hate people who get drunk. I'd have hated you!

RICHARD. Well, it was all your fault, wasn't it? If you hadn't written that letter—

MURIEL. But I've told you I didn't mean— (*Then faltering but fascinated*) But what happened with that Belle—after—before you went home?

RICHARD. Oh, we kept drinking champagne and she said she'd fallen in love with me at first sight and she came and sat on my lap and kissed me.

MURIEL. (*stiffening*) Oh!

RICHARD. (*quickly, afraid he has gone too far*) But it was only all in fun, and then we just kept on drinking champagne, and finally I said good night and came home.

MURIEL. And did you kiss her?

RICHARD. No, I didn't.

MURIEL. (*distractedly*) You did, too! You're lying and you know it. You did, too! (*Then tearfully*) And there I was right at that time lying in bed not able to sleep, wondering how I was ever going to see you again and crying my eyes out, while you—! (*She suddenly jumps to her feet in a tearful fury*) I hate you! I wish you were dead! I'm going home this minute! I never want to lay eyes on you again! And this time I mean it! (*She tries to jump out of the boat but he holds her back. All the pose has dropped from him now and he is in a frightened state of contrition.*)

RICHARD. (*imploringly*) Muriel! Wait! Listen!

MURIEL. I don't want to listen! Let me go! If you don't I'll bite your hand!

RICHARD. I won't let you go! You've got to let me explain! I never—! Ouch! (*For MURIEL has bitten his hand and it hurts, and, stung by the pain, he lets go instinctively, and she jumps quickly out of the boat and starts running toward the path.* RICHARD *calls after her with bitter despair and hurt*) All right! Go if you want to—if you haven't the decency to let me explain! I hate you, too! I'll go and see Belle!

MURIEL. (*seeing he isn't following her, stops at the foot of the path —defiantly*) Well, go and see her—if that's the kind of girl you like! What do I care? (*Then as he only stares before him broodingly, sitting dejectedly in the stern of the boat, a pathetic figure of injured grief*) You can't explain! What can you explain? You owned up you kissed her!

RICHARD. I did not. I said she kissed me.

MURIEL. (*scornfully, but drifting back a step in his direction*) And I suppose you just sat and let yourself be kissed! Tell that to the Marines!

RICHARD. (*injuredly*) All right! If you're going to call me a liar every word I say—

MURIEL. (*drifting back another step*) I didn't call you a liar. I only meant—it sounds fishy. Don't you know it does?

RICHARD. I don't know anything. I only know I wish I was dead!

MURIEL. (*gently reproving*) You oughtn't to say that. It's wicked. (*Then after a pause*) And I suppose you'll tell me you didn't fall in love with her?

RICHARD. (*scornfully*) I should say not! Fall in love with that kind of girl! What do you take me for?

MURIEL. (*practically*) How do you know what you did if you drank so much champagne?

RICHARD. I kept my head—with her. I'm not a sucker, no matter what you think!

MURIEL. (*drifting nearer*) Then you didn't—love her?

RICHARD. I hated her! She wasn't even pretty! And I had a fight with her before I left, she got so fresh. I told her I loved you and never could love anyone else, and for her to leave me alone.

MURIEL. But you said just now you were going to see her—

RICHARD. That was only bluff. I wouldn't—unless you left me. Then

I wouldn't care what I did—any more than I did last night. (*Then suddenly defiant*) And what if I did kiss her once or twice? I only did it to get back at you!

MURIEL. Dick!

RICHARD. You're a fine one to blame me—when it was all your fault! Why can't you be fair? Didn't I think you were out of my life forever? Hadn't you written me you were? Answer me that!

MURIEL. But I've told you a million times that Pa—

RICHARD. Why didn't you have more sense than to let him make you write it? Was it my fault you didn't?

MURIEL. It was your fault for being so stupid! You ought to have known he stood right over me and told me each word to write. If I'd refused, it would only have made everything worse. I had to pretend, so I'd get a chance to see you. Don't you see, Silly? And I had sand enough to sneak out to meet you tonight, didn't I? (*He doesn't answer. She moves nearer*) Still I can see how you felt the way you did—and maybe I am to blame for that. So I'll forgive and forget, Dick—if you'll swear to me you didn't even think of loving that—

RICHARD. (*eagerly*) I didn't! I swear, Muriel. I couldn't. I love you!

MURIEL. Well, then—I still love you.

RICHARD. Then come back here, why don't you?

MURIEL. (*coyly*) It's getting late.

RICHARD. It's not near half-past yet.

MURIEL. (*comes back and sits down by him shyly*) All right—only I'll have to go soon, Dick. (*He puts his arm around her. She cuddles up close to him*) I'm sorry—I hurt your hand.

RICHARD. That was nothing. It felt wonderful—even to have you bite!

MURIEL. (*impulsively takes his hand and kisses it*) There! That'll cure it. (*She is overcome by confusion at her boldness.*)

RICHARD. You shouldn't—waste that—on my hand. (*Then tremblingly*) You said—you'd let me—

286

MURIEL. I said, maybe.

RICHARD. Please, Muriel. You know—I want it so!

MURIEL. Will it wash off—her kisses—make you forget you ever —for always?

RICHARD. I should say so! I'd never remember—anything but it— never want anything but it—ever again.

MURIEL. (*shyly lifting her lips*) Then—all right—Dick. (*He kisses her tremblingly and for a moment their lips remain together. Then she lets her head sink on his shoulder and sighs softly*) The moon *is* beautiful, isn't it?

RICHARD. (*kissing her hair*) Not as beautiful as you! Nothing is! (*Then after a pause*) Won't it be wonderful when we're married?

MURIEL. Yes—but it's so long to wait.

RICHARD. Perhaps I needn't go to Yale. Perhaps Pa will give me a job. Then I'd soon be making enough to—

MURIEL. You better do what your pa thinks best—and I'd like you to be at Yale. (*Then patting his face*) Poor you! Do you think he'll punish you awful?

RICHARD. (*intensely*) I don't know and I don't care! Nothing would have kept me from seeing you tonight—not if I'd had to crawl over red-hot coals! (*Then falling back on Swinburne—but with passionate sincerity*) You have my being between the hands of you! You are "my love, mine own soul's heart, more dear than mine own soul, more beautiful than God!"

MURIEL. (*shocked and delighted*) Ssshh! It's wrong to say that.

RICHARD. (*adoringly*) Gosh, but I love you! Gosh, I love you— Darling!

MURIEL. I love you, too—Sweetheart! (*They kiss. Then she lets her head sink on his shoulder again and they both sit in a rapt trance, staring at the moon. After a pause—dreamily*) Where'll we go on our honeymoon, Dick? To Niagara Falls?

RICHARD. (*scornfully*) That dump where all the silly fools go? I should say not! (*With passionate romanticism*) No, we'll go to some far-off wonderful place! (*He calls on Kipling to help him*) Somewhere out on the Long Trail—the trail that is always new—on the road to Mandalay! We'll watch the dawn come up like thunder out of China!

MURIEL. (*hazily but happily*) That'll be wonderful, won't it?

CURTAIN

ACT FOUR—SCENE THREE

SCENE—*The sitting-room of the Miller house again—about 10 o'clock the same night.* MILLER *is sitting in his rocker at left, front, of table, his wife in the rocker at right, front, of table. Moonlight shines through the screen door at right, rear. Only the green-shaded reading lamp is lit and by its light* MILLER, *his specs on, is reading a book while his wife, sewing basket in lap, is working industriously on a doily.* MRS. MILLER's *face wears an expression of unworried content.* MILLER's *face has also lost its look of harassed preoccupation, although he still is a prey to certain misgivings, when he allows himself to think of them. Several books are piled on the table by his elbow, the books that have been confiscated from* RICHARD.

MILLER. (*chuckles at something he reads—then closes the book and puts it on the table.* MRS. MILLER *looks up from her sewing*) This Shaw's a comical cuss—even if his ideas are so crazy they oughtn't to allow them to be printed. And that Swinburne's got a fine swing to his poetry—if he'd only choose some other subjects besides loose women.

MRS. MILLER. (*smiling teasingly*) I can see where you're becoming corrupted by those books, too—pretending to read them out of duty to Richard, when your nose has been glued to the page!

288

MILLER. No, no—but I've got to be honest. There's something to them. That Rubaiyat of Omar Khayyam, now. I read that over again and liked it even better than I had before—parts of it, that is, where it isn't all about boozing.

MRS. MILLER. (*has been busy with her own thoughts during this last—with a deep sigh of relief*) My, but I'm glad Mildred told me where Richard went off to. I'd have worried my heart out if she hadn't. But now, it's all right.

MILLER. (*frowning a little*) I'd hardly go so far as to say that. Just because we know he's all right tonight doesn't mean last night is wiped out. He's still got to be punished for that.

MRS. MILLER. (*defensively*) Well, if you ask me, I think after the way I punished him all day, and the way I know he's punished himself, he's had about all he deserves. I've told you how sorry he was, and how he said he'd never touch liquor again. It didn't make him feel happy like Sid, but only sad and sick, so he didn't see anything in it for him.

MILLER. Well, if he's really got that view of it driven into his skull, I don't know but I'm glad it all happened. That'll protect him more than a thousand lectures—just horse sense about himself. (*Then frowning again*). Still, I can't let him do such things and go scot-free. And then; besides, there's another side to it— (*He stops abruptly.*)

MRS. MILLER. (*uneasily*) What do you mean, another side?

MILLER. (*hastily*) I mean, discipline. There's got to be some discipline in a family. I don't want him to get the idea he's got a stuffed shirt at the head of the table. No, he's got to be punished, if only to make the lesson stick in his mind, and I'm going to tell him he can't go to Yale, seeing he's so undependable.

MRS. MILLER. (*up in arms at once*) Not go to Yale! I guess he can go to Yale! Every man of your means in town is sending his boys to college! What would folks think of you? You let Wilbur go, and you'd have let Lawrence, only he didn't want to, and you're letting

289

AH, WILDERNESS!

Arthur! If our other children can get the benefit of a college education, you're not going to pick on Richard—

MILLER. Hush up, for God's sake! If you'd let me finish what I started to say! I said I'd *tell* him that now—bluff—then later on I'll change my mind, if he behaves himself.

MRS. MILLER. Oh, well, if that's all— (*Then defensively again*) But it's your duty to give him every benefit. He's got an exceptional brain, that boy has! He's proved it by the way he likes to read all those deep plays and books and poetry.

MILLER. But I thought you— (*He stops, grinning helplessly.*)

MRS. MILLER. You thought I what?

MILLER. Never mind.

MRS. MILLER. (*sniffs, but thinks it better to let this pass*) You mark my words, that boy's going to turn out to be a great lawyer, or a great doctor, or a great writer, or—

MILLER. (*grinning*) You agree he's going to be great, anyway.

MRS. MILLER. Yes, I most certainly have a lot of faith in Richard.

MILLER. Well, so have I, as far as that goes.

MRS. MILLER. (*after a pause—judicially*) And as for his being in love with Muriel, I don't see but what it might work out real well. Richard could do worse.

MILLER. But I thought you had no use for her, thought she was stupid.

MRS. MILLER. Well, so I did, but if she's good for Richard and he wants her— (*Then inconsequentially*) Ma used to say you weren't overbright, but she changed her mind when she saw I didn't care if you were or not.

MILLER. (*not exactly pleased by this*) Well, I've been bright enough to—

MRS. MILLER. (*going on as if he had not spoken*) And Muriel's real cute-looking, I have to admit that. Takes after her mother. Alice Briggs was the prettiest girl before she married.

MILLER. Yes, and Muriel will get big as a house after she's married, the same as her mother did. That's the trouble. A man never can tell what he's letting himself in for— (*He stops, feeling his wife's eyes fixed on him with indignant suspicion.*)

MRS. MILLER. (*sharply*) I'm not too fat and don't you say it!

MILLER. Who was talking about you?

MRS. MILLER. And I'd rather have some flesh on my bones than be built like a string bean and bore a hole in a chair every time I sat down—like some people!

MILLER. (*ignoring the insult—flatteringly*) Why, no one'd ever call you fat, Essie. You're only plump, like a good figure ought to be.

MRS. MILLER. (*childishly pleased—gratefully giving tit for tat*) Well, you're not skinny, either—only slender—and I think you've been putting on weight lately, too. (*Having thus squared matters she takes up her sewing again. A pause. Then MILLER asks incredulously.*)

MILLER. You don't mean to tell me you're actually taking this Muriel crush of Richard's seriously, do you? I know it's a good thing to encourage right now but—pshaw, why, Richard'll probably forget all about her before he's away six months, and she'll have forgotten him.

MRS. MILLER. Don't be so cynical. (*Then, after a pause, thoughtfully*) Well, anyway, he'll always have it to remember—no matter what happens after—and that's something.

MILLER. You bet that's something. (*Then with a grin*) You surprise me at times with your deep wisdom.

MRS. MILLER. You don't give me credit for ever having common sense, that's why. (*She goes back to her sewing.*)

MILLER. (*after a pause*) Where'd you say Sid and Lily had gone off to?

MRS. MILLER. To the beach to listen to the band. (*She sighs sympathetically*) Poor Lily! Sid'll never change, and she'll never marry him. But she seems to get some queer satisfaction out of fussing over him like a hen that's hatched a duck—though Lord knows I wouldn't in her shoes!

291

MILLER. Arthur's up with Elsie Rand, I suppose?

MRS. MILLER. Of course.

MILLER. Where's Mildred?

MRS. MILLER. Out walking with her latest. I've forgot who it is. I can't keep track of them. (*She smiles.*)

MILLER. (*smiling*) Then, from all reports, we seem to be completely surrounded by love!

MRS. MILLER. Well, we've had our share, haven't we? We don't have to begrudge it to our children. (*Then has a sudden thought*) But I've done all this talking about Muriel and Richard and clean forgot how wild old McComber was against it. But he'll get over that, I suppose.

MILLER. (*with a chuckle*) He has already. I ran into him upstreet this afternoon and he was meek as pie. He backed water and said he guessed I was right. Richard had just copied stuff out of books, and kids would be kids, and so on. So I came off my high horse a bit—but not too far—and I guess all that won't bother anyone any more. (*Then rubbing his hands together—with a boyish grin of pleasure*) And I told you about getting that business from Lawson, didn't I? It's been a good day, Essie—a darned good day! (*From the hall beyond the front parlor the sound of the front door being opened and shut is heard.* MRS. MILLER *leans forward to look, pushing her specs up.*)

MRS. MILLER. (*in a whisper*) It's Richard.

MILLER. (*immediately assuming an expression of becoming gravity*) Hmm. (*He takes off his spectacles and puts them back in their case and straightens himself in his chair.* RICHARD *comes slowly in from the front parlor. He walks like one in a trance, his eyes shining with a dreamy happiness, his spirit still too exalted to be conscious of his surroundings, or to remember the threatened punishment. He carries his straw hat dangling in his hand, quite unaware of its existence.*)

RICHARD. (*dreamily, like a ghost addressing fellow shades*) Hello.

MRS. MILLER. (*staring at him worriedly*) Hello, Richard.

MILLER. (*sizing him up shrewdly*) Hello, Son.

(RICHARD *moves past his mother and comes to the far corner, left front, where the light is dimmest, and sits down on the sofa, and stares before him, his hat dangling in his hand.*)

MRS. MILLER. (*with frightened suspicion now*) Goodness, he acts queer! Nat, you don't suppose he's been—?

MILLER. (*with a reassuring smile*) No. It's love, not liquor, this time.

MRS. MILLER. (*only partly reassured—sharply*) Richard! What's the matter with you? (*He comes to himself with a start. She goes on scoldingly*) How many times have I told you to hang up your hat in the hall when you come in! (*He looks at his hat as if he were surprised at its existence. She gets up fussily and goes to him*) Here. Give it to me. I'll hang it up for you this once. And what are you sitting over here in the dark for? Don't forget your father's been waiting to talk to you! (*She comes back to the table and he follows her, still half in a dream, and stands by his father's chair.* MRS. MILLER *starts for the hall with his hat.*)

MILLER. (*quietly but firmly now*) You better leave Richard and me alone for a while, Essie.

MRS. MILLER. (*turns to stare at him apprehensively*) Well—all right. I'll go sit on the piazza. Call me if you want me. (*Then a bit pleadingly*) But you'll remember all I said, Nat, won't you? (MILLER *nods reassuringly. She disappears through the front parlor.* RICHARD, *keenly conscious of himself as the about-to-be-sentenced criminal by this time, looks guilty and a bit defiant, searches his father's expressionless face with uneasy side glances, and steels himself for what is coming.*)

MILLER. (*casually, indicating* MRS. MILLER's *rocker*) Sit down, Richard. (RICHARD *slumps awkwardly into the chair and sits in a self-conscious, unnatural position.* MILLER *sizes him up keenly—then suddenly smiles and asks with quiet mockery*) Well, how are the vine leaves in your hair this evening?

RICHARD. (*totally unprepared for this approach—shamefacedly mutters*) I don't know, Pa.

MILLER. Turned out to be poison ivy, didn't they? (*Then kindly*)

But you needn't look so alarmed. I'm not going to read you any temperance lecture. That'd bore me more than it would you. And, in spite of your damn foolishness last night, I'm still giving you credit for having brains. So I'm pretty sure anything I could say to you you've already said to yourself.

RICHARD. (*his head down—humbly*) I know I was a darned fool.

MILLER. (*thinking it well to rub in this aspect—disgustedly*) You sure were—not only a fool but a downright, stupid, disgusting fool! (RICHARD *squirms, his head still lower*) It was bad enough for you to let me and Arthur see you, but to appear like that before your mother and Mildred—! And I wonder if Muriel would think you were so fine if she ever saw you as you looked and acted then. I think she'd give you your walking papers for keeps. And you couldn't blame her. No nice girl wants to give her love to a stupid drunk!

RICHARD. (*writhing*) I know, Pa.

MILLER. (*after a pause—quietly*) All right. Then that settles—the booze end of it. (*He sizes* RICHARD *up searchingly—then suddenly speaks sharply*) But there is another thing that's more serious. How about that tart you went to bed with at the Pleasant Beach House?

RICHARD. (*flabbergasted—stammers*) You know—? But I didn't! If they've told you about her down there, they must have told you I didn't! She wanted me to—but I wouldn't. I gave her the five dollars just so she'd let me out of it. Honest, Pa, I didn't! She made everything seem rotten and dirty—and—I didn't want to do a thing like that to Muriel—no matter how bad I thought she'd treated me—even after I felt drunk, I didn't. Honest!

MILLER. How'd you happen to meet this lady, anyway?

RICHARD. I can't tell that, Pa. I'd have to snitch on someone—and you wouldn't want me to do that.

MILLER. (*a bit taken aback*) No. I suppose I wouldn't. Hmm. Well, I believe you—and I guess that settles that. (*Then, after a quick furtive glance at* RICHARD, *he nerves himself for the ordeal and begins with a shamefaced, self-conscious solemnity*) But listen here, Richard, it's about time you and I had a serious talk about—hmm—certain matters pertaining to—and now that the subject's come up of its own accord, it's a good time—I mean, there's no use in procrastinating further—so, here goes. (*But it doesn't go smoothly and as he goes on he becomes more and more guiltily embarrassed and self-conscious and his expressions more stilted.* RICHARD *sedulously avoids even glancing at him, his own embarrassment made tenfold more painful by his father's*) Richard, you have now come to the age when— Well, you're a fully developed man, in a way, and it's only natural for you to have certain desires of the flesh, to put it that way— I mean, pertaining to the opposite sex—certain natural feelings and temptations —that'll want to be gratified—and you'll want to gratify them. Hmm —well, human society being organized as it is, there's only one outlet for—unless you're a scoundrel and go around ruining decent girls —which you're not, of course. Well, there are a certain class of women —always have been and always will be as long as human nature is what it is— It's wrong, maybe, but what can you do about it? I mean, girls like that one you—girls there's something doing with—and lots of 'em are pretty, and it's human nature if you— But that doesn't mean to ever get mixed up with them seriously! You just have what you want and pay 'em and forget it. I know that sounds hard and unfeeling, but we're talking facts and— But don't think I'm encouraging you to— If you can stay away from 'em, all the better—but if— why—hmm— Here's what I'm driving at, Richard. They're apt to be whited sepulchres— I mean, your whole life might be ruined if— so, darn it, you've got to know how to—I mean, there are ways and means— (*Suddenly he can go no farther and winds up helplessly*) But, hell, I suppose you boys talk all this over among yourselves and you know more about it than I do. I'll admit I'm no authority. I never had anything to do with such women, and it'll be a hell of a lot better for you if you never do!

RICHARD. (*without looking at him*) I'm never going to, Pa. (*Then shocked indignation coming into his voice*) I don't see how you could think I could—now—when you know I love Muriel and am going to marry her. I'd die before I'd—!

MILLER. (*immensely relieved—enthusiastically*) That's the talk! By God, I'm proud of you when you talk like that! (*Then hastily*) And now that's all of that. There's nothing more to say and we'll forget it, eh?

RICHARD. (*after a pause*) How are you going to punish me, Pa?

MILLER. I *was* sort of forgetting that, wasn't I? Well, I'd thought of telling you you couldn't go to Yale—

RICHARD. (*eagerly*) Don't I have to go? Gee, that's great! Muriel thought you'd want me to. I was telling her I'd rather you gave me a job on the paper because then she and I could get married sooner. (*Then with a boyish grin*) Gee, Pa, you picked a lemon. That isn't any punishment. You'll have to do something besides that.

MILLER. (*grimly—but only half concealing an answering grin*) Then you'll go to Yale and you'll stay there till you graduate, that's the answer to that! Muriel's got good sense and you haven't! (RICHARD *accepts this philosophically*) And now we're finished, you better call your mother. (RICHARD *opens the screen door and calls "Ma," and a moment later she comes in. She glances quickly from son to husband and immediately knows that all is well and tactfully refrains from all questions.*)

MRS. MILLER. My, it's a beautiful night. The moon's way down low —almost setting. (*She sits in her chair and sighs contentedly.* RICHARD *remains standing by the door, staring out at the moon, his face pale in the moonlight.*)

MILLER. (*with a nod at* RICHARD, *winking at his wife*) Yes, I don't believe I've hardly ever seen such a beautiful night—with such a wonderful moon. Have you, Richard?

RICHARD. (*turning to them—enthusiastically*) No! It was wonderful —down at the beach— (*He stops abruptly, smiling shyly.*)

MILLER. (*watching his son—after a pause—quietly*) I can only remember a few nights that were as beautiful as this—and they were

AH, WILDERNESS!

so long ago, when your mother and I were young and planning to get married.

RICHARD. (*stares at him wonderingly for a moment, then quickly from his father to his mother and back again, strangely, as if he'd never seen them before—then he looks almost disgusted and swallows as if an acrid taste had come into his mouth—but then suddenly his face is transfigured by a smile of shy understanding and sympathy. He speaks shyly*) Yes, I'll bet those must have been wonderful nights, too. You sort of forget the moon was the same way back then—and everything.

MILLER. (*huskily*) You're all right, Richard. (*He gets up and blows his nose.*)

MRS. MILLER. (*fondly*) You're a good boy, Richard. (RICHARD *looks dreadfully shy and embarrassed at this. His father comes to his rescue.*)

MILLER. Better get to bed early tonight, Son, hadn't you?

RICHARD. I couldn't sleep. Can't I go out on the piazza and sit for a while—until the moon sets?

MILLER. All right. Then you better say good night now. I don't know about your mother, but I'm going to bed right away. I'm dead tired.

MRS. MILLER. So am I.

RICHARD. (*goes to her and kisses her*) Good night, Ma.

MRS. MILLER. Good night. Don't you stay up till all hours now.

RICHARD. (*comes to his father and stands awkwardly before him*) Good night, Pa.

MILLER. (*puts his arm around him and gives him a hug*) Good night, Richard. (RICHARD *turns impulsively and kisses him—then hurries out the screen door.* MILLER *stares after him—then says huskily*) First time he's done that in years. I don't believe in kissing between fathers and sons after a certain age—seems mushy and silly—but that meant something! And I don't think we'll ever have to worry about his being safe—from himself—again. And I guess no matter what life will do to him, he can take care of it now. (*He sighs with satisfaction and, sitting down in his chair, begins to unlace his shoes*) My darned feet are giving me fits!

MRS. MILLER. (*laughing*) Why do you bother unlacing your shoes now, you big goose—when we're going right up to bed?

MILLER. (*as if he hadn't thought of that before, stops*) Guess you're right. (*Then getting to his feet—with a grin*) Mind if I don't say my prayers tonight, Essie? I'm certain God knows I'm too darned tired.

MRS. MILLER. Don't talk that way. It's real sinful. (*She gets up—then laughing fondly*) If that isn't you all over! Always looking for an excuse to— You're worse than Tommy! But all right. I suppose tonight you needn't. You've had a hard day. (*She puts her hand on the reading-lamp switch*) I'm going to turn out the light. All ready?

MILLER. Yep. Let her go, Gallagher. (*She turns out the lamp. In the ensuing darkness the faint moonlight shines full in through the screen door. Walking together toward the front parlor they stand full in it for a moment, looking out.* MILLER *puts his arm around her. He says in a low voice*) There he is—like a statue of Love's Young Dream. (*Then he sighs and speaks with a gentle nostalgic melancholy*) What's it that Rubaiyat says:

"Yet Ah, that Spring should vanish with the Rose!
That Youth's sweet-scented manuscript should close!"

(*Then throwing off his melancholy, with a loving smile at her*) Well, Spring isn't everything, is it, Essie? There's a lot to be said for Autumn. That's got beauty, too. And Winter—if you're together.

MRS. MILLER. (*simply*) Yes, Nat. (*She kisses him and they move quietly out of the moonlight, back into the darkness of the front parlor.*)

CURTAIN

ALL GOD'S CHILLUN GOT WINGS

CHARACTERS

JIM HARRIS

MRS. HARRIS, *his mother*

HATTIE, *his sister*

ELLA DOWNEY

SHORTY

JOE

MICKEY

Whites and Negroes.

SCENES

ACT ONE

SCENE I: A corner in lower New York—years ago—end of an afternoon in Spring.

SCENE II: The same—nine years later—end of an evening in Spring.

SCENE III: The same—five years later—a night in Spring.

SCENE IV: The street before a church in the same ward—a morning some weeks later.

ACT TWO

SCENE I: A flat in the same ward—a morning two years later.

SCENE II: The same—at twilight some months later.

SCENE III: The same—a night some months later.

ALL GOD'S CHILLUN GOT WINGS

ACT ONE—SCENE ONE

A CORNER *in lower New York, at the edge of a colored district. Three narrow streets converge. A triangular building in the rear, red brick, four-storied, its ground floor a grocery. Four-story tenements stretch away down the skyline of the two streets. The fire escapes are crowded with people. In the street leading left, the faces are all white; in the street leading right, all black. It is hot Spring. On the sidewalk are eight children, four boys and four girls. Two of each sex are white, two black. They are playing marbles. One of the black boys is* JIM HARRIS. *The little blonde girl, her complexion rose and white, who sits behind his elbow and holds his marbles is* ELLA DOWNEY. *She is eight. They play the game with concentrated attention for a while. People pass, black and white, the Negroes frankly participants in the spirit of Spring, the whites laughing constrainedly, awkward in natural emotion. Their words are lost. One hears only their laughter. It expresses the difference in race. There are street noises— the clattering roar of the Elevated, the puff of its locomotives, the ruminative lazy sound of a horse-car, the hooves of its team clacking on the cobbles. From the street of the whites a high-pitched, nasal tenor sings the chorus of "Only a Bird in a Gilded Cage." On the street of the blacks a Negro strikes up the chorus of: "I Guess I'll Have to Telegraph My Baby." As this singing ends, there is laughter, distinctive in quality, from both streets. Then silence. The light in the street begins to grow brilliant with the glow of the setting sun. The game of marbles goes on.*

WHITE GIRL. (*tugging at the elbow of her brother*) Come on, Mickey!

HER BROTHER. (*roughly*) Aw, gwan, youse!

WHITE GIRL. Aw right den. You kin git a lickin' if you wanter. (*Gets up to move off.*)

HER BROTHER. Aw, git off de eart'!

WHITE GIRL. De old woman'll be madder'n hell!

HER BROTHER. (*worried now*) I'm comin', ain't I? Hold your horses.

BLACK GIRL. (*to a black boy*) Come on, you Joe. We gwine git frailed too, you don't hurry.

JOE. Go long!

MICKEY. Bust up de game, huh? I gotta run! (*Jumps to his feet.*)

OTHER WHITE BOY. Me, too! (*Jumps up.*)

OTHER BLACK GIRL. Lawdy, it's late!

JOE. Me for grub!

MICKEY. (*to* JIM HARRIS) You's de winner, Jim Crow. Yeh gotta play tomorrer.

JIM. (*readily*) Sure t'ing, Mick. Come one, come all! (*He laughs.*)

OTHER WHITE BOY. Me, too! I gotta git back at yuh.

JIM. Aw right, Shorty.

LITTLE GIRLS. Hurry! Come on, come on! (*The six start off together. Then they notice that* JIM *and* ELLA *are hesitating, standing awkwardly and shyly together. They turn to mock.*)

JOE. Look at dat Jim Crow! Land sakes, he got a gal! (*He laughs. They all laugh.*)

JIM. (*ashamed*) Ne'er mind, you Chocolate!

MICKEY. Look at de two softies, will yeh! Mush! Mush! (*He and the two other boys take this up.*)

LITTLE GIRLS. (*pointing their fingers at* ELLA) Shame! Shame! Everybody knows your name! Painty Face! Painty Face!

ELLA. (*hanging her head*) Shut up!

LITTLE WHITE GIRL. He's been carrying her books!

COLORED GIRL. Can't you find nuffin' better'n him, Ella? Look at de big feet he got! (*She laughs. They all laugh.* JIM *puts one foot on top of the other, looking at* ELLA.)

ELLA. Mind yer own business, see! (*She strides toward them angrily. They jump up and dance in an ecstasy, screaming and laughing.*)

ALL. Found yeh out! Found yeh out!

MICKEY. Mush-head! Jim Crow de Sissy! Stuck on Painty Face!

JOE. Will Painty Face let you hold her doll, boy?

SHORTY. Sissy! Softy! (ELLA *suddenly begins to cry. At this they all howl.*)

ALL. Cry-baby! Cry-baby! Look at her! Painty Face!

JIM. (*suddenly rushing at them, with clenched fists, furiously*) Shut yo' moufs! I kin lick de hull of you! (*They all run away, laughing, shouting, and jeering, quite triumphant now that they have made him, too, lose his temper. He comes back to* ELLA, *and stands beside her sheepishly, stepping on one foot after the other. Suddenly he blurts out*): Don't bawl no more. I done chased 'em.

ELLA. (*comforted, politely*) T'anks.

JIM. (*swelling out*) It was a cinch. I kin wipe up de street wid any one of dem. (*He stretches out his arms, trying to bulge out his biceps.*) Feel dat muscle!

ELLA. (*does so gingerly—then with admiration*) My!

JIM. (*protectingly*) You mustn't never be scared when I'm hanging round, Painty Face.

ELLA. Don't call me that, Jim—please!

JIM. (*contritely*) I didn't mean nuffin'. I didn't know you'd mind.

ELLA. I do—more'n anything.

JIM. You oughtn't to mind. Dey's jealous, dat's what.

ELLA. Jealous? Of what?

JIM. (*pointing to her face*) Of dat. Red 'n' white. It's purty.

ELLA. I hate it!

JIM. It's purty. Yes, it's—it's purty. It's—outa sight!

ELLA. I hate it. I wish I was black like you.

303

JIM. (*sort of shrinking*) No you don't. Dey'd call you Crow, den —or Chocolate—or Smoke.

ELLA. I wouldn't mind.

JIM. (*somberly*) Dey'd call you nigger sometimes, too.

ELLA. I wouldn't mind.

JIM. (*humbly*) You wouldn't mind?

ELL. No, I wouldn't mind. (*An awkward pause.*)

JIM. (*suddenly*) You know what, Ella? Since I been tuckin' yo' books to school and back, I been drinkin' lots o' chalk 'n' water tree times a day. Dat Tom, de barber, he tole me dat make me white, if I drink enough. (*Pleadingly*) Does I look whiter?

ELLA. (*comfortingly*) Yes—maybe—a little bit—

JIM. (*trying a careless tone*) Reckon dat Tom's a liar, an' de joke's on me! Dat chalk only makes me feel kinder sick inside.

ELLA. (*wonderingly*) Why do you want to be white?

JIM. Because—just because—I lak dat better.

ELLA. I wouldn't. I like black. Let's you and me swap. I'd like to be black. (*Clapping her hands*) Gee, that'd be fun, if we only could!

JIM. (*hesitatingly*) Yes—maybe—

ELLA. Then they'd call me Crow, and you'd be Painty Face!

JIM. They wouldn't never dast call you nigger, you bet! I'd kill 'em! (*A long pause. Finally she takes his hand shyly. They both keep looking as far away from each other as possible.*)

ELLA. I like you.

JIM. I like you.

ELLA. Do you want to be my feller?

JIM. Yes.

ELLA. Then I'm your girl.

JIM. Yes. (*Then grandly*) You kin bet none o' de gang gwine call you Painty Face from dis out! I lam' 'em good! (*The sun has set. Twilight has fallen on the street. An organ grinder comes up to the corner and plays "Annie Rooney." They stand hand-in-hand and listen. He goes away. It is growing dark.*)

ELLA. (*suddenly*) Golly, it's late! I'll git a lickin'!

JIM. Me, too.

ELLA. I won't mind it much.

JIM. Me nuther.

ELLA. See you going to school tomorrow?

JIM. Sure.

ELLA. I gotta skip now.

JIM. Me, too.

ELLA. I like you, Jim.

JIM. I like you.

ELLA. Don't forget.

JIM. Don't you.

ELLA. Good-by.

JIM. So long. (*They run away from each other—then stop abruptly, and turn as at a signal.*)

ELLA. Don't forget.

JIM. I won't, you bet!

ELLA. Here! (*She kisses her hand at him, then runs off in frantic embarrassment.*)

JIM. (*overcome*) Gee! (*Then he turns and darts away as the curtain falls.*)

ACT ONE—SCENE TWO

THE *same corner. Nine years have passed. It is again late Spring at a time in the evening which immediately follows the hour of Scene One. Nothing has changed much. One street is still all white, the other all black. The fire escapes are laden with drooping human beings. The grocery store is still at the corner. The street noises are now more rhythmically mechanical, electricity having taken the place of horse and steam. People pass, white and black. They laugh as in Scene One. From the street of the whites the high-pitched nasal tenor sings: "Gee, I Wish That I Had a Girl," and the Negro replies with "All I Got Was Sympathy." The singing is followed again by laughter from both streets. Then silence. The dusk grows darker. With a spluttering flare the arc-lamp at the corner is lit and sheds a pale glare over the street. Two young roughs slouch up to the corner, as tough in manner as they can make themselves. One is the* SHORTY *of Scene One; the other the Negro,* JOE. *They stand loafing. A boy of seventeen or so passes by, escorting a girl of about the same age. Both are dressed in their best, the boy in black with stiff collar, the girl in white.*

SHORTY. (*scornfully*) Hully cripes! Pipe who's here. (*To the girl, sneeringly*) Wha's matter, Liz? Don't yer recernize yer old fr'ens?

GIRL. (*frightenedly*) Hello, Shorty.

SHORTY. Why de glad rags? Goin' to graduation? (*He tries to obstruct their way, but, edging away from him, they turn and run.*)

JOE. Har-har! Look at dem scoot, will you! (SHORTY *grins with satisfaction.*)

SHORTY. (*looking down other street*) Here comes Mickey.

JOE. He won de semi-final last night easy?

SHORTY. Knocked de bloke out in de thoid.

JOE. Dat boy's suah a-comin'! He'll be de champeen yit.

SHORTY. (*judicially*) Got a good chanct—if he leaves de broads alone. Dat's where he's wide open. (MICKEY *comes in from the left. He is dressed loudly, a straw hat with a gaudy band cocked over one cauliflower ear. He has acquired a typical "pug's" face, with the added viciousness of a natural bully. One of his eyes is puffed, almost closed, as a result of his battle the night before. He swaggers up.*)

BOTH. Hello, Mickey.

MICKEY. Hello.

JOE. Hear you knocked him col'.

MICKEY. Sure. I knocked his block off. (*Changing the subject*) Say Seen 'em goin' past to de graduation racket?

SHORTY. (*with a wink*) Why, you int'rested?

JOE. (*chuckling*) Mickey's gwine roun' git a good conduct medal.

MICKEY. Sure. Dey kin pin it on de seat o' me pants. (*They laugh*) Listen. Seen Ella Downey goin'?

SHORTY. Painty Face? No, she ain't been along.

MICKEY. (*with authority*) Can dat name, see! Want a bunch o' fives in yer kisser? Den nix! She's me goil, understan'?

JOE. (*venturing to joke*) Which one? Yo' number ten?

MICKEY. (*flattered*) Sure. De real K.O. one.

SHORTY. (*pointing right—sneeringly*) Gee! Pipe Jim Crow all dolled up for de racket.

JOE. (*with disgusted resentment*) You mean tell me dat nigger's graduatin'?

SHORTY. Ask him. (JIM HARRIS *comes in. He is dressed in black, stiff white collar, etc.—a quiet-mannered Negro boy with a queerly baffled, sensitive face.*)

JIM. (*pleasantly*) Hello, fellows. (*They grunt in reply, looking over him scornfully.*)

JOE. (*staring resentfully*) Is you graduatin' tonight?

JIM. Yes.

JOE. (*spitting disgustedly*) Fo' Gawd's sake! You *is* gittin' high-falutin'!

JIM. (*smiling deprecatingly*) This is my second try. I didn't pass last year.

JOE. What de hell does it git you, huh? Whatever is you gwine do wid it now you gits it? Live lazy on yo' ol' woman?

JIM. (*assertively*) I'm going to study and become a lawyer.

JOE. (*with a snort*) Fo' Chris' sake, nigger!

JIM. (*fiercely*) Don't you call me that—not before them!

JOE. (*pugnaciously*) Does you deny you's a nigger? I shows you—

MICKEY. (*gives them both a push—truculently*) Cut it out, see!

I'm runnin' dis corner. (*Turning to* JIM *insultingly*) Say you! Painty Face's gittin' her ticket tonight, ain't she?

JIM. You mean Ella—

MICKEY. Painty Face Downey, dat's who I mean! I don't have to be perlite wit' her. She's me goil!

JIM. (*glumly*) Yes, she's graduating.

SHORTY. (*winks at* MICKEY) Smart, huh?

MICKEY. (*winks back—meaningly*) Willin' to loin, take it from me! (JIM *stands tensely as if a struggle were going on in him.*)

JIM. (*finally blurts out*) I want to speak to you, Mickey—alone.

MICKEY. (*surprised—insultingly*) Aw, what de hell—!

JIM. (*excitedly*) It's important, I tell you!

MICKEY. Huh? (*Stares at him inquisitively—then motions the others back carelessly and follows* JIM *down front.*)

SHORTY. Some noive!

JOE. (*vengefully*) I gits dat Jim alone, you wait!

MICKEY. Well, spill de big news. I ain't got all night. I got a date.

JIM. With—Ella?

MICKEY. What's dat to you?

JIM. (*the words tumbling out*) What—I wanted to say! I know—I've heard—all the stories—what you've been doing around the ward —with other girls—it's none of my business, with them—but she— Ella—it's different—she's not that kind—

MICKEY. (*insultingly*) Who told yuh so, huh?

JIM. (*draws back his fist threateningly*) Don't you dare—! (MICKEY *is so paralyzed by this effrontery that he actually steps back.*)

MICKEY. Say, cut de comedy! (*Beginning to feel insulted*) Listen, you Jim Crow! Ain't you wise I could give yuh one poke dat'd knock yuh into next week?

JIM. I'm only asking you to act square, Mickey.

MICKEY. What's it to yuh? Why, yoh lousy goat, she wouldn't spit on yuh even! She hates de sight of a coon.

JIM. (*in agony*) I—I know—but once she didn't mind—we were kids together—

MICKEY. Aw, ferget dat! Dis is *now!*

JIM. And I'm still her friend always—even if she don't like colored people—

MICKEY. *Coons,* why don't yuh say it right! De trouble wit' you is yuh're gittin' stuck up, dat's what! Stay where yeh belong, see! Yer old man made coin at de truckin' game and yuh're tryin' to buy yerself white—graduatin' and law, for Christ sake! Yuh're gittin' yerself in Dutch wit' everyone in de ward—and it ain't cause yer a coon neider. Don't de gang all train wit' Joe dere and lots of others? But yuh're tryin' to buy white and it won't git yuh no place, see!

JIM. (*trembling*) Some day—I'll show you—

MICKEY. (*turning away*) Aw, gwan!

JIM. D'you think I'd change—be you—your dirty white—!

MICKEY. (*whirling about*) What's dat?

JIM. (*with hysterical vehemence*) You act square with her—or I'll show you up—I'll report you—I'll write to the papers—the sporting writers—I'll let them know how white you are!

MICKEY. (*infuriated*) Yuh damn nigger, I'll bust yer jaw in! (*Assuming his ring pose he weaves toward* JIM, *his face set in a cruel scowl.* JIM *waits helplessly but with a certain dignity.*)

SHORTY. Cheese it! A couple bulls! And here's de Downey skoit comin', too.

MICKEY. I'll get yuh de next time! (ELLA DOWNEY *enters from the right. She is seventeen, still has the same rose and white complexion, is pretty but with a rather repelling bold air about her.*)

ELLA. (*smiles with pleasure when she sees* MICKEY) Hello, Mick. Am I late? Say, I'm so glad you won last night. (*She glances from one to the other as she feels something in the air*) Hello! What's up?

MICKEY. Dis boob. (*He indicates* JIM *scornfully.*)

JIM. (*diffidently*) Hello, Ella.

ELLA. (*shortly, turning away*) Hello. (*Then to* MICKEY) Come on, Mick. Walk down with me. I got to hurry.

JIM. (*blurts out*) Wait—just a second. (*Painfully*) Ella, do you hate—colored people?

MICKEY. Aw, shut up!

JIM. Please answer.

ELLA. (*forcing a laugh*) Say! What is this—another exam?

JIM. (*doggedly*) Please answer.

ELLA. (*irritably*) Of course I don't! Haven't I been brought up alongside— Why, some of my oldest—the girls I've been to public school the longest with—

JIM. Do you hate me, Ella?

ELLA. (*confusedly and more irritably*) Say, is he drunk? Why should I? I don't hate anyone.

JIM. Then why haven't you ever hardly spoken to me—for years?

ELLA. (*resentfully*) What would I speak about? You and me've got nothing in common any more.

JIM. (*desperately*) Maybe not any more—but—right on this corner—do you remember once—?

ELLA. I don't remember nothing! (*Angrily*) Say! What's got into you to be butting into my business all of a sudden like this? Because you finally managed to graduate, has it gone to your head?

JIM. No, I—only want to help you, Ella.

ELLA. Of all the nerve! You're certainly forgetting your place! Who's asking you for help, I'd like to know? Shut up and stop bothering me!

JIM. (*insistently*) If you ever need a friend—a true friend—

ELLA. I've got lots of friends among my own—kind, I can tell you. (*Exasperatedly*) You make me sick! Go to the devil! (*She flounces off. The three men laugh.* MICKEY *follows her.* JIM *is stricken. He goes and sinks down limply on a box in front of the grocery store.*)

SHORTY. I'm going to shoot a drink. Come on, Joe, and I'll blow yuh.

310

JOE. (*who has never ceased to follow every move of* JIM's *with angry, resentful eyes*) Go long. I'se gwine stay here a secon'. I got a lil' argument. (*He points to* JIM.)

SHORTY. Suit yerself. Do a good job. See yuh later. (*He goes, whistling.*)

JOE. (*stands for a while glaring at* JIM, *his fierce little eyes peering out of his black face. Then he spits on his hands aggressively and strides up to the oblivious* JIM. *He stands in front of him, gradually working himself into a fury at the other's seeming indifference to his words*) Listen to me, nigger: I got a heap to whisper in yo' ear! Who is you, anyhow? Who does you think you is? Don't yo' old man and mine work on de docks togidder befo' yo' old man gits his own truckin' business? Yo' ol' man swallers his nickels, my ol' man buys him beer wid dem and swallers dat—dat's the on'y diff'rence. Don't you 'n' me drag up togidder?

JIM. (*dully*) I'm your friend, Joe.

JOE. No, you isn't! I ain't no fren' o' yourn! I don't even know who you is! What's all dis schoolin' you doin'? What's all dis dressin' up and graduatin' an' sayin' you gwine study be a lawyer? What's all dis fakin' an' pretendin' and swellin' out grand an' talkin' soft and perlite? What's all dis denyin' you's a nigger—an' wid de white boys listenin' to you say it! Is you aimin' to buy white wid yo' ol' man's dough like Mickey say? What is you? (*In a rage at the other's silence*) You don't talk? Den I takes it out o' yo' hide! (*He grabs* JIM *by the throat with one hand and draws the other fist back*) Tell me befo' I wrecks yo' face in! Is you a nigger or isn't you? (*Shaking him*) Is you a nigger, Nigger? Nigger, is you a nigger?

JIM. (*looking into his eyes—quietly*) Yes. I'm a nigger. We're both niggers. (*They look at each other for a moment.* JOE's *rage vanishes. He slumps onto a box beside* JIM's. *He offers him a cigarette.* JIM *takes it.* JOE *scratches a match and lights both their cigarettes.*)

JOE. (*after a puff, with full satisfaction*) Man, why didn't you 'splain dat in de fust place?

JIM. We're both niggers. (*The same hand-organ man of Scene One comes to the corner. He plays the chorus of "Bon-bon Buddie The Chocolate Drop." They both stare straight ahead listening. Then the organ man goes away. A silence.* JOE *gets to his feet.*)

JOE. I'll go get me a cold beer. (*He starts to move off—then turns*) Time you was graduatin', ain't it? (*He goes.* JIM *remains sitting on his box staring straight before him as the curtain falls.*)

ACT ONE—SCENE THREE

THE *same corner five years later. Nothing has changed much. It is a night in Spring. The arc-lamp discovers faces with a favorless cruelty. The street noises are the same but more intermittent and dulled with a quality of fatigue. Two people pass, one black and one white. They are tired. They both yawn, but neither laughs. There is no laughter from the two streets. From the street of the whites the tenor, more nasal than ever and a bit drunken, wails in high barbershop falsetto the last half of the chorus of "When I Lost You." The Negro voice, a bit maudlin in turn, replies with the last half of "Waitin' for the Robert E. Lee." Silence.* SHORTY *enters. He looks tougher than ever, the typical gangster. He stands waiting, singing a bit drunkenly, peering down the street.*

SHORTY. (*indignantly*) Yuh bum! Ain't yuh ever comin'? (*He begins to sing: "And sewed up in her yellow kimono, She had a blue-barreled forty-five gun, For to get her man Who'd done her wrong." Then he comments scornfully*) Not her, dough! No gat for her. She ain't got de noive. A little sugar. Dat'll fix her. (ELLA *enters. She is dressed poorly, her face is pale and hollow-eyed, her voice cold and tired.*)

SHORTY. Yuh got de message?

ELLA. Here I am.

SHORTY. How yuh been?

ELLA. All right. (*A pause. He looks at her puzzledly.*)

SHORTY. (*a bit embarrassedly*) Well, I s'pose yuh'd like me to give yuh some dope on Mickey, huh?

ELLA. No.

SHORTY. Mean to say yuh don't wanter know where he is or what he's doin'?

ELLA. No.

SHORTY. Since when?

ELLA. A long time.

SHORTY. (*after a pause—with a rat-like viciousness*) Between you'n me, kid, you'll get even soon—you'n all de odder dames he's tossed. I'm on de inside. I've watched him trainin'. His next scrap, watch it! He'll go! It won't be de odder guy. It'll be all youse dames he's kidded—and de ones what's kidded him. Youse'll all be in de odder guy's corner. He won't need no odder seconds. Youse'll trow water on him, and sponge his face, and take de kinks out of his socker— and Mickey'll catch it on de button—and he won't be able to take it no more—'cause all your weight—you and de odders—'ll be behind dat punch. Ha, ha! (*He laughs an evil laugh*) And Mickey'll go— down to his knees first—(*He sinks to his knees in the attitude of a groggy boxer.*)

ELLA. I'd like to see him on his knees!

SHORTY. And den—flat on his pan—dead to de woild—de boidies singin' in de trees—ten—out! (*He suits his action to the words, sinking flat on the pavement, then rises and laughs the same evil laugh.*)

ELLA. He's been out—for me—a long time. (*A pause*) Why did you send for me?

SHORTY. He sent me.

ELLA. Why?

SHORTY. To slip you dis wad o' dough. (*He reluctantly takes a roll of bills from his pocket and holds it out to her.*)

313

ELLA. (*looks at the money indifferently*) What for?

SHORTY. For you.

ELLA. No.

SHORTY. For de kid den.

ELLA. The kid's dead. He took diphtheria.

SHORTY. Hell yuh say! When?

ELLA. A long time.

SHORTY. Why didn't you write Mickey—?

ELLA. Why should I? He'd only be glad.

SHORTY. (*after a pause*) Well—it's better.

ELLA. Yes.

SHORTY. You made up wit yer family?

ELLA. No chance.

SHORTY. Livin' alone?

ELLA. In Brooklyn.

SHORTY. Workin'?

ELLA. In a factory.

SHORTY. You're a sucker. There's lots of softer snaps fer you, kid—

ELLA. I know what you mean. No.

SHORTY. Don't yuh wanter step out no more—have fun—live?

ELLA. I'm through.

SHORTY. (*mockingly*) Jump in de river, huh? T'ink it over, baby. I kin start yuh right in my stable. No one'll bodder yuh den. I got influence.

ELLA. (*without emphasis*) You're a dirty dog. Why doesn't some-one kill you?

SHORTY. Is dat so! What're you? They say you been travelin' round with Jim Crow.

ELLA. He's been my only friend.

SHORTY. A nigger!

ELLA. The only white man in the world! Kind and white. You're all black—black to the heart.

SHORTY. Nigger-lover! (*He throws the money in her face. It falls*

314

to the street) Listen, you! Mickey says he's off of yuh fer keeps. Dis is de finish! Dat's what he sent me to tell you. (*Glances at her searchingly—a pause*) Yuh won't make no trouble?

ELLA. Why should I? He's free. The kid's dead. I'm free. No hard feelings—only—I'll be there in spirit at his next fight, tell him! I'll take your tip—the other corner—second the punch—nine—ten—out! He's free! That's all. (*She grins horribly at* SHORTY) Go away, Shorty.

SHORTY. (*looking at her and shaking his head—maudlinly*) Groggy! Groggy! We're all groggy! Gluttons for punishment! Me for a drink. So long. (*He goes. A Salvation Army band comes toward the corner. They are playing and singing "Till We Meet at Jesus' Feet." They reach the end as they enter and stop before* ELLA. THE CAPTAIN *steps forward.*)

CAPTAIN. Sister—

ELLA. (*picks up the money and drops it in his hat—mockingly*) Here. Go save yourself. Leave me alone.

A WOMAN SALVATIONIST. Sister—

ELLA. Never mind that. I'm not in your line—yet. (*As they hesitate, wonderingly*) I want to be alone. (*To the thud of the big drum they march off.* ELLA *sits down on a box, her hands hanging at her sides. Presently* JIM HARRIS *comes in. He has grown into a quietly-dressed studious-looking Negro with an intelligent yet queerly baffled face.*)

JIM. (*with a joyous but bewildered cry*) Ella! I just saw Shorty—

ELLA. (*smiling at him with frank affection*) He had a message from Mickey.

JIM. (*sadly*) Ah!

ELLA. (*pointing to the box behind her*) Sit down. (*He does so. A pause—then she says indifferently*) It's finished. I'm free, Jim.

JIM. (*wearily*) We're never free—except to do what we have to do.

ELLA. What are you getting gloomy about all of a sudden?

JIM. I've got the report from the school. I've flunked again.

ELLA. Poor Jim.

JIM. Don't pity me. I'd like to kick myself all over the block. Five years—and I'm still plugging away where I ought to have been at the end of two.

ELLA. Why don't you give it up?

JIM. No!

ELLA. After all, what's being a lawyer?

JIM. A lot—to me—what it means. (*Intensely*) Why, if I was a Member of the Bar right now, Ella, I believe I'd almost have the courage to—

ELLA. What?

JIM. Nothing. (*After a pause—gropingly*) I can't explain—just—but it hurts like fire. It brands me in my pride. I swear I know more'n any member of my class. I ought to, I study harder. I work like the devil. It's all in my head—all fine and correct to a T. Then when I'm called on—I stand up—all the white faces looking at me—and I can feel their eyes—I hear my own voice sounding funny, trembling—and all of a sudden it's all gone in my head—there's nothing remembered—and I hear myself stuttering—and give up—sit down— They don't laugh, hardly ever. They're kind. They're good people. (*In a frenzy*) They're considerate, damn them! But I feel branded!

ELLA. Poor Jim.

JIM. (*going on painfully*) And it's the same thing in the written exams. For weeks before I study all night. I can't sleep anyway. I learn it all, I see it, I understand it. Then they give me the paper in the exam room. I look it over, I know each answer—perfectly. I take up my pen. On all sides are white men starting to write. They're so sure—even the ones that I know know nothing. But I know it all—but I can't remember any more—it fades—it goes—it's gone. There's a blank in my head—stupidity—I sit like a fool fighting to remember a little bit here, a little bit there—not enough to pass—not enough for anything—when I know it all!

ELLA. (*compassionately*) Jim. It isn't worth it. You don't need to—

316

JIM. I need it more than anyone ever needed anything. I need it to live.

ELLA. What'll it prove?

JIM. Nothing at all much—but everything to me.

ELLA. You're so much better than they are in every other way.

JIM. (*looking up at her*) Then—you understand?

ELLA. Of course. (*Affectionately*) Don't I know how fine you've been to me! You've been the only one in the world who's stood by me—the only understanding person—and all after the rotten way I used to treat you.

JIM. But before that—way back so high—you treated me good. (*He smiles.*)

ELLA. You've been white to me, Jim. (*She takes his hand.*)

JIM. White—to you!

ELLA. Yes.

JIM. All love is white. I've always loved you. (*This with the deepest humility.*)

ELLA. Even now—after all that's happened!

JIM. Always.

ELLA. I like you, Jim—better than anyone else in the world.

JIM. That's more than enough, more than I ever hoped for. (*The organ grinder comes to the corner. He plays the chorus of "Annie Laurie." They sit listening, hand in hand*) Would you ever want to marry me, Ella?

ELLA. Yes, Jim.

JIM. (*as if this quick consent alarmed him*) No, no, don't answer now. Wait! Turn it over in your mind! Think what it means to you! Consider it—over and over again! I'm in no hurry, Ella. I can wait months—years—

ELLA. I'm alone. I've got to be helped. I've got to help someone—or it's the end—one end or another.

JIM. (*eagerly*) Oh, I'll help—I know I can help—I'll give my life to help you—that's what I've been living for—

ELLA. But can I help you? Can I help you?

JIM. Yes! Yes! We'll go abroad where a man is a man—where it don't make that difference—where people are kind and wise to see the souls under skins. I don't ask you to love me—I don't dare to hope nothing like that! I don't want nothing—only to wait—to know you like me—to be near you—to keep harm away—to make up for the past—to never let you suffer any more—to serve you—to lie at your feet like a dog that loves you—to kneel by your bed like a nurse that watches over you sleeping—to preserve and protect and shield you from evil and sorrow—to give my life and my blood and all the strength that's in me to give you peace and joy—to become your slave! —yes, be your slave—your black slave that adores you as sacred! (*He has sunk to his knees. In a frenzy of self-abnegation, as he says the last words he beats his head on the flagstones.*)

ELLA. (*overcome and alarmed*) Jim! Jim! You're crazy! I want to help you, Jim—I want to help—

CURTAIN

ACT ONE—SCENE FOUR

SOME *weeks or so later. A street in the same ward in front of an old brick church. The church sets back from the sidewalk in a yard enclosed by a rusty iron railing with a gate at center. On each side of this yard are tenements. The buildings have a stern, forbidding look. All the shades on the windows are drawn down, giving an effect of staring, brutal eyes that pry callously at human beings without ac-knowledging them. Even the two tall, narrow church windows on either side of the arched door are blanked with dull green shades. It is a bright sunny morning. The district is unusually still, as if it were waiting, holding its breath.*

318

From the street of the blacks to the right a Negro tenor sings in a voice of shadowy richness—the first stanza with a contented, child-like melancholy—

> *Sometimes I feel like a mourning dove,*
> *Sometimes I feel like a mourning dove,*
> *Sometimes I feel like a mourning dove,*
> *I feel like a mourning dove.*
> *Feel like a mourning dove.*

The second with a dreamy, boyish exultance—

> *Sometimes I feel like an eagle in the air,*
> *Sometimes I feel like an eagle in the air,*
> *Sometimes I feel like an eagle in the air,*
> *I feel like an eagle in the air.*
> *Feel like an eagle in the air.*

The third with a brooding, earthbound sorrow—

> *Sometimes I wish that I'd never been born,*
> *Sometimes I wish that I'd never been born,*
> *Sometimes I wish that I'd never been born,*
> *I wish that I'd never been born.*
> *Wish that I'd never been born.*

As the music dies down there is a pause of waiting stillness. This is broken by one startling, metallic clang of the church-bell. As if it were a signal, people—men, women, children—pour from the two tenements, whites from the tenement to the left, blacks from the one to the right. They hurry to form into two racial lines on each side of the gate, rigid and unyielding, staring across at each other with bitter hostile eyes. The halves of the big church door swing open and JIM *and* ELLA *step out from the darkness within into the sunlight. The doors slam behind them like wooden lips of an idol that has spat*

319

them out. JIM *is dressed in black.* ELLA *in white, both with extreme plainness. They stand in the sunlight, shrinking and confused. All the hostile eyes are now concentrated on them. They become aware of the two lines through which they must pass; they hesitate and tremble; then stand there staring back at the people, as fixed and immovable as they are. The organ grinder comes in from the right. He plays the chorus of "Old Black Joe." As he finishes the bell of the church clangs one more single stroke, insistently dismissing.*

JIM. (*as if the sound had awakened him from a trance, reaches out and takes her hand*) Come. Time we got to the steamer. Time we sailed away over the sea. Come, Honey! (*She tries to answer but her lips tremble; she cannot take her eyes off the eyes of people; she is unable to move. He sees this and, keeping the same tone of profound, affectionate kindness, he points upward in the sky, and gradually persuades her eyes to look up*) Look up, Honey! See the sun! Feel his warm eye lookin' down! Feel how kind he looks! Feel his blessing deep in your heart, your bones! Look up, Honey! (*Her eyes are fixed on the sky now. Her face is calm. She tries to smile bravely back at the sun. Now he pulls her by the hand, urging her gently to walk with him down through the yard and gate, through the lines of people. He is maintaining an attitude to support them through the ordeal only by a terrible effort, which manifests itself in the hysteric quality of ecstasy which breaks into his voice*) And look at the sky! Ain't it kind and blue! Blue for hope. Don't they say blue's for hope? Hope! That's for us, Honey. All those blessings in the sky! What's it the Bible says? Falls on just and unjust alike? No, that's the sweet rain. Pshaw, what am I saying? All mixed up. There's no unjust about it. We're all the same—equally just—under the sky—under the sun—under God— sailing over the sea—to the other side of the world—the side where Christ was born—the kind side that takes count of the soul—over the sea—the sea's blue, too—. Let's not be late—let's get that steamer!

(They have reached the curb now, passed the lines of people. She is looking up to the sky with an expression of trance-like calm and peace. He is on the verge of collapse, his face twitching, his eyes staring. He calls hoarsely): Taxi! Where is he? Taxi!

CURTAIN

ACT TWO—SCENE ONE

Two *years later. A flat of the better sort in the Negro district near
the corner of Act One. This is the parlor. Its furniture is a queer
clash. The old pieces are cheaply ornate, naïvely, childishly gaudy—
the new pieces give evidence of a taste that is diametrically opposed,
severe to the point of somberness. On one wall, in a heavy gold frame,
is a colored photograph—the portrait of an elderly Negro with an
able, shrewd face but dressed in an outlandish lodge regalia, a get-up
adorned with medals, sashes, a cocked hat with frills—the whole effect
as absurd to contemplate as one of Napoleon's Marshals in full uniform. In the left corner, where a window lights it effectively, is a
Negro primitive mask from the Congo—a grotesque face, inspiring
obscure, dim connotations in one's mind, but beautifully done, conceived in a true religious spirit. In this room, however, the mask acquires an arbitrary accentuation. It dominates by a diabolical quality
that contrast imposes upon it.*

*There are two windows on the left looking out in the street. In the
rear, a door to the hall of the building. In the right, a doorway with
red and gold portières leading into the bedroom and the rest of the
flat. Everything is cleaned and polished. The dark brown wallpaper
is new, the brilliantly figured carpet also. There is a round mahogany
table at center. In a rocking chair by the table* MRS. HARRIS *is sitting.
She is a mild-looking, gray-haired Negress of sixty-five, dressed in an
old-fashioned Sunday-best dress. Walking about the room nervously
is* HATTIE, *her daughter,* JIM's *sister, a woman of about thirty with a
high-strung, defiant face—an intelligent head showing both power
and courage. She is dressed severely, mannishly.*

*It is a fine morning in Spring. Sunshine comes through the windows
at the left.*

322

MRS. HARRIS. Time dey was here, ain't it?

HATTIE. (*impatiently*) Yes.

MRS. H. (*worriedly*) You ain't gwine ter kick up a fuss, is you—like you done wid Jim befo' de weddin'?

HATTIE. No. What's done is done.

MRS. H. We mustn't let her see we hold it agin' her—de bad dat happened to her wid dat no-count fighter.

HATTIE. I certainly never give that a thought. It's what she's done to Jim—making him run away and give up his fight—!

MRS. H. Jim loves her a powerful lot, must be.

HATTIE. (*after a pause—bitterly*) I wonder if she loves Jim!

MRS. H. She must, too. Yes, she must, too. Don't you forget dat it was hard for her—mighty, mighty hard—harder for de white dan for de black!

HATTIE. (*indignantly*) Why should it be?

MRS. H. (*shaking her head*) I ain't talkin' of shoulds. It's too late for shoulds. Dey's o'ny one should. (*Solemnly*) De white and de black shouldn't mix dat close. Dere's one road where de white goes on alone; dere's anudder road where de black goes on alone—

HATTIE. Yes, if they'd only leave us alone!

MRS. H. Dey leaves your Pa alone. He comes to de top till he's got his own business, lots o' money in de bank, he owns a building even befo' he die. (*She looks up proudly at the picture.* HATTIE *sighs impatiently—then her mother goes on*) Dey leaves me alone. I bears four children into dis worl', two dies, two lives, I helps you two grow up fine an' healthy and eddicated wid schoolin' and money fo' yo' comfort—

HATTIE. (*impatiently*) Ma!

MRS. H. I does de duty God set for me in dis worl'. Dey leaves me alone. (HATTIE *goes to the window to hide her exasperation. The mother broods for a minute—then goes on*) The worl' done change. Dey ain't no satisfaction wid nuffin' no more.

HATTIE. Oh! (*Then after a pause*) They'll be here any minute now.

MRS. H. Why didn't you go meet 'em at de dock like I axed you?

HATTIE. I couldn't. My face and Jim's among those hundreds of white faces— (*With a harsh laugh*) It would give her too much advantage!

MRS. H. (*impatiently*) Don't talk dat way! What makes you so proud? (*Then after a pause—sadly*) Hattie.

HATTIE. (*turning*) Yes, Ma.

MRS. H. I want to see Jim again—my only boy—but—all de same I'd ruther he stayed away. He say in his letter he's happy, she's happy, dey likes it dere, de folks don't think nuffin' but what's natural at seeing 'em married. Why don't dey stay?

HATTIE. (*vehemently*) No! They were cowards to run away. If they believe in what they've done, then let them face it out, live it out here, be strong enough to conquer all prejudice!

MRS. H. Strong? Dey ain't many strong. Dey ain't many happy neider. Dey was happy ovah yondah.

HATTIE. We don't deserve happiness till we've fought the fight of our race and won it! (*In the pause that follows there is a ring from back in the flat*) It's the door bell! You go, Ma. I—I—I'd rather not. (*Her mother looks at her rebukingly and goes out agitatedly through the portières.* HATTIE *waits, nervously walking about, trying to compose herself. There is a long pause. Finally the portières are parted and* JIM *enters. He looks much older, graver, worried.*)

JIM. Hattie!

HATTIE. Jim! (*They embrace with great affection.*)

JIM. It's great to see you again! You're looking fine.

HATTIE. (*looking at him searchingly*) You look well, too—thinner maybe—and tired. (*Then as she sees him frowning*) But where's Ella?

JIM. With Ma. (*Apologetically*) She sort of—broke down—when we came in. The trip wore her out.

HATTIE. (*coldly*) I see.

JIM. Oh, it's nothing serious. Nerves. She needs a rest.

HATTIE. Wasn't living in France restful?

JIM. Yes, but—too lonely—especially for her.

HATTIE. (*resentfully*) Why! Didn't the people there want to associate—?

JIM. (*quickly*) Oh, no indeedy, they didn't think anything of that. (*After a pause*) But—she did. For the first year it was all right. Ella liked everything a lot. She went out with French folks and got so she could talk a little—and I learned it—a little. We were having a right nice time. I never thought then we'd ever want to come back here.

HATTIE. (*frowning*) But—what happened to change you?

JIM. (*after a pause—haltingly*) Well—you see—the first year—she and I were living around—like friends—like a brother and sister—like you and I might.

HATTIE. (*her face becoming more and more drawn and tense*) You mean—then—? (*She shudders—then after a pause*) She loves you, Jim?

JIM. If I didn't know that I'd have to jump in the river.

HATTIE. Are you sure she loves you?

JIM. Isn't that why she's suffering?

HATTIE. (*letting her breath escape through her clenched teeth*) Ah!

JIM. (*suddenly springs up and shouts almost hysterically*) Why d'you ask me all those damn questions? Are you trying to make trouble between us?

HATTIE. (*controlling herself—quietly*) No, Jim.

JIM. (*after a pause—contritely*) I'm sorry, Hattie. I'm kind of on edge today. (*He sinks down on his chair—then goes on as if something forced him to speak*) After that we got to living housed in. Ella didn't want to see nobody, she said just the two of us was enough. I was happy then—and I really guess she was happy, too—in a way —for a while. (*Again a pause*) But she never did get to wanting to go out any place again. She got to saying she felt she'd be sure to run into someone she knew—from over here. So I moved us out to the

country where no tourist ever comes—but it didn't make any difference to her. She got to avoiding the French folks the same as if they
were Americans and I couldn't get it out of her mind. She lived in
the house and got paler and paler, and more and more nervous and
scary, always imagining things—until I got to imagining things, too.
I got to feeling blue. Got to sneering at myself that I wasn't any better than a quitter because I sneaked away right after getting married,
didn't face nothing, gave up trying to become a Member of the Bar—
and I got to suspecting Ella must feel that way about me, too—that
I wasn't a *real man!*

HATTIE. (*indignantly*) She couldn't!

JIM. (*with hostility*) You don't need to tell me! All this was only
in my own mind. We never quarreled a single bit. We never said
a harsh word. We were as close to each other as could be. We were
all there was in the world to each other. We were alone together!
(*A pause*) Well, one day I got so I couldn't stand it. I could see she
couldn't stand it. So I just up and said: Ella, we've got to have a
plain talk, look everything straight in the face, hide nothing, come out
with the exact truth of the way we feel.

HATTIE. And you decided to come back!

JIM. Yes. We decided the reason we felt sort of ashamed was we'd
acted like cowards. We'd run away from the thing—and taken it
with us. We decided to come back and face it and live it down in ourselves, and prove to ourselves we were strong in our love—and then,
and that way only, by being brave we'd free ourselves, and gain confidence, and be really free inside and able then to go anywhere and
live in peace and equality with ourselves and the world without any
guilty, uncomfortable feeling coming up to rile us. (*He has talked
himself now into a state of happy confidence.*)

HATTIE. (*bending over and kissing him*) Good for you! I admire
you so much, Jim! I admire both of you! And are you going to begin
studying right away and get admitted to the Bar?

JIM. You bet I am!

HATTIE. You must, Jim! Our race needs men like you to come to the front and help— (*As voices are heard approaching she stops, stiffens, and her face grows cold.*)

JIM. (*noticing this—warningly*) Remember Ella's been sick! (*Losing control—threateningly*) You be nice to her, you hear! (MRS. HARRIS *enters, showing* ELLA *the way. The colored woman is plainly worried and perplexed.* ELLA *is pale, with a strange, haunted expression in her eyes. She runs to* JIM *as to a refuge, clutching his hands in both of hers, looking from* MRS. HARRIS *to* HATTIE *with a frightened defiance.*)

MRS. H. Dere he is, child, big's life! She was afraid we'd done kidnapped you away, Jim.

JIM. (*patting her hand*) This place ought to be familiar, Ella. Don't you remember playing here with us sometimes as a kid?

ELLA. (*queerly—with a frown of effort*) I remember playing marbles one night—but that was on the street.

JIM. Don't you remember Hattie?

HATTIE. (*coming forward with a forced smile*) It was a long time ago—but I remember Ella. (*She holds out her hand.*)

ELLA. (*taking it—looking at* HATTIE *with the same queer defiance*) I remember. But you've changed so much.

HATTIE. (*stirred to hostility by* ELLA'S *manner—condescendingly*) Yes, I've grown older, naturally. (*Then in a tone which, as if in spite of herself, becomes bragging*) I've worked so hard. First I went away to college, you know—then I took up post-graduate study—when suddenly I decided I'd accomplish more good if I gave up learning and took up teaching. (*She suddenly checks herself, ashamed, and stung by* ELLA'S *indifference*) But this sounds like stupid boasting. I don't mean that. I was only explaining—

ELLA. (*indifferently*) I didn't know you'd been to school so long. (*A pause*) Where are you teaching? In a colored school, I suppose. (*There is an indifferent superiority in her words that is maddening to* HATTIE.)

HATTIE. (*controlling herself*) Yes. A private school endowed by some wealthy members of our race.

ELLA. (*suddenly—even eagerly*) Then you must have taken lots of examinations and managed to pass them, didn't you?

HATTIE. (*biting her lips*) I always passed with honors!

ELLA. Yes, we both graduated from the same High School, didn't we? That was dead easy for me. Why I hardly even looked at a book. But Jim says it was awfully hard for him. He failed one year, remember? (*She turns and smiles at* JIM—*a tolerant, superior smile but one full of genuine love.* HATTIE *is outraged, but* JIM *smiles.*)

JIM. Yes, it was hard for me, Honey.

ELLA. And the law school examinations Jim hardly ever could pass at all. Could you? (*She laughs lovingly.*)

HATTIE. (*harshly*) Yes, he could! He can! He'll pass them now—if you'll give him a chance!

JIM. (*angrily*) Hattie!

MRS. HARRIS. Hold yo' fool tongue!

HATTIE. (*sullenly*) I'm sorry. (ELLA *has shrunk back against* JIM. *She regards* HATTIE *with a sort of wondering hatred. Then she looks away about the room. Suddenly her eyes fasten on the primitive mask and she gives a stifled scream.*)

JIM. What's the matter, Honey?

ELLA. (*pointing*) That! For God's sake, what is it?

HATTIE. (*scornfully*) It's a Congo mask. (*She goes and picks it up*) I'll take it away if you wish. I thought you'd like it. It was my wedding present to Jim.

ELLA. What is it?

HATTIE. It's a mask which used to be worn in religious ceremonies by my people in Africa. But, aside from that, it's beautifully made, a work of Art by a real artist—as real in his way as your Michael Angelo. (*Forces* ELLA *to take it*) Here. Just notice the workmanship.

ELLA. (*defiantly*) I'm not scared of it if you're not. (*Looking at it with disgust*) Beautiful? Well, some people certainly have queer notions! It looks ugly to me and stupid—like a kid's game—making faces. (*She slaps it contemptuously*) Pooh! You needn't look hard at me. I'll give you the laugh. (*She goes to put it back on the stand.*)

JIM. Maybe, if it disturbs you, we better put it in some other room.

ELLA. (*defiantly aggressive*) No. I want it here where I can give it the laugh! (*She sets it there again—then turns suddenly on* HATTIE *with aggressive determination*) Jim's not going to take any more examinations! I won't let him!

HATTIE. (*bursting forth*) Jim! Do you hear that? There's white justice!—their fear for their superiority!—

ELLA. (*with a terrified pleading*) Make her go away, Jim!

JIM. (*losing control—furiously to his sister*) Either you leave here —or we will!

MRS. H. (*weeping—throws her arms around* HATTIE) Let's go, child! Let's go!

HATTIE. (*calmly now*) Yes, Ma. All right. (*They go through the portières. As soon as they are gone,* JIM *suddenly collapses into a chair and hides his head in his hands.* ELLA *stands beside him for a moment. She stares distractedly about her, at the portrait, at the mask, at the furniture, at* JIM. *She seems fighting to escape from some weight on her mind. She throws this off and, completely her old self for the moment, kneels by* JIM *and pats his shoulder.*)

ELLA. (*with kindness and love*) Don't, Jim! Don't cry, please! You don't suppose I really meant that about the examinations, do you? Why, of course, I didn't mean a word! I couldn't mean it! I want you to take the examinations! I want you to pass! I want you to be a lawyer! I want you to be the best lawyer in the country! I want you to show 'em—all the dirty sneaking, gossiping liars that talk behind our backs—what a man I married. I want the whole world to know you're the whitest of the white! I want you to climb and climb—and step on 'em, stamp right on their mean faces! I love you, Jim! You know that!

JIM. (*calm again—happily*) I hope so, Honey—and I'll make myself worthy.

HATTIE. (*appears in the doorway—quietly*) We're going now, Jim.

ELLA. No. Don't go.

HATTIE. We were going to, anyway. This is your house—Mother's gift to you, Jim.

JIM. (*astonished*) But I can't accept— Where are you going?

HATTIE. We've got a nice flat in the Bronx—(*with bitter pride*) in the heart of the Black Belt—the Congo—among our own people!

JIM. (*angrily*) You're crazy—I'll see Ma— (*He goes out.* HATTIE *and* ELLA *stare at each other with scorn and hatred for a moment, then* HATTIE *goes.* ELLA *remains kneeling for a moment by the chair, her eyes dazed and strange as she looks about her. Then she gets to her feet and stands before the portrait of* JIM'S *father—with a sneer.*)

ELLA. It's his Old Man—all dolled up like a circus horse! Well, they can't help it. It's in the blood, I suppose. They're ignorant, that's all there is to it. (*She moves to the mask—forcing a mocking tone*) Hello, sport! Who d'you think you're scaring? Not me! I'll give you the laugh. He won't pass, you wait and see. Not in a thousand years! (*She goes to the window and looks down at the street and mutters*) All black! Every one of them! (*Then with sudden excitement*) No, there's one. Why, it's Shorty! (*She throws the window open and calls*) Shorty! Shorty! Hello, Shorty! (*She leans out and waves—then stops, remains there for a moment looking down, then shrinks back on the floor suddenly as if she wanted to hide—her whole face in an anguish*) Say! Say! I wonder—No, he didn't hear you. Yes, he did, too! He must have! I yelled so loud you could hear me in Jersey! No, what are you talking about? How would he hear with all the kids yelling down there? He never heard a word, I tell you! He did, too! He didn't want to hear you! He didn't want to let anyone know he knew you! Why don't you acknowledge it? What are you lying about? I'm not! Why shouldn't he? Where does he come in to—for God's sake, who is Shorty, anyway? A pimp! Yes, and a dope-peddler, too! D'you

mean to say he'd have the nerve to hear me call him and then deliberately—? Yes, I mean to say it! I do say it! And it's true, and you
know it, and you might as well be honest for a change and admit it!
He heard you but he didn't want to hear you! He doesn't want to
know you any more. No, not even him! He's afraid it'd get him in
wrong with the old gang. Why? You know well enough! Because
you married a—a—a—well, I won't say it, but you know without my
mentioning names! (ELLA *springs to her feet in horror and shakes
off her obsession with a frantic effort*) Stop! (*Then whimpering like
a frightened child*) Jim! Jim! Jim! Where are you? I want you, Jim!
(*She runs out of the room as the curtain falls.*)

ACT TWO—SCENE TWO

T HE *same. Six months later. It is evening. The walls of the room
appear shrunken in, the ceiling lowered, so that the furniture,
the portrait, the mask look unnaturally large and domineering.* JIM
*is seated at the table studying, law books piled by his elbows. He is
keeping his attention concentrated only by a driving physical effort
which gives his face the expression of a runner's near the tape. His
forehead shines with perspiration. He mutters one sentence from
Blackstone over and over again, tapping his forehead with his fist in
time to the rhythm he gives the stale words. But, in spite of himself,
his attention wanders, his eyes have an uneasy, hunted look, he starts
at every sound in the house or from the street. Finally, he remains
rigid, Blackstone forgotten, his eyes fixed on the portières with tense
grief. Then he groans, slams the book shut, goes to the window and
throws it open and sinks down beside it, his arms on the sill, his head
resting wearily on his arms, staring out into the night, the pale glare
from the arc-lamp on the corner throwing his face into relief. The
portières on the right are parted and* HATTIE *comes in.*

339

HATTIE. (*not seeing him at the table*) Jim! (*Discovering him*) Oh, there you are. What're you doing?

JIM. (*turning to her*) Resting. Cooling my head. (*Forcing a smile*) These law books certainly are a sweating proposition! (*Then anxiously*) How is she?

HATTIE. She's asleep now. I felt it was safe to leave her for a minute. (*After a pause*) What did the doctor tell you, Jim?

JIM. The same old thing. She must have rest, he says, her mind needs rest— (*Bitterly*) But he can't tell me any prescription for that rest—leastways not any that'd work.

HATTIE. (*after a pause*) I think you ought to leave her, Jim—or let her leave you—for a while, anyway.

JIM. (*angrily*) You're like the doctor. Everything's so simple and easy. Do this and that happens. Only it don't. Life isn't simple like that—not in this case, anyway—no, it isn't simple a bit. (*After a pause*) I can't leave her. She can't leave me. And there's a million little reasons combining to make one big reason why we can't. (*A pause*) For her sake—if it'd do her good—I'd go—I'd leave—I'd do anything— because I love her. I'd kill myself even—jump out of this window this second—I've thought it over, too—but that'd only make matters worse for her. I'm all she's got in the world! Yes, that isn't bragging or fooling myself. I know that for a fact! Don't you know that's true? (*There is a pleading for the certainty he claims.*)

HATTIE. Yes, I know she loves you, Jim. I know that now.

JIM. (*simply*) Then we've got to stick together to the end, haven't we, whatever comes—and hope and pray for the best? (*A pause— then hopefully*) I think maybe this is the crisis in her mind. Once she settles this in herself, she's won to the other side. And me—once I become a Member of the Bar—then I win, too! We're both free—by our own fighting down our own weakness! We're both really, truly free! Then we can be happy with ourselves here or anywhere. She'll be proud then! Yes, she's told me again and again, she says she'll be actually proud!

332

HATTIE. (*turning away to conceal her emotion*) Yes, I'm sure—but you mustn't study too hard, Jim. You mustn't study too awfully hard!

JIM. (*gets up and goes to the table and sits down wearily*) Yes, I know. Oh, I'll pass easily. I haven't got any scary feeling about that any more. And I'm doing two years' work in one here alone. That's better than schools, eh?

HATTIE. (*doubtfully*) It's wonderful, Jim.

JIM. (*his spirit evaporating*) If I can only hold out! It's hard! I'm worn out. I don't sleep. I get to thinking and thinking. My head aches and burns like fire with thinking. Round and round my thoughts go chasing like crazy chickens hopping and flapping before the wind. It gets me crazy mad—'cause I can't stop!

HATTIE. (*watching him for a while and seeming to force herself to speak*) The doctor didn't tell you all, Jim.

JIM. (*dully*) What's that?

HATTIE. He told me you're liable to break down too, if you don't take care of yourself.

JIM. (*abjectly weary*) Let 'er come! I don't care what happens to me. Maybe if I get sick she'll get well. There's only so much bad luck allowed to one family, maybe. (*He forces a wan smile.*)

HATTIE. (*hastily*) Don't give in to that idea, for the Lord's sake!

JIM. I'm tired—and blue—that's all.

HATTIE. (*after another long pause*) I've got to tell you something else, Jim.

JIM. (*dully*) What?

HATTIE. The doctor said Ella's liable to be sick like this a very long time.

JIM. He told me that too—that it'd be a long time before she got back her normal strength. Well, I suppose that's got to be expected.

HATTIE. (*slowly*) He didn't mean convalescing—what he told me. (*A long pause.*)

JIM. (*evasively*) I'm going to get other doctors in to see Ella—specialists. This one's a damn fool.

HATTIE. Be sensible, Jim. You'll have to face the truth—sooner or later.

JIM. (*irritably*) I know the truth about Ella better'n any doctor.

HATTIE. (*persuasively*) She'd get better so much sooner if you'd send her away to some nice sanitarium—

JIM. No! She'd die of shame there!

HATTIE. At least until after you've taken your examinations—

JIM. To hell with me!

HATTIE. Six months. That wouldn't be long to be parted.

JIM. What are you trying to do—separate us? (*He gets to his feet—furiously*) Go on out! Go on out!

HATTIE. (*calmly*) No, I won't. (*Sharply*) There's something that's got to be said to you and I'm the only one with the courage— (*Intensely*) Tell me, Jim, have you heard her raving when she's out of her mind?

JIM. (*with a shudder*) No!

HATTIE. You're lying, Jim. You must have—if you don't stop your ears—and the doctor says she may develop a violent mania, dangerous for you—get worse and worse until—Jim, you'll go crazy too—living this way. Today she raved on about "Black! Black!" and cried because she said her skin was turning black—that you had poisoned her—

JIM. (*in anguish*) That's only when she's out of her mind.

HATTIE. And then she suddenly called me a dirty nigger.

JIM. No! She never said that ever! She never would!

HATTIE. She did—and kept on and on! (*A tense pause*) She'll be saying that to you soon.

JIM. (*torturedly*) She don't mean it! She isn't responsible for what she's saying!

HATTIE. I know she isn't—yet she is just the same. It's deep down in her or it wouldn't come out.

JIM. Deep down in her people—not deep in her.

334

HATTIE. I can't make such distinctions. The race in me, deep in me, can't stand it. I can't play nurse to her any more, Jim,—not even for your sake. I'm afraid—afraid of myself—afraid sometime I'll kill her dead to set you free! (*She loses control and begins to cry.*)

JIM. (*after a long pause—somberly*) Yes, I guess you'd better stay away from here. Good-by.

HATTIE. Who'll you get to nurse her, Jim,—a white woman?

JIM. Ella'd die of shame. No, I'll nurse her myself.

HATTIE. And give up your studies?

JIM. I can do both.

HATTIE. You can't! You'll get sick yourself! Why, you look terrible even as it is—and it's only beginning!

JIM. I can do anything for her! I'm all she's got in the world! I've got to prove I can be all to her! I've got to prove worthy! I've got to prove she can be proud of me! I've got to prove I'm the whitest of the white!

HATTIE. (*stung by this last—with rebellious bitterness*) Is that the ambition she's given you? Oh, you soft, weak-minded fool, you traitor to your race! And the thanks you'll get—to be called a dirty nigger—to hear her cursing you because she can never have a child because it'll be born black—!

JIM. (*in a frenzy*) Stop!

HATTIE. I'll say what must be said even though you'll kill me, Jim. Send her to an asylum before you both have to be sent to one together.

JIM. (*with a sudden wild laugh*) Do you think you're threatening me with something dreadful now? Why, I'd like that. Sure, I'd like that! Maybe she'd like it better, too. Maybe we'd both find it all simple then—like you think it is now. Yes. (*He laughs again.*)

HATTIE. (*frightenedly*) Jim!

JIM. Together! You can't scare me even with hell fire if you say she and I go together. It's heaven then for me! (*With sudden savagery*) You go out of here! All you've ever been aiming to do is to separate us so we can't be together!

HATTIE. I've done what I did for your own good.

JIM. I have no own good. I only got a good together with her. I'm all she's got in the world! Let her call me nigger! Let her call me the whitest of the white! I'm all she's got in the world, ain't I? She's all I've got! You with your fool talk of the black race and the white race! Where does the human race get a chance to come in? I suppose that's simple for you. You lock it up in asylums and throw away the key! (*With fresh violence*) Go along! There isn't going to be no more people coming in here to separate—excepting the doctor. I'm going to lock the door and it's going to stay locked, you hear? Go along, now!

HATTIE. (*confusedly*) Jim!

JIM. (*pushes her out gently and slams the door after her—vaguely*) Go along! I got to study. I got to nurse Ella, too. Oh, I can do it! I can do anything for her! (*He sits down at the table and, opening the book, begins to recite the line from Blackstone in a meaningless rhythm, tapping his forehead with his fist.* ELLA *enters noiselessly through the portières. She wears a red dressing-gown over her night-dress but is in her bare feet. She has a carving-knife in her right hand. Her eyes fasten on* JIM *with a murderous mania. She creeps up behind him. Suddenly he senses something and turns. As he sees her he gives a cry, jumping up and catching her wrist. She stands fixed, her eyes growing bewildered and frightened.*)

JIM. (*aghast*) Ella! For God's sake! Do you want to murder me? (*She does not answer. He shakes her.*)

ELLA. (*whimperingly*) They kept calling me names as I was walking along—I can't tell you what, Jim—and then I grabbed a knife—

JIM. Yes! See! This! (*She looks at it frightenedly.*)

ELLA. Where did I—? I was having a nightmare— Where did they go—I mean, how did I get here? (*With sudden terrified pleading—like a little girl*) Oh, Jim—don't ever leave me alone! I have such terrible dreams, Jim—promise you'll never go away!

JIM. I promise, Honey.

ELLA. (*her manner becoming more and more childishly silly*) I'll be a little girl—and you'll be old Uncle Jim who's been with us for years and years— Will you play that?

JIM. Yes, Honey. Now you better go back to bed.

ELLA. (*like a child*) Yes, Uncle Jim. (*She turns to go. He pretends to be occupied by his book. She looks at him for a second—then suddenly asks in her natural woman's voice*) Are you studying hard, Jim?

JIM. Yes, Honey. Go to bed now. You need to rest, you know.

ELLA. (*stands looking at him, fighting with herself. A startling transformation comes over her face. It grows mean, vicious, full of jealous hatred. She cannot contain herself but breaks out harshly with a cruel, venomous grin*) You dirty nigger!

JIM. (*starting as if he'd been shot*) Ella! For the good Lord's sake!

ELLA. (*coming out of her insane mood for a moment, aware of something terrible, frightened*) Jim! Jim! Why are you looking at me like that?

JIM. What did you say to me just then?

ELLA. (*gropingly*) Why, I—I said—I remember saying, are you studying hard, Jim? Why? You're not mad at that, are you?

JIM. No, Honey. What made you think I was mad? Go to bed now.

ELLA. (*obediently*) Yes, Jim. (*She passes behind the portières.* JIM *stares before him. Suddenly her head is thrust out at the side of the portières. Her face is again that of a vindictive maniac*) Nigger! (*The face disappears—she can be heard running away, laughing with cruel satisfaction.* JIM *bows his head on his outstretched arms but he is too stricken for tears.*)

CURTAIN

ACT TWO—SCENE THREE

THE *same, six months later. The sun has just gone down. The Spring twilight sheds a vague, gray light about the room, picking out the Congo mask on the stand by the window. The walls appear shrunken in still more, the ceiling now seems barely to clear the people's heads, the furniture and the characters appear enormously magnified. Law books are stacked in two great piles on each side of the table.* ELLA *comes in from the right, the carving-knife in her hand. She is pitifully thin, her face is wasted, but her eyes glow with a mad energy, her movements are abrupt and spring-like. She looks stealthily about the room, then advances and stands before the mask, her arms akimbo, her attitude one of crazy mockery, fear and bravado. She is dressed in the red dressing-gown, grown dirty and ragged now, and is in her bare feet.*

ELLA. I'll give you the laugh, wait and see! (*Then in a confidential tone*) He thought I was asleep! He called, Ella, Ella—but I kept my eyes shut, I pretended to snore. I fooled him good. (*She gives a little hoarse laugh*) This is the first time he's dared to leave me alone for months and months. I've been wanting to talk to you every day but this is the only chance— (*With sudden violence—flourishing her knife*) What're you grinning about, you dirty nigger, you? How dare you grin at me? I guess you forget what you are! That's always the way. Be kind to you, treat you decent, and in a second you've got a swelled head, you think you're somebody, you're all over the place putting on airs; why, it's got so I can't even walk down the street without seeing niggers, niggers everywhere. Hanging around, grinning, grinning—going to school—pretending they're white—taking examinations— (*She stops, arrested by the word, then suddenly*) That's where he's gone—down to the mail-box—to see if there's a letter from the Board—telling him— But why is he so long? (*She calls pitifully*) Jim! (*Then in a terrified whimper*) Maybe he's passed! Maybe he's passed! (*In a frenzy*) No! No! He can't! I'd kill him! I'd kill myself! (*Threatening the Congo mask*) It's you who're to blame for this! Yes, you! Oh, I'm on to you! (*Then appealingly*) But why d'you want to do this to us? What have I ever done wrong to you? What have you got against me? I married you, didn't I? Why don't you let Jim alone? Why don't you let him be happy as he is—with me? Why don't you let me be happy? He's white, isn't he—the whitest man that ever lived? Where do you come in to interfere? Black! Black! Black as dirt! You've poisoned me! I can't wash myself clean! Oh, I hate you! I hate you! Why don't you let Jim and me be happy? (*She sinks down in his chair, her arms outstretched on the table. The door from the hall is slowly opened and* JIM *appears. His bloodshot, sleepless eyes stare from deep hollows. His expression is one of crushed numbness. He holds an open letter in his hand.*)

JIM. (*seeing* ELLA—*in an absolutely dead voice*) Honey— I thought you were asleep.

ELLA. (*starts and wheels about in her chair*) What's that? You got —you got a letter—?

JIM. (*turning to close the door after him*) From the Board of Examiners for admission to the Bar, State of New York—God's country! (*He finishes up with a chuckle of ironic self-pity so spent as to be barely audible.*)

ELLA. (*writhing out of her chair like some fierce animal, the knife held behind her—with fear and hatred*) You didn't—you didn't— you didn't pass, did you?

JIM. (*looking at her wildly*) Pass? Pass? (*He begins to chuckle and laugh between sentences and phrases, rich, Negro laughter, but heart-breaking in its mocking grief*) Good Lord, child, how come you can ever imagine such a crazy idea? Pass? Me? Jim Crow Harris? Nigger Jim Harris—become a full-fledged Member of the Bar! Why the mere notion of it is enough to kill you with laughing! It'd be against all natural laws, all human right and justice. It'd be miraculous, there'd be earthquakes and catastrophes, the seven Plagues'd come again and locusts'd devour all the money in the banks, the second Flood'd come roaring and Noah'd fall overboard, the sun'd drop out of the sky like a ripe fig, and the Devil'd perform miracles, and God'd be tipped head first right out of the Judgment seat! (*He laughs, maudlinly uproarious.*)

ELLA. (*her face beginning to relax, to light up*) Then you—you didn't pass?

JIM. (*spent—giggling and gasping idiotically*) Well, I should say not! I should certainly say not!

ELLA. (*with a cry of joy, pushes all the law books crashing to the floor—then with childish happiness she grabs* JIM *by both hands and dances up and down*) Oh, Jim, I knew it! I knew you couldn't! Oh, I'm so glad, Jim! I'm so happy! You're still my old Jim—and I'm so glad! (*He looks at her dazedly, a fierce rage slowly gathering on his face. She dances away from him. His eyes follow her. His hands clench. She stands in front of the mask—triumphantly*) There! What did I tell? I told you I'd give you the laugh! (*She begins to laugh with wild unrestraint, grabs the mask from its place, sets it in the middle of the table and plunging the knife down through it pins it to the table*) There! Who's got the laugh now?

JIM. (*his eyes bulging—hoarsely*) You devil! You white devil woman! (*In a terrible roar, raising his fists above her head*) You devil!

ELLA. (*looking up at him with a bewildered cry of terror*) Jim! (*Her appeal recalls him to himself. He lets his arms slowly drop to his sides, bowing his head.* ELLA *points tremblingly to the mask*) It's all right, Jim! It's dead. The devil's dead. See! It couldn't live—unless you passed. If you'd passed it would have lived in you. Then I'd have had to kill you, Jim, don't you see?—or it would have killed me. But

340

now I've killed it. (*She pats his hand*) So you needn't ever be afraid any more, Jim.

JIM. (*dully*) I've got to sit down, Honey. I'm tired. I haven't had much chance for sleep in so long— (*He slumps down in the chair by the table.*)

ELLA. (*sits down on the floor beside him and holds his hand. Her face is gradually regaining an expression that is happy, childlike and pretty*) I know, Jim! That was my fault. I wouldn't let you sleep. I couldn't let you. I kept thinking if he sleeps good then he'll be sure to study good and then he'll pass—and the devil'll win!

JIM. (*with a groan*) Don't, Honey!

ELLA. (*with a childish grin*) That was why I carried that knife around—(*she frowns—puzzled*)—one reason—to keep you from studying and sleeping by scaring you.

JIM. I wasn't scared of being killed. I was scared of what they'd do to you after.

ELLA. (*after a pause—like a child*) Will God forgive me, Jim?

JIM. Maybe He can forgive what you've done to me; and maybe He can forgive what I've done to you; but I don't see how He's going to forgive—Himself.

ELLA. I prayed and prayed. When you were away taking the examinations and I was alone with the nurse, I closed my eyes and pretended to be asleep but I was praying with all my might: O God, don't let Jim pass!

JIM. (*with a sob*) Don't, Honey, don't! For the good Lord's sake! You're hurting me!

ELLA. (*frightenedly*) How, Jim? Where? (*Then after a pause— suddenly*) I'm sick, Jim. I don't think I'll live long.

JIM. (*simply*) Then I won't either. Somewhere yonder maybe— together—our luck'll change. But I wanted—here and now—before you—we—I wanted to prove to you—to myself—to become a full-fledged Member—so you could be proud— (*He stops. Words fail and he is beyond tears.*)

ELLA. (*brightly*) Well, it's all over, Jim. Everything'll be all right now. (*Chattering along*) I'll be just your little girl, Jim—and you'll be my little boy—just as we used to be, remember, when we were beaux; and I'll put shoe-blacking on my face and pretend I'm black and you can put chalk on your face and pretend you're white just as we used to do—and we can play marbles—only you mustn't all the time be a boy. Sometimes you must be my old kind Uncle Jim who's been with us for years and years. Will you, Jim?

JIM. (*with utter resignation*) Yes, Honey.

ELLA. And you'll never, never, never, never leave me, Jim?

JIM. Never, Honey.

ELLA. 'Cause you're all I've got in the world—and I love you, Jim. (*She kisses his hand as a child might, tenderly and gratefully.*)

JIM. (*suddenly throws himself on his knees and raises his shining eyes, his transfigured face*) Forgive me, God—and make me worthy! Now I see Your Light again! Now I hear Your Voice! (*He begins to weep in an ecstasy of religious humility*) Forgive me, God, for blaspheming You! Let this fire of burning suffering purify me of selfishness and make me worthy of the child You send me for the woman You take away!

ELLA. (*jumping to her feet—excitedly*) Don't cry, Jim! You mustn't cry! I've got only a little time left and I want to play. Don't be old Uncle Jim now. Be my little boy, Jim. Pretend you're Painty Face and I'm Jim Crow. Come and play!

JIM. (*still deeply exalted*) Honey, Honey, I'll play right up to the gates of Heaven with you! (*She tugs at one of his hands, laughingly trying to pull him up from his knees as the curtain falls.*)

342

MARCO MILLIONS

CHARACTERS

CHRISTIANS (*in the order in which they appear*):

A TRAVELER

MARCO POLO

DONATA

NICOLO POLO, *Marco's father*

MAFFEO POLO, *Marco's uncle*

TEDALDO, *Legate of Syria (afterward Pope Gregory X)*

A DOMINICAN MONK

A KNIGHT-CRUSADER

A PAPAL COURIER

PAULO LOREDANO, *Donata's father, a gentleman from Venice*

Ladies and gentlemen of Venice, soldiers, people of Acre, musicians, servants, etc.

HEATHEN (*in the order in which they appear*):

A MAGIAN TRAVELER

A BUDDHIST TRAVELER

A MAHOMETAN CAPTAIN OF GHAZAN'S ARMY

THE ALI BROTHERS, *Mahometan merchants*

A PROSTITUTE

A DERVISH

TWO BUDDHIST MERCHANTS

TWO TARTAR MERCHANTS

A MONGOL PRIEST

EMISSARY FROM KUBLAI

KUBLAI, THE GREAT KAAN

PRINCESS KUKACHIN, *his granddaughter*

CHU-YIN, *a Cathayan sage*

GENERAL BAYAN

A MESSENGER FROM PERSIA

GHAZAN, KHAN OF PERSIA

A BUDDHIST PRIEST

A TAOIST PRIEST

A CONFUCIAN PRIEST

A MOSLEM PRIEST

A TARTAR CHRONICLER

People of Persia, India, Mongolia, Cathay, courtiers, nobles, ladies. wives, warriors of KUBLAI's *court, musicians, dancers. Chorus of Mourners.*

SCENES

Prologue: A sacred tree in Persia near the confines of India toward the close of the thirteenth century.

ACT ONE

Scene I: Exterior of DONATA's house, Venice, twenty-three years earlier.

Scene II: Palace of the Papal Legate of Syria at Acre—six months later.

Scene III: Persia—four months later.

Scene IV: India—eight months later.

Scene V: Mongolia—eleven months later.

Scene VI: Cathay—The Grand Throne Rome in KUBLAI's palace at Cambaluc—one month later.

ACT TWO

Scene I: The Little Throne Room in KUBLAI's summer palace at Xanadu, "the city of Peace," fifteen years later.

Scene II: The royal wharf at the seaport of Zayton, several weeks later.

Scene III: Deck of the royal junk of the PRINCESS KUKACHIN at anchor in the harbor of Hormuz, Persia—two years later.

ACT THREE

Scene I: The Grand Throne Room in the Imperial Palace at Cambaluc, one year later—and later the Dining Room of the Polo Home in Venice at the same time.

Scene II: The Grand Throne Room at Cambaluc—one year later.

Epilogue: The theatre.

MARCO MILLIONS

PROLOGUE

Scene—*A sacred tree on a vast plain in Persia near the confines of India. Votive offerings, pieces of cloth torn from clothing, bangles, armlets, ornaments, tapers, have been nailed on the trunk or tied to the branches. The heavy limbs spread out to a great distance from the trunk. Beneath them is deep cool shade, contrasting with the blinding glare of the noon sun on the sandy plain in the background. A merchant, carrying in each hand a strapped box that resembles a modern sample case, plods wearily to the foot of the tree. He puts the boxes down and takes out a handkerchief to mop his forehead. He is a white Christian, middle-aged, average-looking, with a moustache and beard beginning to show gray. His clothes in the style of the Italian merchant class of the thirteenth century are travel-worn. He sighs, tired and hot.*

CHRISTIAN. Phoo!

(*From the left a* MAGIAN, *a Persian, dressed in the fashion of a trader, comes in. He carries a small, square bag. He also is hot, weary, and dust-covered. In age and appearance, making allowance for the difference in race, he closely resembles the* CHRISTIAN. *He and the latter stare at each other, then bow perfunctorily. The* MAGIAN *sets down his bag and wipes his brow.*)

CHRISTIAN. (*sympathetically*) Hot as hell!

MAGIAN. (*grimly*) Hotter! (*They both chuckle. A* BUDDHIST, *a Kashmiri traveling merchant comes in, puffing and sweating, from the right. He has a pack strapped on his back. He resembles the other two*

347

in the essential character of his body and face. He stops on seeing them.
After eyeing him for an appraising second, the two bow and the
BUDDHIST *comes forward to set his pack beside the bags of the others.*)

BUDDHIST. (*with relief*) Phoo! (*Then breaking the ice*) The sun
would cook you!

MAGIAN. It is hot certainly.

CHRISTIAN. (*as they all sit down to rest, looks from one to the other
—jovially*) Funny! you'd think we three had an appointment here.
Your faces look familiar. Haven't I seen you somewheres before?

MAGIAN. In the house of the courtezans at Shiraz. You were drunk.

BUDDHIST. I happened to be there that night, too. You danced and
sang lewd songs.

CHRISTIAN. (*a bit embarrassed, but grinning*) Humn—oh, yes—I
remember. It was my birthday and I'd taken a drop too much—a
very unusual thing for me. (*Then abruptly changing the subject*)
How are conditions down your way?

BUDDHIST. (*pursing his lips*) Slow. I come from Delhi. There is a
new import tax and trade is very unsettled. We make prayer beads.

MAGIAN. (*gloomily*) And I, for my sins, am hawking a novelty, a
block-printed book, for an Arab house. It contains one thousand
Arabian lies, with one over for good measure, all full of lechery—at
least so they instructed me to tell people to get them to buy.

CHRISTIAN. Did your trip take you down around Ispahan way?

MAGIAN. I just came from there. It is a sad city now. All the bazaars
have been closed by an imperial edict in mourning for Queen Kukachin.

CHRISTIAN. (*bounding to his feet as if a wasp had stung him*) Is
Queen Kukachin dead? (*Stunned*) Why, I've got a letter of intro-
duction to her from the head of my firm—Marco Polo of Polo Brothers
and Son, Venice. He acted as her official escort, and took her from
Cathay to Persia to be married! Why, I was counting on selling her
and her husband a whole fleet load of goods!

348

MAGIAN. (*suddenly, pointing off left*) What makes that cloud of dust? (*They all stare and begin to grow worried.*)

CHRISTIAN. It doesn't look like camels.

BUDDHIST. (*fearfully*) It has a strange look!

CHRISTIAN. It's coming directly this way.

MAGIAN. These plains are haunted by evil spirits.

CHRISTIAN. (*very frightened, but striving to put up a brave front*) I've heard those rumors. And I know for a fact that people are sometimes possessed by devils, but I don't believe—

BUDDHIST. (*suddenly, pointing to the tree*) I am going to offer a prayer for protection to this tree sacred to Buddha.

CHRISTIAN. } (*in chorus—irritably*) Sacred to Buddha?
MAGIAN. }

BUDDHIST. Certainly! Do you not know the legend of how the Holy Sakya picked a twig to cleanse his teeth, and then throwing it away, it took root, and sprang up into this mighty tree to testify forever to his miraculous power?

CHRISTIAN. (*resentfully*) You're absolutely all wrong! This tree was the staff of our first father, Adam. It was handed down to Moses who used it to tap water out of stones and finally planted it. The cross our Lord was crucified on was made of this wood. And ever since this tree has been sacred to Him!

MAGIAN. (*cuttingly*) You have both of you been duped by childish lies! This tree is sacred to the founder of the one true religion, Zoroaster, who brought a shoot of the Tree of Life down from Paradise and planted it here!

BUDDHIST. (*scornfully*) You are a pair of superstitious sheep!

CHRISTIAN. You are a couple of idolatrous dogs!

MAGIAN. The two of you are blasphemous hogs! (*They glare at each other insultingly, their hands on their daggers. Suddenly they hear a noise from the left. Their eyes at once are turned in that direction and, forgetting personal animosities, they give a startled exclamation at what they see.*)

349

BUDDHIST. They are pulling a chariot!

CHRISTIAN. They must be slaves. See how the driver lashes them!

BUDDHIST. But what can that be on the wagon—like a coffin!

CHRISTIAN. It must be treasure!

MAGIAN. No. It is a coffin. (*Trembling*) Ssst! I have a foreboding of evil. (*They prostrate themselves, their faces to the ground. A moment later, preceded by shouts, a cracking of whips, and the dull stamping of feet, a double file of thirty men of different ages, stripped to the waist, harnessed to each other waist-to-waist and to the long pole of a two-wheeled wagon, stagger in, straining forward under the lashes of two soldiers who run beside them and the long whips of the* CAPTAIN *and a* CORPORAL *who are riding on the wagon, the* CAPTAIN *driving. As they reach the middle of the shade they stop. Lashed on the wagon is a coffin covered with a white pall.*)

CAPTAIN. (*a brutal, determined-looking man of forty, bellows*) Halt! (*The files of bleeding and sweating men collapse in panting, groaning heaps. The* SOLDIERS *sprawl down beside them. The* CAPTAIN *springs off the wagon*) Phoo! This shade is grateful. (*He looks at the tree—then in an awed tone*) This must be the Holy Tree which was once the staff of Mahomet and, passing down through generations, was buried in the grave of Abu Abdallah where it struck root and grew by the will of Allah into this tree. (*He makes obeisance and prays to the tree as do the* SOLDIERS. *He gets up and takes a gulp of water—then, looking around, notices the three merchants—with startled surprise, drawing his sword*) Ho! What are you? Get up! (*They do so frightenedly. He stares at them and laughs coarsely with relief*) By all the demons, you startled me! But you traders are like fleas, one finds you everywhere! (*Then with a scowl*) Three dogs of unbelievers, too! (*Sharply*) Give an account of yourselves!

BUDDHIST. I was proceeding westward on a business venture, good sir.

MAGIAN. And I to the northward.

CHRISTIAN. And I to the court of Ghazan Khan to present this letter to Queen Kukachin. But I hear she's dead. (*He hands him the letter but the* CAPTAIN *backs away superstitiously*.)

CAPTAIN. Allah forbid I touch what belongs to a corpse! (*Then with forced laughter*) You need not journey farther. She is in there! (*His voice has dropped, he points toward the coffin. The others stare at it, dumbfounded and awed. The* CAPTAIN *goes on dryly*) You cannot cheat her now, Christian! (*Then lowering his voice as if afraid he will be overheard*) And yet, to look at her face you would think her only sleeping.

CHRISTIAN. (*astonished*) What? Can you look at her?

CAPTAIN. Her coffin is glass. Her body was anointed by Egyptians so that she preserves the appearance of life. This was done by command of her grandfather Kublai, the Great Kaan. She is being taken home to Cathay for burial—and under penalty of torture I must transport her over the first stage by dark tonight! (*Suddenly lamenting*) But Allah afflicted me! When I reached the last village with my camels foundering, I found the accursed villagers had driven off their beasts to escape requisition. But the dogs could not balk me. I hitched them to the pole instead. (*He looks at the moaning figures with a cruel appraising eye*) But will they last till night? Hi, there! Water to revive them! (*The soldiers carry around jugs of water which the panting men reach out for avidly, then sink back. But three of the more elderly men are too spent to move*.)

CHRISTIAN. (*timorously—anxious to change the subject*) Was the Queen very beautiful?

CAPTAIN. (*with bravado*) Would you care to see? You had a letter to her. It can do no harm—and it is a very great wonder!

CHRISTIAN. (*reassuringly, because he is now extremely curious*) Dead Queens in the West usually lie in state.

CAPTAIN. You pull back the cloth then, since that is your custom. (*The* CHRISTIAN *goes to the wagon and gingerly pulls back the pall from the head of the coffin—then retreats with an exclamation as* KUKACHIN's *face, that of a beautiful Tartar princess of twenty-three,*

351

is revealed inside the glass. Her calm expression seems to glow with the intense peace of a life beyond death, the eyes are shut as if she were asleep. The men stare fascinatedly.)

CHRISTIAN. (*after a pause—crossing himself awedly*) Are you certain she's dead?

CAPTAIN. (*in an awed whisper*) In the palace I commanded the company who guarded her coffin at night. I could not take my eyes from her face. It seemed that any moment she must awake and speak! (*While they have been speaking, unnoticed by them, it has grown dark. An unearthly glow, like a halo, lights up the face of* KUKACHIN. *From the branches of the tree comes a sound of sweet sad music as if the leaves were tiny harps strummed by the wind. The face of* KUKACHIN *becomes more and more living. Finally her lips part and her eyes open to look up at the tree.*)

CAPTAIN. (*kneeling down to pray*) Allah, be pitiful!

BUDDHIST. Buddha, protect Thy servant!

MAGIAN. Mithra, All-Powerful One!

CHRISTIAN. Jesus, have mercy! (*A voice which is* KUKACHIN's *and yet more musical than a human voice, comes from the coffin as her lips are seen to move.*)

KUKACHIN. Say this, I loved and died. Now I am love, and live. And living, have forgotten. And loving, can forgive. (*Here her lips part in a smile of beautiful pity*) Say this for me in Venice! (*A sound of tender laughter, of an intoxicating, supernatural gaiety, comes from her lips and is taken up in chorus in the branches of the tree as if every harp-leaf were laughing in music with her. The laughter recedes heavenward and dies as the halo of light about her face fades and noonday rushes back in a blaze of baking plain. Everyone is prostrate, the harnessed wretches in the exhausted attitudes of sleep, the others visibly trembling with superstitious horror.*)

CHRISTIAN. (*the first to recover—bewilderedly*) Venice! It must have been a message she wished me to take back to Marco Polo!

CAPTAIN. (*his terror going and rage taking its place, leaps to his feet*) It was the voice of some Christian devil you summoned! It bewitched even me until Allah drove it back to hell! (*He draws his sword*) Cover her face, accursed sorcerer!

CHRISTIAN. (*pulls the covering over the head of the coffin with indecent haste*) I pledge you my word, good Captain—!

CAPTAIN. (*to his* SOLDIERS) Attention! Kick them up! We must get away from here! (*With blows and kicks the* SOLDIERS *get their human beasts to their feet. There are groans and curses and cries of pain. But three cannot be roused. The* CAPTAIN *growls savagely at the* CHRISTIAN *to keep up his courage*) Pig of an infidel! (*Then glaring at the* BUDDHIST *and* MAGIAN) You too! You were in league with him! (*He grips his sword.*)

ALL THREE. (*kneeling—pitiably*) Mercy! Spare us!

A CORPORAL. (*comes up and salutes*) We cannot get three of them up, sir.

CAPTAIN. (*raging*) Lash them!

CORPORAL. They are dead, sir.

CAPTAIN. (*glumly*) Oh. (*Then an idea comes—with cruel satisfaction*) Three, did you say? That is fortunate. Allah has provided! Cut them out and put these in their places! (*At a sign, the* SOLDIERS *fall upon the three merchants, strip off their upper clothes, untie the dead men, and hitch them in their places. All the time the three set up miserable screams of protest, punctuated by the blows and kicks they receive. The others look on with exhausted indifference.*)

CHRISTIAN. (*making himself heard above the tumult*) My letter! It was to the Queen! When Polo Brothers hear of this outrage they'll get the Kaan to flay you alive!

CAPTAIN. (*taken aback for a moment—then craftily*) Show me your letter again!

CHRISTIAN. (*holding it out with frantic eagerness*) Here! Now set me free!

CAPTAIN. (*takes it and calmly tears it up*) I cannot read but I think you are lying. At any rate, now you have no letter! (*The* CHRISTIAN

353

sets up a wailing cry and receives a blow. The CAPTAIN *and* CORPORALS *spring up on the wagon*) And now forward march! (*With a great cracking of whips and shouts of pain the wagon is pulled swiftly away. On the ground under the sacred tree three bodies lie in crumpled heaps. The same sweet sad music comes from the tree again as if its spirit were playing on the leaves a last lamenting farewell to the dead* PRINCESS. *It rises softly and as softly dies away until it is nothing but a faint sound of wind rustling the leaves.*

CURTAIN

ACT ONE—SCENE ONE

SCENE: *Twenty-three years earlier. A fresh boy's voice is heard sing-ing a love song in a subdued tone. The light slowly reveals the exterior of* DONATA'S *home on a canal, Venice.* MARCO POLO, *a boy of fifteen, youthfully handsome and well made, is standing in a gondola beneath a barred window of the house, a guitar over his shoulder. The song finished, he waits anxiously. A hand is thrust out to him through the bars. He kisses it passionately. It is hurriedly withdrawn.* DONATA'S *face appears pressed against the bars. She is a girl of twelve, her face pale and pretty in the moonlight.*

DONATA. (*coyly and tenderly*) You mustn't, Mark.

MARCO. There's no harm in that—just kissing your hand!

DONATA. (*demurely*) It's a sin, I'm sure of it.

MARCO. (*with a quick movement of his own hand, captures hers through the bars*) Then I'll have to steal it, and that's a worse sin. (*He pulls her willing hand down toward his lips.*)

DONATA. You're hurting my fingers.

MARCO. (*boldly now*) Then I know how to cure them. (*He kisses them one by one*) There!

DONATA. (*tenderly*) You silly boy! Why do you do that?

MARCO. (*very seriously*) You know, Donata.

DONATA. Know what? (*Softly*) Go on and tell me, Mark.

MARCO. (*blurts out gruffly*) I love you, that's what. I've loved you ever since I can remember. And you've known it right along, too, so there's no good pretending.

DONATA. (*softly*) I wasn't sure.

MARCO. (*recklessly*) And how about you? Do you love me? You've got to answer me that!

355

DONATA. You know—without my saying it.

MARCO. Please say it!

DONATA. (*in a whisper*) I love you. There, silly!

MARCO. And you'll promise to marry me when I come back?

DONATA. Yes, but you'll have to ask my parents.

MARCO. (*easily*) Don't worry about them. They'll be glad, and my folks, too. It'll bring the two firms into closer contact.

DONATA. (*practically*) Yes, I think so, too. (*A pause. Songs and music come from near and far-off in the night about them.* MARCO *has gained possession of her two hands now and his face is closer to the bars of her window.*)

MARCO. (*with a sigh*) It's beautiful tonight. I wish I didn't have to go away.

DONATA. I wish, too! Do you really have to?

MARCO. Yes. And I want to, too—all but leaving you. I want to travel and see the world and all the different people, and get to know their habits and needs from first-hand knowledge. You've got to do that if you want to become really big and important. That's what Father says—and Uncle.

DONATA. But won't this trip so very far away be full of danger?

MARCO. (*boastfully*) I can take care of myself. Uncle says taking chances—*necessary* chances, of course—is the best schooling for a real merchant and Father has a saying that where there's nothing risked, there's nothing gained. And they ought to know, oughtn't they, after spending nine years at the court of the Great Kaan and traveling there and back?

DONATA. Is that where you're going?

MARCO. Yes. He's the richest king in the world and Uncle and Father are personal friends of his. They did a lot of work for him. I'll be on the right side of him from the start, and Father and Uncle both say there's millions to be made in his service if you're not afraid of work and keep awake to opportunity.

DONATA. I'm sure you'll succeed. But I wish you weren't going for so long.

MARCO. I'll miss you as much as you miss me. (*Huskily*) I hate to leave you, Donata—but I've got to make my own way—so we can marry—

DONATA. (*hurriedly*) Yes—of course—only come back as soon as you can.

MARCO. But you'll wait, won't you, no matter how long?

DONATA. (*solemnly*) Yes, I swear to, Mark.

MARCO. And I swear by God I'll come back and marry you, and I'll always be true and never forget or do anything—

DONATA. (*startled by a noise from within*) Ssshh! There's someone moving inside. You'll have to go. Here. (*She hands him a locket*) It's a medallion of me painted by an artist who owed Father for spices and couldn't pay with money. Will you keep looking at this all the time you're away and never forget me?

MARCO. (*kissing it passionately*) Every day!

DONATA. And you'll write me?

MARCO. I promise. Every chance I get.

DONATA. (*hesitatingly*) Will you write me—a poem? I won't care how short it is if it's only a poem.

MARCO. I'll try, Donata. I'll do my best.

DONATA. I'll just love it to death, Mark! (*Startledly*) Ssshh! I hear it again. It must be Father. I've got to sneak back.

MARCO. (*desperately*) Won't you kiss me—let me really kiss you— just one—for good-bye?

DONATA. I mustn't.

MARCO. Just once—when I'm going so far away? (*Desperately*) I—I—I'll die if you don't!

DONATA. Well—just once. (*The moonlight fades into darkness as their lips meet. Then from the darkness are their voices heard in hushed tones*) Good-bye, Mark.

MARCO. Good-bye, Donata. (*The sentimental singing voices and guitars are heard from all corners of the night in celebration of love. The sound gradually grows fainter and fainter, receding into the distance, as if* MARCO *were already leaving Venice behind him.*)

DARKNESS

ACT ONE—SCENE TWO

Scene—*Six months later. The tolling of a church bell is first heard. Then the interior of the Papal Legate's palace at Acre is revealed —a combination of church and government building.*

The Legate, TEDALDO, *a man of sixty with a strong, intelligent face, is seated on a sort of throne placed against the rear wall. On his right, stands a warrior noble, a* KNIGHT-CRUSADER, *in full armor, leaning on his sword. On his left, a* DOMINICAN MONK, *his adviser. On the left of the room is an altar with candles burning. On the right, an open portal with a sentry pacing up and down, spear in hand.*

The two elder Polos, NICOLO *and* MAFFEO, *stand in attitudes of patient servility before the throne.* MARCO'S *father,* NICOLO, *is a small thin middle-aged man, with a dry, shrewd face.* MAFFEO, MARCO'S *uncle, is around the same age, but he is tall and stout with a round, jovial face and small, cunning eyes. There is a strong general resemblance between both of them and* MARCO. MARCO *is sitting on a stool in the foreground, his body all screwed up into an awkward intensity, striving with all his might to compose a poem to* DONATA, *but constantly distracted in spite of himself.*

TEDALDO. (*bored but tolerantly*) What can I do except advise you to be patient? I'm sure the Conclave of Cardinals must soon select a Pope.

NICOLO. Two years in session! (*Then suddenly—consoled*) Well, it's a new world's record, anyway.

MAFFEO. (*shaking his head*) This uncertainty is bad for trade.

TEDALDO. (*with a bored yawn*) No doubt. (*Then rather impatiently*) Then, when your business so evidently calls you to the East, why delay longer? Why not simply explain to the Great Kaan, Kublai, that there was no Pope to whom you could deliver his message?

NICOLO. He mightn't understand. His instructions to us were pretty emphatic.

MAFFEO. To request the Pope to send him a hundred wise men of the West—

TEDALDO. (*dryly*) This Kublai is an optimist!

MAFFEO. —to argue with his Buddhists and Taoists and Confucians which religion in the world is best.

MONK. (*outraged*) Impudent ignoramus! Does he imagine the Church would stoop to such bickering?

TEDALDO. (*with a weary smile*) I begin to think Kublai is a humorist, too.

MAFFEO. (*craftily*) It'd pay to convert him. He's the richest king in the world. He rules over millions of subjects, his empire covers millions of square miles of great undeveloped natural resources, his personal wealth in cash and jewels and goods alone easily runs into millions of millions!

MARCO. (*stares at his uncle—then mutters fascinatedly*) Millions! (*Then, shaking away this interruption, bends to his writing again.*)

TEDALDO. (*wearily*) I am bored with your millions, Messrs. Polo. Even if they are true, it is too much effort to conceive them. (*They bow humbly and retire backward. His eyes following them listlessly,* TEDALDO *sees* MARCO, *who at this moment is scratching himself, twisting and turning his legs and feet, tearing his hair in a perfect frenzy of balked inspiration.* TEDALDO *smiles and addresses him in an affectionate, humorous tone*) God's mercy on you, Master Marco! Are

359

you suddenly possessed by a devil—or is it only these infernal Mahometan fleas the Almighty sends us for our sins?

MARCO. (*coming out of his fit—sheepishly*) I'm only writing something.

MAFFEO. Mark is surprisingly quick at figures.

NICOLO. But still heedless. A dreamer! (*To* MARCO, *with a condescending paternal air*) What are you writing, son? (*He and* MAFFEO *draw near* MARCO.)

MARCO. (*more confused*) Nothing, sir—just—something. (*He tries to hide it.*)

MAFFEO. Why are you so mysterious? Come, let's see.

MARCO. No—please, Uncle.

MAFFEO. (*with a sudden cunning motion, he snatches it from* MARCO's *hand, glances at it and bursts into laughter*) Look, Nicolo, Look!

MARCO. (*rebelliously*) Give that back!

NICOLO. (*sternly*) Behave yourself, Mark! (*To* MAFFEO) What is it?

MAFFEO. See for yourself. (*He hands it to him*) Did you know you'd hatched a nightingale? (*He laughs coarsely.* NICOLO *reads, a scornful grin coming to his lips.*)

TEDALDO. Surely it cannot be a song he has written?

NICOLO. (*going to him—laughing*) A rhyme! A love poem, no less!

TEDALDO. (*severely, as he takes the poem*) Do not mock at him! Rather be grateful if a thistle can bring forth figs. (MARCO *remains sullenly apart, shamefaced and angry, his fists clenched.* TEDALDO *reads—frowns—laughs—then smilingly to* NICOLO) Your fear that this is a poem is—human—exaggerated! (*He reads amusedly as* MARCO *squirms*):

> "You are lovely as the gold in the sun
> Your skin is like silver in the moon
> Your eyes are black pearls I have won.
> I kiss your ruby lips and you swoon,
> Smiling your thanks as I promise you
> A large fortune if you will be true,

While I am away earning gold
And silver so when we are old
I will have a million to my credit
And in the meantime can easily afford
A big wedding that will do us credit
And start having children, bless the Lord!"

(*There is a roar of laughter in which* TEDALDO *joins.* MARCO *looks about for a hole into which to crawl.* TEDALDO *addresses him amusedly but with kindness*) Come, Marco. Here is your poem. Your lady is a bit too mineral, your heaven of love a trifle monetary—but, never mind, you will be happier as a Polo than as a poet. Here. (*He gives it to* MARCO. *The latter fiercely crumples it up and throws it on the floor and stamps on it.*)

NICOLO. (*approvingly*) Sensibly done, my boy.

TEDALDO. (*looking searchingly at* MARCO'S *face—gently*) Perhaps I was too critical. Your poem had merits of its own. I am sure it would touch your lady's heart.

MARCO. (*with a great bluster of manliness*) Oh, I don't mind your making fun. I can take a joke. It *was* silly. Poetry's all stupid, anyway. I was only trying it for fun, to see if I could. You won't catch me ever being such a fool again!

MONK. (*as a noise of shouting comes toward them*) Ssstt! What's that? (*The* KNIGHT *hurries to the portal.*)

KNIGHT. Someone is running here, and a crowd behind. I hear them shouting "Pope."

MONK. Then the Conclave has chosen!

POLOS. (*joyfully*) At last! (*The cries of many voices. The* SENTINEL *and* KNIGHT *admit the* MESSENGER *but push back the others.*)

MESSENGER. (*exhausted—falls on his knees before* TEDALDO, *holding out a sealed paper*) I come from the Conclave. You were chosen. Your Holiness— (*He falls fainting. The crowds cheer and sweep in.*)

TEDALDO. (*rising—pale and trembling*) What does he say?

361

MONK. (*has picked up the document—joyfully*) See! The official seal! You are the Pope! (*He kneels humbly*) Your Holiness, let me be the first— (*He kisses* TEDALDO's *hand. All are kneeling now, their heads bowed. The bells of the churches begin to ring.*)

TEDALDO. (*raising his hands to heaven—dazedly*) Lord, I am not worthy! (*Then to those about him—tremblingly*) Leave me. I must pray to God for strength—for guidance!

CROWD. (*in a clamor*) Your blessing! (TEDALDO, *with a simple dignity and power, blesses them. They back out slowly, the* MONK *and* KNIGHT *last. The* POLOS *group together in the foreground, holding a whispered conference.* TEDALDO *kneels before the altar.*)

MAFFEO. Now that he's the Pope, if we could get an answer from him, we could start right away.

NICOLO. We couldn't hope for better weather.

MAFFEO. He seems to have taken a fancy to Mark. You speak to him, Mark.

MARCO. (*unwillingly*) He's praying.

MAFFEO. He'll have time enough for that, but with us time is money. (*Giving the unwilling* MARCO *a push*) This will test your nerve, Mark! Don't shirk!

MARCO. (*gritting his teeth*) All right. I'll show you I'm not scared! (*He advances boldly toward the altar, stands there for a moment awkwardly as* TEDALDO *remains oblivious—then he falls on his knees—humbly but insistently*) Your Holiness. Forgive me, Your Holiness—

TEDALDO. (*turns to him and springs to his feet—imperiously*) I wish to be alone! (*Then as* MARCO *is shrinking back—more kindly*) Well, what is it? I owe you a recompense, perhaps—for an injury.

MARCO. (*stammeringly*) Your Holiness—if you could give us some answer to deliver to the Great Kaan—we could start now—with such favorable weather—

TEDALDO. (*amused in spite of himself*) On the last day one of your seed will interrupt Gabriel to sell him another trumpet! (*Then sardonically to the elder* POLOS) I have no hundred wise men—nor one!

Tell the Great Kaan he must have been imposed upon by your patriotic lies, or he could never make such a request.

POLOS. (*terrified*) But, Your Holiness, we dare not repeat— He'd have us killed!

TEDALDO. I will send him a monk or two. That is quite sufficient to convert a Tartar barbarian!

MAFFEO. But, Your Holiness, he's not a barbarian! Why, every plate on his table is solid gold!

TEDALDO. (*smiling*) And has he millions of plates, too? (*Then with a sudden whimsicality*) But if the monks fail, Master Marco can be my missionary. Let him set an example of virtuous Western manhood amid all the levities of paganism, shun the frailty of poetry, have a million to his credit, as he so beautifully phrased it, and I will wager a million of something or other myself that the Kaan will soon be driven to seek spiritual salvation somewhere! Mark my words, Marco will be worth a million wise men—in the cause of wisdom! (*He laughs gaily, raising his hand over* MARCO's *head*) Go with my blessing! But what need have you for a blessing? You were born with success in your pocket! (*With a last gesture he turns, going quickly out the door in rear.*)

MAFFEO. (*as he goes—approvingly*) Mark is making a good impression already!

NICOLO. Well, he's got a head on him!

MARCO. (*beginning to swell out a bit matter-of-factly*) Never mind about me. When do we start?

POLOS. (*hurriedly*) At once. Let's go and pack. (*They go out left*) Come, Mark! Hurry!

MARCO. I'm coming. (*He waits, looks after them, picks up the crumpled poem, starts to hide it in his jacket, stops, mutters with brave self-contempt*) Aw! You damn fool! (*He throws the poem down again, starts to go, hesitates, suddenly turns back, picks it up, crams it into his doublet and runs wildly out the door. The scene fades into darkness. For a time the church bells, which have never ceased ringing,*

363

are heard acclaiming the new Pope; but the POLOS *proceed speedily on their journey and the sound is soon left behind them.)*

DARKNESS

ACT ONE—SCENE THREE

SCENE—*Light comes, gradually revealing the scene. In the rear is the front of a Mahometan mosque. Before the mosque is a throne on which sits a Mahometan ruler. On the right, the inevitable warrior—on his left, the inevitable priest—the two defenders of the State. At the ruler's feet his wives crouch like slaves. Everything is jeweled, high-colored, gorgeous in this background. Squatted against the side walls, forming a sort of semi-circle with the throne at center, counting from left to right consecutively, are a mother nursing a baby, two children playing a game, a young girl and a young man in a loving embrace, a middle-aged couple, an aged couple, a coffin. All these Mahometan figures remain motionless. Only their eyes move, staring fixedly but indifferently at the* POLOS, *who are standing at center.* MARCO *is carrying in each hand bags which curiously resemble modern sample cases. He sets these down and gazes around with a bewildered awe.*

NICOLO. (*turning on him—genially*) Well, son, here we are in Islam.

MARCO. (*round-eyed*) A man told me that Noah's Ark is still somewhere around here on top of a mountain. (*Eagerly*) And he proved it to me, too. Look! (*He shows them a piece of wood*) He broke this off of the Ark. See, it's got Noah's initials on it!

MAFFEO (*grimly*) How much did you pay him for it?

MARCO. Ten soldi in silver.

364

NICOLO. (*dashing it out of* MARCO's *hand—bitterly*) Muttonhead! Do you suppose Almighty God would allow infidels to cut up Noah's Ark into souvenirs to sell to Christians?

MAFFEO. (*teasingly*) Your son and your money are soon parted, Brother. (*Then placatingly*) But he's only a boy. He'll learn. And before we go farther, Nicolo, we better read him from the notes we made on our last trip all there is to remember about this corner of the world.

NICOLO. (*they take out note-books closely resembling a modern business man's date-book and read*) We're now passing through kingdoms where they worship Mahomet.

MAFFEO. There's one kingdom called Musul and in it a district of Baku where there's a great fountain of oil. There's a growing demand for it. (*Then speaking*) Make a mental note of that.

MARCO. Yes, sir.

NICOLO. Merchants make great profits. The people are simple creatures. It's very cold in winter. The women wear cotton drawers. This they do to look large in the hips, for the men think that a great beauty. (*The two* MAHOMETAN MERCHANTS *enter from the left.* MAFFEO *recognizes them immediately—in a swift aside to his brother.*)

MAFFEO. There's those damned Ali brothers. They'll cut under our prices with their cheap junk as usual. (*The* ALI *brothers have seen the* POLOS *and a whispered aside, evidently of the same nature, passes between them. Then simultaneously the two firms advance to meet each other putting on expressions of the utmost cordiality*) Well, well. You folks are a welcome sight!

ONE ALI. My dear, dear friends! Praise be to Allah! (*They embrace.*)

MAFFEO. (*with a cunning smirk*) Selling a big bill of goods hereabouts, I'll wager, you old rascals?

THE OLDER ALI. (*airily*) My dear friend, don't speak of business. But you, you are on a venture to the court of the Great Kaan, we hear?

MAFFEO. What lies get around! Nothing in it—absolutely nothing!

365

NICOLO. For heaven's sake, let's not talk business! Let's have a nice friendly chat. (*The four squat together in a circle.*)

MAFFEO. (*with a wink*) I'll tell you a good one an Armenian doily-dealer told me down in Bagdad. (*They all bend their heads toward him with expectant grins. He looks around—then begins in a cautious lowered tone*) Well, there was an old Jew named Ikey and he married a young girl named Rebecca— (*He goes on telling the rest of the story with much exaggerated Jewish pantomime but in a voice too low to be heard. In the meantime,* MARCO *has slipped off, full of curiosity and wonder, to look at this strange life. He goes first to the left, stops before the mother and baby, smiles down at it uncertainly, then bends down to take hold of its hand.*)

MARCO. Hello! (*Then to the mother*) He's fat as butter! (*Both remain silent and motionless, staring at him from a great distance with indifferent calm.* MARCO *is rebuffed, grows embarrassed, turns away to the children, who, frozen in the midst of their game of jackstraws, are looking at him.* MARCO *adopts a lofty condescending air*) Humph! Do you still play that game here? I remember it—when I was a kid. (*They stare silently. He mutters disgustedly*) Thickheads! (*And turns to the lovers who with their arms about each other, cheek to cheek, stare at him. He looks at them, fascinated and stirred, and murmurs enviously*) She's pretty. I suppose they're engaged—like Donata and me. (*He fumbles and pulls out the locket which is hung around his neck on a ribbon*) Donata's prettier. (*Then embarrassedly, he holds it out for them to see*) Don't you think she's pretty? She and I are going to be married some day. (*They do not look except into his eyes. He turns away, hurt and angry*) Go to the devil, you infidels! (*He stuffs the locket back—stops before the throne—tries to stare insolently at the king but, awed in spite of himself, makes a grudging bow and passes on, stops before the family group, sneers and passes on, stops before the old couple and cannot restrain his curiosity*) Would you tell me how old you are? (*He passes on, rebuffed again, stops fascinatedly before the coffin, leans out and touches it with defiant daring, shudders superstitiously and shrinks away, going to the merchant group who are roaring with laughter as* MAFFEO *ends his story.*)

THE OLDER ALI. (*to* NICOLO) Your son?

NICOLO. Yes, and a chip of the old block.

THE OLDER ALI. Will he follow in your footsteps?

NICOLO. (*jocosely*) Yes, and you better look out then! He's as keen as a hawk already.

THE OLDER ALI. (*with a trace of a biting smile*) He greatly resembles a youth I saw back on the road buying a piece of Noah's Ark from a wayside sharper.

MAFFEO. (*hastily coming to the rescue as* NICOLO *cannot hide his chagrin—boastfully*) It wasn't Mark. Mark would have sold him the lions of St. Mark's for good mousers! (*The* PROSTITUTE *enters from the right. She is painted, half-naked, alluring in a brazen, sensual way. She smiles at* MARCO *enticingly.*)

MARCO. (*with a gasp*) Look! Who's that? (*They all turn, and, recognizing her, laugh with coarse familiarity.*)

MAFFEO. (*jokingly*) So here you are again. You're like a bad coin—always turning up.

PROSTITUTE. (*smiling*) Shut up. You can bet it isn't old fools like you that turn me.

NICOLO. (*with a lecherous grin at her*) No? But it's the old who have the money.

PROSTITUTE. Money isn't everything, not always. Now I wouldn't ask money from him. (*She points to* MARCO.)

NICOLO. (*crossly and jealously*) Leave him alone, you filth!

MAFFEO. (*broad-mindedly*) Come, come, Nicolo. Let the boy have his fling.

PROSTITUTE. (*her eyes on* MARCO) Hello, Handsome.

MARCO. (*bewilderedly*) You've learned our language?

PROSTITUTE. I sell to all nations.

MARCO. What do you sell?

367

PROSTITUTE. (*mockingly*) A precious jewel. Myself. (*Then desir-ously*) But for you I'm a gift. (*Putting her hands on his shoulders and lifting her lips*) Why don't you kiss me?

MARCO. (*terribly confused—strugglingly*) I don't know—I mean, I'm sorry but—you see I promised someone I'd never— (*Suddenly freeing himself—frightenedly*) Leave go! I don't want your kisses. (*A roar of coarse taunting laughter from the men.* MARCO *runs away, off left.*)

NICOLO. (*between his teeth*) What a dolt!

MAFFEO. (*slapping the* PROSTITUTE *on the bare shoulder*) Better luck next time. He'll learn!

PROSTITUTE. (*trying to hide her pique—forcing a cynical smile*) Oh, yes, but I won't be a gift then. I'll make him pay, just to show him! (*She laughs harshly and goes out left. A pause. All four squat again in silence.*)

THE OLDER ALI. (*suddenly*) Many wonders have come to pass in these regions. They relate that in old times three kings from this country went to worship a Prophet that was born and they carried with them three manner of offerings—Gold and Frankincense and Myrrh—and when they had come to the place where the Child was born, they marveled and knelt before him.

MAFFEO. That's written in the Bible. The child was Jesus Christ, our Lord. (*He blesses himself,* NICOLO *does likewise.*)

THE OLDER ALI. Your Jesus was a great prophet.

NICOLO. (*defiantly*) He was the Son of God!

BOTH ALIS. (*stubbornly*) There is no God but Allah! (*A strained pause. A dervish of the desert runs in shrieking and begins to whirl. No one is surprised except the two* POLOS *who get up to gape at him with the thrilled appreciation inspired by a freak in a sideshow.* MARCO *comes back and joins them.*)

MAFFEO. (*with appreciation*) If we had him in Venice we could make a mint of money exhibiting him. (NICOLO *nods.*)

368

MARCO. I'll have to write Donata all about this. (*Wonderingly*) Is he crazy?

MAFFEO. (*in a low aside to him*) My boy, all Mahometans are crazy. That's the only charitable way to look at it. (*Suddenly the call to prayer sounds from Muezzins in the minarets of the mosque. The* DERVISH *falls on his face. Everyone sinks into the attitude of prayer except the* POLOS *who stand embarrassedly, not knowing what to do.*)

MARCO. Are they praying?

NICOLO. Yes, they call it that. Much good it does them!

MAFFEO. Ssshh! Come! This is a good time to move on again. Marco! Wake up! (*They go quickly out right,* MARCO *following with the sample cases. The scene fades quickly into darkness as the call of the Muezzins is heard again.*)

DARKNESS

ACT ONE—SCENE FOUR

SCENE—*The slowly-rising light reveals an Indian snake-charmer squatted on his haunches at center. A snake is starting to crawl from the basket in front of him, swaying its head to the thin, shrill whine of a gourd. Otherwise, the scene, in the placing of its people and the characters and types represented, is the exact duplicate of the last except that here the locale is Indian. The background for the ruler's throne is now a Buddhist temple instead of a mosque. The motionless staring figures are all Indians. Looming directly above and in back of the ruler's throne is an immense Buddha. The* POLOS *stand at center as before,* MARCO *still lugging the sample cases. He is seventeen now. Some of the freshness of youth has worn off.*

They stare at the snake-charmer, the two older men cynically. MARCO *gasps with enthralled horror.*

MARCO. Look at that deadly snake!

MAFFEO. (*cynically*) He's a fake, like everything else here. His fangs have been pulled out.

MARCO. (*disillusioned*) Oh! (*He turns away. The snake-charmer glares at them, stops playing, pushes his snake back into the box and carries it off, after spitting on the ground at their feet with angry disgust.* MARCO *sits on one of the cases and glances about with a forced scorn; looks finally at the Buddha—in a smart-Aleck tone*) So that is Buddha!

NICOLO. (*begins to read from his note-book*) These people are idolaters. The climate is so hot if you put an egg in their rivers it will be boiled.

MAFFEO. (*taking up the reading from his book in the same tone*) The merchants make great profits. Ginger, pepper, and indigo. Largest sheep in the world. Diamonds of great size. The Kings have five hundred wives apiece.

MARCO. (*disgustedly*) It's too darn hot here!

MAFFEO. (*warningly*) Sshhh! Don't let the natives hear you. Remember any climate is healthy where trade is brisk.

MARCO. (*walks sullenly off to left. At the same moment two merchants, this time Buddhists, come in. The same interplay goes on with them as with the* ALI BROTHERS *in the previous scene, only this time it is all done in pantomime until the loud laughter at the end of* MAFFEO's *story. As* MAFFEO *tells the story,* MARCO *is looking at the people but this time he assumes the casual, indifferent attitude of the worldly-wise. He makes a silly gesture to attract the baby's attention, passes by the two children with only a contemptuous glance, but stops and stares impudently at the lovers—finally spits with exaggerated scorn*) Where do you think you are—home with the light out? Why don't you charge admission? (*He stalks on—pauses before the middle-aged couple who have a bowl of rice between them—in astonishment as though this evidence of a humanity common with his struck him as strange*) Real rice! (*He ignores the throne, passes quickly by the old people with a glance of aversion and very obviously averts his head from the coffin. As he returns to the group at center,* MAFFEO *has just finished his story. There is a roar of laughter.*)

MARCO. (*grinning eagerly*) What was it, Uncle?

MAFFEO. (*grinning teasingly*) You're too young.

MARCO.(*boastfully*) Is that so?

NICOLO. (*severely*) Mark! (*The* PROSTITUTE, *the same but now in Indian garb, has entered from left and comes up behind* MARCO.)

PROSTITUTE. A chip of the old block, Nicolo!

NICOLO. (*angrily*) You again!

MARCO. (*pleased to see her—embarrassedly*) Why, hello.

PROSTITUTE. (*cynically*) I knew you'd want to see me. (*She raises her lips*) Will you kiss me now? (*As he hesitates*) Forget your promise. You know you want to.

MAFFEO. (*grinning*) There's no spirit in the youngsters nowadays I'll bet he won't.

PROSTITUTE. (*her eyes on* MARCO'S) How much will you bet?

MAFFEO. Ten— (MARCO *suddenly kisses her.*)

PROSTITUTE. (*turning to* MAFFEO) I win, Uncle.

MARCO. (*with a grin*) No. I kissed you before he said ten what.

MAFFEO. That's right! Good boy, Mark!

PROSTITUTE. (*turning to* MARCO—*cynically*) You're learning, aren't you? You're becoming shrewd even about kisses. You need only me now to make you into a real man—for ten pieces of gold.

MARCO. (*genuinely overcome by a sudden shame*) No, please.—I—I didn't mean it. It was only in fun.

PROSTITUTE. (*with a sure smile*) Later, then—when we meet again, (*She walks off left.*)

MARCO. (*looks after her. As she evidently turns to look back at him, he waves his hand and grins—then abashed*) She's pretty. It's too bad she's—what she is.

MAFFEO. Don't waste pity. Her kind are necessary evils. All of us are human. (*A long pause.*)

371

THE OLDER BUDDHIST MERCHANT. (*suddenly*) The Buddha taught that one's loving-kindness should embrace all forms of life, that one's compassion should suffer with the suffering, that one's sympathy should understand all things, and last that one's judgment should regard all persons and things as of equal importance.

NICOLO. (*harshly*) Who was this Buddha?

THE OLDER BUDDHIST MERCHANT. The Incarnation of God.

NICOLO. You mean Jesus?

THE OLDER BUDDHIST MERCHANT. (*unheedingly*) He was immaculately conceived. The Light passed into the womb of Maya, and she bore a son who, when he came to manhood, renounced wife and child, riches and power, and went out as a beggar on the roads to seek the supreme enlightenment which would conquer birth and death; and at last he attained the wisdom where all desire has ended and experienced the heaven of peace, Nirvana. And when he died he became a God again. (*The temple bells begin to ring in chorus. All except the* POLOS *prostrate themselves before the Buddha.*)

MARCO. (*to his uncle—in a whispered chuckle*) Died and became a God? So that's what they believe about that stone statue, is it?

MAFFEO. They're all crazy, like the Mahometans. They're not responsible.

MARCO. (*suddenly*) I saw two of them with a bowl of rice—

MAFFEO. Oh, yes. They eat the same as we do. (*Then abruptly*) Come on! This is our chance to make a start. Don't forget our cases, Mark. (*They go out left followed by* MARCO *with the sample cases. The scene fades into darkness. The clamor of the temple bells slowly dies out in the distance.*)

DARKNESS

ACT ONE—SCENE FIVE

SCENE—*From the darkness comes the sound of a small Tartar kettle-drum, its beats marking the rhythm for a crooning, nasal voice, rising and falling in a wordless chant.*

The darkness gradually lifts. In the rear is a section of the Great Wall of China with an enormous shut gate. It is late afternoon, just before sunset. Immediately before the gate is a rude throne on which sits a Mongol ruler with warrior and sorcerer to right and left of him. At the sides are Mongol circular huts. The motionless figures sit before these. The MINSTREL, *squatting at center, is the only one whose body moves. In the back of the throne and above it is a small idol made of felt and cloth. The clothes of the ruler and his court are of rich silk stuffs, lined with costly furs. The squatting figures of the people are clothed in rough robes.*

The POLOS *stand at center,* MARCO *still lugging the battered sample cases. He is now nearly eighteen, a brash, self-confident young man, assertive and talky. All the* POLOS *are weary and their clothes shabby and travel-worn.*

MARCO. (*setting down the bags with a thump and staring about with an appraising contempt*) Welcome to that dear old Motherland, Mongolia!

MAFFEO. (*wearily takes out his guide-book and begins to read in the monotone of a boring formula*) Flocks—goats—horses—cattle. The women do all the buying and selling. Business is all in cattle and crops. In short, the people live like beasts.

NICOLO. (*reading from his book*) They have two Gods—a God of Heaven to whom they pray for health of mind, and a God of Earth, who watches over their earthly goods. They pray to him also and do many other stupid things.

373

MARCO. (*boredly*) Well—let them! (*He walks away and makes the circuit of the figures, but now he hardly glances at them. The* TWO TARTAR MERCHANTS *enter and there is the same pantomime of greeting between them and the* POLOS *as with the* BUDDHIST MERCHANTS *in the previous scene.* MARCO *joins them. It is apparent the whole company is extremely weary. They yawn and prepare to lie down.*)

MAFFEO. We'll have time to steal a nap before they open the Gate.

MARCO. (*with an assertive importance*) Just a moment! I've got a good one an idol-polisher told me in Tibet. This is the funniest story you ever heard! It seems an Irishman got drunk in Tangut and wandered into a temple where he mistook one of the female statues for a real woman and— (*He goes on, laughing and chuckling to himself, with endless comic pantomime. The two* TARTAR MERCHANTS *fall asleep.* NICOLO *stares at his son bitterly,* MAFFEO *with contemptuous pity. Finally* MARCO *finishes to his own uproarious amusement.*)

NICOLO. (*bitterly*) Dolt!

MAFFEO. (*mockingly—with a yawn*) Youth will have its laugh! (MARCO *stops open-mouthed and stares from one to the other.*)

MARCO. (*faintly*) What's the matter?

NICOLO. (*pettishly*) Unless your jokes improve you'll never sell anything.

MAFFEO. I'll have to give Marco some lessons in how to tell a short story. (*Warningly*) And until I pronounce you graduated, mum's the word, understand! The people on the other side of that wall may look simple but they're not. (*The* PROSTITUTE *enters dressed now as a Tartar. She comes and puts her hand on* MARCO'S *head.*)

PROSTITUTE. What has this bad boy been doing now?

MAFFEO. He's getting too witty! (*He rests his head on his arms and goes to sleep.*)

PROSTITUTE. Shall I expect you again tonight?

MARCO. No. You've got all my money. (*Suddenly gets to his feet and faces her—disgustedly*) And I'm through with you, anyway.

PROSTITUTE. (*with a scornful smile*) And I with you—now that you're a man. (*She turns away.*)

MARCO. (*angrily*) Listen here! Give me back what you stole! I know I had it on a ribbon around my neck last night and this morning it was gone. (*Threateningly*) Give it to me, you, or I'll make trouble!

PROSTITUTE. (*takes a crumpled paper from her bosom*) Do you mean this?

MARCO. (*tries to snatch it*) No!

PROSTITUTE. (*she unfolds it and reads*)

> "I'll have a million to my credit
> 'And in the meantime can easily afford
> A big wedding that will do us credit
> And start having children, Bless the Lord!"

(*She laughs*) Are you a poet, too?

MARCO. (*abashed and furious*) I didn't write that.

PROSTITUTE. You're lying. You must have. Why deny it? Don't sell your soul for nothing. That's bad business. (*She laughs, waving the poem in her upraised hand, staring mockingly*) Going! Going! Gone! (*She lets it fall and grinds it under her feet into the earth— laughing*) Your soul! Dead and buried! You strong man! (*She laughs.*)

MARCO. (*threateningly*) Give me what was wrapped up in that, d'you hear!

PROSTITUTE. (*scornfully—takes the miniature from her bosom*) You mean this? I was bringing it back to you. D'you think I want her ugly face around? Here! (*She throws it at his feet. He leans down and picks it up, polishing it on his sleeve remorsefully. The* PROSTITUTE, *walking away, calls back over her shoulder*) I kissed it so you'd remember my kiss whenever you kiss her! (*She laughs.* MARCO *starts as if to run after her angrily. Suddenly a shout rises from the lips of all the Tartars, the* MINSTREL *and his drum become silent, and with*

one accord they raise their arms and eyes to the sky. Then the MIN-
STREL *chants.*)

MINSTREL. God of the Heaven, be in our souls! (*Then they all prostrate themselves on the ground as he chants*) God of the Earth, be in
our bodies! (*The Tartars sit up. The* MINSTREL *begins again his drum
beat, crooning in a low monotone. The* POLOS *rise and stretch sleepily.*)

MARCO. (*inquisitively*) Two Gods? Are they in one Person like our
Holy Trinity?

MAFFEO. (*shocked*) Don't be impious! These are degraded pagans—
or crazy, that's a more charitable way to— (*From behind the wall
comes the sound of martial Chinese music. The gate opens. The blinding glare of the setting sun floods in from beyond. A file of soldiers,
accompanying a richly-dressed* COURT MESSENGER, *come through. He
walks directly up to the* POLOS *and bows deeply.*)

MESSENGER. The Great Kaan, Lord of the World, sent me— (*He
looks around*) But where are the hundred wise men of the West?

NICOLO. (*confusedly*) We had two monks to start with—but they
left us and went back.

MAFFEO. (*warningly*) Ssst!

MESSENGER. (*indifferently*) You will explain to the Kaan. I was
ordered to arrange a welcome for them.

MAFFEO. (*claps him on the back*) Well, here we are—and hungry
as hunters! So your welcome will be welcome, Brother. (*The* MESSEN-
GER *bows, starts back, the* POLOS *following him,* MAFFEO *calling*) Get
on the job, Mark! (*They pass through the gate.*)

MARCO. (*wearily picks up the cases—then goading himself on*)
Giddap! Cathay or bust! (*He struggles through the gate. For a second
he is framed in it, outlined against the brilliant sky, tugging a sample
case in each hand. Then the gate shuts, the light fades out. The drum
beat and the chanting recede into the distance.*)

DARKNESS

ACT ONE—SCENE SIX

SCENE—*Music from full Chinese and Tartar bands crashes up to a tremendous blaring crescendo of drums, gongs, and the piercing shrilling of flutes. The light slowly comes to a pitch of blinding brightness. Then, as light and sound attain their highest point, there is a sudden dead silence. The scene is revealed as the Grand Throne Room in the palace of* KUBLAI, THE GREAT KAAN, *in the city of Cambulac, Cathay—an immense octagonal room, the lofty walls adorned in gold and silver. In the far rear wall, within a deep recess like the shrine of an idol, is the throne of the Great Kaan. It rises in three tiers, three steps to a tier. On golden cushions at the top* KUBLAI *sits dressed in his heavy gold robes of state. He is a man of sixty but still in the full prime of his powers, his face proud and noble, his expression tinged with an ironic humor and bitterness yet full of a sympathetic humanity. In his person are combined the conquering indomitable force of a descendant of Chinghiz with the humanizing culture of the conquered Chinese who have already begun to absorb their conquerors.*

On the level of the throne below KUBLAI *are: on his right a Mongol warrior in full armor with shield and spear, his face grim, cruel and fierce. On his left* CHU-YIN, *the Cathayan sage and adviser to the Kaan, a venerable old man with white hair, dressed in a simple black robe. On the main floor, grouped close to the throne are: on the right, the sons of the Kaan. Farther away, the nobles and warriors of all degrees with their wives behind them. On the left, the wives and concubines of the Kaan, then the courtiers, officers, poets, scholars, etc.—all the non-military officials and hangers-on of government, with their women beside them.* MARCO *stands, a sample case in each hand, bewildered and dazzled, gawking about him on every*

*side. His father and uncle, bowing, walk to the foot of the throne and
kneel before the Kaan. They make frantic signals to* MARCO *to do
likewise but he is too dazed to notice. All the people in the room are
staring at him. The Kaan is looking at the two brothers with a stern
air. An usher of the palace comes quietly to* MARCO *and makes violent
gestures to him to kneel down.*

MARCO. (*misunderstanding him—gratefully*) Thank you, Brother.
(*He sits down on one of the sample cases to the gasping horror of all
the Court. The Kaan is still looking frowningly at the two* POLOS *as
he listens to the report of their Messenger escort. He does not notice.
An outraged Chamberlain rushes over to* MARCO *and motions him to
kneel down.*)

MARCO. (*bewilderedly*) What's the trouble now?

KUBLAI. (*dismissing the* MESSENGER, *having heard his report—addresses the* POLOS *coldly*) I bid you welcome, Messrs. Polo. But where
are the hundred wise men of the West who were to dispute with my
wise men of the sacred teachings of Lao-Tseu and Confucius and
the Buddha and Christ?

MAFFEO. (*hurriedly*) There was no Pope elected until just before—

NICOLO. And he had no wise men, anyway. (*The Kaan now sees*
MARCO *and a puzzled expression of interest comes over his face.*)

KUBLAI. Is he with you?

NICOLO. (*hesitantly*) My son, Marco, your Majesty—still young and
graceless.

KUBLAI. Come here, Marco Polo. (MARCO *comes forward, trying
feebly to assume a bold, confident air.*)

MAFFEO. (*in a loud, furious aside*) Kneel, you ass! (MARCO *flounders
to his knees.*)

KUBLAI. (*with a smile*) I bid you welcome, Master Marco.

MARCO. Thank you, sir—I mean, your Lordship—your— (*then
suddenly*) Before I forget—the Pope gave me a message for you, sir.

KUBLAI. (*smiling*) Are you his hundred wise men?

MARCO. (*confidently*) Well—almost. He sent me in their place. He said I'd be worth a million wise men to you.

NICOLO. (*hastily*) His Holiness meant that Marco, by leading an upright life—not neglecting the practical side, of course—might set an example that would illustrate, better than wise words, the flesh and blood product of our Christian civilization.

KUBLAI. (*with a quiet smile*) I shall study this apotheosis with un-wearied interest, I foresee it.

MARCO. (*suddenly—with a confidential air*) Wasn't that just a joke, your asking for the wise men? His Holiness thought you must have a sense of humor. Or that you must be an optimist.

KUBLAI. (*with a smile of appreciation*) I am afraid your Holy Pope is a most unholy cynic. (*Trying to solve a riddle in his own mind—musingly*) Could he believe this youth possesses that thing called soul which the West dreams lives after death—and might reveal it to me? (*Suddenly to* MARCO) Have you an immortal soul?

MARCO. (*in surprise*) Of course! Any fool knows that.

KUBLAI. (*humbly*) But I am not a fool. Can you prove it to me?

MARCO. Why, if you didn't have a soul, what would happen when you die?

KUBLAI. What, indeed?

MARCO. Why, nothing. You'd be dead—just like an animal.

KUBLAI. Your logic is irrefutable.

MARCO. Well, I'm not an animal, am I? That's certainly plain enough. (*Then proudly*) No, sir! I'm a man made by Almighty God in His Own Image for His greater glory!

KUBLAI. (*staring at him for a long moment with appalled apprecia-tion—ecstatically*) So you are the Image of God! There is certainly something about you, something complete and unanswerable—but wait—a test! (*He claps his hands, pointing to* MARCO. *Soldiers with drawn swords leap forward and seize him, trussing him up, his hands behind his back.*)

MAFFEO. (*groveling*) Mercy! He is only a boy!

NICOLO. (*groveling*) Mercy! He is only a fool!

KUBLAI. (*sternly*) Silence! (*To* MARCO, *with inhuman calm*) Since you possess eternal life, it can do you no harm to cut off your head. (*He makes a sign to a soldier who flourishes his sword.*)

MARCO. (*trying to conceal his fear under a quavering, joking tone*) I might—catch—cold!

KUBLAI. You jest, but your voice trembles. What! Are you afraid to die, immortal youth? Well, then, if you will confess that your soul is a stupid invention of your fear and that when you die you will be dead as a dead dog is dead—

MARCO. (*with sudden fury*) You're a heathen liar! (*He glares defiantly. His father and uncle moan with horror.*)

KUBLAI. (*laughs and claps his hand.* MARCO *is freed. The Kaan studies his sullen but relieved face with amusement*) Your pardon, Marco! I suspected a flaw but you are perfect. You cannot imagine your death. You are a born hero. I must keep you near me. You shall tell me about your soul and I will listen as to a hundred wise men from the West! Is it agreed?

MARCO. (*hesitatingly*) I know it's a great honor, sir—but forgetting the soul side of it, I've got to eat.

KUBLAI. (*astonished*) To eat?

MARCO. I mean, I'm ambitious. I've got to succeed, and— (*Suddenly blurts out*) What can you pay me?

KUBLAI. Ha! Well, you will find me a practical man, too. I can start you upon any career you wish. What is your choice?

MAFFEO. (*interposing eagerly*) If I might speak to the boy in private a minute—give him my humble advice—he is young— (MAFFEO *and* NICOLO *hurriedly lead* MARCO *down to the foreground.*)

MAFFEO. You've made a favorable impression—God knows why—but strike while the iron is hot, you ninny! Ask to be appointed a Second Class government commission-agent.

MARCO. (*offendedly*) No! I'll be first-class or nothing!

MAFFEO. Don't be a fool! A First Class agent is all brass buttons and no opportunities. A Second Class travels around, is allowed his expenses, gets friendly with all the dealers, scares them into letting him in on everything—and gets what's rightfully coming to him! (*Then with a crafty look and a nudge in the ribs*) And, being always in the secret, you'll be able to whisper to us in time to take advantage—

MARCO. (*a bit flustered—with bluff assertion*) I don't know. The Kaan's been square with me. After all, honesty's the best policy, isn't it?

MAFFEO. (*looking him over scathingly*) You'd think I was advising you to steal—I, Maffeo Polo, whose conservatism is unquestioned!

MARCO. (*awed*) I didn't mean—

MAFFEO. (*solemnly*) Do you imagine the Kaan is such a Nero as to expect you to live on your salary?

MARCO. (*uncertainly*) No, I suppose not. (*He suddenly looks at Maffeo with a crafty wink*) When I do give you a tip, what do I get from Polo Brothers?

MAFFEO. (*between appreciation and dismay*) Ha! You learn quickly, don't you? (*Then hastily*) Why, we—we've already thought of that—trust us to look after your best interests—and decided to—to make you a junior parner in the firm—eh, Nick?—Polo Brothers and Son—doesn't that sound solid, eh?

MARCO. (*with a sly grin*) It's a great honor—a very great honor. (*Then meaningly*) But as neither of you are Neros, naturally you'll also offer me—

MAFFEO. (*grinning in spite of himself*) Hmm! Hmm! You Judas!

MARCO. A fair commission—

NICOLO. (*blustering—but his eyes beaming with paternal pride* You young scamp!

MAFFEO. (*laughing*) Ha-ha! Good boy, Mark! Polos will be Polos! (*They all embrace laughingly.* KUBLAI, *who has been observing them intently, turns to* CHU-YIN *and they both smile.*)

KUBLAI. Did their Pope mean that a fool is a wiser study for a ruler of fools than a hundred wise men could be? This Marco touches me, as a child might, but at the same time there is something warped, deformed— Tell me, what shall I do with him?

CHU-YIN. Let him develop according to his own inclination and give him also every opportunity for true growth if he so desires. And let us observe him. At least, if he cannot learn, we shall.

KUBLAI. (*smilingly*) Yes. And be amused. (*He calls commandingly*) Marco Polo! (MARCO *turns rather frightenedly and comes to the throne and kneels*) Have you decided?

MARCO. (*promptly*) I'd like to be appointed a commission-agent of the Second Class.

KUBLAI. (*somewhat taken aback, puzzledly*) You are modest enough!

MARCO. (*manfully*) I want to start at the bottom!

KUBLAI. (*with mocking grandeur*) Arise then, Second Class Marco! You will receive your agent's commission at once. (*Then with a twinkle in his eye*) But each time you return from a journey you must relate to me all the observations and comments of your soul on the East. Be warned and never fail me in this!

MARCO. (*confused but cocksuredly*) I won't. I'll take copious notes. (*Then meaningly*) And I can memorize any little humorous incidents—

MAFFEO. (*apprehensively*) Blessed Savior! (*He gives a violent fit of coughing.*)

MARCO. (*looks around at him questioningly*) Hum? (*Misinterpreting his signal*) And may I announce to your Majesty that a signal honor has just been conferred on me? My father and uncle have taken me into the firm. It will be Polo Brothers and Son from now on, and any way we can serve your Majesty—

KUBLAI (*a light coming over his face*) Aha! I begin to smell all the rats in Cathay! (*The two elder* POLOS *are bowed to the ground, trembling with apprehension.* KUBLAI *laughs quietly*) Well, I am sure you wish to celebrate this family triumph together, so you may go. And accept my congratulations, Marco!

MARCO. Thank you, your Majesty. You will never regret it. I will always serve your best interests, so help me God! (*He goes grandly, preceded hurriedly by the trembling* NICOLO *and* MAFFEO. KUBLAI *laughs and turns to* CHU-YIN *who is smiling*.)

CURTAIN

ACT TWO—SCENE ONE

SCENE—*The Little Throne Room in the bamboo summer palace of the Kaan at Xanadu, the City of Peace—smaller, more intimate than the one at Cambaluc, but possessing an atmosphere of aloof dignity and simplicity fitting to the philosopher ruler who retreats here to contemplate in peace the vanity of his authority.*

About fifteen years have elapsed. It is a beautiful sunlit morning in late June. The Kaan reclines comfortably on his cushioned bamboo throne. His face has aged greatly. The expression has grown mask-like, full of philosophic calm. He has the detached air of an idol. KUKACHIN, *a beautiful young girl of twenty, pale and delicate, is sitting at his feet. Her air is grief-stricken. A flute player in the garden is playing a melancholy air.* KUKACHIN *recites in a low tone:*

KUKACHIN.

My thoughts in this autumn are lonely and sad,
A chill wind from the mountain blows in the garden.
The sky is gray, a snowflake falls, the last chrysanthemum
Withers beside the deserted summerhouse.
I walk along the path in which weeds have grown.
My heart is bitter and tears blur my eyes.
I grieve for the days when we lingered together
In this same garden, along these paths between flowers.
In the spring we sang of love and laughed with youth
But now we are parted by many leagues and years,
And I weep that never again shall I see your face.

(*She finishes and relapses into her attitude of broken resignation. The flute player ceases his playing.* KUBLAI *looks down at her tenderly.*)

KUBLAI. (*musingly*) Sing while you can. When the voice fails, listen

384

to song. When the heart fails, be sung asleep. (*Chidingly*) That is a sad poem, Little Flower. Are you sad because you must soon become Queen of Persia? But Arghun is a great hero, a Khan of the blood of Chinghiz. You will be blessed with strong sons able to dare the proud destiny of our blood.

KUKACHIN. (*dully*) Your will is my law.

KUBLAI. Not my will. The will of life to continue the strong. (*Forcing a consoling tone*) Come, Little Flower. You have been fading here. See how pale you have grown! Your eyes are listless! Your lips droop even in smiling! But life at the Court of Persia is gay. There will be feasts, celebrations, diverting pleasures. You will be their Queen of Beauty.

KUKACHIN. (*with a sigh*) A Queen may be only a woman who is unhappy.

KUBLAI. (*teasingly*) What despair! You talk like the ladies in poems who have lost their lovers! (KUKACHIN *gives a violent start which he does not notice and a spasm of pain comes over her face*) But, never mind, Arghun of Persia is a hero no woman could fail to love.

KUKACHIN. (*starting to her feet—desperately*) No! I can bear his children, but you cannot force me to— (*She breaks down, weeping.*)

KUBLAI. (*astonished—gazing at her searchingly*) Have I ever forced you to anything? (*Then resuming his tone of tender teasing*) I would say, rather, that ever since you were old enough to talk, the Ruler of Earth, as they innocently call your grandfather, has been little better than your slave.

KUKACHIN. (*taking his hand and kissing it*) Forgive me. (*Then smiling at him*) Have I been so bad as that? Has my love for you who have been both father and mother to me, brought you no happiness?

KUBLAI. (*with deep emotion*) You have been a golden bird singing beside a black river. You took your mother's place in my heart when she died. I was younger then. The river was not so black—the river of man's life so deep and silent—flowing with an insane obsession—whither?—and why? (*Then suddenly forcing a smile*) Your poem

385

has made me melancholy. And I am too old, if not too wise, to afford anything but optimism! (*Then sadly*) But now you in your turn must leave me, the river seems black indeed! (*Then after a pause—tenderly*) If it will make you unhappy, you need not marry Arghun Khan.

KUKACHIN. (*recovering herself—resolutely*) No. Your refusal would insult him. It might mean war. (*Resignedly*) And Arghun is as acceptable as any other. Forgive my weakness. You once told me a Princess must never weep. (*She forces a smile*) It makes no difference whether I stay or go, except that I shall be homesick for you. (*She kisses his hand again.*)

KUBLAI. (*gratefully*) My little one. (*He strokes her hair. After a pause during which he looks at her thoughtfully—tenderly*) We have never had secrets from each other, you and I. Tell me, can you have fallen in love?

KUKACHIN. (*after a pause—tremblingly*) You must not ask that—if you respect my pride! (*With a pitiful smile*) You see—he does not even know— (*She is blushing and hanging her head with confusion.* CHU-YIN *enters hurriedly from the right. He is very old but still upright. He is a bit breathless from haste but his face is wreathed in smiles.*)

CHU-YIN. (*making an obeisance*) Your Majesty, do you hear that martial music? His Honor, Marco Polo, Mayor of Yang-Chau, seems about to visit you in state! (*The strains of a distant band can be heard.*)

KUBLAI. (*still looking at* KUKACHIN *who has started violently at the mention of* MARCO's *name—worriedly*) Impossible! In love? . . . (*Then to* CHU-YIN—*preoccupiedly*) Eh? Marco? I have given no orders for him to return.

CHU-YIN. (*ironically*) No doubt he comes to refresh your humor with new copious notes on his exploits. Our Marco has made an active mayor. Yang-Chau, according to the petition for mercy you have received from its inhabitants, is the most governed of all your cities. I talked recently with a poet who had fled from there in horror. Yang-

Chau used to have a soul, he said. Now it has a brand new Court House. And another, a man of wide culture, told me, our Christian mayor is exterminating our pleasures and our rats as if they were twin breeds of vermin!

KUBLAI. (*irritably*) He is beginning to weary me with his grotesque antics. A jester inspires mirth only so long as his deformity does not revolt one. Marco's spiritual hump begins to disgust me. He has not even a mortal soul, he has only an acquisitive instinct. We have given him every opportunity to learn. He has memorized everything and learned nothing. He has looked at everything and seen nothing. He has lusted for everything and loved nothing. He is only a shrewd and crafty greed. I shall send him home to his native wallow.

CHU-YIN. (*in mock alarm*) What? Must we lose our clown?

KUKACHIN. (*who has been listening with growing indignation*) How dare you call him a clown? Just because he is not a dull philosopher you think—

KUBLAI. (*astounded—admonishingly*) Princess!

KUKACHIN. (*turns to him—on the verge of tears—rebelliously*) Why are you both so unjust? Has he not done well everything he was ever appointed to do? Has he not always succeeded where others failed? Has he not by his will-power and determination risen to the highest rank in your service? (*Then her anger dying—more falteringly*) He is strange, perhaps, to people who do not understand him, but that is because he is so different from other men, so much stronger! And he has a soul! I know he has!

KUBLAI. (*whose eyes have been searching her face—aghast*) Kukachin! (*She sees he has guessed her secret and at first she quails and shrinks away, then stiffens regally and returns his gaze unflinchingly.* CHU-YIN *looks from one to the other comprehendingly. Finally* KUBLAI *addresses her sternly*) So, because I have allowed this fool a jester's latitude, because I permitted him to amuse you when you were a little girl, and since then, on his returns, to speak with you—a Princess!— (*Then brusquely*) I shall inform the ambassadors you will be

387

ready to sail for Persia within ten days. You may retire. (*She bows with a proud humility and walks off left.* KUBLAI *sits in a somber study, frowning and biting his lips. The blaring of* MARCO'S *band grows steadily nearer.*)

CHU-YIN. (*gently*) Is intolerance wisdom? (*A pause. Then he goes on*) I have suspected her love for him for a long time.

KUBLAI. Why didn't you warn me?

CHU-YIN. Love is to wisdom what wisdom seems to love—a folly. I reasoned, love comes like the breath of wind on water and is gone leaving calm and reflection. I reasoned, but this is an enchanted moment for her and it will remain a poignant memory to recompense her when she is no longer a girl but merely a Queen. And I reasoned, who knows but some day this Marco may see into her eyes and his soul may be born and that will make a very interesting study—for Kukachin, and her grandfather, the Son of Heaven and Ruler of the World! (*He bows mockingly*) And for the old fool who is I!

KUBLAI. (*bewilderedly*) I cannot believe it! Why, since she was a little girl, she has only talked to him once or twice every two years or so!

CHU-YIN. That was unwise, for thus he has remained a strange, mysterious dream-knight from the exotic West, an enigma with something about him of a likable boy who brought her home each time a humble, foolish, touching little gift! And also remember that on each occasion he returned in triumph, having accomplished a task—a victor, more or less, acting the hero. (*The band has crashed and dinned its way into the courtyard*) As now! Listen! (*He goes to the window and looks down—with ironical but intense amusement*) Ah! He wears over his Mayor's uniform the regalia of Cock of Paradise in his secret fraternal order of the Mystic Knights of Confucius! The band of the Xanadu lodge is with him as well as his own! He is riding on a very fat white horse. He dismounts, aided by the steps of your Imperial Palace! He slaps a policeman on the back and asks his name! He chucks a baby under the chin and asks the mother its name. She lies and says "Marco" although the baby is a girl. He smiles. He is talking loudly so everyone can overhear. He gives the baby one yen to start a savings account and encourage its thrift. The mother looks savagely disappointed. The crowd cheers. He keeps his smile frozen as he notices an artist sketching him. He shakes hands with a one-legged veteran of the Manzi campaign and asks his name. The veteran is touched. Tears come to his eyes. He tells him—but the Polo forgets his name even as he turns to address the crowd. He waves one hand for silence. The band stops. It is the hand on which he wears five large jade rings. The other hand rests upon—and pats—the head of a bronze dragon, our ancient symbol of Yang, the celestial, male principle of the Cosmos. He clears his throat, the crowd stands petrified, he is about to draw a deep breath and open his mouth carefully in position one of the five phonetic exercises— (*Here* CHU-CHIN *chuckles*) But I am an old man full of malice and venom and it embitters me to see others unreasonably happy so— (*Here just as* MARCO *is heard starting to speak, he throws open the window and calls in a loud, commanding tone*) Messer Polo, His Imperial Majesty commands that you stop talking, dismiss your followers, and repair to his presence at once!

MARCO'S VOICE. (*very faint and crestfallen*) Oh—all right—I'll be right there.

KUBLAI. (*cannot control a laugh in spite of himself—helplessly*) How can one deal seriously with such a child-actor?

CHU-YIN. (*coming back from the window—ironically*) Most women, including Kukachin, love children—and all women must take acting seriously in order to love at all. (*Just as he finishes speaking,* KUKACHIN *enters from the left. She is terribly alarmed. She throws herself at* KUBLAI'S *feet.*)

KUKACHIN. Why did you summon him? I told you he does not know. It is all my fault! Punish me, if you will! But promise me you will not harm him!

KUBLAI. (*looking down at her—sadly*) Is it my custom to take vengeance? (*Then as people are heard approaching—quickly*) Compose yourself! Remember again, Princesses may not weep! (*She springs to her feet, turns away for a moment, then turns back, her face rigidly calm and emotionless.* KUBLAI *nods with appreciation of her control*) Good. You will make a Queen. (*She bows and retires backward to the left side of the throne. At the same moment,* NICOLO *and* MAFFEO POLO *enter ceremoniously from the right. They wear the regalia of officers in the Mystic Knights of Confucius over their rich merchants' robes.* [*This costume is a queer jumble of stunning effects that recall the parade uniforms of our modern Knights Templar, of Columbus, of Pythias, Mystic Shriners, the Klan, etc.*] *They are absurdly conscious and proud of this get-up—like two old men in a children's play.* KUBLAI *and* CHU-YIN *regard them with amused astonishment. Even* KUKACHIN *cannot restrain a smile. They prostrate themselves at the foot of the throne. Then just at the right moment, preceded by a conscious cough,* MARCO POLO *makes his entrance. Over his gorgeous uniform of Mayor, he wears his childishly fantastic regalia as chief of the Mystic Knights of Confucius. As he steps on, he takes off his gilded, laced hat with its Bird of Paradise plumes and bows with a mechanical dignity on all sides. He has the manner and appearance of a successful movie star at a masquerade ball, disguised so that no one can fail to recognize him. His regular, good-looking, well-groomed face is carefully arranged into the grave responsible expression of a Senator from the South of the United States of America about to propose an amendment to the Constitution restricting the migration of non-Nordic birds into Texas, or prohibiting the practice of the laws of biology within the twelve-mile limit. He moves in stately fashion to the throne and prostrates himself before the* KAAN. KUKACHIN *stares at him with boundless admiration, hoping to catch his eye. The* KAAN *looks from her to him and his face grows stern.* CHU-YIN *is enjoying himself.*)

KUBLAI. Rise. (MARCO *does so.* KUBLAI *continues dryly*) To what do I owe the honor of this unexpected visit?

MARCO. (*hastily, but with full confidence*) Well, I was sending in to your treasury the taxes of Yang-Chau for the fiscal year, and I knew you'd be so astonished at the unprecedented amount I had sweated out of them that you'd want to know how I did it—so here I am. (*An awkward pause.* MARCO *is disconcerted at the* KAAN'S *steady impersonal stare. He glances about—sees the* PRINCESS—*welcomes this opportunity for diverting attention. Bowing with humble respect*) Pardon me, Princess. I didn't recognize you before, you've gotten so grown up. (*Flatteringly*) You look like a Queen.

KUKACHIN. (*flatteringly*) I bid you welcome, Your Honor.

KUBLAI. (*as a warning to* KUKACHIN *to control her emotion*) The Princess will soon be Queen of Persia.

MARCO. (*flustered and awed, bowing to her again—flatteringly*) Then—Your Majesty—if I may be humbly permitted (*Bowing to* KUBLAI)—to offer my congratulations—and before I settle down to discussing business—if her Highness—Majesty—will accept a small token of my esteem— (*Here he stamps his foot. An* AFRICAN SLAVE, *dressed in a pink livery with green hat and shoes and stockings and carrying a golden wicker basket, enters. He kneels, presents the basket to* MARCO, *who lifts the cover and pulls out a small chow puppy with a pink ribbon tied around its neck. He steps forward and offers this to the* PRINCESS, *with a boyish grin*) A contribution to your ZOO —from your most humble servant!

KUKACHIN. (*taking it—flushing with pleasure*) Oh, what a little darling! (*She cuddles the puppy in her arms.*)

MARCO. (*boastfully*) He's a genuine, pedigreed pup. I procured him at great cost—I mean he's extra well-bred.

KUKACHIN. Oh, thank you so much, Marco Polo! (*Stammering*) I mean, Your Honor.

KUBLAI. (*warningly*) His Honor wishes to talk business, Princess.

KUKACHIN. (*controlling herself*) I ask pardon. (*She bows and retires to left, rear, where she stands fondling the puppy and watching* MARCO.)

MARCO. (*plunging in confidently on what he thinks is a sure point of attack*) My tax scheme, Your Majesty, that got such wonderful results is simplicity itself. I simply reversed the old system. For one thing I found they had a high tax on excess profits. Imagine a profit being excess! Why, it isn't humanly possible! I repealed it. And I repealed the tax on luxuries. I found out the great majority in Yang-Chau couldn't afford luxuries. The tax wasn't democratic enough to make it pay! I crossed it off and I wrote on the statute books a law that taxes every necessity in life, a law that hits every man's pocket equally, be he beggar or banker! And I got results!

CHU-YIN. (*gravely*) In beggars?

KUBLAI. (*with a chilling air*) I have received a petition from the inhabitants of Yang-Chau enumerating over three thousand cases of your gross abuse of power!

MARCO. (*abashed only for a moment*) Oh, so they've sent that vile slander to you, have they? That's the work of a mere handful of radicals—

KUBLAI. (*dryly*) Five hundred thousand names are signed to it. (*Still more dryly*) Half a million citizens accuse you of endeavoring to stamp out their ancient culture!

MARCO. What! Why, I even had a law passed that anyone caught interfering with culture would be subject to a fine! It was Section One of a blanket statute that every citizen must be happy or go to jail. I found it was the unhappy ones who were always making trouble and getting discontented. You see, here's the way I figure it; if a man's good, he's happy—and if he isn't happy, it's a sure sign he's no good to himself or anyone else and he better be put where he can't do harm.

KUBLAI. (*a bit helplessly now*) They complain that you have entirely prohibited all free expression of opinion.

MARCO. (*feelingly*) Well, when they go to the extreme of circulating such treasonable opinions against me, isn't it time to protect your sovereignty by strong measures? (KUBLAI *stares at this effrontery with amazement.* MARCO *watches this impression and hurries on with an injured dignity*) I can't believe, Your Majesty, that this minority of malcontents can have alienated your long-standing high regard for me!

KUBLAI. (*conquered—suddenly overpowered by a great smile*) Not so! You are the marvel of mankind! And I would be lost without you!

MARCO. (*flattered but at the same time nonplussed*) I thank you! (*Hesitatingly*) But, to tell the truth, I want to resign anyhow. I've done all I could. I've appointed five hundred committees to carry on my work and I retire confident that with the system I've instituted everything will go on automatically and brains are no longer needed. (*He adds as a bitter afterthought*) And it's lucky they're not or Yang-Chau would soon be a ruin!

KUBLAI. (*with mock seriousness*) In behalf of the population of Yang-Chau I accept your resignation, with deep regret for the loss of your unique and extraordinary services. (*Then suddenly in a strange voice*) Do you still possess your immortal soul, Marco Polo?

MARCO. (*flustered*) Ha-ha! Yes, of course—at least I hope so. But I see the joke. You mean that Yang-Chau used to be a good place to lose one. Well, you wouldn't know the old town now. Sin is practically unseen. (*Hurrying on to another subject—boisterously*) But however much I may have accomplished there, it's nothing to the big surprise I've got in reserve for you. May I demonstrate? (*Without waiting for permission, takes a piece of printed paper like a dollar bill from his pocket*) What is it? Paper. Correct! What is it worth? Nothing. That's where you're mistaken. It's worth ten yen. No, I'm not a liar! See ten yen written on it, don't you? Well, I'll tell you the secret. This is money, legally valued at ten yens' worth of anything you wish to buy, by order of His Imperial Majesty, the Great Kaan! Do you see my point? Its advantages over gold and silver coin are obvious. It's light, easy to carry,— (*Here he gives a prodigious wink*) wears out quickly, can be made at very slight expense and yields enormous profit. Think of getting ten yen for this piece of paper.

Yet it can be done. If you make the people believe it's worth it, it is! After all, when you stop to think, who was it first told them gold was money? I'll bet anything it was some quick-thinker who'd just discovered a gold mine! (KUBLAI *and* CHU-YIN *stare at him in petrified incredulity. He mistakes it for admiration and is flattered. Bows and lays his paper money on the* KAAN's *knee*) You're stunned, I can see that. It's so simple—and yet, who ever thought of it before me? I was amazed myself. Think it over, Your Majesty, and let the endless possibilities dawn on you! And now I want to show another little aid to government that I thought out. (*He makes a sign to his uncle and father. The former takes a mechanical contrivance out of a box and sets it up on the floor. It is a working model of a clumsy cannon.* NICOLO, *meanwhile, takes children's blocks out of his box and builds them into a fortress wall.* MARCO *is talking. His manner and voice have become grave and portentous*) It all came to me, like an inspiration, last Easter Sunday when Father and Uncle and I were holding a little service. Uncle read a prayer which spoke of Our Lord as the Prince of Peace. Somehow, that took hold of me. I thought to myself, well, it's funny, there always have been wars and there always will be, I suppose, because I've never read much in any history about heroes who waged peace. Still, that's wrong. War is a waste of money which eats into the profits of life like thunder! Then why war, I asked myself? But how are you going to end it? Then the flash came! There's only one workable way and that's to conquer everybody else in the world so they'll never dare fight you again! An impossible task, you object? Not any more! This invention you see before you makes conquering easy. Let me demonstrate with these models. On our right, you see the fortress wall of a hostile capital. Under your present system, with battering rams, to make an effective breach in this wall would cost you the lives of ten thousand men. Valuing each life conservatively at ten yen, this amounts to one hundred thousand yen. This makes the cost of breaching prohibitive. But all of this waste can be saved. How? Just keep your eyes on your right and permit my exclusive invention to solve this problem. (*He addresses the fortress in a matter-of-fact tone*) So you won't surrender, eh? (*Then in a mock-heroic falsetto, answering himself like a ventriloquist*) We die but we never surrender! (*Then matter-of-factly*) Well, Brother, those heroic sentiments do you a lot of credit, but this is war and not a tragedy. You're up against new methods this time, and you better give in and avoid wasteful bloodshed. (*Answering himself*) No! Victory or Death! (*Then again*) All right, Brother, don't blame me. Fire! (*His uncle fires the gun. There is a bang, and a leaden ball is shot out which knocks a big breach in the wall of blocks.* MARCO *beams.* KUKACHIN *gives a scream of fright, then a gasp of delight, and claps her hands.* MARCO *bows to her the more gratefully as* KUBLAI *and* CHU-YIN *are staring at him with a queer appalled wonder that puzzles him although he cannot imagine it is not admiration*) I see you are stunned again. What made it do that, you're wondering? This! (*He takes a little package out of his pocket and pours some black powder out of it on his palm*) It's the same powder they've been using here in children's fire works. They've had it under their noses for years without a single soul ever having creative imagination enough to visualize the enormous possibilities. But you can bet I did! It was a lad crying with a finger half blown off where he held a firecracker too long that first opened my eyes. I learned the formula, improved on it, experimented in secret, and here's the gratifying result! (*He takes the cannon ball from his father who has retrieved it*) You see? Now just picture this little ball magnified into one weighing twenty pounds or so and then you'll really grasp my idea. The destruction of property and loss of life would be tremendous! No one could resist you!

KUBLAI. (*after a pause—musingly*) I am interested in the hero of that city who preferred death to defeat. Did you conquer his immortal soul?

MARCO. (*with frankness*) Well, you can't consider souls when you're dealing with soldiers, can you? (*He takes his model and places it on the* KAAN's *knee with the paper money*) When you have time, I wish you'd look this over. In fact—and this is the big idea I've been saving for the last—consider these two inventions of mine in combination. You conquer the world with this— (*He pats the cannon-model*) and you pay for it with this. (*He pats the paper money—rhetorically*) You become the bringer of peace on earth and good-will to men, and it doesn't cost you a yen hardly. Your initial expense—my price—is as low as I can possibly make it out of my deep affection for your Majesty—only a million yen.

KUBLAI. (*quickly*) In paper?

MARCO. (*with a grin and a wink*) No. I'd prefer gold, if you don't mind. (*Silence.* MARCO *goes on meaningly*) Of course, I don't want to force them on you. I'm confident there's a ready market for them elsewhere.

KUBLAI. (*grimly smiling*) Oh, I quite realize that in self-protection I've got to buy them—or kill you!

MARCO. (*briskly*) Then it's a bargain? But I've still got one proviso—that you give us permission to go home. (KUKACHIN *gives a little gasp.* MARCO *goes on feelingly*) We're homesick, Your Majesty. We've served you faithfully, and frankly now that we've made our fortune we want to go home and enjoy it. There's no place like home, Your Majesty! I'm sure even a King in his palace appreciates that.

KUBLAI. (*with smiling mockery*) But—who can play your part? And your mission—your example? What will your Pope say when you tell him I'm still unconverted?

MARCO. (*confidently*) Oh, you will be—on your death-bed, if not before—a man of your common sense.

KUBLAI. (*ironically*) Courtier! (*Then solemnly*) But my last objection is insurmountable. You haven't yet proved you have an immortal soul!

MARCO. It doesn't need proving.

KUBLAI. If you could only bring forward one reliable witness.

MARCO. My Father and Uncle can swear—

KUBLAI. They think it is a family trait. Their evidence is prejudiced.

396

MARCO. (*worried now—looks at* CHU-YIN *hopefully*) Mr. Chu-Yin ought to be wise enough to acknowledge—

CHU-YIN. (*smiling*) But I believe that what can be proven cannot be true. (MARCO *stands puzzled, irritated, looking stubborn, frightened and foolish. His eyes wander about the room, finally resting appealingly on* KUKACHIN.)

KUKACHIN. (*suddenly steps forward—flushed but proudly*) I will bear witness he has a soul. (KUBLAI *looks at her with a sad wonderment,* CHU-YIN *smilingly,* MARCO *with gratitude,* NICOLO *and* MAFFEO *exchange a glance of congratulation.*)

KUBLAI. How can you know, Princess?

KUKACHIN. Because I have seen it—once, when he bound up my dog's leg, once when he played with a slave's baby, once when he listened to music over water and I heard him sigh, once when he looked at sunrise, another time at sunset, another at the stars, another at the moon, and each time he said that Nature was wonderful. And all the while, whenever he has been with me I have always felt—something strange and different—and that something must be His Honor's soul, must it not?

KUBLAI. (*with wondering bitterness*) The eye sees only its own sight.

CHU-YIN. But a woman may feel life in the unborn.

KUBLAI. (*mockingly but sadly*) I cannot contest the profound intuitions of virgins and mystics. Go home, Your Honor, Immortal Marco, and live forever! (*With forced gaiety*) And tell your Pope your example has done much to convert me to wisdom—if I could find the true one!

KUKACHIN. (*boldly now*) And may I humbly request, since His Honor, and his father and uncle, are experienced masters of navigation, that they be appointed, for my greater safety, to attend me and command the fleet on my voyage to Persia?

KUBLAI. (*astonished at her boldness—rebukingly*) Princess!

KUKACHIN. (*returning his look—simply*) It is the last favor I shall

397

ever ask. I wish to be converted to wisdom, too—one or another—before I become a name.

KUBLAI. (*bitterly*) I cannot deny your last request, even though you wish your own unhappiness. (*To the* POLOS) You will accompany the Princess.

MARCO. (*jubilantly*) I'll be only too glad! (*Turning to the* PRINCESS) It'll be a great pleasure! (*Then briskly*) And have we your permission to trade in the ports along the way?

KUKACHIN. (*to* MARCO, *embarrassedly*) As you please, Your Honor.

MARCO. (*bowing low*) I'll promise it won't disturb you. It's really a scheme to while away the hours, for I warn you in advance this is liable to be a mighty long trip.

KUKACHIN. (*impulsively*) I do not care how long— (*She stops in confusion.*)

MARCO. Now if I had the kind of ships we build in Venice to work with I could promise you a record passage, but with your tubby junks it's just as well to expect the worst and you'll never be disappointed. (*Familiarly*) And the trouble with any ship, for a man of action, is that there's so little you can do. I hate idleness where there's nothing to occupy your mind but thinking. I've been so used to being out, overcoming obstacles, getting things done, creating results where there weren't any before, going after the impossible—well— (*Here he gives a little deprecating laugh*) all play and no work makes Jack a dull boy. I'm sure I'd make a pretty dull person to have around if there wasn't plenty to do. You might not believe it, but when I'm idle I actually get gloomy sometimes!

KUKACHIN. (*eagerly*) But we shall have dancers on the ship and actors who will entertain us with plays—

MARCO. (*heartily*) That'll be grand. There's nothing better than to sit down in a good seat at a good play after a good day's work in which you know you've accomplished something, and after you've had a good dinner, and just take it easy and enjoy a good wholesome thrill or a good laugh and get your mind off serious things until it's time to go to bed.

KUKACHIN. (*vaguely*) Yes. (*Then eager to have him pleased*) And there will be poets to recite their poems—

MARCO. (*not exactly overjoyed*) That'll be nice. (*Then very confidentially—in a humorous whisper*) I'll tell you a good joke on me, Your Highness. I once wrote a poem myself; would you ever believe it to look at me?

KUKACHIN. (*smiling at him as at a boy—teasingly*) No?

MARCO. (*smiling back like a boy*) Yes, I did too, when I was young and foolish. It wasn't bad stuff either, considering I'd had no practice. (*Frowning with concentration*) Wait! Let me see if I can remember any—oh, yes—"You are lovely as the gold in the sun." (*He hesitates.*)

KUKACHIN. (*thrilled*) That is beautiful!

MARCO. That's only the first line. (*Then jokingly*) You can consider yourself lucky. I don't remember the rest.

KUKACHIN. (*dropping her eyes—softly*) Perhaps on the voyage you may be inspired to write another.

KUBLAI. (*who has been staring at them with weary amazement*) Life is so stupid, it is mysterious!

DARKNESS

ACT TWO—SCENE TWO

SCENE—*The wharves of the Imperial Fleet at the seaport of Zayton —several weeks later. At the left, stern to, is an enormous junk, the flagship. The wharf extends out, rear, to the right of her. At the right is a warehouse, from a door in which a line of half-naked slaves, their necks, waists, and right ankles linked up by chains, form an endless chain which revolves mechanically, as it were, on sprocket wheels in the interiors of the shed and the junk. As each individual link passes out of the shed it carries a bale on its head, moves with mechanical precision across the wharf, disappears into the junk, and reappears a moment later having dumped its load and moves back into the shed. The whole process is a man-power original of the modern devices with bucket scoops that dredge, load coal, sand, etc. By the side of the shed, a foreman sits with a drum and gong with which he marks a perfect time for the slaves, a four-beat rhythm, three beats of the drum, the fourth a bang on the gong as one slave at each end loads and unloads. The effect is like the noise of a machine. A bamboo stair leads up to the high poop of the junk from front, left. Dawn is just breaking. A forest of masts, spars, sails of woven bamboo laths, shuts out all view of the harbor at the end of the wharf. At the foot of the stairs,* CHU-YIN *stands like a sentinel. Above, on top of the poop, the figures of* KUBLAI *and* KUKACHIN *are outlined against the lightening sky.*

KUBLAI. (*brokenly*) I must go. (*He takes her in his arms*) We have said all we can say. Little Daughter, all rare things are secrets which cannot be revealed to anyone. That is why life must be so lonely. But I love you more dearly than anything on earth. And I know you love me. So perhaps we do not need to understand. (*Rebelliously*) Yet I wish some Power could give me assurance that in granting your desire I am acting for your happiness, and for your eventual deliverance from sorrow to acceptance and peace. (*He notices she is weeping—in self-reproach*) Old fool! I have made you weep again! I am death advising life how to live! Be deaf to me! Strive after what your heart desires! Who can ever know which are the mistakes we make? One should be either sad or joyful. Contentment is a warm sty for the eaters and sleepers! (*Impulsively*) Do not weep! Even now I can refuse your hand to Arghun. Let it mean war!

KUKACHIN. (*looking up and controlling herself—with a sad finality*) You do not understand. I wish to take this voyage.

400

KUBLAI. (*desperately*) But I could keep Polo here. (*With impotent anger*) He shall pray for his soul on his knees before you!

KUKACHIN. (*with calm sadness*) Do I want a slave? (*Dreamily*) I desire a captain of my ship on a long voyage in dangerous, enchanted seas.

KUBLAI. (*with a fierce defiance of fate*) I am the Great Kaan! I shall have him killed! (*A pause.*)

CHU-YIN. (*from below, recites in a calm, soothing tone*) The noble man ignores self. The wise man ignores action. His truth acts without deeds. His knowledge venerates the unknowable. To him birth is not the beginning, nor is death the end. (KUBLAI's *head bends in submission.* CHU-YIN *continues tenderly*) I feel there are tears in your eyes. The Great Kaan, Ruler of the World, may not weep.

KUBLAI. (*brokenly*) Ruler? I am my slave! (*Then controlling himself—forcing an amused teasing tone*) Marco will soon be here, wearing the self-assurance of an immortal soul and his new admiral's uniform! I must fly in retreat from what I can neither laugh away nor kill. Write when you reach Persia. Tell me—all you can tell—particularly what his immortal soul is like! (*Then tenderly*) Farewell, Little Flower! Live. There is no other advice possible from one human being to another.

KUKACHIN. Live—and love!

KUBLAI. (*trying to renew his joking tone*) One's ancestors, particularly one's grandfather. Do not forget me!

KUKACHIN. Never! (*They embrace.*)

KUBLAI. (*chokingly*) Farewell. (*He hurries down the ladder—to* CHU-YIN) You remain—see him—bring me word— (*He turns his head up to* KUKACHIN) For the last time, farewell, Little Flower of my life! May you know happiness! (*He turns quickly and goes.*)

KUKACHIN. Farewell! (*She bows her head on the rail and weeps.*)

CHU-YIN. (*after a pause*) You are tired, Princess. Your eyes are red from weeping and your nose is red. You look old—a little homely, even. The Admiral Polo will not recognize you. (KUKACHIN *dries her eyes hastily.*)

KUKACHIN. (*half smiling and half weeping at his teasing*) I think you are a very horrid old man!

CHU-YIN. A little sleep, Princess, and you will be beautiful. The old dream passes. Sleep and awake in the new. Life is perhaps most wisely regarded as a bad dream between two awakenings, and every day is a life in miniature.

KUKACHIN. (*wearily and drowsily*) Your wisdom makes me sleep. (*Her head sinks back on her arms and she is soon asleep.*)

CHU-YIN. (*after a pause—softly*) Kukachin! (*He sees she is asleep—chuckles*) I have won a convert. (*Then speculatively*) Youth needs so much sleep and old age so little. Is that not a proof that from birth to death one grows steadily closer to complete life? Hum. (*He ponders on this. From the distance comes the sound of* POLO's *band playing the same martial air as in the previous scene.* CHU-YIN *starts—then smiles. The music quickly grows louder. The* PRINCESS *awakes with a start.*)

KUKACHIN. (*startledly*) Chu-Yin! Is that the Admiral coming?

CHU-YIN. (*dryly*) I suspect so. It is like him not to neglect a person in the city when saying good-bye.

KUKACHIN. (*flurriedly*) I must go to my cabin for a moment. (*She hurries back.*)

CHU-YIN. (*listens with a pleased, ironical smile as the band gets rapidly nearer. Finally it seems to turn a corner nearby, and a moment later, to a deafening clangor,* MARCO *enters, dressed in a gorgeous Admiral's uniform. Two paces behind, side by side, walk* MAFFEO *and* NICOLO, *dressed only a trifle less gorgeously as Commodores. Behind them comes the band.* MARCO *halts as he sees* CHU-YIN, *salutes condescendingly, and signals the band to be silent.* CHU-YIN *bows gravely and remarks as if answering an argument in his own mind*) Still, even though they cannot be house-broken, I prefer monkeys because they are so much less noisy.

MARCO. (*with a condescending grin*) What's that—more philosophy? (*Clapping him on the back*) Well, I like your determination. (*He wipes his brow with a handkerchief*) Phew! I'll certainly be glad to get back home where I can hear some music that I can keep step to. My feet just won't give in to your tunes. (*With a grin*) And look at the Old Man and Uncle. They're knock-kneed for life. (*Confidentially*) Still I thought the band was a good idea—to sort of cheer up the Princess, and let people know she's leaving at the same time. (*As people begin to come in and stare at the poop of the ship*) See the crowd gather? I got them out of bed, too!

CHU-YIN. (*ironically*) You also woke up the Princess. You sail at sunrise?

MARCO. (*briskly—taking operations in hand*) Thank you for reminding me. I've got to hurry. (*To his* FATHER *and* UNCLE) You two better get aboard your ships and be ready to cast off when I signal. (*They go off. He suddenly bawls to someone in the ship*) Much more cargo to load?

A VOICE. Less than a hundred bales, sir.

MARCO. Good. Call all hands on deck and stand by to put sail on her.

A VOICE. Aye-aye, sir.

MARCO. And look lively, damn your lazy souls! (*To* CHU-YIN—*complacently*) You've got to impose rigid discipline on shipboard.

CHU-YIN. (*inquisitively*) I suppose you feel your heavy responsibility as escort to the future Queen of Persia?

MARCO. (*soberly*) Yes, I do. I'll confess I do. If she were a million yen worth of silk or spices, I wouldn't worry an instant, but a Queen, that's a different matter. However, when you give my last word to His Majesty, you can tell him that I've always done my duty by him and I won't fail him this time. As long as I've a breath in me, I'll take care of her!

CHU-YIN. (*with genuine appreciation*) That is bravely spoken.

MARCO. I don't know anything about brave speaking. I'm by nature a silent man, and I let my actions do the talking. But, as I've proved to you people in Cathay time and again, when I say I'll do a thing, I do it!

CHU-YIN. (*suddenly with a sly smile to himself*) I was forgetting. His Majesty gave me some secret last instructions for you. You are at some time every day of the voyage, to look carefully and deeply into the Princess's eyes and note what you see there.

MARCO. What for? (*Then brightly*) Oh, he's afraid she'll get fever in the tropics. Well, you tell him I'll see to it she keeps in good condition. I'll do what's right by her without considering fear or favor. (*Then practically*) Then, of course, if her husband thinks at the end of the voyage that my work deserves a bonus—why, that's up to him. (*Inquisitively*) She's never seen him, has she?

CHU-YIN. No.

MARCO. (*with an air of an independent thinker*) Well, I believe in love matches myself, even for Kings and Queens. (*With a grin*) Come to think of it, I'll be getting married to Donata myself when I get home.

CHU-YIN. Donata?

MARCO. (*proudly*) The best little girl in the world! She's there waiting for me.

CHU-YIN. You have heard from her?

MARCO. I don't need to hear. I can trust her. And I've been true to her, too. I haven't ever thought of loving anyone else. Of course, I don't mean I've been any he-virgin. I've played with concubines at odd moments when my mind needed relaxation—but that's only human nature. (*His eyes glistening reminiscently*) Some of them were beauties, too! (*With a sigh*) Well, I've had my fun and I suppose it's about time I settled down.

CHU-YIN. Poor Princess!

MARCO. What's that? Oh, I see, yes, I sympathize with her, too—going into a harem. If there's one thing more than another that proves you in the East aren't responsible, it's that harem notion. (*With a grin*) Now in the West we've learned by experience that one at a time is trouble enough.

CHU-YIN. (*dryly*) Be sure and converse on love and marriage often with the Princess. I am certain you will cure her.

MARCO. (*mystified*) Cure her?

CHU-YIN. Cure her mind of any unreasonable imaginings.

MARCO. (*easily*) Oh, I'll guarantee she'll be contented, if that's what you mean. (*The human chain in back finishes its labors and disappears into the shed. The crowd of people has been steadily augmented by new arrivals, until a small multitude is gathered standing in silence staring up at the poop.* MARCO *says with satisfaction*) Well, cargo's all aboard, before schedule, too. We killed six slaves but, by God, we did it! And look at the crowd we've drawn, thanks to my band!

CHU-YIN. (*disgustedly*) They would have come without noise. They love their Princess.

MARCO. (*cynically*) Maybe, but they love their sleep, too. I know 'em! (*A cry of adoration goes up from the crowd. With one movement they prostrate themselves as the* PRINCESS *comes from the cabin dressed in a robe of silver and stands at the rail looking down.*)

THE CROWD. (*in a long ululating whisper*) Farewell—farewell— farewell—farewell!

KUKACHIN. (*silences them with a motion of her hand*)

I shall know the long sorrow of an exile
As I sail over the green water and the blue water
Alone under a strange sky amid alien flowers and faces.
My eyes shall be ever red with weeping, my heart bleeding,
While I long for the land of my birth and my childhood
Remembering with love the love of my people.

(*A sound of low weeping comes from the crowd*) Farewell!

THE CROWD. Farewell—farewell—farewell—farewell!

MARCO. (*feeling foolish because he is moved*) Damn it! Reciting always makes me want to cry about something. Poetry acts worse on me than wine that way. (*He calls up—very respectfully*) Princess! We'll be sailing at once. Would you mind retiring to your cabin? I'm afraid you're going to catch cold standing bareheaded in the night air.

KUKACHIN. (*tremulously—grateful for his solicitude*) I am in your charge, Admiral. I am grateful that you should think of my health, and I obey. (*She turns and goes back into her cabin. The crowd silently filters away, leaving only the band.*)

MARCO. (*proudly and fussily*) You can't have women around when you're trying to get something done. I can see where I'll have to be telling her what to do every second. Well, I hope she'll take it in good part and not forget I'm acting in her husband's interests, not my own. (*Very confidentially*) You know, apart from her being a Princess, I've always respected her a lot. She's not haughty and she's—well, human, that's what I mean. I'd do anything I could for her, Princess or not! Yes, sir!

CHU-YIN. (*wonderingly*) There may be hope—after all.

MARCO. What's that?

CHU-YIN. Nothing. Enigma!

MARCO. There's always hope! Don't be a damned pessimist! (*Clapping him on the back*) Enigma, eh? Well, if that isn't like a philosopher—to start in on riddles just at the last moment! (*He ascends half-way up the ladder to the poop, then turns back to* CHU-YIN *with a chuckle*) Take a fool's advice and don't think so much or you'll get old before your time! (*More oratorically*) If you look before you leap, you'll decide to sit down. Keep on going ahead and you can't help being right! You're bound to get somewhere! (*He suddenly breaks into a grin again*) There! Don't ever say I never gave you good advice! (*He springs swiftly to the top deck and bellows*) Cast off there amidships! Where the hell are you—asleep? Set that foresail! Hop, you kidney-footed gang of thumb-fingered infidels! (*He turns with a sudden fierceness on the band who are standing stolidly, awaiting orders*) Hey you! Didn't I tell you to strike up when I set foot on the deck? What do you think I paid you in advance for—to wave me good-bye? (*The band plunges madly into it. A frenzied cataract of sound results.* CHU-YIN *covers his ears and moves away, shaking his head, as* MARCO *leans over the rail and bawls after him*) And tell the Kaan—anything he wants—write me—just Venice—they all know me there—and if they don't, by God, they're going to!

DARKNESS

ACT TWO—SCENE THREE

Scene—*Poop deck of the royal junk of the* PRINCESS KUKACHIN *at anchor in the harbor of Hormuz, Persia—a moonlight night some two years later. On a silver throne at center* KUKACHIN *is sitting dressed in a gorgeous golden robe of ceremony. Her beauty has grown more intense, her face has undergone a change, it is the face of a woman who has known real sorrow and suffering. In the shadow of the highest deck in rear her women-in-waiting are in a group, sitting on cushions. On the highest deck in rear* SAILORS *lower and furl the sail of the mizzenmast, every movement being carried out in unison with a machine-like rhythm. The bulwarks of the junk are battered and splintered, the sail is frayed and full of jagged holes and patches. In the foreground (the port side of deck) the two elder* POLOS *are squatting. Each has a bag of money before him from which they are carefully counting gold coins and packing stacks of these into a chest that stands between them.*

MARCO. (*his voice, hoarse and domineering, comes from the left just before the curtain rises*) Let go that anchor! (*A meek "Aye-aye, sir," is heard replying and then a great splash and a long rattling of chains. The curtain then rises discovering the scene as above.* MARCO'S *voice is again heard, "Lower that mizzensail! Look lively now!"*)

407

BOATSWAIN. (*with the sailors*) Aye-aye, sir! (*They lower the sail, and begin to tie it up trimly.*)

MAFFEO. (*looking up and straightening his cramped back—with a relieved sigh*) Here's Persia! I'll be glad to get on dry land again. Two years on this foreign tub are too much.

NICOLO. (*with a grunt, intent on the money*) Keep counting if you want to finish before we go ashore. It's nine hundred thousand now in our money, isn't it?

MAFFEO. (*nods—counting again*) This lot will bring it to a million. (*He begins stacking and packing again.*)

BOATSWAIN. (*chanting as his men work*)
    Great were the waves
    Volcanoes of foam
    Ridge after ridge
    To the rim of the world!
    Great were the waves!

CHORUS OF SAILORS. Great were the waves!

BOATSWAIN.   Fierce were the winds!
    Demons screamed!
    Their claws rended
    Sails into rags,
    Fierce were the winds!

CHORUS.   Fierce were the winds!

BOATSWAIN.   Fire was the sun!
    Boiled the blood black,
    Our veins hummed
    Like bronze kettles.
    Fire was the sun!

CHORUS.   Fire was the sun!

BOATSWAIN.   Long was the voyage!
    Life drifted becalmed,
    A dead whale awash

	In the toil of tides.
	Long was the voyage!
CHORUS.	Long was the voyage!
BOATSWAIN.	Many have died!
	Sleep in green water.
	Wan faces at home
	Pray to the sea.
	Many have died!
CHORUS.	Many have died!

KUKACHIN. (*chants the last line after them—sadly*)

Many have died!

(*After a brooding pause she rises and chants in a low voice*)

If I were asleep in green water,
No pang could be added to my sorrow,
Old grief would be forgotten,
I would know peace.

SAILORS.	There is peace deep in the sea
	But the surface is sorrow.
WOMEN.	Kukachin will be a Queen!
	A Queen may not sorrow
	Save for her King!
KUKACHIN.	When love is not loved it loves Death.
	When I sank drowning, I loved Death.
	When the pirate's knife gleamed, I loved Death.
	When fever burned me I loved Death.
	But the man I love saved me.
SAILORS.	Death lives in a silent sea,
	Gray and cold under cold gray sky,
	Where there is neither sun nor wind
	Nor joy nor sorrow!
WOMEN.	Kukachin will be a wife.
	A wife must not sorrow
	Save for her man.

409

KUKACHIN. A hero is merciful to women.
　　　　　　Why could not this man see or feel or know?
　　　　　　Then he would have let me die.

SAILORS. There are harbors at every voyage-end
　　　　　Where we rest from the sorrows of the sea.

WOMEN. Kukachin will be a mother
　　　　A mother may not sorrow
　　　　Save for her son.

KUKACHIN. (*bows her head in resignation. A pause of silence*) (MARCO POLO *enters briskly from below on the left. He is dressed in full uniform, looking spick and span and self-conscious. His face wears an expression of humorous scorn. He bows ceremoniously to the* PRINCESS, *his attitude a queer mixture of familiarity and an uncertain awe.*)

MARCO. Your Highness— (*Then ingratiatingly*) —or I suppose I'd better say Majesty now that we've reached Persia—I've got queer news for you. A boat just came from the shore with an official notification that your intended husband, Arghun Khan, is dead and I'm to hand you over to his son, Ghazan, to marry. (*He hands her a sealed paper*) See!

KUKACHIN. (*letting the paper slip from her hand without a glance —dully*) What does it matter?

MARCO. (*admiringly—as he picks it up*) I must say you take it coolly. Of course, come to think of it, never having seen either, one's as good as another. (*He winds up philosophically*) And you'll be Queen just the same, that's the main thing.

KUKACHIN. (*with bitter irony*) So you think that is happiness? (*Then as* MARCO *stares at her uncertainly, she turns away and looks out over the sea with a sigh—after a pause*) There, where I see the lights, is that Hormuz?

MARCO. Yes. And I was forgetting, the messenger said Ghazan Khan would come to take you ashore tonight.

KUKACHIN. (*with sudden fear*) So soon? Tonight? (*Then rebel-liously*) Is the granddaughter of the Great Kublai no better than a slave? I will not go until it pleases me!

MARCO. Good for you! That's the spirit! (*Then alarmed at his own temerity—hastily*) But don't be rash! The Khan probably meant whenever you were willing. And don't mind what I just said.

KUKACHIN. (*looks at him with a sudden dawning of hope—gently*) Why should you be afraid of what you said?

MARCO. (*offended*) I'm not afraid of anything—when it comes to the point!

KUKACHIN. What point?

MARCO. (*nonplussed*) Why—well—when I feel someone's trying to steal what's rightfully mine, for instance.

KUKACHIN. And now—here—you do not feel that?

MARCO. (*with a forced laugh, thinking she is joking*) Ha! Well— (*Uncertainly*) That is—I don't catch your meaning— (*Then changing the subject abruptly*) But here's something I want to ask you. Your grandfather entrusted you to my care. He relied on me to prove equal to the task of bringing you safe and sound to your husband. Now I want to ask you frankly if you yourself won't be the first to acknowledge that in spite of typhoons, shipwrecks, pirates and every other known form of bad luck, I've brought you through in good shape?

KUKACHIN. (*with an irony almost hysterical*) More than any one in the world, I can appreciate your devotion to duty! You have been a prodigy of heroic accomplishment! In the typhoon when a wave swept me from the deck, was it not you who swam to me as I was drowning?

MARCO. (*modestly*) It was easy. Venetians make the best swimmers in the world.

KUKACHIN. (*even more ironically*) When the pirates attacked us, was it not your brave sword that warded off their curved knives from my breast and struck them dead at my feet?

411

MARCO. I was out of practice, too. I used to be one of the crack swordsmen of Venice—and they're the world's foremost, as everyone knows.

KUKACHIN. (*with a sudden change—softly*) And when the frightful fever wasted me, was it not you who tended me night and day, watching by my bedside like a gentle nurse, even brewing yourself the medicines that brought me back to life?

MARCO. (*with sentimental solemnity*) My mother's recipes. Simple home remedies—from the best friend I ever had!

KUKACHIN. (*a trifle wildly*) Oh, yes, you have been a model guardian, Admiral Polo!

MARCO. (*quickly*) Thank you, Princess. If I have satisfied you— then if I might ask you a favor, that you put in writing all you've just said in your first letter to the Great Kaan, and also tell your husband?

KUKACHIN. (*suddenly wildly bitter*) I will assuredly! I will tell them both of your heroic cruelty in saving me from death! (*Intensely*) Why could you not let me die?

MARCO. (*confusedly*) You're joking. You certainly didn't want to die, did you?

KUKACHIN. (*slowly and intensely*) Yes!

MARCO. (*puzzled and severe*) Hum! You shouldn't talk that way.

KUKACHIN. (*longingly*) I would be asleep in green water!

MARCO. (*worriedly, suddenly reaches out and takes her hand*) Here now, young lady! Don't start getting morbid!

KUKACHIN. (*with a thrill of love*) Marco!

MARCO. I believe you're feverish. Let me feel your pulse!

KUKACHIN. (*violently*) No! (*She draws her hand from his as if she had been stung.*)

MARCO. (*worriedly*) Please don't be unreasonable. There'd be the devil to pay if you should suffer a relapse of that fever after I sweated blood to pull you through once already! Do you feel hot?

KUKACHIN. (*wildly*) No! Yes! On fire!

MARCO. Are your feet cold?

KUKACHIN. No! Yes! I don't know! (*Gravely* MARCO *kneels, removes a slipper, and feels the sole of her foot—then pats her foot playfully*.)

MARCO. No. They're all right. (*He gets up—professionally*) Any cramps?

KUKACHIN. You fool! No! Yes! My heart feels as if it were bursting!

MARCO. It burns?

KUKACHIN. Like a red ember flaring up for the last time before it chills into gray ash forever!

MARCO. Then something must have disagreed with you. Will you let me see your tongue?

KUKACHIN. (*in a queer hysterical state where she delights in self-humiliation*) Yes! Yes! Anything! I am a Princess of the Imperial blood of Chinghiz and you are a dog! Anything! (*She sticks out her tongue, the tears streaming down her face as he looks at it.*)

MARCO. (*shakes his head*) No sign of biliousness. There's nothing seriously wrong. If you would only try to sleep a while—

KUKACHIN. O Celestial God of the Heavens! What have I done that Thou shouldst torture me? (*Then wildly to* MARCO) I wished to sleep in the depths of the sea. Why did you awaken me?

MARCO. (*worried again*) Perhaps it's brain fever. Does your head ache?

KUKACHIN. No! Does your immortal soul?

MARCO. Don't blaspheme! You're talking as if you were delirious! (*Then pleadingly*) For Heaven's sake, try and be calm, Princess! What if your husband, Ghazan Khan, should find you in such a state?

KUKACHIN. (*calming herself with difficulty—after a pause, bitterly*) I suppose you are relieved to get me here alive and deliver me—like a cow!

MARCO. (*injuredly*) I've only carried out your own grandfather's orders!

KUKACHIN. (*forcing a smile*) Won't you miss being my guardian?

(*Striving pitifully to arouse his jealousy*) When you think of Ghazan protecting me and nursing me when I am sick—and—and loving me? Yes! I will compel him to love me, even though I never love him! He shall look into my eyes and see that I am a woman and beautiful!

MARCO. That's a husband's privilege.

KUKACHIN. Or a man's—a man who has a soul! (*Mockingly but intensely*) And that reminds me, Admiral Polo! You are taking advantage of this being the last day to shirk your duty!

MARCO. Shirk! No one can ever say—!

KUKACHIN. It was my grandfather's special command, given to you by Chu-Yin, you told me, that every day you should look into my eyes.

MARCO. (*resignedly*) Well, it isn't too late yet, is it? (*He moves toward her with a sigh of half-impatience with her whims.*)

KUKACHIN. Wait. This is the one part of your duty in which I shall have to report you incompetent.

MARCO. (*hurt*) I've done my best. I never could discover anything out of the way.

KUKACHIN. There must be something he wished you to find. I myself feel there is something, something I cannot understand, something you must interpret for me! And remember this is your last chance! There is nothing in life I would not give—nothing I would not do—even now it is not too late! See my eyes as those of a woman and not a Princess! Look deeply! I will die if you do not see what is there! (*She finishes hysterically and beseechingly.*)

MARCO. (*worried—soothingly*) There! There! Certainly, Princess! Of course, I'll look. And will you promise me that afterwards you'll lie down?

KUKACHIN. Look! See! (*She throws her head back, her arms outstretched. He bends over and looks into her eyes. She raises her hands slowly above his head as if she were going to pull it down to hers. Her lips part, her whole being strains out to him. He looks for a moment critically, then he grows tense, his face moves hypnotically*

414

toward hers, their lips seem about to meet in a kiss. She murmurs)
Marco!

MARCO. (*his voice thrilling for this second with oblivious passion*)
Kukachin!

MAFFEO. (*suddenly slapping a stack of coins into the chest with a resounding clank*) One million!

MARCO. (*with a start, comes to himself and backs away from the PRINCESS in terror*) What, Uncle? Did you call?

MAFFEO. One million in God's money! (*He and NICOLO lock and fasten the box jubilantly.*)

KUKACHIN. (*in despair*) Marco!

MARCO. (*flusteredly*) Yes, Princess. I saw something queer! It made me feel feverish too! (*Recovering a bit—with a sickly smile*) Oh, there's trouble there, all right! You must be delirious! I advise you to go to sleep.

KUKACHIN. (*with wild despair pulls out a small dagger from the bosom of her dress*) I obey! I shall sleep forever! (*But MARCO, the man of action, springs forward and wresting the dagger from her hand, flings it over the side. She confronts him defiantly, her eyes wild with grief and rage. He stares at her, dumbfounded and bewildered.*)

MARCO. (*bewilderedly*) I never believed people—sane people—ever seriously tried—

KUKACHIN. (*intensely*) I implored an ox to see my soul! I no longer can endure the shame of living!

MARCO. (*sheepishly*) You mean it was a terrible insult when I called you—by your name?

KUKACHIN. (*bursting into hysterical laughter*) Yes! How dared you!

MARCO. (*hastily*) I ask pardon, Princess! Please forgive me! My only excuse is, I forgot myself. I guess I'll have to stop overworking or I'll suffer a nervous breakdown. I felt like one of those figures in a puppet show with someone jerking the wires. It wasn't me, you understand. My lips spoke without me saying a word. And here's the funniest part of it all, and what'll explain matters in full, if you can believe it. It wasn't you I was seeing and talking to, not a Princess at all, you'd changed into someone else, someone I've got a good right to—just a girl—

KUKACHIN. (*again clutching a hope*) A girl—a woman—you saw in me?

MARCO. (*enthusiastically, groping in his shirt front*) Yes. Here she is! (*He jerks the locket out of an under pocket and presents it to her proudly*) The future Mrs. Marco Polo! (*The* PRINCESS *takes it mechanically and stares at it in a stupor as* MARCO *rambles on.*)

MARCO. You may believe it or not but like a flash she was standing there in your place and I was talking to her, not you at all!

KUKACHIN. (*dully*) But it was my name you spoke.

MARCO. (*confusedly*) I meant to say Donata. That's her name. We're going to be married as soon as I get home. (*Then as she stares at the miniature—proudly*) Pretty, isn't she?

KUKACHIN. (*dully*) She may have married another.

MARCO. (*confidently*) No. Her family needs an alliance with our house.

KUKACHIN. She may have had lovers.

MARCO. (*simply*) Oh, no. She's not that kind.

KUKACHIN. (*staring at the picture*) She will be middle-aged—fat—and stupid!

MARCO. (*with a grin*) Well, I don't mind a wife being a bit plump—and who wants a great thinker around the house? Sound common sense and a home where everything runs smooth, that's what I'm after.

KUKACHIN. (*looks from him to the miniature*) There is no soul even in your love, which is no better than a mating of swine! And I—! (*A spasm of pain covers her face—then with hatred and disdain*) Pig of a Christian! Will you return to this sow and boast that a Princess and a Queen—? (*With rage*) Shall I ask as my first wedding present from Ghazan Khan that he have you flayed and thrown into the street to be devoured by dogs?

416

MAFFEO AND NICOLO. (*who have pricked up their ears at this last,* *rush to the* PRINCESS, *dragging their box between them and prostrate themselves at her feet*) Mercy! Mercy! (*She seems not to hear or to see them but stares ahead stonily.* MARCO *beckons* MAFFEO *to one side.*)

MARCO. (*in a whisper*) Don't be afraid. She doesn't mean a word of it. She's hysterical. Listen, I just noticed the royal barge coming. I'll go and meet the Khan. You keep her from doing anything rash until he gets here.

MAFFEO. Yes. (*He goes back and crouches again before the* PRINCESS, *keeping a wary eye on her, but she seems turned to stone.* MARCO *comes down and goes off left. There is the blare of a trumpet, the reflections of lanterns and torches, the sound of running about on deck and* MARCO'S *voice giving commands. The* WOMEN *come out to attend the* PRINCESS. *She remains rigid, giving no sign.*)

WOMEN. (*in chorus*)
>The lover comes,
>Who becomes a husband,
>Who becomes a son,
>Who becomes a father—
>In this contemplation lives the woman.

KUKACHIN. (*her face now a fatalistic mask of acceptance*)
>I am not.
>Life is.
>A cloud hides the sun.
>A life is lived.
>The sun shines again.
>Nothing has changed.
>Centuries wither into tired dust.
>A new dew freshens the grass.
>Somewhere this dream is being dreamed.

(*From the left* MARCO *comes escorting* GHAZAN KHAN, *attended by a train of nobles and slaves with lights. He can be heard saying: "She is a little feverish—the excitement—" All are magnificently dressed, glittering with jewels.* GHAZAN *is a young man, not handsome but noble and manly looking. He comes forward and bows low before her, his attendants likewise. Then he looks into her face and stands fascinated by her beauty. She looks back at him with a calm indifference.*)

GHAZAN. (*after a pause—his voice thrilling with admiration*) If it were possible for a son who loved a noble father to rejoice at that father's death, then I should be that guilty son! (*As she makes no reply*) You have heard? Arghun Khan is dead. You must bear the humiliation of accepting his son for husband, a crow to replace an eagle! Forgive me. But with your eyes to watch I may become at least a shadow of his greatness.

KUKACHIN. (*calmly*) What am I? I shall obey the eternal will which governs your destiny and mine.

GHAZAN. (*impetuously*) You are more beautiful than I had dared to dream! It shall not be I who rules, but you! I shall be your slave! Persia shall be your conquest and everywhere where songs are sung they shall be in praise of your beauty! You shall be Queen of Love—!

KUKACHIN. (*sharply with pain*) No! (*She drops the locket on the floor and grinds it into pieces under her foot.*)

MARCO. (*excitedly*) Princess! Look out! You're stepping on— (*She kicks it away from her.* MARCO *stoops on his knees and begins picking up the wreckage in his handkerchief.* KUKACHIN *turns to* GHAZAN *and points to* MARCO) My first request of you, my lord, is that you reward this Christian who has brought me here in safety. I ask, as a fitting tribute to his character, that you give an immense feast in his honor. Let there be food in tremendous amounts! He is an exquisite judge of quantity. Let him be urged to eat and drink until he can hold no more, until he becomes his own ideal figure, an idol of stuffed self-satisfaction! Will you do this? (*She is a trifle hectic now and her manner has grown wilder.*)

GHAZAN. Your wish is my will!

KUKACHIN. (*pointing to a magnificent lion in diamonds on his breast*) What is that wonderful glittering beast?

GHAZAN. It is the emblem of the Order of the Lion which only great heroes and kings of men may wear.

KUKACHIN. (*gives a laugh of wild irony*) Great heroes—kings of men? (*Then eagerly*) Will you give it to me? I implore you! (GHAZAN, *fascinated, yet with a wondering glance, unpins it and hands it to her without a word. She prods* MARCO, *who is still collecting the pieces of the locket with her foot*) Arise! Let me give you the noble Order of the Lion! (*She pins the blazing diamond figure on the breast of the stunned* MARCO, *laughing with bitter mockery*) How well it is set off on the bosom of a sheep! (*She laughs more wildly*) Kneel again! Bring me a chest of gold! (GHAZAN *makes a sign. Two slaves bring a chest of gold coins to her. She takes handfuls and throws them over the kneeling forms of the* POLOS, *laughing*) Here! Guzzle! Grunt! Wallow for our amusement! (*The two elder are surreptitiously snatching at the coins but* MARCO *jumps to his feet, his face flushing.*)

MARCO. (*in a hurt tone*) I don't see why you're trying to insult me—just at the last moment. What have I done? (*Then suddenly forcing a smile*) But I realize you're not yourself.

GHAZAN. (*sensing something*) Has this man offended you? Shall he be killed?

KUKACHIN. (*wearily*) No. He has amused me. Let him be fed. Stuff him with food and gold and send him home. And you, my lord, may I ask that this first night I be allowed to remain on board alone with my women? I am weary!

GHAZAN. Again your wish is my will, even though I will not live until I see you again!

KUKACHIN. (*exhaustedly*) I am humbly grateful. Good night, my lord. (*She bows.* GHAZAN *and the Court bow before her. They retire toward the left,* MARCO *talking earnestly to the oblivious* GHAZAN *whose eyes are riveted on the* PRINCESS, *who has turned away from them. The two elder* POLOS, *carrying their chest, their pockets stuffed, trudge along last.*)

MARCO. The close confinement of a long voyage. I think probably her spleen is out of order. (*They are gone from sight.* KUKACHIN'S *shoulders quiver as, her head bowed in her hands, she sobs quietly. The ship can be heard making off.*)

WOMEN.   Weep, Princess of the Wounded Heart,
                      Weeping heals the wounds of sorrow
                      Till only the scars remain
                      And the heart forgets.

KUKACHIN. (*suddenly runs up to the upper deck and stands outlined against the sky, her arms outstretched—in a voice which is a final, complete renunciation, calls*) Farewell, Marco Polo!

MARCO. (*his voice comes from over the water cheery and relieved*) Good-bye, Your Majesty—and all best wishes for long life and happiness! (*The* PRINCESS *sinks to her knees, her face hidden in her arms on the bulwark.*)

CURTAIN

ACT THREE—SCENE ONE

SCENE—*One year later.*

The Grand Throne Room in the Imperial palace at Cambaluc.
KUBLAI *squats on his throne, aged and sad, listening with an impassive face to* GENERAL BAYAN *who, dressed in the full military uniform and armor of the Commander-in-Chief is explaining earnestly with several maps in his hand. On* KUBLAI's *left stands* CHU-YIN, *who is reading. Behind* BAYAN *are grouped at attention all the generals of his army with a multitude of young staff officers, all gorgeously uniformed and armored. From the room on the right, the ballroom, a sound of dance music and laughter comes through the closed doors.*

BAYAN. (*impressively—pointing to the map*) Here, Your Majesty, is the line of the river Danube which marks the Western boundary of your Empire. Beyond it, lies the West. Our spies report their many petty states are always quarreling. So great is their envy of each other that we could crush each singly and the rest would rejoice. We can mobilize one million horsemen on the Danube within a month. (*Proudly*) We would ride their armies down into the sea! Your Empire would extend from ocean to ocean!

KUBLAI. (*wearily*) It is much too large already. Why do you want to conquer the West? It must be a pitiful land, poor in spirit and material wealth. We have everything to lose by contact with its greedy hypocrisy. The conqueror acquires first of all the vices of the conquered. Let the West devour itself.

BAYAN. (*helplessly*) But—everywhere in the East there is peace!

KUBLAI. (*with hopeless irony*) Ah! And you are becoming restless?

BAYAN. (*proudly*) I am a Mongol—a man of action!

KUBLAI. (*looking at him with musing irony*) Hum! You have already conquered the West, I think.

421

BAYAN. (*puzzled*) What, Your Majesty? (*Then persuasively*) The West may not be strong but it is crafty. Remember how that Christian, Polo, invented the engine to batter down walls? It would be better to wipe out their cunning now before they make too many engines to weaken the power of men. (*Then with a sudden inspiration*) And it would be a righteous war! We would tear down their Christian Idols and set up the image of the Buddha!

KUBLAI. Buddha, the Prince of Peace?

BAYAN. (*bowing his head as do all his retinue*) The Gentle One, The Good, The Kind, The Pitiful, The Merciful, The Wise, The Eternal Contemplative One!

KUBLAI. In His Name?

BAYAN. (*fiercely*) Death to those who deny Him!

ALL. (*with a great fierce shout and a clanking of swords*) Death!

KUBLAI. (*looks up at the ceiling quizzically*) A thunderbolt? (*Waits*) No? Then there is no God! (*Then to* BAYAN *with a cynical bitter smile*) August Commander, if you must have war, let it be one without fine phrases—a practical war of few words, as that Polo you admire would say. Leave the West alone. Our interests do not conflict —yet. But there is a group of islands whose silk industry is beginning to threaten the supremacy of our own. Lead your gallant million there —and see to it your war leaves me in peace!

BAYAN. I hear and obey! (*He turns to his staff exultantly*) His Majesty has declared war!

ALL. (*with a fierce cheer*) Down with the West!

BAYAN. (*hastily*) No. Not yet. Down with Japan! (*They cheer with equal enthusiasm—then he harangues them with the air of a patriotic exhorter*) His Majesty's benevolence and patience have been exhausted by the continued outrages against our silk nationals perpetrated by unscrupulous Japanese trade-pirates who, in spite of his protests, are breeding and maintaining silkworms for purposes of aggression! We fight in the cause of moral justice, that our silk-makers may preserve their share of the eternal sunlight! (*A long cheer.*)

KUBLAI. (*smiling—distractedly*) War without rhetoric, please! Polo has infected you with cant! The West already invades us! Throw open the doors! Music! (*The doors are thrown open. The dance music sounds loudly*) Go in and dance, everyone! You, too, General! I revoke my declaration of war—unless you learn to dance and be silent! (*They all go into the ballroom,* BAYAN *stalking majestically with an injured mien*) But dancing makes me remember Kukachin whose little dancing feet—! Shut the doors! Music brings back her voice singing! (*Turning to* CHU-YIN—*harshly*) Wisdom! No, do not read! What good are wise writings to fight stupidity? One must have stupid writings that men can understand. In order to live even wisdom must be stupid!

A CHAMBERLAIN. (*enters hurriedly and prostrates himself*) A courier from Persia!

KUBLAI. (*excitedly*) From Kukachin! Bring him here! (*The* CHAMBERLAIN *dashes to the door and a moment later the* COURIER *enters, travel-stained and weary. He sinks into a heap before the throne.* KUBLAI *shouts at him impatiently*) Have you a letter?

COURIER. (*with a great effort holds out a letter*) Here! (*He collapses.* CHU-YIN *hands the letter up to* KUBLAI *who takes it eagerly from him. He begins to read at once. The* CHAMBERLAIN *comes back with a cup of wine. The* COURIER *is revived and gets to his knees, waiting humbly.*)

CHU-YIN. (*goes back to* KUBLAI *who has finished reading the short note and is staring somberly before him*) And did the Little Flower save his Immortal Soul? (KUBLAI *does not look at him but mutely hands him the letter.* CHU-YIN *becomes grave. He reads aloud*) "Arghun had died. I am the wife of his son, Ghazan. It does not matter. He is kind but I miss my home and you. I doubt if I shall be blessed with a son. I do not care. I have lost my love of life. My heart beats more and more wearily. Death woos me. You must not grieve. You wish me to be happy, do you not? And my body may resist Death for a long time yet. Too long. My soul he has already possessed. I wish

423

to commend the unremitting attention to his duty of Admiral Polo. He saved my life three times at the risk of his own. He delivered me to Ghazan. Send him another million. You were right about his soul. What I had mistaken for one I discovered to be a fat woman with a patient virtue. By the time you receive this they will be married in Venice. I do not blame him. But I cannot forgive myself—nor forget —nor believe again in any beauty in the world. I love you the best in life. And tell Chu-Yin I love him too." (*He lets the letter in his hand drop to his side, his eyes filling, his voice grown husky.* KUBLAI *stares bleakly ahead of him.*)

KUBLAI. (*at last rouses himself—harshly to the* COURIER) Did the Queen give you this in person?

COURIER. Yes, Your Majesty—with a generous gift.

KUBLAI. I can be generous too. Did she appear—ill?

COURIER. Yes. I could scarcely hear her voice.

KUBLAI. You brought no other word?

COURIER. Not from the Queen. I came privately from her. But Admiral Polo suspected my departure and gave me a verbal message which he caused me to memorize.

KUBLAI. (*harshly—his eyes beginning to gleam with anger*) Ha! Go on! Repeat!

COURIER. (*stopping for a moment to freshen his memory*) He said, tell the Great Kaan that "in spite of perils too numerous to relate, I have delivered my charge safely to Ghazan Khan. In general, she gave but little trouble on the voyage, for although flighty in temper and of a passionate disposition, she never refused to heed my advice for her welfare and as I informed His Majesty, King Ghazan, the responsibilities of marriage and the duties of motherhood will sober her spirit and she will settle down as a sensible wife should. This much I further add, that in humble obedience to your final instructions given me by Mr. Chu-Yin, I looked daily into her eyes."

KUBLAI. (*bewilderedly to* CHU-YIN) What? Did you—?

424

CHU-YIN. (*miserably*) Forgive an old fool! I meant it partly in jest as a last chance—to cure her—or to awaken him.

COURIER. (*continuing*) "But I have never noted any unnatural change in them except toward the termination of our trip, particularly on the last day, when I noticed a rather strained expression but this I took to be fever due to her Highness's spleen being sluggish after the long confinement on shipboard."

KUBLAI. (*choking with wrath*) O God of the Somber Heavens!

COURIER. And he gave me no money for delivering the message but he promised that you would reward me nobly.

KUBLAI. (*with wild laughter*) Ha-ha-ha! Stop! Do you dare to madden me? (*Then suddenly raging*) Out of my sight, dog, before I have you impaled! (*The terror-stricken* COURIER *scrambles out like a flash.* KUBLAI *stands up with flashing eyes—revengefully.*) I have reconsidered! I shall conquer the West! I shall lead my armies in person! I shall not leave one temple standing nor one Christian alive who is not enslaved! Their cities shall vanish in flame, their fields shall be wasted! Famine shall finish what I leave undone! And of the city of Venice not one vestige shall remain! And of the body of Marco Polo there shall not be a fragment of bone nor an atom of flesh which will not have shrieked through ten days' torture before it died!

CHU-YIN. Master! (*He throws himself on his face at* KUBLAI's *feet*) Do not torture yourself! Is this Wisdom? Is this the peace of the soul?

KUBLAI. (*distractedly*) To revenge oneself—that brings a kind of peace!

CHU-YIN. To revenge equally the wrong of an equal perhaps, but this—? Can you confess yourself weaker than his stupidity?

KUBLAI. He has murdered her!

CHU-YIN. She does not accuse him. What would be her wish?

KUBLAI. (*his anger passing—wearily and bitterly, after a pause*) Rise, my old friend, it is I who should be at your feet, not you at mine! (*He sinks dejectedly on his throne again. After a pause, sadly*)

425

She will die. Why is this? What purpose can it serve? My hideous suspicion is that God is only an infinite, insane energy which creates and destroys without other purpose than to pass eternity in avoiding thought. Then the stupid man becomes the Perfect Incarnation of Omnipotence and the Polos are the true children of God! (*He laughs bitterly*) Ha! How long before we shall be permitted to die, my friend? I begin to resent life as the insult of an ignoble inferior with whom it is a degradation to fight! (*Broodingly—after a pause*) I have had a foreboding she would die. Lately, to while away time, I experimented with the crystal. I do not believe the magic nonsense about it but I do consider that, given a focus, the will can perhaps overcome the limits of the senses. Whatever the explanation be, I looked into the crystal and willed to see Kukachin in Persia and she appeared, sitting alone in a garden, beautiful and sad, apart from life, waiting— (*Brokenly*) My eyes filled with tears. I cried out to her— and she was gone! (*Then suddenly—to the* CHAMBERLAIN) Bring me the crystal! (*To* CHU-YIN *as the* CHAMBERLAIN *goes*) Marco, the true ruler of the world, will have come to Venice by this time. My loathing grows so intense I feel he must jump into the crystal at my bidding. And—in the cause of wisdom, say—we must see what he is doing now. (*The* CHAMBERLAIN *returns with the crystal.* KUBLAI *takes it eagerly from his hand and stares fixedly into it.*)

CHU-YIN. (*protestingly*) Why do you wish to hurt yourself further?

KUBLAI. (*staring fixedly*) I shall observe dispassionately. It is a test of myself I want to make as a penalty for my weakness a moment ago. (*He sees something*) Ah—it begins. (*A pause. The light grows dimmer and dimmer on the stage proper as it begins to come up on the extreme foreground*) I see—a city whose streets are canals—it is evening—a house. I begin to see through the walls— Ah! (*The lights come up again on the back stage as the forestage is fully revealed. The* KAAN *on his throne and* CHU-YIN *are seen dimly, behind and above, like beings on another plane. At the center of the forestage is a great banquet table garishly set with an ornate gold service. A tall major-*

domo in a gorgeous uniform enters and stands at attention as the procession begins. First come the Guests, male and female, a crowd of good substantial bourgeois, who stare about with awe and envy and are greatly impressed by the gold plate.)

A MAN. They've laid out a pile of money here!

A WOMAN. Is that gold service really gold?

ANOTHER. Absolutely. I can tell without biting it.

A MAN. They must have cash, whoever they are.

A WOMAN. Do you think they're really the Polos?

ANOTHER. They looked like greasy Tartars to me.

ANOTHER. That was their queer clothes.

A MAN. And remember they've been gone twenty-odd years.

ANOTHER. In spite of that, I thought I could recognize Maffeo.

A WOMAN. Will Donata know Marco, I wonder?

A MAN. What's more to her point, will he recognize her?

A WOMAN. Imagine her waiting all this time!

ANOTHER. How romantic! He must be terribly rich—if it's really him.

A MAN. We'll soon know. That's why we were invited.

A WOMAN. Ssshh! Here comes Donata now. How old she's getting to look!

ANOTHER. And how fat in the hips!

A MAN. (*jokingly*) That's the way I like 'em, and perhaps Marco— (DONATA *enters on the arm of her father, a crafty, wizened old man. She has grown into a stout middle age but her face is unlined and still pretty in a bovine, good-natured way. All bow and they return this salutation.*)

ALL. Congratulations, Donata! (*She blushes and turns aside in an incongruous girlish confusion.*)

FATHER. (*proud but pretending querulousness*) Don't tease her now! The girl's nervous enough already. And it may not be Marco after all but only a joke someone's put up on us.

A WOMAN. No one could be so cruel!

ALL. (*suddenly with a great gasp*) Oh, listen! (*An orchestra vigorously begins a flowery, sentimental Italian tune. This grows into quite a blare as the musicians enter from the right, six in number, in brilliant uniforms*) Oh, look! (*The musicians form a line, three on each side by the stairs on right*) Oh, see! (*A procession of servants begins to file one by one through the ranks of musicians, each carrying on his head or upraised hand an enormous platter on which are whole pigs, fowl of all varieties, roasts, vegetables, salads, fruits, nuts, dozens of bottles of wines. The servants arrange these on the table, in symmetrical groups, with the trained eye for display of window-dressers, until the table, with the bright light flooding down on it, closely resembles the front of a pretentious delicatessen store. Meanwhile*) See! What a turkey! Such a goose! The fattest pig I ever saw! What ducks! What vegetables! Look at the wine! A feast for the Gods! And all those servants! An army! And the orchestra! What expense! Lavish! They must be worth millions! (*The three* POLOS *make their grand entrance from the stairs on right, walking with bursting self-importance between the files of musicians who now blare out a triumphant march. The two elder precede* MARCO. *All three are dressed in long robes of embroidered crimson satin reaching almost to the ground. The guests give a new united gasp of astonishment*) Is it they? Is that old Nicolo? That's Maffeo's nose! No! It isn't them at all! Well, if it's a joke, I don't see the point. But such robes! Such hand embroidery! Such material! They must be worth millions.

DONATA. (*falteringly*) Is that him, father? I can't tell. (*She calls faintly*) Marco! (*But he pretends not to hear. He gives a sign at which the three take off their robes and hand them to the servants. They have even more gorgeous blue ones underneath.* MARCO *addresses the servants in a false voice.*)

MARCO. My good men, you may sell these rich robes and divide the proceeds among yourselves! And here is a little something extra. (*He tosses a handful of gold to the servants and another to the musicians.*

428

A mad scramble results. The guests gasp. They seem inclined to join in the scramble.)

GUESTS. How generous! What prodigality! What indifference to money! They throw it away like dirt. They must be worth millions!

MARCO. (*in the same false voice*) Our guests look thirsty. Pass around the wine. (*The servants do so. The guests gaze, smell, taste.*)

ALL. What a vintage! What flavor! What bouquet! How aged! It must have cost twenty lire a bottle! (*At another signal the three* POLOS *take off their blue robes.*)

MARCO. (*regally*) Give those to the musicians! (*They are revealed now in their old dirty, loose Tartar traveling dress and look quite shabby. The guests gape uncertainly. Then* MARCO *declares grandly*) You look astonished, good people, but this is a moral lesson to teach you not to put too much faith in appearances, for behold! (*He slits up the wide sleeves of his own robe, as do his father and uncle, and now the three, standing beside a big empty space which has been purposely left at the very center of the table at the front, lower their opened sleeves, and, as the musicians, obeying this signal, start up a great blare, let pour from them a perfect stream of precious stones which forms a glittering multicolored heap. This is the final blow. The guests stare pop-eyed, open-mouthed, speechless for a second. Then their pent-up admiration breaks forth.*)

ALL. Extraordinary! Jewels! Gems! Rubies! Emeralds! Diamonds! Pearls! A king's ransom! Millions!

MARCO. (*suddenly with his hail-fellow-well-met joviality*) Well, folks, are you all tongue-tied? Isn't one of you going to say welcome home? And Miss Donata, don't I get a kiss? I'm still a bachelor! (*Immediately with mad shouts of "Bravo!" "Welcome home!" "Hurrah for the Polos!" etc., etc., the guests bear down on them in a flood. There is a confused whirl of embraces, kisses, back-slaps, handshakes and loud greetings of all sorts.* MARCO *manages to get separated and pulls* DONATA *down front to the foreground.*)

DONATA. (*half swooning*) Marco!

MARCO. (*moved*) My old girl! (*They kiss, then he pushes her away*) Here! Let me get a good look at you! Why, you're still as pretty as a picture and you don't look a day older!

DONATA. (*exaltedly*) My beloved prince!

MARCO. (*jokingly*) No, if I was a prince I'd never have remained single all these years in the East! I'm a hero, that's what! And all the twenty-odd years I kept thinking of you, and I was always intending to write— (*He pulls the pieces of the miniature wrapped in the handkerchief out of his pocket*) Here's proof for you! Look at yourself! You're a bit smashed but that was done in a hand-to-hand fight with pirates. Now don't I deserve another kiss?

DONATA. (*giving it*) My hero! (*Then jealously*) But I know all the heathen women must have fallen in love with you.

MARCO. Oh, maybe one or two or so—but I didn't have time to waste on females. I kept my nose to the grindstone every minute. (*Proudly*) And I gots results. I don't mind telling you, Donata, I'm worth over two millions! How's that for keeping my promise? Worth while your waiting, eh? (*He slaps her on the back.*)

DONATA. Yes, my wonder boy! (*Then worriedly*) You said there were one or two women? But you were true in spite of them, weren't you?

MARCO. I tell you I wouldn't have married the prettiest girl in Cathay! (*This with emphasis. Then abruptly*) But never mind any other girl. (*He chucks her under the chin*) What I want to know is when this girl is going to marry me?

DONATA. (*softly*) Any time! (*They hug. The guests group about them kittenishly, pointing and murmuring, "What a romance! What a romance!"*)

DONATA'S FATHER. (*seizing the opportunity*) Friends, I take this opportunity to publicly announce the betrothal of my daughter, Donata, to Marco Polo of this City! (*Another wild round of congratulations, kisses, etc.*)

MARCO. (*his voice sounding above the hubbub*) Let's eat, friends!

(*They swirl to their places behind the long table. When they stand their faces can be seen above the piles of food but when they sit they are out of sight*) No ceremony among friends. Just pick your chair. All ready? Let's sit down then! (*With one motion they disappear.*)

VOICE OF DONATA'S FATHER. But first, before we regale ourselves with your cheer, won't you address a few words to your old friends and neighbors who have gathered here on this happy occasion? (*Applause.* MARCO *is heard expostulating but finally he gives in.*)

MARCO. All right, if you'll promise to go ahead and eat and not wait for me. (*His head appears, his expression full of importance. Servants flit about noisily. He coughs and begins with dramatic feeling*) My friends and neighbors of old, your generous and whole-hearted welcome touches me profoundly. I would I had the gift of oratory to thank you fittingly, but I am a simple man, an ordinary man, I might almost say,—a man of affairs used to dealing in the hard facts of life, a silent man given to deeds, not words— (*Here he falters fittingly*) And so now—forgive my emotion—words fail me— (*Here he clears his throat with an important cough and bursts forth into a memorized speech in the grand Chamber of Commerce style*) But I'll be glad to let you have a few instructive facts about the silk industry as we observed it in the Far East, laying especial emphasis upon the key-stone of the whole silk business—I refer to the breeding of worms! (*A few hungry guests start to eat. Knives and forks and spoons rattle against plates. Soup is heard.* MARCO *strikes a good listening attitude so he will be sure not to miss a word his voice utters and warms to his work*) Now, to begin with, there are millions upon millions of capital invested in this industry, millions of contented slaves labor unremittingly millions of hours per annum to obtain the best results in the weaving and dyeing of the finished product, but I don't hesitate to state that all this activity is relatively unimportant beside the astounding fact that in the production of the raw material there are constantly employed millions upon millions upon millions of millions of worms!

ONE VOICE. (*rather muffled by roast pig*) Hear! (*But the rest are all*

absorbed in eating and a perfect clamor of knives and forks resounds.
MARCO *begins again but this time the clamor is too great, his words*
are lost, only the one he lays such emphasis upon can be distinguished.)

MARCO. Millions! . . . millions! . . . millions! . . . millions!

KUBLAI. (*who from the height of his golden throne, crystal in hand,*
has watched all this with fascinated disgust while CHU-YIN *has sat*
down to read again, now turns away with a shudder of loathing—and,
in spite of himself, a shadow of a smile—and lets the crystal fall from
his hand and shatter into bits with a loud report. Instantly there is
darkness and from high up in the darkness KUBLAI's *voice speaking*
with a pitying scorn.) The Word became their flesh, they say. Now all
is flesh! And can their flesh become the Word again?

DARKNESS

ACT THREE—SCENE TWO

SCENE—*Grand Throne Room in the Imperial Palace at Cambaluc,*
about two years later. The walls tower majestically in shadow,
their elaborate detail blurred into a background of half-darkness.

KUBLAI *sits at the top of his throne, cross-legged in the posture of*
an idol, motionless, wrapped in contemplation. He wears a simple
white robe without adornment of any sort. A brilliant light floods
down upon him in one concentrated ray. His eyes are fixed on a cata-
falque, draped in heavy white silk, which stands in the center of the
room, emphasized by another downpouring shaft of light.

CHU-YIN *stands on the level below, on* KUBLAI's *left. On the main*
floor are the nobles and people of the court, grouped as in Act One,
Scene Six.

There is a long pause clamorous with the pealing of the thousands
of bells in the city, big and little, near and far. Every figure in the

room is as motionless as the KAAN himself. Their eyes are kept on him with the ardent humility and respect of worship. Behind their impassive faces, one senses a tense expectancy of some sign from the throne. At last, KUBLAI makes a slight but imperious motion of command with his right hand. Immediately the women all turn with arms outstretched toward the catafalque. Their voices rise together in a long, rhythmic wail of mourning; their arms with one motion move slowly up; their voices attain a prolonged note of unbearable poignancy; their heads are thrown back, their arms appeal to Heaven in one agonized gesture of despair. Here the KAAN makes the same barely perceptible sign of command again. The voices are instantly silenced. With one motion, the women throw themselves prostrate on the floor. The bells, except for one slow deep-toned one in the palace itself, are almost instantly hushed. At the same instant, from outside, at first faint, but growing momentarily in volume, comes the sound of funeral music. A moment later the funeral procession enters. The men sink to the cross-legged position of prayer, their heads bowed.

First come the musicians, nine in number, men in robes of bright red. They are followed by the chorus of nine singers, five men and four women, all of them aged, with bent bodies, their thin, cracked voices accompanying the music in queer, breaking waves of lamentation. These are masked, the men with a male mask of grief, the women with a female. All are dressed in deep black with white edging to their robes. After them comes a troupe of young girls and boys, dressed in white with black edging, moving slowly backward in a gliding, interweaving dance pattern. Their faces are not masked but are fixed in a disciplined, traditional expression of bewildered, uncomprehending grief that is like a mask. They carry silver censers which they swing in unison toward the corpse of the PRINCESS KUKACHIN, carried on a bier directly behind them on the shoulders of eight princes of the blood in black armor.

Accompanying the bier, one at each corner, are four priests—the foremost two, a Confucian and a Taoist, the latter two, a Buddhist

433

and a Moslem. Each walks with bent head reading aloud to himself from his Holy Book.

The princes lift the bier of KUKACHIN *to the top of the catafalque. Her body is wrapped in a winding sheet of deep blue, a jeweled golden head-dress is on her black hair, her face is white and clear as a statue's. The young boys and girls place their smoking censers about the catafalque, the incense ascending in clouds about the Princess as if it were bearing her soul with it. The music and the singing cease as the dancers, singers, and musicians form on each side, and to the rear, of the catafalque and sink into attitudes of prayer.*

KUBLAI *speaks to the priests in a voice of command in which is weariness and disbelief.*

KUBLAI. Peace! She does not need your prayers. She was a prayer! (*With one motion they shut their books, raise their heads and stare before them in silence.* KUBLAI *continues—sadly*) Can words recall life to her beauty? (*To the* PRIEST OF TAO) Priest of Tao, will you conquer death by your mystic Way?

PRIEST OF TAO. (*bowing his head in submission—fatalistically*) Which is the greater evil, to possess or to be without? Death is.

CHORUS. (*in an echo of vast sadness*) Death is.

KUBLAI. (*to the* CONFUCIAN) Follower of Confucius, the Wise, have you this wisdom?

PRIEST OF CONFUCIUS. (*slowly*) Before we know life, how can we know death? (*Then as the* TAOIST, *submissively*) Death is.

CHORUS. (*as before*) Death is.

KUBLAI. (*to the* BUDDHIST PRIEST) Worshiper of Buddha, can your self-overcoming overcome that greatest overcomer of self?

BUDDHIST PRIEST. This is a thing which no god can bring about: that what is subject to death should not die. (*Then as the others, submissively*) Death is.

CHORUS. (*as before*) Death is.

KUBLAI. (*wearily*) And your answer, priest of Islam?

434

PRIEST OF ISLAM. It is the will of Allah! (*Submissively*) Death is.

CHORUS. Death is. Death is. Death is. (*Their voices die away.*)

KUBLAI. (*after a pause*) What is death? (*A long pause. His eyes rest in loving contemplation on the body of* KUKACHIN. *Finally he speaks tenderly to her with a sad smile*) Girl whom we call dead, whose beauty is even in death more living than we, smile with infinite silence upon our speech, smile with infinite forbearance upon our wisdom, smile with infinite remoteness upon our sorrow, smile as a star smiles! (*His voice appears about to break. A muffled sound of sobbing comes from the prostrate women.* KUBLAI *regains control over his weakness and rises to his feet—with angry self-contempt*) No more! That is for poets! (*With overstressed arrogance—assertively*) I am the Great Kaan! (*Everyone in the room rises with one motion of assertion.*)

CHORUS. (*accompanied by a clangor of brass from the musicians—recite with discordant vigor*)

> Greatest of the Great!
> Son of Heaven!
> Lord of Earth!
> Sovereign of the World!
> Ruler over Life and Death!

KUBLAI. (*silences them by an imperious gesture— and now even the great palace bell is stilled—half mockingly but assertively*) The Son of Heaven? Then I should know a prayer. Sovereign of the World? Then I command the World to pray! (*With one motion all sink to the position of prayer*) In silence! Prayer is beyond words! Contemplate the eternal life of Life! Pray thus! (*He himself sinks to the position of prayer—a pause—then slowly*) In silence—for one concentrated moment—be proud of life! Know in your heart that the living of life can be noble! Know that the dying of death can be noble! Be exalted by life! Be inspired by death! Be humbly proud! Be proudly grateful! Be immortal because life is immortal. Contain the harmony of womb and grave within you! Possess life as a lover—then sleep

435

requited in the arms of death! If you awake, love again! If you sleep on, rest in peace! Who knows which? What does it matter? It is nobler not to know! (*A pause of silence. He rises to his feet. With one motion all do likewise.* KUBLAI *sits back on his cushions again, withdrawing into contemplation. The Mongol* CHRONICLER *comes forward to fulfill his function of chanting the official lament for the dead. He declaims in a high wailing voice accompanied by the musicians and by the* CHORUS *who sway rhythmically and hum a rising and falling mourning accompaniment.*)

CHRONICLER. We lament the shortness of life. Life at its longest is brief enough.

Too brief for the wisdom of joy, too long for the knowledge of sorrow.

Sorrow becomes despair when death comes to the young, untimely.

Oh, that her beauty could live again, that her youth could be born anew.

Our Princess was young as Spring, she was beautiful as a bird or flower.

Cruel when Spring is smitten by Winter, when birds are struck dead in full song, when the budding blossom is blighted!

Alas that our Princess is dead, she was the song of songs, the perfume of perfumes, the perfect one!

Our sobs stifle us, our tears wet the ground, our lamentations sadden the wind from the West.

(*Bows submissively—speaks*)

Yet we must bow humbly before the Omnipotent.

CHORUS. We must be humble.

CHRONICLER. Against Death all Gods are powerless.

CHORUS. All Gods are powerless. (*Their voices die into silence.*)

KUBLAI. (*after a pause—wearily*) Leave her in peace. Go. (*The Court leaves silently at his command in a formal, expressionless order. The four priests go first, beginning to pray silently again. They are followed by the nobles and officials with their women coming after.*

Finally the young boys and girls take up their censers and dance their pattern out backward, preceded by the musicians. Only the CHORUS *remain, grouped in a semi-circle behind the catafalque, motionless, and* CHU-YIN *who stays at the left hand of* KUBLAI. *The music fades away.* KUBLAI *takes his eyes from the dead girl with a sigh of bitter irony.)*

KUBLAI. Oh, Chu-Yin, my Wise Friend, was the prayer I taught them wisdom?

CHU-YIN. It was the wisdom of pride. It was thy wisdom.

CHORUS. (*echoing sadly*) Thy wisdom.

KUBLAI. Was it not truth?

CHU-YIN. It was the truth of power. It was thy truth.

CHORUS. (*as before*) Thy truth.

KUBLAI. My pride, my power? My wisdom, my truth? For me there remains only—her truth! (*Then after staring at* KUKACHIN *for a second, bitterly*) Her truth! She died for love of a fool!

CHU-YIN. No. She loved love. She died for beauty.

KUBLAI. Your words are hollow echoes of the brain. Do not wound me with wisdom. Speak to my heart! (*Sadly—his eyes again on* KU-KACHIN) Her little feet danced away the stamp of armies. Her smile made me forget the servile grin on the face of the World. In her eyes' mirror I watched myself live protected from life by her affection—a simple old man dying contentedly a little, day after pleasant day.

CHU-YIN. (*bowing—compassionately*) Then weep, old man. Be humble and weep for your child. The old should cherish sorrow. (*He bows again and goes out silently.*)

KUBLAI. (*after a pause, gets up and, descending from his throne, slowly approaches the catafalque, speaking to the dead girl softly as he does so—with a trembling smile*) I think you are hiding your eyes, Kukachin. You are a little girl again. You are playing hide and seek. You are pretending. Did we not once play such games together, you and I? You have made your face still, you have made your face cold, you have set your lips in a smile so remote—you are pretending even that you are dead! (*He is very near her now. His voice breaks—more and more intensely*) Let us stop playing! It is late. It is time you were asleep. Open your eyes and laugh! Laugh now that the game is over. Take the blindfold from my dim eyes. Whisper your secret in my ear. I—I am dead and you are living! Weep for me, Kukachin! Weep for the dead! (*He stretches his arms out to her beseechingly—pauses, standing beside the body, staring down at her; then, after a moment, he passes his hand over her face—tremblingly—with a beautiful tenderness of grief*) So, little Kukachin—so, Little Flower—you have come back—they could not keep you—you were too homesick—you wanted to return—to gladden my last days— (*He no longer tries to control his grief. He sobs like a simple old man, bending and kissing his granddaughter on the forehead—with heart-breaking playfulness*) I bid you welcome home, Little Flower! I bid you welcome home! (*He weeps, his tears falling on her calm white face.*)

CURTAIN

EPILOGUE

THE *play is over. The lights come up brilliantly in the theatre. In an aisle seat in the first row a* MAN *rises, conceals a yawn in his palm, stretches his legs as if they had become cramped by too long an evening, takes his hat from under the seat and starts to go out slowly with the others in the audience. But although there is nothing out of the ordinary in his actions, his appearance excites general comment and surprise for he is dressed as a Venetian merchant of the later Thirteenth Century. In fact, it is none other than* MARCO POLO *himself, looking a bit sleepy, a trifle puzzled, and not a little irritated as his thoughts, in spite of himself, cling for a passing moment to the play just ended. He appears quite unaware of being unusual and walks in the crowd without self-consciousness, very much as one of them. Arrived in the lobby his face begins to clear of all disturbing memories of what had happened on the stage. The noise, the lights of the streets, recall him at once to himself. Impatiently he waits for his car, casting a glance here and there at faces in the groups around him, his eyes impersonally speculative, his bearing stolid with the dignity of one who is sure of his place in the world. His car, a luxurious limousine, draws up at the curb. He gets in briskly, the door is slammed, the car edges away into the traffic and* MARCO POLO, *with a satisfied sigh at the sheer comfort of it all, resumes his life.*

439

WELDED

A Play in Three Acts

CHARACTERS

MICHAEL CAPE

ELEANOR

JOHN

A WOMAN

SCENES

ACT ONE
Scene: Studio apartment.

ACT TWO
Scene I: Library.
Scene II: Bedroom.

ACT THREE
Scene: Same as Act I.

WELDED

ACT ONE

Scene—*Studio apartment. In the rear, a balcony with a stairway at center leading down to the studio floor.*

The room is in darkness. Then a circle of light reveals ELEANOR *lying back on a chaise longue. She is a woman of thirty. Her figure is tall. Her face, with its high, prominent cheek-bones, lacks harmony. It is dominated by passionate, blue-gray eyes, restrained by a high forehead from which the mass of her dark brown hair is combed straight back. The first impression of her whole personality is one of charm, partly innate, partly imposed by years of self-discipline.*

She picks up a letter from the table, which she opens and reads, an expression of delight and love coming over her face. She kisses the letter impulsively—then gives a gay laugh at herself. She lets the letter fall on her lap and stares straight before her, lost in a sentimental reverie.

A door underneath the balcony is noiselessly opened and MICHAEL *comes in. (A circle of light appears with him, follows him into the room. These two circles of light, like auras of egoism, emphasize and intensify* ELEANOR *and* MICHAEL *throughout the play. There is no other lighting. The two other people and the rooms are distinguishable only by the light of* ELEANOR *and* MICHAEL.)

MICHAEL *is thirty-five, tall and dark. His unusual face is a harrowed battlefield of supersensitiveness, the features at war with one another —the forehead of a thinker, the eyes of a dreamer, the nose and mouth of a sensualist. One feels a powerful imagination tinged with somber sadness—a driving force which can be sympathetic and cruel at the*

443

*same time. There is something tortured about him—a passionate ten-
sion, a self-protecting, arrogant defiance of life and his own weakness,
a deep need for love as a faith in which to relax.*

*He has a suitcase, hat, and overcoat which he sets inside on the floor,
glancing toward* ELEANOR, *trying not to make the slightest noise. But
she suddenly becomes aware of some presence in the room and turns
boldly to face it. She gives an exclamation of delighted astonishment
when she sees* MICHAEL *and jumps up to meet him as he strides toward
her.*

ELEANOR. Michael!

CAPE. (*with a boyish grin*) You've spoiled it, Nelly; I wanted a kiss
to announce me. (*They are in each other's arms. He kisses her tenderly.*)

ELEANOR. (*joyously*) This *is* a surprise!

CAPE. (*straining her in his arms and kissing her passionately*) Own
little wife!

ELEANOR. Dearest! (*They look into each other's eyes for a long moment.*)

CAPE. (*tenderly*) Happy?

ELEANOR. Yes, yes! Why do you always ask? You know. (*Suddenly
pushing him at arms' length—with a happy laugh*) It's positively
immoral for an old married couple to act this way. (*She leads him by
the hand to the chaise longue*) And you must explain. You wrote not
to expect you till the end of the week. (*She sits down*) Get a cushion.
Sit down here. (*He puts a cushion on the floor beside the chaise longue
and sits down*) Tell me all about it.

CAPE. (*notices the letter lying on the floor*) Were you reading my
letter? (*She nods. He gives a happy grin*) Do you mean to say you
still read them over—after five years of me?

ELEANOR. (*with a tender smile*) Oh—sometimes.

CAPE. Sweetheart! (*Smiling*) What were you dreaming about when
I intruded?

444

ELEANOR. Never mind. You're enough of an egotist already. (*Her hand caressing his face and hair*) I've been feeling so lonely—and it's only been a few weeks, hasn't it? (*She laughs*) How was everything in the country? (*Suddenly kissing him*) Oh, I'm so happy you're back. (*With mock severity*) But ought I? Have you finished the fourth act? You know you promised not to return until you did.

CAPE. This afernoon!

ELEANOR. You're sure you didn't force it—(*with a tender smile at him*)—because you were lonely, too?

CAPE. (*with a sudden change in manner that is almost stern*) No. I wouldn't. I couldn't. You know that.

ELEANOR. (*her face showing a trace of hurt in spite of herself*) I was only fooling. (*Then rousing herself as if conquering a growing depression*) I'm terribly anxious to hear what you've done.

CAPE. (*enthusiastically*) You'll see when I read you— And you're going to be marvelous! It's going to be the finest thing we've ever done!

ELEANOR. I love you for saying "we." But the "we" is you. I only— (*with a smile of ironical self-pity*)—act a part you've created.

CAPE. (*impetuously*) Nonsense! You're an artist. Each performance of yours has taught me something. Why, my women used to be— death masks. But now they're as alive as you are—(*with a sudden grin*)—at least, when you play them.

ELEANOR. (*her eyes shining with excited pleasure*) You don't know how much it means to have you talk like that! Oh, I'm going to work so hard, Michael! (*Impetuously*) You've simply got to read me that last act right now!

CAPE. (*jumping to his feet eagerly*) All right. (*He walks toward his bag—then stops when he is half-way and, hesitating, turns slowly and comes back. He bends down and lifts her face to his—with a smile*) No. I won't.

ELEANOR. (*disappointed*) Oh. Why not, dear?

CAPE. Because—

ELEANOR. Plagiarist!

CAPE. Because I've been hoping for this night as our own. Let's forget the actress and playwright. Let's just be—us—lovers.

ELEANOR. (*with a tender smile—musingly*) We *have* remained lovers, haven't we?

CAPE. (*with a grin*) Fights and all?

ELEANOR. (*with a little frown*) We don't fight so much.

CAPE. (*frowning himself*) Too much.

ELEANOR. (*forcing a smile*) Perhaps that's the price.

CAPE. Don't grow fatalistic—just when I was about to propose reform.

ELEANOR. (*smiling—quickly*) Oh, I'll promise to be good—if you will. (*Gently reproachful*) Do you think I enjoy fighting with you?

CAPE. (*with sudden passion*) It's wrong, Nelly. It's evil!

ELEANOR. Ssshh! We promised.

CAPE. (*hesitatingly*) We've been taking each other too much for granted. That may do very well with the common loves of the world —but ours—! (*He suddenly pulls her head down and kisses her impulsively*) But you understand! Oh, Nelly, I love you with all my soul!

ELEANOR. (*deeply moved*) And I love you, Michael—always and forever! (*They sit close, she staring dreamily before her, he watching her face.*)

CAPE. (*after a pause*) What are you thinking?

ELEANOR. (*with a tender smile*) Of the first time we met—at rehearsal, remember? I was thinking of how mistakenly I'd pictured you before that. (*She pauses—then frowning a little*) I'd heard such a lot of gossip about your love affairs.

CAPE. (*with a wry grin*) You must have been disappointed if you expected Don Juan. (*A pause—then forcing a short laugh*) I also had heard a lot of rumors about your previous— (*He stops abruptly with an expression of extreme bitterness.*)

ELEANOR. (*sharply*) Don't! (*A pause—then she goes on sadly*) It was only our past together I wanted to remember. (*A pause—then with a trace of scornful resentment*) I was forgetting your morbid obsession—

CAPE. (*with gloomy irritation*) Obsession? Why—? (*Then determinedly throwing off this mood—reproachfully forcing a joking tone*) We're not "starting something" now, are we—after our promise?

ELEANOR. (*impulsively pressing his hand*) No, no—of course not!

CAPE. (*after a pause—a bit awkwardly*) But you guessed my desire, at that. I wanted to dream with you in our past—to find there—a new faith—

ELEANOR. (*smiling*) Another Grand Ideal for our marriage?

CAPE. (*frowning*) Don't mock.

ELEANOR. (*teasingly*) But you're such a relentless idealist. You needn't frown. That was exactly what drew me to you in those first days. (*Earnestly*) I'd lost faith in everything. Your love saved me. Your work saved mine. I owe you myself, Michael! (*She kisses him*) Do you remember—our first night together?

CAPE. Do you imagine I could've forgotten?

ELEANOR. (*continuing as if she hadn't heard*) The play was such a marvelous success! I knew I had finally won—through your work! I loved myself! I loved you! You came to me— (*More and more intensely*) Oh, it was beautiful madness! I lost myself. I began living in you. I wanted to die and become you!

CAPE. (*passionately*) And I, you!

ELEANOR. (*softly*) And do you remember the dawn creeping in—and how we began to plan our future? (*She exclaims impulsively*) Oh, I'd give anything in the world to live those days over again!

CAPE. Why? Hasn't our marriage kept the spirit of that time—with a growth of something deeper—finer—

ELEANOR. Yes,—but— Oh, you know what I mean! It was revelation then—a miracle out of the sky!

CAPE. (*insistently*) But haven't we realized the ideal of our marriage— (*Smiling but with deep earnestness nevertheless*) Not for us

447

the ordinary family rite, you'll remember! We swore to have a true sacrament—or nothing! Our marriage must be a consummation demanding and combining the best in each of us! Hard, difficult, guarded from the commonplace, kept sacred as the outward form of our inner harmony! (*With an awkward sense of having become rhetorical he adds self-mockingly*) We'd tend our flame on an altar, not in a kitchen range! (*He forces a grin—then abruptly changing again, with a sudden fierce pleading*) It has been what we dreamed, hasn't it, Nelly?

ELEANOR. Our ideal was difficult. (*Sadly*) Sometimes I think we've demanded too much. Now there's nothing left but that something which can't give itself. And I blame you for this—because I can neither take more nor give more—and you blame me! (*She smiles tenderly*) And then we fight!

CAPE. Then let's be proud of our fight! It began with the splitting of a cell a hundred million years ago into you and me, leaving an eternal yearning to become one life again.

ELEANOR. At moments—we do.

CAPE. Yes! (*He kisses her—then intensely*) You and I—year after year—together—forms of our bodies merging into one form; rhythm of our lives beating against each other, forming slowly the one rhythm —the life of Us—created by us!—beyond us, above us! (*With sudden furious anger*) God, what I feel of the truth of this—the beauty!— but how can I express it?

ELEANOR. (*kissing him*) I understand.

CAPE. (*straining her to him with fierce passion*) Oh, my own, my own—and I your own—to the end of time!

ELEANOR. I love you!

CAPE. (*with passionate exultance*) Why do you regret our first days? Their fire still burns in us—deeper! Don't you feel that? (*Kissing her again and again*) I've become you! You've become me! One heart! One blood! Ours! (*He pulls her to her feet*) My wife! Come!

448

ELEANOR. (*almost swooning in his arms*) My lover—yes— My lover—

CAPE. Come! (*With his arms around her he leads her to the stairway. As they get to the foot, there is a noise from the hall. She hears it, starts, seems suddenly brought back to herself.* CAPE *is oblivious and continues up the stairs. She stands swaying, holding on to the bannister as if in a daze. At the top,* CAPE *turns in surprise at not finding her, as if he had felt her behind him. He looks down passionately, stretching out his arms, his eyes glowing*) Come!

ELEANOR. (*weakly*) Ssshh! A moment— Listen!

CAPE. (*bewilderedly*) What? What is it?

ELEANOR. Ssshh—Listen—Someone— (*She speaks in an unnatural, mechanical tone. A knock comes at the door. She gives a sort of gasp of relief*) There!

CAPE. (*still bewilderedly as if something mysterious were happening that he cannot grasp*) What—what—? (*Then as she takes a slow, mechanical step toward the door—with tense pleading*) Nelly! Come here! (*She turns to look at him and is held by his imploring eyes. She sways irresolutely toward him, again reaching to the bannister for support. Then a sharper knock comes at the door. It acts like a galvanic shock on her. Her eyes move in that direction, she takes another jerky step.* CAPE *stammers in a fierce whisper*) No! Don't go!

ELEANOR. (*without looking at him—mechanically*) I must.

CAPE. (*frantically*) They'll go away. Nelly, don't! Don't! (*Again she stops irresolutely like a hypnotized person torn by two conflicting suggestions. The knock is repeated, this time with authority, assurance. Her body reacts as if she were throwing off a load.*)

ELEANOR. (*with a return to her natural tone—but hysterical*) Please—don't be silly, Michael. It might be—something important. (*She hurries to the door.*)

CAPE. (*rushing down the stairs—frantically*) No! No! (*He just gets to the bottom as she opens the door. He stands there fixed, disorganized, trembling all over.*)

ELEANOR. (*as she sees who it is—in a relieved tone of surprise*) Why hello, John. Come in! Here's Michael. Michael, it's John. (JOHN *steps into the room. He is a man of about fifty, tall, loose-limbed, a bit stoop-shouldered, with iron-gray hair, and a gaunt, shrewd face. He is not handsome but his personality compels affection. His eyes are round and child-like. He has no nerves. His voice is low and calming.*)

JOHN. (*shaking* ELEANOR *by the hand*) Hello, Nelly. I was on my way home from the theater and I thought I'd drop in for a second. Hello, Michael. When'd you get in? Glad to see you back. (*He comes to him and shakes his hand which* CAPE *extends jerkily, as if in spite of himself, without a word.*)

ELEANOR. (*after a glance at her husband—in a forced tone*) We're so glad you've come. Sit down.

JOHN. (*he becomes aware of the disharmonious atmosphere his appearance has created*) I can't stay a second. (*To* CAPE) I wanted some news. I thought Nelly'd probably have heard from you. (*He slaps* CAPE *on the back with jovial familiarity*) Well, how's it coming?

CAPE. (*in a frozen tone*) Oh,—all right—all right.

ELEANOR. (*uneasily*) Won't you have a cigarette, John? (*She takes the box from the table and holds it out to him.*)

JOHN. (*taking one*) Thanks, Nelly. (*He half-sits on the arm of a chair. She holds out a light to him*) Thanks.

ELEANOR. (*nervously*) Why don't you sit down, Michael? (*He doesn't answer. She goes to him with the cigarettes*) Don't you want a cigarette? (CAPE *stares at her with a hot glance of scorn. She recoils from it, turning quickly away from him, visibly shaken. Without appearing to notice,* JOHN *scrutinizes their faces keenly, sizing up the situation.*)

JOHN. (*breaking in matter-of-fact*) You look done up, Michael.

CAPE. (*with a guilty start*) I—I'm tired out.

ELEANOR. (*with a forced air*) He's been working too hard. He finished the last act only this afternoon.

JOHN. (*with a grunt of satisfaction*) Glad to hear it. (*Abruptly*) When can I see it?

CAPE. In a day or so—I want to go over—

JOHN. All right. (*Getting to his feet*) Well, that's that. I'll run along.

ELEANOR. (*almost frightenedly*) Do stay. Why don't you read us the last act now, Michael?

CAPE. (*fiercely*) No! It's rotten! I hate the whole play!

JOHN. (*easily*) Reaction. This play's the finest thing you've done. (*He comes to* CAPE *and slaps him on the back reassuringly*) And it's the biggest chance the lady here has ever had. It'll be a triumph for you both, wait and see. So cheer up—and get a good night's rest. (CAPE *smiles with bitter irony*) Well, good-night. (CAPE *nods without speaking,* JOHN *goes to the door,* ELEANOR *accompanying him*) Good-night, Nelly. Better start on your part—only don't you overdo it, too. (*He pats her on the back*) Good-night.

ELEANOR. Good-night. (*She closes the door after him. She remains there for a moment staring at the closed door, afraid to turn and meet* CAPE'S *fiercely accusing eyes which she feels fixed upon her. Finally, making an effort of will, she walks back to the table, avoiding his eyes, assuming a careless air.*)

CAPE. (*suddenly explodes in furious protest*) Why did you do that?

ELEANOR. (*with an assumed surprise but with a guilty air, turning over the pages of a magazine*) Do what?

CAPE. (*tensely, clutching her by the arm*) You know what I mean! (*Unconsciously he grips her tighter, almost shaking her.*)

ELEANOR. (*coldly*) You're hurting me. (*A bit shamefacedly,* CAPE *lets go of her arm. She glances quickly at his face, then speaks with a kind of dull remorse*) I suppose I can guess—my going to the door?

CAPE. He would've gone away— (*With anguish*) Nelly, why did you?

ELEANOR. (*defensively*) Wasn't it important you see John?

451

CAPE. (*with helpless anger*) Don't evade! (*With deep feeling*) I should think you'd be ashamed.

ELEANOR. (*after a pause—dully*) Perhaps—I am. (*A pause*) I couldn't help myself.

CAPE. (*intensely*) You should've been oblivious to everything! (*Miserably*) I—I can't understand!

ELEANOR. That's you, Michael. The other is me—or a part of me— I hardly understand myself.

CAPE. (*sinking down on a chair, his head in his hands*) After all we'd been to each other tonight—! (*With bitter despondency*) Ruined now—gone—a rare moment of beauty! It seems at times as if some jealous demon of the commonplace were mocking us. (*With a violent gesture of loathing*) Oh, how intolerably insulting life can be! (*Then brokenly*) Nelly, why, why did you?

ELEANOR. (*dully*) I—I don't know. (*Then after a pause she comes over and puts her hand on his shoulder*) Don't brood, dear. I'm sorry. I hate myself. (*A pause. She looks down at him, seeming to make up her mind to something—in a forced tone*) But—why is it gone—our beautiful moment? (*She strokes his hair*) We have the whole night— (*He stares up at her wonderingly. She forces a smile, half turning away.*)

CAPE. (*in wild protest*) Nelly, what are you offering me—a sacrifice? Please!

ELEANOR. (*revolted*) Michael! (*Then hysterically*) No, forgive me! I'm the disgusting one! Forgive me! (*She turns away from him and throws herself on a chair, staring straight before her. Their chairs are side by side, each facing front, so near that by a slight movement each could touch the other, but during the following scene they stare straight ahead and remain motionless. They speak, ostensibly to the other, but showing by their tone it is a thinking aloud to oneself, and neither appears to hear what the other has said.*)

CAPE. (*after a long pause*) More and more frequently. There's always some knock at the door, some reminder of the life outside which calls you away from me.

ELEANOR. It's so beautiful—and then—suddenly I'm being crushed. I feel a cruel presence in you paralyzing me, creeping over my body, possessing it so it's no longer my body—then grasping at some last inmost thing which makes me me—my soul—demanding to have that, too! I have to rebel with all my strength—seize any pretext! Just now at the foot of the stairs—the knock on the door was—liberation. (*In anguish*) And yet I love you! It's because I love you! If I'm destroyed, what is left to love you, what is left for you to love?

CAPE. I've grown inward into our life. But you keep trying to escape as if it were a prison. You feel the need of what is outside. I'm not enough for you.

ELEANOR. Why is it I can never know you? I try to know you and I can't. I desire to take all of you into my heart, but there's a great alien force— I hate that unknown power in you which would destroy me. (*Pleadingly*) Haven't I a right to myself as you have to yourself?

CAPE. You fight against me as if I were your enemy. Every word or action of mine which affects you, you resent. At every turn you feel your individuality invaded—while at the same time, you're jealous of any separateness in me. You demand more and more while you give less and less. And I have to acquiesce. Have to? Yes, because I can't live without you! You realize that! You take advantage of it while you despise me for my helplessness! (*This seems to goad him to desperation*) But look out! I still have the strength to—! (*He turns his head and stares at her challengingly.*)

ELEANOR. (*as before*) You insist that I have no life at all outside you. Even my work must exist only as an echo of yours. You hate my need of easy, casual associations. You think that weakness. You hate my friends. You're jealous of everything and everybody. (*Resentfully*) I have to fight. You're too severe. Your ideal is too inhuman. Why can't you understand and be generous—be just! (*She turns to meet his eyes, staring back with resentful accusation. They look at each other in this manner for a long moment.*)

CAPE. (*averting his eyes and addressing her directly in a cold, sarcastic tone*) Strange—that John should pop in on us suddenly like that.

ELEANOR. (*resentfully*) I don't see anything strange about it.

CAPE. It's past twelve—

ELEANOR. You're in New York now.

CAPE. (*sharply*) I'm quite aware of that. Nevertheless—

ELEANOR. (*shortly*) He explained. Didn't you hear him? He wanted news of the play and thought I might have a letter—

CAPE. That's just the point. He had no idea he would find me here.

ELEANOR. (*about to fly at him, checks herself after a pause, coldly*) Why shouldn't he come to see me? He's the oldest friend I've got. He gave me my first chance and he's always helped me since. I owe whatever success I've made to his advice and direction.

CAPE. (*stung—sarcastically*) Oh, undoubtedly!

ELEANOR. I suppose you think I ought to have said it's to you I owe everything?

CAPE. (*dryly*) I'd prefer to say it was to yourself, and no one else. (*After a pause—attempting a casual tone*) Has he been in the habit of calling here while I've been gone? (*Hurriedly*) Don't misunderstand me. I'm merely asking a question.

ELEANOR. (*scornfully*) Oh! (*A pause. She bites her lips—then coldly*) Yes, he's been here once before. (*Mockingly*) And after the theater, too! Think of that!

CAPE. (*sneeringly*) The same insatiable curiosity about my play?

ELEANOR. (*angrily*) Michael! (*A pause—then scornfully*) Don't tell me you're becoming jealous of John again!

CAPE. (*meaningly*) Again. That's just it.

ELEANOR. (*springing from her chair—excitedly*) This is insufferable! (*Then calming herself with an effort—with a forced laugh*) Please don't be so ridiculous, Michael. I'll only lose my temper if you

454

keep on. (*Then suddenly she makes up her mind and comes to him*) Please stop, dear. We've made up our minds not to quarrel. Let's drop it. (*She pats his head with a friendly smile.*)

CAPE. (*impulsively takes her hand and kisses it*) All right. Forgive me. I'm all unstrung. His breaking in on us like that— (*He relapses into frowning brooding again. She sits down, this time facing him, and looks at him uneasily.*)

ELEANOR. (*after a pause—rather irritably*) It's too absolutely silly, your being jealous of John.

CAPE. I'm not jealous of him. I'm jealous of you—the something in you that repulses our love—the stranger in you.

ELEANOR. (*with a short laugh*) I should think after five years—

CAPE. (*unheeding*) And what makes me hate you at those times is that I know you like to make me jealous, that my suffering pleases you, that it satisfies some craving in you—for revenge!

ELEANOR. (*scornfully*) Can't you realize how absurd you are? (*Then with a forced placating laugh*) No, really, Michael, it'd be funny— if it weren't so exasperating.

CAPE. (*after a pause—somberly*) You mentioned our years together as proof. What of the years that preceded?

ELEANOR. (*challengingly*) Well, what of them?

CAPE. By their light, I have plausible grounds for jealousy in John's case. Or don't you acknowledge that?

ELEANOR. I deny it absolutely!

CAPE. Why, you've told me yourself he was in love with you for years, and that he once asked you to marry him!

ELEANOR. Well, did I marry him?

CAPE. But he still loves you.

ELEANOR. Don't be stupid!

CAPE. He does, I tell you!

ELEANOR. If you had any sense you'd know that his love has become purely that of an old friend. And I refuse to give up his friendship for your silly whims.

CAPE. (*after a pause in which they each brood resentfully—sarcastically*) You were a shining exception, it appears. The other women he helped could hardly claim he had remained—merely their friend.

ELEANOR. (*vehemently*) It's a lie! And even if it were true, you'd find it was they who offered themselves!

CAPE. (*significantly*) Ah! (*Then after a pause*) Perhaps because they felt it necessary for their careers.

ELEANOR. (*dryly*) Perhaps. (*Then after a pause*) But they discovered their mistake, then. John isn't that type.

CAPE. (*suddenly*) Why do you act so jealous—of those others?

ELEANOR. (*flushing angrily*) I don't. It's your imagination.

CAPE. Then why lose your temper?

ELEANOR. Because I resent your superior attitude that John had to bribe women to love him. Isn't he as worthy of love—as you are?

CAPE. (*sarcastically*) If I am to believe your story, you didn't think so.

ELEANOR. (*irritably*) Then let's stop arguing, for heaven's sake! Why do you always have to rake up the past? For the last year or so you've begun to act more and more as you did when we first lived together—jealous and suspicious of everything and everybody! (*Hysterically*) I can't bear it, Michael!

CAPE. (*ironically*) You used to love me for it then.

ELEANOR. (*calming herself*) Well, I can't endure it now. It's too degrading. I have a right to your complete faith. (*Reaching over and grasping his hands—earnestly*) You know I have in your heart of hearts. You know that there can never be anyone but you. Forget the past. It wasn't us. For your peace—and mine, Michael!

CAPE. (*moved—pressing her hands*) All right. Let's stop. It's only that I've thought I've felt you drawing away—! Perhaps it's all my supersensitiveness— (*Patting her hand and forcing a smile*) Let's talk of something else. (*Cheerfully—after a pause*) You can't imagine how wonderful it's been up in the country. There's just enough winter in the air to make one energetic. No summer fools about. Solitude and work. I was happy—that is, as happy as I ever can be without you.

ELEANOR. (*withdrawing her hands from his with a quick movement—sarcastically*) Thanks for that afterthought—but do you expect me to believe it? When you're working I might die and you'd never know it.

CAPE. (*amused but irritated*) There you go! You denounce my jealousy, but it seems to me your brand of it is much more ridiculous.

ELEANOR. (*sharply*) You imagine I'm jealous of your work? You—you flatter yourself!

CAPE. (*stung—bitingly*) It's an unnatural passion certainly—in your case. And an extremely ungrateful passion, I might add!

ELEANOR. (*losing her temper completely*) You mean I ought to be grateful for— I suppose you think that without your work I— (*Springing to her feet*) Your egotism is making a fool of you! You're becoming so exaggeratedly conceited no one can stand you! Everyone notices it!

CAPE. (*angrily*) You know that's untrue. You only say it to be mean. As for my work, you've acknowledged a million times—

ELEANOR. If I have—but please remember there are other playwrights in the world!

CAPE. (*bitingly*) You were on the stage seven years before I met you. Your appearance in the work of other playwrights—you must admit you were anything but successful!

ELEANOR. (*with a sneer of rage*) And I suppose you were?

CAPE. Yes! Not in your commercial sense, perhaps, but—

ELEANOR. You're contemptible! You know that's the very last thing you can say of me. It was exactly because I wasn't that kind—because I was an artist—that I found it so hard!

CAPE. (*unheeding*) My plays had been written. The one you played in first was written three years before. The work was done. That's the proof.

ELEANOR. (*scathingly*) That's absurd! You know very well if it hadn't been for John, you—

CAPE. (*violently*) Nonsense! There were other managers who—

ELEANOR. They didn't want your work, you know it!

CAPE. (*enraged*) I see what you're driving at! You'd like to pretend I was as much dependent on John as you were! (*Trembling all over with the violence of his passion*) I should think you'd be ashamed to boast so brazenly—to me!—of what he had done for you!

ELEANOR. Why should I be ashamed of my gratitude?

CAPE. To drag that relationship out of the past and throw it in my face!

ELEANOR. (*very pale—tensely*) What relationship?

CAPE. (*incoherently, strangled by his passion*) Ask anyone! (*Then suddenly with anguished remorse*) No, no! I don't mean that! (*Torturedly*) Wounds! Wounds! For God's sake!

ELEANOR. (*trembling with rage*) I'll never forget you said that!

CAPE. (*stung—in a passion again at once*) Because I resent that man's being here—late at night—when I was away? Oh, I don't mean I suspect you—now—

ELEANOR. (*viciously*) What noble faith! Maybe you're going to discover I don't deserve it!

CAPE. (*unheeding*) But there was scandal enough about you and him, and if you had any respect for me—

ELEANOR. I've lost it now!

CAPE. You wouldn't deliberately open the way—

ELEANOR. (*tensely*) So you believe—that gutter gossip? You think I—? Then all these years you've really believed—? Oh, you mean hypocrite!

CAPE. (*stung—bitingly*) Don't act moral indignation! What else could I have thought? When we first fell in love, you confessed frankly you had had lovers—not John but others—

ELEANOR. (*brokenly—with mingled grief and rage*) I was an idiot! I should have lied to you! But I thought you'd understand—that I'd been searching for something—that I needed love—something I found in you! I tried to make you see—the truth—that those experiences had

458

only made me appreciate you all the more when I found you! I told you how little these men had meant to me, that in the state of mind I had been in they had no significance either one way or the other, and that such an attitude is possible for a woman without her being low. I thought you understood. But you didn't, you're not big enough for that! (*With a wild ironical laugh*) Now I know why the women in your plays are so wooden! You ought to thank me for breathing life into them!

CAPE. (*furiously*) Good God, how dare you criticize creative work, you actress!

ELEANOR. (*violently*) You deny that I create—? Perhaps if I'd have children and a home, take up knitting—! (*She laughs wildly*) I'd be safe then, wouldn't I—reliable, guaranteed not to— (*Her face seems suddenly to congeal*) So you think that I was John's mistress—that I loved him—or do you believe I just sold myself?

CAPE. (*in agony*) No, no! For God's sake, not that! I may have thought you once loved—

ELEANOR. (*frozenly*) Well, it was—that—just that! When he first engaged me—I'd heard the gossip—I thought he expected—and I agreed with myself—it meant nothing to me one way or the other—nothing meant anything then but a chance to do my work—yes, I agreed—but you see he didn't, he didn't agree. He loved me but he saw I didn't love him—that way—and he's a finer man than you think!

CAPE. (*hoarsely*) You're lying! (*Bewilderedly*) I can't believe—

ELEANOR. (*fiercely*) Oh yes, you can! You want to! You do! And you're glad! It makes me lower than you thought, but you're glad to know it just the same! You're glad because now you can really believe that—nothing ever happened between us! (*She stares into his eyes and seems to read some confirmation of her statement there, for she cries with triumphant bitterness*) You can't deny it!

CAPE. (*wildly*) No! You devil, you, you read thoughts into my mind!

ELEANOR. (*with wild hysterical scorn*) It's true! How could I ever love you?

CAPE. (*clutching her in his arms fiercely*) You do! (*He kisses her frantically. For a moment she submits, appears even to return his kisses in spite of herself.* CAPE *cries triumphantly*) You do! (*She suddenly pushes him away and glares at him at arms' length. Her features are working convulsively. Her whole tortured face expresses an abysmal self-loathing, a frightful hatred for him.*)

ELEANOR. (*as if to herself—in a strangled voice*) No! You can't crush—me! (*Her face becomes deadly calm. She speaks with intense, cold hatred*) Don't kiss me. I love him. He was—my lover—here—when you were away!

CAPE. (*stares dumbly into her eyes for a long moment—hoarsely, in agony*) You lie! You only want to torture—

ELEANOR. (*deathly calm*) It's true! (CAPE *stares at her another second—then, with a snarl of fury like an animal's he seizes her about the throat with both hands. He chokes her, forcing her down to her knees. She does not struggle but continues to look into his eyes with the same defiant hate. At last he comes to himself with a shudder and steps away from her. She remains where she is, only putting out her hand on the floor to support herself.*)

CAPE. (*in a terrible state, sobbing with rage and anguish*) Gone! All our beauty gone! And you don't love him! You lie! You did this out of hatred for me! You dragged our ideal in the gutter—with delight! (*Wildly*) And you pride yourself you've killed it, do you, you actress, you barren soul? (*With savage triumph*) But I tell you only a creator can really destroy! (*With a climax of frenzy*) And I will! I will! I won't give your hatred the satisfaction of seeing our love live on in me—to torture me! I'll drag it lower than you! I'll stamp it into the vilest depths! I'll leave it dead! I'll murder it—and be free! (*Again he threatens her, his hands twitching back toward her neck—then he rushes out of the door as if furies were pursuing him, slamming it shut behind him.*)

460

ELEANOR. (*with a cry of despair*) Michael! (*She stops as hatred and* *rage overpower her again—leaps up and runs to the door—opens it* *and screams after him violently*) Go! Go! I'm glad! I hate you. I'll go, too! I'm free! I'll go— (*She turns and runs up the stairs. She disappears for a moment, then comes back with a hat and coat on and, hurrying down the stairs again, rushes out leaving the door open behind her.*)

CURTAIN

ACT TWO—SCENE ONE

LIBRARY. *A door is in the rear, toward right. A large couch facing front. On the wall, a framed portrait study of* ELEANOR.

At first the room is in darkness. As the curtain rises, JOHN *can be dimly distinguished sitting, bent over wearily, his shoulders bowed, his long arms resting on his knees, his hands dangling. He sits on the extreme edge in the exact middle of the big couch, and this heightens the sense of loneliness about him.*

Suddenly he stares as the sound of a motor comes from the driveway. The car is heard driving up; it stops before the front door; its door is slammed, it drives off; a ringing of the doorbell sounds from somewhere back in the house. JOHN *has gotten up, gone toward the door in the rear, exclaiming irritably as the bell continues to ring—* All right, damn it! Who the devil—? (*He is heard opening the front door —in blank amazement*) Nelly! (*Then her voice in a strained, hysterical pitch*) John, I— (*The rest is lost incoherently. Then his voice soothingly*) Come in! Come in. (*He follows her into the room. Her face is pale, distraught, desperate. She comes quickly to the couch and flings herself down in one corner. He stands nearby uncertainly, watching her. His face holds a confused mixture of alarm, tenderness, perplexity, passionate hope.*)

JOHN. You're trembling.

ELEANOR. (*with a startled movement*) No—I—I'm— (*A pause. He waits for her to speak, not knowing what to think. She gradually collects herself. Memory crowds back on her and her face twitches with pain which turns to hatred and rage. She becomes conscious of* JOHN's *eyes, forces this back, her face growing mask-like and determined. She looks up at* JOHN *and forces the words out slowly*) John—you said, if ever— You once said I might always come—

462

JOHN. (*his face lights up for a second with a joy that is incongruously savage—at once controlling this—simply*) Yes, Nelly.

ELEANOR. (*a bit brokenly now*) I hope—you meant that.

JOHN. (*simply*) Yes, I meant it.

ELEANOR. I mean—that you still mean it—?

JOHN. (*forcing an awkward smile*) Then—now—forever after, amen—any old time at all, Nelly. (*Then overcome by a rush of bewildered joy—stammering*) Why—you ought to know—!

ELEANOR. (*smiling tensely*) Would I still be welcome if I'd come—to stay?

JOHN. (*his voice quivering*) Nelly! (*He stares toward her, then stops—in a low, uncertain voice*) And Michael?

ELEANOR. (*with an exclamation of pain*) Don't! (*Quickly recovering herself—in a cold, hard voice*) That's—dead! (JOHN *lets a held-back breath of suspense escape him.* ELEANOR *stammers a bit hysterically*) Don't talk of him! I've forgotten—as if he'd never lived! Do you still love me? Do you? Then tell me! I must know someone—

JOHN. (*still uncertain, but coming nearer to her—simply*) You knew once. Since then— My God, you've guessed, haven't you?

ELEANOR. I need to hear. You've never spoken—for years—

JOHN. There was—Michael.

ELEANOR. (*wildly, putting her hands up to her ears as if to shut out the name*) Don't! (*Then, driven by a desperate determination, forces a twisted smile*) Why do you stand there? Are you afraid? I'm beginning to suspect—perhaps, you've only imagined—

JOHN. Nelly! (*He seizes one of her hands awkwardly and covers it with kisses—confusedly, with deep emotion*) I— You know— You know—

ELEANOR. (*with the same fixed smile*) You must put your arms around me—and kiss me—on the lips—

JOHN. (*takes her in his arms awkwardly and kisses her on the lips—with passionate incoherence*) Nelly! I'd given up hoping—I—I can't believe— (*She submits to his kisses with closed eyes, her face like a mask, her body trembling with revulsion. Suddenly he seems to sense something disharmonious—confusedly*) But you—you don't care for me.

ELEANOR. (*still with closed eyes—dully*) Yes. (*With a spurt of desperate energy she kisses him wildly several times, then sinks back again closing her eyes*) I'm so tired, John—so tired!

JOHN. (*immediately all concern*) You're trembling all over. I'm an idiot not to have seen— Forgive me. (*He puts his hand on her forehead*) You're feverish. You'd better go to bed, young lady, right away. Come. (*He raises her to her feet.*)

ELEANOR. (*wearily*) Yes, I'm tired. (*Bitterly*) Oh, it's good to be loved by someone who is unselfish and kind—

JOHN. Ssshh! (*Forcing a joking tone*) I'm cast for the Doctor now. Doctor's orders: don't talk, don't think, sleep. Come, I'll show you your room.

ELEANOR. (*dully*) Yes. (*As if she were not aware of what she is doing, she allows him to lead her to the door at right, rear. There she suddenly starts as if awakening—frightenedly.*) Where are we going?

JOHN. (*with gentle bullying*) You're going upstairs to bed.

ELEANOR. (*with a shudder—incoherently*) No, no! Not now—no—wait—you must wait— (*Then calming herself and trying to speak matter-of-factly*) I'd rather stay up and sit with you.

JOHN. (*worriedly, but giving in to her at once*) All right. Whatever suits you. (*They go back. She sits in a chair. He puts a cushion in back of her*) How's that?

ELEANOR. (*with a wan, grateful smile*) You're so kind, John. You've always been kind. You're so different— (*She checks herself, her face growing hard.* JOHN *watches her. There is a long pause.*)

JOHN. (*finally—in a gentle tone*) Nelly, don't you think it'd help if you told me—everything that's happened?

ELEANOR. (*with a shudder*) No! It was all horror and disgust! (*Wildly resentful*) Why do you make me remember? I've come to you. Why do you ask for reasons? (*With a harsh laugh*) Are you jealous—of him?

JOHN. (*quietly*) I've always envied Michael.

ELEANOR. If you'd seen him tonight, you wouldn't envy him. He's mean and contemptible! He makes everything as low as he is! He went away threatening, boasting he'd— (*Hysterically*) Why do you make me think of him? I want to be yours! (*She throws herself into his arms.*)

JOHN. (*straining her to him—with awkward passion*) Nelly! (*Under his kisses her face again becomes mask-like, her body rigid, her eyes closed.* JOHN *suddenly grows aware of this. He stares down at her face, his own growing bewildered and afraid. He stammers*) Nelly! What is it?

ELEANOR. (*opening her eyes—in alarm*) What—?

JOHN. (*with a sigh of relief*) You gave me a scare. You were like a corpse.

ELEANOR. (*breaks away from him*) I—I believe I do feel ill. I'll go to bed. (*She moves toward the door.*)

JOHN. (*uneasily—with a forced heartiness*) Now you're talking sense. Come on. (*He leads the way into the hall. She goes as far as the doorway—then stops. A queer struggle is apparent in her face, her whole body, as if she were fighting with all her will to overcome some invisible barrier which bars her way.* JOHN *is watching her keenly now, a sad foreboding coming into his eyes. He steps past her back into the room, saying kindly but with a faint trace of bitterness*) It's the first door upstairs on your right—if you'd rather go alone. (*He walks still further away, then turns to watch her, his face growing more and more aware and melancholy.*)

ELEANOR. (*vaguely*) No—you don't understand— (*She stands swaying, reaching out her hand to the side of the doorway for support—dully*) The first door to the right—upstairs?

JOHN. Yes.

ELEANOR. (*struggles with herself, confused and impotent, trying to*

465

will—finally turns to JOHN *like a forlorn child*) John. Can't you help me?

JOHN. (*gravely*) No—not now when I do understand. You must do it alone.

ELEANOR. (*with a desperate cry*) I can! I'm as strong as he! (*This breaks the spell which has chained her. She grows erect and strong. She walks through the doorway.*)

JOHN. (*with a triumphant exclamation of joy*) Ah! (*He strides toward the doorway—then stops as he notices that she also has stopped at the bottom of the stairs, one foot on the first stair, looking up at the top. Then she wavers and suddenly bolts back ino the room, gropingly, her face strained and frightened.* JOHN *questions her with fierce disappointment*) What is it? Why did you stop?

ELEANOR. (*forcing a twisted smile—wildly*) You're right. I must be feverish. (*Trying to control herself—self-mockingly*) Seeing spooks, that's pretty far gone, isn't it? (*Laughing hysterically*) Yes—I swear I saw him—standing at the head of the stairs waiting for me—just as he was standing when you knocked at our door, remember? (*She laughs*) Really, it was too ridiculous—so plain—

JOHN. Ssshh! (*glancing at her worriedly*) Won't you lie down here? Try and rest.

ELEANOR. (*allowing him to make her comfortable on the couch before the fire*) Yes. (*Her eyes glance up into his bewilderedly.*)

JOHN. (*after a long pause—slowly*) You don't love me, Nelly.

ELEANOR. (*pitifully protesting*) But I do, John! I do! You're kind! You're unselfish and fine!

JOHN. (*with a wry smile*) That isn't me.

ELEANOR. (*desperately defiant, leaps to her feet*) I do! (*She takes his face between her hands and bringing her own close to it stares into his eyes. He looks back into hers. She mutters fiercely between her clenched teeth*) I do! (*For a long moment they remain there, as she brings her face nearer and nearer striving with all her will to kiss him on the lips. Finally, her eyes falter, her body grows limp, she turns away and throws herself on the couch in a fit of abandoned sobbing.*)

JOHN. (*with a sad smile*) You see?

ELEANOR. (*her voice muffled—between sobs*) But I—want to! And I will—I know—some day—I promise!

JOHN. (*forcing a light tone*) Well, I'll be resigned to wait and hope then—and trust in your good intentions. (*After a pause—in a calming, serious tone*) You're calmer now? Tell me what happened between you and Michael.

ELEANOR. No! Please!

JOHN. (*smiling but earnestly*) It'll relieve your mind, Nelly—and besides, how can I help you otherwise?

ELEANOR. (*after a pause—with resigned dullness*) We've quarreled, but never like this before. This was final. (*She shudders—then suddenly bursts out wildly*) Oh, John, for God's sake don't ask me! I want to forget! We tore each other to pieces. I realized I hated him! I couldn't restrain my hate! I had to crush him as he was crushing me! (*After a pause—dully again*) And so that was the end.

JOHN. (*tensely, hoping again now—pleadingly*) You're sure, Nelly?

ELEANOR. (*fiercely*) I hate him!

JOHN. (*after a pause—earnestly*) Then stay here. I think I can help you forget. Never mind what people say. Make this your home—and maybe—in time— (*He forces a smile*) You see, I'm already starting to nurse along that crumb of hope you gave. (*She is looking down, preoccupied with her own thoughts. He looks at her embarrassedly, then goes on gently, timidly persuasive*) I don't mind waiting. I'm used to it. And I've been hoping ever since I first met you. (*Forcing a half laugh*) I'll admit when you married him the waiting and hoping seemed excess labor. I tried to fire them—thought I had—but when you came tonight—they were right onto the job again! (*He laughs—then catching himself awkwardly*) But hell! I don't want to bother you now. Forget me.

ELEANOR. (*in a bland, absent-minded tone which wounds him*) You're so kind, John. (*Then following her own line of thought, she breaks out savagely*) I told him I'd been your mistress while he was away!

JOHN. (*amazed*) Nelly!

ELEANOR. I had to tell that lie! He was degrading me! I had to revenge myself!

JOHN. But certainly he could never believe—

ELEANOR. (*with fierce triumph*) Oh, I made him believe! (*Then dully*) He went away. He said he'd kill our love as I had—worse— (*With a twisted smile*) That's what he's doing now. He's gone to one of those women he lived with before— (*Laughing harshly*) No! They wouldn't be vile enough—for his beautiful revenge on me! He has a wonderful imagination. Everyone acknowledges that! (*She laughs with wild bitterness*) My God, why do I think—? Help me, John! Help me to forget.

JOHN. (*after a pause—with a sad, bitter helplessness*) You mean— help you—to revenge yourself! But don't you realize I can't—you can't because you still love him!

ELEANOR. (*fiercely*) No! (*After a pause—brokenly*) Don't! I know! (*She sobs heartbrokenly.*)

JOHN. (*after a pause, as her sobbing grows quieter—sadly*) Go home.

ELEANOR. No! (*After a pause, brokenly*) He'll never come back now.

JOHN. (*with a bitter humor*) Oh, yes he will; take my word for it. I know—because I happen to love you, too.

ELEANOR. (*faintly*) And do you—hate me?

JOHN. (*after a pause—with melancholy self-disgust*) No. I'm too soft. (*Bitterly*) I ought to hate you! Twice now you've treated my love with the most humiliating contempt— Once when you were willing to endure it as the price of a career—again tonight, when you try to give yourself to me out of hate for him! (*In sudden furious revolt*) Christ! What am I, eh? (*Then checking his anger and forcing a wry smile*) I think your treatment has been rather hard to take, Nelly—

458

and even now I'm not cured, at that! (*He laughs harshly and turns away to conceal his real hurt.*)

ELEANOR. (*with a deep grief*) Forgive me.

JOHN. (*as if to himself—reassuringly*) Still—I'd have been the poorest slave. I couldn't have fought you like Michael. Perhaps, deep down, I'm glad— (*Then bluntly*) You'd better go home right away.

ELEANOR. (*dully*) Even if he—

JOHN. (*brusquely*) No matter what! Face the truth in yourself. Must you—or mustn't you?

ELEANOR. (*after a moment's defiant struggle with herself—forlornly*) Yes. (*After a pause, with a gesture toward the door and a weary, beaten smile*) Upstairs—if I could have gone—I might have been free. But he's trained me too well in his ideal. (*Then shrugging her shoulders, fatalistically*) It's broken me. I'm no longer anything. So what does it matter how weak I am? (*A slight pause*) I begin to know —something. (*With a sudden queer, exultant pride*) My love for him is my own, not his! That he can never possess! It's *my* own. It's *my* life! (*She turns to* JOHN *determinedly*) I must go home now.

JOHN. (*wonderingly*) Good. I'll drive you back. (*He starts for the door.*)

ELEANOR. (*suddenly grasping his arm*) Wait. (*Affectionately*) I was forgetting you—as usual. What can I do—?

JOHN. (*with a wry smile*) Study your part; help Michael; and we'll all three be enormously successful! (*He laughs mockingly.*)

ELEANOR. (*tenderly*) I'll always believe Fate should have let me love you, instead.

JOHN. (*with the same wry smile*) While I begin to suspect that in a way I'm lucky—to be heartbroken. (*With a laugh*) Curtain! You'll want to go upstairs and powder your nose. There's no angel with a flaming sword there now, is there? (*He points to the doorway.*)

ELEANOR. (*with a tired smile*) No. (*She goes to the doorway. He follows her. They both stop there for a moment instinctively and smile forlornly at each other.*)

JOHN. (*impulsively*) That time you stood here and called to me for help—if I could have given you a push, mental, moral, physical—?

ELEANOR. It wouldn't have helped. The angel was here. (*She touches her breast.*)

JOHN. (*with a sigh*) Thanks. That saves me a life-long regret.

ELEANOR. (*earnestly—gripping his right hand in hers and holding his eyes*) There must be no regrets—between old friends.

JOHN. (*gripping her hand in turn*) No, I promise, Nelly. (*Then letting her hand drop and turning away to conceal his emotion— forcing a joking tone*) After all, friendship is sounder, saner—more in the picture for my type, eh?

ELEANOR. (*absent-mindedly again now—vaguely*) I don't know. (*Then briskly*) We must hurry. I'll be right down. (*She goes out and up the stairway in the hall.*)

JOHN. (*Stares up after her for a second, then smiling grimly*) Well, business of living on as usual. (*He walks out, calling up the stairs*) I'm going to get the car, Nelly.

CURTAIN

ACT TWO—SCENE TWO

A BEDROOM. *In the rear, center, a door. A chair to left of door. In the left corner, a washstand. In the left wall, center, a small window with a torn dark shade pulled down. On the right, a bed. Ugly wall-paper, dirty, stained, criss-crossed with match-strokes.*

When the curtain rises, the room is in darkness except for a faint glow on the window shade from some street lamp. Then the door is opened and a woman's figure is silhouetted against the dim, yellow light of a hall. She turns and speaks to someone who is following her. Her voice is heavy and slow with the strong trace of a foreign intona-

*tion, although the words are clearly enough defined. A man's figure
appears behind hers. The* WOMAN *is fairly young. Her face, rouged,
powdered, penciled, is broad and stupid. Her small eyes have a glazed
look. Yet she is not ugly—rather pretty for her bovine, stolid type—
and her figure is still attractive although its movements just now are
those of a tired scrubwoman. She takes off her coat, hangs it on a
hook, and removes her hat.*

The man is MICHAEL. *He is bare-headed, his hair disheveled, his eyes
wild, his face has a feverish, mad expression. He stands in the doorway
watching each movement of the* WOMAN'S *with an unnatural preoccupied concentration.)*

WOMAN. (*having removed her hat and put it on the washstand, turns
to him impatiently*) Ain't you comin' in? (*He starts and nods stupidly, moving his lips as if answering but not making a sound*) Come
in! Shut the door. (*He does so and locks it mechanically—then looks
from her around the room with a frightened, puzzled glance as if he
were aware of his surroundings for the first time.*)

WOMAN. (*forcing a trade smile—with an attempt at lightness*) Well,
here we are, dearie. (*Then with a sigh of physical weariness as she sits
on the side of the bed*) Gawd, I'm tired! My feet hurt fierce! I been
walkin' miles. I got corns, too. (*She sighs again, this time with a sort
of restful content*) It's good 'n' warm in this dump, I'll hand it that.
(*A pause*) I'd gave up hope and was beatin' it home when you come
along. (*A pause during which she takes him in calculatingly*) How'd
you lose your hat? (*He starts, passes a trembling hand through his
hair bewilderedly but does not answer. A pause—then the* WOMAN
sighs and yawns wearily—bored) Can't you say nothin'? You was
full enough of bull when you met me. Gawd, I thought you'd get us
both pinched. You acted like you was crazy. Remember kissing me
on the corner with a whole mob pipin' us off?

CAPE. (*with a start—evidently answering some train of thought in his mind—with a wild laugh*) Remember? (*He sinks on the chair with his head in his hands. There is a pause.*)

WOMAN. (*insinuatingly*) Goin' to stay all night? (*He glances up at her stupidly but doesn't answer. The* WOMAN *insists dully*) Say, you got ear-muffs on? I ast you, d'you wanta stay all night?

CAPE. (*after a moment's groping, nods emphatically again and again, swallowing hard several times as if he were striving to get control of his voice—finally blurts out in a tone of desperation*) Yes— yes—of course!— Where else would I go?

WOMAN. Home. (*Indifferently*) That's where most of 'em goes— afterwards.

CAPE. (*with a sudden burst of wild laughter*) Ha-ha-ha. Home! Is that your private brand of revenge—to go with men with homes? I congratulate you! (*He laughs to himself with bitter irony—then suddenly deadly calm*) Yes, I have a home, come to think of it—from now on Hell is my home! I suspect we're fellow-citizens. (*He laughs.*)

WOMAN. (*superstitiously*) You oughtn't to say them things.

CAPE. (*with dull surprise*) Why?

WOMAN. Somep'n might happen. (*A pause*) Don't you believe in no God?

CAPE. I believe in the devil!

WOMAN. (*frightened*) Say! (*Then after a pause, forcing a smile*) I'm wise to what's wrong with you. You been lappin' up some bum hooch.

CAPE. (*jerkily*) No. I'm not drunk. I thought of that—but it's evasion. (*Wildly*) And I must be conscious—fully conscious, do you understand? I will this as a symbol of release—of the end of all things! (*He stops, shuddering. She looks at him stolidly. A pause. He presses his hands to his forehead*) Stop thinking, damn you! (*Then after a pause—dully*) How long—? What time is it?

WOMAN. Little after two, I guess.

CAPE. (*amazed*) Only that? (*She nods*) Only two hours—? (*A pause*) I remember streets—lights—dead faces— Then you—your face

472

alone was alive for me, alive with my deliverance! That was why I kissed you.

WOMAN. (*looking up at him queerly*) Say, you talk nutty. Been dopin' up on coke, I bet you.

CAPE. (*with an abrupt exclamation*) Ha! (*He stares at her with unnatural intensity*) You seem to take it quite casually that men must be either drunk or doped—otherwise—! Marvelous! You,—you're the last depth— (*With a strange, wild exultance, leaps to his feet*) You're my salvation! You have the power—and the right—to murder love! You can satisfy hate! Will you let me kiss you again? (*He strides over to her.*)

WOMAN. (*in a stupid state of bewilderment, feeling she has been insulted but not exactly knowing by what or how to resent it— angrily, pushing him away*) No! Get away from me! (*Then afraid she may lose his trade by this rebuff*) Aw, all right. Sure you can. (*Making a tremendous visible effort he kisses her on the lips, then shrinks back with a shudder and forces a harsh laugh. She stares at him and mutters resentfully*) On'y don't get so fresh, see? I don't like your line of talk. (*He slumps down on the chair again, sunk in a somber stupor. She watches him. She yawns. Finally she asks insinuatingly*) Ain't you gettin' sleepy?

CAPE. (*starting—with wild scorn*) Do you think I—! (*Staring at her*) Oh—I see—you mean, what did I come here for?

WOMAN. (*in same tone*) It's gettin' late.

CAPE. (*dully, with no meaning to his question—like an automaton*) A little after two?

WOMAN. Yes. (*She yawns*) You better let me go to bed and come yourself.

CAPE. (*again staring at her with strange intensity—suddenly with a queer laugh*) How long have you and I been united in the unholy bonds of—bedlock? (*He chuckles sardonically at his own play on words.*)

WOMAN. (*with a puzzled grin*) Say!

CAPE. Ten thousand years—about—isn't it? Or twenty? Don't you remember?

WOMAN. (*keeping her forced grin*) Tryin' to kid me, ain't you?

CAPE. Don't lie about your age! You were beside the cradle of love, and you'll dance dead drunk on its grave!

WOMAN. I'm only twenty-six, honest.

CAPE. (*with a wild laugh*) A fact! You're right. Thoughts keep alive. Only facts kill—deeds! (*He starts to his feet*) Then hate will let me alone. Love will be dead. I'll be as ugly as the world. My dreams will be low dreams. I'll "lay me down among the swine." Will you promise me this, you?

WOMAN. (*vaguely offended—impatiently*) Sure, I'll promise anything. (*She gets up to start undressing. She has been pulling the pins out of her hair and, as she rises, it falls over her shoulders in a peroxided flood. She turns to him, smiling with childish pride*) D'you like my hair, kid? I got a lot of it, ain't I?

CAPE. (*laughing sardonically*) "O love of mine, let down your hair and I will make my shroud of it."

WOMAN. (*coquettishly pleased*) What's that—po'try? (*Then suddenly reminded of something she regards him calculatingly—after a pause, coldly*) Say, you ain't broke, are you? Is that what's troubling you?

CAPE. (*startled—then with bitter mockery*) Ha! I see you're a practical person. (*He takes a bill from his pocket and holds it out to her—contemptuously*) Here!

WOMAN. (*stares from the bill to him, flushing beneath her rouge*) Say! I don't like the way you act. (*Proudly*) I don't take nothin' for nothin'—not from you, see!

CAPE. (*surprised and ashamed*) I'll leave it here, then. (*He puts it on top of the washstand and turns to her—embarrassedly*) I didn't mean—to offend you.

WOMAN. (*her face clearing immediately*) Aw, never mind. It's all right.

474

CAPE. (*staring at her intently—suddenly deeply moved*) Poor woman!

WOMAN. (*stung—excitedly*) Hey, none of that! Nix! Cut it out! I don't stand for that from nobody! (*She sits down on the bed angrily.*)

CAPE. (*with unnatural intensity*) Do you know what you are? You're a symbol. You're all the tortures man inflicts on woman—and you're the revenge of woman! You're love revenging itself upon itself! You're the suicide of love—of my love—of all love since the world began! (*Wildly*) Listen to me! Two hours ago— (*Then he beats his head with both clenched hands—distractedly*) Leave me alone! Leave me alone, damn you! (*He flings himself on the chair in a violent outburst of dry sobbing.*)

WOMAN. (*bewilderedly*) Say! Say! (*Then touched, she comes to him and puts her arms around his shoulders, on the verge of tears herself*) Aw, come on, kid. Quit it. It's all right. Everything's all right, see. (*As his sobbing grows quieter—helpfully*) Say, maybe you ain't ate nothin', huh? Maybe soup'd fix you. S'posin' I go round the corner, huh? Sure, all I got to do is put up my hair—

CAPE. (*controlling hysterical laughter—huskily*) No—thanks. (*Then his bitter memories rush back agonizingly. He stammers wildly*) She confessed! She was proud of her hate! She was proud of my torture. She screamed: "I'll go too." Go where? Did she go? Yes, she must—! Oh, my God! Stop! Stop! (*He springs up, his face distorted, and clutches the* WOMAN *fiercely in his arms*) Save me, you! Help me to kill! Help me to gain peace! (*He kisses her again and again frenziedly. She submits stolidly. Finally with a groan he pushes her away, shuddering with loathing, and sinks back on the chair*) No! I can't—I can't!

WOMAN. (*wiping her lips with the back of her hand—a vague comprehension coming into her face—scornfully*) Huh! I got a hunch now what's eatin' you. (*Then with a queer sort of savage triumph*) Well, I'm glad one of youse guys got paid back like you oughter!

CAPE. (*with dull impotent rage*) I can't! I can't. I'm the weaker. Our love must live on in me. There's no death for it. There's no freedom—while I live. (*Struck by a sudden thought*) Then, why—? (*A pause*) An end of loathing—no wounds, no memories—sleep!

WOMAN. (*with a shudder*) Say, you're beginning to give me the creeps.

CAPE. (*startled—with a forced laugh*) Am I? (*He shakes his head as if to drive some thought from his mind and forces a trembling, mocking smile*) That's over. The great temptation, isn't it? I suppose you've known it. But also the great evasion. Too simple for the complicated,—too weak for the strong, too strong for the weak. One must go on, eh?—even wounded, on one's knees—if only out of curiosity to see what will happen—to oneself. (*He laughs harshly and turns with a quick movement toward the door*) Well, good-by, and forgive me. It isn't you, you know. You're the perfect death—but I'm too strong, or weak—and I can't, you understand—can't! So, good-by. (*He goes to the door.*)

WOMAN. (*frightenedly*) Say! What're you goin' to do?

CAPE. Go on in the dark.

WOMAN. You better beat it home, that's what.

CAPE. (*violently*) No!

WOMAN. (*wearily*) Aw, forget it. She's your wife, ain't she?

CAPE. How do you know? (*He comes back to her, curiously attracted.*)

WOMAN. (*cynically*) Aw, I'm wise. Stick to her, see? You'll get over it. You can get used to anything, take it from me!

CAPE. (*in anguish*) Don't! But it's true—it's the insult we all swallow as the price of life. (*Rebelliously*) But I—!

WOMAN. (*with a sort of forlorn chuckle*) Oh, you'll go back aw right! Don't kid yourself. You'll go back no matter what, and you'll loin to like it. Don't I know? You love her, don't you? Well, then! There's no use buckin' that game. Go home. Kiss and make up.

476

Ferget it! It's easy to ferget—when you got to! (*She finishes up with a cynical, weary scorn.*)

CAPE. (*very pale—stammering*) You—you make life despicable.

WOMAN. (*angrily*) Say! (*Then with groping, growing resentment*) I don't like your talk! You've pulled a lot of bum cracks about— about—never mind, I got you, anyhow! You ain't got no right— What'd you wanter pick me up for, anyway? Wanter just get me up here to say rotten things? Wanter use me to pay her back? Say! Where do I come in? Guys go with me 'cause they like my looks, see?—what I am, understand?—but you, you don't want nothin'. You ain't drunk, neither! You just don't like me. And you was beatin' it leavin' your money there—without nothin'. I was goin' to let you then. I ain't now. (*She suddenly gives him a furious push which sends him reeling back against the wall*) G'wan! Take your lousy coin and beat it! I wouldn't take nothin', nor have nothin' to do with you if you was to get down on your knees!

CAPE. (*stares at her—an expression comes as if he were seeing her for the first time—with great pity*) So—it still survives in you. They haven't killed it—that lonely life of one's own which suffers in solitude. (*Shame-facedly*) I should have known. Can you forgive me?

WOMAN. (*defensively*) No!

CAPE. Through separate ways love has brought us both to this room. As one lonely human being to another, won't you—?

WOMAN. (*struggling with herself—harshly*) No!

CAPE. (*gently*) Not even if I ask it on my knees? (*He kneels before her, looking up into her face.*)

WOMAN. (*bewildered, with hysterical fierceness*) No! Git up, you—! Don't do that, I tell you! Git up or I'll brain yuh! (*She raises her fist threateningly over his head.*)

CAPE. (*gently*) Not until you—

WOMAN. (*exhaustedly*) Aw right—aw right—I forgive—

CAPE. (*gets up and takes her face between his hands and stares into her eyes—then he kisses her on the forehead*) Sister.

WOMAN. (*with a half sob*) Nix! Lay off of me, can't you?

CAPE. But I learned that from you.

WOMAN. (*stammering*) What?—loined what? (*She goes away from him and sinks on the bed exhaustedly*) Say, you better beat it.

CAPE. I'm going. (*He points to the bill on the washstand*) You need this money. You'll accept it from me now, won't you?

WOMAN. (*dully*) Sure. Leave it there.

CAPE. (*in the same gentle tone*) You'll have to give it to him in the morning?

WOMAN. (*dully*) Sure.

CAPE. All of it?

WOMAN. Sure.

CAPE. Or he'd beat you?

WOMAN. Sure. (*Then suddenly grinning*) Maybe he'll beat me up, anyway—just for the fun of it.

CAPE. But you love him, don't you?

WOMAN. Sure. I'm lonesome.

CAPE. Yes. (*After a slight pause*) Why did you smile when you said he'd beat you, anyway?

WOMAN. I was thinkin' of the whole game. It's funny, ain't it?

CAPE. (*slowly*) You mean—life?

WOMAN. Sure. You got to laugh, ain't you? You got to loin to like it!

CAPE. (*this makes an intense impression on him. He nods his head several times*) Yes! That's it! That's exactly it! That goes deeper than wisdom. To learn to love life—to accept it and be exalted—that's the one faith left to us! (*Then with a tremulous smile*) Good-by. I've joined your church. I'm going home.

WOMAN. (*with a grin that is queerly affectionate*) Sure. That's the stuff. Close your eyes and your feet'll take you there.

CAPE. (*impressed again*) Yes! Yes! Of course they would! They've been walking there for thousands of years—blindly. However, now, I'll keep my eyes open—(*he smiles back at her affectionately*)—and learn to like it!

478

WOMAN. (*grinning*) Sure. Good luck.

CAPE. Good-by. (*He goes out, closing the door after him. She stares at the door listening to his footsteps as they die out down the stairs.*)

WOMAN. (*confusedly*) Say—?

CURTAIN

ACT THREE

SCENE—*Same as Act One.* ELEANOR *is standing by the table, leaning her back against it, facing the door, her whole attitude strained, expectant but frightened, tremblingly uncertain whether to run and hide from, or run forward and greet* CAPE, *who is standing in the doorway. For a long, tense moment they remain fixed, staring into each other's eyes with an apprehensive questioning. Then, as if unconsciously, falteringly, with trembling smiles, they come toward each other. Their lips move as if they were trying to speak. When they come close, they instinctively reach out their hands in a strange conflicting gesture of a protective warding off and at the same time a seeking possession. Their hands clasp and they again stop, searching each other's eyes. Finally their lips force out words.*

ELEANOR. (*penitently*) Michael!

CAPE. (*humbly*) Nelly! (*They smile with a queer understanding, their arms move about each other, their lips meet. They seem in a forgetful, happy trance at finding each other again. They touch each other testingly as if each cannot believe the other is really there. They act for the moment like two persons of different races, deeply in love but separated by a barrier of language.*)

ELEANOR. (*rambling tenderly*) Michael—I— I was afraid—

CAPE. (*stammeringly*) Nelly—it's no good!—I thought— (*They stare at each other—a pause.*)

ELEANOR. (*beginning to be aware—a bit bewilderedly, breaking away from him with a little shiver—stupidly*) I feel—there's a draught, isn't there?

CAPE. (*becoming aware in his turn—heavily*) I'll shut the door. (*He goes and does so. She walks to her chair and sits down. He comes and sits beside her. They are now side by side as in Act One. A pause.*

480

They stare ahead, each frowningly abstracted. Then each, at the same moment, steals a questioning side glance at the other. Their eyes meet, they look away, then back, they stare at each other with a peculiar dull amazement, recognition yet non-recognition. They seem about to speak, then turn away again. Their faces grow sad, their eyes begin to suffer, their bodies become nervous and purposeless. Finally CAPE *exclaims with a dull resentment directed not at her but at life*) What is—it? (*He makes a gesture of repulsing something before him.*)

ELEANOR. (*in his tone*) I don't know.

CAPE. (*harshly*) A moment ago—there— (*He indicates where they had stood in an embrace*) We knew everything. We understood!

ELEANOR. (*eagerly*) Oh, yes!

CAPE. (*bitterly*) Now—we must begin to think—to continue going on, getting lost—

ELEANOR. (*sadly*) It was happy to forget. Let's not think—yet.

CAPE. (*grimly*) We've begun. (*Then with a harsh laugh*) Thinking explains. It eliminates the unexplainable—by which we live.

ELEANOR. (*warningly*) By which we love. Sssh! (*A pause.*)

CAPE. (*wonderingly—not looking at her*) You have learned that, too?

ELEANOR. (*with a certain exultance*) Oh, yes, Michael—yes! (*She clasps his hand. A pause. Then she murmurs*) Now—we know peace. (*Their hands drop apart. She sighs.*)

CAPE. (*slowly*) Peace isn't our meaning.

ELEANOR. (*suddenly turns and addresses him directly in a sad, sympathetic tone*) You've something you want to ask me, Michael?

CAPE. (*turns to her with an immediate affirmative on his lips, checks it as he meets her eyes, turns away—a pause—then he turns back humbly*) No.

ELEANOR. (*her head has been averted since he turned away—without looking at him*) Yes.

CAPE. (*decisively*) No, Nelly. (*She still keeps her head averted.*

481

After a pause he asks simply) Why? Is there something you want to ask me?

ELEANOR. No. (*After a pause—with a trace of bitter humor*) I can't be less magnanimous than you, can I?

CAPE. Then there is something—?

ELEANOR. Haven't you something you want to tell?

CAPE. (*looks at her. Their eyes meet again*) Yes—the truth—if I can. And you?

ELEANOR. Yes, I wish to tell you the truth. (*They look into each other's eyes. Suddenly she laughs with a sad self-mockery*) Well, we've both been noble. I haven't asked you; you haven't asked me; and yet— (*She makes a helpless gesture with her hands. A pause. Then abruptly and mechanically*) I'll begin at the beginning. I left here right after you did.

CAPE. (*with an involuntary start*) Oh! (*He checks himself.*)

ELEANOR. (*her eyes reading his—after a pause—a bit dryly*) You thought I'd stayed here all the time? (*Mockingly*) Waiting for you?

CAPE. (*wounded*) Don't! (*After a pause—painfully*) When I found you—perhaps I hoped—

ELEANOR. (*dully*) I had only been back a few minutes. (*After a pause*) Was that why you seemed so happy—there—? (*She points to the spot where they had stood embraced.*)

CAPE. (*indignantly*) No, no! Don't think that! I'm not like that— not any more! (*Without looking at her he reaches out and clasps her hand.*)

ELEANOR. (*looks at him—after a pause, understandingly*) I'm sorry—

CAPE. (*self-defensively*) Of course, I knew you must have gone, you'd have been a fool to stay. (*Excitedly*) And it doesn't matter—not a damn! I've gotten beyond that.

ELEANOR. (*misunderstanding—coldly*) I'm glad. (*A pause. She asks coldly*) Shall I begin again?

CAPE. (*struggling with himself—disjointedly*) No—not unless—I

482

don't need— I've changed. That doesn't matter. I— (*With a sudden twisted grin*) I'm learning to like it, you see.

ELEANOR. (*looks at him, strangely impressed—a pause—slowly*) I think I know what you mean. We're both learning.

CAPE. (*wonderingly*) You—? (*She has turned away from him. He turns to stare at her.*)

ELEANOR. (*after a pause, taking up her story matter-of-factly*) I went to John.

CAPE. (*trying with agony to take this stoically—mumbling stupidly*) Yes—of course—I supposed—

ELEANOR. (*in the same mechanical tone*) He drove me back here in his car. He predicted you'd be back any moment, so he went right home again.

CAPE. (*a wild, ironical laugh escapes his control*) Shrewd—Ha!

ELEANOR. (*after a pause—rebukingly*) John is a good man.

CAPE. (*startled, turns and stares at her averted face—then miserably humble, stammers*) Yes, yes—I know—I acknowledge—good— (*He breaks down, cursing pitiably at himself*) God damn you!

ELEANOR. Oh!

CAPE. Not you! Me! (*Then he turns to her—with fierce defiance*) I love John!

ELEANOR. (*moved, without looking at him, reaches and clasps his hand*) That—is fine, Michael. (*A pause.*)

CAPE. (*begins to frown somberly—lets go of her hand*) It's hard— after what you confessed—

ELEANOR. (*frightenedly*) Ssshh! (*Then calmly*) That was a lie. I lied to make you suffer more than you were making me suffer. (*A pause—then she turns to him*) Can you believe this?

CAPE. (*humbly*) I want to believe—

ELEANOR. (*immediately turning away—significantly*) Oh!

CAPE. (*fiercely as if to himself*) I will believe! But what difference does it make—believing or not believing? I've changed, I tell you! I accept!

ELEANOR. I can't be a lie you live with!

CAPE. (*turning to her resentfully*) Well, then— (*As if she were goading him to something against his will—threateningly*) Shall I tell you what happened to me?

ELEANOR. (*facing him defiantly*) Yes. (*He turns away. Immediately her brave attitude crumbles. She seems about to implore him not to speak.*)

CAPE. (*after a pause—hesitatingly*) You said that years ago you had offered yourself—to him— (*He turns suddenly—hopefully*) Was that a lie, too?

ELEANOR. No.

CAPE. (*turns away with a start of pain*) Ah. (*A pause. Suddenly his face grows convulsed. He turns back to her, overcome by a craving for revenge—viciously*) Then I may as well tell you I— (*He checks himself and turns away.*)

ELEANOR. (*defensively—with feigned indifference*) I don't doubt— you kept your threat.

CAPE. (*glares at her wildly*) Oho, you don't doubt that, do you? You saw I'd changed, eh?

ELEANOR. I saw—something.

CAPE. (*with bitter irony*) God! (*A pause.*)

ELEANOR. (*turning on him doggedly as if she were impersonally impelled to make the statement*) I want to tell you that tonight—John and I—nothing you may ever suspect— (*She falters, turns away with a bitter smile*) I only tell you this for my own satisfaction. I don't expect you to believe it.

CAPE. (*with a wry grin*) No. How could you? (*Then turning to her—determinedly—after a pause*) But it doesn't matter.

ELEANOR. I wanted revenge as much as you. I wanted to destroy— and be free of you forever! (*After a pause—simply*) I couldn't.

CAPE. (*turns and stares at her—a pause—then he asks wonderingly, eagerly*) Why couldn't you? Tell me that.

ELEANOR. (*simply*) Something stronger.

CAPE. (*with a passionate triumph*) Love! (*With intense pleading*) Nelly! Will you believe that I, too—? (*He tries to force her eyes to return to his.*)

ELEANOR. (*after a pause—looking before her—sadly*) You should have been generous sooner.

CAPE. It's the truth, Nelly! (*Desperately*) I swear to you—!

ELEANOR. (*after a pause—wearily*) We've sworn to so much.

CAPE. Everything is changed, I tell you! Something extraordinary happened to me—a revelation!

ELEANOR. (*with bitter cynicism*) A woman?

CAPE. (*wounded, turns away from her*) Don't. (*Then after a pause—with deep feeling*) Yes—she was a woman. And I had thought of her only as revenge—the lowest of the low!

ELEANOR. (*with a shudder*) Ah!

CAPE. Don't judge, Nelly. She was—good!

ELEANOR. Not her! You!

CAPE. (*desperately*) I tell you I—! (*He checks himself helplessly. She gives no sign. Then he asks sadly*) If you can think that, how could you come back?

ELEANOR. (*stammering hysterically*) How? How! (*Bursting into tears*) Because I love you!

CAPE. (*starting up from his chair and trying to take her in his arms—exultantly*) Nelly!

ELEANOR. (*pushing him away—violently*) No! I didn't come back to you! It conquered me, not you! Something in me—mine—not you! (*She stares him in the eyes defiantly, triumphantly.*)

CAPE. (*gently*) It doesn't matter. (*After a pause*) Did I come back to you?

ELEANOR. (*taken aback, turning away*) No, I suppose— (CAPE *stares at her uncertainly, then sits down in his chair again.*)

CAPE. (*after a pause, looking before him—assertively, as if taking a pledge*) But I have faith!

ELEANOR. (*wearily*) Now—for a moment.

485

CAPE. No!

ELEANOR. Yes. We'll believe—and disbelieve. We are—that.

CAPE. (*protesting*) Nelly! (*For a time they both sit staring bleakly before them. Suddenly he turns to her—desperately*) If there's nothing left but—resignation!—what use is there? How can we endure having our dream perish in this?

ELEANOR. Have we any choice?

CAPE. (*intensely—he seems to collect all his forces and turns on her with a fierce challenge*) We can choose—an end!

ELEANOR. (*shudders instinctively as she reads his meaning*) Michael! (*A pause—then looking into his eyes—as a calm counter-challenge*) Yes—if *you* wish.

CAPE. (*with passionate self-scorn*) We! We have become ignoble.

ELEANOR. As *you* wish. (*She again accents the you.*)

CAPE. I?

ELEANOR. I accept. (*A pause—gently*) You must not suffer too much. (*She reaches out her hand and clasps his comfortingly*) It's I who have changed most, Michael. (*Then she speaks sadly but firmly as if she had come to a decision*) There's only one way we can give life to each other.

CAPE. (*sharply*) How?

ELEANOR. By releasing each other.

CAPE. (*with a harsh laugh*) Are you forgetting we tried that once tonight?

ELEANOR. With hate. This would be because we loved.

CAPE. (*violently*) Don't be a fool! (*Controlling himself—forcing a smile*) Forgive me. (*Excitedly*) But, my God, what solution—?

ELEANOR. It will give you peace for your work—freedom—

CAPE. Nonsense!

ELEANOR. I'll still love you. I'll work for you! We'll no longer stand between one another. Then I can really give you my soul—

CAPE. (*controlling himself with difficulty*) You're talking rot!

ELEANOR. (*hurt*) Michael!

486

CAPE. (*suddenly glaring at her suspiciously*) Why did you come back? Why do you want to go? What are you hiding behind all this?

ELEANOR. (*wounded*) Your faith? You see?

CAPE. (*brokenly*) I—I didn't mean— (*Then after a struggle—with desperate bitterness*) Well—I accept! Go—if you want to!

ELEANOR. (*hurt*) Michael! It isn't— (*Then determinedly*) But even if you misunderstand, I must be strong for you!

CAPE. (*almost tauntingly*) Then go now—if you're strong enough. (*Harshly*) Let me see you act nobility! (*Then suddenly remorseful, catching her hand and covering it with kisses*) No! Go now before— Be strong! Be free! I—I can't!

ELEANOR. (*brokenly*) We can try— (*She bends down swiftly and kisses his head, turns away quickly*) Good-by.

CAPE. (*in a strangled voice*) Good-by. (*He sits in anguish, in a tortured restraint. She grabs her cloak from the chair, goes quickly to the door, puts her hand on the knob—then stops as tense as he. Suddenly he can stand it no longer, he leaps to his feet and jumps toward the door with a pleading cry*) Nelly! (*He stands fixed as he sees her before the door as if he had expected to find her gone. She does not turn but remains staring at the door in front of her. Finally she raises her hand and knocks on the door softly—then stops to listen.*)

ELEANOR. (*in a queer far-away voice*) No. Never again "come out." (*She opens the door and turns to* CAPE *with a strange smile*) It opens inward, Michael. (*She closes it again, smiles to herself and walks back to the foot of the stairway. Then she turns to face* CAPE. *She looks full of some happy certitude. She smiles at him and speaks with a tender weariness*) It must be nearly dawn. I'll say good-night instead of good-by. (*They stare into each other's eyes. It is as if now by a sudden flash from within they recognized themselves, shorn of all the ideas, attitudes, cheating gestures which constitute the vanity of personality. Everything, for this second, becomes simple for them—*

DIFF'RENT

A Play in Two Acts

CHARACTERS

Captain Caleb Williams
Emma Crosby
Captain John Crosby, *her father*
Mrs. Crosby, *her mother*
Jack Crosby, *her brother*
Harriet Williams, *Caleb's sister* (*later* Mrs. Rogers)
Alfred Rogers
Benny Rogers, *their son*

SCENES

ACT ONE

Parlor of the Crosby home on a side street of a seaport village in New England—mid-afternoon of a day in late spring in the year 1890.

ACT TWO

The same. Late afternoon of a day in the early spring of the year 1920.

DIFF'RENT

ACT ONE

Scene—*Parlor of the* CROSBY *home. The room is small and low-ceilinged. Everything has an aspect of scrupulous neatness. On the left, forward, a stiff plush-covered chair. Farther back, in order, a window looking out on a vegetable garden, a black horsehair sofa, and another window. In the far left corner, an old mahogany chest of drawers. To the right of it, in rear, a window looking out on the front yard. To the right of this window is the front door, reached by a dirt path through the small lawn which separates the house from the street. To the right of door, another window. In the far right corner, a diminutive, old-fashioned piano with a stool in front of it. Near the piano on the right, a door leading to the next room. On this side of the room are also a small bookcase half filled with old volumes, a big open fireplace, and another plush-covered chair. Over the fireplace a mantel with a marble clock and a Rogers group. The walls are papered a brown color. The floor is covered with a dark carpet. In the center of the room there is a clumsy, marble-topped table. On the table, a large china lamp, a bulky Bible with a brass clasp, and several books that look suspiciously like cheap novels. Near the table, three plush-covered chairs, two of which are rockers. Several enlarged photos of strained, stern-looking people in uncomfortable poses are hung on the walls.*

It is mid-afternoon of a fine day in late spring of the year 1890. Bright sunlight streams through the windows on the left. Through the window and the screen door in the rear the fresh green of the lawn and of the elm trees that line the street can be seen. Stiff, white curtains are at all the windows.

493

As the curtain rises, EMMA CROSBY *and* CALEB WILLIAMS *are discovered.* EMMA *is a slender girl of twenty, rather under the medium height. Her face, in spite of its plain features, gives an impression of prettiness, due to her large, soft blue eyes which have an incongruous quality of absent-minded romantic dreaminess about them. Her mouth and chin are heavy, full of a self-willed stubbornness. Although her body is slight and thin, there is a quick, nervous vitality about all her movements that reveals an underlying constitution of reserve power and health. She has light brown hair, thick and heavy. She is dressed soberly and neatly in her black Sunday best, style of the period.*

CALEB WILLIAMS *is tall and powerfully built, about thirty. Black hair, keen, dark eyes, face rugged and bronzed, mouth obstinate but good-natured. He, also, is got up in black Sunday best and is uncomfortably self-conscious and stiff therein.*

They are sitting on the horsehair sofa, side by side. His arm is about her waist. She holds one of his big hands in both of hers, her head leaning back against his shoulder, her eyes half closed in a dreamy contentedness. He stares before him rigidly, his whole attitude wooden and fixed as if he were posing for a photograph; yet his eyes are expressively tender and protecting when he glances down at her diffidently out of the corners without moving his head.

EMMA. (*sighing happily*) Gosh, I wish we could sit this way forever! (*Then after a pause, as he makes no comment except a concurring squeeze*) Don't you, Caleb?

CALEB. (*with another squeeze—emphatically*) Hell, yes! I'd like it, Emmer.

EMMA. (*softly*) I do wish you wouldn't swear so awful much, Caleb.

CALEB. S'cuse me, Emmer, it jumped out o' my mouth afore I thought. (*Then with a grin*) You'd ought to be used to that part o' men's wickedness—with your Pa and Jack cussin' about the house all the time.

494

EMMA. (*with a smile*) Oh, I haven't no strict religious notions about it. I'm hardened in sin so far's they're concerned. Goodness me, how would Ma and me ever have lived in the same house with them two if we wasn't used to it? I don't even notice their cussing no more. And I don't mind hearing it from the other men, either. Being sea-faring men, away from their women folks most of the time, I know it just gets to be part of their natures and they ain't responsible. (*Decisively*) But you're diff'rent. You just got to be diff'rent from the rest.

CALEB. (*amused by her seriousness*) Diff'rent? Ain't I a sea-farin' man, too?

EMMA. You're diff'rent just the same. That's what made me fall in love with you 'stead of any of them. And you've got to stay diff'rent. Promise me, Caleb, that you'll always stay diff'rent from them—even after we're married years and years.

CALEB. (*embarrassed*) Why—I promise to do my best by you, Emmer. You know that, don't ye? On'y don't git the notion in your head I'm any better'n the rest. They're all good men—most of 'em, anyway. Don't tell me, for instance, you think I'm better'n your Pa or Jack—'cause I ain't. And I don't know as I'd want to be, neither.

EMMA. (*excitedly*) But you got to want to be—when I ask it.

CALEB. (*surprised*) Better'n your Pa?

EMMA. (*struggling to convey her meaning*) Why, Pa's all right. He's a fine man—and Jack's all right, too. I wouldn't hear a bad word about them for anything. And the others are all right in their way, too, I s'pose. Only—don't you see what I mean?—I look on you as diff'rent from all of them. I mean there's things that's all right for them to do that wouldn't be for you—in my mind, anyway.

CALEB. (*puzzled and a bit uneasy*) Sailors ain't plaster saints, Emmer,—not a darn one of 'em ain't!

EMMA. (*hurt and disappointed*) Then you won't promise me to stay diff'rent for my sake?

495

CALEB. (*with rough tenderness*) Oh, hell, Emmer, I'll do any cussed thing in the world you want me to, and you know it!

EMMA. (*lovingly*) Thank you, Caleb. It means a lot to me—more'n you think. And don't you think I'm diff'rent, too—not just the same as all the other girls hereabouts?

CALEB. 'Course you be! Ain't I always said that? You're wo'th the whole pack of 'em put together.

EMMA. Oh, I don't mean I'm any better. I mean I just look at things diff'rent from what they do—getting married, for example, and other things, too. And so I've got it fixed in my head that you and me ought to make a married couple—diff'rent from the rest—not that they ain't all right in their way.

CALEB. (*puzzled—uncertainly*) Waal—it's bound to be from your end of it, you bein' like you are. But I ain't so sure o' mine.

EMMA. Well, I am!

CALEB. (*with a grin*) You got me scared, Emmer. I'm scared you'll want me to live up to one of them high-fangled heroes you been readin' about in them books. (*He indicates the novels on the table.*)

EMMA. No, I don't. I want you to be just like yourself, that's all.

CALEB. That's easy. It ain't hard bein' a plain, ordinary cuss.

EMMA. You are not!

CALEB. (*with a laugh*) Remember, I'm warnin' you, Emmer; and after we're married and you find me out, you can't say I got you under no false pretenses.

EMMA. (*laughing*) I won't. I won't ever need to. (*Then after a pause*) Just think, it's only two days more before you and me'll be man and wife.

CALEB. (*squeezing her*) Waal, it's about time, ain't it?—after waitin' three years for me to git enough money saved—and us not seein' hide or hair of each other the last two of 'em. (*With a laugh*) Shows ye what trust I put in you, Emmer, when I kin go off on a two-year whalin' vige and leave you all 'lone for all the young fellers in town to make eyes at.

496

EMMA. But lots and lots of the others does the same thing without thinking nothing about it.

CALEB. (*with a laugh*) Yes, but I'm diff'rent, like you says.

EMMA. (*laughing*) Oh, you're poking fun now.

CALEB. (*with a wink*) And you know as well's me that some o' the others finds out some funny things that's been done when they was away.

EMMA. (*laughing at first*) Yes, but you know I'm diff'rent, too. (*Then frowning*) But don't let's talk about that sort o' ructions. I hate to think of such things—even joking. I ain't like that sort.

CALEB. Thunder, I know you ain't, Emmer. I was on'y jokin'.

EMMA. And I never doubted you them two years; and I won't when you sail away again, neither.

CALEB. (*with a twinkle in his eye*) No, even a woman'd find it hard to git jealous of a whale!

EMMA. (*laughing*) I wasn't thinking of whales, silly! But there's plenty of diversion going on in the ports you touched, if you'd a mind for it.

CALEB. Waal, I didn't have no mind for it, that's sartin. My fust vige as skipper, you don't s'pose I had time for no monkey-shinin', do ye? Why, I was that anxious to bring back your Pa's ship with a fine vige that'd make him piles o' money, I didn't even think of nothin' else.

EMMA. 'Cepting me, I hope?

CALEB. O' course! What was my big aim in doin' it if it wasn't so's wed git married when I come to home? And then, s'far as ports go, we didn't tech at one the last year—'ceptin' when that durn tempest blowed us south and we put in at one o' the Islands for water.

EMMA. What island? You never told me nothing about that.

CALEB. (*growing suddenly very embarrassed as if some memory occurred to him*) Ain't nothin' to tell, that's why. Just an island near the Line, that's all. O'ny naked heathen livin' there—brown colored savages that ain't even Christians. (*He gets to his feet abruptly and pulls out his watch*) Gittin' late, must be. I got to go down to the store and git some things for Harriet afore I forgets 'em.

EMMA. (*rising also and putting her hands on his shoulders*) But you did think of me and miss me all the time you was gone, didn't you?—same as I did you.

CALEB. 'Course I did. Every minute.

EMMA. (*nestling closer to him—softly*) I'm glad of that, Caleb. Well, good-by for a little while.

CALEB. I'll step in again for a spell afore supper—that is, if you want me to.

EMMA. Yes, of course I do, Caleb. Good-by. (*She lifts her face to his.*)

CALEB. Good-by, Emmer. (*He kisses her and holds her in his arms for a moment.* JACK *comes up the walk to the screen door. They do not notice his approach.*)

JACK. (*peering in and seeing them—in a joking bellow*) Belay, there! (*They separate with startled exclamations.* JACK *comes in grinning. He is a hulking, stocky-built young fellow of 25. His heavy face is sunburned, handsome in a coarse, good-natured animal fashion. His small blue eyes twinkle with the unconsciously malicious humor of the born practical joker. He wears high seaboots turned down from the knee, dirty cotton shirt and pants, and a yellow sou'wester pushed jauntily on the back of his head, revealing his disheveled, curly blond hair. He carries a string of cod heads.*)

JACK. (*laughing at the embarrassed expression on their faces*) Caught ye that time, by gum! Go ahead! Kiss her again, Caleb. Don't mind me.

EMMA. (*with flurried annoyance*) You got a head on you just like one of them cod heads you're carrying—that stupid! I should think you'd be ashamed at your age—shouting to scare folks as if you was a little boy.

JACK. (*putting his arm about her waist*) There, kitty, don't git to spittin'. (*Stroking her hair*) Puss, puss, puss! Nice kitty! (*He laughs.*)

EMMA. (*forced to smile—pushing him away*) Get away! You'll never get sense. Land sakes, what a brother to have!

JACK. Oh, I dunno. I ain't so bad, as brothers go—eh, Caleb?

CALEB. (*smiling*) I reckon you'll do, Jack.

JACK. See there! Listen to Caleb. You got to take his word—love, honor, and *obey,* ye know, Emmer.

EMMA. (*laughing*) Leave it to men folks to stick up for each other, right or wrong.

JACK. (*cockily*) Waal, I'm willin' to leave it to the girls, too. Ask any of 'em you knows if I ain't a jim-dandy to have for a brother. (*He winks at* CALEB *who grins back at him.*)

EMMA. (*with a sniff*) I reckon you don't play much brother with them—the kind you knows. You may fool 'em into believing you're some pumpkins but they'd change their minds if they had to live in the same house with you playing silly jokes all the time.

JACK. (*provokingly*) A good lot on 'em 'd be on'y too damn glad to git me in the same house—if I was fool enough to git married.

EMMA. "Pride goeth before a fall." But shucks, what's the good paying any attention to you. (*She smiles at him affectionately.*)

JACK. (*exaggeratedly*) You see, Caleb? See how she misuses me—her lovin' brother. Now you know what you'll be up against for the rest o' your natural days.

CALEB. Don't see no way but what I got to bear it, Jack.

EMMA. Caleb needn't fear. He's diff'rent.

JACK. (*with a sudden guffaw*) Oh, hell, yes! I was forgittin'. Caleb's a Sunday go-to-meetin' Saint, ain't he? Yes, he is!

EMMA. (*with real resentment*) He's better'n what you are, if that's what you mean.

JACK. (*with a still louder laugh*) Ho-ho! Caleb's one o' them goody-goody heroes out o' them story books you're always readin', ain't he?

CALEB. (*soberly—a bit disturbed*) I was tellin' Emmer not to take me that high.

JACK. No use, Caleb. She won't hear of it. She's got her head sot

499

t'other way. You ought to heard her argyin' when you was gone about what a parson's pet you was. Butter won't melt in your mouth, no siree! Waal, love is blind—and deaf, too, as the feller says—and I can't argy no more 'cause I got to give Ma these heads. (*He goes to the door on right—then glances back at his sister maliciously and says meaningly*) You ought to have a talk with Jim Benson, Emmer. Oughtn't she, Caleb? (*He winks ponderously and goes off laughing uproariously.*)

CALEB. (*his face worried and angry*) Jack's a durn fool at times, Emmer—even if he is your brother. He needs a good lickin'.

EMMA. (*staring at him—uneasily*) What'd he mean about Jim Benson, Caleb?

CALEB. (*frowning*) I don't know—ezactly. Makin' up foolishness for a joke, I reckon.

EMMA. You don't know—*exactly?* Then there is—something?

CALEB. (*quickly*) Not as I know on. On'y Jim Benson's one o' them slick jokers, same's Jack; can't keep their mouths shet or mind their own business.

EMMA. Jim Benson was mate with you this last trip, wasn't he?

CALEB. Yes.

EMMA. Didn't him and you get along?

CALEB. (*a trifle impatiently*) 'Course we did. Jim's all right. We got along fust rate. He just can't keep his tongue from waggin', that's all's the matter with him.

EMMA. (*uneasily*) What's it got to wag about? You ain't done nothing wrong, have you?

CALEB. Wrong? No, nothin' a man'd rightly call wrong.

EMMA. Nothing you'd be ashamed to tell me?

CALEB. (*awkwardly*) Why—no, Emmer.

EMMA. (*pleadingly*) You'd swear that, Caleb?

CALEB. (*hesitating for a second—then firmly*) Yes, I'd swear. I'd own up to everything fair and square I'd ever done, if it comes to that

500

p'int. I ain't ashamed o' anything I ever done, Emmer. On'y—women folks ain't got to know everything, have they?

EMMA. (*turning away from him—frightenedly*) Oh, Caleb!

CALEB. (*preoccupied with his own thoughts—going to the door in rear*) I'll see you later, Emmer. I got to go up street now more'n ever. I want to give that Jim Benson a talkin' to he won't forget in a hurry—that is, if he's been tellin' tales. Good-by, Emmer.

EMMA. (*faintly*) Good-by, Caleb. (*He goes out. She sits in one of the rockers by the table, her face greatly troubled, her manner nervous and uneasy. Finally she makes a decision, goes quickly to the door on the right and calls*) Jack! Jack!

JACK. (*from the kitchen*) What you want?

EMMA. Come here a minute, will you?

JACK. Jest a second. (*She comes back by the table, fighting to conceal her agitation. After a moment, JACK comes in from the right. He has evidently been washing up, for his face is red and shiny, his hair wet and slicked in a part. He looks around for CALEB*) Where's Caleb?

EMMA. He had to go up street. (*Then coming to the point abruptly—with feigned indifference*) What's that joke about Jim Benson, Jack? It seemed to get Caleb all riled up.

JACK. (*with a chuckle*) You got to ask Caleb about that, Emmer.

EMMA. I did. He didn't seem to want to own up it was anything.

JACK. (*with a laugh*) 'Course he wouldn't. He don't 'preciate a joke when it's on him.

EMMA. How'd you come to hear of it?

JACK. From Jim. Met him this afternoon and me and him had a long talk. He was tellin' me all 'bout their vige.

EMMA. Then it was on the vige this joke happened?

JACK. Yes. It was when they put in to git water at them South Sea Islands where the tempest blowed 'em.

EMMA. Oh. (*Suspiciously*) Caleb didn't seem willing to tell me much about their touching there.

JACK. (*chuckling*) 'Course he didn't. Wasn't I sayin' the joke's on him? (*Coming closer to her—in a low, confidential tone, chucklingly*) We'll fix up a joke on Caleb, Emmer, what d'ye say?

EMMA. (*tortured by foreboding—resolved to find out what is back of all this by hook or crook—forcing a smile*) All right, Jack. I'm willing.

JACK. Then I'll tell you what Jim told me. And you put it up to Caleb, see, and pertend you're madder'n hell. (*Unable to restrain his mirth*) Ho-ho! It'll git him wild if you do that. On'y I didn't tell ye, mind. You heard it from someone else. I don't want to git Caleb down on me. And you'd hear about it from someone sooner or later 'cause Jim and the rest o' the boys has been tellin' the hull town.

EMMA. (*taken aback—frowning*) So all the town knows about it?

JACK. Yes, and they're all laffin' at Caleb. Oh, it ain't nothin' so out o' the ordinary. Most o' the whalin' men hereabout have run up against it in their time. I've heard Pa and all the others tellin' stories like it out o' their experience. On'y with Caleb it ended up so damn funny! (*He laughs*) Ho-ho! Jimminy!

EMMA. (*in a strained voice*) Well, ain't you going to tell me?

JACK. I'm comin' to it. Waal, seems like they all went ashore on them islands to git water and the native brown women, all naked a'most, come round to meet 'em same as they always does—wantin' to swap for terbaccer and other tradin' stuff with straw mats and whatever other junk they got. Them brown gals was purty as the devil, Jim says—that is, in their heathen, outlandish way—and the boys got makin' up to 'em; and then, o' course, everything happened like it always does, and even after they'd got all the water they needed aboard, it took 'em a week to round up all hands from where they was foolin' about with them nigger women.

EMMA. (*in anguish*) Yes—but Caleb—he ain't like them others. He's diff'rent.

JACK. (*with a sly wink*) Oho, is he? I'm comin' to Caleb. Waal, seems 's if he kept aboard mindin' his own business and winkin' at what the boys was doin'. And one o' them gals—the purtiest on 'em,

Jim says—she kept askin', where's the captain? She wouldn't have nothin' to do with any o' the others. She thought on'y the skipper was good enough for her, I reckon. So one night jest afore they sailed some o' the boys, bein' drunk on native rum they'd stole, planned to put up a joke on Caleb and on that brown gal, too. So they tells her the captain had sent for her and she was to swim right out and git aboard the ship where he was waitin' for her alone. That part of it was true enough 'cause Caleb was alone, all hands havin' deserted, you might say.

EMMA. (*letting an involuntary exclamation escape her*) Oh!

JACK. Waal, that fool brown gal b'lieved 'em and she swum right off, tickled to death. What happened between 'em when she got aboard, nobody knows. Some thinks one thing and some another. And I ain't sayin' nothin' 'bout it—(*With a wink*) but I know damn well what I'd 'a done in Caleb's boots, and I guess he ain't the cussed old woman you makes him out. But that part of it's got nothin' to do with the joke nohow. The joke's this: that brown gal took an awful shine to Caleb and when she saw the ship was gittin' ready to sail she raised ructions, standin' on the beach howlin' and screamin', and beatin' her chest with her fists. And when they ups anchors, she dives in the water and swims out after 'em. There's no wind hardly and she kin swim like a fish and catches up to 'em and tries to climb aboard. At fust, Caleb tries to treat her gentle and argy with her to go back. But she won't listen, she gits wilder and wilder, and finally he gits sick of it and has the boys push her off with oars while he goes and hides in the cabin. Even this don't work. She keeps swimmin' round and yellin' for Caleb. And finally they has to p'int a gun at her and shoot in the water near her afore the crazy cuss gives up and swims back to home, howlin' all the time. (*With a chuckle*) And Caleb lyin' low in the cabin skeered to move out, and all hands splittin' their sides! Gosh, I wish I'd been there! It must have been funnier'n hell! (*He laughs loudly—then noticing his sister's stony expression,*

503

stops abruptly) What're you pullin' that long face for, Emmer?
(*Offendedly*) Hell, you're a nice one to tell a joke to!

EMMA. (*after a pause—forcing the words out slowly*) Caleb's comin'
back here, Jack. I want you to see him for me. I want you to tell him—

JACK. Not me! You got to play this joke on him yourself or it won't
work.

EMMA. (*tensely*) This ain't a joke, Jack—what I mean. I want you
to tell him I've changed my mind and I ain't going to marry him.

JACK. What!

EMMA. I been thinking things over, tell him—and I take back my
promise—and he can have back his ring—and I ain't going to marry
him.

JACK. (*flabbergasted—peering into her face anxiously*) Say—what
the hell—? Are you tryin' to josh me, Emmer? Or are you gone crazy
all of a sudden?

EMMA. I ain't joking nor crazy neither. You tell him what I said.

JACK. (*vehemently*) I will like— Say, what's come over you, anyhow?

EMMA. My eyes are opened, that's all, and I ain't going to marry
him.

JACK. Is it—'count of that joke about Caleb I was tellin' you?

EMMA. (*her voice trembling*) It's 'count of something I got in my
own head. What you told only goes to prove I was wrong about it.

JACK. (*greatly perturbed now*) Say, what's the matter? Can't you
take a joke? Are you mad at him 'count o' that brown gal?

EMMA. Yes, I am—and I ain't going to marry him and that's all
there is to it.

JACK. (*argumentatively*) Jealous of a brown, heathen woman that
ain't no better'n a nigger? God sakes, Emmer, I didn't think you was
that big a fool. Why, them kind o' women ain't women like you. They
don't count like folks. They ain't Christians—nor nothin'!

EMMA. That ain't it. I don't care what they are.

JACK. And it wasn't Caleb anyhow. It was all her fixin'. And how'd you know he had anything to do with her—like that? I ain't said he did. Jim couldn't swear he did neither. And even if he did—what difference does it make? It ain't rightly none o' your business what he does on a vige. He didn't ask her to marry him, did he?

EMMA. I don't care. He'd ought to have acted diff'rent.

JACK. Oh golly, there you go agen makin' a durned creepin'-Jesus out of him! What d'you want to marry, anyhow—a man or a sky-pilot? Caleb's a man, ain't he?—and a damn good man and as smart a skipper as there be in these parts! What more d'you want, anyhow?

EMMA. (*violently*) I want you to shet up! You're too dumb stupid and bad yourself to ever know what I'm thinking.

JACK. (*resentfully*) Go to the devil, then! I'm goin' to tell Ma and sic her onto you. You'll maybe listen to her and git some sense. (*He stamps out, right, while he is speaking.* EMMA *bursts into sobs and throws herself on a chair, covering her face with her hands.* HARRIET WILLIAMS *and* ALFRED ROGERS *come up the path to the door in rear. Peering through the screen and catching sight of* EMMA, HARRIET *calls*) Emmer! (EMMA *leaps to her feet and dabs at her eyes with a hand-kerchief in a vain effort to conceal traces of her tears.* HARRIET *has come in, followed by* ROGERS. CALEB'S *sister is a tall, dark girl of twenty. Her face is plainly homely and yet attracts the eye by a certain boldly-appealing vitality of self-confident youth. She wears an apron and has evidently just come out of the kitchen.* ROGERS *is a husky young fisherman of twenty-four, washed and slicked up in his ill-fitting best.*)

ROGERS. Hello, Emmer.

EMMA. (*huskily, trying to force a smile*) Hello, Harriet. Hello, Alfred. Won't you set?

HARRIET. No, I jest run over from the house a second to see if— Where's Caleb, Emmer?

EMMA. He's gone up street.

HARRIET. And here I be waitin' in the kitchen for him to bring back the things so's I can start his supper. (*With a laugh and a roguish look at* ROGERS) Dearie me, it ain't no use dependin' on a man to remember nothin' when he's in love.

ROGERS. (*putting his arm about her waist and giving her a squeeze—grinning*) How 'bout me? Ain't I in love and ain't I as reliable as an old hoss?

HARRIET. Oh, you! You're the worst of 'em all.

ROGERS. You don't think so. (*He tries to kiss her.*)

HARRIET. Stop it. Ain't you got no manners? What'll Emmer think?

ROGERS. Emmer can't throw stones. Her and Caleb is worser at spoonin' than what we are. (HARRIET *breaks away from him laughingly and goes to* EMMA.)

HARRIET. (*suddenly noticing the expression of misery on* EMMA's *face—astonished*) Why, Emmer Crosby, what's the matter? You look as if you'd lost your last friend.

EMMA. (*trying to smile*) Nothing. It's nothing.

HARRIET. It is, too! Why, I do believe you've been crying!

EMMA. No, I ain't.

HARRIET. You have, too! (*Putting her arms about* EMMA) Goodness, what's happened? You and Caleb ain't had a spat, have you, with your weddin' only two days off?

EMMA. (*with quick resentful resolution*) There ain't going to be any wedding.

HARRIET. What!

ROGERS. (*pricking up his ears—inquisitively*) Huh?

EMMA. Not in two days nor no time.

HARRIET. (*dumbfounded*) Why, Emmer Crosby! Whatever's got into you? You and Caleb must have had an awful spat!

ROGERS. (*with a man-of-the-world attitude of cynicism*) Don't take her so dead serious, Harriet. Emmer'll git over it like you all does.

EMMA. (*angrily*) You shet up, Alf Rogers! (MRS. CROSBY *enters bustlingly from the right. She is a large, fat, florid woman of fifty. In spite of her two hundred and more pounds she is surprisingly active, and the passive, lazy expression of her round moon face is belied by her quick, efficient movements. She exudes an atmosphere of motherly good nature. She wears an apron on which she is drying her hands as she enters.* JACK *follows her into the room. He has changed to a dark suit, is ready for "up street."*)

MRS. CROSBY. (*smiling at* HARRIET *and* ROGERS) Afternoon, Harriet— and Alf.

HARRIET. Afternoon, Ma.

ROGERS. Afternoon.

JACK. (*grinning*) There she be, Ma. (*Points to* EMMA) Don't she look like she'd scratch a feller's eyes out! Phew! Look at her back curve! Meow? Sptt-sptt! Nice puss! (*He gives a vivid imitation of a cat fight at this last. Then he and* ROGERS *roar with laughter and* HARRIET *cannot restrain a giggle and* MRS. CROSBY *smiles.* EMMA *stares stonily before her as if she didn't hear.*)

MRS. CROSBY. (*good-naturedly*) Shet up your foolin', Jack.

JACK. (*pretending to be hurt*) Nobody in this house kin take a joke. (*He grins and beckons to* ROGERS) Come along, Alf. You kin 'preciate a joke. Come on in here till I tell you. (*The grinning* ROGERS *follows him into the next room where they can be heard talking and laughing during the following scene.*)

MRS. CROSBY. (*smiling, puts her arms around* EMMA) Waal, Emmer, what's this foolishness Jack's been tellin' about—

EMMA. (*resentfully*) It ain't foolishness, Ma. I've made up my mind, I tell you that right here and now.

MRS. CROSBY. (*after a quick glance at her face—soothingly*) There, there! Let's set down and be comfortable. Me, I don't relish roostin' on my feet. (*She pushes* EMMA *gently into a rocker—then points to a chair on the other side of the table*) Set down, Harriet.

HARRIET. (*torn between curiosity and a sense of being one too many*) Maybe I'd best go to home and leave you two alone?

MRS. CROSBY. Shucks! Ain't you like one o' the family—Caleb's sister and livin' right next door ever since you was all children playin' to-gether. We ain't got no secrets from you. Set down. (HARRIET *does so*

507

with an uncertain glance at the frozen EMMA. MRS. CROSBY *has effi-
ciently bustled another rocker beside her daughter's and sits down
with a comfortable sigh*) There. (*She reaches over and takes one of
her daughter's hands in hers*) And now, Emmer, what's all this fuss
over? (*As* EMMA *makes no reply*) Jack says as you've sworn you was
breakin' with Caleb. Is that true?

EMMA. Yes.

MRS. CROSBY. Hmm. Caleb don't know this yet, does he?

EMMA. No. I asked Jack to tell him when he comes back.

MRS. CROSBY. Jack says he won't.

EMMA. Then I'll tell him myself. Maybe that's better, anyhow.
Caleb'll know what I'm driving at and see my reason—(*Bitterly*)
which nobody else seems to.

MRS. CROSBY. Hmm. You ain't tried me yet. (*After a pause*) Jack
was a dumb fool to tell you 'bout them goin's-on at them islands they
teched. Ain't no good repeatin' sech things.

EMMA. (*surprised*) Did you know about it before Jack—

MRS. CROSBY. Mercy, yes. Your Pa heard it from Jim Benson fust
thing they landed here, and Pa told me that night.

EMMA. (*resentfully*) And you never told me!

MRS. CROSBY. Mercy, no. 'Course I didn't. They's trouble enough in
the world without makin' more. If you was like most folks I'd told
it to you. Me, I thought it was a good joke on Caleb.

EMMA. (*with a shudder*) It ain't a joke to me.

MRS. CROSBY. That's why I kept my mouth shet. I knowed you was
touchy and diff'rent from most.

EMMA. (*proudly*) Yes, I am diff'rent—and that's just what I thought
Caleb was, too—and he ain't.

HARRIET. (*breaking in excitedly*) Is it that story about Caleb and that
heathen brown woman you're talking about? Is that what you're mad
at Caleb for, Emmer?

MRS. CROSBY. (*as* EMMA *remains silent*) Yes, Harriet, that's it.

HARRIET. (*astonished*) Why, Emmer Crosby, how can you be so silly? You don't s'pose Caleb took it serious, do you, and him makin' them fire shots round her to scare her back to land and get rid of her? Good gracious! (*A bit resentfully*) I hope you ain't got it in your head my brother Caleb would sink so low as to fall in love serious with one of them critters?

EMMA. (*harshly*) He might just as well.

HARRIET. (*bridling*) How can you say sech a thing! (*Sarcastically*) I ain't heard that Caleb offered to marry her, have you? Then you might have some cause— But d'you s'pose he's ever give her another thought? Not Caleb! I know him better'n that. He'd forgot all about the hull thing before they was out o' sight of land, I'll bet, and if them fools hadn't started this story going, he'd never remembered it again.

MRS. CROSBY. (*nodding*) That's jest it. Harriet's right, Emmer.

EMMA. Ma!

MRS. CROSBY. Besides, you don't know they was nothin' wrong happened. Nobody kin swear that for sartin. Ain't that so, Harriet?

HARRIET. (*hesitating—then frankly*) I don't know. Caleb ain't no plaster saint and I reckon he's as likely to sin that way as any other man. He wasn't married then and I s'pose he thought he was free to do as he'd a mind to 'til he was hitched up. Goodness sakes, Emmer, all the men thinks that—and a lot of 'em after they're married, too.

MRS. CROSBY. Harriet's right, Emmer. If you've been wide awake to all that's happened in this town since you was old enough to know, you'd ought to realize what men be.

HARRIET. (*scornfully*) Emma'd ought to have fallen in love with a minister, not a sailor. As for me, I wouldn't give a durn about a man that was too goody-goody to raise Cain once in a while—before he married me, I mean. Why, look at Alf Rogers, Emmer. I'm going to marry him some day, ain't I? But I know right well all the foolin' he's done—and still is doing, I expect. I ain't sayin' I like it but I do like him and I got to take him the way he is, that's all. If you're looking for saints, you got to die first and go to heaven. A girl'd never git married hereabouts if she expected too much.

MRS. CROSBY. Harriet's right, Emmer.

EMMA. (*resentfully*) Maybe she is, Ma, from her side. I ain't claiming she's wrong. Her and me just looks at things diff'rent, that's all. And she can't understand the way I feel about Caleb.

HARRIET. Well, there's one thing certain, Emmer. You won't find a man in a day's walk is any better'n Caleb—or as good.

EMMA. (*wearily*) I know that, Harriet.

HARRIET. Then it's all right. You'll make up with him, and I s'pose I'm a fool to be takin' it so serious. (*As* EMMA *shakes her head*) Oh, yes, you will. You wouldn't want to get him all broke up, would you? (*As* EMMA *keeps silent—irritably*) Story-book notions, that's the trouble with you, Emmer. You're gettin' to think you're better'n the rest of us.

EMMA. (*vehemently*) No, I don't! Can't you see—

MRS. CROSBY. Thar, now! Don't you two git to fightin'—to make things worse.

HARRIET. (*repentantly, coming and putting her arms around* EMMA *and kissing her*) I'm sorry, Emmer. You know I wouldn't fall out with you for nothing or nobody, don't you? Only it gits me riled to think of how awful broke up Caleb'd be if— But you'll make it all up with him when he comes, won't you? (EMMA *stares stubbornly before her. Before she has a chance to reply a roar of laughter comes from the next room as* JACK *winds up his tale.*)

ROGERS. (*from the next room*) Gosh, I wished I'd been there! (*He follows* JACK *into the room. Both are grinning broadly.* ROGERS *says teasingly*) Reckon I'll take to whalin' 'stead o' fishin' after this. You won't mind, Harriet? From what I hears o' them brown women, I'm missin' a hull lot by stayin' to home.

HARRIET. (*in a joking tone—with a meaning glance at* EMMA) Go on, then! There's plenty of fish in the sea. Anyhow, I'd never git jealous of your foolin' with one o' them heathen critters. They ain't worth notice from a Christian.

JACK. Oho, ain't they! They're purty as pictures, Benson says. (*With*

510

a wink) And mighty accommodatin' in their ways. (*He and* ROGERS *roar delightedly.* EMMA *shudders with revulsion.*)

MRS. CROSBY. (*aware of her daughter's feelings—smilingly but firmly*) Get out o' this, Jack. You, too, Alf. Go on up street if you want to joke. You're in my way.

JACK. Aw right, Ma. Come on up street, Alf.

HARRIET. Wait. I'll go with you a step. I got to see if Caleb's got back with them supper things. (*They all go to the door in rear.* JACK *and* ROGERS *pass out, talking and laughing.* HARRIET *turns in the doorway—sympathetically*) I'll give Caleb a talking-to before he comes over. Then it'll be easy for you to finish him. Treat him firm but gentle and you'll see he won't never do it again in a hurry. After all, he wasn't married, Emmer—and he's a man—and what can you expect? Good-by. (*She goes.*)

EMMA. (*inaudibly*) Good-by.

MRS. CROSBY. (*after a pause in which she rocks back and forth studying her daughter's face—placidly*) Harriet's right, Emmer. You give him a good talkin'-to and he won't do it again.

EMMA. (*coldly*) I don't care whether he does or not. I ain't going to marry him.

MRS. CROSBY. (*uneasy—persuasively*) Mercy, you can't act like that, Emmer. Here's the weddin' on'y two days off, and everythin' fixed up with the minister, and your Pa and Jack has bought new clothes speshul for it, and I got a new dress—

EMMA. (*turning to her mother—pleadingly*) You wouldn't want me to keep my promise to Caleb if you knew I'd be unhappy, would you, Ma?

MRS. CROSBY. (*hesitatingly*) N-no, Emmer. (*Then decisively*) 'Course I wouldn't. It's because I know he'll make you happy. (*As* EMMA *shakes her head*) Pshaw, Emmer, you can't tell me you've got over all likin' for him jest 'count o' this one foolishness o' hisn.

EMMA. I don't love him—what he is now. I loved—what I thought he was.

MRS. CROSBY. (*more and more uneasy*) That's all your queer notions, and I don't know where you gits them from. Caleb ain't changed, neither have you. Why, Emmer, it'd be jest like goin' agen an act of Nature for you not to marry him. Ever since you was children you been livin' side by side, goin' round together, and neither you nor him ever did seem to care for no one else. Shucks, Emmer, you'll git me to lose patience with you if you act that stubborn. You'd ought to remember all he's been to you and forget this one little wrong he's done.

EMMA. I can't, Ma. It makes him another person—not Caleb, but someone just like all the others.

MRS. CROSBY. Waal, is the others so bad? Men is men the world over, I reckon.

EMMA. No, they ain't bad. I ain't saying that. Don't I like 'em all? If it was one of the rest—like Jim Benson or Jack, even—had done this I'd thought it was a joke, too. I ain't strict in judging 'em and you know it. But—can't you see, Ma?—Caleb always seemed diff'rent—and I thought he was.

MRS. CROSBY. (*somewhat impatiently*) Wall, if he ain't, he's a good man jest the same, as good as any sensible girl'd want to marry.

EMMA. (*slowly*) I don't want to marry nobody no more. I'll stay single.

MRS. CROSBY. (*tauntingly*) An old maid! (*Then resentfully*) Emmer, d'you s'pose if I'd had your high-fangled notions o' what men ought to be when I was your age, d'you s'pose you'd ever be settin' there now?

EMMA. (*slowly*) No. I know from what I can guess from his own stories Pa never was no saint.

MRS. CROSBY. (*in a tone of finality as if this settled the matter*) There, now! And ain't he been as good a husband to me as ever lived, and a good father to you and Jack? You'll find out Caleb'll turn out the same. You think it over. (*She gets up—bustlingly*) And now I got to git back in the kitchen.

EMMA. (*wringing her hands—desperately*) Oh, Ma, why can't you see what I feel? Of course, Pa's good—as good as good can be—

CAPTAIN CROSBY. (*from outside the door which he has approached without their noticing him—in a jovial bellow*) What's that 'bout Pa bein' good? (*He comes in laughing. He is a squat, bow-legged, powerful man, almost as broad as he is long—sixty years old but still in the prime of health and strength, with a great, red, weather-beaten face seamed by sun wrinkles. His sandy hair is thick and disheveled. He is dressed in an old baggy suit much the worse for wear—striped cotton shirt open at the neck. He pats* EMMA *on the back with a playful touch that almost jars her off her feet*) Thunderin' Moses, that's the fust time ever I heerd good o' myself by listenin'! Most times it's: "Crosby? D'you mean that drunken, good-for-nothin', mangy old cuss?" That's what I hears usual. Thank ye, Emmer. (*Turning to his wife*) What ye got to say now, Ma? Here's Emmer tellin' you the truth after you hair-pullin' me all these years 'cause you thought it wa'n't. I always told ye I was good, ain't I—good as hell I be! (*He shakes with laughter and kisses his wife a resounding smack.*)

MRS. CROSBY. (*teasing lovingly*) Emmer don't know you like I do.

CROSBY. (*turning back to* EMMA *again*) Look-a-here, Emmer, I jest seen Jack. He told me some fool story 'bout you fallin' out with Caleb. Reckon he was joshin', wa'nt he?

MRS. CROSBY. (*quickly*) Oh, that's all settled, John. Don't you go stirrin' it up again. (EMMA *seems about to speak but stops helplessly after one glance at her father.*)

CROSBY. An' all 'count o' that joke they're tellin' 'bout him and that brown female critter, Jack says. Hell, Emmer, you ain't a real Crosby if you takes a joke like that serious. Thunderin' Moses, what the hell d'you want Caleb to be—a durned, he-virgin, sky-pilot? Caleb's a man wo'th ten o' most and, spite o' his bein' on'y a boy yit, he's the smartest skipper out o' this port and you'd ought to be proud you'd got him. And as for them islands, all whalin' men knows 'em. I've teched thar for water more'n once myself, and I know them brown females like a book. And I tells you, after a year or more aboard ship, a man'd have to be a goll-durned geldin' if he don't—

MRS. CROSBY. (*glancing uneasily at* EMMA) Ssshh! You come out in the kitchen with me, Pa, and leave Emmer be.

CROSBY. God A'mighty, Ma, I ain't sayin' nothin' agen Emmer, be I? I knows Emmer ain't that crazy. If she ever got religion that bad, I'd ship her off as female missionary to the damned yellow Chinks. (*He laughs.*)

MRS. CROSBY. (*taking his arm*) You come with me. I want to talk with you 'bout somethin'.

CROSBY. (*going*) Aye-aye, skipper! You're boss aboard here. (*He goes out right with her, laughing.* EMMA *stands for a while, staring stonily before her. She sighs hopelessly, clasping and unclasping her hands, looking around the room as if she longed to escape from it. Finally she sits down helplessly and remains fixed in a strained attitude, her face betraying the conflict that is tormenting her. Slow steps sound from the path in front of the house.* EMMA *recognizes them and her face freezes into an expression of obstinate intolerance.* CALEB *appears outside the screen door. He looks in, coughs—then asks uncertainly*) It's me, Emmer. Kin I come in?

EMMA. (*coldly*) Yes.

CALEB. (*comes in and walks down beside her chair. His face is set emotionlessly but his eyes cannot conceal a worried bewilderment, a look of uncomprehending hurt. He stands uncomfortably, fumbling with his hat, waiting for her to speak or look up. As she does neither, he finally blurts out*) Kin I set a spell?

EMMA. (*in the same cold tone*) Yes. (*He lowers himself carefully to a wooden posture on the edge of a rocker near hers.*)

CALEB. (*after a pause*) I seen Jim Benson. I give him hell. He won't tell no more tales, I reckon. (*Another pause*) I stopped to home on the way back from the store. I seen Harriet. She says Jack'd told you that story they're all tellin' as a joke on me. (*Clenching his fists—angrily*) Jack's a durn fool. He needs a good lickin' from someone.

EMMA. (*resentfully*) Don't try to put the blame on Jack. He only told me the truth, didn't he? (*Her voice shows that she hopes against hope for a denial.*)

CALEB. (*after a long pause—regretfully*) Waal, I guess what he told is true enough.

EMMA. (*wounded*) Oh!

CALEB. But that ain't no good reason for tellin' it. Them sort o' things ought to be kept among men. (*After a pause—gropingly*) I didn't want nothin' like that to happen, Emmer. I didn't mean it to. I was thinkin' o' how you might feel—even down there. That's why I stayed aboard all the time when the boys was ashore. I wouldn't have b'lieved it could happen—not to me. (*A pause*) I wish you could see them Islands, Emmer, and be there for a time. Then you might see— It's hard 's hell to explain, and you havin' never seen 'em. Everything is diff'rent down there—the weather—and the trees and water. You git lookin' at it all, and you git to feel diff'rent from what you do to home here. It's purty hereabouts sometimes—like now, in spring— but it's purty there all the time—and down there you notice it and you git feelin'—diff'rent. And them native women—they're diff'rent. A man don't think of 'em as women—like you. But they're purty—in their fashion—and at night they sings—and it's all diff'rent like something you'd see in a painted picture. (*A pause*) That night when she swum out and got aboard when I was alone, she caught me by s'prise. I wasn't expectin' nothin' o' that sort. I tried to make her git back to land at fust—but she wouldn't go. She couldn't understand enough English for me to tell her how I felt—and I reckon she wouldn't have seed my p'int anyhow, her bein' a native. (*A pause*) And then I was afeerd she'd catch cold goin' round all naked and wet in the moonlight—though it was warm—and I wanted to wrap a blanket round her. (*He stops as if he had finished.*)

EMMA. (*after a long, tense pause—dully*) Then you own up—there really was something happened?

CALEB. (*after a pause*) I was sorry for it, after. I locked myself in the cabin and left her to sleep out on deck.

EMMA. (*after a pause—fixedly*) I ain't going to marry you, Caleb.

CALEB. Harriet said you'd said that; but I didn't b'lieve you'd let a slip like that make—such a diff'rence.

EMMA. (*with finality*) Then you can believe it now, Caleb.

CALEB. (*after a pause*) You got queer, strict notions, Emmer. A man'll never live up to 'em—with never one slip. But you got to act accordin' to your lights, I expect. It sort o' busts everythin' to bits for me— (*His voice betrays his anguish for a second but he instantly regains his iron control*) But o' course, if you ain't willin' to take me the way I be, there's nothin' to do. And whatever you think is best, suits me.

EMMA. (*after a pause—gropingly*) I wish I could explain my side of it—so's you'd understand. I ain't got any hard feelings against you, Caleb—not now. It ain't plain jealousy—what I feel. It ain't even that I think you've done nothing terrible wrong. I think I can understand —how it happened—and make allowances. I know that most any man would do the same, and I guess all of 'em I ever met has done it.

CALEB. (*with a glimmer of eager hope*) Then—you'll forgive it, Emmer?

EMMA. Yes, I forgive it. But don't think that my forgiving is going to make any diff'rence—'cause I ain't going to marry you, Caleb. That's final. (*After a pause—intensely*) Oh, I wish I could make you see—my reason. You don't. You never will, I expect. What you done is just what any other man would have done—and being like them is exactly what'll keep you from ever seeing my meaning. (*After a pause—in a last effort to make him understand*) Maybe it's my fault more'n your'n. It's like this, Caleb. Ever since we was little I guess I've always had the idea that you was—diff'rent. And when we growed up and got engaged I thought that more and more. And you was diff'rent, too! And that was why I loved you. And now you've proved you ain't. And so how can I love you any more? I don't, Caleb, and that's all there is to it. You've busted something way down inside me —and I can't love you no more.

CALEB. (*gloomily*) I've warned you often, ain't I, you was settin' me up where I'd no business to be. I'm human like the rest and always was. I ain't diff'rent. (*After a pause—uncertainly*) I reckon there ain't no use sayin' nothin' more. I'll go home. (*He starts to rise.*)

EMMA. Wait. I don't want you to go out of here with no hard feelings. You 'n' me, Caleb, we've been too close all our lives to ever get to be enemies. I like you, Caleb, same's I always did. I want us to stay friends. I want you to be like one of the family same's you've always been. There's no reason you can't. I don't blame you—as a man—for what I wouldn't hold against any other man. If I find I can't love you —that way—no more or be your wife, it's just that I've decided— things being what they be and me being what I am—I won't marry no man. I'll stay single. (*Forcing a smile*) I guess there's worse things than being an old maid.

CALEB. I can't picture you that, Emmer. It's natural in some, but it ain't in you. (*Then with a renewal of hope*) And o' course I want to stay friends with you, Emmer. There's no hard feelin's on my side. You got a right to your own way—even if— (*hopefully*) And maybe if I show you what I done wasn't natural to me—by never doin' it again—maybe the time'll come when you'll be willin' to forget—

EMMA. (*shaking her head—slowly*) It ain't a question of time, Caleb. It's a question of something being dead. And when a thing's died, time can't make no diff'rence.

CALEB. (*sturdily*) You don't know that for sure, Emmer. You're human, too, and as liable to make mistakes as any other. Maybe you on'y think it's dead, and when I come back from the next vige and you've had two years to think it over, you'll see diff'rent and know I ain't as bad as I seem to ye now.

EMMA. (*helplessly*) But you don't seem bad, Caleb. And two years can't make no change in me—that way.

CALEB. (*feeling himself somehow more and more heartened by hope*) I ain't givin' up hope, Emmer, and you can't make me. Not by a hell of a sight. (*With emphasis*) I ain't never goin' to marry no woman but you, Emmer. You can trust my word for that. And I'll wait for ye to change your mind, I don't give a durn how long it'll take—till I'm sixty years old—thirty years if it's needful! (*He rises to his feet as he is speaking this last.*)

EMMA. (*with a mournful smile*) You might just as well say for life, Caleb. In thirty years we'll both be dead and gone, probably. And I don't want you to think it's needful for you to stay single 'cause I—

CALEB. I ain't goin' to stay single. I'm goin' to wait for you. And some day when you realize men was never cut out for angels you'll—

EMMA. (*helplessly*) Me 'n' you'll never understand each other, Caleb, so long as we live. (*Getting up and holding out her hand*) Good-by, Caleb. I'm going up and lie down for a spell.

CALEB. (*made hopeless again by her tone—clasps her hand mechanically—dully*) Good-by, Emmer. (*He goes to the door in the rear, opens it, then hesitates and looks back at her as she goes out the door on the right without turning around. Suddenly he blurts out despairingly*) You'll remember what I told ye 'bout waitin', Emmer? (*She is gone, makes no reply. His face sets in its concealment mask of emotionlessness and he turns slowly and goes out the door as the curtain falls.*)

ACT TWO

Scene—*Thirty years after—the scene is the same but not the same. The room has a grotesque aspect of old age turned flighty and masquerading as the most empty-headed youth. There is an obstreperous newness about everything. Orange curtains are at the windows. The carpet has given way to a varnished hardwood floor, its glassy surface set off by three small, garish-colored rugs, placed with precision in front of the two doors and under the table. The wallpaper is now a cream color sprayed with pink flowers. Seascapes, of the painted-to-order quality, four in number, in gilded frames, are hung on the walls at mathematically-spaced intervals. The plush-covered chairs are gone, replaced by a set of varnished oak. The horsehair sofa has been relegated to the attic. A cane-bottomed affair with fancy cushions serves in its stead. A Victrola is where the old mahogany chest had been. A brand new piano shines resplendently in the far right corner by the door, and a bookcase with glass doors that pull up and slide in flanks the fireplace. This bookcase is full of installment-plan sets of uncut volumes. The table at center is of varnished oak. On it are piles of fashion magazines and an electric reading lamp. Only the old Bible, which still preserves its place of honor on the table, and the marble clock on the mantel, have survived the renovation and serve to emphasize it all the more by contrast.*

It is late afternoon of a day in the early spring of the year 1920.

As the curtain rises, EMMA *and* BENNY ROGERS *are discovered. She is seated in a rocker by the table. He is standing by the Victrola on which a jazz band record is playing. He whistles, goes through the motions of dancing to the music. He is a young fellow of twenty-three, a replica of his father in Act One, but coarser, more hardened and cocksure. He is dressed in the khaki uniform of a private in the United States Army. The thirty years have transformed* EMMA *into a with-*

ered, scrawny woman. But there is something revoltingly incongruous about her, a pitiable sham, a too-apparent effort to cheat the years by appearances. The white dress she wears is too frilly, too youthful for her; so are the high-heeled pumps and clocked silk stockings. There is an absurd suggestion of rouge on her tight cheeks and thin lips, of penciled make-up about her eyes. The black of her hair is brazenly untruthful. Above all there is shown in her simpering, self-consciously coquettish manner that laughable—and at the same time irritating and disgusting—mockery of undignified age snatching greedily at the empty simulacra of youth. She resembles some passé stock actress of fifty made up for a heroine of twenty.

BENNY. (*as the record stops—switches off the machine*) Oh, baby! Some jazz, I'll tell the world!

EMMA. (*smiling lovingly at his back*) I'm glad you like it. It's one of them you picked out on the list.

BENNY. Oh, I'm a swell little picker, aw right. (*Turning to her*) Say, you're a regular feller—gettin' them records for me.

EMMA. (*coquettishly*) Well, if that ain't just like a man! Who told you I got them just for you?

BENNY. Well, didn't you?

EMMA. No indeedy! I only took your advice on what to get. I knew you'd know, being growed to a man of the world now since you was overseas. But I got 'em because I like them jazz tunes myself. They put life and ginger in an old lady like me—not like them slow, old-timey tunes.

BENNY. (*bends over chair—kiddingly*) You ain't old. That's all bunk.

EMMA. (*flattered*) Now, now, Benny!

BENNY. You ain't. You're a regular, up-to-date sport—the only live one in this dead dump. (*With a grin*) And if you fall for that jazz stuff, all you got to do now is learn to dance to it.

EMMA. (*giggling*) I will—if you'll teach me.

520

BENNY. (*struggling with a guffaw*) Oh, oui! Sure I will! We'll have a circus, me an' you. Say, you're sure one of the girls aw right, Aunt Emmer.

EMMA. Oh, you needn't think we're *all* so behind the times to home here just because you've been to France and all over.

BENNY. *You* ain't, I'll say, Aunt Emmer.

EMMA. And how often have I got to tell you not to call me Aunt Emmer?

BENNY. (*with a grin*) Oh, oui! My foot slipped. 'Scuse me, Emmer.

EMMA. (*delighted by his coarse familiarity*) That's better. Why, you know well enough I ain't your aunt anyway.

BENNY. I got to get used to the plain Emmer. They taught me to call you "aunt" when I was a kid. (EMMA *looks displeased at this remark and* BENNY *hastens to add cajolingly*) And you almost was my aunt-in-law one time from what I've heard. (*Winks at her cunningly.*)

EMMA. (*flustered*) That was ages ago. (*Catching herself quickly*) Not so awful long really, but it's all so dead and gone it seems a long while.

BENNY. (*unthinkingly*) It was before I was born, wasn't it? (*Seeing her expression he hurries on*) Well, that ain't so darned long. Say, here's something I never could make out—how did you ever come to fall for Uncle Caleb?

EMMA. (*bridling quickly*) I never did. That's all talk, Benny. We was good friends and still are. I was young and foolish and got engaged to him—and then discovered I didn't like him that way. That's all there ever was to it.

BENNY. (*resentfully*) I can't figure how anybody'd ever like him anyway. He's a darn stingy, ugly old cuss, if you want my dope on him. I can't see him at all. I've hated him ever since Pa died and Ma and me had to go live next door with him.

EMMA. You oughtn't to say that. He's kind at bottom, spite of his rough ways, and he's brought you up.

BENNY. (*grumpily*) Dragged me up, you mean. (*With a calculat-*

ing look at her out of the corners of his eyes) He's a tight-wad and I hate folks that're tight with their coin. Spend and be a good sport, that's my motto. (*Flattering*) He'd ought to be more like you that way, Emmer.

EMMA. (*pleased—condescendingly*) Your Uncle Caleb's an old man, remember. He's sot in his ways and believes in being strict with you— too strict, I've told him.

BENNY. He's got piles of money hoarded in the bank but he's too mean even to retire from whalin' himself—goes right on makin' vige after vige to grab more and never spends a nickel less'n he has to. It was always like pryin' open a safe for me to separate him from a cent. (*With extreme disgust*) Aw, he's a piker. I hate him and I always did!

EMMA. (*looking toward the door apprehensively*) Ssshh!

BENNY. What you scared of? He don't get in from New Bedford till the night train and even if he's got to the house by this he'll be busy as a bird dog for an hour getting himself dolled up to pay you a call.

EMMA. (*perfunctorily*) I hope he's had a good vige and is in good health.

BENNY. (*roughly*) You needn't worry. He's too mean ever to get real sick. Gosh, I wish Pa'd lived—or Uncle Jack. They wasn't like him. I was only a kid when they got drowned, but I remember enough about 'em to know they was good sports. Wasn't they?

EMMA. (*rather primly*) They was too sporty for their own good.

BENNY. Don't you hand me that. That don't sound like you. You're a sport yourself. (*After a pause*) Say, it's nutty when you come to think of it—Uncle Caleb livin' next door all these years and comin' to call all the time when he ain't at sea.

EMMA. What's funny about that? We've always been good friends.

BENNY. (*with a grin*) It's just as if the old guy was still mashin' you. And I'll bet anything he's as stuck on you as he ever was—the old fool!

EMMA. (*with a coquettish titter*) Land sakes, Benny, a body'd think you were actually jealous of your uncle the way you go on.

BENNY. (*with a mocking laugh*) Jealous! Oh, oui! Sure I am! Kin you blame me? (*Then seriously, with a calculating look at her*) No, all kiddin' aside, I know he'll run me down first second he sees you. Ma'll tell him all her tales, and he'll be sore at me right off. He's always hated me anyway. He was glad when I enlisted, 'cause that got him rid of me. All he was hopin' was that some German'd get me for keeps. Then when I come back he wouldn't do nothin' for me so I enlisted again.

EMMA. (*chiding—playfully*) Now, Benny! Didn't you tell me you enlisted again 'cause you were sick o' this small place and wanted to be out where there was more fun?

BENNY. Well, o' course it was that, too. But I could have a swell time even in this dump if he'd loosen up and give me some kale. (*Again with the calculating look at her*) Why, look here, right now there's a buddy of mine wants me to meet him in Boston and he'll show me a good time, and if I had a hundred dollars—

EMMA. A hundred dollars! That's an awful pile to spend, Benny.

BENNY. (*disgustedly*) Now you're talkin' tight like him.

EMMA. (*hastily*) Oh, no, Benny. You know better'n that. What was you sayin'—if you had a hundred dollars—?

BENNY. That ain't such a much these days with everything gone up so. If I went to Boston I'd have to get dolled up and everything. And this buddy of mine is a sport and a spender. Easy come, easy go is his motto. His folks ain't tight-wads like mine. And I couldn't show myself up as a cheap skate by travelin' 'round with him without a nickel in my jeans and just spongin' on him. (*With the calculating glance to see what effect his words are having—pretending to dismiss the subject*) But what's the good of talkin'? I got a swell chance tellin' that to Uncle Caleb. He'd give me one look and then put a double padlock on his roll. But it ain't fair just the same. Here I'm sweatin' blood in the army after riskin' my life in France and when I get a leave to home, everyone treats me like a wet dog.

EMMA. (*softly*) Do you mean me, too, Benny?

BENNY. No, not you. You're diff'rent from the rest. You're regular

—and you ain't any of my real folks, either, and ain't got any reason.

EMMA. (*coquettishly*) Oh, yes, I have a reason. I like you very, very much, Benny—better than anyone in the town—especially since you've been to home these last few times and come to call so often and I feel I've growed to know you. When you first came back from France I never would have recognized you as Harriet's Benny, you was so big and strong and handsome.

BENNY. (*uncomfortably*) Aw, you're kiddin'. But you can tell how good I think you are from me bein' over here so much—so you know I ain't lyin'. (*Made more and more uncomfortable by the ardent looks* EMMA *is casting at him*) Well, guess I'll be movin' along.

EMMA. (*pleadingly*) Oh, you mustn't go yet! Just when we're gettin' so friendly!

BENNY. Uncle Caleb'll be over soon and I don't want him to catch me here—nor nowhere else till he gets calmed down after hearin' Ma's kicks about me. So I guess I better beat it up street.

EMMA. He won't come for a long time yet. I know when to expect him. (*Pleading ardently and kittenishly*) Do set down a spell, Benny! Land sakes, I hardly get a sight of you before you want to run away again. I'll begin to think you're only pretending to like me.

BENNY. (*seeing his calculations demand it*) Aw right—jest for a second. (*He looks about him, seeking a neutral subject for conversation*) Gee, you've had this old place fixed up swell since I was to home last.

EMMA. (*coquettishly*) Guess who I had it all done for, mostly?

BENNY. For yourself, of course.

EMMA. (*shaking her head roguishly*) No, not for me, not for me! Not that I don't like it but I'd never have gone to the trouble and expense for myself. (*With a sigh*) I s'pose poor Ma and Pa turned over in their graves when I ordered it done.

BENNY. (*with a sly grin*) Who d'you have it done for, then?

EMMA. For you! Yes, for you, Benny—so's you'd have a nice, up-to-date place to come to when you was on vacation from the horrid old army.

BENNY. (*embarrassed*) Well, it's great aw right. And it sure looks swell—nothing cheap about it.

EMMA. (*delighted*) As long as you like it, I'm satisfied. (*Then suddenly, wagging an admonishing finger at him and hiding beneath a joking manner an undercurrent of uneasiness*) I was forgetting I got a bone to pick with you, young man! I heard them sayin' to the store that you'd been up callin' on that Tilly Small evenin' before last.

BENNY. (*with a lady-killer's carelessness*) Aw, I was passin' by and she called me in, that's all.

EMMA. (*frowning*) They said you had the piano goin' and was singing and no end of high jinks.

BENNY. Aw, these small town boobs think you're raising hell if you're up after eleven.

EMMA. (*excitedly*) I ain't blamin' you. But her—she ought to have better sense—at her age, too, when she's old enough to be your mother.

BENNY. Aw, say, she ain't half as old— (*Catching himself*) Oh, she's an old fool, you're right there, Emmer.

EMMA. (*severely*) And I hope you know the kind of woman she is and has been since she was a girl.

BENNY. (*with a wink*) I wasn't born yesterday. I got her number long ago. I ain't in my cradle, get me! I'm in the army! Oui! (*Chuckles.*)

EMMA. (*fidgeting nervously*) What'd you—what'd you do when you was there?

BENNY. Why, nothin'. I told her to cut the rough work and behave—and a nice time was had by all. (*He grins provokingly.*)

EMMA. (*springs to her feet nervously*) I don't know what to think—when you act so queer about it.

BENNY. (*carelessly*) Well, don't think nothing wrong—'cause there wasn't. Bill Tinker was with me and we was both wishin' we had a drink. And Bill says, "Let's go see Tilly Small. She always has some

525

buried and if we hand her a line of talk maybe she'll drag out the old bottle." So we did—and she did. We kidded her for a couple of drinks. (*He snickers.*)

EMMA. (*standing in front of him—fidgeting*) I want you to promise you won't go to see her no more. If you—if you want liquor now and again maybe I—maybe I can fix it so's I can get some to keep here for you.

BENNY. (*eagerly*) Say, that'd be great! Will you? (*She nods. He goes on carelessly*) And sure I'll promise not to see Tilly no more. Gosh, what do you think I care about her? Or about any dame in this town, for that matter—'ceptin' you. These small town skirts don't hand me nothin'. (*With a grin*) You forgot I was in France— and after the dames over there these birds here look some punk.

EMMA. (*sits down—wetting her lips*) And what—what are those French critters like?

BENNY. (*with a wink*) Oh, boy! They're some pippins! It ain't so much that they're better lookin' as that they've got a way with 'em— lots of ways. (*He laughs with a lascivious smirk.*)

EMMA. (*unconsciously hitches her chair nearer his. The turn the conversation has taken seems to have aroused a hectic, morbid intensity in her. She continually wets her lips and pushes back her hair from her flushed face as if it were stifling her*) What do you mean, Benny? What kind of ways have they got—them French girls?

BENNY. (*smirking mysteriously*) Oh, ways of dressin' and doin' their hair—and lots of ways.

EMMA. (*eagerly*) Tell me! Tell me all about 'em. You needn't be scared—to talk open with me. I ain't as strict as I seem—about hearin' things. Tell me! I've heard French girls was awful wicked.

BENNY. I don't know about wicked, but they're darned good sports. They'd do anything a guy'd ask 'em. Oui, tooty sweet! (*Laughs foolishly.*)

EMMA. And what—what'd you ask 'em, for instance?

526

BENNY. (*with a wink*) Curiosity killed a cat! Ask me no questions and I'll tell you no lies.

EMMA. (*with queer, stupid insistence*) But won't you tell me? Go on!

BENNY. Can't be did, Aunt Emmer, can't be did! (*With a silly laugh*) You're too young. No, all I'll say is, that to the boys who've knocked around over there the girls in town here are just rank amateurs. They don't know how to love and that's a fact. (*He gets to his feet*) And as for an old bum like Tilly—not me! Well, I guess I'll hike along—

EMMA. (*getting up and putting a hand on his arm—feverishly*) No, don't go. Not yet—not yet. No, don't go.

BENNY. (*stepping away with an expression of repulsion*) Why not? What's the matter with you, Aunt Emmer? You look 's if you was gettin' sick. (*Before she can reply,* HARRIET's *voice is heard calling.*)

HARRIET. Benny! Benny! (*This acts like a pail of cold water on* EMMA *who moves away from* BENNY *quickly.*)

EMMA. That's Harriet. It's your Ma calling, Benny.

BENNY. (*impatiently*) I know. That means Uncle Caleb has come and she's told him her stories and it's up to me to catch hell. (*Stopping* EMMA *as she goes toward the door as if to answer* HARRIET's *hail*) Don't answer, Aunt Emmer. Let her come over here to look. I want to speak to her and find out how I stand before he sees me.

EMMA. (*doubtfully*) I don't know as she'll come. She's been actin' funny to me lately, Harriet has, and she ain't put her foot in my door the last month.

BENNY. (*as his mother's voice is heard much nearer, calling "Benny!"*) There! Sure she's comin'.

EMMA. (*flustered*) Land sakes, I can't let her see me this way. I got to run upstairs and tidy myself a little. (*She starts for the door at right.*)

BENNY. (*flatteringly*) Aw, you look swell. Them new duds you got looks great.

527

EMMA. (*turning in the doorway—coquettishly*) Oh, them French girls ain't the only ones knows how to fix up. (*She flounces out.* BENNY *stands looking after her with a derisive grin of contempt. There is a sharp knock on the door in the rear.* BENNY *goes to open it, his expression turning surly and sullen.* HARRIET *enters. She wears an apron over her old-fashioned black dress with a brooch at the neck. Her hair is gray, her face thin, lined and careworn, with a fretful, continuously irritated expression. Her shoulders stoop, and her figure is flabby and ugly. She stares at her son with resentful annoyance.*)

HARRIET. Ain't you got sense enough, you big lump, to answer me when I call, and not have me shouting my lungs out?

BENNY. I never heard you callin'.

HARRIET. You're lyin' and you know it. (*Then severely*) Your uncle's to home. He's waitin' to talk to you.

BENNY. Let him wait. (*In a snarling tone*) I s'pose you've been givin' him an earful of lies about me?

HARRIET. I told him the truth, if that's what you mean. How you stole the money out of the bureau drawer—

BENNY. (*alarmed but pretending scorn*) Aw, you don't know it was me. You don't know nothin' about it.

HARRIET. (*ignoring this*) And about your disgracin' him and me with your drunken carryin's-on with that harlot, Tilly Small, night after night.

BENNY. Aw, wha'd you know about that?

HARRIET. And last but not least, the sneakin' way you're makin' a silly fool out of poor Emmer Crosby.

BENNY. (*with a grin*) You don't notice her kickin' about it, do you? (*Brusquely*) Why don't you mind your own business, Ma?

HARRIET. (*violently*) It's a shame, that's what it is! That I should live to see the day when a son of mine'd descend so low he'd tease an old woman to get money out of her, and her alone in the world. Oh, you're low, you're low all through like your Pa was—and since you

528

been in the army you got bold so you ain't even ashamed of your dirtiness no more!

BENNY. (*in a snarling whisper*) That's right! Blame it all on me. I s'pose she ain't got nothin' to do with it. (*With a wink*) You oughter see her perform sometimes. You'd get wise to something then.

HARRIET. Shut up! You've got the same filthy mind your Pa had. As for Emmer, I don't hold her responsible. She's been gettin' flighty the past two years. She couldn't help it, livin' alone the way she does, shut up in this house all her life. You ought to be 'shamed to take advantage of her condition—but shame ain't in you.

BENNY. Aw, give us a rest!

HARRIET. (*angrily*) Your Uncle Caleb'll give you a rest when he sees you! Him and me's agreed not to give you another single penny if you was to get down on your knees for it. So there! You can git along on your army pay from this out.

BENNY. (*worried by the finality in her tone—placatingly*) Aw, say, Ma, what's eatin' you? What've I done that's so bad? Gosh, you oughta know some of the gang I know in the army. You'd think I was a saint if you did. (*Trying a confidential tone*) Honest, Ma, this here thing with Aunt Emmer ain't my fault. How can I help it if she goes bugs in her old age and gets nutty about me? (*With a sly grin—in a whisper*) Gee, Ma, you oughta see her today. She's a scream, honest! She's upstairs now gettin' calmed down. She was gettin' crazy when your callin' stopped her. Wait till she comes down and you git a look! She'll put your eye out—all dolled up like a kid of sixteen and enough paint on her mush for a Buffalo Bill Indian—

HARRIET. (*staring at him with stern condemnation*) You're a worthless loafer, Benny Rogers, same as your Pa was.

BENNY. (*frustrated and furious*) Aw, g'wan with that bunk! (*He turns away from her.*)

HARRIET. And I'm goin' to tell Emma about you and try to put some sense back into her head.

BENNY. Go ahead. You'll get fat runnin' me down to her!

HARRIET. And if my word don't have no influence, I'll tell your Uncle Caleb everything, and get him to talk to her. She'll mind him.

BENNY. (*defiantly*) You just try it, that's all!

HARRIET. I've been scared to do more'n hint about it to him. I'm hopin' any day Emma'll come out of this foolishness, and he'll never know.

BENNY. Aw!

HARRIET. If shame was in you, you'd remember your Uncle Caleb's been in love with Emma all his life and waited for her year after year hopin' in the end she'd change her mind and marry him. And she will, too, I believe, if she comes out of this fit in her sane mind—which she won't if you keep fussin' with her.

BENNY. (*with revengeful triumph*) She'll never marry the old cuss—I'll fix that!

HARRIET. Now you're showin' yourself up for what you are! And I kin see it's come to the p'int where I got to tell your Uncle Caleb everythin' no matter how it breaks him up. I got to do it for Emmer's sake as well as his'n. We got to get her cured of your bad influence once and for all. It's the only hope for the two of 'em.

BENNY. You just try it!

HARRIET. And as for you, you get back to the army where you b'long! And don't never expect another cent from me or Caleb 'cause you won't get it! And don't never come to see us again till you've got rid of the meanness and filth that's the Rogers part of you and found the honesty and decency that's the Williams part—if you got any of me in you at all, which I begin to doubt. (*Goes to the door in rear*) And now I'm goin' back to Caleb—and you better not let him find you here when he comes less'n you want a good hidin' for once in your life. (*She goes out.*)

BENNY. (*stammering between fear and rage—shouting after her*) G'wan! Tell him! What the hell do I care? I'll fix him! I'll spill the beans for both of you, if you try to gum me! (*He stands in the middle of the room hesitating whether to run away or stay, concentrating his thoughts on finding some way to make good his bluff. Suddenly his face lights up with a cruel grin and he mutters to himself with savage satisfaction*) By God, that's it! I'll bet I kin work it, too! By God, that'll fix 'em! (*He chuckles and goes quickly to the door on right and calls up to the floor above*) Emmer! Emmer!

EMMA. (*her voice faintly heard answering*) Yes, Benny, I'm coming.

BENNY. (*he calls quickly*) Come down! Come down quick! (*He comes back to the center of the room where he stands waiting, planning his course of action.*)

EMMA. (*appears in the doorway. Her face is profusely powdered—with nervous excitement*) Benny! What's the matter? You sounded so— Why, where's your Ma?

BENNY. Gone. Gone back to home.

EMMA. (*offendedly*) Without waiting to see me? Why, I only sat down for a minute to give you a chance to talk to her. I was coming right down. Didn't she want to see me? Whatever's got into Harriet lately?

BENNY. She's mad as thunder at you 'cause I come over here so much 'stead of stayin' to home with her.

EMMA. (*pleased*) Oh, is that why? Well, if she ain't peculiar! (*She sits in a rocker by the table.*)

BENNY. (*with a great pretense of grief, taking one of her hands in his*) Say, Emmer—what I called you down for was—I want to say good-by and thank you for all you've done—

EMMA. (*frightenedly*) Good-by? How you say that! What—?

BENNY. Good-by for good this time.

EMMA. For good?

BENNY. Yep. I've got to beat it. I ain't got no home here no more. Ma and Uncle Caleb, they've chucked me out.

EMMA. Good gracious, what're you saying?

BENNY. That's what Ma come over to tell me—that Uncle Caleb'd said I'd never get another cent from him, alive or after he's dead, and she said for me to git back to the army and never come home again.

EMMA. (*gaspingly*) She was only joking. She—they couldn't mean it.

BENNY. If you'd heard her you wouldn't think she was joking.

EMMA. (*as he makes a movement as if to go away*) Benny! You can't go! Go, and me never see you again, maybe! You can't! I won't have it!

BENNY. I got to, Emmer. What else is there for me to do when they've throwed me out? I don't give a damn about leaving them—but I hate to leave you and never see you again.

EMMA. (*excitedly—grabbing his arm*) You can't! I won't let you go!

BENNY. I don't want to—but what can I do?

EMMA. You can stay here with me.

BENNY. (*his eyes gleaming with satisfaction*) No, I couldn't. You know this dump of a town. Folks would be sayin' all sorts of bad things in no time. I don't care for myself. They're all down on me anyway because I'm diff'rent from small-town boobs like them and they hate me for it.

EMMA. Yes, you are diff'rent. And I'll show 'em I'm diff'rent, too. You can stay with me—and let 'em gossip all they've a mind to!

BENNY. No, it wouldn't be actin' square with you. I got to go. And I'll try to save up my pay and send you back what I've borrowed now and again.

EMMA. (*more and more wrought up*) I won't hear of no such thing. Oh, I can't understand your Ma and your Uncle Caleb bein' so cruel!

BENNY. Folks have been lyin' to her about me, like I told you, and she's told him. He's only too glad to believe it, too, long as it's bad.

EMMA. I can talk to your Uncle Caleb. He's always minded me more'n her.

BENNY. (*hastily*) Don't do that, for God's sake! You'd only make it worse and get yourself in Dutch with him, too!

EMMA. (*bewilderedly*) But—I—don't see—

BENNY. (*roughly*) Well, he's still stuck on you, ain't he?

EMMA. (*with a flash of coquetry*) Now, Benny!

BENNY. I ain't kiddin'. This is dead serious. He's stuck on you and you know it.

EMMA. (*coyly*) I haven't given him the slightest reason to hope in thirty years.

BENNY. Well, he hopes just the same. Sure he does! Why Ma said when she was here just now she'd bet you and him'd be married some day yet.

EMMA. No such thing! Why, she must be crazy!

BENNY. Oh, she ain't so crazy. Ain't he spent every durn evenin' of the time he's to home between trips over here with you—for the last thirty years?

EMMA. When I broke my engagement I said I wanted to stay friends like we'd been before, and we always have; but every time he'd even hint at bein' engaged again I'd always tell him we was friends only and he'd better leave it be that way. There's never been nothing else between us. (*With a coy smile*) And besides, Benny, you know how little time he's had to home between viges.

BENNY. I kin remember the old cuss marchin' over here every evenin' he was to home since I was a kid.

EMMA. (*with a titter of delight*) D'you know, Benny, I do actually believe you're jealous!

BENNY. (*loudly—to lend conviction*) Sure I'm jealous! But that ain't the point just now. The point is *he's* jealous of me—and you can see what a swell chance you've got of talkin' him over now, can't you! You'd on'y make him madder.

EMMA. (*embarrassedly*) He's getting foolish. What cause has he got—

BENNY. When Ma tells him the lies about us—

EMMA. (*excitedly*) What lies?

BENNY. I ain't goin' to repeat 'em to you but you kin guess, can't you, me being so much over here?

EMMA. (*springing to her feet—shocked but pleased*) Oh!

533

BENNY. (*turning away from her*) And now I'm going to blow. I'll stay at Bill Grainger's tonight and get the morning train.

EMMA. (*grabbing his arm*) No such thing! You'li stay right here!

BENNY. I can't—Emmer. If you was really my aunt, things'd be diff'rent and I'd tell 'em all to go to hell.

EMMA. (*smiling at him coquettishly*) But I'm glad I ain't your aunt.

BENNY. Well, I mean if you was related to me in some way. (*At some noise he hears from without, he starts frightenedly*) Gosh, that sounded like our front door slamming. It's him and he's coming over. I got to beat it out the back way. (*He starts for the door on the right.*)

EMMA. (*clinging to him*) Benny! Don't go! You mustn't go!

BENNY. (*inspired by alarm and desire for revenge suddenly blurts out*) Say, let's me 'n' you git married, Emmer—tomorrow, eh? Then I kin stay! That'll stop 'em, damn 'em, and make 'em leave me alone.

EMMA. (*dazed with joy*) Married? You 'n' me? Oh, Benny, I'm too old. (*She hides her head on his shoulder.*)

BENNY. (*hurriedly, with one anxious eye on the door*) No, you ain't! Honest, you ain't! You're the best guy in this town! (*Shaking her in his anxiety*) Say yes, Emmer! Say you will—first thing tomorrow.

EMMA. (*choking with emotion*) Yes—I will—if I'm not too old for you.

BENNY. (*jubilantly*) Tell him. Then he'll see where he gets off! Listen! I'm goin' to beat it to the kitchen and wait. You come tell me when he's gone. (*A knock comes at the door. He whispers*) That's him. I'm goin'.

EMMA. (*embracing him fiercely*) Oh, Benny! (*She kisses him on the lips. He ducks away from her and disappears off right. The knock is repeated.* EMMA *dabs tremblingly at her cheeks with a handkerchief. Her face is beaming with happiness and looks indescribably silly. She trips lightly to the door and opens it—forcing a light, careless tone*) Oh, it's you, Caleb. Come right in and set. I was kind of expecting you. Benny—I'd heard you was due to home tonight. (*He comes in and shakes the hand she holds out to him in a limp, vague,*

534

absent-minded manner. In appearance, he has changed but little in the thirty years save that his hair is now nearly white and his face more deeply lined and wrinkled. His body is still erect, strong and vigorous. He wears dark clothes, much the same as he was dressed in Act One.)

CALEB. (*mechanically*) Hello, Emmer. (*Once inside the door, he stands staring about the room, frowning. The garish strangeness of everything evidently repels and puzzles him. His face wears its set expression of an emotionless mask but his eyes cannot conceal an inward struggle, a baffled and painful attempt to comprehend, a wounded look of bewildered hurt.*)

EMMA. (*blithely indifferent to this—pleasantly*) Are you looking at the changes I've made? You ain't seen this room since, have you? Of course not. What am I thinking of? They only got through with the work two weeks ago. Well, what d' you think of it?

CALEB. (*frowning—hesitatingly*) Why—it's—all right, I reckon.

EMMA. It was so gloomy and old-timey before, I just couldn't bear it. Now it's light and airy and young-looking, don't you think? (*With a sigh*) I suppose Pa and Ma turned over in their graves.

CALEB. (*grimly*) I reckon they did, too.

EMMA. Why, you don't mean to tell me you don't like it neither, Caleb? (*Then as he doesn't reply,—resentfully*) Well, you always was a sot, old-fashioned critter, Caleb Williams, same as they was. (*She plumps herself into a rocker by the table—then, noticing the lost way in which he is looking about him*) Gracious sakes, why don't you set, Caleb? You give me the fidgets standing that way! You ain't a stranger that's got to be invited, are you? (*Then suddenly realizing the cause of his discomfiture, she smiles pityingly, not without a trace of malice*) Are you looking for your old chair you used to set in? Is that it? Well, I had it put up in the attic. It didn't fit in with them new things.

CALEB. (*dully*) No, I s'pose it wouldn't.

EMMA. (*indicating a chair next to hers*) Do set down and make yourself to home. (*He does so gingerly. After a pause she asks per-functorily*) Did you have good luck this voyage?

CALEB. (*again dully*) Oh, purty fair. (*He begins to look at her as if he were seeing her for the first time, noting every detail with a numb, stunned astonishment.*)

EMMA. You're looking as well as ever.

CALEB. (*dully*) Oh, I ain't got nothin' to complain of.

EMMA. You're the same as me, I reckon. (*Happily*) Why I seem to get feelin' younger and more chipper every day, I declare I do. (*She becomes uncomfortably aware of his examination—nervously*) Land sakes, what you starin' at so?

CALEB. (*brusquely blurting out his disapproval*) You've changed, Emmer—changed so I wouldn't know you, hardly.

EMMA. (*resentfully*) Well, I hope you think it's for the best.

CALEB. (*evasively*) I ain't enough used to it yet—to tell.

EMMA. (*offended*) I ain't old-timey and old-maidy like I was, I guess that's what you mean. Well, I just got tired of mopin' alone in this house, waiting for death to take me and not enjoyin' anything. I was gettin' old before my time. And all at once, I saw what was happenin' and I made up my mind I was going to get some fun out of what Pa'd left me while I was still in the prime of life, as you might say.

CALEB. (*severely*) Be that paint and powder you got on your face, Emmer?

EMMA. (*embarrassed by this direct question*) Why, yes—I got a little mite—it's awful good for your complexion, they say—and in the cities now all the women wears it.

CALEB. (*sternly*) The kind of women I've seed in cities wearin' it— (*He checks himself and asks abruptly*) Wa'n't your hair turnin' gray last time I was to home?

EMMA. (*flustered*) Yes—yes—so it was—but then it started to come in again black as black all of a sudden.

536

CALEB. (*glancing at her shoes, stockings, and dress*) You're got up in them things like a young girl goin' to a dance.

EMMA. (*forcing a defiant laugh*) Maybe I will go soon's I learn—and Benny's goin' to teach me.

CALEB. (*keeping his rage in control—heavily*) Benny—

EMMA. (*suddenly bursting into hysterical tears*) And I think it's real mean of you, Caleb—nasty mean to come here on your first night to home—and—make—fun—of—my—clothes—and everything. (*She hides her face in her hands and sobs.*)

CALEB. (*overcome by remorse—forgetting his rage instantly—gets up and pats her on the shoulder—with rough tenderness*) Thar, thar, Emmer! Don't cry, now! I didn' mean nothin'. Don't pay no 'tention to what I said. I'm a durned old fool! What the hell do I know o' women's fixin's anyhow? And I reckon I be old-fashioned and sot in my ideas.

EMMA. (*reassured—pressing one of his hands gratefully*) It hurts—hearing you say—me 'n' you such old friends and—

CALEB. Forgit it, Emmer. I won't say no more about it. (*She dries her eyes and regains her composure. He goes back to his seat, his face greatly softened, looking at her with the blind eyes of love. There is a pause. Finally, he ventures in a gentle tone*) D'you know what time this be, Emmer?

EMMA. (*puzzled*) I don't know exactly, but there's a clock in the next room.

CALEB. (*quickly*) Hell, I don't mean that kind o' time. I mean—it was thirty years ago this spring.

EMMA. (*hastily*) Land sakes, don't let's talk of that. It only gets me thinking how old I am.

CALEB. (*with an affectionate smile*) We both got to realize now and then that we're gettin' old.

EMMA. (*bridling*) That's all right for you to say. You're twelve years older 'n me, don't forget, Caleb.

CALEB. (*smiling*) Waal, even that don't make you out no spring chicken, Emmer.

EMMA. (*stiffly*) A body's as old as they feels—and I feel right young.

CALEB. Waal, so do I as far as health goes. I'm as able and sound as ever. (*After a pause*) But, what I meant was, d'you remember what happened thirty years back?

EMMA. I suppose I do.

CALEB. D'you remember what I said that day?

EMMA. (*primly*) You said a lot that it's better to forget, if you ask me.

CALEB. I don't mean—that part of it. I mean when I was sayin' good-by, I said— (*He gasps—then blurts it out*) I said I'd wait thirty years—if need be. (*After a pause*) I know you told me time and again not to go back to that. On'y—I was thinkin' all this last vige—that maybe—now when the thirty years are past—I was thinkin' that maybe— (*He looks at her humbly, imploring some encouragement. She stares straight before her, her mouth set thinly. He sighs forlornly and blunders on*) Thirty years—that's a hell of a long time to wait, Emmer—makin' vige after vige always alone—and feelin' even more alone in between times when I was to home livin' right next door to you and callin' on you every evenin'. (*A pause*) I've made money enough, I know—but what the hell good's that to me—long as you're out of it? (*A pause*) Seems to me, Emmer, thirty o' the best years of a man's life ought to be proof enough to you to make you forget—that one slip o' mine.

EMMA. (*rousing herself—forcing a careless tone*) Land sakes, I forgot all about that long ago. And here you go remindin' me of it!

CALEB. (*doggedly*) You ain't answered what I was drivin' at, Emmer. (*A pause; then, as if suddenly afraid of what her answer will be, he breaks out quickly*) And I don't want you to answer right now, neither. I want you to take time to think it all over.

EMMA. (*feebly evasive*) All right, Caleb, I'll think it over.

CALEB. (*after a pause*) Somehow—seems to me 's if—you might really *need* me now. You never did before.

EMMA. (*suspiciously*) Why should I need you now any more'n any other time?

CALEB. (*embarrassedly*) Oh, I just feel that way.

EMMA. It ain't count o' nothin' Harriet's been tellin' you, is it? (*Stiffly*) Her 'n' me ain't such good friends no more, if you must know.

CALEB. (*frowning*) Her 'n' me nearly had a fight right before I came over here. (EMMA *starts*) Harriet lets her tongue run away with her and says dumb fool things she don't really mean. I didn't pay much 'tention to what she was sayin'—but it riled me jest the same. She won't repeat such foolishness after the piece o' my mind I gave her.

EMMA. What did she say?

CALEB. Oh, nothin' worth tellin'. (*A pause*) But neither you nor me ought to get mad at Harriet serious. We'd ought, by all rights, to make allowances for her. You know 's well as me what a hard time she's had. Bein' married to Alf Rogers for five years'd pizin' any woman's life.

EMMA. No, he wasn't much good, there's no denyin'.

CALEB. And now there's Benny drivin' her crazy.

EMMA. (*instantly defensive*) Benny's all right!

CALEB. (*staring at her sharply—after a pause*) No, that's jest it. He ain't all right, Emmer.

EMMA. He is, too! He's as good as gold!

CALEB. (*frowning—with a trace of resentment*) You kin say so, Emmer, but the facts won't bear you out.

EMMA. (*excitedly*) What facts, Caleb Williams? If you mean the nasty lies the folks in this town are mean enough to gossip about him, I don't believe any of 'em. I ain't such a fool.

CALEB. (*bitterly*) Then you've changed, Emmer. You didn't stop about believin' the fool stories they gossiped about me that time.

539

EMMA. You owned up yourself that was true!

CALEB. And Benny'd own up if he was half the man I was! (*Angrily;*) But he ain't a man noways. He's a mean skunk from truck to keelson!

EMMA. (*springing to her feet*) Oh!

CALEB. (*vehemently*) I ain't judged him by what folks have told me. But I've watched him grow up from a boy and every time I've come to home I've seed he was gittin' more 'n' more like his Pa—and you know what a low dog Alf Rogers turned out to be, and what a hell he made for Harriet. Waal, I'm sayin' this boy Benny is just Alf all over again—on'y worse!

EMMA. Oh!

CALEB. They ain't no Williams' blood left in Benny. He's a mongrel Rogers! (*Trying to calm himself a little and be convincing*) Listen, Emmer. You don't suppose I'd be sayin' it, do you, if it wasn't so? Ain't he Harriet's boy? Ain't I brought him up in my own house since he was knee-high? Don't you know I got some feelin's 'bout it and I wouldn't hold nothing agen him less'n I knowed it was true?

EMMA. (*harshly*) Yes, you would! You're only too anxious to believe all the bad you can about him. You've always hated him, he says—and I can see it's so.

CALEB. (*roughly*) You know damned well it ain't, you mean! Ain't I talked him over with you and asked your advice about him whenever I come to home? Ain't I always aimed to do all I could to help him git on right? You know damned well I never hated him! It's him that's always hated me! (*Vengefully*) But I'm beginning to hate him now— and I've good cause for it!

EMMA. (*frightenedly*) What cause?

CALEB. (*ignoring her question*) I seed what he was comin' to years back. Then I thought when the war come, and he was drafted into it, that the army and strict discipline'd maybe make a man o' him. But it ain't! It's made him worse! It's killed whatever mite of decency was left in him. And I reckon now that if you put a coward in one of them there uniforms, he thinks it gives him the privilege to be a bully! Put a sneak in one and it gives him the courage to be a thief! That's why when the war was over Benny enlisted again 'stead o' goin' whalin' with me. He thinks he's found a good shield to cover up his natural-born laziness—and crookedness!

EMMA. (*outraged*) You can talk that way about him that went way over to France to shed his blood for you and me!

CALEB. I don't need no one to do my fightin' for me—against German or devil. And you know durned well he was only in the Quartermaster's Department unloadin' and truckin' groceries, as safe from a gun as you and me be this minute. (*With heavy scorn*) If he shed any blood, he must have got a nose bleed.

EMMA. Oh, you do hate him, I can see it! And you're just as mean as mean, Caleb Williams! All you've said is a wicked lie and you've got no cause—

CALEB. I ain't, eh? I got damned good cause, I tell ye! I ain't minded his meanness to me. I ain't even give as much heed to his meanness to Harriet as I'd ought to have, maybe. But when he starts in his sneakin' thievery with you, Emmer, I put my foot down on him for good and all!

EMMA. What sneakin' thievery with me? How dare you say such things?

CALEB. I got proof it's true. Why, he's even bragged all over town about bein' able to borrow all the money from you he'd a mind to—boastin' of what an old fool he was makin' of you, with you fixin' up your house all new to git him to comin' over.

EMMA. (*scarlet—blazing*) It's a lie! He never said it! You're makin' it all up—'cause you're—'cause you're—

CALEB. 'Cause I'm what, Emmer?

EMMA. (*flinging it at him like a savage taunt*) 'Cause you're jealous of him, that's what! Any fool can see that!

CALEB. (*getting to his feet and facing her—slowly*) Jealous? Of Benny? How—I don't see your meanin' rightly.

541

EMMA. (*with triumphant malice*) Yes, you do! Don't pretend you don't! You're jealous 'cause you know I care a lot about him.

CALEB. (*slowly*) Why would I be jealous 'count o' that? What kind o' man d'you take me for? Don't I know you must care for him when you've been a'most as much a mother to him for years as Harriet was?

EMMA. (*wounded to the quick—furiously*) No such thing! You're a mean liar! I ain't never played a mother to him. He's never looked at me that way—never! And I don't care for him that way at all. Just because I'm a mite older 'n him—can't them things happen just as well as any other—what d'you suppose—can't I care for him same as any woman cares for a man? And I do! I care more'n I ever did for you! And that's why you're lying about him! You're jealous of that!

CALEB. (*staring at her with stunned eyes—in a hoarse whisper*) Emmer! Ye don't know what you're sayin', do ye?

EMMA. I do too!

CALEB. Harriet said you'd been actin' out o' your right senses.

EMMA. Harriet's mad because she knows Benny loves me better 'n her. And he does love me! He don't mind my bein' older. He's said so! And I love him, too!

CALEB. (*stepping back from her in horror*) Emmer!

EMMA. And he's asked me to marry him tomorrow. And I'm going to! Then you can all lie all you've a mind to!

CALEB. You're—going to—marry Benny?

EMMA. First thing tomorrow. And since you've throwed him out of his house in your mad jealousness, I've told him he can stay here with me tonight. And he's going to!

CALEB. (*his fists clenching—tensely*) Where—where is the skunk now?

EMMA. (*hastily*) Oh, he ain't here. He's gone up street.

CALEB. (*starting for the door in rear*) I'm goin' to find the skunk.

EMMA. (*seizing his arms—frightenedly*) What're you going to do?

CALEB. (*between his clenched teeth*) I don't know, Emmer—I don't know— On'y he ain't goin' to marry you, by God!

542

EMMA. Caleb! (*She tries to throw her arms about him to stop his going. He pushes her firmly but gently aside. She shrieks*) Caleb! (*She flings herself on her knees and wraps her arms around his legs in supplicating terror*) Caleb! You ain't going to kill him, Caleb? You ain't going to hurt him, be you? Say you ain't! Tell me you won't hurt him! (*As she thinks she sees a relenting softness come into his face as he looks down at her*) Oh, Caleb, you used to say you loved me! Don't hurt him then, Caleb,—for my sake! I love him, Caleb! Don't hurt him—just because you think I'm an old woman ain't no reason—and I won't marry you, Caleb. I won't—not even if you have waited thirty years. I don't love you. I love him! And I'm going to marry him—tomorrow. So you won't hurt him, will you, Caleb— not when I ask you on my knees!

CALEB. (*breaking away from her with a shudder of disgust*) No, I won't touch him. If I was wantin' to git even with ye, I wouldn't dirty my hands on him. I'd let you marry the skunk and set and watch what happened—or else I'd offer him money not to marry ye—more money than the little mite you kin bring him—and let ye see how quick he'd turn his back on ye!

EMMA. (*getting to her feet—frenziedly*) It's a lie! He never would!

CALEB. (*unheeding—with a sudden ominous calm*) But I ain't goin' to do neither. You ain't worth it—and he ain't—and no one ain't, nor nothin'. Folks be all crazy and rotten to the core and I'm done with the whole kit and caboodle of 'em. I kin only see one course out for me and I'm goin' to take it. "A dead whale or a stove boat!" we says in whalin'—and my boat is stove! (*He strides away from her, stops, and turns back—savagely*) Thirty o' the best years of my life flung for a yeller dog like him to feed on. God! You used to say you was diff'rent from the rest o' folks. By God, if you are, it's just you're a mite madder'n they be! By God, that's all! (*He goes, letting the door slam to behind him.*)

EMMA. (*in a pitiful whimper*) Caleb! (*She sinks into a chair by the table sobbing hysterically. Benny sneaks through the door on right, hesitates for a while, afraid that his uncle may be coming back*.)

BENNY. (*finally, in a shrill whisper*) Aunt Emmer!

EMMA. (*raising her face to look at him for a second*) Oh, Benny! (*She falls to weeping again*.)

BENNY. Say, you don't think he's liable to come back, do you?

EMMA. No—he'll—never come back here—no more. (*Sobs bitterly*.)

BENNY. (*his courage returning, comes forward into the room*) Say, he's way up in the air, ain't he? (*With a grin*) Say, that was some bawlin' out he give you!

EMMA. You—you heard what he said?

BENNY. Sure thing. When you got to shoutin' I sneaked out o' the kitchen into there to hear what was goin' on. (*With a complacent grin*) Say, you certainly stood up for me all right. You're a good old scout at that, d'you know it?

EMMA. (*raising her absurd, besmeared face to his, as if expecting him to kiss her*) Oh, Benny, I'm giving up everything I've held dear all my life for your sake.

BENNY. (*turning away from her with a look of aversion*) Well, what about it? Ain't I worth it? Ain't I worth a million played-out old cranks like him? (*She stares at him bewilderedly. He takes a handful of almonds from his pocket and begins cracking and eating them, throwing the shells on the floor with an impudent carelessness*) Hope you don't mind my havin' a feed? I found them out in the kitchen and helped myself.

EMMA. (*pitifully*) You're welcome to anything that's here, Benny.

BENNY. (*insolently*) Sure, I know you're a good scout. Don't rub it in. (*After a pause—boastfully*) Where did you get that stuff about askin' him not to hurt me? He'd have a swell chance! There's a lot of hard guys in the army have tried to get funny with me till I put one over on 'em. I'd like to see him start something! I could lick him with my hands handcuffed.

EMMA. (*revolted*) Oh!

544

BENNY. (*resentfully*) Think I'm bluffin'? I'll show you sometime. (*He swaggers about the room—finally stopping beside her. With a cunning leer*) Say, I been thinkin' it over and I guess I'll call his bluff.

EMMA. (*confusedly*) What—do you mean?

BENNY. I mean what he said just before he beat it—that he could get me not to marry you if he offered me more coin than you got. (*Very interestedly*) Say, d'you s'pose the old miser really was serious about that?

EMMA. (*dazedly—as if she could not realize the significance of his words*) I—I—don't know, Benny.

BENNY. (*swaggering about again*) If I was only sure he wasn't stallin'! If I could get the old cuss to shell out that way! (*With a tickled chuckle*) Gosh, that'd be the real stunt aw right, aw right. Oui, oui! Maybe he wasn't kiddin' at that, the old simp! It's worth takin' a stab at, damned if it ain't. I ain't got nothin' to lose.

EMMA. (*frightenedly*) What—what're you talkin' about, Benny?

BENNY. Say, I think I'll go over and talk to Ma after a while. You can go over first to make sure he ain't there. I'll get her to put it up to him straight. If he's willin' to dig in his jeans for some real coin—real dough, this time!—I'll agree to beat it and not spill the beans for him with you. (*Threateningly*) And if he's too tight, I'll go right through with what I said I would, if only to spite him! That's me!

EMMA. You mean—if he's willing to bribe you with money, you won't marry me tomorrow?

BENNY. Sure! If he'll put up enough money. I won't stand for no pikin'.

EMMA. (*whimpering*) Oh, Benny, you're only jokin', ain't you? You can't—you can't mean it!

BENNY. (*with careless effrontery*) Why can't I? Sure I mean it!

EMMA. (*hiding her face in her hands—with a tortured moan*) Oh, Benny!

BENNY. (*disgustedly*) Aw, don't go bawlin'! (*After a pause—a bit

545

embarrassedly) Aw, say, what d'you think, anyway? What're you takin' it so damned serious for—me askin' you to marry me, I mean? I was on'y sort of kiddin' anyway—just so you'd tell him and get his goat right. (*As she looks up at him with agonized despair. With a trace of something like pity showing in his tone*) Say, honest, Aunt Emmer, you didn't believe—you didn't think I was really stuck on you, did you? Ah, say, how could I? Have a heart! Why, you're as old as Ma is, ain't you, Aunt Emmer? (*He adds ruthlessly*) And I'll say you look it, too!

EMMA. (*cowering—as if he had struck her*) Oh! Oh!

BENNY. (*a bit irritated*) What's the use of blubberin', for God's sake? Can't you take it like a sport? Hell, I ain't lookin' to marry no one, if I can help it. What do I want a wife for? There's too many others. (*After a pause—as she still sobs—calculatingly*) Aw, come on, be a sport—and say, listen, if he ain't willin' to come across, I'll marry you all right, honest I will. (*More and more calculatingly*) Sure! If they mean that stuff about kickin' me out of home—sure I'll stay here with you! I'll do anything you want. If you want me to marry you, all you've got to do is say so—anytime! Only not tomorrow, we'd better wait and see—

EMMA. (*hysterically*) Oh, go away! Go away!

BENNY. (*looking down at her disgustedly*) Aw, come up for air, can't you? (*He slaps her on the back*) Buck up! Be a pal! Tell me what your dope is. This thing's got me so balled up I don't know how I stand. (*With sudden fury*) Damn his hide! I'll bet he'll go and leave all he's got to some lousy orphan asylum now.

EMMA. Oh, go away! Go away!

BENNY. (*viciously*) So you're givin' me the gate, too, eh? I'd like to see you try it! You asked me to stay and I'll stick. It's all your fool fault that's got me in wrong. And now you want to shake me! This is what I get for foolin' around with an old hen like you that oughta been planted in the cemetery long ago! Paintin' your old mush and dressin' like a kid! Christ A'mighty!

546

EMMA. (*in a cry of despair*) Don't! Stop! Go away.

BENNY. (*suddenly alert—sharply*) Sh! I hear someone coming. (*Shaking her*) Stop—now, Emmer! Damn it, you gotta go to the door. Maybe it's him. (*He scurries into the room on right. There is a faint knock at the door.* EMMA *lifts her head. She looks horribly old and worn out. Her face is frozen into an expressionless mask, her eyes are red-rimmed, dull and lifeless. The knock is repeated more sharply.* EMMA *rises like a weary automaton and goes to the door and opens it.* HARRIET *is revealed standing outside.*)

HARRIET. (*making no movement to come in—coldly*) I want to speak to Caleb.

EMMA. (*dully*) He ain't here. He left a while back—said he was goin' up street—I think.

HARRIET. (*worriedly*) Oh, land sakes! (*Then hostilely*) Do you know where Benny is?

EMMA. (*dully*) Yes, he's here.

HARRIET. (*contemptuously*) I might have guessed that! (*Icily formal*) Would you mind tellin' him I want to see him?

EMMA. (*turns and calls*) Benny! Here's your Ma!

BENNY. (*comes from the next room*) Aw right. (*In a fierce whisper as he passes* EMMA) What d'you tell her I was here for, you old fool?

EMMA. (*gives no sign of having heard him but comes back to her chair and sits down.* BENNY *slouches to the door—sullenly*) What d'you want, Ma?

HARRIET. (*coldly*) I wanted your Uncle Caleb, not you, but you'll have to do, bein' the only man about.

BENNY. (*suspiciously*) What is it?

HARRIET. (*a bit frightenedly*) I just heard a lot of queer noises down to the barn. Someone's in there, Benny, sure as I'm alive. They're stealin' the chickens, must be.

BENNY. (*carelessly*) It's only the rats.

HARRIET. (*angrily*) Don't play the idiot! This was a big thumpin' noise no rat'd make.

BENNY. What'd any guy go stealin' this earlv— (*As* HARRIET *turns away angrily—placatingly*) Aw right, I'm coming. I'll have a look if that'll satisfy you. Don't go gettin' sore at me again. (*While he is speaking he goes out and disappears after his mother.* EMMA *sits straight and stiff in her chair for a while, staring before her with waxy eyes. Then she gets to her feet and goes from window to window taking down all the curtains with quick mechanical movements. She throws them on a pile in the middle of the floor. She lifts down the framed pictures from the walls and piles them on the curtains. She takes the cushions and throws them on; pushes the rugs to the pile with her feet; sweeps everything off the table onto the floor. She does all this without a trace of change in her expression—rapidly, but with no apparent effort. There is the noise of running footsteps from outside and* BENNY *bursts into the room panting for breath. He is terribly excited and badly frightened.*)

BENNY. (*stops short as he sees the pile on the floor*) What the hell—

EMMA. (*dully*) The junk man's coming for them in the morning.

BENNY. (*too excited to be surprised*) To hell with that! Say, listen, Aunt Emmer, he's hung himself—Uncle Caleb—in the barn—he's dead!

EMMA. (*slowly letting the words fall—like a beginner on the typewriter touching two new letters*) Caleb—dead!

BENNY. (*voluble now*) Dead as a door nail! Neck's busted. I just cut him down and carried him to home. Say, you've got to come over and help look after Ma. She's goin' bugs. I can't do nothin' with her.

EMMA. (*as before*) Caleb hanged himself—in the barn?

BENNY. Yes—and made a sure job of it. (*With morbid interest in the details*) He got a halter and made a noose of the rope for his neck and climbed up in the loft and hitched the leather end to a beam and then let himself drop. He must have kicked in that quick! (*He snaps his fingers—then urgently*) Say, come on. Come on over 'n' help me with Ma, can't you? She's goin' wild. I can't do nothin'!

EMMA. (*vaguely*) I'll be over—in a minute. (*Then with a sudden air of having decided something irrevocably*) I got to go down to the barn.

BENNY. Barn? Say, are you crazy? He ain't there now. I told you I carried him home.

EMMA. I mean—my barn. I got to go down—

BENNY. (*exasperated*) Oh hell! You're as bad as Ma! Everyone's lost their heads but me. Well, I got to get someone else, that's all. (*He rushes out rear, slamming the door behind him.*)

EMMA. (*after a tense pause—with a sudden outburst of wild grief*) Caleb! (*Then in a strange whisper*) Wait, Caleb, I'm going down to the barn. (*She moves like a sleepwalker toward the door in the rear as the curtain falls.*)

THE FIRST MAN

A Play in Four Acts

CHARACTERS

CURTIS JAYSON
MARTHA, *his wife*
JOHN JAYSON, *his father, a banker*
JOHN, JR., *his brother*
RICHARD, *his brother*
ESTHER (MRS. MARK SHEFFIELD), *his sister*
LILY, *his sister*
MRS. DAVIDSON, *his father's aunt*
MARK SHEFFIELD, *a lawyer*
EMILY, JOHN JR.'s *wife*
EDWARD BIGELOW
A MAID
A TRAINED NURSE

SCENES

ACT ONE

Living-room in the house of CURTIS JAYSON, Bridgetown, Conn.—an afternoon in early Fall.

ACT TWO

CURTIS' study—morning of the following day.

ACT THREE

The same—three o'clock in the morning of a day in early spring of the next year.

ACT FOUR

Same as Act One—three days later.

THE FIRST MAN

ACT ONE

S CENE—*Living-room of* CURTIS JAYSON'S *house in Bridgetown, Conn. A large, comfortable room. On the left, an armchair, a big open fireplace, a writing desk with chair in far left corner. On this side there is also a door leading into* CURTIS' *study. In the rear, center, a double doorway opening on the hall and the entryway. Bookcases are built into the wall on both sides of this doorway. In the far right corner, a grand piano. Three large windows looking out on the lawn, and another armchair, front, are on this right side of the room. Opposite the fireplace is a couch, facing front. Opposite the windows on the right is a long table with magazines, reading lamp, etc. Four chairs are grouped about the table. The walls and ceiling are in a French gray color. A great rug covers most of the hardwood floor.*

As the curtain rises, MARTHA, CURTIS *and* BIGELOW *are discovered.* MARTHA *is a healthy, fine-looking woman of thirty-eight. She does not appear this age for her strenuous life in the open has kept her young and fresh. She possesses the frank, clear, direct quality of out-doors, outspoken and generous. Her wavy hair is a dark brown, her eyes blue-gray.* CURTIS JAYSON *is a tall, rangy, broad-shouldered man of thirty-seven. Though spare, his figure has an appearance of rugged health, of great nervous strength held in reserve. His square-jawed, large-featured face retains an eager boyish enthusiasm in spite of its prevailing expression of thoughtful, preoccupied aloofness. His crisp dark hair is graying at the temples.* EDWARD BIGELOW *is a large, handsome man of thirty-nine. His face shows culture and tolerance, a sense of humor, a lazy unambitious contentment.* CURTIS *is reading an article in some scientific periodical, seated by the table.* MARTHA *and* BIGELOW *are sitting nearby, laughing and chatting.*

BIGELOW. (*is talking with a comically worried but earnest air*) Do you know, I'm getting so I'm actually afraid to leave them alone with that governess. She's too romantic. I'll wager she's got a whole book full of ghost stories, superstitions, and yellow-journal horrors up her sleeve.

MARTHA. Oh, pooh! Don't go milling around for trouble. When I was a kid I used to get fun out of my horrors.

BIGELOW. But I imagine you were more courageous than most of us.

MARTHA. Why?

BIGELOW. Well, Nevada—the Far West at that time—I should think a child would have grown so accustomed to violent scenes—

MARTHA. (*smiling*) Oh, in the mining camps; but you don't suppose my father lugged me along on his prospecting trips, do you? Why, I never saw any rough scenes until I'd finished with school and went to live with father in Goldfield.

BIGELOW. (*smiling*) And then you met Curt.

MARTHA. Yes—but I didn't mean he was a rough scene. He was very mild even in those days. Do tell me what he was like at Cornell.

BIGELOW. A romanticist—and he still is!

MARTHA. (*pointing at* CURTIS *with gay mischief*) What! That sedate man! Never!

CURTIS. (*looking up and smiling at them both affectionately—lazily*) Don't mind him, Martha. He always was crazy.

BIGELOW. (*to* CURT—*accusingly*) Why did you elect to take up mining engineering at Cornell instead of a classical degree at the Yale of your fathers and brothers? Because you had been reading Bret Harte in prep school and mistaken him for a modern realist. You devoted four years to grooming yourself for another outcast of Poker Flat. (MARTHA *laughs.*)

CURTIS. (*grinning*) It was you who were hypnotized by Harte—so

554

much so that his West of the past is still your blinded New England-movie idea of the West at present. But go on. What next?

BIGELOW. Next? You get a job as engineer in that Goldfield mine—but you are soon disillusioned by a laborious life where six-shooters are as rare as nuggets. You try prospecting. You find nothing but different varieties of pebbles. But it is necessary to your nature to project romance into these stones, so you go in strong for geology. As a geologist, you become a slave to the Romance of the Rocks. It is but a step from that to anthropology—the last romance of all. There you find yourself—because there is no further to go. You win fame as the most proficient of young skull-hunters—and wander over the face of the globe, digging up bones like an old dog.

CURTIS. (*with a laugh*) The man is mad, Martha.

BIGELOW. Mad! What an accusation to come from one who is even now considering setting forth on a five-year excavating contest in search of the remains of our gibbering ancestor, the First Man!

CURTIS. (*with sudden seriousness*) I'm not considering it any longer. I've decided to go.

MARTHA. (*starting—the hurt showing in her voice*) When did you decide?

CURTIS. I only really came to a decision this morning. (*With a seriousness that forces* BIGELOW's *interested attention*) It's a case of got to go. It's a tremendous opportunity that it would be a crime for me to neglect.

BIGELOW. And a big honor, too, isn't it, to be picked as a member of such a large affair?

CURTIS. (*with a smile*) I guess it's just that they want all the men with considerable practical experience they can get. There are bound to be hardships and they know I'm hardened to them. (*Turning to his wife with an affectionate smile*) We haven't roughed it in the queer corners for the last ten years without knowing how it's done, have we, Martha?

MARTHA. (*dully*) No, Curt.

CURTIS. (*with an earnest enthusiasm*) And this expedition *is* what you call a large affair, Big. It's the largest thing of its kind ever undertaken. The possibilities, from the standpoint of anthropology, are limitless.

BIGELOW. (*with a grin*) Aha! Now we come to the Missing Link.

CURTIS. (*frowning*) Darn your Barnum and Bailey circus lingo, Big. This isn't a thing to mock at. I should think the origin of man would be something that would appeal even to your hothouse imagination. Modern science believes—knows—that Asia was the first home of the human race. That's where we're going, to the great Central Asian plateau north of the Himalayas.

BIGELOW. (*more soberly*) And there you hope to dig up—our first ancestor?

CURTIS. It's a chance in a million, but I believe we may, myself—at least find authentic traces of him so that we can reconstruct his life and habits. I was up in that country a lot while I was mining advisor to the Chinese government—did some of my own work on the side. The extraordinary results I obtained with the little means at my disposal convinced me of the riches yet to be uncovered. The First Man may be among them.

BIGELOW. (*turning to* MARTHA) And you were with him on that Asian plateau?

MARTHA. Yes, I've always been with him.

CURTIS. You bet she has. (*He goes over and puts his hand on his wife's shoulder affectionately*) Martha's more efficient than a whole staff of assistants and secretaries. She knows more about what I'm doing than I do half the time. (*He turns toward his study*) Well, I guess I'll go in and work some.

MARTHA. (*quietly*) Do you need me now, Curt?

BIGELOW. (*starting up*) Yes, if you two want to work together, why just shoo me—

CURTIS. (*puts both hands on his shoulders and forces him to his seat again*) No. Sit down, Big. I don't need Martha now. (*Coming over to her, bends down and kisses her—rather mockingly*) I couldn't deprive Big of an audience for his confessions of a fond parent.

BIGELOW. Aha! Now it's you who are mocking at something you know nothing about. (*An awkward silence follows this remark.*)

CURTIS. (*frowning*) I guess you're forgetting, aren't you, Big? (*He turns and walks into his study, closing the door gently behind him.*)

MARTHA. (*after a pause—sadly*) Poor Curt.

BIGELOW. (*ashamed and confused*) I had forgotten—

MARTHA. The years have made me reconciled. They haven't Curt. (*She sighs—then turns to* BIGELOW *with a forced smile*) I suppose it's hard for any of you back here to realize that Curt and I ever had any children.

BIGELOW. (*after a pause*) How old were they when—?

MARTHA. Three years and two—both girls. (*She goes on sadly*) We had a nice little house in Goldfield. (*Forcing a smile*) We were very respectable home folks then. The wandering came later, after— It was a Sunday in winter when Curt and I had gone visiting some friends. The nurse girl fell asleep—or something—and the children sneaked out in their underclothes and played in the snow. Pneumonia set in—and a week later they were both dead.

BIGELOW. (*shocked*) Good heavens!

MARTHA. We were real lunatics for a time. And then when we'd calmed down enough to realize—how things stood with us—we swore we'd never have children again—to steal away their memory. It wasn't what you thought—romanticism—that set Curt wandering —and me with him. It was a longing to lose ourselves—to forget. He flung himself with all his power into every new study that interested him. He couldn't keep still, mentally or bodily—and I followed. He needed me—then—so dreadfully!

BIGELOW. And is it that keeps driving him on now?

MARTHA. Oh, no. He's found himself. His work has taken the place of the children.

BIGELOW. And with you, too?

MARTHA. (*with a wan smile*) Well, I've helped—all I could. His work has me in it, I like to think—and I have him.

BIGELOW. (*shaking his head*) I think people are foolish to stand by such an oath as you took—forever. (*With a smile*) Children are a great comfort in one's old age, I've tritely found.

MARTHA. (*smiling*) Old age!

BIGELOW. I'm knocking at the door of fatal forty.

MARTHA. (*with forced gayety*) You're not very tactful, I must say. Don't you know I'm thirty-eight?

BIGELOW. (*gallantly*) A woman is as old as she looks. You're not thirty yet.

MARTHA. (*laughing*) After that nice remark I'll have to forgive you everything, won't I? (LILY JAYSON *comes in from the rear. She is a slender, rather pretty girl of twenty-five. The stamp of college student is still very much about her. She rather insists on a superior, intellectual air, is full of nervous, thwarted energy. At the sight of them sitting on the couch together, her eyebrows are raised.*)

LILY. (*coming into the room—breezily*) Hello, Martha. Hello, Big. (*They both get up with answering "Hellos"*) I walked right in regardless. Hope I'm not interrupting.

MARTHA. Not at all.

LILY. (*sitting down by the table as* MARTHA *and* BIGELOW *resume their seats on the lounge*) I must say it sounded serious. I heard you tell Big you'd forgive him everything, Martha. (*Dryly—with a mocking glance at* BIGELOW) You're letting yourself in for a large proposition.

BIGELOW. (*displeased but trying to smile it off*) The past is never past for a dog with a bad name, eh, Lily? (LILY *laughs.* BIGELOW *gets up*) If you want to reward me for my truthfulness, Mrs. Jayson, help me take the kids for an airing in the car. I know it's an imposition but they've grown to expect you. (*Glancing at his watch*) By Jove, I'll have to run along. I'll get them and then pick you up here. Is that all right?

MARTHA. Fine.

BIGELOW. I'll run, then. Good-by, Lily. (*She nods.* BIGELOW *goes out rear.*)

MARTHA. (*cordially*) Come on over here, Lily.

LILY. (*sits on couch with* MARTHA—*after a pause—with a smile*) You were forgetting, weren't you?

MARTHA. What?

LILY. That you'd invited all the family over here to tea this afternoon. I'm the advance guard.

MARTHA. (*embarrassed*) So I was! How stupid!

LILY. (*with an inquisitive glance at* MARTHA'S *face but with studied carelessness*) Do you like Bigelow?

MARTHA. Yes, very much. And Curt thinks the world of him.

LILY. Oh, Curt is the last one to be bothered by anyone's morals. Curt and I are the unconventional ones of the family. The trouble with Bigelow, Martha, is that he was too careless to conceal his sins— and that won't go down in this Philistine small town. You have to hide and be a fellow hypocrite or they revenge themselves on you. Bigelow didn't. He flaunted his love-affairs in everyone's face. I used to admire him for it. No one exactly blamed him, in their secret hearts. His wife was a terrible, strait-laced creature. No man could have endured her. (*Disgustedly*) After her death he suddenly acquired a bad conscience. He'd never noticed the children before. I'll bet he didn't even know their names. And then, presto, he's about in our midst giving an imitation of a wet hen with a brood of ducks. It's a bore, if you ask me.

MARTHA. (*flushing*) I think it's very fine of him.

LILY. (*shaking her head*) His reform is too sudden. He's joined the hypocrites, I think.

MARTHA. I'm sure he's no hypocrite. When you see him with the children—

LILY. Oh, I know he's a good actor. Lots of women have been in

{ove with him. (*Then suddenly*) You won't be furious if I'm very,
very frank, will you, Martha?

MARTHA. (*surprised*) No, of course not, Lily.

LILY. Well, I'm the bearer of a message from the Jayson family.

MARTHA. (*astonished*) A message? For me?

LILY. Don't think that I have anything to do with it. I'm only a
Victor record of their misgivings. Shall I switch it going? Well, then,
Father thinks, brother John and wife, sister Esther and husband all
think that you are unwisely intimate with this same Bigelow.

MARTHA. (*stunned*) I? Unwisely intimate—? (*Suddenly laughing
with amusement*) Well, you sure are funny people!

LILY. No, we're not funny. We'd be all right if we were. On the
contrary, we're very dull and deadly. Bigelow really has a villainous
rep. for philandering. But, of course, you didn't know that.

MARTHA. (*beginning to feel resentful—coldly*) No, I didn't and I
don't care to know it now.

LILY. (*calmly*) I told them you wouldn't relish their silly advice.
(*In a very confidential, friendly tone*) Oh, I hate their narrow small-
town ethics as much as you do, Martha. I sympathize with you, indeed
I do. But I have to live with them and so, for comfort's sake, I've had
to make compromises. And you're going to live in our midst from
now on, aren't you? Well then, you'll have to make compromises.
too—if you want any peace.

MARTHA. But—compromises about what? (*Forcing a laugh*) I
refuse to take it seriously. How anyone could think—it's too absurd.

LILY. What set them going was Big's being around such an awful
lot the weeks Curt was in New York, just after you'd settled down
here. You must acknowledge he was—very much present then, Martha.

MARTHA. But it was on account of his children. They were always
with him.

LILY. The town doesn't trust this sudden fond parenthood, Martha.
We've known him too long, you see.

MARTHA. But he's Curt's oldest and best friend.

LILY. We've found they always are.

MARTHA. (*springing to her feet—indignantly*) It's a case of evil minds, it seems to me—and it would be extremely insulting if I didn't have a sense of humor. (*Resentfully*) You can tell your family, that as far as I'm concerned, the town may—

LILY. Go to the devil. I knew you'd say that. Well, fight the good fight. You have all my best wishes. (*With a sigh*) I wish I had something worth fighting for. Now that I'm through with college, my occupation's gone. All I do is read book after book. The only live people are the ones in books, I find, and the only live life.

MARTHA. (*immediately sympathetic*) You're lonely, that's what, Lily.

LILY. (*dryly*) Don't pity me, Martha—or I'll join the enemy.

MARTHA. I'm not. But I'd like to help you if I could. (*After a pause*) Have you ever thought of marrying?

LILY. (*with a laugh*) Martha! How banal! The men I see are enough to banish that thought if I ever had it.

MARTHA. Marriage isn't only the man. It's children. Wouldn't you like to have children?

LILY. (*turning to her bluntly*) Wouldn't you?

MARTHA. (*confused*) But—Lily—

LILY. Oh, I know it wasn't practicable as long as you elected to wander with Curt—but why not now when you've definitely settled down here? I think that would solve things all round. If you could present Father with a grandson, I'm sure he'd fall on your neck. He feels piqued at the John and Esther families because they've had a run of girls. A male Jayson! Aunt Davidson would weep with joy. (*Suddenly*) You're thirty-eight, aren't you, Martha?

MARTHA. Yes.

LILY. Then why don't you—before it's too late? (MARTHA, *struggling with herself, does not answer.* LILY *goes on slowly*) You won't want to tag along with Curt to the ends of the earth forever, will

561

you? (*Curiously*) Wasn't that queer life like any other? I mean, didn't it get to pall on you?

MARTHA. (*as if confessing it reluctantly*) Yes—perhaps—in the last two years.

LILY. (*decisively*) It's time for both of you to rest on your laurels. Why can't Curt keep on with what he's doing now—stay home and write his books?

MARTHA. Curt isn't that kind. The actual work—the romance of it—that's his life.

LILY. But if he goes and you have to stay, you'll be lonesome—(*meaningly*) alone.

MARTHA. Horribly. I don't know what I'll do.

LILY. Then why—why? Think, Martha. If Curt knew—that was to happen—he'd want to stay here with you. I'm sure he would.

MARTHA. (*shaking her head sadly*) No. Curt has grown to dislike children. They remind him of—ours that were taken. He adored them so. He's never become reconciled.

LILY. If you confronted Curt with the actual fact, he'd be reconciled soon enough, and happy in the bargain.

MARTHA. (*eagerly*) Do you really think so?

LILY. And you, Martha—I can tell from the way you've talked that you'd like to.

MARTHA. (*excitedly*) Yes, I—I never thought I'd ever want to again. For many years after they died I never once dreamed of it— But lately—the last years—I've felt—and when we came to live here—and I saw all around me—homes—and children, I—(*She hesitates as if ashamed of having confessed so much.*)

LILY. (*putting an arm around her—affectionately*) I know. (*Vigorously*) You must, that's all there is to it! If you want my advice, you go right ahead and don't tell Curt until it's a fact he'll have to learn to like, willy-nilly. You'll find, in his inmost heart, he'll be tickled to death.

MARTHA. (*forcing a smile*) Yes, I—I'll confess I thought of that. In spite of my fear, I—I've—I mean—I— (*She flushes in a shamed confusion.*)

LILY. (*looking at her searchingly*) Why, Martha, what— (*Then suddenly understanding—with excited pleasure*) Martha! I know! It is so, isn't it? It is!

MARTHA. (*in a whisper*) Yes.

LILY. (*kissing her affectionately*) You dear, you! (*Then after a pause*) How long have you known?

MARTHA. For over two months. (*There is a ring from the front door bell in the hall.*)

LILY. (*jumping up*) I'll bet that's we Jaysons now. (*She runs to the door in the rear and looks down the hall to the right*) Yes, it's Esther and husband and Aunt Davidson. (*She comes back to* MARTHA *laughing excitedly. The* MAID *is seen going to the door*) The first wave of attack, Martha! Be brave! The Young Guard dies but never surrenders!

MARTHA. (*displeased but forcing a smile*) You make me feel terribly ill at ease when you put it that way, Lily. (*She rises now and goes to greet the visitors, who enter.* MRS. DAVIDSON *is seventy-five years old—a thin, sinewy old lady, old-fashioned, unbending and rigorous in manner. She is dressed aggressively in the fashion of a bygone age.* ESTHER *is a stout, middle-aged woman with the round, unmarked, sentimentally contented face of one who lives unthinkingly from day to day, sheltered in an assured position in her little world.* MARK, *her husband, is a lean, tall, stooping man of about forty-five. His long face is alert, shrewd, cautious, full of the superficial craftiness of the lawyer mind.* MARTHA *kisses the two women, shakes hands with* MARK, *uttering the usual meaningless greetings in a forced tone. They reply in much the same spirit. There is the buzz of this empty chatter while* MARTHA *gets them seated.* LILY *stands looking on with a cynical smile of amusement.* MRS. DAVIDSON *is in the chair at the end of table, left,* ESTHER *sits by* MARTHA *on coach,* MARK *in chair at front of table*) Will you have tea now or shall we wait for the others?

ESTHER. Let's wait. They ought to be here any moment.

LILY. (*maliciously*) Just think, Martha had forgotten you were coming. She was going motoring with Bigelow. (*There is a dead silence at this—broken diplomatically by* SHEFFIELD.)

SHEFFIELD. Where is Curt, Martha?

MARTHA. Hard at work in his study. I'm afraid he's there for the day.

SHEFFIELD. (*condescendingly*) Still plugging away at his book, I suppose. Well, I hope it will be a big success.

LILY. (*irritated by his smugness*) As big a success as the brief you're writing to restrain the citizens from preventing the Traction Company robbing them, eh, Mark? (*Before anyone can reply, she turns suddenly on her aunt who is sitting rigidly on her chair, staring before her stonily like some old lady in a daguerreotype—in a loud challenging tone*) You don't mind if I smoke, Aunt? (*She takes a cigarette out of case and lights it.*)

ESTHER. (*smiling*) Lily!

MRS. DAVIDSON. (*fixes* LILY *with her stare—in a tone of irrevocable decision*) We'll get you married, young lady, and that very soon. What you need to bring you down to earth is a husband and the responsibility of children. (*Turning her glance to* MARTHA, *a challenge in her question*) Every woman who is able should have children. Don't you believe that, Martha Jayson? (*She accentuates the full name.*)

MARTHA. (*taken aback for a moment but restraining her resentment —gently*) Yes, I do, Mrs. Davidson.

MRS. DAVIDSON. (*seemingly placated by this reply—in a milder tone*) You must call me aunt, my dear. (*Meaningly*) All the Jaysons do.

MARTHA. (*simply*) Thank you, Aunt.

LILY. (*as if all of this aroused her irritation—in a nervous fuming*) Why don't the others come, darn 'em? I'm dying for my tea. (*The door from the study is opened and* CURT *appears. They all greet him.*)

CURTIS. (*absent-mindedly*) Hello, everybody. (*Then with a pre-*

occupied air to MARTHA) Martha, I don't want to interrupt you—but—

MARTHA. (*getting up briskly*) You want my help?

CURTIS. (*with the same absent-minded air*) Yes—not for long—
just a few notes before I forget them. (*He goes back into the study.*)

MARTHA. (*seemingly relieved by this interruption and glad of the
chance it gives to show them her importance to* CURT) You'll excuse
me for a few moments, all of you, won't you? (*They all nod.*)

MRS. DAVIDSON. (*rather harshly*) Why doesn't Curt hire a secretary?
That is no work for his wife.

MARTHA. (*quietly*) A paid secretary could hardly give the sympathy
and understanding Curt needs, Mrs. Davidson. (*Proudly*) And she
would have to study for years, as I have done, in order to take my
place. (*To* LILY) If I am not here by the time the others arrive, will you
see about the tea, Lily—?

LILY. (*eagerly*) Sure. I love to serve drinks. If I were a man, I'd be
a bartender—in Mexico or Canada.

MARTHA. (*going toward the study*) I'll be with you again in a minute, I hope. (*She goes in and shuts the door behind her.*)

ESTHER. (*pettishly*) Even people touched by a smattering of science
seem to get rude, don't they?

MRS. DAVIDSON. (*harshly*) I have heard much silly talk of this being
an age of free women, and I have always said it was tommyrot. (*Pointing to the study*) She is an example. She is more of a slave to Curt's
hobbies than any of my generation were to anything but their children. (*Still more harshly*) Where are her children?

LILY. They died, Aunt, as children have a bad habit of doing. (*Then,
meaningly*) However, I wouldn't despair if I were you. (MRS. DAVID-
SON *stares at her fixedly.*)

ESTHER. (*betraying a sudden frightened jealousy*) What do you
mean, Lily? What are you so mysterious about? What did she say?
What—?

LILY. (*mockingly*) Mark, your frau seems to have me on the stand.
Can I refuse to answer? (*There is a ring at the bell.* LILY *jumps to her*

feet excitedly) Here comes the rest of our Grand Fleet. Now I'll have my tea. (*She darts out to the hallway.*)

ESTHER. (*shaking her head*) Goodness, Lily is trying on the nerves.

JAYSON, *his two sons,* JOHN *and* DICK, *and* JOHN's *wife,* EMILY, *enter from hallway in rear.* JAYSON, *the father, is a short, stout bald-headed man of sixty. A typical, small-town, New England best-family banker, reserved in pose, unobtrusively important—a placid exterior hiding querulousness and a fussy temper.* JOHN JUNIOR *is his father over again in appearance, but pompous, obtrusive, purse-and-family-proud, extremely irritating in his self-complacent air of authority, emptily assertive and loud. He is about forty.* RICHARD, *the other brother, is a typical young Casino and country club member, college-bred, good-looking, not unlikable. He has been an officer in the war and has not forgotten it.* EMILY, JOHN JR.'s *wife, is one of those small, mouse-like women who conceal beneath an outward aspect of gentle, unprotected innocence a very active envy, a silly pride, and a mean malice. The people in the room with the exception of* MRS. DAVIDSON *rise to greet them. All exchange familiar, perfunctory greetings.* SHEFFIELD *relinquishes his seat in front of the table to* JAYSON, *going to the chair, right front, himself.* JOHN *and* DICK *take the two chairs to the rear of table.* EMILY *joins* ESTHER *on the couch and they whisper together excitedly,* ESTHER *doing most of the talking. The men remain in uncomfortable silence for a moment.*)

DICK. (*with gay mockery*) Well, the gang's all here. Looks like the League of Nations. (*Then with impatience*) Let's get down to cases, folks. I want to know why I've been summoned here. I'm due for tournament mixed-doubles at the Casino at five. Where's the tea— and has Curt a stick in the cellar to put in it?

LILY. (*appearing in the doorway*) Here's tea—but no stick for you, sot. (*The* MAID *brings in tray with tea things.*)

JOHN. (*heavily*) It seems it would be more to the point to inquire where our hostess—

JAYSON. (*rousing himself again*) Yes. And where is Curt?

LILY. Working at his book. He called Martha to take notes on something.

ESTHER. (*with a trace of resentment*) She left us as if she were glad of the excuse.

LILY. Stuff, Esther! She knows how much Curt depends on her— and we don't.

EMILY. (*in her quiet, lisping voice—with the most innocent air*) Martha seems to be a model wife. (*But there is some quality to the way she says it that makes them all stare at her uneasily.*)

LILY. (*insultingly*) How well you say what you don't mean, Emily! Twinkle, twinkle, little bat! But I'm forgetting to do the honors. Tea, everybody? (*Without waiting for any answer*) Tea, everybody! (*The tea is served.*)

JAYSON. (*impatiently*) Stop fooling, Lily. Let's get to our muttons. Did you talk with Martha?

LILY. (*briskly*) I did, sir.

JAYSON. (*in a lowered voice*) What did she say?

LILY. She said you could all go to the devil! (*They all look shocked and insulted.* LILY *enjoys this, then adds quietly*) Oh, not in those words. Martha is a perfect lady. But she made it plain she will thank you to mind your own business.

ESTHER. (*volubly*) And just imagine, she'd even forgotten she'd asked us here this afternoon and was going motoring with Bigelow.

LILY. With his three children, too, don't forget.

EMILY. (*softly*) They have become such well-behaved and intelligent children, they say. (*Again all the others hesitate, staring at her suspiciously.*)

LILY. (*sharply*) You'd better let Martha train yours for a while, Emily. I'm sure she'd improve their manners—though, of course, she couldn't give them any intelligence.

EMILY. (*with the pathos of outraged innocence*) Oh!

DICK. (*interrupting*) So it's Bigelow you're up in the air about? (*He gives a low whistle—then frowns angrily*) The deuce you say!

567

LILY. (*mockingly*) Look at our soldier boy home from the wars getting serious about the family honor! It's too bad this is a rough, untutored country where they don't permit dueling, isn't it, Dick?

DICK. (*his pose crumbling—angrily*) Go to the devil!

SHEFFIELD. (*with a calm, judicious air*) This wrangling is getting us nowhere. You say she was resentful about our well-meant word to the wise?

JAYSON. (*testily*) Surely she must realize that some consideration is due the position she occupies in Bridgetown as Curt's wife.

LILY. Martha is properly unimpressed by big frogs in tiny puddles. And there you are.

MRS. DAVIDSON. (*outraged*) The idea! She takes a lot upon herself—the daughter of a Wild Western coal-miner.

LILY. (*mockingly*) Gold miner, Aunt.

MRS. DAVIDSON. It makes no difference—a common miner!

SHEFFIELD. (*keenly inquisitive*) Just before the others came, Lily, you gave out some hints—very definite hints, I should say.

ESTHER. (*excitedly*) Yes, you did, Lily. What did you mean?

LILY. (*uncertainly*) Perhaps I shouldn't have. It's not my secret. (*Enjoying herself immensely now that she holds the spotlight—after a pause, in a stage whisper*) Shall I tell you? Yes, I can't help telling. Well, Martha is going to have a son. (*They are all stunned and flabbergasted and stare at her speechlessly.*)

MRS. DAVIDSON. (*her face lighting up—joyously*) A son! Curt's son!

JAYSON. (*pleased by the idea but bewildered*) A son?

DICK. (*smartly*) Lily's kidding you. How can she know it's a son—unless she's a clairvoyant.

ESTHER. (*with glad relief*) Yes, how stupid!

LILY. I am clairvoyant in this case. Allah is great and it will be a son—if only to make you and Emily burst with envy among your daughters.

ESTHER. Lily!

EMILY. Oh!

568

JAYSON. (*testily*) Keep still for a moment, Lily, for God's sake. This is no subject to joke about, remember.

LILY. Martha told me. I know that.

JAYSON. And does Curt know this?

LILY. No, not yet. Martha has been afraid to tell him.

JAYSON. Ah, that explains matters. You know I asked Curt some time ago—and he said it was impossible.

EMILY. (*with a lift of her eyebrows*) Impossible? Why, what a funny thing to say.

SHEFFIELD. (*keenly lawyer-like*) And why is Martha afraid to tell him, Lily?

LILY. It's all very simple. When the two died years ago, they said they would never have one again. Martha thinks Curt is still haunted by their memory and is afraid he will resent another as an intruder. I told her that was all foolishness—that a child was the one thing to make Curt settle down for good at home here and write his books.

JAYSON. (*eagerly*) Yes, I believe that myself. (*Pleased*) Well, this is fine news.

EMILY. Still it was her duty to tell Curt, don't you think? I don't see how she could be afraid of Curt—for those reasons. (*They all stare at her.*)

ESTHER. (*resentfully*) I don't, either. Why, Curt's the biggest-hearted and kindest—

EMILY. I wonder how long she's known—this?

LILY. (*sharply*) Two months, she said.

EMILY. Two months? (*She lets this sink in.*)

JOHN. (*quickly scenting something—eagerly*) What do you mean, Emily? (*Then as if he read her mind*) Two months? But before that —Curt was away in New York almost a month!

LILY. (*turning on* EMILY *fiercely*) So! You got someone to say it for you as you always do, Poison Mind! Oh, I wish the ducking stool had never been abolished!

EMILY. (*growing crimson—falteringly*) I—I didn't mean—

569

JOHN. (*furiously*) Where the honor of the family is at stake—

LILY. (*fiercely*) Ssshh, you empty barrel! I think I hear— (*The door from the study is opened and* MARTHA *comes in in the midst of a heavy silence. All the gentlemen rise stiffly.* MARTHA *is made immediately self-conscious and resentful by the feeling that they have been discussing her unfavorably.*)

MARTHA. (*coming forward—with a forced cordiality*) How do you do, everybody? So sorry I wasn't here when you came. I hope Lily made proper excuses for me. (*She goes from one to the other of the four latest comers with "So glad you came," etc. They reply formally and perfunctorily.* MARTHA *finally finds a seat on the couch between* EMILY *and* ESTHER) I hope Lily—but I see you've all had tea.

LILY. (*trying to save the situation—gaily*) Yes. You can trust me as understudy for the part of hostess any time.

MARTHA. (*forcing a smile*) Well, I'm glad to know I wasn't missed.

EMILY. (*sweetly*) We were talking about you—at least, we were listening to Lily talk about you.

MARTHA. (*stiffening defensively*) About me?

EMILY. Yes—about how devoted you were to Curt's work. (LILY *gives her a venomous glance of scorn.*)

MARTHA. (*pleased but inwardly uneasy*) Oh, but you see I consider it my work, too, I've helped him with it so long now.

JAYSON. (*in a forced tone*) And how is Curt's book coming, Martha?

MARTHA. (*more and more stung by their strained attitudes and inquisitive glances. Coldly and cuttingly*) Finely, thank you. The book will cause quite a stir, I believe. It will make the name of Jayson famous in the big world outside of Bridgetown.

MRS. DAVIDSON. (*indignantly*) The name of Jayson has been—

JAYSON. (*pleadingly*) Aunt Elizabeth!

LILY. Aunt means it's world famous already, Martha. (*Pointing to the sullen* JOHN) John was once a substitute on the Yale Freshman soccer team, you know. If it wasn't for his weak shins he would have made the team, fancy!

DICK. (*this tickles his sense of humor and he bursts into laughter*) Lily wins! (*As his brother glares at him—looking at his watch*) Heavens, I'll have to hustle! (*Gets to his feet*) I'm due at the Casino. (*Comes and shakes* MARTHA's *hand formally*) I'm sorry I can't stay.

MARTHA. So glad you came. Do come in again any time. We keep open house, you know—Western fashion. (*She accentuates this.*)

DICK. (*hurriedly*) Delighted to. (*He starts for the door in rear.*)

LILY. (*as if suddenly making up her mind*) Wait a second! I'm coming with you—

DICK. Sure thing—only hurry, darn you! (*He goes out.*)

LILY. (*stops at the door in rear and catching* MARTHA's *eye, looks meaningly at the others*) Phew! I need fresh air! (*She makes an encouraging motion as if pummeling someone to* MARTHA, *indicating her assembled family as the victim—then goes out laughing. A motor is heard starting—running off.*)

ESTHER. (*with a huge sigh of relief*) Thank goodness, she's gone. What a vixen! What would you do if you had a sister like that, Martha?

MARTHA. I'd love her—and try to understand her.

SHEFFIELD. (*meaningly*) She's a bad ally to rely on—this side of the fence one day, and that the next.

MARTHA. Is that why you advised her to become a lawyer, Mr. Sheffield?

SHEFFIELD. (*stung but maintaining an unruffled front*) Now, now, that remark must be catalogued as catty.

MARTHA. (*defiantly*) It seems to be in the Bridgetown atmosphere. I never was—not the least bit—in the open air.

JAYSON. (*conciliatingly*) Oh, Bridgetown isn't so bad, Martha, once you get used to us.

JOHN. It's one of the most prosperous and wealthy towns in the U. S. —and that means in the world, nowadays.

EMILY. (*with her sugary smile*) That isn't what Martha means, you silly. I know what she's thinking about us, and I'm not sure that

I don't agree with her—partly. She feels that we're so awfully strict—about certain things. It must be so different in the Far West—I suppose—so much freer.

MARTHA. (*acidly*) Then you believe broadmindedness and clean thinking are a question of locality? I can't agree with you. I know nothing of the present Far West, not having lived there for ten years, but Curt and I have lived in the Far East and I'm sure he'd agree with me in saying that Chinese ancestor worship is far more dignified than ours. After all, you know, theirs is religion, not snobbery. (*There is a loud honking of an auto horn before the house.* MARTHA *starts, seems to come to a quick decision, and announces with studied carelessness*) That must be Mr. Bigelow. I suppose Lily told you I had an engagement to go motoring with him. So sorry I must leave. But I'm like Lily. I need fresh air. (*She walks to the study door as she is talking*) I'll call Curt. (*She raps loudly on the door and calls*) Curt! Come out! It's important. (*She turns and goes to the door, smiling fixedly*) He'll be out when he's through swearing. (*She goes out, rear.*)

JOHN. (*exploding*) Well, of all the damned cheek!

ESTHER. She shows her breeding, I must say.

EMILY. (*with horror*) Oh, how rude—and insulting!

MRS. DAVIDSON. (*rising rigidly to her feet*) I will never set foot in this house again!

JAYSON. (*jumping up to restrain her—worriedly*) Now, Aunt Elizabeth, do keep your head! We must have no scandal of any sort. Remember there are servants about. Do sit down. (*The old lady refuses in stubborn silence.*)

SHEFFIELD. (*judiciously*) One must make allowances for one in her condition, Aunt.

JAYSON. (*snatching at this*) Exactly. Remember her condition, Aunt (*Testily*) and do sit down. (*The old lady plumps herself down again angrily.*)

EMILY. (*in her lisp of hidden meanings*) Yes, the family mustn't forget—her condition. (*The door from the study is opened and* CURTIS *appears. His face shows his annoyance at being interrupted, his eyes are preoccupied. They all turn and greet him embarrassedly. He nods silently and comes slowly down front.*)

CURTIS. (*looking around*) Where's Martha? What's the important thing she called me out for?

ESTHER. (*forcing gaiety*) To play host, you big bear, you! Don't you think we came to see you, too? Sit down here and be good. (*He sits on sofa.*)

EMILY. (*softly*) Martha had to leave us to go motoring with Mr. Bigelow.

ESTHER. (*hastily*) And the three children.

CURTIS. (*frowning grumpily*) Hm! Big and his eternal kids. (*He sighs. They exchange meaning glances.* CURTIS *seems to feel ashamed of his grumpiness and tries to fling it off—with a cheerful smile*) But what the deuce! I must be getting selfish to grudge Martha her bit of fresh air. You don't know what it means to outdoor animals like us to be pent up. (*He springs to his feet and paces back and forth nervously*) We're used to living with the sky for a roof— (*Then interestedly*) Did Martha tell you I'd definitely decided to go on the five year Asian expedition?

ESTHER. Curt! You're not!

EMILY. And leave Martha here—all alone—for five years?

JAYSON. Yes, you can't take Martha with you this time, you know.

CURTIS. (*with a laugh*) No? What makes you so sure of that? (*As they look mystified, he continues confidentially*) I'll let you in on the secret—only you must all promise not to breathe a word to Martha— until tomorrow. Tomorrow is her birthday, you know, and this is a surprise I've saved for her. (*They all nod*) I've been intriguing my damnedest for the past month to get permission for Martha to go with me. It was difficult because women are supposed to be barred. (*Happily*) But I've succeeded. The letter came this morning. How tickled to death she'll be when she hears! I know she's given up hope.

573

(*Thoughtfully*) I suppose it's that has been making her act so out-of-sorts lately.

JAYSON. (*worriedly*) Hmm! But would you persist in going—alone—if you knew it was impossible for her—?

CURTIS. (*frowning*) I can't imagine it without her. You people can't have any idea what a help—a chum—she's been. You can't believe that a woman could be—so much that—in a life of that kind, how I've grown to depend on her. The thousand details—she attends to them all. She remembers everything. Why, I'd be lost. I wouldn't know how to start. (*With a laugh*) I know this sounds like a confession of weakness but it's true just the same. (*Frowning again*) However, naturally my work must always be the first consideration. Yes, absolutely! (*Then with glad relief*) But what's the use of rambling on this way? We can both go, thank heaven!

MRS. DAVIDSON. (*sternly*) No. She cannot go. And it is *your* duty—

CURTIS. (*interrupting her with a trace of impatience*) Oh, come! That's all nonsense, Aunt. You don't understand the kind of woman Martha is.

MRS. DAVIDSON. (*harshly*) The women I understand prefer rearing their children to selfish gallivanting over the world.

CURTIS. (*impatiently*) But we have no children now, Aunt.

MRS. DAVIDSON. I know that, more's the pity. But later—

CURTIS. (*emphatically*) No, I tell you! It's impossible!

MRS. DAVIDSON. (*grimly*) I have said my last word. Go your own road and work your own ruin.

CURTIS. (*brusquely*) I think I'll change my togs and go for a walk. Excuse me for a second. I'll be right down again. (*He goes out, rear.*)

EMILY. (*with her false air of innocence*) Curt acts so funny, doesn't he? Did you notice how emphatic he was about it's being impossible? And he said Martha seemed to him to be acting queer lately—with him, I suppose he meant.

ESTHER. He certainly appeared put out when he heard she'd gone motoring with Big.

574

JAYSON. (*moodily*) This dislike of the very mention of children. It isn't like Curt, not a bit.

JOHN. There's something rotten in Denmark somewhere. This family will yet live to regret having accepted a stranger—

SHEFFIELD. (*mollifyingly—with a judicial air*) Come now! This is all only suspicion. There is no evidence; you have no case; and the defendant is innocent until you have proved her guilty, remember. (*Getting to his feet*) Well, let's break up. Esther, you and I ought to be getting home. (*They all rise.*)

JAYSON. (*testily*) Well, if I were sure it would all blow over without any open scandal, I'd offer up a prayer of thanks.

CURTAIN

ACT TWO

SCENE—CURTIS JAYSON's *study. On the left, forward, a gun rack in which are displayed several varieties of rifles and shotguns. Farther back, three windows looking out on the garden. In the rear wall, an open fireplace with two leather armchairs in front of it. To right of fireplace, a door leading into the living-room. In the far right corner, another chair. In the right wall, three windows looking out on the lawn and garden. On this side, front, a typewriting table with machine and chair. Opposite the windows on the right, a bulky leather couch, facing front. In front of the windows on the left, a long table with stacks of paper piled here and there on it, reference books, etc. On the left of table, a swivel chair. Gray oak bookcases are built into the cream rough plaster walls which are otherwise almost hidden from view by a collection of all sorts of hunter's trophies, animal heads of all kinds. The floor is covered with animal skins—tiger, polar bear, leopard, lion, etc. Skins are also thrown over the backs of the chairs. The sections of the bookcase not occupied by scientific volumes have been turned into a specimen case for all sorts of zoölogical, geographical, anthropological oddities.*

It is mid-morning, sunny and bright, of the following day.

CURTIS *and* BIGELOW *are discovered.* CURTIS *is half-sitting on the corner of the table, left, smoking a pipe.* BIGELOW *is lying sprawled on the couch. Through the open windows on the right come the shouts of children playing.* MARTHA's *voice joins in with theirs.*

BIGELOW. Listen to that rumpus, will you! The kids are having the time of their lives. (*He goes to the window and looks out—delightedly*) Your wife is playing hide and seek with them. Come and look.

CURTIS. (*with a trace of annoyance*) Oh, I can see well enough from here.

BIGELOW. (*with a laugh*) She seems to get as much fun out of it as they do. (*As a shriek comes from outside—excitedly*) Ah, Eddy discovered her behind the tree. Isn't he tickled now! (*He turns back from the window and lights a cigarette—enthusiastically*) Jove, what a hand she is with children!

CURTIS. (*as if the subject bored him*) Oh, Martha gets along well with anyone.

BIGELOW. (*sits on the couch again—with a sceptical smile*) You think so? With everyone?

CURTIS. (*surprised*) Yes—with everyone we've ever come in contact with—even aboriginal natives.

BIGELOW. With the aboriginal natives of Bridgetown? With the well-known Jayson family, for example?

CURTIS. (*getting to his feet—frowning*) Why, everything's all right between Martha and them, isn't it? What do you mean, Big? I certainly imagined—but I'll confess this damn book has had me so preoccupied—

BIGELOW. Too darn preoccupied, if you'll pardon my saying so. It's not fair to leave her to fight it alone.

CURTIS. (*impatiently*) Fight what? Martha has a sense of humor. I'm sure their petty prejudices merely amuse her.

BIGELOW. (*sententiously*) A mosquito is a ridiculous, amusing creature, seen under a microscope; but when a swarm has been stinging you all night—

CURTIS. (*a broad grin coming over his face*) You speak from experience, eh?

BIGELOW. (*smiling*) You bet I do. Touch me anywhere and you'll find a bite. This, my native town, did me the honor of devoting its entire leisure attention for years to stinging me to death.

CURTIS. Well, if I am to believe one-tenth of the family letters I used to receive on the subject of my old friend, Bigelow, they sure had just cause.

BIGELOW. Oh, I'll play fair. I'll admit they did—then. But it's exas-

577

perating to know they never give you credit for changing—I almost said, reforming. One ought to be above the gossip of a town like this —but say what you like, it does get under your skin.

CURTIS. (*with an indulgent smile*) So you'd like to be known as a reformed character, eh?

BIGELOW. (*rather ruefully*) Et tu! Your tone is sceptical. But I swear to you, Curt, I'm an absolutely new man since my wife's death, since I've grown to love the children. Before that I hardly knew them. They were hers, not mine, it seemed. (*His face lighting up*) Now we're the best of pals, and I've commenced to appreciate life from a different angle. I've found a career at last—the children—the finest career a man could have, I believe.

CURTIS. (*indifferently*) Yes, I suppose so—if you're made that way.

BIGELOW. Meaning you're not?

CURTIS. Not any more. (*Frowning*) I tried that once.

BIGELOW. (*after a pause—with a smile*) But we're wandering from the subject of Martha versus the mosquitoes.

CURTIS. (*with a short laugh*) Oh, to the deuce with that! Trust Martha to take care of herself. Besides, I'll have her out of this stagnant hole before so very long—six months, to be exact.

BIGELOW. Where do you think of settling her then?

CURTIS. No settling about it. I'm going to take her with me.

BIGELOW. (*surprised*) On the Asian expedition?

CURTIS. Yes. I haven't told her yet but I'm going to today. It's her birthday—and I've been saving the news to surprise her with.

BIGELOW. Her birthday? I wish the children and I had known—but it's not too late yet.

CURTIS. (*with a grin*) Thirty-nine candles, if you're thinking of baking a cake!

BIGELOW. (*meaningly*) That's not old—but it's not young either, Curt.

CURTIS. (*disgustedly*) You talk like an old woman, Big. What have years to do with it? Martha is young in spirit and always will be.

(*There is a knock at the door and* MARTHA's *voice calling:* "May I come in, people?") Sure thing! (BIGELOW *jumps to open the door and* MARTHA *enters. She is flushed, excited, full of the joy of life, panting from her exertions.*)

MARTHA. (*laughing*) I've had to run away and leave them with the governess. They're too active for me. (*She throws herself on the couch*) Phew! I'm all tired out. I must be getting old.

CURTIS. (*with a grin*) Big was just this minute remarking that, Martha. (BIGELOW *looks embarrassed.*)

MARTHA. (*laughing at him*) Well, I declare! Of all the horrid things to hear—

BIGELOW. (*still embarrassed but forcing a joking tone*) He—prevaricates, Mrs. Jayson.

MARTHA. There now, Curt! I'm sure it was you who said it. It sounds just like one of your horrid facts.

BIGELOW. And how can I offer my felicitations now? But I do, despite your husband's calumny. May your shadow never grow less.

MARTHA. Thank you. (*She shakes his proffered hand heartily.*)

BIGELOW. And now I'll collect my flock and go home.

CURTIS. So long, Big. Be sure you don't mislay one of your heirs!

BIGELOW. No fear—but they might mislay me. (*He goes.* CURTIS *sits down on couch.* MARTHA *goes to the window right, and looks out—after a pause, waving her hand.*)

MARTHA. There they go. What darlings they are! (CURTIS *grunts perfunctorily.* MARTHA *comes back and sits beside* CURTIS *on the couch —with a sigh*) Whoever did say it was right, Curt. I am getting old.

CURTIS. (*taking one of her hands and patting it*) Nonsense!

MARTHA. (*shaking her head and smiling with a touch of sadness*) No. I feel it.

CURTIS. (*puts his arms around her protectingly*) Nonsense! You're not the sort that ever grows old.

MARTHA. (*nestling up to him*) I'm afraid we're all that sort, dear. Even you. (*She touches the white hair about his temples playfully*)

Circumstantial evidence. I'll have to dye it when you're asleep some time—and then nobody'll know.

CURTIS. (*looking at her*) You haven't any silver threads. (*Jokingly*) Am I to suspect—

MARTHA. No, I don't. Honest, cross my heart, I wouldn't even conceal that from you, if I did. But gray hairs prove nothing. I am actually older than you, don't forget.

CURTIS. One whole year! That's frightful, isn't it?

MARTHA. I'm a woman, remember; so that one means at least six. Ugh! Let's not talk about it. Do you know, it really fills me with a queer panic sometimes?

CURTIS. (*squeezing her*) Silly girl!

MARTHA. (*snuggling close to him*) Will you always love me—even when I'm old and ugly and feeble and you're still young and strong and handsome?

CURTIS. (*kisses her—tenderly*) Martha! What a foolish question, sweetheart! If we ever have to grow old, we'll do it together just as we've always done everything.

MARTHA. (*with a happy sigh*) That's my dream of happiness, Curt. (*Enthusiastically*) Oh, it has been a wonderful, strange life we've lived together, Curt, hasn't it? You're sure you've never regretted, never had the weest doubt that it might have been better with— someone else?

CURTIS. (*kisses her again—tenderly reproachful*) Martha!

MARTHA. And I have helped—really helped you, haven't I?

CURTIS. (*much moved*) You've been the best wife a man could ever wish for, Martha. You've been—you are wonderful. I owe everything to you—your sympathy and encouragement. Don't you know I realize that? (*She kisses him gratefully.*)

MARTHA. (*musing happily*) Yes, it's been a wonderful, glorious life. I'd live it over again if I could, every single second of it—even the terrible suffering—the children.

CURTIS. (*wincing*) Don't. I wouldn't want that over again. (*Then changing the subject abruptly*) But why have you been putting all our life into the past tense? It seems to me the most interesting part is still ahead of us.

MARTHA. (*softly*) I mean—together—Curt.

CURTIS. So do I!

MARTHA. But you're going away—and I can't go with you this time.

CURTIS. (*smiling to himself over her head*) Yes, that does complicate matters, doesn't it?

MARTHA. (*hurt—looking up at him*) Curt! How indifferently you say that—as if you didn't care!

CURTIS. (*avoiding her eyes—teasingly*) What do you think you'll do all the time I'm gone?

MARTHA. Oh, I'll be lost—dead—I won't know what to do. I'll die of loneliness—(*yearning creeping into her voice*) unless—

CURTIS. (*inquisitively*) Unless what?

MARTHA. (*burying her face on his shoulders—passionately*) Oh, Curt, I love you so! Swear that you'll always love me no matter what I do—no matter what I ask—

CURTIS. (*vaguely uneasy now, trying to peer into her face*) But, sweetheart—

MARTHA. (*giving way weakly to her feelings for a moment—entreatingly*) Then don't go!

CURTIS. (*astonished*) Why, I've got to go. You know that.

MARTHA. Yes, I suppose you have. (*Vigorously, as if flinging off a weakness*) Of course you have!

CURTIS. But, Martha, you said you'd be lonely unless—unless what?

MARTHA. Unless I— (*She hesitates, blushing and confused*) I mean we—oh, I'm so afraid of what you'll—hold me close, very close to you and I'll whisper it. (*She pulls his head down and whispers in his ear. A look of disappointment and aversion forces itself on his face.*)

CURTIS. (*almost indignantly*) But that's impossible, Martha!

MARTHA. (*pleadingly*) Now don't be angry with me, Curt—not till you've heard everything. (*With a trace of defiance*) It isn't impossible,

Curt. It's so! It's happened! I was saving it as a secret—to tell you today—on my birthday.

CURTIS. (*stunned*) You mean it's a fact?

MARTHA. Yes. (*Then pitifully*) Oh, Curt, don't look that way! You seem so cold—so far away from me. (*Straining her arms about him*) Why don't you hold me close to you? Why don't you say you're glad —for my sake?

CURTIS. (*agitatedly*) But Martha, you don't understand. How can I pretend gladness when— (*Vehemently*) Why, it would spoil all our plans!

MARTHA. Plans? *Our* plans? What do you mean?

CURTIS. (*excitedly*) Why, you're going with me, of course! I've obtained official permission. I've been working for it for months. The letter came yesterday morning.

MARTHA. (*stunned*) Permission—to go with you—?

CURTIS. (*excitedly*) Yes. I couldn't conceive going without you. And I knew how you must be wishing—

MARTHA. (*in pain*) Oh!

CURTIS. (*distractedly—jumping to his feet and staring at her bewilderedly*) Martha! You don't mean to tell me you weren't!

MARTHA. (*in a crushed voice*) I was wishing you'd finally decide not to go—

CURTIS. (*betraying exasperation*) But you must realize that's impossible. Martha, are you sure you've clearly understood what I've told you? You can go with me, do you hear? Everything is arranged. And I've had to fight so hard—I was running the risk of losing my own chance by my insistence that I couldn't go without you.

MARTHA. (*weakly and helplessly*) I understand all that, Curt.

CURTIS. (*indignantly*) And yet you hesitate! Why, this is the greatest thing of its kind ever attempted! There are unprecedented possibilities! A whole new world of knowledge may be opened up, the very origin of Man himself! And you will be the only woman—

MARTHA. I realize all that, Curt.

CURTIS. You can't—and hesitate! And then—think, Martha!—it will mean that you and I won't have to be separated. We can go on living the old, free life together.

MARTHA. (*growing calm now*) You are forgetting—what I told you, Curt. You must face the fact. I can't go.

CURTIS. (*overwhelmed by the finality of her tone—after a pause*) How long have you known this?

MARTHA. Two months, about.

CURTIS. But why didn't you tell me before?

MARTHA. I was afraid you wouldn't understand—and you haven't, Curt. But why didn't you tell me before what you were planning?

CURTIS. (*eagerly*) You mean—then you would have been glad to go —before this had happened?

MARTHA. I would have accepted it.

CURTIS. (*despairingly*) Martha, how could you ever have allowed this to happen? Oh, I suppose I'm talking foolishness. It wasn't your seeking, I know.

MARTHA. Yes, it was, Curt.

CURTIS. (*indignantly*) Martha! (*Then in a hurt tone*) You have broken the promise we made when they died. We were to keep their memories inviolate. They were to be always—our only children.

MARTHA. (*gently*) They forgive me, Curt. And you'll forgive me, too, when you see him—and love him.

CURTIS. Him?

MARTHA. I know it will be a boy.

CURTIS. (*sinking down on the couch beside her—dully*) Martha! You have blown my world to bits.

MARTHA. (*taking one of his hands in hers—gently*) You must make allowances for me, Curt, and forgive me. I *am* getting old. No, it's the truth. I've reached the turning point. Will you listen to my side of it, Curt, and try to see it—with sympathy—with true understanding— (*With a trace of bitterness*)—forgetting your work for the moment?

CURTIS. (*miserably*) That's unfair, Martha. I think of it as *our* work—and I always have believed you did, too.

MARTHA. (*quickly*) I did, Curt! I do! All in the past is our work. It's my greatest pride to think so. But, Curt, I'll have to confess frankly—during the past two years I've felt myself feeling as if I wasn't complete—with that alone.

CURTIS. Martha! (*Bitterly*) And all the time I believed that more and more it was becoming the aim of your life, too.

MARTHA. (*with a sad smile*) I'm glad of that, dear. I tried my best to conceal it from you. It would have been so unfair to let you guess while we were still in harness. But oh, how I kept looking forward to the time when we would come back—and rest—in our own home! You know, you said that was your plan—to stay here and write your books—and I was hoping—

CURTIS. (*with a gesture of aversion*) I loathe this book writing. It isn't my part, I realize now. But when I made the plans you speak of, how could I know that then?

MARTHA. (*decisively*) You've got to go. I won't try to stop you. I'll help all in my power—as I've always done. Only—I can't go with you any more. And you must help me—to do my work—by understanding it. (*He is silent, frowning, his face agitated, preoccupied. She goes on intensely*) Oh, Curt, I wish I could tell you what I feel, make you feel with me the longing for a child. If you had just the tiniest bit of feminine in you—! (*Forcing a smile*) But you're so utterly masculine, dear! That's what made me love you, I suppose—so I've no right to complain of it. (*Intensely*) I don't. I wouldn't have you changed one bit! I love you! And I love the things you love—your work—because it's a part of you. And that's what I want you to do—to reciprocate—to love the creator in me—to desire that I, too, should complete myself with the thing nearest my heart!

CURTIS. (*intensely preoccupied with his own struggle—vaguely*) But I thought—

MARTHA. I know; but, after all, your work is yours, not mine. I have been only a helper, a good comrade, too, I hope, but—somehow—outside of it all. Do you remember two years ago when we were camped in Yunnan, among the aboriginal tribes? It was one night there when we were lying out in our sleeping-bags up in the mountains along the Tibetan frontier. I couldn't sleep. Suddenly I felt oh, so tired—utterly alone—out of harmony with you—with the earth under me. I became horribly despondent—like an outcast who suddenly realizes the whole world is alien. And all the wandering about the world, and all the romance and excitement I'd enjoyed in it, appeared an aimless, futile business, chasing around in a circle in an effort to avoid touching reality. Forgive me, Curt. I meant myself, not you, of course. Oh, it was horrible, I tell you, to feel that way. I tried to laugh at myself, to fight it off, but it stayed and grew worse. It seemed as if I were the only creature alive—who was not alive. And all at once the picture came of a tribeswoman who stood looking at us in a little mountain village as we rode by. She was nursing her child. Her eyes were so curiously sure of herself. She was horribly ugly, poor woman, and yet —as the picture came back to me—I appeared to myself the ugly one while she was beautiful. And I thought of our children who had died —and such a longing for another child came to me that I began sobbing. You were asleep. You didn't hear. (*She pauses—then proceeds slowly*) And when we came back here—to have a home at last, I was so happy because I saw my chance of fulfillment—before it was too late. (*In a gentle, pleading voice*) Now can you understand, dear? (*She puts her hand on his arm.*)

CURTIS. (*starting as if awaking from a sleep*) Understand? No, I can't understand, Martha.

MARTHA. (*in a gasp of unbearable hurt*) Curt! I don't believe you heard a word I was saying.

CURTIS. (*bursting forth as if releasing all the pent-up struggle that has been gathering within him*) No, I can't understand. I can't! It seems like treachery to me.

MARTHA. Curt!

CURTIS. I've depended on you. This is the crucial point—the biggest thing of my life—and you desert me!

MARTHA. (*resentment gathering in her eyes*) If you'd listened to me —if you'd even tried to feel—

CURTIS. I feel that you're deliberately ruining my highest hope. How can I go on without you? I've been trying to imagine myself alone. I can't! Even with my work—whom can I get to take your place? Oh, Martha, why do you have to bring this new element into our lives at this late day? Haven't we been sufficient, you and I together? Isn't that a more difficult, beautiful happiness to achieve than—children? Everyone has children. Don't I love you as much as any man could love a woman? Isn't that enough for you? Doesn't it mean anything to you that I need you so terribly—for myself, for my work—for everything that is best and worthiest in me? Can you expect me to be glad when you propose to introduce a stranger who will steal away your love, your interest—who will separate us and deprive me of you! No, no, I can't! It's asking the impossible. I'm only human.

MARTHA. If you were human you'd think of my life as well as yours.

CURTIS. I do! It's *our* life I am fighting for, not mine—*our* life that you want to destroy.

MARTHA. Our life seems to mean your life to you, Curt—and only your life. I have devoted fifteen years to that. Now I must fight for my own.

CURTIS. (*aghast*) You talk as if we were enemies, Martha! (*Striding forward and seizing her in his arms*) No, you don't mean it! I love you so, Martha! You've made yourself part of my life, my work—I need you so! I can't share you with anyone! I won't! Martha, my own! Say that you won't, dear? (*He kisses her passionately again and again.*)

MARTHA. (*all her love and tenderness aroused by his kisses and passionate sincerity—weakening*) Curt! Curt! (*Pitiably*) It won't separate us, dear. Can't you see he will be a link between us—even when

586

we're away from each other—that he will bring us together all the closer?

CURTIS. But I can't be away from you!

MARTHA. (*miserably*) Oh, Curt, why won't you look the fact in the face—and learn to accept it with joy? Why can't you for my sake? I would do that for you.

CURTIS. (*breaking away from her—passionately*) You will not do what I have implored you—for me! And I am looking the fact in the face—the fact that there must be no fact! (*Avoiding her eyes—as if defying his own finer feelings*) There are doctors who—

MARTHA. (*shrinking back from him*) Curt! You propose that—to me! (*With overwhelming sorrow*) Oh, Curt! When I feel him—his life within me—like a budding of my deepest soul—you say what you have just said! (*Grief-stricken*) Oh, you never, never, never will understand!

CURTIS. (*shamefacedly*) Martha,—I (*Distractedly*) I don't know what I'm saying! This whole situation is so unbearable! Why does it have to happen now?

MARTHA. (*gently*) It must be now—or not at all—at my age, dear. (*Then after a pause—staring at him frightenedly—sadly*) You've changed, Curt. I remember it used to be your happiness to sacrifice yourself for me.

CURTIS. I had no work then—no purpose beyond myself. To sacrifice oneself is easy. But when your only meaning comes as a searcher for knowledge—you can't sacrifice that, Martha. You must sacrifice everything for that or lose all sincerity.

MARTHA. I wonder where your work leaves off and you begin. Hasn't your work become you?

CURTIS. Yes and no. (*Helplessly*) You can't understand, Martha! . . .

MARTHA. Nor you.

CURTIS. (*with a trace of bitter irony*) And you and your work? Aren't they one and the same?

MARTHA. So you think mine is selfish, too? (*After a pause—sadly*) I can't blame you, Curt. It's all my fault. I've spoiled you by giving up my life so completely to yours. You've forgotten I have one. Oh, I don't mean that I was a martyr. I know that in you alone lay my happiness in those years—after the children died. But we are no longer what we were then. We must, both of us, relearn to love and respect —what we have become.

CURTIS. (*violently*) Nonsense! You talk as if love were an intellectual process— (*Taking her into his arms—passionately*) I love you — You are me and I am you! What use is all this vivisecting? (*He kisses her fiercely. They look into each other's eyes for a second— then instinctively fall back from one another.*)

MARTHA. (*in a whisper*) Yes, you love me. But who am I? You don't know.

CURTIS. (*frightfully*) Martha! Stop! This is terrible! (*They continue to be held by each other's fearfully questioning eyes.*)

CURTAIN

ACT THREE

SCENE—*Same as Act Two. As the curtain rises,* JAYSON *is discovered sitting in an armchair by the fireplace, in which a log fire is burning fitfully. He is staring into the flames, a strained, expectant expression on his face. It is about three o'clock in the morning. There is no light but that furnished by the fire which fills the room with shifting shadows. The door in the rear is opened and* RICHARD *appears, his face harried by the stress of unusual emotion. Through the open doorway, a low muffled moan of anguish sounds from the upper part of the house.* JAYSON *and* RICHARD *both shudder. The latter closes the door behind him quickly as if anxious to shut out the noise.*

JAYSON. (*looking up anxiously*) Well?

RICHARD. (*involuntarily straightening up as if about to salute and report to a superior officer*) No change, sir. (*Then, as if remembering himself, comes to the fireplace and slumps down in a chair—agitatedly*) God, Dad, I can't stand her moaning and screaming! It's got my nerves shot to pieces. I thought I was hardened. I've heard them out in No Man's Land—dying by inches—when you couldn't get to them or help—but this is worse—a million times! After all, that was war—and they were men—

JAYSON. Martha is having an exceptionally hard ordeal.

RICHARD. Since three o'clock this morning—yesterday morning, I should say. It's a wonder she isn't dead.

JAYSON. (*after a pause*) Where is Curt?

RICHARD. (*harshly*) Still out in the garden, walking around like a lunatic.

JAYSON. Why didn't you make him come in?

589

RICHARD. Make him! It's easy to say. He's in a queer state, Dad, I can tell you! There's something torturing him besides her pain—

JAYSON. (*after a pause*) Yes, there's a lot in all this we don't know about.

RICHARD. I suppose the reason he's so down on the family is because we've rather cut her since that tea affair.

JASON. He shouldn't blame us. She acted abominably and has certainly caused enough talk since then—always about with Bigelow—

RICHARD. (*with a sardonic laugh*) And yet he keeps asking everyone to send for Bigelow—says he wants to talk to him—not us. *We* can't understand! (*He laughs bitterly.*)

JAYSON. I'm afraid Curt knows we understand too much. (*Agitatedly*) But why does he want Bigelow, in God's name? In his present state—with the suspicions he must have—there's liable to be a frightful scene.

RICHARD. Don't be afraid of a scene. (*With pitying scorn*) The hell of it is he seems to regard Bigelow as his best friend. Damned if I can make it out.

JAYSON. I gave orders that they were always to tell Curt Bigelow was out of town and couldn't be reached. (*With a sigh*) What a frightful situation for all of us! (*After a pause*) It may sound cruel of me—but —I can't help wishing for all our sakes that this child will never—

RICHARD. Yes, Dad, I know what you're thinking. It would be the best thing for it, too—although I hate myself for saying it. (*There is a pause. Then the door in rear is opened and* LILY *appears. She is pale and agitated. Leaving the door open behind her she comes forward and flings herself on the lounge.*)

JAYSON. (*anxiously*) Well?

LILY. (*irritably, getting up and switching on the lights*) Isn't everything gloomy enough? (*Sits down*) I couldn't bear it upstairs one second longer. Esther and Emily are coming down, too. It's too much for them—and they've had personal experience. (*Trying to mask her agitation by a pretense at flippancy*) I hereby become a life-member

590

of the Birth Control League. Let's let humanity cease—if God can't manage its continuance any better than that!

RICHARD. (*seriously*) Second the motion.

JAYSON. (*peevishly*) You're young idiots. Keep your blasphemous nonsense to yourself, Lily!

LILY. (*jumping up and stamping her foot—hysterically*) I can't stand it. Take me home, Dick, won't you? We're doing no good waiting here. I'll have a fit—or something—if I stay.

RICHARD. (*glad of the excuse to go himself—briskly*) That's how I feel. I'll drive you home. Come along. (ESTHER *and* EMILY *enter, followed by* JOHN.)

LILY. (*excitedly*) I'll never marry or have a child! Never, never! I'll go into Mark's office tomorrow and make myself independent of marriage.

ESTHER. Sssh! Lily! Don't you know you're shouting? And what silly talk!

LILY. I'll show you whether it's silly! I'll—

RICHARD. (*impatiently*) Are you coming or not?

LILY. (*quickly*) Yes—wait—here I am. (*She pushes past the others and follows* RICHARD *out rear.* ESTHER *and* EMILY *sit on couch—*JOHN *on chair, right rear.*)

ESTHER. (*with a sigh*) I thought I went through something when mine were born—but this is too awful.

EMILY. And according to John, Curt actually says he hates it! Isn't that terrible? (*After a pause—meaningly*) It's almost as if her suffering was a punishment, don't you think?

ESTHER. If it is, she's being punished enough, Heaven knows. It can't go on this way much longer or something dreadful will happen.

EMILY. Do you think the baby—

ESTHER. I don't know. I shouldn't say it but perhaps it would be better if—

EMILY. That's what I think.

ESTHER. Oh, I wish I didn't have such evil suspicions—but the way

Curt goes on—how can you help feeling there's something wrong?

JAYSON. (*suddenly*) How is Curt?

EMILY. John just came in from the garden. (*Turning around to where* JOHN *is dozing in his chair—sharply*) John! Well I never! If he isn't falling asleep! John! (*He jerks up his head and stares at her, blinking stupidly. She continues irritably*) A nice time to pick out for a nap, I must say.

JOHN. (*surlily*) Don't forget I have to be at the bank in the morning.

JAYSON. (*testily*) I have to be at the bank, too—and you don't notice me sleeping. Tell me about Curt. You just left him, didn't you?

JOHN. (*irritably*) Yes, and I've been walking around that damned garden half the night watching over him. Isn't that enough to wear anyone out? I can feel I've got a terrible cold coming on—

ESTHER. (*impatiently*) For goodness' sake, don't you start to pity yourself!

JOHN. (*indignantly*) I'm not. I think I've showed my willingness to do everything I could. If Curt was only the least bit grateful! He isn't. He hates us all and wishes we were out of his home. I would have left long ago if I didn't want to do my part in saving the family from disgrace.

JAYSON. (*impatiently*) Has he quieted down, that's what I want to know?

JOHN. (*harshly*) Not the least bit. He's out of his head—and I'd be out of mine if a child was being born to my wife that—

JAYSON. (*angrily*) Keep that to yourself! Remember you have no proof. (*Morosely*) Think all you want—but don't talk.

EMILY. (*pettishly*) The whole town knows it, anyway; I'm sure they must.

JAYSON. There's only been gossip—no real scandal. Let's do our united best to keep it at that. (*After a pause*) Where's Aunt Elizabeth? We'll have to keep an eye on her, too, or she's quite liable to blurt out the whole business before all comers.

ESTHER. You needn't be afraid. She's forgotten all about the scandalous part. No word of it has come to her out in the country and she hasn't set foot in town since that unfortunate tea, remember. And at present she's so busy wishing the child will be a boy, that she hasn't a thought for another thing. (*The door in the rear is opened and* MARK SHEFFIELD *enters. He comes up to the fire to warm himself. The others watch him in silence for a moment.*)

JAYSON. (*impatiently*) Well, Mark? Where's Curt?

SHEFFIELD. (*frowning*) Inside. I think he'll be with us in a minute. (*With a scornful smile*) Just now he's phoning to Bigelow. (*The others gasp.*)

JAYSON. (*furiously*) For God's sake, couldn't you stop him?

SHEFFIELD. Not without a scene. Your Aunt persuaded him to come into the house—and he rushed for the phone. I think he guessed we had been lying to him—

JAYSON. (*after a pause*) Then he—Bigelow—will be here soon?

SHEFFIELD. (*dryly*) It depends on his sense of decency. As he seems lacking in that quality, I've no doubt he'll come.

JOHN. (*rising to his feet—pompously*) Then I, for one, will go. Come, Emily. Since Curt seems bound to disgrace everyone concerned, I want it thoroughly understood that we wash our hands of the whole disgraceful affair.

EMILY. (*snappishly*) Go if you want to! I won't! (*Then with a sacrificing air*) I think it is our duty to stay.

JAYSON. (*exasperated*) Sit down. Wash your hands indeed! Aren't you as much concerned as any of us?

SHEFFIELD. (*sharply*) Sshh! I think I hear Curt now. (JOHN *sits down abruptly. All stiffen into stony attitudes. The door is opened and* CURTIS *enters. He is incredibly drawn and haggard, a tortured, bewildered expression in his eyes. His hair is disheveled, his boots caked with mud. He stands at the door staring from one to the other of his family with a wild, contemptuous scorn and mutters.*)

CURTIS. Liars! Well, he's coming now. (*Then bewilderedly*) Why didn't you want him to come, eh? He's my oldest friend. I've got to

593

talk to someone—and I can't to you. (*Wildly*) What do you want here, anyway? Why don't you go? (*A scream of* MARTHA'S *is heard through the doorway.* CURT *shudders violently, slams the door to with a crash, putting his shoulders against it as if to bar out the sound inexorably —in anguish*) God, why must she go through such agony? Why? Why? (*He goes to the fireplace as* MARK *makes way for him, flings himself exhaustedly on a chair, his shoulders bowed, his face hidden in his hands. The others stare at him pityingly. There is a long silence. Then the two women whisper together, get up and tiptoe out of the room, motioning for the others to follow them.* JOHN *does so.* SHEFFIELD *starts to go, then notices the preoccupied* JAYSON *who is staring moodily into the fire.*)

SHEFFIELD. Sstt! (*As* JAYSON *looks up—in a whisper*) Let's go out and leave him alone. Perhaps he'll sleep.

JAYSON. (*starting to follow* SHEFFIELD, *hesitates and puts a hand on his son's shoulder*) Curt. Remember I'm your father. Can't you confide in me? I'll do anything to help.

CURTIS. (*harshly*) No, Dad. Leave me alone.

JAYSON. (*piqued*) As you wish. (*He starts to go.*)

CURTIS. And send Big in to me as soon as he comes.

JAYSON. (*stops, appears about to object—then remarks coldly*) Very well—if you insist. (*He switches off the lights. He hesitates at the door uncertainly, then opens it and goes out. There is a pause. Then* CURTIS *lifts his head and peers about the room. Seeing he is alone he springs to his feet and begins to pace back and forth, his teeth clenched, his features working convulsively. Then, as if attracted by an irresistible impulse, he goes to the closed door and puts his ear to the crack. He evidently hears his wife's moans for he starts away—in agony.*)

CURTIS. Oh, Martha, Martha! Martha, darling! (*He flings himself in the chair by the fireplace—hides his face in his hands and sobs bitterly. There is a ring from somewhere in the house. Soon after there is a knock at the door.* CURTIS *doesn't hear at first but when it is repeated he mutters huskily*) Come in. (BIGELOW *enters.* CURTIS *looks up at him*) Close that door, Big, for God's sake!

BIGELOW. (*does so—then taking off his overcoat, hat, and throwing them on the lounge comes quickly over to* CURTIS) I got over as soon as I could. (*As he sees* CURTIS' *face he starts and says sympathetically*) By Jove, old man, you look as though you'd been through hell!

CURTIS. (*grimly*) I have. I am.

BIGELOW. (*slapping his back*) Buck up! (*Then anxiously*) How's Martha?

CURTIS. She's in hell, too—

BIGELOW. (*attempting consolation*) You're surely not worrying, are you? Martha is so strong and healthy there's no doubt of her pulling through in fine shape.

CURTIS. She should never have attempted this. (*After a pause*) I've a grudge against you, Big. It was you bringing your children over here that first planted this in her mind.

BIGELOW. (*after a pause*) I've guessed you thought that. That's why you haven't noticed me—or them—over here so much lately. I'll confess that I felt you— (*Angrily*) And the infernal gossip—I'll admit I thought that you—oh, damn this rotten town, anyway!

CURTIS. (*impatiently*) Oh, for God's sake! (*Bitterly*) I didn't want you here to discuss Bridgetown gossip.

BIGELOW. I know, old man, forgive me. (*In spite of the closed door one of* MARTHA'S *agonized moans is heard. They both shudder.*)

CURTIS. (*in a dead, monotonous tone*) She has been moaning like that hour after hour. I'll have those sounds in my ears until the day I die.

BIGELOW. (*trying to distract him*) Deuce take it, Curt, I never thought you'd turn morbid.

CURTIS. (*darkly*) I've changed, Big—I hardly know myself any more.

BIGELOW. Once you're back on the job again, you'll be all right. You're still determined to go on this expedition, aren't you?

CURTIS. Yes. I was supposed to join them this week in New York but I've arranged to catch up with them in China—as soon as it's possible for us to go.

BIGELOW. Us?

CURTIS. (*angrily aggressive*) Yes, certainly! Why not? Martha ought to be able to travel in a month or so.

BIGELOW. Yes, but—do you think it would be safe to take the child?

CURTIS. (*with a bitter laugh*) Yes—I was forgetting the child, wasn't I? (*Viciously*) But perhaps— (*Then catching himself with a groan*) Oh, damn all children, Big!

BIGELOW. (*astonished*) Curt!

CURTIS. (*in anguish*) I can't help it—I've fought against it. But it's there—deep down in me—and I can't drive it out. I can't!

BIGELOW. (*bewildered*) What, Curt?

CURTIS. Hatred! Yes, hatred! What's the use of denying it? I must tell someone and you're the only one who might understand. (*With a wild laugh*) For you—hated your wife, didn't you?

BIGELOW. (*stunned*) Good God, you don't mean you hate—Martha?

CURTIS. (*raging*) Hate Martha? How dare you, you fool! I love Martha—love her with every miserable drop of blood in me—with all my life—all my soul! She is my whole world—everything! Hate Martha! God, man, have you gone crazy to say such a mad thing? (*Savagely*) No. I hate it. It!

BIGELOW. (*shocked*) Curt! Don't you know you can't talk like that —now—when—

CURTIS. (*harshly*) It has made us both suffer torments—not only now—every day, every hour, for months and months. Why shouldn't I hate it, eh?

BIGELOW. (*staring at his friend's wild, distorted face with growing horror*) Curt! Can't you realize how horrible—

CURTIS. Yes, it's horrible. I've told myself that a million times. (*With emphasis*) But it's true!

596

BIGELOW. (*severely*) Shut up! What would Martha feel if she heard you going on this way? Why—it would kill her!

CURTIS. (*with a sobbing groan*) Oh, I know, I know! (*After a pause*) She read it in my eyes. Yes, it's horrible, but when I saw her there suffering so frightfully—I couldn't keep it out of my eyes. I tried to force it back—for her sake—but I couldn't. I was holding her hands and her eyes searched mine with such a longing question in them—and she read only my hatred there, not my love for her. And she screamed and seemed to try to push me away. I wanted to kneel down and pray for forgiveness—to tell her it was only my love for her—that I couldn't help it. And then the doctors told me to leave— and now the door is locked against me— (*He sobs.*)

BIGELOW. (*greatly moved*) This is only your damned imagination. They put you out because you were in their way, that's all. And as for Martha, she was probably suffering so much—

CURTIS. No. she read it in my eyes. I saw that look in hers—of hor- ror—horror of me!

BIGELOW. (*gruffly*) You're raving, damn it!

CURTIS. (*unheeding*) It came home to her then—the undeniable truth. (*With a groan*) Isn't it fiendish that I should be the one to add to her torture—in spite of myself—in spite of all my will to conceal it! She'll never forgive me, never! And how can I forgive myself?

BIGELOW. (*distractedly*) For God's sake, don't think about it! It's ridiculous!

CURTIS. (*growing more calm—in a tone of obsession*) She's guessed it ever since that day when we quarreled—her birthday. Oh, you can have no idea of the misery there has been in our lives since then. You haven't seen or guessed the reason. No one has. It's been—the thought of *it*.

BIGELOW. Curt!

CURTIS. (*unheeding*) For years we two were sufficient, each to each. There was no room for a third. And it was a fine, free life we had made.

BIGELOW. But that life was your life, Curt—

CURTIS. (*vehemently*) No, it was her life, too—her work as well as mine. She had made the life, our life—the work, our work. Had she the right to repudiate what she'd built because she suddenly has a fancy for a home, children, a miserable ease?

BIGELOW. Curt!

CURTIS. Oh, I tried to become reconciled. I tried my damnedest. But I couldn't. I grew to dread the idea of this intruder. She saw this. I denied it—but she knew. There was something in each of us the other grew to hate. And still we loved as never before, perhaps, for we grew to pity each other's helplessness.

BIGELOW. Curt! Are you sure you ought to tell anyone this?

CURTIS. (*waving his remark aside*) One day a thought suddenly struck me—a horrible but fascinating possibility that had never occurred to me before. (*With feverish intensity*) Can you guess what it was?

BIGELOW. No. And I think you've done enough morbid raving, if you ask me.

CURTIS. The thought came to me that if a certain thing happened, Martha could still go with me. And I knew, if it did happen, that she'd want to go, that she'd fling herself into the spirit of our work to forget, that she'd be mine more than ever.

BIGELOW. (*afraid to believe the obvious answer*) Curt!

CURTIS. Yes. My thought was that the child might be born dead.

BIGELOW. (*repelled—sternly*) Damn it, man, do you know what you're saying? (*Relentingly*) No, Curt, old boy, do stop talking. If you don't I'll send for a doctor, damned if I won't. That talk belongs in an asylum. God, man, can't you realize this is your child—yours as well as hers?

CURTIS. I've tried. I can't. There is some force in me—

BIGELOW. (*coldly*) Do you realize how contemptible this confession makes you out? (*Angrily*) Why, if you had one trace of human kindness in you—one bit of unselfish love for your wife—one particle of pity for her suffering—

CURTIS. (*anguished*) I have—all the love and pity in the world for her! That's why I can't help hating—the cause of her suffering.

BIGELOW. Have you never thought that you might repay Martha for giving up all her life to you by devoting the rest of yours to her?

CURTIS. (*bitterly*) She can be happy without me. She'll have this child—to take my place. (*Intensely*) You think I wouldn't give up my work for her? But I would! I'll stay here—do anything she wishes —if only we can make a new beginning again—together—*alone!*

BIGELOW. (*agitated*) Curt, for God's sake, don't return to that! Why, good God, man—even now—don't you realize what may be happening? And you can talk as if you were wishing—

CURTIS. (*fiercely*) I can't help but wish it!

BIGELOW. (*distractedly*) For the love of God, if you have such thoughts, keep them to yourself. (*The door in the rear is opened and* JAYSON *enters, pale and unnerved. A succession of quick, piercing shrieks is heard before he can close the door behind him. Shuddering*) My God! My God! (*With a fierce cry*) Will—this—never—end!

JAYSON. (*tremblingly*) Sh-h-h, they say this is the crisis. (*Puts his arm around* CURTIS) Bear up, my boy, it'll soon be over now. (*He sits down in the chair* BIGELOW *has vacated, pointedly ignoring the latter. The door is opened again and* EMILY, ESTHER, JOHN *and* SHEFFIELD *file in quickly as if escaping from the cries of the woman upstairs. They are all greatly agitated.* CURTIS *groans, pressing his clenched fists against his ears. The two women sit on the lounge.* MARK *comes forward and stands by* JAYSON's *chair,* JOHN *sits by the door as before.* BIGELOW *retreats behind* CURTIS' *chair, aware of their hostility. There is a long pause.*)

ESTHER. (*suddenly*) She's stopped— (*They all listen.*)

JAYSON. (*huskily*) Thank God, it's over at last. (*The door is opened and* MRS. DAVIDSON *enters. The old lady is radiant, weeping tears of joy.*)

599

MRS. DAVIDSON. (*calls out exultantly between sobs*) A son, Curt—a son. (*With rapt fervor—falling on her knees*) Let us all give thanks to God!

CURTIS. (*in a horrible cry of rage and anguish*) No! No! (*They all cry in fright and amazement:* "Curt!" *The door is opened and the* NURSE *appears.*)

NURSE. (*looking at* CURTIS, *in a low voice*) Mr. Jayson, your wife is asking for you.

BIGELOW. (*promptly slapping* CURTIS *on the back*) There! What did I tell you? Run, you chump!

CURTIS. (*with a gasp of joy*) Martha! (*He rushes out after the* NURSE.)

BIGELOW. (*comes forward to get his hat and coat from the sofa—coldly*) Pardon me, please. (*They shrink away from him.*)

EMILY. (*as he goes to the door—cuttingly*) Some people seem to have no sense of decency!

BIGELOW. (*stung, stops at the door and looks from one to the other of them—bitingly*) No, I quite agree with you. (*He goes out, shutting the door. They all gasp angrily.*)

JOHN. Scoundrel!

JAYSON. (*testily—going to* MRS. D., *who is still on her knees praying*) Do get up, Aunt Elizabeth! How ridiculous! What a scene if anyone should see you like that! (*He raises her to her feet and leads her to a chair by the fire. She obeys unresistingly, seemingly unaware of what she is doing.*)

ESTHER. (*unable to restrain her jealousy*) So it's a boy.

EMILY. Did you hear Curt—how he yelled out "No"? It's plain as the nose on your face he didn't want—

ESTHER. How awful!

JOHN. Well, can you blame him?

EMILY. And the awful cheek of that Bigelow person coming here—

ESTHER. They appeared as friendly as ever when we came in.

JOHN. (*scornfully*) Curt is a blind simpleton—and that man is a dyed-in-the-wool scoundrel.

JAYSON. (*frightenedly*) Shhh! Suppose we were overheard!

EMILY. When Curt leaves we can put her in her proper place. I'll soon let her know she hasn't fooled me, for one. (*While she is speaking* MRS. D. *has gotten up and is going silently toward the door.*)

JAYSON. (*testily*) Aunt Elizabeth, where are you going?

MRS. D. (*tenderly*) I must see him again, the dear! (*She goes out.*)

ESTHER. (*devoured by curiosity—hesitatingly*) I think I—come on, Emily. Let's go up and see—

EMILY. Not I! I never want to lay eyes on it.

JOHN. Nor I.

ESTHER. I was only thinking—everyone will think it funny if we don't.

JAYSON. (*hastily*) Yes, yes. We must keep up appearances. (*Getting to his feet*) Yes, I think we had better all go up—make some sort of inquiry about Martha, you know. It's expected of us and— (*They are all standing, hesitating, when the door in the rear is opened and the* NURSE *appears, supporting* CURTIS. *The latter is like a corpse. His face is petrified with grief, his body seems limp and half-paralyzed.*)

NURSE. (*her eyes flashing, indignantly*) It's a wonder some of you wouldn't come up—here, help me! Take him, can't you? I've got to run back! (JAYSON *and* SHEFFIELD *spring forward and lead* CURTIS *to a chair by the fire.*)

JAYSON. (*anxiously*) Curt! Curt, my boy! What is it, son?

EMILY. (*catching the* NURSE *as she tries to go*) Nurse! What is the matter?

NURSE. (*slowly*) His wife is dead. (*They are all still, stunned*) She lived just long enough to recognize him.

EMILY. And—the baby?

NURSE. (*with a professional air*) Oh, it's a fine, healthy baby—eleven pounds—that's what made it so difficult. (*She goes. The others all stand in silence.*)

601

ESTHER. (*suddenly sinking on the couch and bursting into tears*) Oh, I'm so sorry I said—or thought—anything wrong about her. Forgive me, Martha!

SHEFFIELD. (*honestly moved but unable to resist this opportunity for Latin—solemnly*) De mortuis nil nisi bonum.

JAYSON. (*who has been giving all his attention to his son*) Curt! Curt!

EMILY. Hadn't the doctor better—

JAYSON. Shhh! He begins to recognize me. Curt!

CURTIS. (*looking around him bewilderedly*) Yes. (*Suddenly remembrance comes and a spasm of intolerable pain contracts his features. He presses his hands to the side of his head and groans brokenly*) Martha! (*He appeals wildly to the others*) Her eyes—she knew me—she smiled—she whispered—Forgive me, Curt!— Forgive her—when it was I who should have said forgive me—but before I could—she— (*He falters brokenly.*)

EMILY. (*looking from one to the other meaningly as if this justified all their suspicions*) Oh!

CURTIS. (*a sudden triumph in his voice*) But she loved me again—only me—I saw it in her eyes! She had forgotten—*it.* (*Raging*) It has murdered her! (*Springing to his feet*) I hate it—I will never see it—never—never—I take my oath! (*As his father takes his arm—shaking him off*) Let me go! I am going back to her! (*He strides out of the door in a frenzy of grief and rage. They all stand transfixed, looking at each other bewilderedly.*)

EMILY. (*putting all her venomous gratification into one word*) Well!

CURTAIN

ACT FOUR

SCENE—*Same as Act One. It is afternoon of a fine day three days later. Motors are heard coming up the drive in front of the house. There is the muffled sound of voices. The* MAID *is seen going along the hall to the front door. Then the family enter from the rear. First come* JAYSON *and* ESTHER *with* MRS. DAVIDSON—*then* LILY, DICK *and* SHEFFIELD—*then* JOHN *and his wife. All are dressed in mourning. The only one who betrays any signs of sincere grief is* MRS. DAVIDSON. *The others all have a strained look, irritated, worried, or merely gloomy. They seem to be thinking "The worst is yet to come."*

JAYSON. (*leading* MRS. D., *who is weeping softly, to the chair at left of table—fretfully*) Please do sit down, Aunt. (*She does so mechanically*) And do stop crying. (*He sits down in front of table.* ESTHER *goes to couch where she is joined by* EMILY. MARK *goes over and stands in back of them.* DICK *and* JOHN *sit at rear of table.* LILY *comes down front and walks about nervously. She seems in a particularly fretful, upset mood.*)

LILY. (*trying to conceal her feelings under a forced flippancy*) What ridiculous things funerals are, anyway! That stupid minister—whining away through his nose! Why does the Lord show such a partiality for men with adenoids, I wonder!

JAYSON. (*testily*) Sshhh! Have you no respect for anything?

LILY. (*resentfully*) If I had, I'd have lost it when I saw all of you pulling such long faces in the church where you knew you were under observation. Pah! Such hypocrisy! And then, to cap it all, Emily has to force out a few crocodile tears at the grave!

EMILY. (*indignantly*) When I saw Curt—that's why I cried—not for her!

603

JAYSON. What a scene Curt made! I actually believe he wanted to throw himself into the grave!

DICK. You *believe* he wanted to! Why, it was all Mark and I could do to hold him, wasn't it, Mark? (SHEFFIELD *nods.*)

JAYSON. I never expected he'd turn violent like that. He's seemed calm enough the past three days.

LILY. Calm! Yes, just like a corpse is calm.

JAYSON. (*distractedly*) And now this perfectly mad idea of going away today to join that infernal expedition—leaving that child on our hands—the child he has never even looked at! Why, it's too monstrously flagrant! He's deliberately flaunting this scandal in everyone's face!

JOHN. (*firmly*) He must be brought to time.

SHEFFIELD. Yes, we must talk to him—quite openly, if we're forced to. After all, I guess he realizes the situation more keenly than any of us.

LILY. (*who has wandered to window on right*) You mean you think he believes— Well, I don't. And you had better be careful not to let him guess what you think. (*Pointing outside*) There's my proof. There he is walking about with Bigelow. Can you imagine Curt doing that—if he thought for a moment—

DICK. Oh, I guess Curt isn't all fool. He knows that's the very best way to keep people from suspecting.

ESTHER. (*indignantly*) But wouldn't you think that Bigelow person— It's disgusting, his sticking to Curt like this.

SHEFFIELD. Well, for one, I'm becoming quite resigned to Bigelow's presence. In the first place, he seems to be the only one who can bring Curt to reason. Then again, I feel that it is to Bigelow's own interest to convince Curt that he mustn't provoke an open scandal by running away without acknowledging this child.

LILY. (*suddenly bursting forth hysterically*) Oh, I hate you, all of you! I loathe your suspicions—and I loathe myself because I'm beginning to be poisoned by them, too.

604

EMILY. Really, Lily, at this late hour—after the way Curt has acted —and her last words when she was dying—

LILY. (*distractedly*) I know! Shut up! Haven't you told it a million times already? (MRS. DAVIDSON *gets up and walks to the door, rear. She has been crying softly during this scene, oblivious to the talk around her.*)

JAYSON. (*testily*) Aunt Elizabeth! Where are you going? (*As she doesn't answer but goes out into the hall*) Esther, go with her and see that she doesn't—

ESTHER. (*gets up with a jealous irritation*) She's only going up to see the baby. She's simply forgotten everything else in the world!

LILY. (*indignantly*) She probably realizes what we are too mean to remember—that the baby, at least, is innocent. Wait, Esther. I'll come with you.

JAYSON Yes, hurry, she shouldn't be left alone. (ESTHER *and* LILY *follow the old lady out, rear.*)

DICK. (*after a pause—impatiently*) Well, what next? I don't see what good we are accomplishing. May I run along? (*He gets up restlessly as he is speaking and goes to the window.*)

JAYSON. (*severely*) You will stay, if you please. There's to be no shirking on anyone's part. It may take all of us to induce Curt—

SHEFFIELD. I wouldn't worry. Bigelow is taking that job off our hands, I imagine.

DICK. (*looking out of the window*) He certainly seems to be doing his damnedest. (*With a sneer*) The stage missed a great actor in him.

JAYSON. (*worriedly*) But, if Bigelow should fail—

SHEFFIELD. Then we'll succeed. (*With a grim smile*) By God, we'll have to.

JAYSON. Curt has already packed his trunks and had them taken down to the station—told me he was leaving on the five o'clock train.

SHEFFIELD. But didn't you hint to him there was now this matter of the child to be considered in making his plans?

605

THE FIRST MAN

JAYSON. (*lamely*) I started to. He simply flared up at me with insane rage.

DICK. (*looking out the window*) Say, I believe they're coming in.

JAYSON. Bigelow?

DICK. Yes, they're both making for the front door.

SHEFFIELD. I suggest we beat a retreat to Curt's study and wait there.

JAYSON. Yes, let's do that—come on, all of you. (*They all retire grumblingly but precipitately to the study, closing the door behind them. The front door is heard opening and a moment later* CURTIS *and* BIGELOW *enter the room.* CURTIS' *face is set in an expression of stony grief.* BIGELOW *is flushed, excited, indignant.*)

BIGELOW. (*as* CURTIS *sinks down on the couch—pleading indignantly*) Curt, damn it, wake up! Are you made of stone? Has everything I've said gone in one ear and out the other? I know it's hell for me to torment you at this particular time but it's your own incredibly unreasonable actions that force me to. I know how terribly you must feel but—damn it, man, postpone this going away! Face this situation like a man! Be reconciled to your child, stay with him at least until you can make suitable arrangements—

CURTIS. (*fixedly*) I will never see it! Never!

BIGELOW. How can you keep repeating that—with Martha hardly cold in her grave? I ask you again, what would she think, how would she feel— If you would only consent to see this baby, I know you'd realize how damnably mad and cruel you are. Won't you—just for a second?

CURTIS. No. (*Then raging*) If I saw it I'd be tempted to— (*Then brokenly*) No more of that talk, Big. I've heard enough. I've reached the limit.

BIGELOW. (*restraining his anger with difficulty—coldly*) That's your final answer, eh? Well, I'm through. I've done all I could. If you want to play the brute—to forget all that was most dear in the world to Martha—to go your own damn selfish way—well, there's nothing more to be said. (*He takes a step toward the door*) And I—I want you to understand that all friendship ceases between us from this day. You're not the Curt I thought I knew—and I have nothing but a feeling of repulsion—good-by. (*He starts for the door.*)

CURTIS. (*dully*) Good-by, Big.

BIGELOW. (*stops, his features working with grief, and looks back at his friend—then suddenly goes back to him—penitently*) Curt! Forgive me! I ought to know better. This isn't you. You'll come to yourself when you've had time to think it over. The memory of Martha—she'll tell you what you must do. (*He wrings* CURTIS' *hand*) Good-by, old scout!

CURTIS. (*dully*) Good-by. (BIGELOW *hurries out, rear.* CURTIS *sits in a dumb apathy for a while—then groans heartbrokenly*) Martha! Martha! (*He springs to his feet distractedly. The door of the study is slowly opened and* SHEFFIELD *peers out cautiously—then comes into the room, followed by the others. They all take seats as before.* CURTIS *ignores them.*)

SHEFFIELD. (*clearing his throat*) Curt—

CURTIS. (*suddenly*) What time is it, do you know?

SHEFFIELD. (*looking at his watch*) Two minutes to four.

CURTIS. (*impatiently*) Still an hour more of this!

JAYSON. (*clearing his throat*) Curt— (*Before he starts what he intends to say, there is the sound of voices from the hall.* ESTHER *and* LILY *help in* MRS. DAVIDSON *to her former chair. The old lady's face is again transformed with joy.* ESTHER *joins* EMILY *on the couch.* LILY *sits in chair—front right. There is a long, uncomfortable pause during which* CURTIS *paces up and down.*)

MRS. DAVIDSON. (*suddenly murmuring aloud to herself—happily*) He's such a dear! I could stay watching him forever.

JAYSON. (*testily*) Sshhh! Aunt! (*Then clearing his throat again*) Surely you're not still thinking of going on the five o'clock train, are you, Curt?

CURTIS. Yes.

SHEFFIELD. (*dryly*) Then Mr. Bigelow didn't persuade you—

CURTIS. (*coldly and impatiently*) I'm not to be persuaded by Big or anyone else. And I'll thank you not to talk any more about it. (*They all stiffen resentfully at his tone.*)

JAYSON. (*to* CURTIS—*in a pleading tone*) You mustn't be unreasonable, Curt. After all we are your family—your best friends in the world—and we are only trying to help you—

CURTIS. (*with nervous vehemence*) I don't want your help. You'll help me most by keeping silent.

EMILY. (*with a meaning look at the others—sneeringly*) Yes, no doubt.

ESTHER. Sshhh, Emily!

JAYSON. (*helplessly*) But, you see, Curt—

SHEFFIELD. (*with his best judicial air*) If you'll all allow me to be the spokesman, I think perhaps that I— (*They all nod and signify their acquiescence*) Well, then, will you listen to me, Curt? (*This last somewhat impatiently as* CURTIS *continues to pace, eyes on the floor.*)

CURTIS. (*without looking at him—harshly*) Yes, I'm listening. What else can I do when you've got me cornered? Say what you like and let's get this over.

SHEFFIELD. First of all, Curt, I hope it is needless for me to express how very deeply we all feel for you in your sorrow. But we sincerely trust that you are aware of our heartfelt sympathy. (*They all nod. A bitter, cynical smile comes over* LILY's *face.*)

ESTHER. (*suddenly breaking down and beginning to weep*) Poor Martha! (SHEFFIELD *glances at his wife, impatient at this interruption. The others also show their irritation.*)

EMILY. (*pettishly*) Esther! For goodness' sake! (CURTIS *hesitates, stares at his sister frowningly as if judging her sincerity—then bends down over her and kisses the top of her bowed head impulsively—seems about to break down himself—grits his teeth and forces it back—glances around at the others defiantly and resumes his pacing.* ESTHER *dries her eyes.*)

608

SHEFFIELD. (*clearing his throat*) I may truthfully say we all feel—as Esther does—even if we do not give vent— (*With an air of sincere sympathy*) I know how terrible a day this must be for you, Curt. We all do. And we feel guilty in breaking in upon the sanctity of your sorrow in any way. But, if you will pardon my saying so, your own course of action—the suddenness of your plans—have made it imperative that we come to an understanding about certain things—about one thing in particular, I might say. (*He pauses.* CURTIS *goes on pacing back and forth as if he hadn't heard.*)

JAYSON. (*placatingly*) Yes, it is for the best, Curt.

ESTHER. Yes, Curt dear, you mustn't be unreasonable.

DICK. (*feeling called upon to say something*) Yes, old man, you've got to face things like a regular. Facts are facts. (*This makes everybody uneasy.*)

LILY. (*springing to her feet*) Phew! it's close in here. I'm going out in the garden. You can call me when these—orations—are finished. (*She sweeps out scornfully.*)

JAYSON. (*calling after her imperiously*) Lily! (*But she doesn't answer and he gives it up with a hopeless sigh.*)

CURTIS. (*harshly*) What time is it?

SHEFFIELD. You have plenty of time to listen to what I—I should rather say we—have to ask you, Curt. I promise to be brief. But first let me again impress upon you that I am talking in a spirit of the deepest friendliness and sympathy with you—as a fellow-member of the same family, I may say—and with the highest ideals and the honor of that family always in view. (CURTIS *makes no comment.* SHEFFIELD *unconsciously begins to adopt the alert keenness of the cross-examiner*) First, let me ask you, is it your intention to take that five o'clock train today?

CURTIS. (*harshly*) I've told you that.

SHEFFIELD. And then you'll join this expedition in Asia?

CURTIS. You know that.

SHEFFIELD. To be gone five years?

609

CURTIS. (*shrugging his shoulders*) More or less.

SHEFFIELD. Is it your intention to return here at any time before you leave for Asia?

CURTIS. No.

SHEFFIELD. And your determination on these plans is irrevocable?

CURTIS. Irrevocable! Exactly. Please remember that.

SHEFFIELD. (*sharply*) That being your attitude, I will come bluntly to the core of the whole matter—the child whose coming into the world cost Martha her life.

CURTIS. (*savagely*) Her murderer! (*They all look shocked, suspicious.*)

SHEFFIELD. (*remonstratingly but suspiciously*) You can hardly hold the child responsible for the terrible outcome. Women die every day from the same cause. (*Keenly*) Why do you attribute guilt to the child in this case, Curt?

CURTIS. It lives and Martha is gone— But I've said I never wanted it mentioned to me. Will you please remember that?

SHEFFIELD. (*sharply*) Its name is Jayson, Curt—in the eyes of the law. Will *you* please remember that?

CURTIS. (*distractedly*) I don't want to remember anything! (*Wildly*) Please, for God's sake, leave me alone!

SHEFFIELD. (*coldly*) I am sorry, Curt, but you can't act as if you were alone in this affair.

CURTIS. Why not? Am I not alone—more alone this minute than any creature on God's earth?

SHEFFIELD. (*soothingly*) In your great grief. Yes, yes, of course. We all appreciate—and we hate to— (*Persuasively*) Yes, it would be much wiser to postpone these practical considerations until you are in a calmer mood. And if you will only give us the chance—why not put off this precipitate departure—for a month, say—and in the meantime—

CURTIS. (*harshly*) I am going when I said I was. I must get away from this horrible hole—as far away as I can. I must get back to my work for only in it will I find Martha again. But you—you can't understand that. What is the good of all this talking which leads nowhere?

SHEFFIELD. (*coldly*) You're mistaken. It leads to this: Do you understand that your running away from this child—on the very day of its mother's funeral!—will have a very queer appearance in the eyes of the world?

EMILY. And what are you going to do with the baby, Curt? Do you think you can run off regardless and leave it here—on our hands?

CURTIS. (*distractedly*) I'll give it this home. And someone—anyone—Esther, Lily—can appoint a nurse to live here and— (*Breaking down*) Oh, don't bother me!

SHEFFIELD. (*sharply*) In the world's eyes, it will appear precious like a desertion on your part.

CURTIS. Oh, arrange it to suit yourselves—anything you wish—

SHEFFIELD. (*quickly*) I'll take you at your word. Then let us arrange it this way. You will remain here a month longer at least—

CURTIS. No!

SHEFFIELD. (*ignoring the interruption*) You can make plans for the child's future in that time, become reconciled to it—

CURTIS. No!

JAYSON. (*pleadingly*) Curt—please—for all our sakes—when the honor of the family is at stake.

DICK. Yes, old man, there's that about it, you know.

CURTIS. No.

EMILY. Oh, he's impossible!

SHEFFIELD. Perhaps Curt misunderstood me. (*Meaningly*) Be reconciled to it in the eyes of the public, Curt. That's what I meant. Your own private feelings in the matter—are no one's business but your own, of course.

CURTIS. (*bewilderedly*) But—I don't see— Oh, damn your eyes of the public!

EMILY. (*breaking in*) It's all very well for you to ignore what people in town think—you'll be in China or heaven knows where. The scandal won't touch you—but we've got to live here and have our position to consider.

CURTIS. (*mystified*) Scandal? What scandal? (*Then with a harsh laugh*) Oh, you mean the imbecile busy-bodies will call me an unnatural father. Well, let them! I suppose I am. But they don't know—

EMILY. (*spitefully*) Perhaps they know more than you think they do.

CURTIS. (*turning on her—sharply*) Just what do you mean by that, eh?

ESTHER. Emily! Shhh!

JAYSON. (*flurriedly*) Be still, Emily. Let Mark do the talking.

SHEFFIELD. (*interposing placatingly*) What Emily means is simply this, Curt: You haven't even been to look at this child since it has been born—not once, have you?

CURTIS. No, and I never intend—

SHEFFIELD. (*insinuatingly*) And don't you suppose the doctors and nurses—and the servants—have noticed this? It is not the usual procedure, you must acknowledge, and they wouldn't be human if they didn't think your action—or lack of action—peculiar and comment on it outside.

CURTIS. Well, let them! Do you think I care a fiddler's curse how people judge me?

SHEFFIELD. It is hardly a case of their judging—you. (*Breaking off as he catches* CURTIS' *tortured eyes fixed on him wildly*) This is a small town, Curt, and you know as well as I do, gossip is not the least of its faults. It doesn't take long for such things to get started. (*Persuasively*) Now I ask you, frankly, is it wise to provoke deliberately what may easily be set at rest by a little—I'll be frank—a little pretense on your part?

JAYSON. Yes, my boy. As a Jayson, I know you don't wish—

ESTHER. (*with a sigh*) Yes, you really must think of us, Curt.

CURTIS. (*in an acute state of muddled confusion*) But—I—you—

how are you concerned? Pretense? You mean you want me to stay and pretend—in order that you won't be disturbed by any silly tales they tell about me? (*With a wild laugh*) Good God, this is too much! Why does a man have to be maddened by fools at such a time! (*Raging*) Leave me alone! You're like a swarm of poisonous flies.

JAYSON. Curt! This is—really—when we've tried to be so considerate—

JOHN. (*bursting with rage*) It's an outrage to allow such insults!

DICK. You're not playing the game, Curt.

EMILY. (*spitefully*) It seems to me it's much more for Martha's sake we're urging you than for our own. After all, the town can't say anything against us.

CURTIS. (*turning on her*) Martha's sake? (*Brokenly*) Martha is gone. Leave her out of this.

SHEFFIELD. (*sharply*) But unfortunately, Curt, others will not leave her out of this. They will pry and pry—you know what they are—and—

EMILY. Curt couldn't act the way he is doing if he ever really cared for her.

CURTIS. You dare to say that! (*Then controlling himself a bit—with scathing scorn*) What do you know of love—women like you! You call your little rabbit-hutch emotions love—your bread-and-butter passions—and you have the effrontery to judge—

EMILY. (*shrinking from him frightenedly*) Oh! John!

JOHN. (*getting to his feet*) I protest! I cannot allow my own brother—

DICK. (*grabbing his arm*) Keep your head, old boy.

SHEFFIELD. (*peremptorily*) You are making a fool of yourself, Curt —and you are damned insulting in the bargain. I think I may say that we've all about reached the end of our patience. What Emily said is for your own best interest, if you had the sense to see it. And I put it to you once and for all: Are you or are you not willing to act like a man of honor to protect your own good name, the family name, the name of this child, and your wife's memory? Let me tell you, your wife's good name is more endangered by your stubbornness than anything else.

CURTIS. (*trembling with rage*) I—I begin to think—you—all of you—are aiming at something against Martha in this. Yes—in back of your words—your actions—I begin to feel— (*Raging*) Go away! Get out of this house—all of you! Oh, I know your meanness! I've seen how you've tried to hurt her ever since we came—because you resented in your small minds her evident superiority—

EMILY. (*scornfully*) Superiority, indeed!

CURTIS. Her breadth of mind and greatness of soul that you couldn't understand. I've guessed all this, and if I haven't interfered it's only because I knew she was too far above you to notice your sickening malice—

EMILY. (*furiously*) You're only acting—acting for our benefit because you think we don't—

CURTIS. (*turning on her—with annihilating contempt*) Why, you— poor little nonentity! (JOHN *struggles to get forward but* DICK *holds him back.*)

EMILY. (*insane with rage—shrilly*) But we know—and the whole town knows—and you needn't pretend you've been blind. You've given the whole thing away yourself—the silly way you've acted— telling everyone how you hated that baby—letting everyone see—

JAYSON. Emily! (*The others are all frightened, try to interrupt her.* CURTIS *stares at her in a stunned bewilderment.*)

EMILY. (*pouring forth all her venom regardless*) But you might as well leave off your idiotic pretending. It doesn't fool us—or anyone else—your sending for Bigelow that night—your hobnobbing with him ever since—your pretending he's as much your friend as ever. They're all afraid of you—but I'm not! I tell you to your face—it's all acting you're doing—just cheap acting to try and pull the wool over our eyes until you've run away like a coward—and left us to face the disgrace for you with this child on our hands!

614

ESTHER. (*trying to silence her—excitedly*) Emily! Keep still, for Heaven's sake! (*The others all utter exclamations of caution, with fearful glances at* CURTIS.)

EMILY. (*becoming exhausted by her outburst—more faintly*) Well, someone had to show him his place. He thinks he's so superior to us just because—telling us how much better she was than— But I won't stand for that. I've always had a clean name—and always will— and my children, too, thank God! (*She sinks down on the couch exhausted, panting but still glaring defiantly at* CURTIS.)

CURTIS. (*an awareness of her meaning gradually forcing itself on his mind*) Bigelow! Big? Pretending he's as much my friend— (*With a sudden gasp of sickened understanding*) Oh! (*He sways as if he were about to fall, shrinking away from* EMILY, *all horror*) Oh, you— you—you—filth!

JOHN. (*his fists clenched, tries to advance on his brother*) How dare you insult my wife! (*He is restrained, held back by his remonstrating father and* DICK.)

MRS. DAVIDSON. (*as if suddenly coming out of a dream—frightenedly*) What is the matter? Why is John mad at Curt?

CURTIS. (*his hands over his eyes, acting like a person stricken with a sudden attack of nausea, weakly*) So—that's—what has been in your minds. Oh, this is bestial—disgusting! And there is nothing to be done. I feel defenseless. One would have to be as low as you are— She would have been defenseless, too. It is better that she's dead. (*He stares about him—wildly*) And you think—you all think—

ESTHER. (*pityingly*) Curt, dear, we don't think anything except what you've made us think with your crazy carrying-on.

CURTIS. (*looking from one to the other of them*) Yes—all of you— it's on your faces. (*His eyes fix themselves on his aunt*) No, you don't —you don't—

MRS. DAVIDSON. I? Don't what, Curtis? My, how sick you look, poor boy!

CURTIS. You don't believe—this child—

615

MRS. DAVIDSON. (*proudly*) He's the sweetest baby I ever saw!

CURTIS. Ah, I know you— (*Looking around at the others with loathing and hatred*) But look at them— (*With a burst of fierce determination*) Wait! I'll give you the only answer— (*He dashes for the door in rear, shakes off his father and* DICK, *who try to stop him, and then is heard bounding up the stairs in hall.* DICK *runs after him,* JAYSON *as far as the doorway.* ESTHER *gives a stifled scream. There is a tense pause. Then* DICK *reappears.*)

DICK. It's all right. I saw him go in.

JAYSON. (*frightenedly*) But—good God—he's liable—why didn't you follow him?

DICK. The doctor and nurse are there. They would have called out, wouldn't they, if—

MRS. DAVIDSON. (*getting angrier and angrier as her puzzlement has grown greater—in a stern tone*) I understand less and less of this. Where has Curtis gone? Why did he act so sick? What is the matter with all of you?

ESTHER. Nothing, Aunt dear, nothing!

MRS. DAVIDSON. No, you'll not hush me up! (*Accusingly*) You all look guilty. Have you been saying anything against Curt's baby? That was what Curtis seemed to think. A fine time you've picked out—with his wife not cold in her grave!

JAYSON. Aunt!

MRS. DAVIDSON. I never liked that woman. I never understood her. But now—now I love her and beg her forgiveness. She died like a true woman in the performance of her duty. She died gloriously— and I will always respect her memory. (*Suddenly flying into a passion*) I feel that you are all hostile to her baby—poor, little, defenseless creature! Yes, you'd hate the idea of Curtis' having a son—you and your girls! Well, I'll make you bitterly regret the day you— (*She plumps herself down in her chair again, staring stubbornly and angrily before her.*)

EMILY. (*spitefully*) I fear it will be necessary to tell Aunt--

616

JAYSON. Sshh! You have made enough trouble with your telling already! (*Miserably*) It should never have come to this pass. Curt will never forgive us, never!

ESTHER. (*resentfully to* EMILY) See what not holding your tongue has done—and my children will have to suffer for it, too!

SHEFFIELD. (*severely*) If Emily had permitted me to conduct this business uninterruptedly, this would never have occurred.

EMILY. That's right! All pick on me! Cowards! (*She breaks down and sobs.*)

DICK. (*from the doorway. Coming back into the room*) Sstt! Here he comes!

CURTIS. (*Reënters. There is a look of strange exultation on his face. He looks from one to the other of them. He stammers*) Well—my answer to you—your rotten world—I kissed him—he's mine! He looked at me—it was as if Martha looked at me—through his eyes.

ESTHER. (*voicing the general relief. Joyfully*) Oh, Curt! You won't go now? You'll stay?

CURTIS. (*staring at her, then from one to another of the rest with a withering scorn*) Ha! Now you think you've conquered, do you? No, I'm not going to stay. Do you think your vile slander could influence me to give up my work? And neither shall you influence the life of my son. I leave him here. I must. But not to your tender mercies. No, no! Thank God, there still remains one Jayson with unmuddled integrity to whom I can appeal. (*He goes to* MRS. DAVIDSON) I'll leave him in your care, Aunt—while I'm gone.

MRS. DAVIDSON. (*delighted*) It will be a great happiness. He will be— the one God never granted me. (*Her lips trembling*) God has answered my prayer at last.

CURTIS. I thank you, Aunt. (*Kisses her reverentially.*)

MRS. DAVIDSON. (*pleased but morally bound to grumble at him*) But I cannot approve of your running away like this. It isn't natural. (*Then with selfish haste, fearing her words may change his mind*

617

and she will lose the baby) But you always were a queer person—and a man must do faithfully the work ordained for him.

CURTIS. (*gladly*) Yes, I must go! What good would I be for him—or anyone—if I stayed? Thank God, you understand. But I'll come back. (*The light of an ideal beginning to shine in his eyes*) When he's old enough, I'll teach him to know and love a big, free life. Martha used to say that he would take her place in time. Martha shall live again for me in him. And you, Aunt, swear to keep him with you—out there in the country—never to let him know this obscene little world. (*He indicates his relatives.*)

MRS. DAVIDSON. Yes, I promise, Curtis. Let anyone dare—! (*She glares about her. The noise of a motor is heard from the drive. It stops in front of the house.*)

CURTIS. I must go. (*He kisses his aunt*) Teach him his mother was the most beautiful soul that ever lived. Good-by, Aunt.

MRS. DAVIDSON. Good-by, Curtis! (*Without looking at the others, he starts for the door, rear. They all break out into conscience-stricken protestations.*)

JAYSON. (*miserably*) Curt! You're not leaving us that way?

ESTHER. Curt—you're going—without a word! (*They all say this practically together and crowd toward him.* JOHN *and* EMILY *remain sullenly apart.* CURTIS *turns to face them.*)

LILY. (*enters from the rear*) You're not going, Curt?

CURTIS. (*turning to her*) Yes. Good-by, Lily. (*He kisses her*) You loved her, didn't you? You're not like— Take my advice and get away before you become— (*He has been staring into her face. Suddenly he pushes her brusquely away from him—coldly*) But I see in your face it's too late.

LILY. (*Miserably*) No, Curt—I swear—

CURTIS. (*facing them all defiantly*) Yes, I am going without a word—because I can't find the fitting one. Be thankful I can't. (*He again turns and strides to the door.*)

618

JAYSON. (*his grief overcoming him*) My boy! We are wrong—we know—but—at least say you forgive us.

CURTIS. (*wavers with his back towards them—then turns and forces the words out*) Ask forgiveness of her. She—yes—she was so fine—I feel she—so you are forgiven. Good-by. (*He goes. The motor is heard driving off. There is a tense pause.*)

LILY. Then he did find out? Oh, a fine mess you've made of everything! But no—I should say "we," shouldn't I? Curt guessed that. Oh, I hate you—and myself! (*She breaks down.*)

(*There is a strained pause during which they are all silent, their eyes avoiding each other, fixed in dull, stupid stares. Finally, DICK fidgets uncomfortably, heaves a noisy sigh, and blurts out with an attempt at comforting reassurance:*)

DICK. Well, it isn't as bad as it might have been, anyway. He did acknowledge the kid—before witnesses, too.

JAYSON. (*testily*) Keep your remarks to yourself, if you please! (*But most of his family are already beginning to look relieved.*)

CURTAIN

GOLD

A Play in Four Acts

CHARACTERS

CAPTAIN ISAIAH BARTLETT, *of the whaling ship "Triton"*

SILAS HORNE, *boatswain of the "Triton"*

BEN CATES

JIMMY KANAKA, *an Islander* } *of the "Triton's" crew*

BUTLER, *cook of the "Triton"*

ABEL, *the ship's boy*

SARAH ALLEN BARTLETT, *the captain's wife*

SUE, *their daughter*

NAT, *their son*

DANIEL DREW, *officer of a freight steamer*

DOCTOR BERRY

GOLD

ACT ONE

Scene—*A small, barren coral island on the southern fringe of the Malay Archipelago. The coral sand, blazing white under the full glare of the sun, lifts in the right foreground to a long hummock a few feet above sea-level. A stunted coco palm rises from the center of this elevation, its bunch of scraggly leaves drooping motionlessly, casting a small circular patch of shadow directly beneath on the ground about the trunk. About a hundred yards in the distance the lagoon is seen, its vivid blue contrasting with the white coral beach which borders its circular outline. The far horizon to seaward is marked by a broad band of purplish haze which separates the bright blue of the water from the metallic gray-blue of the sky. The island bakes. The intensity of the sun's rays is flung back skyward in a quivering mist of heat-waves which distorts the outlines of things, giving the visible world an intangible eerie quality, as if it were float-ing submerged in some colorless molten fluid.*

As the curtain rises, ABEL *is discovered lying asleep, curled up in the patch of shade beneath the coco palm. He is a runty, undersized boy of fifteen, with a shrivelled old face, tanned to parchment by the sun. He has on a suit of dirty dungarees, man's size, much too large for him, which hang in loose folds from his puny frame. A thatch of brown hair straggles in limp wisps from under the peaked canvas cap he wears. He looks terribly exhausted. His dreams are evidently fraught with terror, for he twitches convulsively and moans with fright.* BUTLER *enters hurriedly, panting, from the right, rear. He is a tall man of over middle age, dressed in the faded remainder of what*

623

was once a brown suit. The coat, the buttons of which have been torn off, hangs open, revealing his nakedness beneath. A cloth cap covers his bald head, with its halo of dirty thin gray hair. His body is emaciated. His face, with its round, blue eyes, is weathered and cracked by the sun's rays. The wreck of a pair of heavy shoes flop about his bare feet. He looks back cautiously, as if he were afraid of being followed; then satisfied that he is not, he approaches the sleeping boy, and bending down, puts his hand on ABEL's *forehead.* ABEL *groans and opens his eyes. He stares about furtively, as if seeking someone whose presence he dreads to find.*

ABEL. (*in a husky voice*) Where's Capt'n and the rest, Butts?

BUTLER. (*in a hoarse, cracked whisper*) On the beach—down there. (*He makes an exhausted gesture, right, and then sinks with a groan at the foot of the tree, leaning back against the trunk, trying vainly to hunch his long legs up so as to be completely in the shade.*)

ABEL. (*with avid eyes*) They ain't found no water yet?

BUTLER. (*shaking his head, his eyes closing wearily*) No. How would they—when there ain't any—not on this devil's island—dry as a bone, my sonny—sand and sun—that's all.

ABEL. (*with a sudden, shrill agony—his lips twitching*) I need a drink of water—something awful! (*With tremulous pleading*) Say, ain't you got 'nother drink left?—honest, ain't you?

BUTLER. (*looking around him cautiously*) Not so loud! (*Fixing his eyes sternly on the boy*) This is a dead secret, mind! You'll swear you won't blab—not to him?

ABEL. Sure, Butts, sure! Gawd strike me dead!

BUTLER. (*takes a pint bottle from the hip-pocket of his pants. It is about half full of water*) He—and the rest—they'd kill me like a dog—and you too, sonny—remember that!

ABEL. Sure! I ain't goin' to tell 'em, Butts. (*Stretching out his hands frenziedly*) Aw, give it to me, Butts! Give me a drink, for Christ's sake!

BUTLER. No, you don't! Only a few drops. It's got to last 'til a ship comes past that'll pick us up. That's the only hope. (*Holding the bottle at arm's length from the boy*) Hands down, now—or you don't get a drop! (*The boy lets his hands drop to his sides.* BUTLER *puts the bottle carefully to his lips, and allows the boy two gulps—then snatches it away*) That's all now. More later. (*He takes one gulp himself, and making a tremendous effort of will, jerks the bottle from his lips, and corking it quickly, thrusts it back in his pocket and heaves a shuddering sigh.*)

ABEL. Aw, more! Just another swaller—

BUTLER. (*determinedly*) No!

ABEL. (*crying weakly*) Yuh dirty mutt!

BUTLER. (*quietly*) Don't get riled. It only makes you hotter—and thirstier. (*The boy sinks back exhausted and closes his eyes.* BUTLER *begins to talk in a more assured voice, as if the sip of water had renewed his courage*) That'll save us yet, that bit of water. A lucky notion of mine to think of it—at the last moment. They were just lowering the boats. I could hear you calling to me to hurry and come. But I thought of filling this bottle. It'd been lying there in the galley for two years almost. I'd had it on my hip, full of whisky, that night in Oakland when I was shanghaied. So I filled it out of a bucket before I ran to the boat. Lucky I did, son—for you and me—not for them— damn 'em! (*As if in self-justification*) Why should I tell 'em, eh? Did I ever get anything better than a kick or a curse from one of them? (*Vindictively*) Would they give it to me if they had it? They'd see me in hell first! And besides, it's too late for them. They're mad as hatters right now, the four of them. They ain't had a drop since three nights back, when the water in the cask gave out and we rowed up against this island in the dark. (*Suddenly he laughs queerly*) Didn't you hear them shouting and yelling like lunatics just before I came?

ABEL. I thought I heard something—on'y maybe I was dreamin'.

BUTLER. It's them that are doing the dreaming. I was with them.

(*With rising anger*) He kicked me awake—and every time I tried to get away he beat me back. He's strong yet—(*with threatening vindictiveness*)—but he can't last long, damn him! (*Controlling himself, goes on with his story excitedly*) We went looking for water. Then Jimmy Kanaka saw a boat sunk half under down inside the reef—a Malay canoe, only bigger. They thought there might be something to drink on her. All of a sudden they gave an awful yell. They was all standing about a box they'd forced open, yelling and cursing and out of their heads completely. When I looked I seen the box was full of all sorts of metal junk—bracelets and bands and necklaces that I guess the Malays wear. Nothing but brass and copper, and bum imitations of diamonds and things—not worth a damn! I picked up some of the stuff to make sure. Then I told him straight. "This ain't gold. It's brass and copper—not worth a damn." God, he got wild! I had to run, or he'd knifed me. (*With sudden violence*) It serves 'em right, all that's happened and going to happen. Me shanghaied when I was drunk—taken away from a good job and forced to cook the swill on a rotten whaler! Oh, I'll pay him back for it! His damn ship is wrecked and lost to him—that's the first of it. I'll see him rot and die—and the three with him! But you and me'll be saved! D'you know why I've let you go halves on this water? It's because they kicked and beat you, too. And now we'll get even! (*He sinks back, exhausted by this outburst. They are both silent, leaning with closed eyes against the bole of the tree. A murmur of men's voices comes from the right, rear, and gradually gets nearer.*)

ABEL. (*opening his eyes with a start*) Butts! I hear 'em comin'!

BUTLER. (*listening, wide-eyed, for a moment*) Yes, it's them. (*He gets up weakly.* ABEL *staggers to his feet. They both move to the left.* BUTLER *shades his eyes with his hands and looks toward the beach*) Look! They're dragging along that box of junk with 'em, the damn fools! (*Warningly*) They're crazy as hell. Don't give 'em no chance to pick on you, d'you hear? (*There is a scuffling of heavy footsteps in the sand, and* CAPTAIN BARTLETT *appears, followed by* HORNE, *who in turn is followed by* CATES *and* JIMMY KANAKA. BARTLETT *is a tall, huge-framed figure of a man, dressed in a blue double-breasted coat, pants of the same material, and rubber sea-boots turned down from the knees. In spite of the ravages of hunger and thirst there is still a suggestion of immense strength in his heavy-muscled body. His head is massive, thickly covered with tangled, iron-gray hair. His face is large, bony, and leather-tanned, with a long aquiline nose and a gash of a mouth shadowed by a bristling gray mustache. His broad jaw sticks out at an angle of implacable stubbornness. Bushy gray brows overhang the obsessed glare of his somber dark eyes.* SILAS HORNE *is a thin, parrot-nosed, angular old man, his lean face marked by a lifetime of crass lusts and mean cruelty. He is dressed in gray cotton trousers, and a singlet torn open across his hairy chest. The exposed skin of his arms and shoulders and chest has been blistered and seared by the sun. A cap is on his head.* CATES *is squat and broad chested, with thick, stumpy legs and arms. His square, stupid face, with its greedy pig's eyes, is terribly pock-marked. He is gross and bestial, an unintelligent brute. He is dressed in dungaree pants and a dirty white sailor's blouse, and wears a brown cap.* JIMMY KANAKA *is a tall, sinewy, bronzed young Islander. He wears only a loin cloth and a leather belt with a sheath-knife. The last two are staggering beneath the weight of a heavy inlaid chest. The eyes of the three white men are wild. They pant exhaustedly, their legs trembling with weakness beneath them. Their lips are puffed and cracked, their voices muffled by their swollen tongues. But there is a mad air of happiness, of excitement, about their scorched faces.*)

BARTLETT. (*in a crooning, monotonous voice*) It's heavy, I know, heavy—that chest. Up, bullies! Up with her! (He *flings himself in the shade, resting his back against the tree, and points to the sand at his feet.*) Put 'er there, bullies—there where I kin see!

HORNE. (*echoing his words mechanically*) Put 'er there!

CATES. (*in thick, stupid tones*) Aye-aye, sir! Down she goes, Jimmy. (*They set the chest down.*)

BARTLETT. Sit down, lads, sit down. Ye've earned your spell of rest. (*The three men throw themselves on the sand in attitudes of spent weariness.* BARTLETT's *eyes are fixed gloatingly on the chest. There is a silence suddenly broken by* CATES, *who leaps to a kneeling position with a choked cry.*)

CATES. (*his eyes staring at the* CAPTAIN *with fierce insistence*) I want a drink—water! (*The others are startled into a rigid, dazed attention.* HORNE's *lips move painfully in a soundless repetition of the word. There is a pause. Then* BARTLETT *strikes the sides of his head with his fist, as if to drive this obsession from his brain.* BUTLER *and* ABEL *stand looking at them with frightened eyes.*)

BARTLETT. (*having regained control over himself, in a determined voice, deep-toned and menacing*) If ye speak that word again, Ben Cates—if ye say it once again—ye'll be food for the sharks! Ye hear?

CATES. (terrified) Yes, sir. (*He collapses limply on the sand again.* HORNE *and the* KANAKA *relax hopelessly.*)

BARTLETT. (*with heavy scorn*) Are ye a child to take on like a sick woman—cryin' for what ye know we've not got? Can't ye stand up under a little thirst like a man? (*Resolutely*) There'll be water enough —if ye'll wait and keep a stiff upper lip on ye. We'll all be picked up today. I'll stake my word on it. This state o' things can't last. (*His eyes fall on the chest*) Ye ought to be singin' 'stead o' cryin'—after the find we've made. What's the lack of water amount to—when ye've gold before you? (*With mad exultation*) Gold! Enough of it is your share alone to buy ye rum, and wine, and women, too, for the rest o' your life.

CATES. (*straightening up to a sitting posture—his small eyes staring at the box fascinatedly—in a stupid mumble*) Aye—aye—rum and wine!

BARTLETT. (*half closing his eyes as if the better to enjoy his vision*) Aye, rum and wine and women for you and Horne and Jimmy. No more hard work on the dirty sea for ye, bullies, but a full payday in your pockets to spend each day o' the year. (*The three strain their ears, listening eagerly. Even* BUTLER *and* ABEL *advance a step or two toward him, as if they, too, were half hypnotized*) And Cates grumbling because he's thirsty! I'd be the proper one to complain—if complainin' there was to do! Ain't I lost my ship and the work o' two years with her? And what have ye lost, all three, but a few rags o' clothes? (*With savage emphasis*) I tell ye, I be glad the "Triton" went down! (*He taps the box with his fingers*) They's more in this than ever was earned by all the whalin' ships afloat. They's gold—heavy and solid—and diamonds and emeralds and rubies!—red and green, they be.

CATES. (*licking his lips*) Aye, I seen 'em there—and emeralds be green, I know, and sell for a ton of gold!

BARTLETT. (*as if he hadn't heard and was dreaming out loud to himself*) Rum and wine for you three, and rest for me. Aye, I'll rest to home 'til the day I die. Aye, woman, I be comin' home now. Aye, Nat and Sue, your father be comin' home for the rest o' his life! I'll give up whalin' like ye've always been askin' me, Sarah. Aye, I'll go to meetin' with ye on a Sunday like ye've always prayed I would. We'll make the damn neighbors open their eyes, curse 'em! Carriages and silks for ye—they'll be nothin' too good—and for Sue and the boy. I've been dreamin' o' this for years. I never give a damn 'bout the oil—that's just trade—but I always hoped on some voyage I'd pick up ambergris—a whole lot of it—and that's worth gold!

HORNE. (*his head bobbing up from his chest drowsily*) Aye, ambergris! It's costly truck.

BUTLER. (*in a whisper to the boy—cautiously*) There! Wasn't I right? Mad as hatters, all of 'em!

BARTLETT. (*his voice more and more that of a somnambulist*) It's time I settled down to home with ye, Sarah. They's plenty o' big trees on my place, bullies, and shade and green grass, and a cool wind off the sea. (*He shakes off the growing drowsiness and glares about him in a rage*) Hell's fire! What crazy truck be I thinkin' of? (*But he and the others sink back immediately into stupor. After a pause*

629

he begins to relate a tale in a droning voice) Years ago, when I was whalin' out o' New Bedford, a man come to me—Spanish-looking, he was—and wanted to charter my ship and me go shares. He showed me a map o' some island off the coast of South America somewhere. They was a cross marked on it where treasure had been buried by the old pirates. But I was a fool. I didn't believe him. He got old Scott's schooner—finally. She sailed and never was heard o' since. But I've never forgot him and his ma. And often I've thought if I'd 'a' went that vige— (*He straightens up and shouts with aggressive violence*) But here she be! Run right into it—without no map nor nothin'. Gold and diamonds and all—there they be in front o' our eyes! (*To the now alert* JIMMY) Open 'er up, Jimmy!

JIMMY. (*getting up—in his soft voice*) Aye, Captain. (*He reaches down to lift the lid.*)

BARTLETT. (*a sudden change of feeling comes over him, and he knocks* JIMMY's *arm aside savagely*) Hands off, ye dog! I'm takin' care o' this chest, and no man's hand's goin' to touch it but mine!

JIMMY. (*stepping back docilely—in the same unmoved, soft tone*) Aye, Captain. (*He squats down to the left of the chest.*)

BARTLETT. (*seeming suddenly to notice the cook for the first time*) So there you be, eh? (*His voice growing thick with rage*) I ain't forgot what ye said down by the shore there! Lucky for ye I didn't catch ye then! "Brass and copper—junk," ye said—"not gold! Not worth a damn," ye said! Ye blasted son of a liar! (*Looking at* ABEL) Ye've been tellin' that boy your lies too, I kin tell by the look o' him. (*Sternly*) Come here, boy!

ABEL. (*advances with faltering steps*) Y-yes, s-sir?

BARTLETT. Open up that chest! Open it up, ye brat! (*With a desperate movement of fear* ABEL *reaches down and flings open the lid of the chest. As he does so,* BARTLETT's *huge hand fastens on the collar of his coat, and holds him with face bent over the box.* HORNE, CATES, *and* JIMMY KANAKA *pull themselves close, their necks craning for a look inside.*)

BARTLETT. (*shaking the terror-stricken boy*) What d'ye see there, ye little swab? What d'ye see there?

ABEL. Aw—leggo—I'm chokin'!

BARTLETT. (*grimly*) Ye'll choke in earnest if ye don't answer me. What d'ye see? Is it gold? Answer me—is it gold?

ABEL. (*stutteringly*) Yes—sure—gold—I see it!

BARTLETT. (*thrusts him away. The boy staggers and falls to the sand. BARTLETT turns to BUTLER triumphantly*) Ye see, ye liar? Gold! Gold! Even a child can tell it at a look. (*With a somber menace in his tone*) But ye—don't believe—do ye?

BUTLER. (*frightenedly*) Maybe I was wrong, sir. I—didn't—look very careful.

BARTLETT. Come here! (*He stands up, his back against the tree*) Come here!

BUTLER. Yes, sir. (*But he looks about him shiftily, as if to run away.*)

BARTLETT. Jimmy! (*The KANAKA leaps to his feet*) Knife him, Jimmy, if he tries to run.

JIMMY. (*his hand goes to his knife, his dark eyes lighting up with savagery—in his soft voice*) Aye, Captain!

BARTLETT. (*to the trembling cook*) Come here!

BUTLER. (*goes to him with the courage of desperation*) Yes, sir.

BARTLETT. (*pointing to the contents of the chest*) Is it gold—or no?

BUTLER. If I can feel of one—

BARTLETT. Pick one up.

BUTLER. (*picks up a heavy anklet encrusted with colored glass, looks at it for a minute—then feigning great assurance*) I was wrong, Captain. It's gold all right enough—worth all kinds of money, I bet.

BARTLETT. (*with mad triumph*) Ha! Ye've come to your senses, have ye? Too late, ye swab! No share for ye! And here's to teach ye for lyin' to me before! (*His fist jerks out from his side, and BUTLER is knocked sprawling on the sand, where he lies groaning for a moment, the anklet still clutched in his hand. The boy gives a gasp of fright and scampers off, left.*)

631

BARTLETT. That'll learn ye! (*He sits down beside the chest. The others crouch close.* BARTLETT *shoves in both of his hands—in a tone of mad gloating*) Gold! Better'n whaling, ain't she, boys? Better'n ambergris, even if I ever had luck to find any! (BUTLER *staggers to his feet. He examines the anklet with contemptuous scorn and even bites it to make sure. Then he edges stealthily toward the left. A sudden transformation comes over his face and he glowers at the Captain with hatred, his features distorted with fury.*)

JIMMY KANAKA. (*pointing to* BUTLER) He got him, Captain!

BARTLETT. (*glancing at the cook with contemptuous scorn*) Sneakin' away with that piece o' the gold, be ye? Ye thievin' swine! Ye know right enough it's gold now, don't ye? Well, ye kin keep it—for your share for speakin' the truth that once.

HORNE. (*his cupidity protesting*) Don't give it to him, sir! It's so much the less for us that worked for it when he did nothin'!

BUTLER. (*overcome by hysterical rage—stammering*) Who asked you for it—eh? Who—wants the damn thing? Not me! No! (*Holding the anklet out contemptuously*) Gold? Ha-ha! Gold? Brass, that's what—and pieces of glass! Junk! Not worth a damn. Here! Take it! (*He flings it on the sand before them.* BARTLETT *snatches it up protectingly.*)

BARTLETT. (*in a frenzy*) Jimmy! (*But* BUTLER *runs off left with a terrified cry.* JIMMY *springs to his feet and stands with his hand on his knife, waiting for a further order.*)

JIMMY. (*eagerly*) I go catch—go stick him, Captain?

BARTLETT. (*pausing—with a frown*) No. They's time enough for that—if need be. Sit down. (JIMMY *sits down again with a childish air of sulking.* BARTLETT *stares at the treasure, continuing to frown, as if* BUTLER's *action had made him uneasy, bewildered and confused him. He mutters half to himself*) Queer! Queer! He threw it back as if 'twas a chunk of mud! He knew—and yet he said he didn't want it. Junk, he called it—and he knows it's gold! He said 'twas gold himself a second back. He's queer. Why would he say junk when he knows it's gold? D'ye think—he don't believe?

HORNE. He was mad because you knocked him down.

BARTLETT. (*shaking his head grimly*) It ain't the first time I've knocked him down; but he never spoke up to me—like that—before. No, it's somethin' else is wrong with him—somethin'.

HORNE. No share for him, you told him, sir. That's what's wrong with him.

BARTLETT. (*again shaking his head*) No. His eyes—It's somethin' he's got in his head—somethin' he's hidin'! His share—maybe he thinks he'll get his share anyway, in spite o' us! Maybe he thinks his share wouldn't be all he wants! Maybe he thinks we'll die o' hunger and thirst before we get picked up—and he'll live—and then—he'll come in for the whole chestful! (*Suddenly springing to his feet in a rage*) Hell's fire! That's it, bullies! That's his sneakin' plan! To watch us die—and steal it from us!

CATES. (*rising to his knees and shaking his hand threateningly above his head*) Tell Jimmy to knife him, sir! Tell Jimmy—I ain't got a knife, or I'd do it myself. (*He totters weakly to his feet.*)

JIMMY. (*eagerly*) You speak, I stick him, Captain. I stick boy, too.

CATES. (*weakening*) I'm weak, but I kin do for him yet. I'm weak— (*His knees sag under him. He pleads piteously*) If I'd only a drink to put some strength in me! If I'd only a sup o' water, I'd do for him! (*Turning, as if to stagger down toward the beach*) There must be water. Let's look again. I'll go look— (*But the effort he makes is too much for his strength and he falls to the sand, panting with open mouth*).

BARTLETT. (*summoning his will—sternly*) Put a clapper on that jaw of yours, Cates, or I'll do it for ye!

CATES. (*blubbering*) If we don't find water—he'll watch us die.

JIMMY. (*insinuatingly*) Better me knife cook fella—kill boy, too!

BARTLETT. Will killin' 'em give us drink, ye fools? (*After a pause, he shakes his head as if to drive off some thought, and mutters*) No

633

more o' that! (*Suddenly, in a tone of sharp command*) No more o' that, I say! We're keepin' no right watch for ships. Go aloft on that tree, Jimmy—and damn quick! (KANAKA *climbs quickly up the bole of the coco palm to the top and looks out on all sides of him. The others rise painfully to their feet and gaze up at him with awakened hope.*)

JIMMY. (*suddenly, in a glad voice*) I see um—see sail, Captain.

CATES. (*waving his arms frenziedly*) Sail—ho!

JIMMY. Look plenty like trade schooner, Captain. She no change course she fetch plenty close by here. She make full sail, she got plenty fella wind out there, she come quick.

HORNE. (*clapping* CATES *on the back*) Headin' straight for us, Cates, d'you hear?

BARTLETT. Come down. (*The Islander slides down.* BARTLETT *exclaims exultantly*) Didn't I tell ye? In the nick o' time. When she makes in close we'll go down to the reef and yell and wave at her. They'll see! The luck's with us today! (*His eyes fall on the treasure and he starts*) But now—what's to do with this chest—the gold?

HORNE. (*quickly*) You ain't going to tell them on the schooner about it?

CATES. They'd claim to share with us.

BARTLETT. (*scornfully*) D'ye think I'm cracked? No, we'll bury it here.

CATES. (*regretfully*) Leave it behind for anyone to find?

BARTLETT. We'll bury it deep, where hell itself won't find it—and we'll make a map o' this island. (*He takes a piece of paper and a stub of pencil from his pocket—pointing to the foot of the tree*) Dig a hole here—you, Horne and Jimmy—and dig it deep. (*The two bend down and commence to hollow out the sand with their hands.* BARTLETT *draws on the paper*) There's the lagoon—and the reef— (*To* CATES, *who is peering over his shoulder*) And here where the tree is, d'ye see, Cates, I'll make a cross where the gold is hid. (*Exultantly*) Oh, all hell'd not stop me from findin' this place again! Let us once get home and I'll fit out a small schooner the four of us can sail, and we'll come back here to dig it up. It won't be long, I swear to ye!

HORNE. (*straightening up*) This deep enough, sir?

JIMMY. (*who has straightened up and is looking off left—suddenly points excitedly*) He look, Captain! Cook fella, he look here! Boy he look, too! They look plenty too much, Captain! (*All four stand staring off at* BUTLER *and the boy, whose presence on the island they have forgotten in their mad excitement.*)

CATES. (*in stupid dismay*) They'll know where it's hid, sir!

HORNE. They'll tell 'em on the schooner!

CATES. (*wildly*) We've got to do for 'em, Captain! Gimme your knife, Jimmy—your knife— (*He stumbles toward the Islander, who pushes him aside brusquely, looking questioningly toward the Captain.*)

BARTLETT. (*who has been standing motionless, as if stunned by this forgotten complication—slowly*) There they be watchin' us, the sneakin' dogs! I was forgettin' they was here. (*Striking his knee with clenched fist*) We've got to do somethin' damn quick! That schooner'll be up soon where they kin sight her—and they'll wave and yell then—and she'll see 'em!

HORNE. And good-by to the gold for us!

JIMMY. (*eagerly*) You say fella word, Captain, me kill um quick. They no make plenty cry for schooner! They keep dam still plenty too much!

BARTLETT. (*looking at the Islander with mad cunning but replying only to* HORNE) Aye, it's good-by to the gold, Horne. That scum of a cook—he's made a mock o' us—sayin' it wasn't gold when he knew it was—he'll tell 'em—he'll get joy o' tellin' 'em!

HORNE. And that scrub of a boy—he's no better. He'll be in with him neck and crop.

CATES. (*hoarsely*) Knife 'em—and be done with it—I say!

BARTLETT. Or, if they don't tell the schooner's skipper it'll only be because they're plannin' to come back themselves—before we kin—

635

and dig it up. That cook—there's somethin' queer in his mind—somethin' he was hidin'—pretendin' not to believe. What d'ye think, Horne?

HORNE. I think—time's gettin' short—and talkin' won't do no good. (*Insinuatingly*) They'd do for us soon enough if *they* was able.

BARTLETT. Aye, murder was plain in his eyes when he looked at me.

HORNE. (*lowering his voice to a whisper*) Tell Jimmy—Captain Bartlett—is what I say!

BARTLETT. It's agin the law, Silas Horne!

HORNE. The law don't reach to this island.

BARTLETT. (*monotonously*) It's agin the law a captain's sworn to keep wherever he sails. They ain't refused duty—nor mutinied.

HORNE. Who'll know they ain't? They're trying to steal what's yours—that's worse'n mutiny. (*As a final persuasion*) And Jimmy's a heathen and under no laws. And he's stronger'n you are. You couldn't stop 'im.

BARTLETT. Aye—I couldn't prevent—

JIMMY. (*eagerly*) I fix um, Captain, they no tell! (BARTLETT *doesn't answer, but stares at the treasure.* HORNE *makes violent motions to* JIMMY *to go. The Islander stares at his master's face. Then, seeming to read the direct command there, he grunts with satisfaction, and pulling his knife from his sheath, he goes stealthily off left.* CATES *raises himself on his haunches to watch the Islander's movements.* HORNE *and* BARTLETT *sit still in a strained immobility, their eyes on the chest.*)

CATES. (*in an excited whisper*) I see 'em! They're sittin' with their backs this way! (*A slight pause*) There's Jimmy. He's crawlin' on his hands behind 'em. They don't notice—he's right behind—almost atop o' them. (*A pause.* CATES *gives a fiendish grunt*) Ugh! (BUTLER's *muffled cry comes from the left*) Right in the middle of the back! The cook's done! The boy's runnin'! (*There is a succession of quick screams from the boy, the padding of feet running toward them, the fall of a body, and the boy's dying groan.*)

HORNE. (*with satisfaction*) It's done, sir!

BARTLETT. (*slowly*) I spoke no word, remember that, Silas Horne!

HORNE. (*cunningly*) Nor me neither, sir. Jimmy took it on himself. If blame there is—it's on him.

BARTLETT. (*gloomily*) I spoke no word! (JIMMY *returns noiselessly from the left.*)

JIMMY. (*grinning with savage pride*) I fix um fella plenty, Captain. They no tell. They no open mouth plenty too much!

CATES. (*maudlinly*) You're a man, Jimmy—a man with guts to him —even if you're a— (*He babbles incoherently.*)

JIMMY. (*as the Captain does not look at him*) I go climb fella tree, Captain? I make look for schooner?

BARTLETT. (*rousing himself with an effort*) Aye. (*The Islander climbs the tree.*)

HORNE. (*getting to his feet—eagerly*) Where away, Jimmy?

JIMMY. She come, Captain, she come plenty quick.

HORNE. (*looking in the direction* JIMMY *indicates*) I kin see her tops'ls from here, sir. Look!

BARTLETT. (*getting to his feet—stares out to sea*) Aye! There she be —and makin' towards us fast. (*In a flash his somber preoccupation is gone, and he is commander once more. He puts the anklet in his hand into his coat pocket—harshly*) Come down o' that! They's work to do. (JIMMY *clambers down*) Did ye leave—them—lyin' in plain sight on the open sand?

JIMMY. Yes. I no touch um, Captain.

BARTLETT. Then ye'll touch 'em now. Go, bury 'em, cover 'em up with sand. And mind ye make a good job o' it that none'll see. Jump now!

JIMMY. (*obediently*) I go, Captain. (*He hurries off left.*)

BARTLETT. Down to the reef with ye, Horne! (*Giving the prostrate* CATES *a kick*) Up out o' that, Cates! Go with Horne, and when ye see the schooner hull up, wave to 'em, and yell like mad, d'ye hear?

HORNE. Aye, aye, sir!

637

BARTLETT. I'll stay here and bury the gold. It's best to be quick about it! They may turn a spyglass on us when they raise the island from deck! Off with ye! (*He gives* CATES *another kick.*)

CATES. (*groaning*) I'm sick! (*Incoherently*) Can't—report for duty —this watch. (*With a shout*) Water!

BARTLETT. (*contemptuously*) Ye dog! Give him a hand, Horne.

HORNE. (*putting a hand under his shoulder*) Up, man! We're to signal the schooner. There'll be water on board o' her—barrels of it!

CATES. (*aroused, scrambles to his feet, violently shaking off Horne's hand*) Water aboard o' her! (*His staring eyes catch the schooner's sails on the horizon. He breaks into a staggering run and disappears down toward the beach, right rear, waving his arms wildly and shouting*) Ahoy! Ahoy! Water! (HORNE *walks out quickly after him.*)

BARTLETT. (*after a quick glance around, sinks on his knees beside the chest and shoves both hands into it. From the chest comes a metallic clink as he fingers the pieces in his hands gloatingly*) Ye're safe now! (*In a dreaming tone, his eyes fixed before him in an ecstatic vision*) No more whalin' on the dirty seas! Rest to home! Gold! I've been dreamin' o' it all my life! (*Shaking himself—savagely*) Ye fool! Losin' your senses, be ye? Time ye was pickd up! Lucky! (*He shoves down the lid and places the chest in the hole. He pushes the sand in on top of it, whispering hoarsely*) Lay safe, d'ye hear! For I'll be back for ye! Aye—in spite of hell I'll dig ye up again. (*The voices of* HORNE *and* JIMMY *can be heard from the distance shouting as the curtain falls.*)

ACT TWO

SCENE—*Interior of an old boat-shed on the wharf of the Bartlett place on the California coast. In the rear, a double doorway looking out over the end of the wharf to the bay with the open sea beyond. On the left, two windows, and another door, opening on the dock. Near this door, a cot with blankets and a pillow without a slip. In the center, front, a table with a bottle and glasses on it, and three cane-bottomed chairs. On the right, a fishing dory. Here and there about the shed all sorts of odds and ends pertaining to a ship—old anchors, ropes, tackle, paint-pots, old spars, etc.*

It is late afternoon of a day six months later. Sunlight filters feebly through the stained, cobwebby window panes.

As the curtain rises, BARTLETT *and* SILAS HORNE *are discovered.* HORNE *is in working clothes of paint-stained dungaree. If his sufferings on the island have left any marks on his dry wizened face, they are undiscoverable. In* BARTLETT, *however, the evidence is marked. His hair has turned white. There are deep hollows under his cheek-bones. His jaw and tight-lipped mouth express defiant determination, as if he were fighting back some weakness inside himself, a weakness found in his eyes, which have something in them of fear, of a wishing to avoid other eyes. He is dressed much the same as when on the island. He sits by the table, center, his abstracted gaze bent on the floor before him.*

HORNE. (*who is evidently waiting for the Captain to say something —after a pause, glancing at him uneasily*) I'd best be getting back aboard the schooner, sir. (*Receiving no answer he starts for the door on the left.*)

BARTLETT. (*rousing himself with an effort*) Wait. (*After a pause*)

The full tide's at dawn tomorrow. They know we'll be sailin' then, don't they—Cates and Jimmy?

HORNE. Yes, sir. Oh, they'll be glad o' the word—and me, too, sir. (*With a greedy grin*) It's all we've been talkin' of since ye brought us down here—diggin' up the gold!

BARTLETT. (*passionately*) Aye, the gold! We'll have it before long, now, I reckon. That schooner—the way we've fitted her up—she'd take a man safe to the Pole and back! We'll drop anchor here with the chest on board in six months, unless— (*Hesitates.*)

HORNE. (*uneasily*) What, sir?

BARTLETT. (*brusquely*) The weather, ye fool!

HORNE. We'll trust to luck for that. (*Glancing at the Captain curiously*) And speakin' o' luck, sir—the schooner ain't been christened yet.

BARTLETT. (*betraying a sudden, fierce determination*) She will be!

HORNE. There'd be no luck for a ship sailin' out without a name.

BARTLETT. She'll have a name, I tell ye! She'll be named the "Sarah Allen," and Sarah'll christen her herself.

HORNE. It oughter been done, by rights, when we launched her a month back.

BARTLETT. (*sternly*) I know that as well as ye. (*After a pause*) She wasn't willin' to do it then. Women has queer notions—when they're sick, like. (*Defiantly—as if he were addressing someone outside of the room*) But Sarah'll be willin' now!

HORNE. Yes, sir. (*He again turns to go, as if he were anxious to get away.*)

BARTLETT. Wait! There's somethin' else I want to ask ye. Nat, he's been hangin' round the schooner all his spare time o' late. (*With rising anger*) I hope ye've remembered what I ordered ye, all three. Not a word o' it to him!

HORNE. (*retreating a step—hastily*) No fear o' that, sir!

BARTLETT. It ain't that I'm afeerd to tell him o' the gold, Silas Horne. (*Slowly*) It's them—other things—I'd keep him clear of.

640

HORNE. (*immediately guessing what he means—reassuringly*) We was all out o' our heads when them things happened, sir.

BARTLETT. Mad? Aye! But I ain't forgot—them two. (*He represses a shudder—then goes on slowly*) Do they ever come back to you— when you're asleep, I mean?

HORNE. (*pretending mystification*) Who's that, sir?

BARTLETT. (*with somber emphasis*) That cook and that boy. They come to me. I'm gettin' to be afeered o' goin' to sleep—not 'feered o' them, I don't mean. (*With sudden defiant bravado*) Not all the ghosts out o' hell kin keep me from a thing I've set my mind on. (*Collecting himself*) But I've waked up talkin' out loud—and I'm afeerd there might be someone hear me.

HORNE. (*uneasily—with an attempt to be reassuring*) You ain't all cured o' that sun and thirst on the island yet, sir.

BARTLETT. (*evidently reassured—with an attempt at conviviality*) Sit down a bit, Horne, and take a grog. (HORNE *does so.* BARTLETT *pours out a half-tumbler full of rum for himself and shoves the bottle over to* HORNE.)

HORNE. Luck to our vige, sir.

BARTLETT. Aye, luck! (*They drink.* BARTLETT *leans over and taps* HORNE *on the arm*) Aye, it takes time to get cured o' thirst and sun! (*Somberly—after a pause*) I spoke no word, Silas Horne, d'ye remember?

HORNE. Nor me. Jimmy did it alone. (*Craftily*) We'd all three swear Bible oaths to that in any court. And even if ye'd given the word, there ain't no good thinkin' more o' it, sir. Didn't they deserve all they got? Wasn't they plottin' on the sly to steal the gold?

BARTLETT. (*his eyes gleaming*) Aye!

HORNE. And when you said he'd get no share of it, didn't he lie to your face that it wasn't gold?

BARTLETT. (*with sudden rage*) Aye, brass and junk, he said, the lyin' scum! That's what he keeps sayin' when I see him in sleep! He didn't believe—an' then he owned up himself 'twas gold! He knew! He lied a-purpose! (*Rising to his feet—with confident defiance*) They deserved no better nor they got. Let 'em rot! (*Pours out another drink for himself and* HORNE.)

HORNE. Luck, sir! (*They drink. There is a knock at the door on the left followed by* MRS. BARTLETT'S *voice calling feebly,* "Isaiah! Isaiah!" BARTLETT *starts but makes no answer.* HORNE *turns to him questioningly*) It's Mrs. Bartlett, sir. Shall I open the door?

BARTLETT. No. I ain't aimin' to see her—yet awhile. (*Then with sudden reasonless rage*) Let her in, damn ye! (HORNE *goes and unhooks the door.* MRS. BARTLETT *enters. She is a slight, slender little woman of fifty. Sickness, or the inroads of a premature old age, have bowed her shoulders, whitened her hair, and forced her to walk feebly with the aid of a cane. A resolute spirit still flashes from her eyes, however, and there is a look of fixed determination on her face. She stands gazing at her husband. There is something accusing in her stare.*)

BARTLETT. (*avoiding her eyes—brusquely*) Well? What is it ye want o' me, Sarah?

MRS. B. I want to speak with you alone, Isaiah.

HORNE. I'll be gettin' back aboard, sir. (*Starts to go.*)

BARTLETT. (*in a tone almost of fear*) Wait. I'm goin' with ye. (*Turning to his wife—with a certain rough tenderness*) Ye oughtn't to walk down the hill here, Sarah. The doctor told ye to rest in the house and save your strength.

MRS. B. I want to speak to you alone, Isaiah.

BARTLETT. (*very uneasily*) I've got to work on the schooner, Sarah.

MRS. B. She'll be sailin' soon?

BARTLETT. (*suddenly turning on her defiantly*) Tomorrow at dawn!

MRS. B. (*with her eyes fixed accusingly on his*) And you be goin' with her?

BARTLETT. (*in the same defiant tone*) Yes, I be! Who else'd captain her?

MRS. B. On a craft without a name.

BARTLETT. She'll have that name!

MRS. B. No.

BARTLETT. She'll have that name, I tell ye!

MRS. B. No.

BARTLETT. (*thoroughly aroused, his will tries to break hers, but finds her unbending. He mutters menacingly*) Ye'll see! We'll talk o' that later, you and me. (*Without a further glance at his wife he strides past her and disappears through the doorway, followed by* HORNE. MRS. BARTLETT *sinks down in the chair by the table. She appears suddenly weak and crushed. Then from outside comes a girl's laughing voice.* MRS. BARTLETT *does not seem to hear, nor to notice* SUE *and* DREW *when they enter.* SUE *is a slender, pretty girl of about twenty, with large blue eyes, reddish-brown hair, and a healthy, sun-tanned, out-of-door complexion. In spite of the slightness of her figure there is a suggestion of great vitality and nervous strength about her.* DREW *is a well-set-up, tall young fellow of thirty. Not in any way handsome, his boyish face, tanned to a deep brown, possesses an engaging character of healthy, cheerful forcefulness that has its compelling charm. There would be no chance of mistaking him for anything but the ship's officer he is. It is written on his face, his walk, his voice, his whole bearing.*)

SUE. (*as they enter*) He'll either be here or on the schooner, Danny. (*Then she sees her mother, with startled amazement*) Ma! Good heavens, what are you doing here? Don't you know you shouldn't—

MRS. B. (*with a start—turning to her daughter with a forced smile*) There, Sue, now! Don't go scoldin' me! (*Then seeing* DREW—*in a tone of forced gayety*) And if there ain't Danny Drew—back home to port at last! You can kiss an old woman, Danny—without makin' her jealous, I reckon.

DREW. (*kissing her—with a smile*) It certainly seems good to see you again—and be back again myself.

MRS. B. We read in the paper where your ship'd reached San Francisco. Sue's been on pins and needles ever since.

SUE. (*protestingly*) Ma!

DREW. (*with a grin*) It's a long time to be away from Sue—four

643

months. You remember, Ma, I left just after the big excitement here
—when Captain Bartlett turned up after we'd all heard the "Triton"
was wrecked and given him up for lost.

MRS. B. (*her face clouding—in a tone of deep sorrow*) Yes. (DREW
is surprised and glances at SUE *questioningly. She sighs.* MRS. BARTLETT
gets to her feet with difficulty, assisted by DREW.)

SUE. We'll help you back to the house.

MRS. B. Shucks! I'm sick o' the house. I need sun and fresh air, and
today's so nice I couldn't stay indoors. I'm goin' to set out on the wharf
and watch your Pa workin' on the schooner. Ain't much time left to
see her, Sue. They're sailin' tomorrow at dawn, your Pa says.

SUE. Tomorrow? Then you're going to christen her?

MRS. B. (*with grim determination*) No, I ain't, Sue! (*Catching*
DREW's *glance fixed on her with puzzled curiosity, she immediately
attempts to resume her joking tone*) Shucks! Here's Danny wonderin'
what silliness we're talkin' of. It's just this, Danny. Captain Bartlett,
he's got a crazy notion in his head that just because his ship was
wrecked last vige he'll give up whalin' for life. He's fitted out this
little schooner for tradin' in the Islands. More money in that, he says.
But I don't agree with no such lunatic notions, and I'm not goin' to
set my approval on his craziness by christenin' his ship with my name,
like he wants me to. He'd ought to stick to whalin', like he's done all
his life. Don't you think so, Danny?

DREW. (*embarrassed*) Why, sure—he's rated one of the smartest
whaling skippers here on the coast—and I should think—

MRS. B. Just what I tell him—only he's that stubborn. I'd best get
out quick while it's still sunny and warm. It's damp in here for an old
body. (DREW *helps her to the door on the left, opens it, and the two go
out, followed by* SUE, *who carries a chair. After a pause,* SUE *and* DREW
return. SUE *carefully shuts the door after them. Her face is troubled.*)

DREW. (*looks at her for a minute, then comes and puts his arm
around her and kisses her*) What's the trouble, Sue?

SUE. (*trying to force a smile*) Nothing, Danny.

DREW. Oh, yes there is! No use putting me off that way. Why, I felt it hanging about in the air ever since I looked at your Ma.

SUE. Yes, she's failed terribly since you saw her last.

DREW. Oh, I don't mean just sickness—only—did you notice how she had to—force herself—to joke about things? She used to be so cheerful natural. (*Scratching his head in honest puzzlement*) But—that ain't what I mean, either. What is it, Sue? Maybe I can help somehow. You look worried, too. Pshaw! You can tell me, can't you?

SUE. Why, yes, Danny—of course—only I'm just as puzzled as you over what it comes from. It's something between Pa and Ma—something only the two of them know. It all seemed to start one morning after you'd left—about a week after he'd come home with those three awful men. During that first week he acted all right—just like he used to—only he'd get talking kind of wild now and then about being glad the Triton was lost, and promising we'd all be millionaires once he started making trips on the schooner. Ma didn't seem to mind his going in for trading then. Then, the night of the day he bought the schooner, something must have happened between them. Neither of them came down to breakfast. I went up to Ma, and found her so sick we sent for the doctor. He said she'd suffered a great shock of some kind, although she wouldn't tell him a word. I found Pa down in this shed. He'd moved that cot down here, and said he'd have to sleep here after that because he wanted to be near the schooner. It's been that way ever since. He's slept down here and never come up to the house except at mealtimes. He's never been alone with Ma one second since then, I don't believe. And she—she's been trying to corner him, to get him alone. I've noticed it, although she does her best to hide it from Nat and me. And she's been failing, growing weaker and sicker looking every day. (*Breaking down*) Oh, Danny, these last months have been terrible!

DREW. (*soothing her*) There! It'll all come out right.

SUE. I'm sure that's why she's crept down here today. She's bound she'll see him alone.

645

DREW. (*frowning*) Seems to me it must be all your Pa's fault, Sue— whatever it is. Have you tried to talk to him?

SUE. Yes—a good many times; but all he's ever said was: "There's things you wouldn't take interest in, Sue. You'll know when it's time to know"—and then he'd break off by asking me what I'd like most to have in the world if he had piles of money. And then, one time, he seemed to be terribly afraid of something, and he said to me: "You hustle up and marry Danny, Sue. You marry him and get out of this."

DREW. (*with an affectionate grin*) I surely wish you'd take his advice, Sue! (*He kisses her.*)

SUE. (*with intense longing*) Oh, I wish I could, Danny.

DREW. I've quite considerable saved now, Sue, and it won't be so long before I get my own ship, I'm hoping, now that I've got my master's certificate. I was hoping at the end of this voyage—

SUE. So was I, Danny—but it can't be this time. With Ma so weak, and no one to take care of her but me— (*Shaking her head—in a tone of decision*) I couldn't leave home now, Danny. It wouldn't be right. I couldn't feel really happy—until this thing—whatever it is—is settled between Pa and Ma and they're just as they used to be again. (*Pleadingly*) You understand, don't you, Danny?

DREW. (*soberly*) Why—surely I do, Sue. (*He pats her hand*) Only, it's hard waiting. (*He sighs.*)

SUE. I know. It's just as hard for me.

DREW. I thought maybe I could help; but this isn't anything anyone outside your family could mix in. (SUE *shakes her head. He goes on gloomily after a pause*) What's the matter with Nat? Seems as if he ought to be able to step in and talk turkey to your Pa.

SUE. (*slowly*) You'll find Nat changed, too, Danny—changed terribly. He's caught the disease—whatever it is. You know how interested in his work he's been ever since they put him in the designing department down in the shipyard?

DREW. Yes.

SUE. (*with emphasis*) Well, all that's changed. He hates it now, or at

646

least he says he does. And when he comes home, he spends all his time prowling around the dock here, talking with those three awful men. And what do you think he told me only the other day? That he was bound he'd throw up his job and make this voyage on the schooner. He even asked me to ask Pa to let him go.

DREW. Your Pa don't want him to, eh?

SUE. Why, of course not! Leave a fine position he worked so hard to get just for this crazy notion! The terrible part is, he's got Ma worried to death—as if she wasn't upset enough already. She's so afraid he'll go—that Pa'll let him at the last moment.

DREW. Maybe I can help after all. I can talk to Nat.

SUE. (*shaking her head*) He's not the same Nat, Danny.

DREW. (*trying to be consoling*) Pshaw, Sue! I think you just get to imagining things. (*As he finishes speaking, the door in the rear opens and* NAT *appears. He is a tall, loose-framed boy of eighteen, who bears a striking resemblance to his father. His face, like his father's, is large and bony, with deepset black eyes, an aquiline nose, and a wide, thin-lipped mouth. There is no suggestion in* NAT, *however, of the older man's physical health and great strength. He appears an indoor product, undeveloped in muscle, with a sallow complexion and stooped shoulders. His thick hair is a deep black. His voice recalls his father's, hollow and penetrating. He is dressed in a gray flannel shirt and cor-duroy trousers.* DREW *calls out to him heartily*) Hello, Nat! Speak of the Devil! Sue and I were just talking about you. (*He goes toward* NAT, *his hand outstretched.*)

NAT. (*comes toward them, meets* DREW, *and shakes his hand with evident pleasure*) Hello, Danny! You're a sight for sore eyes! (*His manner undergoes a sudden change. He casts a quick, suspicious glance from* DREW *to his sister*) You were talking about me? what about?

SUE. (*quickly—with a warning glance at* DREW) About your work down at the shipyard.

NAT. (*disgustedly*) Oh, that. (*In a tone of reasonless irritation*) For

God's sake, Sue, let me alone about my work. Don't I have to live with the damn thing all day, without your shoving it in my face the minute I get home? I want to forget it—get away!

DREW. Go to sea, eh?

NAT. (*suspiciously*) Maybe. Why? What do you mean? (*Turning to his sister—angrily*) What have you been telling Danny?

SUE. I was talking about the schooner—telling him she sails tomorrow.

NAT. (*dumfounded*) Tomorrow? (*Overcome by sudden, nervous excitement*) It can't be. How do you know? Who told you?

SUE. Ma. Pa told her.

NAT. Then she's been talking to him—telling him not to take me, I'll bet. (*Angrily*) Oh, I wish Ma'd mind her own business!

SUE. Nat!

NAT. Well, Sue, how would you like it? I'm not a little boy any more. I know what I want to do. I want to go with them. I want to go more than I've ever wanted anything else in my life before. He—he doesn't want me. He's afraid I— But I think I can force him to— (*He glances at* DREW's *amazed face and stops abruptly—sullenly*) Where is Pa?

SUE. He's aboard the schooner.

NAT. (*disappointedly*) Then it's no good trying to see him now.

DREW. Sounds funny to hear you talking about going to sea. Why, you always used—

NAT. This is different.

DREW. You want to see the Islands, I suppose?

NAT. (*suspiciously*) Maybe. Why not?

DREW. What group is your Pa heading for first?

NAT. (*more suspiciously*) You'll have to ask him. Why do you want to know? (*Abruptly*) You better be getting up to the house, Sue— if we're to have any supper. Danny must be hungry. (*He turns his back on them. They exchange meaning glances.*)

SUE. (*with a sigh*) It must be getting late. Come on, Danny. You

648

can see Pa later on. (*They go toward the door in the rear*) Aren't you coming, Nat?

NAT. No. I'll wait. (*Impatiently*) Go ahead. I'll be up before long.

DREW. See you later, then, Nat.

NAT. Yes. (*They go out, rear.* NAT *paces up and down in a great state of excitement. The door on the left is opened and* BARTLETT *enters. Father and son stand looking at one another for a second.* NAT *takes a step backward as if in fear, then straightens up defiantly.*)

BARTLETT. (*slowly*) Is this the way ye mind my orders, boy? I've told ye time an' again not to be sneakin' and spyin' around this wharf.

NAT. I'm not sneaking and spying. I wanted to talk to you, Pa.

BARTLETT. (*sits down by the table*) Well, here I be.

NAT. Sue said the schooner sails tomorrow.

BARTLETT. Aye!

NAT. (*resolutely*) I want to go with you, Pa.

BARTLETT. (*briefly—as if dismissing the matter*) Ye can't. I've told ye that before. Let this be the last time ye ask it.

NAT. But why? Why can't I go?

BARTLETT. Ye've your own work to do—good work. Attend to that and leave me to mine.

NAT. But you always wanted me to go on voyages to learn whaling with you.

BARTLETT. This be different.

NAT. (*with excited indignation*) Yes, this is different! Don't I know it? Do you think you can hide that from me? It is different, and that's why I want to go.

BARTLETT. Ye can't, I say.

NAT. (*pleadingly*) But why not, Pa? I can do a man's work on a ship, or anywhere else.

BARTLETT. (*roughly*) Your place is here, with Sue and your Ma, and here you'll stay.

NAT. (*angrily*) That isn't any reason. But I know your real one. You're afraid—

BARTLETT. (*with a touch of uneasiness—forcing a scornful laugh*) Afeerd! Afeerd o' what? Did ye ever know me to be afeerd?

NAT. Afraid of what I might find out if I went with you.

BARTLETT. (*with the same forced, uneasy scorn*) And what d'ye think ye'd find out, Nat?

NAT. First of all that it's not a trading venture you're going on. Oh, I'm not a fool! That story is all right to fool the neighbors and girls like Sue. But I know better.

BARTLETT. What d'ye know?

NAT. You're going for something else.

BARTLETT. What would that be?

NAT. I don't know—exactly. Something—on that island.

BARTLETT. (*he gets to his feet with a forced burst of laughter*) Ye fool of a boy! Ye got that notion out o' some fool book ye've been reading, didn't ye? And I thought ye'd growed to be a man! (*More and more wild in his forced scorn*) Ye'll be tellin' me next it's buried treasure I be sailin after—pirates' gold buried on that island—all in a chest— and a map to guide me with a cross marked on it where the gold is hid! And then they be ghosts guardin' it, ben't they—spirits o' murdered men? They always be, in the books. (*He laughs scornfully.*)

NAT. (*gazing at him with fascinated eyes*) No, not that last. That's silly—but I did think you might have found—

BARTLETT. (*laughing again*) Treasure? Gold? (*With forced sternness*) Nat, I be ashamed of ye. Ye've had schoolin', and ye've been doin' a man's work in the world, and doin' it well, and I'd hoped ye'd take my place here to home when I be away, and look after your Ma and Sue. But ye've owned up to bein' a little better nor a boy in short britches, dreamin' o' pirates' gold that never was 'cept in books.

NAT. But you—you're to blame. When you first came home you did nothing but talk mysteriously of how rich we'd all be when the schooner got back.

BARTLETT. (*roughly*) But what's that to do with silly dreams? It's in the line o' trade I meant.

650

NAT. But why be so mysterious about trade? There's something you're hiding. You can't say no because I feel it.

BARTLETT. (*insinuatingly—with a crafty glance at his son*) Supposin' in one of them Eastern trading ports I'd run across a bit o' business with a chance for a fortune in it for a man that wasn't afeerd of the law, and could keep his mouth shut?

NAT. (*disappointed*) You mean illegal trading?

BARTLETT. I mean what I mean, Nat—and I'd be a fool to tell an overgrown boy, or two women—or any man in the world, for the matter o' that—what I do mean.

NAT. (*turning toward the door in the rear—disgustedly*) If it's only that, I don't want to hear it. (*He walks toward the door—stops and turns again to his father*) No, I don't believe it. That's not like you. You're not telling the truth, Pa.

BARTLETT. (*rising to his feet—with a savage sternness in which there is a wild note of entreaty*) I've listened to your fool's talk enough. Get up to the house where ye belong! I'll stand no more o' your meddling in business o' mine. I've been patient with ye, but there's an end to that! Take heed o' what I'm sayin', if ye know what's good for ye! (*With a sort of somber pride*) I'll stand alone in this business and finish it out alone if I go to hell for it. Ye hear me?

NAT. (*alarmed by this outburst—submissively*) Yes, Pa.

BARTLETT. Then see that ye heed. (*After a pause—as* NAT *lingers*) They'll be waitin' for ye at the house.

NAT. All right. I'll go. (*He turns to the doorway on the left, but before he gets to it, the door is pushed open and* MRS. BARTLETT *enters.* NAT *stops, startled*) Ma!

MRS. BARTLETT. (*with a forced smile*) Run along, Nat. It's all right. I want to speak with your Pa.

BARTLETT. (*uneasily*) Ye'd best go up with Nat, Sarah. I've work to do.

MRS. BARTLETT. (*fixing her eyes on her husband*) I want to talk with you alone, Isaiah.

BARTLETT. (*grimly—as if he were accepting a challenge*) As ye like, then.

MRS. BARTLETT. (*dismissing* NAT *with a feeble attempt at a smile*) Tell Sue I'll be comin' up directly, Nat.

NAT. (*hesitates for a moment, looking from one to the other uneasily*) All right, Ma. (*He goes out.*)

BARTLETT. (*waits for* NAT *to get out of hearing*) Won't ye set, Sarah? (*She comes forward and sits by the table. He sits by the other side.*)

MRS. BARTLETT. (*shuddering as she sees the bottle on the table*) Will drinkin' this poison make you forget, Isaiah?

BARTLETT. (*gruffly*) I've naught to forget—leastways naught that's in your mind. But they's things about the stubborn will o' woman I'd like to forget. (*They look at each other across the table. There is a pause. Finally he cannot stand her accusing glance. He looks away, gets to his feet, walks about, then sits down again, his face set determinedly—with a grim smile*) Well, here we be, Sarah—alone together for the first time since—

MRS. BARTLETT. (*quickly*) Since that night, Isaiah.

BARTLETT. (*as if he hadn't heard*) Since I come back to you, almost. Did ye ever stop to think o' how strange it be we'd ever come to this? I never dreamed a day 'd come when ye'd force me to sleep away from ye, alone in a shed like a mangy dog!

MRS. BARTLETT. (*gently*) I didn't drive you away, Isaiah. You came o' your own will.

BARTLETT. Because o' your naggin' tongue, woman—and the wrong ye thought o' me.

MRS. BARTLETT. (*shaking her head, slowly*) It wasn't me you ran from, Isaiah. You ran away from your own self—the conscience God put in you that you think you can fool with lies.

BARTLETT. (*starting to his feet—angrily*) Lies?

MRS. BARTLETT. It's the truth, Isaiah, only you be too weak to face it.

BARTLETT. (*with defiant bravado*) Ye'll find I be strong enough to face anything, true or lie! (*Then protestingly*) What call have ye to think evil o' me, Sarah? It's mad o' ye to hold me to account for things I said in my sleep—for the damned nightmares that set me talkin' wild when I'd just come home and my head was still cracked with the thirst and the sun I'd borne on that island. Is that right, woman, to be blamin' me for mad dreams?

MRS. BARTLETT. You confessed the rest of what you said was true— of the gold you'd found and buried there.

BARTLETT. (*with a sudden fierce exultation*) Aye—that be true as Bible, Sarah. When I've sailed back in the schooner, ye'll see for yourself. There be a big chest o' it, yellow and heavy, and fixed up with diamonds, emeralds and sech, that be worth more, even, nor the gold. We'll be rich, Sarah—rich like I've always dreamed we'd be! There'll be silks and carriages for ye—all the woman's truck in the world ye've a mind to want—and all that Nat and Sue'll want, too.

MRS. BARTLETT. (*with a shudder*) Are you tryin' to bribe me, Isaiah— with a treasure that's cursed by God?

BARTLETT. (*as if he hadn't heard*) D'ye remember long ago, how I'd talk to ye o' findin' ambergris, a pile o' it on one vige that'd make us rich? Ye used to take interest then, and all the vige with me ye'd be hopin' I'd find it, too.

MRS. BARTLETT. That was my sin o' greed that I'm bein' punished for now.

BARTLETT. (*again as if he hadn't heard*) And now when the gold's come to us at last—bigger nor I ever dreamed on—ye drive me away from ye and say it's cursed.

MRS. BARTLETT. (*inexorably*) Cursed with the blood o' the man and boy ye murdered!

BARTLETT. (*in a mad rage*) Ye lie, woman! I spoke no word!

MRS. BARTLETT. That's what you kept repeatin' in your sleep, night after night that first week you was home, till I knew the truth, and could bear no more. "I spoke no word!" you kept sayin', as if 'twas your own soul had you at the bar of judgment. And "That cook, he didn't believe 'twas gold," you'd say, and curse him.

BARTLETT. (*wildly*) He was lyin', the thief! Lyin' so's he and the boy could steal the gold. I made him own up he was lyin'. What if it's all true, what ye heard? Hadn't we the right to do away with two thieves? And we was all mad with thirst and sun. Can ye hold madmen to account for the things they do?

MRS. BARTLETT. You wasn't so crazed but you remember.

BARTLETT. I remember I spoke no word, Sarah—as God's my judge!

MRS. BARTLETT. But you could have prevented it with a word, couldn't you, Isaiah? That heathen savage lives in the fear of you. He'd not have done it if—

BARTLETT. (*gloomily*) That's woman's talk. There be three o' us can swear in any court I spoke no word.

MRS. BARTLETT. What are courts? Can you swear it to yourself? You can't, and it's that's drivin' you mad, Isaiah. Oh, I'd never have believed it of you for all you said in sleep, if it wasn't for the way you looked and acted out of sleep. I watched you that first week, Isaiah, till the fear of it had me down sick. I had to watch you, you was so strange and fearful to me. At first I kept sayin', 'twas only you wasn't rid o' the thirst and the sun yet. But then, all to once, God gave me sight, and I saw 'twas guilt written on your face, in the queer stricken way you acted, and guilt in your eyes. (*She stares into them*) I see it now, as I always see it when you look at me. (*She covers her face with her hands with a sob.*)

BARTLETT. (*his face haggard and drawn—hopelessly, as if he were too beaten to oppose her further—in a hoarse whisper*) What would ye have me do, Sarah?

MRS. BARTLETT. (*taking her hands from her face—her eyes lighting up with religious fervor*) Confess your sin, Isaiah! Confess to God and men, and make your peace and take your punishment. Forget that gold that's cursed and the voyage you be settin' out on, and make your peace. (*Passionately*) I ask you to do this for my sake and the children's, and your own most of all! I'll get down on my knees, Isaiah, and pray you to do it, as I've prayed to God to send you His

grace! Confess and wash your soul of the stain o' blood that's on it.
I ask you that, Isaiah—and God asks you—to make your peace with
Him.

BARTLETT. (*his face tortured by the inward struggle—as if the word
strangled him*) Confess and let someone steal the gold! (*This thought
destroys her influence over him in a second. His obsession regains possession of him instantly, filling him with rebellious strength. He laughs
harshly*) Ye'd make an old woman o' me, would ye, Sarah?—an old,
Sunday go-to-meetin' woman snivelin' and prayin' to God for pardon? Pardon for what? Because two sneakin' thieves are dead and
done for? I spoke no word, I tell ye—but if I had, I'd not repent it.
What I've done I've done, and I've never asked pardon o' God or men
for ought I've done, and never will. Confess, and give up the gold
I've dreamed of all my life that I've found at last? By thunder, ye must
think I'm crazed!

MRS. BARTLETT. (*seeming to shrivel up on her chair as she sees she
has lost—weakly*) You be lost, Isaiah—and no one can stop you.

BARTLETT. (*triumphantly*) Aye, none'll stop me. I'll go my course
alone. I'm glad ye see that, Sarah.

MRS. BARTLETT. (*feebly trying to get to her feet*) I'll go to home.

BARTLETT. Ye'll stay, Sarah. Ye've had your say, and I've listened to
ye; now I'll have mine and ye listen to me. (MRS. BARTLETT *sinks back
in her chair exhaustedly.* BARTLETT *continues slowly*) The schooner
sails at dawn on the full tide. I ask ye again and for the last time, will
ye christen her with your name afore she sails?

MRS. BARTLETT. (*firmly*) No.

BARTLETT. (*menacingly*) Take heed, Sarah, o' what ye're sayin'!
I'm your husband ye've sworn to obey. By right I kin order ye, not
ask.

MRS. BARTLETT. I've never refused in anything that's right—but this
be wicked wrong.

BARTLETT. It's only your stubborn woman's spite makes ye refuse.
Ye've christened every ship I've ever been skipper on, and it's brought

655

me luck o' a kind, though not the luck I wanted. And ye'll christen this one with your own name to bring me the luck I've always been seekin'.

MRS. BARTLETT. (*resolutely*) I won't, Isaiah.

BARTLETT. Ye will, Sarah, for I'll make ye. Ye force me to it.

MRS. BARTLETT. (*again trying to get up*) Is this the way you talk to me who've been a good wife to you for more than thirty years?

BARTLETT. (*commandingly*) Wait! (*Threateningly*) If ye don't christen her afore she sails, I'll take Nat on the vige along with me. (MRS. BARTLETT *sinks back in her chair, stunned*) He wants to go, ye know it. He's asked me a hundred times. He s'spects—'bout the gold —but he don't know for sartin. But I'll tell him the truth o' it, and he'll come with me, unless—

MRS. BARTLETT. (*looking at him with terror-stricken eyes—imploringly*) You won't do that, Isaiah? You won't take Nat away from me and drag him into sin? I know he'll go if you give him the word, in spite of what I say. (*Pitifully*) You be only frightenin' me! You can't be so wicked cruel as that.

BARTLETT. I'll do it, I take my oath—unless—

MRS. BARTLETT. (*with hysterical anger*) Then I'll tell him myself—of the murders you did, and—

BARTLETT. (*grimly*) And I'll say 'twas done in fair fight to keep them from stealin' the gold! I'll tell him yours is a woman's notion, and he'll believe me, not you. He's his father's son, and he's set to go. Ye know it, Sarah. (*She falls back in the chair hopelessly staring at him with horrified eyes. He turns away and adds after a pause*) So ye'll christen the "Sarah Allen" in the mornin' afore she sails, won't ye, Sarah?

MRS. BARTLETT. (*in a terrified tone*) Yes—if it's needful to save Nat— and God'll forgive me when He sees my reason. But you— Oh, Isaiah! (*She shudders and then breaks down, sobbing.*)

BARTLETT. (*after a pause, turns to her humbly as if asking forgiveness*) Ye mustn't think hard o' me that I want your name. It's because

656

it's a good woman's name, and I know it'll bring luck to our vige. I'd find it hard to sail without it—the way things be.

MRS. BARTLETT. (*getting to her feet—in a state of feverish fear of him*) I'm going to home.

BARTLETT. (*going to her*) I'll help ye to the top o' the hill, Sarah.

MRS. BARTLETT. (*shrinking from him in terror*) No. Don't you touch me! Don't you touch me! (*She hobbles quickly out of the door in the rear, looking back frightenedly over her shoulder to see if he is following as the curtain falls.*)

ACT THREE

SCENE—*Dawn of the following morning—exterior of the* BARTLETT *home, showing the main entrance, facing left, toward the harbor. On either side of the door, two large windows, their heavy green shutters tightly closed. In front of the door, a small porch, the roof supported by four white columns. A flight of three steps goes up to this porch from the ground. Two paths lead to the steps through the straggly patches of grass, one around the corner of the house to the rear, the other straight to the left to the edge of the cliff where there is a small projecting iron platform, fenced in by a rail. The top of a steel ladder can be seen. This ladder leads up the side of the cliff from the shore below to the platform. The edge of the cliff extends from the left corner front, half-diagonally back to the right, rear center.*

In the gray half-light of the dawn, HORNE, CATES, *and* JIMMY KANAKA *are discovered.* HORNE *is standing on the steel platform looking down at the shore below.* CATES *is sprawled on the ground nearby.* JIMMY *squats on his haunches, his eyes staring out to sea as if he were trying to pierce the distance to the warm islands of his birth.* CATES *wears dungarees,* JIMMY *dungaree pants and a black jersey,* HORNE *the same as in Act Two.*

CATES. (*with sluggish indifference*) Ain't she finished with it yet?

HORNE. (*irritably*) No, damn her! I kin see 'em all together on the wharf at the bow o' the schooner.

CATES. (*after a pause*) Funny, ain't it—his orderin' us to come up here and wait till it's all done.

HORNE. There's nothin' funny to me that he does no more. He's still out o' his head, d'ye know that, Cates?

CATES. (*stupidly*) I ain't noticed nothin' diff'rent 'bout him.

658

HORNE. (*scornfully*) He axed me if I ever seen them two in my sleep—that cook and the boy o' the "Triton." Said he did often.

CATES. (*immediately protesting uneasily as if he had been accused*) They was with us in the boat b'fore we fetched the island, that's all 'bout 'em I remember. I was crazy, after.

HORNE. (*looking at him with contempt*) I'll not call ye a liar, Cates, but—a hell of a man ye be! You wasn't so out o' your head that ye forgot the gold, was ye?

CATES. (*his eyes glistening*) Any man'd remember that, even if he was crazy.

HORNE. (*with a greedy grin*) Aye. That's the one thing I see in my sleep. (*There is the faint sound of cries from the beach below.* HORNE *starts and turns to look down again*) They must 'a' finished it. (CATES *and* JIMMY *come to the edge to look down.*)

JIMMY. (*suddenly—with an eager childish curiosity*) That falla wife Captain she make strong falla spell on ship, we sail fast, plenty good wind?

HORNE. (*contemptuously*) Aye, that's as near as ye'll come to it. She's makin' a spell. Ye stay here, Jimmy, and tell us when the Old Man is comin'. (JIMMY *remains looking down.* HORNE *motions* CATES *to follow him, front—then in a low voice, disgustedly*) Did ye hear that damn fool nigger?

CATES. (*grumblingly*) Why the hell is the Old Man givin' him a full share? One piece o' it'd be enough for a nigger like him.

HORNE. (*craftily*) There's a way to get rid o' him—if it comes to that. He knifed them two, ye remember.

CATES. Aye.

HORNE. The two o' us can take oath to that.

CATES. Aye.

HORNE. (*after a calculating look into his companion's greedy eyes— meaningly*) We're two sane men, Cates—and the other two to share is a lunatic and a nigger. The skipper's showed me where there's a copy o' this map o' the island locked up in the cabin—in case anything happens to him I'm to bring back the gold to his woman, he says. (*He laughs harshly*) Catch me! The fool! I'll be open with ye, Cates. If I could navigate and find the island myself I wouldn't wait for a cracked man to take me there. No, be damned if I would! Me and you'd chance it alone some way or other.

CATES. (*greedily*) The two o' us—share and share alike! (*Then shaking his head warningly*) But he's a hard man to git the best on.

HORNE. (*grimly*) And I be a hard man, too.

JIMMY. (*turning to them*) Captain, he come. (CATES *and* HORNE *separate hastily.* BARTLETT *climbs into sight up the ladder to the platform. He is breathing heavily but his expression is one of triumphant exultation.*)

BARTLETT. (*motions with his arms*) Down with ye and git aboard. The schooner's got a name now—a name that'll bring us luck. We'll sail on this tide.

HORNE. Aye—aye, sir.

BARTLETT. I got to wait here till they climb up the path. I'll be aboard afore long. See that ye have her ready to cast off by then.

HORNE. Aye—aye, sir. (*He and* CATES *disappear down the ladder.* JIMMY *lingers, looking sidewise at his Captain.*)

BARTLETT. (*noticing him—gruffly*) What are ye waitin' for?

JIMMY. (*volubly*) That old falla wife belong you, Captain, she make strong falla spell for wind blow plenty? She catch strong devil charm for schooner, Captain?

BARTLETT. (*scowling*) What's that, ye brown devil? (*Then suddenly laughing harshly*) Yes—a strong spell to bring us luck. (*Roughly*) Git aboard, ye dog! Don't let her find ye here with me. (JIMMY *disappears hurriedly down the ladder.* BARTLETT *remains at the edge looking down after him. There is a sound of voices from the right and presently* MRS. BARTLETT, SUE, DREW *and* NAT *enter, coming around the house from the rear.* NAT *and* DREW *walk at either side of* MRS. BARTLETT, *who is in a state of complete collapse, so that they are practically carrying her.* SUE *follows, her handkerchief to her eyes.*

NAT *keeps his eyes on the ground, his expression fixed and gloomy.* DREW *casts a glance of angry indignation at the Captain, who, after one indifferent look at them, has turned back to watch the operations on the schooner below.*)

BARTLETT. (*as they reach the steps of the house—intent on the work below—makes a megaphone of his hands and shouts in stentorian tones*) Look lively there, Horne!

SUE. (*protestingly*) Pa!

BARTLETT. (*wheels about. When he meets his daughter's eyes he controls his angry impatience and speaks gently*) What d'ye want, Sue?

SUE. (*pointing to her mother who is being assisted through the door —her voice trembling*) You mustn't shout. She's very sick.

BARTLETT. (*dully, as if he didn't understand*) Sick?

SUE. (*turning to the door*) Wait. I'll be right back. (*She enters the house. As soon as she is gone all of* BARTLETT'S *excitement returns. He paces up and down with nervous impatience.* NAT *comes out of the house.*)

NAT. (*in a tone of anxiety*) Ma seems bad. I'm going for the doctor.

BARTLETT. (*as if he hadn't heard—draws* NAT's *attention to the schooner*) Smart lines on that schooner, boy. She'll sail hell bent in a breeze. I knowed what I was about when I bought her.

NAT. (*staring down fascinatedly*) How long will the voyage take?

BARTLETT. (*preoccupied*) How long?

NAT. (*insinuatingly*) To get to the island.

BARTLETT. Three months at most—with fair luck. (*Exultantly*) And I'll have luck now!

NAT. Then in six months you may be back—with *it?*

BARTLETT. Aye, with— (*Stopping abruptly, turns and stares into his son's eyes—angrily*) With what? What boy's foolishness be ye talkin'?

NAT. (*pleading fiercely*) I want to go, Pa! There's no good in my staying here any more. I can't think of anything but—

BARTLETT. (*sternly, to conceal his uneasiness*) Keep clear o' this, boy, I've warned ye!

SUE. (*appearing in doorway—indignantly*) Nat! Haven't you gone for the doctor yet?

NAT. (*shamefacedly*) I forgot.

SUE. Forgot!

NAT. (*starting off*) I'm going, Sue. (*Then over his shoulder*) You won't sail before I come back, Pa. (BARTLETT *does not answer.* NAT *stands miserably hesitating.*)

SUE. Nat! For heaven's sake! (NAT *hurries off around the corner of the house, rear.* SUE *comes to her father who is watching her with a queer, humble, hunted expression.*)

BARTLETT. Well, Sue?

SUE. (*her voice trembling*) Oh, Pa, how could you drag Ma out of bed to christen your old boat—when you knew how sick she's been!

BARTLETT. (*avoiding her eyes*) It's only weakness. She'll get well o' it soon.

SUE. Pa! How can you say things like that—as if you didn't care! (*Accusingly*) The way you've acted ever since you've been home almost, anyone would think—you *hated* her!

BARTLETT. (*wincing*) No!

SUE. Oh, Pa, what is it that has come between you? Can't you tell me? Can't I help to set things right again?

BARTLETT. (*mumblingly*) Nothin'—nothin' ye kin help—nor me.

SUE. But things can't go on like this. Don't you see it's killing Ma?

BARTLETT. She'll forget her stubborn notions, now I be sailin' away.

SUE. But you're not—not going for a while now, are you?

BARTLETT. Ain't I been sayin' I'd sail at dawn today?

SUE. (*looking at him for a moment with shocked amazement*) But —you can't mean—right now!

BARTLETT. (*keeping his face averted*) Aye—or we'll miss this tide.

SUE. (*putting her hands on his shoulders and trying to look into his face*) Pa! You can't mean that! (*His face is set with his obsessed deter-*

662

mination. She lets her hands fall with a shudder) You can't be as cruel as that! Why, I thought, of course, you'd put off— (*Wildly*) You have, haven't you, Pa? You did tell those men you couldn't sail when you saw how sick Ma was, didn't you—when she fainted down on the wharf?

BARTLETT. (*implacably*) I said I was sailin' by this tide!

SUE. Pa! (*Then pleadingly*) When the doctor comes and you hear what he says—

BARTLETT. (*roughly*) I ain't stoppin' on his word nor any man's. (*Intensely*) That schooner's been fit to sail these two weeks past. I been waitin' on her stubborn will, (*He gestures toward the house*) eatin' my heart out day and night. Then I swore I'd sail today. I tell ye, Sue, I got a feelin' in my bones if I don't put out now I never will. Aye, I feel it deep down inside me. (*In a tone of superstitious awe*) And when she christened the schooner—jest to the minute, mind ye!— a fair breeze sprung up and come down out o' the land to blow her out to sea—like a sign o' good luck.

SUE. (*aroused to angry indignation*) Oh, I can't believe you're the same man who used to be my father!

BARTLETT. Sue!

SUE. To talk cold-bloodedly of sailing away on a long voyage when Ma's inside—dying for all you seem to know or care! You're not the father I love! You've changed into someone else—hateful and cruel— and I hate him, I hate him! (*She breaks down, sobbing hysterically.*)

BARTLETT. (*who has listened to her with a face suddenly stricken by fear and torturing remorse*) Sue! Ye don't know what ye be sayin', do ye?

SUE. I do! And I hate those three awful men who make you act this way. I hate the schooner! I wish she and they were at the bottom of the sea!

BARTLETT. (*frenziedly—putting his hand over her mouth to stop her words*) Stop, girl! Don't ye dare—

SUE. (*shrinking away from him—frightenedly*) Pa!

BARTLETT. (*bewilderedly, pleading for forgiveness*) Don't heed that, Sue—I didn't mean—ye git me so riled—I'd not hurt ye for all the gold in the world. But don't ye talk wrong o' things ye can't know on.

SUE. Oh, Pa, what kind of things must they be—when you're ashamed to tell them!

BARTLETT. Ye'll know all they be to know—and your Ma and Nat, too—when I come back from this vige. Oh, ye'll be glad enough then—when ye see with your own eyes! Ye'll bless me then 'stead o' turning agin me! (*Hesitating for a second—then somberly*) On'y now—till it's all over and done—ye'd best keep clear o' it.

SUE. (*passionately*) I don't want to know anything about it. What I do know is that you can't sail now. Haven't you any heart at all? Can't you see how bad Ma is?

BARTLETT. It's the sight o' me sickens her.

SUE. No. She called your name just a while ago—the only word she's spoken since she christened the ship.

BARTLETT. (*desperately*) I got to git away from her, I tell ye, Sue! She's been houndin' me ever since I got back—houndin' me with her stubborn tongue till she's druv me mad, a'most! Ye've been on'y givin' thought to her, not me. It's for her sake as much as my own I'm goin'—for her and you and Nat. (*With a sudden return of his old resolution*) I've made up my mind, I tell ye, and in the end ye'll know I be right. (*A hail in* HORNE's *voice comes thinly up from the shore below.* BARTLETT *starts, his eyes gleaming*) Ye hear! It's Horne hailin' me to come. They be ready to cast off. I'll git aboard. (*He starts for the ladder.*)

SUE. Pa! After all I've said—without one word of good-by to Ma! (*Hysterically*) Oh, what can I do, what can I say to stop you! She hasn't spoken but that one call for you. She hardly seems to breathe. If it weren't for her eyes I'd believe she was dead—but her eyes look for you. She'll die if you go, Pa!

BARTLETT. No!

SUE. (*meaningly*) And you told me, didn't you, that you'd just got your master's papers.

DREW. (*looking at her with stunned astonishment*) Sue! D'you mean—

SUE. (*a light coming over her face*) Oh, Danny, we could trust you! He'd trust you! And after he'd calmed down I know he wouldn't mind so much. Oh, Danny, it'll break my heart to have you go, to send you away just after you've come back. But I don't see any other way. I wouldn't ask—if it wasn't for Ma being this way—and him—Oh, Danny, can't you see your way to do it—for my sake?

DREW. (*bewilderedly*) Why, Sue, I—I never thought— (*Then as he sees the look of disappointment which comes over her face at his hesitancy—resolutely*) Why sure, Sue, I'll do it—if you want me to. I'll do it if it can be done. But we've got to hustle. You've got to keep him in the house some way if he aims to come out. And I'll talk to them. (SUE *goes to the doorway.* DREW *goes over to* HORNE *and* CATES.)

SUE. (*after listening*) He's still in with Ma. It's all right.

DREW. (*to* HORNE) How would you like me for skipper on this one voyage? Listen here. Miss Sue's decided her father isn't in a fit state to captain this trip.

HORNE. That's no lie.

CATES. (*to* HORNE *protestingly*) But if we git ketched the Old Man'll take it out o' our hides, not his'n.

HORNE. (*savagely—with a meaning look at* CATES) Shut up, ye fool!

DREW. (*impatiently*) I'll shoulder all that risk, man!

SUE. (*earnestly*) No harm will come to any of you, I promise you.

HORNE. (*in the tone of one clinching a bargain*) Then we'll chance it. (*Warningly*) But it's got to be done smart, sir.

DREW. I've got to get my dunnage. I'll be right back and we'll tumble aboard. (*He goes into the house.* SUE *follows him in.*)

CATES. (*with stupid anger*) This is a hell of a mess we're gettin' in, if ye axe me.

HORNE. And I tell ye it's a great stroke o' luck.

SUE. You might just as well kill her now in cold blood as murder her that way!

BARTLETT. (*shaken—raising his hands as if to put them over his ears to shut out her words—hoarsely*) No! Ye lie!

DREW. (*appearing at the doorway, his face working with grief and anger—harshly*) Captain Bartlett! (*Then lowering his voice as he sees* SUE) Mrs. Bartlett is asking to see you, Captain, before you go.

SUE. There! Didn't I tell you, Pa!

BARTLETT. (*struggling with himself—dully*) She's wantin' to hound me again, that be all.

SUE. (*seeing him weakening—grasps his hand persuasively*) Pa! Come with me. She won't hound you. How silly you are! Come! (*Hesitatingly, head bowed, he follows her toward the door.*)

BARTLETT. (*As he comes to* DREW *he stops and looks into the young man's angry, accusing face. He mutters half mockingly*) So ye, too, be agin me, Danny!

DREW. (*unable to restrain his indignation*) What man that's a real man wouldn't be against you, sir?

SUE. (*frightenedly*) Danny! Pa!

BARTLETT. (*in a sudden rage draws back his fist threateningly.* DREW *stares into his eyes unflinchingly—*BARTLETT *controls himself with an effort and lets his arm fall to his side—scornfully*) Big words from a boy, Danny. I'll forget them this time—on account o' Sue. (*He turns to her*) I'm goin' in to her to please ye, Sue—but if ye think any words that she kin say'll change my mind, ye make a mistake—for I be sailin' out as I planned I would in spite o' all hell! (*He walks resolutely into the house.* SUE *follows him after exchanging a hopeless glance with* DANNY.)

DREW. (*to himself—with a shudder*) He's mad, damn him! (*He paces up and down.* HORNE *appears on the ladder from below, followed by* CATES.)

HORNE. (*coming forward and addressing* DREW) Is the skipper about?

DREW. (*curtly*) He's in the house. You can't speak to him now.

HORNE. She's ready to cast off. I hailed him from below but I s'pect he didn't hear. (*As* DREW *makes no comment—impatiently*) If he don't shake a leg, we'll miss the tide. There's a bit o' fair breeze, too.

DREW. (*glancing at him resentfully*) Don't count on his sailing today. It's just as likely he'll change his mind.

HORNE. (*angrily*) Change his mind again? After us waitin' and wastin' time for weeks! (*To* CATES *in a loud tone so* DREW *can hear*) What did I tell ye, Cates? He's crazy as hell.

DREW. (*sharply*) What's that?

HORNE. I was tellin' Cates the skipper's not right in his head. (*Angrily*) What man in his senses'd do the way he does?

DREW. (*letting his resentment escape him*) That's no lie, damn it!

HORNE. (*surprised*) Aye, ye've seen it, too, have ye? (*After a pause*) Now I axe ye, as a sailor, how'd ye like to be puttin' out on a vige with a cracked man for skipper? (SUE *comes out of the door, stops with a shudder of disgust as she sees the two sailors, and stands listening. They do not notice her presence.*)

DREW. It seems to me a crazy voyage all round. (*With sudden interest as if a new idea had come to him*) But you know all about it, don't you—what the Captain plans to do on this voyage—and all that?

HORNE. (*dryly*) Aye, as well as himself—but I'm tellin' no man.

DREW. And I'm not asking. What I want to find out is: Do you know enough about this business to make this one voyage alone and attend to everything—in case the Captain can't go?

HORNE. (*exchanging a quick glance with* CATES—*trying to hide his eagerness*) Aye, I could do as well as any many alive. He could trust me for it—and I'd make more money for him than he's likely to make with his head out o' gear. (*Then scowling*) On'y trouble is, who'd captain her if he ain't goin'?

DREW. (*disappointedly*) Then you don't know navigation enough for that?

HORNE. I've never riz above bo'sun. (*Then after a pause in which he appears to be calculating something—curiously*) Why d'ye ask me them questions? (*Insinuatingly—almost in a whisper*) It can't be done 'less we got an officer like you aboard.

DREW. (*angrily*) Eh? What're you driving at?

SUE. (*who has been listening with aroused interest*) Danny! (*She comes down to him.* HORNE *and* CATES *bob their heads respectfully and move back near the platform.* HORNE *watches* SUE *and* DREW *out of the corner of his eye*) Danny, I've been listening to what you were saying, but I don't understand. What are you thinking of?

DREW. (*excitedly*) I was thinking— Listen, Sue! Seems to me your Pa's out of his right mind. Something's got to be done to keep him home in spite of himself. Even leaving your Ma out of it, he's not in any fit state to take a ship to sea; and I was thinking if we could fix it some way so that fellow Horne could take her out on this voyage—

SUE. But, Danny, Pa'd never give in to that.

DREW. I wasn't thinking he would. We—you'd have to give the word—and keep him in the house somehow—and then when he did come out it'd be too late. The schooner'd be gone.

SUE. (*disturbed, but showing that this plan has caught her mind*) But—he'd never forgive—

DREW. When he's back in his right mind again, he would. (*Earnestly*) You can't let him sail, and wreck his ship and himself in the bargain, likely. Then, there's your Ma—

SUE. No, no, we can't let him. (*With a glance at* HORNE *and* CATES) But I don't trust those men.

DREW. No more do I; but it would be better to chance them than— (*Suddenly interrupting himself—with a shrug of his shoulders*) But I was forgetting. None of them can navigate.

SUE. But didn't I hear him say—if they had an officer on board— like you—

DREW. Yes, but where'll you find one at a second's notice?

CATES. He'll be aboard to spy on us.

HORNE. Leave me to fool him. And when the time comes to git rid o' him, I'll find a means some way or other.

CATES. (*stupidly*) S'long as he don't git no share o' the gold—

HORNE. (*contemptuously*) Share, ye dumbhead! I'd see him in hell first—and send him there myself. (DREW *comes out of the house carrying his bag which he hands to* CATES. SUE *follows him.*)

DREW. Look lively now!

HORNE. Aye—aye, sir. (*He and* CATES *clamber hurriedly down the ladder.*)

SUE. (*throwing her arms around his neck and kissing him*) Good-by, Danny. It's so fine of you to do this for us! I'll never forget—

DREW. (*tenderly*) Ssssh! It's nothing, Sue.

SUE. (*tearfully*) Oh, Danny, I hope I'm doing right! I'll miss you so dreadfully! But you'll come back just as soon as you can—

DREW. Of course!

SUE. Danny! Danny! I love you so!

DREW. And I guess you know I love you, don't you? (*Kisses her*) And we'll be married when I come back this time *sure?*

SUE. Yes—yes—Danny—sure!

DREW. I've got to run. Good-by, Sue.

SUE. Good-by, dear. (*They kiss for the last time and he disappears down the ladder. She stands at the top, sobbing, following him with her eyes.* NAT *comes around the house from the rear and goes to the front door.*)

NAT. (*seeing his sister*) Sue! He hasn't gone yet, has he? (*She doesn't hear him. He hesitates in the doorway for a moment, listening for the sound of his father's voice from inside. Then, very careful to make no noise, he tiptoes carefully into the house.* SUE *waves her hand to* DREW *who has evidently now got aboard the ship. Then she covers her face with her hands, sobbing.* NAT *comes out of the house again and goes to his sister. As she sees him approaching, she dries her eyes hastily, trying to smile.*)

SUE. Did you get the doctor, Nat?

NAT. Yes, he's coming right away, he promised. (*Looking at her face*) What—have you been crying?

SUE. No. (*She walks away from the edge of the cliff, drawing him with her.*)

NAT. Yes, you have. Look at your eyes.

SUE. Oh, Nat, everything's so awful. (*She breaks down again.*)

NAT. (*trying to comfort her in an absent-minded way*) There, don't get worked up. Ma'll be all right as soon as the doctor comes. (*Then curiously*) Pa's inside with her. They were arguing—have they made it up, d'you think?

SUE. Oh, Nat, I don't know.

NAT. The strain's been too much for him—waiting and hiding his secret from all of us. What do you suppose it is, Sue?

SUE. (*wildly*) I don't know and I don't care!

NAT. Well, there's something— (*Starts for the platform.* SUE *does her best to interpose to hold him back*) Are they all ready on the schooner? He'll have to hurry if she's going to sail on this tide. (*With sudden passion*) Oh, I've got to go! I can't stay here! (*Pleadingly*) Don't you think, Sue, if you were to ask him for me he'd— You're the only one he seems to act sane with or care about any more.

SUE. No! I won't! I can't!

NAT. (*angrily*) Haven't you any sense? Wouldn't it be better for everyone if I went in his place?

SUE. No. You know that's a lie. Ma would lose her mind if you went.

NAT. And I'll lose mine if I stay! (*Half aware of* SUE's *intention to keep him from looking down at the schooner—irritably*) What are you holding my arm for, Sue? I want to see what they're doing. (*He pushes her aside and goes to the platform—excitedly*) Hello, they've got the fores'l and mains'l set. They're setting the stays'l. (*In amazement*) Why—they're casting off! She's moving away from the wharf! (*More and more excitedly*) I see four of them on board! Who—who is that, Sue?

SUE. It's Danny.

NAT. (*furiously*) Danny! What right has he—when I can't! Sue, call Pa! They're sailing, I tell you, you little fool!

SUE. (*trying to calm him—her voice trembling*) Nat! Don't be such a donkey! Danny's only going a little way—just trying the boat to see how she sails while they're waiting for Pa.

NAT. (*uncertainly*) Oh. (*Then bitterly*) I was never allowed to do even that—his own son! Look, Sue, that must be Danny at the stern waving.

SUE. (*brokenly*) Yes. (*She waves her handkerchief over her head— then breaks down, sobbing again. There is the noise of* BARTLETT's *voice from inside and a moment later he appears in the doorway. He seems terribly shattered, at the end of his tether. He hesitates uncertainly, looking about him wildly as if he didn't know what to do or where to go.*)

SUE. (*after one look at his face, runs to him and flings her arms about his neck*) Pa! (*She weeps on his shoulder.*)

BARTLETT. Sue, ye did wrong beggin' me to see her. I knowed it'd do no good. Ye promised she'd not hound me—"Confess," she says— when they be naught to tell that couldn't be swore to in any court. "Don't go on this vige," she says, "there be the curse o' God on it." (*With a note of baffled anguish*) She kin say that after giving the ship her own name! (*With wild, haggard defiance*) But curse or no curse, I be goin'! (*He moves toward the platform,* SUE *clinging to his arm.*)

SUE. (*frightenedly*) Pa! Go back in the house, won't you?

BARTLETT. I be sorry to go agin your will, Sue, but it's got to be. Ye'll know the reason some day—and be glad o' it. And now good-by to ye. (*With a sudden strange tenderness he bends and kisses his daughter. Then as she seems about to protest further, his expression becomes stern and inflexible*) No more o' talk, Sue! I be bound out. (*He takes her hand off his arm and strides to the platform. One look down at the harbor and he stands transfixed—in a hoarse whisper*)

GOLD

What damned trick be this? (*He points to the schooner and turns to* NAT *bewilderedly*) Ain't that my schooner, boy—the "Sarah Allen"—reachin' toward the p'int?

NAT. (*surprised*) Yes, certainly. Didn't you know? Danny's trying her to see how she sails while they're waiting for you.

BARTLETT. (*with a tremendous sigh of relief*) Aye. (*Then angrily*) He takes a lot o' rope to himself without askin' leave o' me. Don't he know they's no time to waste on boy's foolin'? (*Then with admiration*) She sails smart, don't she, boy? I knowed she'd show a pair o' heels.

NAT. (*with enthusiasm*) Yes, she's a daisy! Say, Danny's taking her pretty far out, isn't he?

BARTLETT. (*anxiously*) He'd ought to come about now if he's to tack back inside the p'int. (*Furiously*) Come about, damn ye! The swab! That's what comes o' steamer trainin'. I'd sooner trust Sue to sail her nor him. (*Waves his arm and shouts*) Come about!

NAT. (*bitterly*) He seems to be heading straight for the open sea. He's taking quite a sail, it seems to me.

BARTLETT. (*as if he couldn't believe his eyes*) He's passed the p'int—and now—headin' her out to sea—so'east by east. By God, that be the course I charted for her! (SUE *bursts out sobbing. He wheels on her, his mouth fallen open, his face full of a stupid despair*) They be somethin' wrong here. What be it, Sue? What be it, Nat? (*His voice has begun to quiver with passion*) That schooner—she's sailin' without me— (*He suddenly springs at* NAT *and grabs him by the throat—with hoarse fury, shaking him*) What be it, ye whelp? It's your doin'—because I wouldn't let ye go. Answer me!

SUE. (*rushing to them with a scream*) Pa! (*She tugs frantically at his hands.* BARTLETT *lets them fall to his side, stepping back from* NAT *who sinks weakly to the ground, gasping for breath.* BARTLETT *stands looking at him wildly.*)

SUE. Nat didn't know it, Pa. It's all my fault. I had to do it. There was no other way—

672

BARTLETT. (*raging*) What d'ye mean, girl? What is it ye've done? Tell me, I say! Tell me or I'll—

SUE. (*unflinchingly*) You had to be stopped from going some way. So I asked Danny if he wouldn't make the trip in your place. He's just got his captain's papers—and oh, Pa, you can trust him, you know that! That man Horne said he knows about everything you wanted done, and he promised to tell Danny, and Danny'll come back—

BARTLETT. (*chokingly*) So—that be it— (*Shaking his clenched fist at the sky as if visualizing the fate he feels in all of this*) Curse ye! Curse ye! (*He subsides weakly, his strength spent, his hand falls limply at his side.*)

MRS. BARTLETT. (*appears in the doorway. Her face is pale with anguish. She gives a cry of joy when she sees her son*) Nat! (*Then with a start of horror as her eyes fall on her husband*) Isaiah! (*He doesn't seem to hear*) Then—you ain't sailed yet?

SUE. (*going to her—gently*) No, Ma, he isn't going to sail. He's going to stay home with you. But the schooner's gone. See. (*She points and her mother's eyes turn seaward.*)

BARTLETT. (*aloud to himself—in a tone of groping superstitious awe and bewildered fear*) They be somethin' queer—somethin' wrong— they be a curse in this somewhere—

MRS. BARTLETT. (*turning accusing eyes on him—with a sort of fanatical triumph*) I'm glad to hear you confess that, Isaiah. Yes, there be a curse—God's curse on the wicked sinfulness o' men—and I thank God He's saved you from the evil of that voyage, and I'll pray Him to visit His punishment and His curse on them three men on that craft you forced me to give my name— (*She has raised her hand as if calling down retribution on the schooner she can dimly see.*)

SUE. (*terrified*) Ma!

BARTLETT. (*starting toward his wife with an insane yell of fury*) Stop it, I tell ye! (*He towers over her with upraised fist as if to crush her.*)

SUE. Pa!

NAT. (*starting to his feet from where he has been sitting on the ground—hoarsely*) Pa! For God's sake!

MRS. BARTLETT. (*gives a weak, frightened gasp*) Would you murder me too, Isaiah? (*She closes her eyes and collapses in* SUE's *arms.*)

SUE. (*tremblingly*) Nat! Help me! Quick! We must carry her to bed. (*They take their mother in their arms, carrying her inside the house.*)

BARTLETT. (*while they are doing this, rushes in his mad frenzy to the platform over the edge of the cliff. He puts his hands to his mouth, megaphone-fashion, and yells with despairing rage*) Ahoy! Ahoy! "Sarah Allen!" Put back! Put back! (*As the curtain falls.*)

ACT FOUR

SCENE—*About nine o'clock of a moonlight night one year later—* CAPTAIN BARTLETT'S *"cabin," a room erected on the top of his house as a lookout post. The interior is fitted up like the cabin of a sailing vessel. On the left, forward, a porthole. Farther back, the stairs of the companionway. Still farther, two more portholes. In the rear, left, a marble-topped sideboard. In the rear, center, a door opening on stairs which lead to the lower house. A cot with a blanket is placed against the wall to the right of door. In the right wall, five portholes. Directly under them, a wooden bench. In front of the bench, a long table with two chairs placed, one in front, one to the left of it. A cheap, dark-colored rug is on the floor. In the ceiling, midway from front to rear, a skylight extending from opposite the door to above the left edge of the table. In the right extremity of the skylight is placed a floating ship's compass. The light from the binnacle sheds down over this and seeps into the room, casting a vague globular shadow of the compass on the floor. Moonlight creeps in through the portholes on the right. A lighted lantern is on the table.*

As the curtain rises, SUE *and* DOCTOR BERRY *are discovered sitting by the table. The doctor is a man of sixty or so, hale and hearty-looking, his white hair and mustache setting off his ruddy complexion. His blue eyes have a gentle expression, his smile is kindly and sympathetic. His whole manner toward* SUE *is that of the old family doctor and friend, not the least of whose duties is to play father-confessor to his patients. She is dressed in deep mourning. She looks much older. But there is an excited elation in her face at present, her eyes are alight with some unexpected joy.*

675

SUE. (*excitedly*) And here is Danny's letter, Doctor—to prove it's all true. (*She takes a letter from the bosom of her dress and holds it out to him.*)

DOCTOR. (*takes it with a smile, patting her hand*) I can't say how glad I am, Susan. Coming after we'd all given him up for lost—it's like a miracle.

SUE. (*smiling happily*) Read what he says.

DOCTOR. (*hesitating—playfully*) I don't know that it's right for me— love letters at my age!

SUE. I want you to read it. (*He reaches in his pocket for his spectacles.* SUE *continues gratefully*) As if I could have any secrets from you after all you've done for us since Ma died. You've been the only friend— (*She stops, her lips trembling.*)

DOCTOR. Tut-tut. (*He adjusts his spectacles and peers at her over them*) Who wouldn't be of all the service he could to a brave girl like you? This past year—with your mother's death—and then the news of the schooner being reported lost—not many could have stood it—living in this house with him the way he is—even if he was their father.

SUE. (*glancing up at the skylight—apprehensively*) Ssshh! He might hear you.

DOCTOR. (*listening intently*) Not him. There he goes pacing up and down, looking out to sea for that ship that will never come back! (*Shaking himself*) Brrr! This house of mad dreams!

SUE. Don't you think Pa'll come to realize the schooner is lost as time goes by and she doesn't come back?

DOCTOR. No, your father won't let himself look the facts in the face. If he did, probably the shock of it would kill him. That darn dream of his has become his life. No, Susan, as time goes on he'll believe in it harder and harder. After observing him for the past year—and I speak for his own sake, too, as his good friend for twenty years or more—my final advice is the same: Send him to an asylum.

SUE. (*with a shudder*) No, Doctor.

676

DOCTOR. (*shaking his head*) You'll have to come to it in time. He's getting worse. No one can tell—he might get violent—

SUE. How can you say that? You know how gentle and sane he is with me.

DOCTOR. You're his one connecting link with things as they are—but that can't last. Eh, well, my dear, one thing you've got to realize: Your father and Nat must be separated somehow. Nat's going to pieces. I'll bet he doesn't believe that schooner is lost any more than your father does.

SUE. You mean he still hopes it may not be true. That's only natural. He's in San Francisco now tracing down the report again. He saw in the papers where the British freighter that found the derelict was there and he went to talk with the people on board. I'm hoping he'll come back fully convinced, with the whole thing out of his mind.

DOCTOR. (*shaking his head—gravely*) I've watched him and talked with him. You've got to persuade Nat to go away, Susan.

SUE. (*helplessly*) I don't know— (*Then brightening*) Just now it's enough to know Danny's alive and coming back. Read his letter, Doctor.

DOCTOR. Yes, yes, let's see. (*He takes the letter from the envelope.*)

SUE. Poor Danny! He's been through terrible things.

DOCTOR. Hmm! Rangoon.

SUE. Yes, he's still in the hospital there. You'll see.

DOCTOR. (*reads the letter—grunts with astonishment—angrily*) By Gad! The damn scoundrels!

SUE. (*shuddering*) Yes, wasn't it hideous—those awful men stabbing him and leaving him for dead in that out of the way native settlement! And then he was laid up for four months there waiting for a vessel to touch and take him back to civilization. And then, think of it, getting the fever on top of all that and nearly dying in the hospital in Rangoon!

DOCTOR. A terrible time of it! He's lucky to be alive. Hmm. I see he foresaw the wreck of the schooner. (*Folding the letter and putting*

GOLD

it back) He doesn't seem to have found out what the purpose of that mad trip was. Horne hid it from him to the last, he says. Well, it's queer—damn queer. But I'm glad to know those wretches have gone to their final accounting.

SUE. (*with a shudder*) I was always afraid of them. They looked like—murderers. (*At a noise from below they both start. Steps can be heard climbing the stairs.* SUE *jumps to her feet frightenedly*) Why—do you hear—who can that be? (*There is a soft rap on the door. The* DOCTOR *jumps to his feet.* SUE *turns to him with a half-hysterical laugh*) Shall I open? I don't know why—but I'm afraid.

DOCTOR. Tut-tut! I'll see who it is. (*He opens the door and* NAT *is discovered on the stairs outside*) Why hello, boy. You gave us a scare. Susan thought it was a ghost knocking.

NAT. (*comes into the room. He has aged, grown thin, his face gaunt and drawn from continual mental strain, his eyes moody and pre-occupied. He glances up at the skylight apprehensively, then turns to* SUE) I didn't find you downstairs so I— (*Then to the* DOCTOR) Yes, you do grow to look for ghosts in this house, don't you? (*Again glancing upward*) He's up there as usual, I suppose—looking for a ship that'll never, never come now!

DOCTOR. (*with a grunt of approval*) I'm glad to hear you acknowl-edge that.

SUE. (*who is just recovering from her fright*) But, Nat, I didn't expect you— Did you find out—?

NAT. Yes, I talked with several of the men who were on board at the time. They said they steamed in so close to the schooner it was easy to read the name with the naked eye. All agreed—"Sarah Allen," Harborport. They even remembered how her taffrail was painted. There's no chance for mistake. The "Sarah Allen" is gone. (*With great emphasis*) And I'm glad—damn glad! I feel free again, and I can go back to work—but not here. I've got to go away—start new alto-gether.

SUE. (*happily, coming and putting her arms around him*) It's so good to hear you talk like your old self again.

DOCTOR. (*earnestly*) Yes, Nat, by Gad, that's sound sense. Get out of this.

NAT. (*giving him a queer look*) I suppose you thought I was doomed, eh?—like him. (*He makes a motion upward—then with an uncertain laugh*) A doctor's always looking for trouble where there isn't any. (*In a tone of finality*) Well, it's all over, anyway.

SUE. (*snatching the letter from the table*) Oh, I was forgetting, Nat. Read this. I got it yesterday.

NAT. (*turns it over in his hands suspiciously*) Who from?

SUE. Open it and see.

NAT. (*does so and turns over the pages to read the signature—he gives a start—hoarsely*) Danny! It can't be! But it's his writing sure enough! (*He exclaims with a sudden wild exultation*) Then they must have been lying to me!

SUE. No, the "Sarah Allen" was wrecked all right, but that was afterwards. Read it. You'll see. (NAT *sinks back on a chair, evidently depressed by this information. He starts to read the letter with unconcealed indifference, then becomes engrossed, excited, the paper trembling in his hands. The* DOCTOR *shakes his head at* SUE *indicating his disapproval of her giving him the letter.* NAT *finishes and springs to his feet—angrily.*)

NAT. The stupid fool! He let Horne pull the wool over his eyes in fine shape.

SUE. (*indignantly*) Nat!

NAT. (*unheedingly*) Oh, if I could only have gone in his place! I knew the kind Horne was. He couldn't have played that trick on me. I'd have forced the secret out of him if I had to— (*He raises his clenched fist in a gesture of threat like his father's—then lets it fall and sits down again—disgustedly*) But what's the use? And what's the use of this? (*Tosses the letter contemptuously on the table*) He might just as well not have written.

SUE. (*snatching up the letter—deeply hurt*) Aren't you even glad to hear Danny's alive?

NAT. (*turning to her at once—with remorseful confusion*) Yes—yes —of course, Sue—I don't have to say that, do I? What I mean is, he never found out from Horne—and we're no wiser.

DOCTOR. (*briskly—with a significant glance at* SUE) Well, Susan— Nat—I've got to run along— (*Meaningly*) I'll be over again tomorrow, Susan.

SUE. Yes, do come. (*Goes with him to the door*) Can you see your way?

DOCTOR. Yes. Good night.

SUE. Good night. (*She closes the door and comes back to* NAT. *The* DOCTOR'S *footsteps die out.*)

NAT. (*savagely*) That damned old fool! What is he doing, sneaking around here all the time? I've grown to hate the sight of him.

SUE. Nat! You can't mean that. Think of how kind he's been.

NAT. Yes—kindness with a purpose.

SUE. Don't be silly. What purpose could he have except wanting to help us?

NAT. To find out things, of course, you simpleton. To pump Pa when he's not responsible for what he's saying.

SUE. (*indignantly*) Nat!

NAT. Much good it's done him! I know Pa. Sane or not, he won't tell *that* to anyone—not even you or me, Sue. (*With sudden fury*) I'm going away—but before I go I'm going to make him tell me! He's been so afraid I'd find out, so scared to speak to me even—locking himself up here. But I'll make him tell—yes, I will!

SUE. Careful, Nat. He'll hear you if you shout like that.

NAT. But we have a right to know—his own children. What if he dies without ever speaking?

SUE. (*uneasily*) Be sensible, Nat. There's nothing to tell except in your imagination. (*Taking his arm—persuasively*) Come on downstairs. I'll get you something to eat. You must be starved, aren't you?

NAT. No—I don't know—I suppose I ought to be. (*He gets to his feet and glances around with a shudder*) What a place for him to build to wait in—like the cabin of a ship sunk deep under the sea— like the "Sarah Allen's" cabin as it is now, probably. (*With a shiver*) There's a chill comes over you. No wonder he's mad. (*He listens*) Hear him. A year ago today she sailed. I wonder if he knows that. Back and forth, always staring out to sea for the "Sarah Allen." Ha-ha! God! It would be funny if it didn't make your flesh creep. (*Brusquely*) Come on. Let's leave him and go down where there's light and warmth. (*They go down the stairs, closing the door behind them. There is a pause. Then the door of the companionway above is heard being opened and shut. A gust of wind sweeps down into the room.* BARTLETT *stamps down the stairs. The madness which has taken almost complete possession of him in the past year is clearly stamped on his face, particularly in his eyes which seem to stare through and beyond objects with a hunted, haunted expression. His movements suggest an automaton obeying invisible wires. They are quick, jerky, spasmodic. He appears to be laboring under a state of extraordinary excitement. He stands for a second at the foot of the stairs, peering about him suspiciously. Then he goes to the table and sits down on the edge of a chair, his chin supported on his hands.*)

BARTLETT. (*takes a folded piece of paper from his pocket and spreads it out on the table in the light of the lantern—pointing with his finger—mumblingly*) Where the cross be—ye'll not forget that, Silas Horne. Ye had a copy o' this—no chance for a mistake, bullies— the gold's there, restin' safe—back to me and we'll share it fair and square. A year ago today—ye remember the orders I wrote ye, Horne. (*Threateningly*) Ye'll not be gone more nor a year or I'll—and if ye make port to home here at night, hang a red and a green light at the mainm'st head so I'll see ye comin'. A red and a green— (*He springs up suddenly and goes to a porthole to look out at the sea—disappointedly*) No lights be there—but they'll come. The year be up today and ye've got to come or I'll— (*He sinks back on the chair, his head in his hands. Suddenly he starts and stares straight in front of him as if he saw something in the air—with angry defiance*) Aye, there ye be again—the two o' ye! Makin' a mock o' me! Brass and junk, ye say, not worth a damn! Ye don't believe, do ye? I'll show ye! (*He springs to his feet and makes a motion as if grabbing someone by the throat and shaking them—savagely*) Ye lie! Is it gold or no? Answer me! (*With a mocking laugh*) Aye, ye own up to it now, right enough. Too late, ye swabs! No share for ye! (*He sinks back on the chair again—after a pause, dully*) Jimmy's gone. Let them rot. But I spoke no word, Silas Horne, remember! (*Then in a tone of fear*) Be ye dyin', Sarah? No, ye must live—live to see your ship come home with the gold—and I'll buy ye all in the world ye set your heart on. No, not ambergris, Sarah—gold and diamonds and sech! We're rich at last! (*Then with great anguish*) What woman's stubborn talk be this? Confess, ye say? But I spoke no word, I swear to ye! Why will ye hound me and think evil o' what I done? Men's business, I tell ye. They would have killed us and stolen the gold, can't ye see? (*Wildly*) Enough o' talk, Sarah! I'll sail out in spite o' ye! (*He gets to his feet and paces up and down the room. The door in the rear is opened and* NAT *re-enters. He glances at his father, then looks down the stairs behind him cautiously to see if he is followed. He comes in and closes the door behind him carefully.*)

NAT. (*in a low voice*) Pa! (*Then as his father does not appear to notice his presence—louder*) Pa!

BARTLETT. (*stops short and stares at his son as if he were gradually awakening from a dream—slowly*) Be that ye, Nat?

NAT. (*coming forward*) Yes. I want to talk with you.

BARTLETT. (*struggling to bring his thoughts under control*) Talk? Ye want to talk—to me? Men's business—no room for a boy in it— keep clear o' this.

NAT. (*defiantly*) That's what you've always said. But I won't be put off any longer. I won't, do you hear?

BARTLETT. (*angrily*) I've ordered ye not to set foot in this cabin o' mine. Git below where ye belong. Where's Sue? I told her to keep ye away.

NAT. She can't prevent me this time. I've made up my mind. Listen, Pa. I'm going away tomorrow.

BARTLETT. (*uncertainly*) Goin' away?

NAT. Yes, and I'm never coming back. I'm going to start a new life. That's why I want a final talk with you—before I go.

BARTLETT. (*dully*) I've naught to say to ye.

NAT. You will have. Listen. I've absolute proof the "Sarah Allen" is lost.

BARTLETT. (*fiercely*) Ye lie!

NAT. (*curiously*) Why do you say that? You know it's true. It's just that you *won't believe*.

BARTLETT. (*wanderingly—the word heading his mind into another channel*) Believe? Aye, he wouldn't believe. Brass and junk, he said, not worth a damn—but in the end I made him own up 'twas gold.

NAT. (*repeating the word fascinatedly*) Gold?

BARTLETT. A year ago today she sailed. Ye lie! Ye don't believe either, do ye?—like him. But I'll show ye! I'll make ye own up as I made him! (*With mad exultation*) She's comin' home tonight as I ordered Horne she must! I kin feel her makin' for home, I tell ye! A red an' a green at the mainm'st head if ye make port o' night, I ordered Horne. Ye'll see! (*He goes to look out of a porthole.* NAT, *as if under a spell, goes to another.*)

NAT. (*turning away disappointedly—making an effort to throw off his thoughts—without conviction*) Nonsense. There's nothing there— no lights—and I don't believe there ever will be.

BARTLETT. (*his wild eyes fixed on his son's with an intense effort of will as if he were trying to break down his resistance*) Ye'll see, I tell ye—a red and a green! It ain't time yet, boy, but when it be they'll be plain in the night afore your eyes. (*He goes and sits down by the table.* NAT *follows him and sits down in the other chair. He sees the map and stares at it fascinatedly.*)

NAT. What is this—the map of the island? (*He reaches out his hand for it.*)

BARTLETT. (*snatching it up—with a momentary return to reason—frightenedly*) Not for ye, boy. Keep clear o' this for your own good. (*Then with a crazed triumph*) Aye! Ye'd believe this soon enough, wouldn't ye?

NAT. (*intensely*) I've always believed there was something—and a moment ago you mentioned gold. (*Triumphant in his turn*) So you needn't try to hide the secret any longer. I know now. It's gold—gold you found on that island—gold you fitted out the "Sarah Allen" to sail back for—gold you buried where I saw that cross marked on the map! (*Passionately*) Why have you been afraid to confide in me, your own son? Did you think I wouldn't believe—?

BARTLETT. (*with a mad chuckle*) Aye, ye believe now, right enough.

NAT. I always believed, I tell you. (*Pleadingly*) And now that I know so much why can't you tell me the rest? I must know! I have a right to be heir to the secret. Why don't you confess—

BARTLETT. (*interrupting—his brain catching at the word*) Confess? Confess, did ye say, Sarah? To Nat, did ye mean? Aye, Sarah, I'll tell him all and leave it to him to say if I did wrong. (*His gleaming eyes fixed on his son's*) I'll tell ye, boy, from start to finish of it. I been eatin' my heart to tell someone—someone who'd believe—someone that 'd say I did no wrong. Listen, boy, ye know o' our four days in an open boat after the "Triton" went down. I told ye o' that when I come home. But what I didn't tell ye was they was six o' us in that boat, not four.

NAT. Six? There were you and Horne and Cates and Jimmy—

BARTLETT. The cook o' the "Triton" and the ship's boy. We'd been on the island two days—an island barren as hell, mind—without food or drink. We was roasted by the sun and nigh mad with thirst. Then, on the second day, I seed a Malay canoe—a proper war canoe such as the pirates use—sunk down inside the reef. I sent Jimmy down to go over her thinkin' they might be some cask o' water in her the sea'd not got to. (*With impressive emphasis*) He found no water, boy, but he did find—d'ye know what, boy?

NAT. (*exultantly*) The gold, of course!

BARTLETT. (*laughing harshly*) Ha-ha! Ye do believe right enough, don't ye! Aye, the gold—in a chest. We hauled her up ashore and forced the lid open. (*Gloatingly*) And there it was afore our eyes in the sun—gold bracelets and rings and ornaments o' all sorts fixed up fancy with diamonds and emeralds and rubies and sech—red and green—shinin' in the sun! (*He stops impressively.*)

NAT. (*fascinatedly*) Diamonds and— But how did they get there?

BARTLETT. Looted treasure o' some Chinese junk, likely. What matter how it come about? There it was afore our eyes. And then, mind ye, that thief o' a cook came runnin' up from where he'd been shirkin' to look at what we'd found. "No share for ye, ye swab," I yelled at him; and then he says: "It ain't gold—brass and junk," he says and run off for fear o' me. Aye, he run off to the boy and told him to jine with his sneakin' plan to steal the gold from us!

NAT. (*savagely*) But why didn't you stop him? Why didn't you—?

BARTLETT. I be comin' to that, boy, and ye'll see if I did wrong. We carried the chest to the shade o' a palm and there was that thief o' a cook an' the boy waitin'. I collared 'em both and made 'em look at the gold. "Look and tell me if it's gold or no," I says. (*Triumphantly*) They was afeered to lie. Even that thief o' a cook owned up 'twas gold. Then when I turned 'em loose, because he knowed he'd git no share, he shouted again: "Brass and junk. Not worth a damn."

NAT. (*furiously*) But why did you allow— Why didn't you—

BARTLETT. (*with mad satisfaction*) Aye, ye be seein' the way o' it, boy. It was just then we sighted the schooner that picked us up after. We made a map and was buryin' the gold when we noticed them two thieves sneakin' about to see where we'd hide it. I saw 'em plain, the scum! That thief o' a cook was thinkin' he'd tell the folks on the schooner and go shares with them—and leave us on the island to rot; or he was thinkin' he and the boy'd be able to come back and dig it up afore I could. We had to do somethin' quick to spile their plan afore the schooner come. (*In a tone of savage satisfaction*) And so—though I spoke no word to him—Jimmy knifed 'em both and covered 'em up with sand. But I spoke no word, d'ye hear? Their deaths be on Jimmy's head alone.

NAT. (*passionately*) And what if you had? They deserved what they got.

BARTLETT. Then ye think I did no wrong?

NAT. No! Any man—I'd have done the same myself.

BARTLETT. (*gripping his son's hand tensely*) Ye be true son o' mine, Nat. I ought to told ye before. (*Exultantly*) Ye hear, Sarah? Nat says I done no wrong.

NAT. The map! Can I see it?

BARTLETT. Aye. (*He hands it to* NAT *who spreads it out on the table and pores over it.*)

NAT. (*excitedly*) Why, with this I—we—can go back—even if the "Sarah Allen" is lost.

BARTLETT. She ain't lost, boy—not her. Don't heed them lies ye been hearin'. She's due now. I'll go up and look. (*He goes up the companionway stairs.* NAT *does not seem to notice his going, absorbed in the map. Then there is a loud muffled hail in* BARTLETT's *voice*) " 'Sarah Allen,' ahoy!" (NAT *starts, transfixed—then rushes to one of the portholes to look. He turns back, passing his hand over his eyes, frowning bewilderedly. The door above is flung open and slammed shut and* BARTLETT *stamps down the stairs.*)

BARTLETT. (*fixing* NAT *hypnotically with his eyes—triumphantly*) What did I tell ye? D'ye believe now she'll come back? D'ye credit your own eyes?

NAT. (*vaguely*) Eyes? I looked. I didn't see—

BARTLETT. Ye lie! The "Sarah Allen," ye blind fool, come back from the Southern Seas as I swore she must! Loaded with gold as I swore she would be!—makin' port!—droppin' her anchor just when I hailed her.

NAT. (*feebly, his will crumbling*) But—how do you know?—some other schooner—

BARTLETT. Not know my own ship—and the signal I'd ordered Horne to make!

NAT. (*mechanically*) I know—a red and a green at the mainm'st head.

BARTLETT. Then look out if ye dare! (*He goes to a porthole*) Ye kin see it plain from here. (*Commandingly*) Will ye believe your eyes? Look! (NAT *comes to him slowly—looks through the porthole—and starts back, a possessed expression coming over his face.*)

NAT. (*slowly*) A red and a green—clear as day!

BARTLETT. (*his face is now transfigured by the ecstasy of a dream come true*) They've lowered a boat—the three—Horne an' Cates and Jimmy Kanaka. They're rowin' ashore. Listen. I hear the oars in the locks. Listen!

NAT. (*staring into his father's eyes—after a pause during which he appears to be straining his hearing to the breaking point—excitedly*) I hear!

BARTLETT. Listen! They've landed. They'll be comin' up the path now. (*In a crooning, monotonous tone*) They move slowly—slowly. It be heavy, I know—that chest. (*After a pause*) Hark! They're below at the door in front.

NAT. I hear!

BARTLETT. Ye'll see it now in a moment, boy—the gold. Up with it, bullies! Up ye come! Up, bullies! It's heavy, heavy!

NAT. (*madly*) I hear them! They're on the floor below! They're coming! I'll open the door. (*He springs to the door and flings it open, shouting*) Welcome home, boys! (SUE *is discovered outside just climbing up the stairs from below. She steps inside, then stops, looking with amazement and horror from father to brother.* NAT *pushes her roughly aside to look behind her down the stairs.*)

SUE. Nat!

NAT. (*Turning to his father*) I'll go down to the wharf. They must be there or— (*The rest of his words are lost as he hurries down the stairs.* BARTLETT *steps back, shrinking away from his daughter, and sinks on a chair by the table with a groan, his hands over his eyes.*)

SUE. (*comes to him and shakes him by the shoulder—alarmed*) Pa! What has happened? What is the matter with Nat? What have you told him? (*With bitter despair*) Oh, can't you see you're driving him mad, too?

BARTLETT. (*letting his hands fall and staring at her haggardly—falteringly, as if reason were slowly filtering back into his brain*) Sue— ye said--drivin' him mad, *too!* Then ye think I be—? (*He staggers to his feet.* SUE *breaks down, sobbing.* BARTLETT *falters on*) But I seen her—the "Sarah Allen"—the signal lights—

SUE. Oh, Pa, there's nothing there! You know it! She was lost months ago.

BARTLETT. Lost? (*He stumbles over to a porthole and looks out. His body sags as if he were going to fall. He turns away and cries hopelessly in a tone of heart-rending grief*) Lost! Aye, they be no "Sarah Allen" there—no lights—nothin'!

SUE. (*pleading fiercely*) Pa, you've got to save Nat! He won't heed anyone else. Can't you tell him the truth—the whole truth whatever it is—now when I'm here and you're yourself again—and set him free from this crazy dream!

BARTLETT. (*with wild grief*) Confess, ye mean? Sue, ye be houndin' me like your Ma did to her dyin' hour! Confess—that I spoke the word to Jimmy—in my mind! Confess—brass and junk—not worth a damn! (*In frenzied protest*) No! Ye lie!

SUE. Oh, Pa, I don't know what you mean. Tell Nat the truth! Save him!

BARTLETT. The truth? It's a lie! (*As* SUE *tries to bar his way to the companionway—sternly*) Out o' my way, girl! (*He pulls himself feebly up the stairs. The door is heard slamming above.* SUE *sits down in a chair in a hopeless, exhausted attitude. After a pause* NAT *re-enters.*

He is panting heavily from his exertions. His pale face is set in an expression of despair.)

NAT. (*looking about the room wildly*) Where is he? Sue! (*He comes forward and falls on his knees beside her chair, hiding his face in her lap like a frightened child. He sobs hoarsely*) Sue! What does it all mean? I looked. There was nothing there—no schooner—nothing.

SUE. (*soothing him as if he were a little boy*) Of course there wasn't. Did you expect there would be, you foolish boy? Come, you know better than that. Why, Nat, you told the doctor and me that you were absolutely convinced the "Sarah Allen" was lost.

NAT. (*dully*) Yes, I know—but I don't believe—like him—

SUE. Sshhhh! You know the state Pa is in. He doesn't realize what he's saying half the time. You ought to have better sense than to pay any attention—

NAT. (*excitedly*) But he told me all he's been hiding from us—all about the gold!

SUE. (*looking at him with alarm—mystified*) Gold? (*Then forcing a smile*) Don't be silly, Nat. It doesn't exist except in his poor, deranged mind.

NAT. (*fiercely*) That's a lie, Sue! I saw the map, I tell you—the map of the island with a cross marked on it where they buried the gold.

SUE. He showed a map to you—a real map? (*Gently*) Are you sure you're not just imagining that, too?

NAT. I had it in my hands, you fool, you! There—on the table. (*He springs to his feet, sees the map on the table, and snatches it up with an exclamation of joy—showing it to* SUE) See! Now will you believe me? (*She examines the map perplexedly.* NAT *paces up and down—excitedly*) I tell you it's all true. You can't deny it now. It's lucky for us I forced him to confess. He might have died keeping the secret and then we'd have lost—I'll tell you what I'm going to do now, Sue. I'm going to raise the money somewhere, somehow, and fit out another schooner and this time I'll sail on her myself. No trusting to Danny or anyone else! Yes, Sue, we'll come into our own yet, even if the

"Sarah Allen" is lost— (*He stops—then in accents of bewildered fear*) But—she can't be lost—I saw the lights, Sue—as plain as I see you now— (*He goes to one of the portholes again.*)

SUE. (*who has been watching him worriedly, puts the map back on the table, gets up and, assuming a brisk, matter-of-fact tone, she goes over and takes him by the arm*) Come downstairs, Nat. Don't think any more about it tonight. It's late and you're worn out. You need rest and a good sleep.

NAT. (*following her toward the door—confusedly*) But Sue—I saw them— (*From above in the night comes the muffled hail in* BARTLETT's *voice*) "Sarah Allen," ahoy! (NAT *stops, tortured, his hands instinctively raised up to cover his ears.* SUE *gives a startled cry. The door above is slammed and* BARTLETT *comes down the stairs, his face revealing that the delusion has again full possession of his mind.*)

BARTLETT. (*pointing his finger at his son and fixing him with his eyes—in ringing, triumphant tones*) The "Sarah Allen," boy—in the harbor below! Come back from the Southern Seas as I swore she must! Loaded with gold as I swore she would be! (NAT *again seems to crumble—to give way to the stronger will. He takes a step toward his father, his eyes lighting up.* SUE *looks at his face—then rushes to her father.*)

SUE. (*putting her hands to her father's head and forcing him to look down into her face—intensely*) Pa! Stop, do you hear me! It's all mad! You're driving Nat mad, too! (*As she sees her father hesitate, the wild light dying out of his eyes, she summons all her power to a fierce pleading*) For my sake, Pa! For Ma's sake! Think of how she would feel if she were alive and saw you acting this way with Nat! Tell him! Tell him now—before me—tell him it's all a lie!

BARTLETT. (*trying in an agony of conflict to get hold of his reason—incoherently*) Yes, Sue—I hear ye—confess—aye, Sarah, your dyin' words—keep Nat clear o' this—but—red and green—I seen 'em plain— (*Then suddenly after a tremendous struggle, lifting his tortured face to* NAT's—*in tones of despair*) Nothin' there, boy! Don't ye believe! No red and green! She'll never come! Derelict and lost, boy, the "Sarah Allen." (*After another struggle with himself*) And I lied to ye, boy. I gave the word—in my mind—to kill them two. I murdered 'em in cold blood.

SUE. (*shrinking from him in horror*) Pa! You don't know what you're saying.

BARTLETT. The truth, girl. Ye said—confess—

NAT. (*bewilderedly*) But—it was right. They were trying to steal—

BARTLETT. (*overcome by the old obsession for a moment—savagely*) Aye, that's it! The thievin' scum! They was tryin'— (*He stops short, throwing his head back, his whole body tense and quivering with the effort he makes to force this sustaining lie out of his brain—then, broken but self-conquering, he looks again at* NAT—*gently*) No, Nat. That be the lie I been tellin' myself ever since. That cook—he said 'twas brass— But I'd been lookin' for ambergris—gold—the whole o' my life—and when we found that chest—I *had* to believe, I tell ye! I'd been dreamin' o' it all my days! But he said brass and junk, and told the boy—and I give the word to murder 'em both and cover 'em up with sand.

NAT. (*very pale—despairingly*) But he lied, didn't he? It is gold— real gold—isn't it?

BARTLETT. (*slowly takes the studded anklet from his pocket and holds it out to* NAT. *The latter brings it to the light of the lantern.* BART- LETT *sits on a chair, covering his face with his hands—in a tone of terrible suffering*) Ye'll tell me, boy—if it's gold or no. I've had it by me all this time—but I've been afeerd to show—

NAT. (*in a tone of wild scorn*) Why, it's brass, of course! The cheapest kind of junk—not worth a damn! (*He flings it savagely into a corner of the room.* BARTLETT *groans and seems to shrink up and turn into a figure of pitiable feebleness.*)

SUE. (*pityingly*) Don't, Nat. (*She puts her arms around her father's shoulders protectingly.*)

NAT. (*in a stifled voice*) What a damned fool I've been! (*He flings himself down on the cot, his shoulders heaving.*)

BARTLETT. (*uncovers his gray face on which there is now settling an expression of strange peace—stroking his daughter's hand*) Sue— don't think hard o' me. (*He takes the map*) An end to this! (*He slowly tears it into small pieces, seeming to grow weaker and weaker as he does so. Finally as he lets the fragments filter through his fingers, his whole frame suddenly relaxes. He sighs, his eyes shut, and sags back in his chair, his head bent forward limply on his chest.*)

SUE. (*alarmed*) Pa! (*She sinks to her knees beside him and looks up into his face*) Pa! Speak to me! It's Sue! (*Then turning toward her brother—terrifiedly*) Nat! Run—get the doctor— (NAT *starts to a sitting position.* SUE *tries with trembling hands to feel of her father's pulse, his heart—then begins to sob hysterically*) Oh, Nat—he's dead. I think—he's dead!

CURTAIN